CRITICAL SURVEY
OF
SHORT FICTION

Fourth Edition

CRITICAL SURVEY
OF
SHORT FICTION
Fourth Edition

Volume 1
American Writers

Lee K. Abbott - Moira Crone

Editor
Charles E. May
California State University, Long Beach

SALEM PRESS
Ipswich, Massachusetts   Hackensack, New Jersey

Some of the essays in this work, which have been updated, originally appeared in the following Salem Press publications, *Critical Survey of Short Fiction* (1981); *Critical Survey of Short Fiction, Supplement* (1987); *Critical Survey of Short Fiction: Revised Edition*, (1993; preceding volumes edited by Frank N. Magill); *Critical Survey of Short Fiction Second Revised Edition* (2001; edited by Charles E. May).

The paper used in these volumes conforms to the American National Standard for Permanence of Paper for Printed Library Materials, X39.48-1992 (R1997).

LIBRARY OF CONGRESS CATALOGING-IN-PUBLICATION DATA

Critical survey of short fiction / editor, Charles E. May. -- 4th ed.
    p. cm.

Includes bibliographical references and index.
ISBN 978-1-58765-789-4 (set : alk. paper) -- ISBN 978-1-58765-790-0 (set, american : alk. paper) --
ISBN 978-1-58765-791-7 (vol. 1, american : alk. paper) -- ISBN 978-1-58765-792-4 (vol. 2, american : alk. paper) --
ISBN 978-1-58765-793-1 (vol. 3, american : alk. paper) -- ISBN 978-1-58765-794-8 (vol. 4, american : alk. paper) --
ISBN 978-1-58765-795-5 (set, british : alk. paper) -- ISBN 978-1-58765-796-2 (vol. 1, british : alk. paper) --
ISBN 978-1-58765-797-9 (vol. 2, british : alk. paper) -- ISBN 978-1-58765-798-6 (european : alk. paper) --
ISBN 978-1-58765-799-3 (world : alk. paper) -- ISBN 978-1-58765-800-6 (topical essays : alk. paper) --
ISBN 978-1-58765-803-7 (cumulative index : alk. paper)

1. Short story. 2. Short story--Bio-bibliography. I. May, Charles E. (Charles Edward), 1941-
PN3321.C7 2011
809.3'1--dc23

2011026000

First Printing

PRINTED IN THE UNITED STATES OF AMERICA

CONTENTS

PUBLISHER'S NOTE

American Writers is part of Salem Press's greatly expanded and redesigned *Critical Survey of Short Fiction, Fourth Edition*. This edition presents profiles of major short-story writers, with sections on other literary forms, achievements, biography, general analysis, and analysis of the writer's most important stories or collections. Although the profiled writers may have written in other genres as well, sometimes to great acclaim, the focus of this set is on their most important works of short fiction.

The *Critical Survey of Short Fiction* was originally published in 1981, with a supplement in 1987, a revised edition in 1993, and a second revised edition in 2001. The *Fourth Edition* includes all writers from the previous edition and adds 145 new ones, covering 625 writers in total. The writers covered in this set represent 44 countries and their short fiction dates from antiquity to the present. The set also offers 53 informative overviews; 24 of these essays were added for this edition. In addition, six resources are provided, one of them new. More than 400 images of writers have been included.

For the first time, the material in the *Critical Survey of Short Fiction* has been organized into five subsets by geography and essay type: a four-volume subset on *American Writers*, a two-volume subset on *British, Irish, and Commonwealth Writers*, a single-volume subset on *European Writers*, a single-volume subset on *World Writers*, and a single-volume subset of *Topical Essays*. Each writer appears in only one subset. *Topical Essays* is organized under the categories "Theories, Themes, and Types," "History of Short Fiction," and "Short Fiction Around the World." A *Cumulative Indexes* volume covering all five subsets is free with purchase of more than one subset.

AMERICAN WRITERS

The four-volume *American Writers* contains 349 writer profiles, arranged alphabetically. For this edi-

tion, 92 new essays have been added, and 63 have been significantly updated with analysis of recently published books or stories. Each volume begins with a list of contents for that volume, a complete contents list covering the entire subset, and a pronunciation key. The writer essays follow in alphabetical order, divided among the four volumes. The fourth volume contains the "Resources" section, which features a glossary, bibliography, guide to online resources, time line, list of major awards, and chronological list of writers, providing guides for further research and additional information on American writers; comprehensive versions appear in *Cumulative Indexes*. The guide to online resources and time line were newly created for this edition.

American Writers contains a categorized index of writers, in which writers are grouped by culture or group identity, literary movement, historical period, and forms and themes, and a subject index. The *Cumulative Indexes* volume contains comprehensive versions of the categorized and subject indexes.

UPDATING THE ESSAYS

All essays in the previous edition were scrutinized for currency and accuracy: The writer's latest works of short fiction and other significant publications were added to the listings, new translations were added to listings for any foreign-language works, and deceased writer's listings were rechecked for accuracy and currency. All essays' bibliographies—lists of sources for further consultation—were revised to provide readers with the latest information.

Updated essays received more thorough attention. All new publications were added to listings, then each section of text was reviewed to ensure that recently received major awards were noted, that new biographical details were incorporated for still-living authors, and that analysis of works included recently published books or stories. The updating experts' names were added to essays. Original articles were reedited and checked for accuracy.

ONLINE ACCESS

Salem Press provides access to its award-winning content both in traditional, printed form and online. Any school or library that purchases *American Writers* is entitled to free, complimentary access to Salem's fully supported online version of the content. Features include a simple intuitive interface, user profile areas for students and patrons, sophisticated search functionality, and complete context, including appendixes. Access is available through a code printed on the inside cover of the first volume, and that access is unlimited and immediate. Our online customer service representatives, at (800) 221-1592, are happy to help with any questions. E-books are also available.

ORGANIZATION OF ESSAYS

The essays in *American Writers* vary in length, with none shorter than 2,000 words and most significantly longer. The profiles are arranged alphabetically, under the name by which the writer is best known. The format of the essays is standardized to allow predictable and easy access to the types of information of interest to a variety of users. Each writer essay contains ready-reference top matter, including full birth and (where applicable) death data, any alternate names used by the writer, and a list of "Principal short fiction," followed by the main text, which is divided into "Other literary forms," "Achievements," "Biography," and "Analysis." A list of "Other major works," a bibliography, and bylines complete the essay.

Principal short fiction lists the titles of the author's major collections of short fiction in chronological order, by date of original appearance. If an author has published works in another language and the works have been translated into English, the titles and dates of the first translations are provided.

Other literary forms describes the author's work in other genres and notes whether the author is known primarily as a short-story writer or has achieved equal or greater fame in another genre. If the writer's last name is unlikely to be familiar to most users, phonetic pro-

nunciation is provided in parentheses after his or her name. A "Key to Pronunciation" appears at the beginning of all volumes.

Achievements lists honors, awards, and other tangible recognitions, as well as a summation of the writer's influence and contributions to short fiction in particular and literature in general, where appropriate.

Biography provides a condensed biographical sketch with vital information from birth through (if applicable) death or the author's latest activities.

Analysis presents an overview of the writer's themes, techniques, style, and development, leading into subsections on major short-story collections, stories, or aspects of the person's work as a writer. Although this set focuses on Americans, some of the profiled writers were born in other countries and have written works in languages other than English. As an aid to students, those foreign-language titles that have not yet appeared in translation are often followed by a "literal translation" when these titles are mentioned in the text. If a title has been published in English, the English-language title is used in the text.

Other major works contains the writer's principal works in genres other than short fiction, listed by genre and by year of publication. English translations are again used for titles and publication dates.

Bibliography lists secondary print sources for further study, annotated to assist users in evaluating focus and usefulness.

Byline notes the original contributor of the essay. If the essay was updated, the name of the updater also appears.

APPENDIXES

The "Resources" section provides tools for further research.

Terms and Techniques is a lexicon of literary terms pertinent to the study of short fiction.

Bibliography identifies general reference works and other secondary sources.

Guide to Online Resources, new to this edition, provides Web sites pertaining to fiction and its writers.

Time Line, also new to this edition, lists major milestones and events in American short fiction and literature in the order in which they occurred.

Major Awards lists the recipients of major short fiction-specific awards in the areas covered by *American Writers* and general awards where applicable to writers or short fiction, from inception of the award to the present day.

Chronological List of Writers lists all 349 writers covered in *American Writers* by birth, in chronological order.

INDEXES

The "Categorized Index of Writers" lists the writers profiled in *American Writers* by culture or group identity, literary movements and historical periods, and forms and themes. The subject index lists all titles, authors, subgenres, and literary movements or terms that receive substantial discussion in *American Writers*.

ACKNOWLEDGMENTS

Salem Press is grateful for the efforts of the original contributors of these essays and those of the outstanding academicians who took on the task of updating or writing new material for this set. Their names and affiliations are listed in the "Contributors" section that follows. Finally, we are indebted to our editor, Professor Charles E. May of California State University, Long Beach, for his development of the table of contents for the *Critical Survey of Short Fiction, Fourth Edition* and his advice on updating the original articles to make this comprehensive and thorough revised edition an indispensable tool for students, teachers, and general readers alike.

CONTRIBUTORS

Randy L. Abbott
University of Evansville

Michael Adams
CUNY Graduate Center

Patrick Adcock
Henderson State University

Thomas P. Adler
Purdue University

A. Owen Aldridge
University of Illinois

Charmaine Allmon-Mosby
Western Kentucky University

Emily Alward
College of Southern Nevada

Andrew J. Angyal
Elon University

Jacob M. Appel
The Mount Sinai Medical School

Gerald S. Argetsinger
Rochester Institute of Technology

Karen L. Arnold
Columbia, Maryland

Marilyn Arnold
Brigham Young University

Leonard R. N. Ashley
*Brooklyn College, City University
of New York*

Bryan Aubrey
Fairfield, Iowa

Stephen Aubrey
Brooklyn College

Edmund August
McKendree College

Jane L. Ball
Wilberforce University

David Barratt
Montreat College

Melissa E. Barth
Appalachian State University

Martha Bayless
University of Oregon

Alvin K. Benson
Utah Valley University

Stephen Benz
Barry University

Margaret Boe Birns
New York University

Nicholas Birns
*Eugene Lang College,
The New School*

Elizabeth Blakesley
*Washington State University
Libraries*

Richard Bleiler
University of Connecticut

Lynn Z. Bloom
University of Connecticut

Julia B. Boken
Indiana University, Southeast

Jo-Ellen Lipman Boon
Buena Park, California

William Boyle
University of Mississippi

Virginia Brackett
Park University

Harold Branam
Savannah State University

Gerhard Brand

California State University, Los Angeles

Alan Brown

Livingston University

Mary Hanford Bruce

Monmouth College

Carl Brucker

Arkansas Tech University

John C. Buchanan

Original Contributor

Stefan Buchenberger

Kanagawa University

Louis J. Budd

Original Contributor

Rebecca R. Butler

Dalton College

Susan Butterworth

Salem State College

Edmund J. Campion

University of Tennessee, Knoxville

Larry A. Carlson

Original Contributor

Amee Carmines

Hampton University

Thomas Gregory Carpenter

Lipscomb University

John Carr

Original Contributor

Warren J. Carson

University of South Carolina, Spartanburg

Mary LeDonne Cassidy

South Carolina State University

Thomas J. Cassidy

South Carolina State University

Hal Charles

Eastern Kentucky University

C. L. Chua

California State University, Fresno

David W. Cole

University of Wisconsin Colleges

Laurie Coleman

Original Contributor

Richard Hauer Costa

Texas A&M University

Ailsa Cox

Edge Hill University

Lisa-Anne Culp

Nuclear Regulatory Commission

Heidi K. Czerwiec

Univeristy of North Dakota

Dolores A. D'Angelo

American University

Anita Price Davis

Converse College

Frank Day

Clemson University

Danielle A. DeFoe

Sierra College

Bill Delaney

San Diego, California

Joan DelFattore

University of Delaware

Kathryn Zabelle Derounian

University of Arkansas- Little Rock

Joseph Dewey

University of Pittsburgh

Marcia B. Dinneen

Bridgewater State University

Thomas Du Bose

Louisiana State University- Shreveport

Stefan Dziemianowicz

Bloomfield, New Jersey

Wilton Eckley

Colorado School of Mines

K Edgington

Towson University

Robert P. Ellis

Northborough Historical Society

Sonia Erlich
Lesley University

Thomas L. Erskine
Salisbury University

Christopher Estep
Original Contributor

Walter Evans
Augusta College

Jack Ewing
Boise, Idaho

Kevin Eyster
Madonna University

Nettie Farris
University of Louisville

Howard Faulkner
Original Contributor

James Feast
Baruch College

Thomas R. Feller
Nashville, Tennessee

John W. Fiero
*University of Louisiana
 at Lafayette*

Edward Fiorelli
St. John's University

Rebecca Hendrick Flannagan
Rrancis Marion University

James K. Folsom
Original Contributor

Ben Forkner
Original Contributor

Joseph Francavilla
Columbus State University

Timothy C. Frazer
Western Illinois University

Kathy Ruth Frazier
Original Contributor

Tom Frazier
Cumberland College

Rachel E. Frier
Rockville, Maryland

Terri Frongia
Santa Rosa Junior College

Miriam Fuchs
University of Hawaii-Manoa

Jean C. Fulton
Landmark College

Louis Gallo
Radford University

Ann Davison Garbett
Averett University

Marshall Bruce Gentry
Georgia College & State University

Jill B. Gidmark
University of Minnesota

M. Carmen Gomez-Galisteo
*Esne-Universidad Camilo
Jose Cela*

Linda S. Gordon
Worcester State College

Julian Grajewski
Tuscon, Arizona

Charles A. Gramlich
Xavier University of Louisiana

James L. Green
Arizona State University

Glenda I. Griffin
Sam Houston State University

John L. Grigsby
*Appalachian Research & Defense
Fund of Kentucky, Inc.*

William E. Grim
Ohio University

Elsie Galbreath Haley
*Metropolitan State College of
Denver*

David Mike Hamilton
Original Contributor

Katherine Hanley
*St. Bernard's School of Theology
and Ministry*

Michele Hardy
Prince George's Community College

Betsy Harfst
Kishwaukee College

Alan C. Haslam
Sierra College

CJ Hauser
Brooklyn College

Peter B. Heller
Manhattan College

Terry Heller
Coe College

Diane Andrews Henningfeld
Adrian College

DeWitt Henry
Emerson College

Cheryl Herr
Original Contributor

Allen Hibbard
Middle Tennessee State University

Cynthia Packard Hill
University of Massachusetts at Amherst

Jane Hill
Original Contributor

Nika Hoffman
Crossroads School for Arts & Sciences

William Hoffman
Fort Myers, Florida

Hal Holladay
Simon's Rock College of Bard

Kimberley M. Holloway
King College

Gregory D. Horn
Southwest Virginia Commmunity College

Sylvia Huete
Original Contributor

Edward Huffstetler
Bridgewater College

Theodore C. Humphrey
California State Polytechnic University, Pomona

Robert Jacobs
Central Washington University

Shakuntala Jayaswal
University of New Haven

Clarence O. Johnson
Joplin, Missouri

Eunice Pedersen Johnston
North Dakota State University

Theresa Kanoza
Lincoln Land Community College

William P. Keen
Washington & Jefferson College

Fiona Kelleghan
South Miami, Florida

Cassandra Kircher
Elon College

Paula Kopacz
Eastern Kentucky University

Uma Kukathas
Seattle, Washingtom

Rebecca Kuzins
Pasadena, California

Marvin Lachman
Santa Fe, New Mexico

Thomas D. Lane
Original Contributor

John Lang
Emory & Henry College

Carlota Larrea
Pennsylvania State University

Donald F. Larsson
Mankato State University

William Laskowski
Jamestown College

Norman Lavers
Arkansas State University

David Layton
*University of California,
Santa Barbar*

Allen Learst
Oklahome State University

James Ward Lee
University of North Texas

Katy L. Leedy
Marquette University

Leon Lewis
Appalachian State University

Elizabeth Johnston Lipscomb
*Randolph-Macon
Women's College*

Douglas Long
Pasadena, California

Michael Loudon
Eastern Illinois University

Robert M. Luscher
*University of Nebraska
at Kearney*

Carol J. Luther
*Pellissippi State Community
College*

R. C. Lutz
CII Group

Laurie Lykken
Century College

Andrew F. Macdonald
Loyola University

Joanne McCarthy
Tacoma Washington

Richard D. McGhee
Arkansas State University

S. Thomas Mack
University of South Carolina-Aiken

Victoria E. McLure
Texas Tech University

Robert J. McNutt
*University of Tennessee
at Chattanooga*

Bryant Mangum
Original Contributor

Barry Mann
Alliance Theatre

Mary E. Markland
Argosy University

Patricia Marks
Valdosta State College

Wythe Marschall
Brooklyn College

Karen M. Cleveland Marwick
*Hemel Hempstead,
Hertfordshire, England*

Charles E. May
*California State University,
Long Beach*

Laurence W. Mazzeno
Alvernia College

Patrick Meanor
SUNY College at Oneonta

Martha Meek
Original Contributor

Ann A. Merrill
Emory University

Robert W. Millett
Original Contributor

Christian H. Moe
*Southern Illinois University at
Carbondale*

Robert A. Morace
Daemen College

Christina Murphy
Original Contributor

Earl Paulus Murphy
Harris-Stowe State College

John M. Muste
Ohio State University

Donna B. Nalley
South University

Keith Neilson
California State University, Fullerton

William Nelles
University of Massachusetts-Dartmouth

John Nizalowski
Mesa State College

Martha Nochimson
Mercy College

Emma Coburn Norris
Troy State University

Bruce Olsen
Austin Peay State University

Brian L. Olson
Kalamazoo Valley Community College

James Norman O'Neill
Bryant College

Keri L. Overall
University of South Carolina

Janet Taylor Palmer
Caldwell Community College & Technical Institute

Sally B. Palmer
South Dakota School of Mines & Technology

Robert J. Paradowski
Rochester Institute of Technology

David B. Parsell
Furman University

Susie Paul
Auburn University, Montgomery

Leslie A. Pearl
San Diego, California

David Peck
Laguna Beach, California

William Peden
University of Missouri-Columbia

Chapel Louise Petty
Blackwell, Oklahoma

Susan L. Piepke
Bridgewater College

Constance Pierce
Original Contributor

Mary Ellen Pitts
Rhodes College

Victoria Price
Lamar University

Jere Real
Lynchburg, Virginia

Peter J. Reed
University of Minnesota

Rosemary M. Canfield Reisman
Sonoma, California

Martha E. Rhynes
Oklahoma East Central University

James Curry Robison
Original Contributor

Mary Rohrberger
New Orleans, Louisiana

Douglas Rollins
Dawson College

Carl Rollyson
Baruch College, CUNY

Paul Rosefeldt
Delgado Community College

Ruth Rosenberg
Brooklyn, New York

Irene Struthers Rush
Boise, Idaho

David Sadkin
Hamburg, New York

David N. Samuelson
California State University, Long Beach

Elizabeth D. Schafer
Loachapoka, Alabama

Barbara Kitt Seidman
Linfield College

D. Dean Shackelford
Concord College

M. K. Shaddix
Dublin University

Allen Shepherd
Original Contributor

Nancy E. Sherrod
Georgia Southern University

Thelma J. Shinn
Arizona State University

R. Baird Shuman
*University of Illinois at
Urbana-Champaign*

Paul Siegrist
Fort Hays State University

Charles L. P. Silet
Iowa State University

Karin A. Silet
University of Wisconsin-Madison

Genevieve Slomski
New Britain, Connecticut

Roger Smith
Portland, Oregon

Ira Smolensky
Monmouth College

Katherine Snipes
Spokane, Washington

Sandra Whipple Spanier
Original Contributor

Brian Stableford
Reading, United Kingdom

John Stark
Original Contributor

Joshua Stein
Los Medanos College

Karen F. Stein
University of Rhode Island

Judith L. Steininger
Milwaukee School of Engineering

Ingo R. Stoehr
Kilgore College

Louise M. Stone
Bloomsburg University

William B. Stone
Chicago, Illinois

Theresa L. Stowell
Adrian College

Gerald H. Strauss
Bloomsburg University

Ryan D. Stryffeler
Western Nevada College

W. J. Stuckey
Purdue University

Catherine Swanson
Austin, Texas

Philip A. Tapley
Louisiana College

Terry Theodore
*University of North Carolina
at Wilmington*

Maxine S. Theodoulou
The Union Institute

David J. Thieneman
Original Contributor

Lou Thompson
Texas Woman's University

Michael Trussler
University of Regina

Richard Tuerk
Texas A&M University-Commerce

Scott Vander Ploeg
Madisonville Community College

Dennis Vannatta
*University of Arkansas at Little
Rock*

Jaquelyn W. Walsh
McNeese State University

Shawncey Webb
Taylor University

James Michael Welsh
Salisbury State University

James Whitlark
Texas Tech University

Barbara Wiedemann
Auburn University at Montgomery

CONTRIBUTORS

Albert Wilhelm

Tennessee Technological University

Donna Glee Williams

North Carolina Center for the Advancement of Teaching

Patricia A. R. Williams

Original Contributor

Judith Barton Williamson

Sauk Valley Community College

Michael Witkoski

University of South Carolina

Jennifer L. Wyatt

Civic Memorial High School

Scott D. Yarbrough

Charleston Southern University

Mary F. Yudin

State College, Pennsylvania

Hasan Zia

Original Contributor

Gay Pitman Zieger

Santa Fe College

COMPLETE LIST OF CONTENTS

American Volume 1

American Volume 2

American Volume 3

American Volume 4

CRITICAL SURVEY
OF
SHORT FICTION

Fourth Edition

A

LEE K. ABBOTT

Born: Panama Canal Zone; October 17, 1947

OTHER LITERARY FORMS

Insisting that he lacks the energy to write a novel, Lee K. Abbott sticks to the short story as his genre of choice. However, he did write a chapter of the novel *The Putt at the End of the World* (2000).

ACHIEVEMENTS

Lee K. Abbott's stories have been selected to appear in *The Best American Short Stories* ("The Final Proof of Fate and Circumstances," 1984, and "Dreams of Distant Lives," 1987), *Prize Stories: The O. Henry Awards* ("The Final Proof of Fate and Circumstances," 1984, and "Living Alone in Iota," 1984), and *The Pushcart Prize* (1984, 1987, and 1989). He has twice received a National Endowment for the Arts Fellowship (1979 and 1985), and he is also the recipient of the St. Lawrence Award for Fiction (1981), the Editors Choice Award from Wampeter-Doubleday (1986), the National Magazine Award for Fiction (1986), a Major Artist Fellowship from the Ohio Arts Council (1991-1992), a Governor's Award for the Arts from the Ohio Arts Council (1993), and the Syndicated Fiction Award (1995).

BIOGRAPHY

Lee Kittredge Abbott was born in the Panama Canal Zone on October 17, 1947, to a military father and an alcoholic mother, whom he has fictionalized in such stories as "The End of Grief" and "Time and Fear and Somehow Love." He received his bachelor's degree in English from New Mexico State University in 1970. He married Pamela Jo Dennis in 1969, after which he and his new wife moved to New York City, where he attended Columbia University. He returned to New Mexico State University, where he received an M.A. degree in English in 1973. He went on to earn an M.F.A. from the University of Arkansas in 1977.

Abbott published a number of stories in various literary magazines while working on his M.A. and M.F.A. After accepting a position as an assistant professor of English at Case Western Reserve University, he published his first collection of stories, *The Heart Never Fits Its Wanting.* In 1990, Abbott began teaching writing as a professor at Ohio State University. He has held visiting professor positions at Wichita State University, Southwest Texas State University, and Yale University. He has also taught writing at Rice University, Colorado College, and the Iowa Writers' Workshop.

ANALYSIS

When asked to comment on minimalism for a special issue of *Mississippi Review,* Abbott disavowed any relationship to that style of writing, insisting he was a "mossback prose-writer who prefers stories with all the parts hanging out and whirling." Abbott once said, "I ride with the Wild Bunch," identifying himself with John Cheever, Peter Taylor, and Eudora Welty. He is most clearly connected, however, to the wild bunch of prose writers of the 1970's and 1980's that includes Barry Hannah, Richard Bausch, and Larry Brown-- writers who create the voice of a down-and-out rural male from the South or the West who chases liquor, women, and enough money to get by. In the game of creating rough, redneck lyrical narrative, Abbott is one of the best.

"LIVING ALONE IN IOTA"

Reese, the protagonist in this story, has been dumped by his girlfriend and feels desolate: "She makes my ears bleed," he tells the boys where he works. "I mean when she starts kissing my neck, I go off into a dark land. It's like death, only welcome." As a result of his loss, the protagonist is "love-sawed." If the story has any specific statement of theme, it is when Reese tells the members of his crew, "Boys, I am being sand-bagged by memory." He goes to Deming, New Mexico, a small town featured in a number of Abbott's stories, to find his girlfriend. Drinking two six-packs of beer on the way, he arrives, "his face yellow with hope" and in a "state as pure and unbecoming as loneliness."

In this wonderfully comic, laugh-out-loud story, Reese tries desperately to win Billy Jean La Took back, but she will have none of it, granting him only one chaste kiss. However, as Abbott says in his typical rural romanticism, "You could tell that kiss really ripped the spine out of him." He tries to forget her with other women, but to no avail. Although he tries one last time to get her back, she remains as "distant from him as he from his ancestral fishes." Three months later, in a flash of unmotivated insight, he says, "Boys I'm a fool." This is one of Abbott's purest lyrical love stories, creating a roughneck Romeo full of poor-boy poetry.

"THE FINAL PROOF OF FATE AND CIRCUMSTANCE"

This prize-winning story is a lyrical account of a man's masculine identification with his father as he listens to the older man tell stories about his past. As the father tells of driving through the desert when he was in his twenties and accidentally hitting and killing a man, the son imagines the father in such detail that he identifies with him completely. When the father finds the body in the darkness, he feels the kind of tranquility that one feels at the end of a drama when, after the ruin is dealt out fairly, one goes off to drink.

The sense of catharsis felt at the end of a tragedy is continued by the narrator as he listens to more of his father's stories "in which the hero, using luck and ignorance, manages to avoid the base and its slick companion, the wanton." He senses he is in a warm place that few get to experience, where a father admits to being a lot like his son, a place "made habitable by age and self-absorption and fatigue that says much about those heretofore pantywaist emotions like pity and fear."

The father's final story is about the death of his first wife, which occurred so unexpectedly that it was like a death in a fairy tale that left him numb, "no more sentient than a clock." The "sad part" of the story, the father says, occurs during the funeral procession, when he orders the car to stop, gets out, and walks to an ice cream parlor. After eating three cones of the best ice cream he has ever had, he is struck with an insight of such force that he feels lightheaded, thinking that if he faints, his last thought, like that of the man he killed in the desert, would be long and complex, featuring "a scene of hope followed by misfortune and doom."

The story ends with the narrator telling his father's stories to his wife, trying to make her see what he only vaguely understands himself. He plans to tell her a story of his own, of wandering through his father's house once and standing over his bed while he slept; this is the part that has the truth in it, he says, about how "a fellow such as me invites a fellow such as him out to do a thing--I'm not sure what--that involves effort and sacrifice and leads, in an hour or a day, to that throb and swell fellows such as you call triumph."

"THE TALK TALKED BETWEEN WORMS"

In this story from Abbott's 1997 collection *Wet Places at Noon*, he focuses once again on the relationship between a father and a son. This time the basis of the relationship is the historical/cultural fact of the report of a flying saucer having landed in the small New Mexico town of Roswell in 1947. Although the official account is that a cowhand named Mac Brazel found the pieces of metal that were reported to be remnants of a crashed flying saucer, Abbott's story is based on the fictional observation of the spacecraft and aliens by Tot Hamsey, the father of the narrator of the story.

Although accounts from the father's journals and recorded tapes of his sighting of the aliens that occurred in 1947 appear throughout the story, the primary events occur in the early 1980's, when the narrator goes to visit his father, who has been institutionalized.

The father has extensive records of his knowledge of the aliens: where they live, what they do in space, their beliefs and conquests. Insisting that he is not mad, the father says he is simply a man who has died and come back. The son perceives him as a figure out of a fairy tale, reading his records so often and so thoroughly that he memorizes whole sections.

As he does in other stories, Abbott projects himself into the mind of the father, imagining he is inside his head, feeling the present overwhelmed by the past. The father says, "There's no power, son, no glory. There's nothing--just them and us and the things we walk on. I have proof. . . . My files." Abbott's cultural reference here is to the popular television show *The X-Files*, which is based on the premise of secret government cover-ups and the obsessive belief in the reality of aliens having invaded earth.

When the father dies, the narrator goes to his house looking for evidence of the truth of his father's hallucinations, feeling like a juvenile on a scavenger hunt. Finding a box of papers hidden under the floorboards, he realizes that just as thousands of days ago "a terrible thing had crashed in my father's life . . . something equally impossible had landed in mine." Although he tells his new wife that what he found is trash, just a lot of talk, he recalls his father's admonition about "the talk talked between worms"--the confrontation of human beings with ultimate mystery.

The story is an interesting exploration of basic human choices among logic, common sense, and everyday reality and obsessive commitment to the unknown mysteries of life. Abbott uses the cultural clichés of alien spacecrafts to embody a basic sense that human beings are surrounded by mysteries that they can never fully know, mysteries that they can either ignore or become so captured by that their lives are dominated by them.

ALL THINGS, ALL AT ONCE

In a half-dozen new stories in this collection, Abbott continues to focus on a typical middle-class American male whose qualities seldom change. He is a man who either played football in high school or wished he had, mainly because of a cheerleader named Bonnie Jo or Peggy Sue. He is a man who missed the Vietnam War because of a bad back or fallen arches and has mixed feelings of relief and regret about that. He became a high school teacher or a real estate agent or a store manager, who both loves his job and hates it. He married his college sweetheart, but he cannot resist his fellow teacher or secretary, or just a woman he met, who embodies something he thinks he missed along the way. He has a son in whom he sees himself and a daughter who scares him. Although some readers may think he is always the same man, as Abbott creates him, he is always a different man.

"GRAVITY"

In "Gravity," one of the best of the new stories in *All Things, All At Once*, Lonnie Nees, a resident of Abbott's favorite fictional town, Deming, New Mexico, is another one of his typical male characters. The story begins with Lonnie, a county manager, hearing that his fourteen-year-old daughter, Tanya, has been kidnapped on the sidewalk in front of the J. C. Penney's store at the mall. Lonnie describes himself in typical self-effacing Abbott style as a practical man with only a few half-baked ideas, who brushes his teeth three times a day and changes his drawers in the morning-- "as ordinary a citizen as you can find in the funny pages." Lonnie shares custody of Tanya with his former wife Ginny, and they maintain what Lonnie calls a "civilized" relationship.

Much of the story focuses on the investigation of the suspected kidnapping by the sheriff, nicknamed Milty, with whom Lonnie plays golf. Much to Lonnie's surprise, Milty first finds drug-making paraphernalia in Tanya's closet and then a cluster of pornographic pictures of Tanya and some friends in her locker at school. Lonnie also finds out that the parents of Tanya's friends have forbidden their children to talk to her. All these surprising revelations come to a climax when Lonnie, bound for revenge, takes a gun to the home of a man Tanya has been seeing. However, he discovers that he was naïve to think the man had corrupted his little girl, for Tanya has gone off to California on her own. "Gravity" is no by means a serious cautionary tale for adults too busy to know what their children are doing. Rather, it is a typical Abbott comedic story with that familiar bewildered male voice he has been creating for years.

OTHER MAJOR WORKS

LONG FICTION: *The Putt at the End of the World*, 2000 (with Richard Bausch, Tim O'Brien, and others).

EDITED TEXT: *Best of the Web 2009*, 2009.

BIBLIOGRAPHY

Abbott, Lee K. "An Interview with Lee K. Abbott." Interview by George Myers. *High Plains Literary Review* 7 (Winter, 1992): 95-108. Abbott rejects being classified as a regional writer, a distinction he says was created for the convenience of reviewers. He discusses how the story "How Love Is Lived in Paradise" came into being. Abbott says he is a realist of the "modernist stripe," and that character is the center of his fiction. He criticizes such popular writers as Danielle Steel and Sidney Sheldon for trivializing literature by putting formula before fact.

_____. "A Short Note on Minimalism." *Mississippi Review*, nos. 40/41 (Winter, 1985): 23. In this special issue on minimalism, Abbott argues that minimalists are basically journalists. He claims he is a "sort of mossback prose-writer who prefers stories with all the parts hanging out and whirling." He says he rides with "Wild Bunch" writers, who include John Updike, John Cheever, Peter Taylor, Walker Percy, and Eudora Welty.

_____. "A Stubborn Sense of Place." *Harper's* 273 (August, 1986): 35-45. Abbott argues that a writer's voice--which he says has to do with character, spirit, custom, practice, habit, and morality--is a function of place, because its authority comes from the crossroads at which the writer learned what he or she knows. He says that literary matters, such as voice, are really cultural matters; he insists that language is culture and that in literature ethos is lingo.

Drury, Tom. "All the Wrong Places." Review of *Wet Places at Noon*, by Lee K. Abbott. *The New York Times*, November 16, 1997, p. 78. Drury says that Abbott draws on American cultural standards to create his own mythology. He argues that Abbott's characters ramble, skip ahead, backtrack, string the reader along, and go on and on as if there is no tomorrow. Notes that recklessness and comic futility are persistent themes in Abbott's fiction; says the theme of how stories hold people together, as well as hold them back, is at work in a number of stories, particularly his best, "The Talk Talked Between Worms."

Giraldi, William. "Next Stop Abbottland: The Stories of Lee K. Abbott." *Georgia Review* 61 (Spring, 2007): 69-79. Summary analysis of Abbott's style, character types, and voice. Calls Abbott primarily a comedic writer who delights in the "folly that is man." Compares Abbott's work with that of Barry Hannah, the American writer with whom he most shares a sensibility. Giraldi argues that Abbott has a vision uniquely suited to the short story.

Pope, Dan. "The Post-Minimalist American Story or What Comes After Carver?" *Gettysburg Review* 1 (Spring, 1988): 331-342. Discusses Abbott's *Strangers in Paradise* and *Love Is the Crooked Thing* to show that the minimalist trap can be avoided and that the American short story is diverse and rich. Argues that Abbott is more influenced by John Cheever than Raymond Carver and that, in contrast to the minimalists, Abbott is a wordsmith whose love of the rhythm of language is akin to that of Stanley Elkin and Barry Hannah.

Written and updated by Charles E. May

ALICE ADAMS

Born: Fredericksburg, Virginia; August 14, 1926
Died: San Francisco, California; May 27, 1999

PRINCIPAL SHORT FICTION
Beautiful Girl, 1979
To See You Again, 1982
Molly's Dog, 1983
Return Trips, 1985
After You've Gone, 1989
The Last Lovely City: Stories, 1999
The Stories of Alice Adams, 2002

OTHER LITERARY FORMS

Though Alice Adams was first successful in short fiction, she also published several novels during her lifetime, including *Careless Love* (1966), *Families and Survivors* (1974), *Listening to Billie* (1978), *Rich Rewards* (1980), *Superior Women* (1984), *Second Chances* (1988), *Caroline's Daughters* (1991), *Almost Perfect* (1993), *A Southern Exposure* (1995), and *Medicine Men* (1997); *After the War* was published posthumously in 2000. In addition, her story "Roses, Rhododendrons" has appeared as an illustrated gift book.

ACHIEVEMENTS

Alice Adams did not publish her first collection of stories until she was in her fifties, but she quickly assumed a place among the leading practitioners of the genre. Twenty-two of her stories have appeared in *Prize Stories: The O. Henry Awards.* In 1976, Adams received a grant from the National Endowment for the Arts and, in 1978, she received a John Simon Guggenheim Memorial Foundation Fellowship. In 1982, Adams received the O. Henry Special Award for Continuing Achievement, given for only the third time; her predecessors were Joyce Carol Oates (in 1970) and John Updike (in 1976). She also received the American Academy of Arts and Letters Award in literature in 1992.

BIOGRAPHY

Alice Boyd Adams was born in Fredericksburg, Virginia, on August 14, 1926, the daughter of Nicholson Adams, a professor, and Agatha (née Boyd) Adams, a writer. Shortly after her birth, the family moved to Chapel Hill, North Carolina, where Adams spent her first sixteen years. After receiving her B.A. degree from Radcliffe College in 1946, she married Mark Linenthal, Jr. Two years later, they moved to California, and in 1951, their only child, Peter, was born. Their marriage ended in divorce in 1958, following which Adams held a number of part-time clerical, secretarial, and bookkeeping jobs while rearing her son and writing short stories.

It was not until 1969 that she broke into the magazine market when *The New Yorker* bought her story "Gift of Grass." After that point, her stories continued to appear in *The New Yorker,* as well as *Redbook, McCall's,* and *The Paris Review.* In addition, Adams taught at the University of California at Davis, the University of California at Berkeley, and Stanford University. She died on May 27, 1999, in San Francisco after being treated for heart problems.

ANALYSIS

Most of Alice Adams's stories revolve around common themes, and her characters, mostly educated, upper-middle-class women, are defined by a set of common traits and situations that reappear in somewhat different combinations. They find their lives flawed, often by unhappy relationships with lovers, husbands, parents, and friends, sometimes with combinations of these, usually with a living antagonist, occasionally with one already dead. Often, they resolve these problems, but sometimes they do not.

Frequently, the tensions of Adams's plots are resolved when her central female characters learn something new or find a new source of strength, which enables them to part with unsatisfactory husbands, lovers, or friends. Claire, in "Home Is Where" (in *Beautiful Girl*), leaves both an unsatisfactory marriage and a miserable love affair in San Francisco, where she feels "ugly--drained, discolored, old," to spend the summer with her parents in her North Carolina hometown, where she had been young and "if not beautiful, sought after." Refreshed and stimulated by the sensual landscape and a summertime affair, Claire returns to San Francisco to divorce her husband, take leave of her unpleasant lover, and, eventually, remarry, this time happily. Cynthia, in "The Break-In" (*To See You Again*), finds herself so different from her fiancé Roger, when he automatically blames the burglary of his home on "Mexicans," that she leaves him without a word. The narrator of "True Colors" (*To See You Again*) discovers, in Las Vegas, David's ugly side as an obsessive gambler and leaves him: "From then on I was going to be all right, I thought." Clover Baskerville in "The Party-Givers" (*To See You Again*) leaves behind her malicious friends when she realizes that she need not call them if she does not want to see them. All these characters have learned that "home is where the heart" not only "is" but also chooses to be.

Adams's heroines sometimes reach out from their lonely and isolated lives to find sympathetic bonds with poor or troubled people from other cultures. In "Greyhound People" (*To See You Again*), a divorced, middle-aged woman's discovery of kinship with her (mostly black and poor) fellow commuters, along with her discovery that her commuter ticket will take her anywhere in California, is so liberating that she can finally break free of her repressive, domineering roommate and friend Hortense. In "Verlie I Say unto You" (*Beautiful Girl*), Jessica Todd's sensitivity to her black maid Verlie's humanity underscores a fundamental difference between herself and her insensitive husband (see also "The Break-In" in this regard). In "Mexican Dust" (*To See You Again*), Marian comes to prefer the company of the Mexican peasants to that of her husband, friends, and other Americans as they bus through Mexico on vacation; she abandons her party and

returns to Seattle, where she plans to study Spanish, presumably to prepare for a return to Mexico alone. In fact, one sign of a strong character in Adams's stories is a marked sensitivity to other cultures. Elizabeth, in the story by that name, purchases her Mexican beach house in the name of her Mexican servant Aurelia and leaves Aurelia in full possession of the house at her death. The central focus in "La Señora" (*Return Trips*) is the friendship between a wealthy, elderly American woman, who vacations annually at a Mexican resort, and Teodola, the Mexican maid in charge of her hotel room. Adams's own concern for the human plight of those of other cultures can be seen in "Teresa," in *Return Trips*, a story about the privation, terror, and grief of a Mexican peasant woman.

"MOLLY'S DOG" AND "A PUBLIC POOL"

In two of Adams's most effective stories, female protagonists learn to live confidently with themselves: "Molly's Dog" and "A Public Pool" (both from *Return Trips*). In the former story, Molly returns with her homosexual friend Sandy to a small cabin by the ocean, where she experienced a love affair so intense she cannot think of it without weeping. A friendly dog attaches itself to them on the beach and follows them as they leave; Molly pleads with Sandy to go back for the dog, but he drives faster, and the dog, though running, falls back and shrinks in the distance. Molly and Sandy quarrel over the dog, and Molly, realizing that she is much too dependent on men, comes to see less of Sandy back in San Francisco. She finally learns to think of the dog without pain but cannot forget it, and the place by the ocean becomes in her memory "a place where she had lost, or left something of infinite value. A place to which she would not go back."

In "A Public Pool," the protagonist, though working class, neither part of the literary or artistic world nor so well educated as many of Adams's female characters, shares with many of them a dissatisfaction with her body and a sense of being cut off and alone. She cannot bear to meet people or even look for a job ("We wouldn't even have room for you," she imagines an employer saying), so that life at age thirty is a grim existence in a cold apartment with a penurious mother. Though swimming offers an escape from home and a chance for meeting new people, it also has its fears: of exposing her body in the locker room and enduring the rebukes of strangers, of the faster swimmers whose lane she blocks, of the blond-bearded man who goes by so swiftly that he splashes her, and of a large black woman who tells her that she should stay by the side of the pool.

After a few months of lap swimming, her body changes and her fear of others lessens. An early remark of the blond-bearded man made her babble nervously, but now she responds to his conventional questions with brief assent. On the day the black lady compliments her on her stroke and they leave the pool together, she is finally able to find a job and thinks of moving out of her mother's apartment. She walks happily about the neighborhood, thinking that she and the black woman might become friends. At that moment, she meets in the street the blond-bearded man, who smells of chewing gum and is wearing "sharp" clothes from Sears. He invites her for coffee, but, "overwhelmed" by the smell of gum and realizing that "I hate sharp clothes," she makes her excuses. Like other Adams women, she has felt loneliness, but, also like many other women in these stories, she finds new strength that will mitigate her isolation by giving her independence. However, this strength is primarily achieved by herself, and Adams's always masterful use of language here is especially striking. As Adams's character goes off independently from the blond-bearded man, she says confidently, "I leave him standing there. I swim away."

"YOU ARE WHAT YOU OWN" AND "TO SEE YOU AGAIN"

Not all these stories, however, end so conclusively; in others, it is unclear whether the heroines' chosen resolutions to the problems confronting them will be satisfactory. The young housewife of "You Are What You Own: A Notebook" (*Return Trips*) lives in a house crammed with her domineering mother's furniture, which the girl seems doomed to polish for all eternity. Her boring graduate-student husband complains that she does not polish the furniture enough and even starts to do it himself. She escapes in fantasy, fictionalizing the artists who live in a house down the street from her, assigning them her own names (not knowing their real ones), and indulging in imagined conversations with

them. At the end of the story--recorded in her notebook--she tells her husband in a letter that she is leaving him the furniture and going to look for a job in San Francisco. Does she go? Is she capable? Similarly, the lonely young wife in "To See You Again" uses the image of a beautiful adolescent boy in her class to re-create the image of her husband as he was when they fell in love--slim and energetic, not as he is now, overweight and frequently paralyzed by chronic, severe depression. The story ends with her fantasizing that somehow she has escaped her grim life with him, that things are as they once were, her husband somehow reclaimed in the body of the young student.

"BEAUTIFUL GIRL"

The story plots summarized here raise a possible objection to Adams's fiction--that many of her female characters are too obsessed with the attention of men, even to the point where the women's own highly successful careers seem to matter little. This issue, however, must be placed in historical perspective. Most of the women in her stories, like Adams herself, grew up and entered adulthood during the period after World War II, when women's roles in American society were constricted, when women were sent home from their wartime jobs to take on what then seemed an almost patriotic duty: submitting themselves to the roles of wife and mother. From this point of view, Adams's female characters are victims of that culture, dependent on men and falling desperately in love with them because they were expected to do just that. Given these crushing expectations, it is no wonder that Adams's heroines feel lost when bereft, by divorce or widowhood, of the men in their lives. The young people in these stories often reach out to surrogate parents, usually mothers, when the incredible strain on the postwar nuclear family cracks and splinters it (a character in "Roses, Rhododendrons," in *Beautiful Girl*, says "we all need more than one set of parents--our relations with the original set are too intense, and need dissipating").

Emblematic of the plight of this generation is Ardis Bascombe in "Beautiful Girl," an ironic title because Ardis, though in her youth beautiful and popular, is now fleshy, drinking herself to death in her San Francisco apartment. She has failed as a wife and, as her filthy kitchen attests, failed as a homemaker. She had been independent enough to leave her unhappy marriage, but, like other women of her generation, despite her intelligence, idealism, courage, and sophistication, she was unable to make a new life. The life of this beautiful girl demonstrates graphically the destructive pressures on postwar women.

THE LAST LOVELY CITY

In this, her final collection of stories, Alice Adams also focuses on sophisticated contemporary women dealing with wandering husbands, belligerent children, and the tribulations of being divorced or widowed; however, because Adams was in her late sixties when she wrote most of these stories, her protagonists are older, albeit not always wiser, veterans of the domestic wars of the 1960's and 1970's.

Adams has always been a favorite of the judges of *Prize Stories: The O. Henry Awards*, and three of these stories were chosen for that prestigious collection: "The Islands" in 1993, "The Haunted Beach" in 1995, and "His Women" in 1996. Two of these are among the best stories in the collection, for they economically and without self-indulgence focus on futile efforts to repeat the past. What "haunts" the beach in "The Haunted Beach" is one woman's previous marriage. Penelope Jaspers, a San Francisco art dealer, takes her new lover, a middle-aged superior court judge, to a West Coast Mexican resort that she and her dead husband used to visit. Although she remembers it as charming, she now sees it as "unspeakable shabby" and returns to San Francisco, having decided not to marry the judge.

The persistence of the past also haunts "His Women," as a university professor cannot reconcile with his lover because of memories of the previous women in his life. In the title story, Benito Zamora, a Mexican cardiologist and "sadhearted widow," is forced to dredge up unpleasant moments from his past by an attractive young reporter whom he mistakenly thinks is interested in him sexually. In "Old Love Affairs," a woman's living room is filled with keepsakes that remind her only that she is growing old and can no longer hope for love in her life.

The last four stories in the book-- "The Drinking Club," "Patients," "The Wrong Mexico," and "Earthquake Damage"--are linked stories, somewhat like

chapters of a novella, in which two Bay Area psychiatrists, who are sometimes lovers, move in and out of various affairs. Both are passive professionals, as are many Adams characters--watchers rather than active participants, caught in a recurrent round of unhappy marriages and unfulfilling affairs.

The weakest stories in the collection-- "The Islands," "Raccoons," and "A Very Nice Dog"--are simple paeans to pets. The most interesting, "The Islands," begins with the sentence: "What does it mean to love an animal, a pet, in my case a cat, in the fierce, entire and unambivalent way that some of us do?" Although readers who share such a pet passion might find the question intriguing, many others will view this story about the death of a beloved cat as sentimental rather than sensitive. Although the fact that Adams died at age seventy-two, a few months after this book appeared, gives it some poignancy, on a purely critical level these stories represent a falling off from the crisp and sophisticated stories of the writer in her prime.

OTHER MAJOR WORKS

LONG FICTION: *Careless Love*, 1966; *Families and Survivors*, 1974; *Listening to Billie*, 1978; *Rich Rewards*, 1980; *Superior Women*, 1984; *Second Chances*, 1988; *Caroline's Daughters*, 1991; *Almost Perfect*, 1993; *A Southern Exposure*, 1995; *Medicine Men*, 1997; *After the War*, 2000.

NONFICTION: *Mexico: Some Travels and Some Travelers There*, 1990.

BIBLIOGRAPHY

Adams, Alice. Interview by Patricia Holt. *Publishers Weekly* 213 (January 16, 1978): 8-9. In talking about her life with interior designer Robert McNee, Adams emphasizes the importance of her work as the foundation for the self-respect necessary in a long-term relationship.

Blades, L. T. "Order and Chaos in Alice Adams' *Rich Rewards*." *Critique: Studies in Modern Fiction* 27 (Summer, 1986): 187-195. In an issue devoted to four women writers--Adams, Ann Beattie, Mary Gordon, and Marge Piercy--Blades explores the artificially imposed order created by Adams's female characters and the world of chaos that threatens it. Like Jane Austen's characters, Adams's women enter into unstable relationships but eventually realize that they must concentrate on work and friendships, not romance, to have a healthy self-respect.

Bolotin, Susan. "Semidetached Couples." Review of *The Last Lovely City: Stories. The New York Times*, February 14, 1999. A detailed review of Adams's collection, commenting on several of the stories, particularly the characters and the social world in which they live.

Chell, Cara. "Succeeding in Their Times: Alice Adams on Women and Work." *Soundings* 68 (Spring, 1985): 62-71. Work is the catalyst that enables Adams's characters to realize their self-worth. Chell provides an interesting treatment of this theme throughout Adams's career.

Flower, Dean. "Picking Up the Pieces." *The Hudson Review* 32 (Summer, 1979): 293-307. Flower sets Adams among other American storytellers who look to the past for explanations and intensification of feelings. He explores how this orientation leads to a preoccupation with growing old.

Gelfant, Blanche H., ed. *The Columbia Companion to the Twentieth-Century American Short Story*. New York: Columbia University Press, 2000. Includes a chapter in which Adams's short stories are analyzed.

Herman, Barbara A. "Alice Adams." In *Contemporary Fiction Writers of the South*, edited by Joseph M. Flora and Robert Bain. Westport, Conn.: Greenwood, 1993. A brief biography and discussion of Adams's novels and short stories. Suggests her two major themes are the maturation of middle-class women seeking self-respect, identity, and independence and women's relationships with husbands, lovers, and friends. Includes a survey of Adams's criticism and a bibliography of works by and about her.

Navratil, Chris. "Writer by the Bay: Alice Adams's Collected Stories Prove Her a Keen Observer of Class, Character, and West Coast Culture." *Boston Globe*, December 29, 2002, p. D8. Navratil reviews a posthumously published collection of fifty-three short stories, praising Adams's ability to "quickly and seamlessly" convey characterization, social class, and the cultural, as well as the physical, landscape. Describes how Adams explores "life's quiet disappointments" in "minute detail."

Papinchak, Robert Allen. "The Building Blocks of a Modern Short-Story Master: Alice Adams." *Writer* 120, no. 6 (June, 2007): 26-27. Papinchak demonstrates how to outline a short story based on his discussion with Adams, who insisted she needed to outline her stories in order to"know where she was going." Includes a brief analysis of "To See You Again."

Pritchard, William H. "Fictive Voices." *The Hudson Review* 38 (Spring, 1985): 120-132. Pritchard examines Adams's narrative voice in the context of other contemporary writers. Though the section on Adams is not long, it provides a useful approach to analyzing her stories.

Upton, Lee. "Changing the Past: Alice Adams' Revisionary Nostalgia." *Studies in Short Fiction* 26 (Winter, 1989): 33-41. In the collection of stories *Return Trips*, Adams's female characters turn to memories of the past as their most valued possessions. Upton isolates three different relationships with the past and shows how each enables Adams's characters to interpret nostalgic images so they can produce more satisfying relationships with the present.

Woo, Elaine. "Alice Adams." *Los Angeles Times*, May 29, 1999, p. B8. Biographical and critical sketch and tribute. Notes Adams's specialization in contemporary relationships among white, urban, middle- and upper-class females. Charts her career and her critical reception.

Timothy C. Frazer
Updated by Louise M. Stone and Charles E. May

JAMES AGEE

Born: Knoxville, Tennessee; November 27, 1909
Died: New York, New York; May 16, 1955

PRINCIPAL SHORT FICTION

"A Mother's Tale," 1952
Four Early Stories by James Agee, 1964
The Collected Short Prose of James Agee, 1968
    (Robert Fitzgerald, editor)

OTHER LITERARY FORMS

James Agee (AY-jee) is best known for his posthumous novel *A Death in the Family* (1957) and his collection of essays *Let Us Now Praise Famous Men* (1941). He wrote the screenplays for *The Red Badge of Courage* (1951), *The African Queen* (1952), *The Bride Comes to Yellow Sky* (1952), and several other films.

ACHIEVEMENTS

James Agee's greatest literary achievement is his posthumous novel *A Death in the Family*, of which 194 handwritten pages, along with 114 pages of working notes, were completed before his death in 1955. The novel was awarded the Pulitzer Prize in 1958. His collection of essays, *Let Us Now Praise Famous Men*, which included photographs by Walker Evans and has since come to be regarded as a highly perceptive work about tenant farmers, received little notice immediately after its publication because Americans were preoccupied with World War II. In 1949, Agee won an American Academy of Arts and Letters Award, and, in 1952, his screenplay for *The African Queen* was nominated for an Academy Award.

BIOGRAPHY

A defining moment in the life of James Rufus Agee occurred in May, 1916, when his father, Hugh James Agee, was killed in an automobile accident.

Hugh's widow, Laura Tyler Agee, recited the details of the accident so often that her children, James and Emma, could repeat them verbatim. These are the details that Agee employed successfully in his most celebrated work, the novel entitled *A Death in the Family*.

In 1919, Laura moved her family to Sewanee, Tennessee, where James attended St. Andrew's Episcopal School, there developing a lifelong friendship with Father James Harold Flye. Agee cycled through Europe with Flye and his wife in 1925 before entering Phillips Exeter Academy, where, as editor of the *Phillips Exeter Monthly*, he gained editorial experience that proved invaluable to him during his seven years as a reporter for *Fortune*. Agee also published some of his earliest writing in the *Phillips Exeter Monthly*.

Continuing his education at Harvard University, from which he was graduated in 1932, Agee worked during the Great Depression as a journalist. Between 1942 and 1948, Agee, starstruck since childhood, wrote the film column for *The Nation*. In 1949 and 1950, he contributed several long film essays on Charlie Chaplin, D. W. Griffith, and John Huston to *Life* magazine. This experience was the catapult he needed to embark on a career of writing screenplays. A consistently productive writer, Agee was most successful when he wrote autobiographically oriented fiction. His novella *The Morning Watch* (1951) recounts a young boy's religious experience in the chapel of a boys' school much like St. Andrew's. His early sketch "Knoxville: Summer of 1915" (1936) recounts the innocent days in the year before his father's death and serves as a prelude to *A Death in the Family*. Suffering for several years from heart trouble, Agee died at age forty-five in a New York City taxicab on his way to his doctor's office. His greatest popular recognition followed his death.

ANALYSIS

Despite his prolonged absence from the South after 1925, James Agee had internalized the details of the area and its people well enough to write about them with exceptional conviction and authenticity. In some of his earliest short prose pieces, such as "Minerva Farmer" (1925), he uses Knoxville, in this case the University of Tennessee, as a backdrop. "A Sentimental Journey" (1928) recounts details about the life of a young widow not unlike his mother, whose marriage had been frowned on by her socially prominent family. "Bound for the Promised Land" (1928) recounts an African American funeral in Tennessee.

In his later work, Agee sometimes writes outside his southern milieu, but he is most convincing in the loosely autobiographical mode that often characterizes his work. His best writing is based on facts that he modifies and embellishes to suit his artistic objectives. The resulting stories, such as the posthumously published "Dream Sequence" (1968), focus on characters who have figured in Agee's life, but he imbues them with a universality, creating archetypes that represent concepts stretching far beyond the narrow geographical range in which his stories take place.

In his novella *The Morning Watch*, Richard, the protagonist, at times is reminiscent of one of James Joyce's protagonists. Agee reveals Richard's subconscious in such a way as to make the reader question whether the twelve-year-old's peak of religious fervor and spiritual insight will last. A master of subtle suggestion, Agee hints that it will not.

Agee brought to his prose poetic qualities that elevated it above the ordinary events about which he wrote. Almost magically, he transformed the commonplace into the extraordinary. His comments about modern society and the inroads it makes on individuality, reflected especially in *Let Us Now Praise Famous Men* and *The Morning Watch*, combine with his preoccupation with innocence and death, as seen so clearly in "Knoxville: Summer of 1915," to produce a body of work unique in modern American literature.

THE COLLECTED SHORT PROSE OF JAMES AGEE

This collection, edited by Robert Fitzgerald, who starts the volume with an extensive memoir, presents four finished pieces of short fiction in the sections "Early

James Agee (Library of Congress)

Stories" and "Satiric Pieces," along with four fragments and other miscellaneous items. Among the last group, "A Mother's Tale" (1952), a fable, is most interesting. "Death in the Desert" (1930) is reprinted from *The Harvard Advocate*, in which it first appeared during Agee's junior year at Harvard. In the following year, *The Harvard Advocate* published "They That Sow in Sorrow Shall Reap" (1931). The satiric pieces include "Formletter 7G3" (1934), previously unpublished, and "Dedication Day" (1946). The fragments, undated but likely written in the early 1930's, include "Run Over," "Give Him Air," "Now as Awareness . . . ," and "A Birthday." Each of these pieces is incomplete and brief, seldom occupying more than two pages.

The stories as a whole reveal an author bent on creating believable characters that suggest archetypes. This is particularly true in the allegorical "A Mother's Tale." Agee is very much concerned with the functioning of the subconscious mind, as demonstrated notably in "Death in the Desert." The seeds of his novel *A Death in the Family* and his novella *The Night Watch* are also found in these early stories.

"KNOXVILLE"

This story, found in the opening pages of *A Death in the Family*, as a prelude to the novel, overflows with innocence and nostalgia. Its protagonist reflects on the last summer of his father's life, soon cut short by an automobile accident. The boy Rufus, through whose eyes the story is told, looks back to a time when his life was secure and comfortable, a time when his father, as is shown in the beginning of *A Death in the Family*, would take his family to an evening's picture show. The tone reminds one of the poet Robert Browning's lines, "God's in his heaven--/ All's right with the world."

Such complacency, however, is not to last. Although this story in itself does not allude to the impending accident that will kill Rufus's father, readers are soon aware that the equilibrium marking the lives of Rufus and his family is about to be disturbed. Included in the original version of the story, which was written in 1936, long before Agee began work on *A Death in the Family*, is a segment that was eventually removed and became a separate entity entitled "Dream Sequence," first published in 1968, thirteen years after Agee's death.

"DREAM SEQUENCE"

"Dream Sequence" begins with a nightmare about a writer who is compelled to write an autobiographical novel in order to sort out his feelings and end the torment of the nightmare, which is based upon a horrible, terrifying event. Whereas in "Knoxville: Summer of 1915" the author returns to his childhood memories and gains a degree of peace by that return, the protagonist in "Dream Sequence" has yet to come to grips with what troubles him and preoccupies his subconscious mind.

When Rufus and his father are brought together in Rufus's dream, the atmosphere of the story changes drastically, and peace descends on the troubled boy. Agee is writing about the inevitability of death while celebrating, simultaneously, the joys of living. He finally brings the two opposites, life and death, into harmony, suggesting that one is the natural outcome of the other.

This story seems in some ways a more valid introduction to *A Death in the Family* than was "Knoxville: Summer of 1915." Rufus's isolation and loneliness pervade much of "Dream Sequence," although the story is resolved quietly and peacefully when the nightmare is finally exorcized.

"DEATH IN THE DESERT"

Written while he was a student at Harvard and first published in *The Harvard Advocate* in 1930, this story might have come directly from the experience of Agee or someone like him: a young man who hits the road for the summer, hitchhiking across a daunting expanse of desert. The young man, on his way to Maine, is picked up by an Oklahoma couple in a five- or six-year-old Buick. He gets into the back seat beside their sleeping son.

As the trip progresses and the characters begin to exhaust their store of things to talk about, the protagonist lapses into a stream-of-consciousness mode. He mentally undresses his hosts, imagining them as skeletons propelling the Buick across the lonely desert. Midway into their journey, they see a desperate African American man stranded in the middle of the desert, facing possible death if he does not get a ride. They pass him by, all of them in their own ways justifying the decision not to pick him up. The social complexities of this situation intrigue Agee and provide his story with the kind of dilemma that forces his readers to wrestle with the ideas he puts before them.

OTHER MAJOR WORKS

LONG FICTION: *The Morning Watch*, 1951; *A Death in the Family*, 1957.

SCREENPLAYS: *The Red Badge of Courage*, 1951 (based on Stephen Crane's novel); *The African Queen*, 1952 (based on C. S. Forester's novel); *The Bride Comes to Yellow Sky*, 1952 (based on Crane's short story); *Noa Noa*, 1953; *White Mane*, 1953; *Green Magic*, 1955; *The Night of the Hunter*, 1955; *Agee on Film: Five Film Scripts*, 1960.

POETRY: *Permit Me Voyage*, 1934; *The Collected Poems of James Agee*, 1968; *Selected Poems*, 2008 (Andrew Hudgins, editor).

NONFICTION: *Let Us Now Praise Famous Men*, 1941 (with photography by Walker Evans); *Agee on Film: Reviews and Comments*, 1958; *Letters of James Agee to Father Flye*, 1962; *James Agee: Selected Journalism*, 1985; *Brooklyn Is: Southeast of the Island, Travel Notes*, 2005 (wr. 1939).

BIBLIOGRAPHY

Bergreen, Laurence. *James Agee: A Life*. New York: E. P. Dutton, 1984. This is one of the best biographies of Agee, thorough and well researched. Its critical analyses are cogent and thoughtful, and Bergreen's writing style is appealing.

Davis, Hugh. *The Making of James Agee*. Knoxville: University of Tennessee Press, 2008. An analysis of Agee's literary career, demonstrating how he expressed his interrelated concerns throughout his work. Discusses the political nature of Agee's writing and his debt to various sources, particularly to European Surrealism.

Kramer, Victor A. *Agee and Actuality: Artistic Vision in His Work*. Troy, N.Y.: Whitston, 1991. Kramer delves into the aesthetics of Agee's writing. This study is valuable for identifying controlling themes that pervade Agee's writing.

_____. *James Agee*. Boston: Twayne, 1975. Although this well-written book is now dated, it remains one of the more valuable sources available to the general reader, useful for its analyses, its bibliography, and its chronology of Agee's life.

Lofaro, Michael A., ed. *Agee Agonistes: Essays on the Life, Legend, and Works of James Agee*. Knoxville: University of Tennessee Press, 2007. Compilation of seventeen essays from the James Agee Celebration, which was held at the University of Tennessee in April, 2005. The essays are divided into four parts, addressing Agee's influences and syntheses, Agee's films, his literature, and his correspondence.

Includes new photographs, previously unknown correspondence, and a remembrance by Agee's daughter.

_____. *James Agee: Reconsiderations*. Knoxville: University of Tennessee Press, 1992. The nine essays in this slim volume are carefully considered. Mary Moss's bibliography of secondary sources is especially well crafted and eminently useful, as are penetrating essays by Linda Wagner-Martin and Victor A. Kramer.

Madden, David, and Jeffrey J. Folks, eds. *Remembering James Agee*. 2d ed. Athens: University of Georgia Press, 1979. The twenty-two essays in this book touch on every important aspect of Agee's life and work. They range from the reminiscences of Father Flye to those of his third wife, Mia Agee. The interpretive essays on his fiction and films are particularly illuminating, as are the essays on his life as a reporter and writer for *Fortune* and *Time*.

Spiegel, Alan. *James Agee and the Legend of Himself*. Columbia: University of Missouri Press, 1998. In this critical study of Agee's writing, Spiegel offers especially sound insights into the role that childhood reminiscence plays in Agee's fiction and into the uses that Agee makes of nostalgia. The hundred pages on *Let Us Now Praise Famous Men* represent one of the best interpretations of this important early work. Teachers will appreciate the section entitled "Agee in the Classroom."

Valiunas, Algis. "What James Agee Achieved." *Commentary* 121, no. 2 (February, 2006): 49-53. Written after the Library of America published two volumes of Agee's work. Focuses on Agee's achievements as a writer, providing an overview of his life and describing how his literary reputation was restored after his death.

R. Baird Shuman.

CONRAD AIKEN

Born: Savannah, Georgia; August 5, 1889
Died: Savannah, Georgia; August 17, 1973
Also known as: Samuel Jeake, Jr.

PRINCIPAL SHORT FICTION
The Dark City, 1922
Bring! Bring!, and Other Stories, 1925
Costumes by Eros, 1928
"Silent Snow, Secret Snow," 1932
Impulse, 1933
Among the Lost People, 1934
"Round by Round," 1935
Short Stories, 1950
Collected Short Stories, 1960
Collected Short Stories of Conrad Aiken, 1966

OTHER LITERARY FORMS

Best-known as a poet, Conrad Aiken (AY-kuhn) published dozens of volumes of poetry from 1914 until his death in 1973. He also published novels, essays, criticism, and a play. In addition, he edited a considerable number of anthologies of poetry.

ACHIEVEMENTS

Conrad Aiken's reputation as a writer of short fiction rests on two frequently anthologized short stories: "Silent Snow, Secret Snow," which has twice been adapted to film, and "Mr. Arcularis," which was adapted to a play. Although he published several collections of short stories--they were collected in one volume in 1950--he did not contribute significantly to the development of the short story. Instead, the fictional "voice" so closely approximates Aiken's poetic "voice" that the stories are often seen as extensions of his more famous poems. Both are "poetic" expressions of characters' psychological states. "Silent Snow, Secret Snow," in fact, is often read as the story of a creative

artist, a "poet" in a hostile environment. Aiken's Freudian themes, his depiction of a protagonist's inner struggle and journey, and his portrait of the consciousness--these are perhaps better expressed in lengthy poetic works than in prose or in individual poems, which are rarely anthologized because they are best read in the context of his other poems.

BIOGRAPHY

When Conrad Potter Aiken was eleven, his father killed his mother and then committed suicide. This incident could very well have influenced the subject matter of a great number of his stories, where one step more may take a character to an immense abyss of madness or death. Graduating from Harvard University in 1911, Aiken became a member of the famous Harvard group that included T. S. Eliot, Robert Benchley, and Van Wyck Brooks. He published his first volume of poems in 1914. A contributing editor of *The Dial* from 1917 to 1919, Aiken later worked as London correspondent for *The New Yorker*. Through the course of his career he was the recipient of many awards, including the Pulitzer Prize in 1930 for *Selected Poems* (1929), the National Book Award in 1954 for *Collected Poems* (1953), and the Bollingen Prize in Poetry in 1956. He died in 1973 at the age of eighty-four.

ANALYSIS
"SILENT SNOW, SECRET SNOW"

In "Silent Snow, Secret Snow," a story once included in almost every anthology of short fiction, Conrad Aiken describes a young boy's alienation and withdrawal from his world. The story begins one morning in December when Paul Hasleman, aged twelve, thinks of the postman, whom the boy hears every morning. The progress of the postman as he turns the corner at the top of the hill and makes his way down the street with a double knock at each door is familiar to the boy, and, as he slowly awakens, he begins to listen for the sounds on the cobblestones of the street of heavy boots as they come around the corner. When he hears the sounds this morning, however, they are closer than the corner and muffled and faint. Paul understands at once: "Nothing could have been simpler--there had been snow during the night, such as all winter he had been longing for." With his eyes still closed, Paul imagines the snow--how it sounds and how it will obliterate the familiar sights of the street--but when he opens his eyes and turns toward the window, he sees only the bright morning sun. The miracle of snow has not transformed anything.

The moment and his feelings about the snow, however, remain with him, and later in the classroom as his geography teacher, Miss Buell, twirls the globe with her finger and talks about the tropics, Paul finds himself looking at the arctic areas, which are colored white on the globe. He recalls the morning and the moment when he had a sense of falling snow, and immediately he undergoes the same experience of seeing and hearing the snow fall.

Conrad Aiken (Library of Congress)

As the days go by, Paul finds himself between two worlds--the real one and a secret one of peace and remoteness. His parents become increasingly concerned by his "daydreaming," inattentive manner, but more and more he is drawn into the incomprehensible beauty of the world of silent snow. His secret sense of possession and of being protected insulates him both from the world of the classroom where Deidre, with the freckles on the back of her neck in a constellation exactly like the Big Dipper, waves her brown flickering hand, and from the world at home where his parents' concern and questions have become an increasingly difficult matter with which to cope.

Aiken's presentation of the escalation of Paul's withdrawal is skillfully detailed through the use of symbols. The outside world becomes for Paul fragmented: scraps of dirty newspapers in a drain, with the word Eczema as the addressee and an address in Fort Worth, Texas; lost twigs from parent trees; bits of broken egg shells; the footprints of a dog who long ago "had made a mistake" and walked on the river of wet cement which in time had frozen into rock; the wound in an elm tree. In the company of his parents Paul neither sees them nor feels their presence. His mother is a voice asking questions, his father a pair of brown slippers. These images cluster together in such a way as to foreshadow the inevitable and relentless progress of Dr. Howells down the street to Paul's house, a visit that replicates the progress of the postman.

The doctor, called by the parents because their concern has now grown into alarm over Paul's behavior, examines the boy, and, as the examination and questioning by the adults accelerate, Paul finds the situation unbearable. He retreats further into his secret world where he sees snow now slowly filling the spaces in the room--highest in the corners, under the sofa--the snow's voice a whisper, a promise of peace, cold and restful. Reassured by the presence of the snow and seduced by its whisperings and promises, Paul begins to laugh and to taunt the adults with little hints. He believes they are trying to corner him, and there is something malicious in his behavior:

> He laughed a third time--but this time, happening to
> glance upward toward his mother's face, he was ap-
> palled at the effect his laughter seemed to have upon

her. Her mouth had opened in an expression of horror. This was too bad! Unfortunate! He had known it would cause pain, of course--but he hadn't expected it to be quite as bad as this. . . .

The hints, however, explain nothing to the adults, and, continuing to feel cornered, Paul pleads a headache and tries to escape to bed. His mother follows him, but it is too late. "The darkness was coming in long white waves," and "the snow was laughing; it spoke from all sides at once." His mother's presence in the room is alien, hostile, and brutal. He is filled with loathing, and he exorcizes her: "Mother! Mother! Go away! I hate you!" With this effort, everything is solved, "everything became all right." His withdrawal is now complete. All contact with the real world is lost, and he gives himself over to a "vast moving screen of snow--but even now it said peace, it said remoteness, it said cold, it said sleep." Paul's withdrawal is, as the snow tells him, a going inward rather than an opening outward: "It is a flower becoming a seed," it is a movement toward complete solipsism and a closure of his life.

"STRANGE MOONLIGHT"

"Strange Moonlight," another story of a young boy's difficulty in dealing with the realities of life and death, could be a prelude to "Silent Snow, Secret Snow." In "Strange Moonlight" a young boy filches a copy of Edgar Allan Poe's tales from his mother's bookshelf and in consequence spends a "delirious night in inferno." The next day the boy wins a gold medal at school that he later carries in his pocket, keeping it a secret from his mother and father. The desire to keep a secret recalls Paul's need to keep from his parents his first hallucination of snow. The gold medal is "above all a secret," something to be kept concealed; it is like a particularly beautiful trinket to be carried unmentioned in his trouser pocket.

The week's events include a visit to a friend's house where the boy meets Caroline Lee, an extraordinarily strange and beautiful child with large pale eyes. Both Caroline Lee and the house in which she lives with its long, dark, and winding stairways excite and fascinate him. Within a few days, however, the boy learns that Caroline Lee is dead of scarlet fever. He is stunned: "How did it happen that he, who was so profoundly

concerned, had not been consulted, had not been invited to come and talk with her, and now found himself so utterly and hopelessly and forever excluded--from the house as from her?" This becomes a thing he cannot understand.

The same night he is confronted with another disturbing mystery. He overhears an intimate conversation between his father and mother. Filled with horror, the boy begins at once to imagine a conversation with Caroline Lee in which she comes back from the grave to talk with him. The next day his father unexpectedly takes the family to the beach, and the boy wanders away and finds a snug, secret hiding place on a lonely hot sand dune. He lies there surrounded by tall whispering grass, and Caroline's imagined visit of the night before becomes real for him. Rather than ending in unreality as one would expect, however, Aiken inexplicably brings the boy back to reality without resolving any of the problems set up in the story. He thus leaves a gap between the protagonist's conflicts with sexuality, reality, and unreality, and their final resolution.

"YOUR OBITUARY, WELL WRITTEN"

In another story, however, "Your Obituary, Well Written," Aiken presents a young man identified only as Mr. Grant who confronts a similar circumstance. Told in the first person by the protagonist, Mr. Grant, the story repeats what is basically the same pattern of events. Although supposedly a portrait of writer Katherine Mansfield, to whom Aiken is strongly indebted for the forms his stories take, the character of Reiner Wilson is also strongly reminiscent of Caroline Lee, the little girl in "Strange Moonlight." The narrator says of Reiner Wilson: "I was struck by the astonishing frailty of her appearance, an otherworld fragility, almost a transparent spiritual quality--as if she were already a disembodied soul." Knowing from the first that she is not only married but also fatally ill, he manages to see her one time and fall in love with her, and then he almost simultaneously withdraws. "At bottom, however, it was a kind of terror that kept me away. . . . The complications and the miseries, if we did allow the meetings to go further might well be fatal to both of us."

The same conflicts that Paul, the child in "Silent Snow, Secret Snow," experienced are again faced by the man who is not able to resolve the riddles of sex and love, life and death. The narrator never sees Reiner again, and at her death he is left on a park bench under a Judas tree wanting to weep, but unable to: "But Reiner Wilson, the dark-haired little girl with whom I had fallen in love was dead, and it seemed to me that I too was dead." Another similarity between "Silent Snow, Secret Snow" and "Your Obituary, Well Written" is Aiken's use of a natural element as major metaphor. In "Your Obituary, Well Written," rain functions in the same manner as snow does in "Silent Snow, Secret Snow." During Grant's one meeting alone with Reiner Wilson, the room had suddenly darkened, and rain fell, sounding to him as though it were inside the room. The sensations the man feels in response to the rain are similar to those Paul feels in response to the snow. Grant tells Reiner about a time when as a boy he went swimming and it began to rain:

> The water was smooth--there was no sound of waves--and all about me arose a delicious *seething* . . . [T]here was something sinister in it, and also something divinely soothing. I don't believe I was ever happier in my life. It was as if I had gone into another world.

Reiner calls Grant "the man who loves rain," and her estimate of him is correct. Unable to open up himself, unable to make himself vulnerable and live in the real world, he is at the end of the story as withdrawn from reality as is Paul, who chooses the silent and secret snow.

"THISTLEDOWN"

Besides dealing with various subconscious desires projected by means of hallucinating visions, many of Aiken's stories reflect the preoccupations of the times in which the stories were written. Chief among these themes is the changing roles of women and sexual mores of the 1920's. In most of Aiken's stories, these conflicts are presented through the male point of view.

"Thistledown," a first-person narrative told by a man who is married and living with his wife, opens with the private musings of the narrator, wherein he associates a young woman named Coralyn with thistledown, which is being swept in every direction by the

wind but which is ultimately doomed for extinction. Coralyn had been his wife's secretary, and, attracted to her, Phillip, the narrator, became bent on seduction. Far from being "frighteningly unworldly," Coralyn is a "new woman" who has had numerous lovers. He finds her cynical and detached, she finds him an old-fashioned and sentimental fool. The affair is brief. Coralyn leaves, and as the years pass she is in and out of his life, until she disappears altogether, leaving him bitter, disappointed, and angry. The irony that marks "Thistledown" is characteristic of the stories in which Aiken examines the conventional sexual mores, holding a double-faced mirror to reflect the double standard by which men and women are judged.

"A CONVERSATION"

In "A Conversation," this theme of double standards is examined within the framework of a conversation between two men, probably professors, taking place on a train in a sleeping car. The conversation is overheard by a visiting lecturer at the university who occupies the adjacent sleeping car. The lecturer is tired of "being polite to fools" and wants desperately to go to sleep; but the conversation he overhears keeps him awake, as do clock bells that ring marking every quarter hour. The conversation concerns the fiancé of one of the men, and the other is trying to convince his friend that the woman is not as innocent as she looks; indeed, she has been "manhandled." The engaged man keeps trying to protect his own views of the woman: her central idealism, her essential holiness--views that attach themselves to women who are not prostitutes. By the end of the story, however, the point is made; the engagement will not last, and the woman will be put aside like a used razor or a cork that has been tampered with, images used earlier in the story. The clock bells do not ask a question; they simply continue to toll. In the end, the men cannot accept a female sexuality that is not exclusively directed toward a husband although there is never a question about their own sexual behavior.

OTHER MAJOR WORKS

LONG FICTION: *Blue Voyage*, 1927; *Great Circle*, 1933; *King Coffin*, 1935; *A Heart for the Gods of Mexico*, 1939; *Conversation: Or, Pilgrim's Progress*, 1940; *The Collected Novels of Conrad Aiken*, 1964.

PLAYS: *Fear No More*, 1946, pb. 1957 (as *Mr. Arcularis: A Play*).

POETRY: *Earth Triumphant, and Other Tales in Verse*, 1914; *The Jig of Forslin*, 1916; *Turns and Movies, and Other Tales in Verse*, 1916; *Nocturne of Remembered Spring, and Other Poems*, 1917; *Senlin: A Biography, and Other Poems*, 1918; *The Charnel Rose*, 1918; *The House of Dust*, 1920; *Punch: The Immortal Liar*, 1921; *Priapus and the Pool*, 1922; *The Pilgrimage of Festus*, 1923; *Changing Mind*, 1925; *Priapus and the Pool, and Other Poems*, 1925; *Prelude*, 1929; *Selected Poems*, 1929; *Gehenna*, 1930; *John Deth: A Metaphysical Legend, and Other Poems*, 1930; *Preludes for Memnon*, 1931; *The Coming Forth by Day of Osiris Jones*, 1931; *And in the Hanging Gardens*, 1933; *Landscape West of Eden*, 1934; *Time in the Rock: Preludes to Definition*, 1936; *And in the Human Heart*, 1940; *Brownstone Eclogues, and Other Poems*, 1942; *The Soldier: A Poem by Conrad Aiken*, 1944; *The Kid*, 1947; *Skylight One: Fifteen Poems*, 1949; *The Divine Pilgrim*, 1949; *Wake II*, 1952; *Collected Poems*, 1953, 1970; *A Letter from Li Po, and Other Poems*, 1955; *The Fluteplayer*, 1956; *Sheepfold Hill: Fifteen Poems*, 1958; *Selected Poems*, 1961; *The Morning Song of Lord Zero*, 1963; *A Seizure of Limericks*, 1964; *Cats and Bats and Things with Wings*, 1965; *The Clerk's Journal*, 1971; *A Little Who's Zoo of Mild Animals*, 1977.

NONFICTION: *Skepticisms: Notes on Contemporary Poetry*, 1919; *Ushant: An Essay*, 1952; *A Reviewer's ABC: Collected Criticism of Conrad Aiken from 1916 to the Present*, 1958; *Selected Letters of Conrad Aiken*, 1978 (Joseph Killorin, editor).

EDITED TEXTS: *A Comprehensive Anthology of American Poetry*, 1929, 1944; *Twentieth Century American Poetry*, 1944.

BIBLIOGRAPHY

Aiken, Conrad. *Selected Letters of Conrad Aiken.* Edited by Joseph Killorin. New Haven, Conn.: Yale University Press, 1978. Killorin includes a representative sample of 245 letters (from some three thousand) written by Aiken. A cast of correspondents, among them T. S. Eliot and Malcolm Lowry, indexes to Aiken's works and important personages, and a wealth of illustrations, mostly photographs, add considerably to the value of the volume.

Butscher, Edward. *Conrad Aiken: Poet of White Horse Vale.* Athens: University of Georgia Press, 1988. This critical biography emphasizes Aiken's literary work, particularly the poetry. Butscher's book nevertheless contains analyses of about fifteen Aiken short stories, including his most famous ones, "Silent Snow, Secret Snow" and "Mr. Arcularis." Includes many illustrations, copious notes, and an extensive bibliography that is especially helpful in psychoanalytic theory.

Dirda, Michael. "Selected Letters of Conrad Aiken." *The Washington Post*, June 25, 1978, p. G5. A review of Aiken's *Selected Letters*, with a brief biographical sketch. Suggests that the letters will help redress the neglect Aiken has suffered.

Hoffman, Frederick J. *Conrad Aiken.* New York: Twayne, 1962. The best overview of Aiken's short fiction. Hoffman's volume contains careful analyses of several individual stories, including "Mr. Arcularis," which receives extensive discussion. Hoffman, who believes Aiken's short stories are more successful than his novels, stresses Aiken's attitude toward New England, his obsession with "aloneness," and his concern about human relationships. Contains a chronology, a biographical chapter, and an annotated bibliography.

Lorenz, Clarissa M. *Lorelei Two: My Life with Conrad Aiken.* Athens: University of Georgia Press, 1983. Lorenz, Aiken's second wife, discusses the years 1926-1938, the period when he wrote his best work, including the short stories "Mr. Arcularis" and "Silent Snow, Secret Snow." She covers his literary acquaintances, his work habits, and the literary context in which he worked. The book is well indexed and contains several relevant photographs.

Seigal, Catharine. *The Fictive World of Conrad Aiken: A Celebration of Consciousness.* De Kalb: Northern Illinois University Press, 1993. Includes chapters on the Freudian foundation of Aiken's fiction, on his New England roots, and on many of his novels. The concluding chapters cover Aiken's autobiography, *Ushant*, and an overview of his fiction. Includes notes, selected bibliography, and index.

Spivey, Ted R. *Time's Stop in Savannah: Conrad Aiken's Inner Journey.* Macon, Ga.: Mercer University Press, 1997. Explores Aiken's thought processes and how they translate to his fiction.

Spivey, Ted R., and Arthur Waterman, eds. *Conrad Aiken: A Priest of Consciousness.* New York: AMS Press, 1989. Though their focus is on Aiken's poetry, Spivey and Waterman include essays on the short stories and a review of criticism of the short stories. Contains an extensive chronology of Aiken's life and a lengthy description of the Aiken materials in the Huntington Library.

Womack, Kenneth. "Unmasking Another Villain in Conrad Aiken's Autobiographical Dream." *Biography* 19 (Spring, 1996): 137. Examines the role of British poet and novelist Martin Armstrong as a fictionalized character in Aiken's *Ushant.* Argues that Aiken's attack on Armstrong is motivated by revenge for Armstrong's marriage to Aiken's first wife.

Mary Rohrberger
Updated by Thomas L. Erskine

THOMAS BAILEY ALDRICH

Born: Portsmouth, New Hampshire; November 11, 1836
Died: Boston, Massachusetts; March 19, 1907

PRINCIPAL SHORT FICTION

Out of His Head: A Romance, 1862
Marjorie Daw, and Other People, 1873
Two Bites at a Cherry, with Other Tales, 1893
A Sea Turn and Other Matters, 1902

OTHER LITERARY FORMS

In addition to short stories, Thomas Bailey Aldrich wrote poems, essays, and novels. His best-known novel is *The Story of a Bad Boy* (1869). He was one of the most prominent men of letters in America in the 1880's, serving as editor of the prestigious *Atlantic Monthly* from 1881 to 1890.

ACHIEVEMENTS

A great popular success during his lifetime, with his collected poems being published in a highly respected series while he was still in his late twenties, Thomas Bailey Aldrich was one of the most influential editors and men of letters of late nineteenth century America. His short story "Marjorie Daw" was one of the most famous stories of his era, earning him an international reputation.

BIOGRAPHY

Born in Portsmouth, New Hampshire, on November 11, 1836, Thomas Bailey Aldrich spent his early years in New York City and New Orleans. Although he returned to Portsmouth in 1849 to prepare for Harvard University, the death of his father made it necessary for him to go to work as a clerk for his uncle in New York instead. During this period, he wrote poetry, became a member of a group of writers that included Walt Whitman, and took a job as a reporter for the *Home Journal.* The popularity of his sentimental verse, "The Ballad of Babie Bell" (1854), encouraged him to quit his clerkship and to devote himself to writing full time.

Aldrich got a job as a literary critic for the *Evening Mirror* in 1855, after which he was soon made an editor. He lived in New York for ten years and was part of a bohemian literary circle that centered on the aestheticism of Fitz-James O'Brien. He was invited to Boston after the publication of his popular collection *Marjorie Daw and Other People* in 1873 to assume the editorship of *Every Saturday*, which reprinted European fiction and poetry for American audiences.

Aldrich published a number of stories and poems in *The Atlantic Monthly*, including his widely popular story "Marjorie Daw," and eventually succeeded William Dean Howells as its editor in 1881, a position he held until 1890. In the last years of his life, he traveled and wrote travel literature, sketches, poems, and short prose. He died in Boston on March 19, 1907.

ANALYSIS

Thomas Bailey Aldrich is primarily remembered in literary histories because of the effect of one story; however, that one story, "Marjorie Daw," like those of other "one-story" writers--such as Frank Stockton, who wrote "The Lady or the Tiger," and Shirley Jackson, who wrote "The Lottery"--brilliantly manages to exploit a basic human fascination with the blurring of fiction and reality. Often called a masterpiece of its type, "Marjorie Daw" clearly epitomizes the kind of story that O. Henry popularized more than half a century later--a story that seduces the reader into believing that a purely fictional creation is actually reality, only to reveal the ruse in a striking surprise reversal at the end.

Aldrich's remaining stories, like much of his vers de société, are lightweight and romantic. Generally, they are witty and amusing sketches and tales that do not pretend to have any submerged meaning or symbolic significance. They are so unremarkable, in fact, that Aldrich's restrained and self-consciously literary creation of "Marjorie Daw" seems like a fortunate inspirational accident. It is so well crafted, so controlled, and so aware of itself as a self-reflexive play with the basic nature of fiction that it will always remain a favorite anthology piece to represent the surprise-ending story so widely popular during the last half of the nineteenth century.

"MARJORIE DAW"

This story achieved its initial popularity and has remained a representative of the well-made, surprise-ending story because Aldrich so masterfully manipulates reader fascination with imaginative creation taken as reality. Aldrich achieves this deception, which lies at the heart of all fictional creation, by setting up a situation in which the fictional "reader," Flemming, cannot test the reality of the story his friend Delaney sends him via letters because of a broken leg.

Throughout the story, Aldrich makes use of various conventions of fiction-making, beginning with Delaney's first letter apologizing that there is nothing to write about because he is living out in the country with no one around. Claiming he wishes he were a novelist so he could write Flemming a "summer romance," Delaney then begins composing by asking Flemming to "imagine" the reality he recounts. After beginning a description of the house across the road from him, Delaney shifts to present tense, as if describing something he sees in reality: "A young woman appears on the piazza with some mysterious Penelope web of embroidery in her hand, or a book." Although the description begins generally, it is enough to catch Flemming, who writes back wanting to know more about the girl, telling Delaney he has "a graphic descriptive touch."

Delaney begins then to create a family for the girl and a name--Marjorie Daw. Although he provides various clues that what he is describing does not exist in the real world, such as noting that it was like "seeing a picture" to see Marjorie hovering around her invented father, Flemming is already convinced. Echoing the experience of many readers who encounter the objectification of a fantasy, Flemming writes back to Delaney, "You seem to be describing a woman I have known in some previous state of existence, or dreamed of in

Thomas Bailey Aldrich (Library of Congress)

this," claiming that if he saw a photo of her he would recognize her at once. When Delaney writes that, if he himself were on a desert island with Marjorie, he would be like a brother to her, he once again provides a clue to the imaginative nature of the story by saying, "Let me suggest a tropical island, for it costs no more to be picturesque."

Throughout the story Delaney is baffled and fascinated by the strange obsessive effect his account is having on his friend, asking, "Do you mean to say that you are seriously half in love with a woman whom you have never seen--with a shadow, a chimera? for what else can Miss Daw be to you? I do not understand it at all." Later Delaney makes another oblique reference to fiction-making by noting that he accepts things "as people do in dreams." When Flemming insists on writing to Marjorie, Delaney reverses the fictional process by reminding him that because she knows Flemming only through him he is an abstraction to her, a figure in a dream--a dream from which the faintest shock would awaken her. When Flemming threatens to come to see Marjorie, Delaney's letters become increasingly urgent, urging Flemming to stay where he is, for his presence would only "complicate matters."

In the only bit of straight narrative in the story, Flemming arrives to find Delaney gone to Boston and no Marjorie Daw to be found. In the final letter, Delaney, filled with horror at what he has done, says he just wanted to make a little romance to interest Flemming and is regretful that he did it all too well. The story ends with these famous lines: "There isn't any colonial mansion on the other side of the road, there isn't any piazza, there isn't any hammock--there isn't any Marjorie Daw!"

The story is a classic one about the power of fiction to create a convincing sense of reality. Emulating the method of composition described by Edgar Allan Poe, Aldrich once said that he wrote the last paragraph of the story first and then worked up to it, avoiding digressions and side issues. Indeed, "Marjorie Daw" is solely dependent on its final, single effect: surprising and delighting the reader, who has been taken in as completely as Flemming has.

"A Struggle for Life"

This is the only other Aldrich story that has received continued reading and commentary. It depends on a surprise ending, the manipulation of time, and gothic conventions more successfully exploited later by Ambrose Bierce; it also capitalizes on the power of fiction-making, although not in as complex a way as "Marjorie Daw." The frame of this story-within-a-story focuses on an external narrator who, passing a man on the street whose body looks thirty while his face looks sixty, says, half-aloud, "That man has a story, and I should like to know it." When a voice at his side says he knows the man's story, the inner story begins.

The story-within-the-story is about an American in Paris, Philip Wentworth, in love with a young French woman, who is found dead in her bed chamber. During her burial in the family vault, Wentworth faints and is locked in the tomb. The remainder of the story focuses on his efforts to remain alive by dividing his single candle into bite-sized pieces which he portions out to himself to eat until he can be rescued. The minutes pass like hours in the total darkness of the tomb, until two days later when Wentworth is down to his last piece of candle. The door of the tomb is flung open and he is led out, his hair gray and his eyes dimmed like an old man's. The storyteller concludes by revealing that Wentworth had been in the tomb for only an hour and twenty minutes.

However, this is not Aldrich's final surprise. The story so haunts the listener that a few days later, he approaches the old-faced man he thinks is Philip Wentworth. When the man says his name is Jones, the narrator realizes he has been duped by the teller, a gentleman of "literary proclivities" who is trying to write the Great American Novel.

OTHER MAJOR WORKS

LONG FICTION: *Daisy's Necklace and What Came of It*, 1857; *The Story of a Bad Boy*, 1869; *Prudence Palfrey*, 1874; *The Queen of Sheba*, 1877; *The Stillwater Tragedy*, 1880; *The Second Son*, 1888 (with Margaret Oliphant).

POETRY: *The Bells: A Collection of Chimes*, 1855; *The Ballad of Babie Bell, and Other Poems*, 1859; *Cloth of Gold, and Other Poems*, 1874; *Flower and Thorn: Later Poems*, 1877; *Mercedes and Later Lyrics*, 1884; *Wyndham Towers*, 1890; *Judith and Holofernes*, 1896; *Unguarded Gates, and Other Poems*, 1896; *The Poems of Thomas Bailey Aldrich: The Revised and Complete Household Edition*, 1897.

NONFICTION: *From Ponkapog to Pesth*, 1883; *An Old Town by the Sea*, 1893; *Ponkapog Papers*, 1903.

MISCELLANEOUS: *The Works of Thomas Bailey Aldrich*, 1970.

BIBLIOGRAPHY

Bellman, Samuel I. "Riding on Wishes: Ritual Make-Believe Patterns in Three Nineteenth-Century American Authors: Aldrich, Hale, Bunner." In *Ritual in the United States: Acts and Representations*. Tampa, Fla.: American Studies Press, 1985. Discusses Aldrich's creation of an imaginary individual in three stories, "A Struggle for Life," "Marjorie Daw," and "Miss Mehetabel's Son." Argues that "things are not what they seem" is the principle of these three stories, which are presented ritualistically in the form of a hoax or tall tale intended to trap the unwary.

Cohoon, Lorinda B. "Necessary Badness: Reconstructing Post-bellum Boyhood Citizenships in *Our Young Folks* and *The Story Of a Bad Boy*." *Children's Literature Association Quarterly* 29 (Spring, 2004): 5-31. Analyzes Aldrich's novel *The Story of a Bad Boy* and *Our Young Folks*, a nineteenth century children's magazine, to demonstrate how post-Civil War children's literature began promoting the idea that American boyhood was a time when boys rebelled and rejected contemporary concepts of citizenship by engaging in pranks or taking trips into the wilderness.

Canby, Henry Seidel. *The Short Story in English*. New York: Henry Holt and Company, 1909. Canby discusses Aldrich, Frank R. Stockton, and H. C. Bunner as the masters of the short story of the "absurd situation" and incongruity. Calls Aldrich a stylist who infused his personality into tales of trivia and made them delightful. Argues Says that in "Marjorie Daw," Aldrich was the first American to duplicate the French conte of Guy de Maupassant.

Cowie, Alexander. *The Rise of the American Novel*. New York: American Book, 1951. Although Cowie discusses Aldrich's novels, his comments on narrative style apply equally well to Aldrich's short stories. Calls Aldrich a vital writer whose contribution to American literature can be measured in terms of authenticity.

Davidson, Cathy N. *Revolution and the Word: The Rise of the Novel in America*. New York: Oxford University Press, 2004. Comprehensive history of American fiction, including a chapter on nineteenth century Gothic fiction and individualism. Extremely useful for contextualizing Aldrich's work. Bibliographic references and index.

Greenslet, Ferris. *Thomas Bailey Aldrich*. Boston: Houghton Mifflin, 1908. This is the official Aldrich biography; it contains numerous letters not available anywhere else. Describes Aldrich's friendship with William Dean Howells, his influence on American literary life in the last half of the nineteenth century, and his editorship of *The Atlantic Monthly*. Makes passing remarks about his short stories throughout, noting how "Marjorie Daw" was the basis of Aldrich's international reputation as a humorist.

O'Brien, Edward J. *The Advance of the American Short Story*. New York: Dodd, Mead, 1931. The originator of *The Best American Short Stories* series discusses Aldrich's responsibility for the vogue of the surprise-ending story in the early twentieth century. Maintains that although "Marjorie Daw" is flawless, many of Aldrich's stories are "pure sleight of hand." Discusses Aldrich's relationship to Frank Stockton and H. C. Bunner and how all three learned their tricks from Maupassant, Alphonse Daudet, and Prosper Mérimée.

Pattee, Fred Lewis. *The Development of the American Short Story: An Historical Survey*. New York: Harper and Brothers, 1923. In this important early history of the American short story, Pattee summarizes Aldrich's career and discusses the importance of "Marjorie Daw" in establishing an influential short-story type. Maintains that the story stood for art that is artless and that it has a

Daudet-like grace and brilliance with the air of careless improvisation.

Samuels, Charles E. *Thomas Bailey Aldrich*. New York: Twayne, 1965. A general introduction to Aldrich's life and art. Includes a chapter on his short stories and sketches in which "Marjorie Daw" is described as a masterpiece of compression that won Aldrich an instant international reputation. Discusses Aldrich's stories of the fanciful gothic and his taste for the macabre.

Charles E. May

SHERMAN ALEXIE

Born: Spokane Indian Reservation, Wellpinit, Washington; October 7, 1966

PRINCIPAL SHORT FICTION

The Lone Ranger and Tonto Fistfight in Heaven, 1993
The Toughest Indian in the World, 2000
Ten Little Indians, 2003
War Dances, 2010

OTHER LITERARY FORMS

A prolific writer, Sherman Alexie (SHUR-muhn AH-lehks-ee) has published well more than three hundred stories and poems. His poetry and poetry-short fiction works include *The Business of Fancydancing* (1992), *I Would Steal Horses* (1992), *First Indian on the Moon* (1993), *Old Shirts and New Skins* (1993), *Seven Mourning Songs for the Cedar Flute I Have Yet to Learn to Play* (1994), *Water Flowing Home* (1994), *The Summer of Black Widows* (1996), *Dangerous Astronomy* (2005), and *Face* (2009). He has also written the novels *Reservation Blues* (1995) and *Indian Killer* (1996). Alexie's young adult novel, *The Absolutely True Diary of a Part-Time Indian*, appeared in 2007; his novel, *Flight*, came out in 2007. He was writer and director of the film *The Business of Fancydancing* in 2002.

ACHIEVEMENTS

While he was in college, Sherman Alexie began accruing numerous accolades and awards, including a Washington State Arts Commission poetry fellowship (1991) and a National Endowment for the Arts poetry fellowship (1992). He also won Slipstream's fifth annual Chapbook Contest (1992), an Ernest Hemingway Foundation Award Citation (1993), the Ernest Hemingway Foundation/PEN Award for First Fiction (1993), and the Lila Wallace-*Reader's Digest* Writer's Award (1994). His first novel, *Reservation Blues* (1995), won the Before Columbus Foundation's American Book Award and the Murray Morgan Prize and prompted Alexie to be named one of *Granta*'s Best of Young American Novelists. *Indian Killer* (1996), his second novel, was listed as a *New York Times* notable book. Alexie won a National Book Award for Young People's Literature in 2007 for *The Absolutely True Diary of a Part-Time Indian*, the 2010 PEN/Faulkner Award for Fiction for *War Dances*, and the Lifetime Achievement Award of the Native Writers' Circle of the Americas in 2010.

BIOGRAPHY

A self-described Spokane-Coeur d'Alene Indian who believes "Native American" is a "guilty white liberal term," Sherman Joseph Alexie, Jr., grew up in Wellpinit, Washington, on the Spokane Indian Reservation. His father, an alcoholic, spent little time at home, and his mother supported the family by selling hand-sewn quilts at the local trading post. Born hydrocephalic, Alexie spent most of his childhood at home, voraciously reading books from the local library. He later attended high school outside the reservation. His academic achievements secured him a place at Spokane's Jesuit Gonzaga University in 1985. While there, he turned to alcohol as a means of coping with the pressure he felt to succeed. His goal to become a medical

Critical Survey of Short Fiction

doctor was derailed by his fainting spells in human anatomy class, and Alexie later transferred to Washington State University in 1987, where he began writing and then publishing his poetry and short stories. During a 1992 National Endowment for the Arts fellowship, he wrote his award-winning *The Business of Fancydancing* and *The Lone Ranger and Tonto Fistfight in Heaven*. With this success came sobriety.

Using a script he wrote based on his short stories in *The Lone Ranger and Tonto Fistfight in Heaven*, Alexie directed the award-winning *Smoke Signals* (1998), the first feature film ever made with an all-Native American cast and crew. Alexie settled in Seattle, Washington, with his wife Diana, a member of the Hidatsa Nation and college counselor, and their child.

ANALYSIS

According to Sherman Alexie in an interview with *Cineaste*, the five major influences on his writing are "my father, for his nontraditional Indian stories; my grandmother, for her traditional Indian stories; Stephen King; John Steinbeck; and *The Brady Bunch*." It is no wonder that Alexie's work, in particular the short stories in *The Lone Ranger and Tonto Fistfight in Heaven*, has been described by *American Indian Quarterly* as resembling a "casebook of postmodernist theory" that revels in such things as irony, parody of traditions, and the mingling of popular and native cultures. The result is a body of work that allows Alexie to challenge and subvert the stereotypes of Native Americans seen in the mass media (the warrior, the shaman, the drunk) and explore what it means to be a contemporary Native American.

In commenting on Native American writers and poets, Leslie Marmon Silko describes how Native American artists often create their strongest work when they write from a position of social responsibility. In Alexie's case, his work is designed often to effect change by exposing other Indians and whites to the harsh realities of reservation life. In Alexie's early work--work influenced by his own alcoholism and his father's abandonment (as seen in *The Lone Ranger and Tonto Fistfight in Heaven*)--he uses the Spokane Indian community as a backdrop for his characters, who often suffer from poverty, despair, and substance abuse.

However, it is his use of dark humor and irony that enables these characters to survive both their own depressions and self-loathing and the attitudes and activities of the often ignorant and apathetic white society. Alexie writes in his short story "Because My Father Always Said He Was the Only Indian Who Saw Jimi Hendrix Play 'The Star-Spangled Banner' at Woodstock":

On a reservation, Indian men who abandon their children are treated worse than white fathers who do the same thing. It's because white men have been doing that forever and Indian men have just learned how. That's how assimilation works.

With sobriety, Alexie claims that from *The Business of Fancydancing* in 1992 to *Smoke Signals* in 1998, his vision of Indian society has brightened and his writing has moved from focusing on the effects to the causes of substance abuse and other self-destructive behaviors. In *Cineaste*, Alexie describes his growth as a writer in this way:

As I've been in recovery over the years and stayed sober, you'll see the work gradually freeing itself of alcoholism and going much deeper, exploring the emotional, sociological, and psychological reasons for any kind of addictions or dysfunctions within the [Indian] community. . . . It's more of a whole journey, you get there and you get back.

THE LONE RANGER AND
TONTO FISTFIGHT IN HEAVEN

Alexie's first collection of (only) short stories, *The Lone Ranger and Tonto Fistfight in Heaven*, received much critical acclaim. Many of the Native American characters that he introduced in his earlier poetry--such as the storyteller Thomas Builds-the-Fire and his friend Victor Joseph--appear as vehicles through which Alexie illustrates how Indians survive both the hardships they face on reservations and the gulfs between cultures, time periods, and men and women.

In a number of the twenty-two often autobiographical stories in this collection, Alexie infuses irony to illustrate the destructive effects of alcohol on both children and adults on reservations. For example, in "The Only Traffic Signal on the Reservation Doesn't Flash Red Any More" he weaves the tradition of storytelling with the contemporary issue of how cultures create their heroes. In this story, the narrator and his friend

Sherman Alexie (AP Photo/Jim Cooper)

Adrian, both recovering alcoholics, are sitting on a porch playing Russian roulette with a BB gun. They stop and watch a local high school basketball player walk by with his friends. As the narrator talks, the reader learns that contemporary heroes on the reservation are often basketball players, and stories about their abilities are retold year after year. Yet, these heroes, including the narrator himself, often succumb to alcoholism and drop off the team. From the narrator's reminisces, it becomes clear that, while all people need heroes in their lives, creating heroes on a reservation can be problematic.

In "A Drug Called Tradition," the narrator tells the story of Thomas Builds-the-Fire and the "second-largest party in reservation history," for which he pays with money he receives from a large utility company land lease. While the narrator claims that "we can all hear our ancestors laughing in the trees" when Indians profit in this way, who the ancestors are truly laughing at is unclear. Are they laughing at the white people for spending a lot of money to put ten telephone poles across some land or at the Indians for spending that

money on large quantities of alcohol? Later in the story, Victor, Junior, and Thomas go off and experience a night of drug-induced hallucinations about the faraway past, the present, and the future. In the present, the boys return to a time before they ever had their first drink of alcohol. From this story, the reader learns that it is better for people to stay in the present and keep persevering than become stuck in the past or an imagined future.

Several of the stories in *The Lone Ranger and Tonto Fistfight in Heaven* that were adapted for the film *Smoke Signals* explore the connections and fissures between people of different genders and cultures. In "Every Little Hurricane," the reader is introduced to nine-year-old Victor, who is awakened often from his frequent nightmares by family fights, this one occurring between his uncles during a New Year's Eve party. Memories of other seasonal alcohol and poverty-induced "hurricanes" ensue, such as that of the Christmas his father could not afford any gifts. At the end of the story, as all the relatives and neighbors pick themselves up and go home, Victor lies down between his father and mother, hoping that the alcohol in their bodies will seep into his and help him sleep. This story is about how Indians continue to be "eternal survivors" of many types of storms.

In "Because My Father Always Said He Was the Only Indian Who Saw Jimi Hendrix Play 'The Star-Spangled Banner' at Woodstock," the narrator details the love-hate relationship between his mother and his father (who would later leave the family), while using a popular music icon to illustrate how Native Americans and whites share at least one common culture. The narrator of this story, the abandoned Victor, later teams up with former childhood friend and storyteller Thomas in "This Is What It Means to Say Phoenix, Arizona," to collect Victor's father's ashes in Phoenix. In their ensuing journey, the characters grow spiritually and emotionally, while exploring what it means today to be a Native American.

TEN LITTLE INDIANS

One opens an Alexie collection with the expectation of the writer's predictable barrage of satiric barbs, comic one-liners, performance posturing, polemical rants, and guilt assaults against the white man's mistreatment of Native Americans. It may be a pleasant surprise for the reader to find himself or herself responding positively to the adult man, rather than the tortured adolescent, at the center of most of these nine stories in *Ten Little Indians*. Instead of making the reader feel guilty for the reader's ancestors' exploitation of Native Americans, Alexie may move the reader, even as he makes the reader laugh.

In "Flight Patterns," during a conversation with an immigrant cabbie on the way to a business trip, the recurring persona of these Alexie stories faces some of the fears of a post-9/11 world, learns something about the losses of others, and experiences a sudden appreciation of his family. When he takes the credit for his future wife's rescue of a lost cat in "Do You Know Where I Am?" and years later must cope with her infidelity, he understands that honesty is the only thing that holds two people together. Even though he struggles with his demons as he futilely tries to raise enough money to buy back his grandmother's stolen regalia, he is able to dance in final celebration in "What You Pawn I Will Redeem." Alexie seems to outgrow his adolescent stand-up comic routines in this collection.

Although it is possible that Alexie cynically manipulates the reader in these stories, playing for tears rather than laughs, it works. The reader likes these men and believes their stories. Even the story that sounds like the former wisecracking Alexie, "The Life and Times of Estelle Walks Above"--filled with the rules of adolescence, the rituals of the reservation, and the self-deceptions of guilty white liberals--concerns the complex relationship between a young man and his mother and ends with a tragicomic rescue.

The engaging indications of Alexie's possible maturation (or his shameless manipulation) are the two stories that open and close the collection. In "The Search Engine," a female college student seeks out an aging forklift operator whose one book of poetry she accidentally discovers in the library. His story of why it is his only book, although predictable, leaves the young woman, and perhaps the reader, smiling wistfully. "What Ever Happened to Frank Snake Church?" is an unlikely but irresistible parable of an aging, overweight, ex-basketball player with a heart problem who makes an improbable but delightful comeback to kick

the butt of an arrogant young point guard. Although the reader rightfully may be wary that Alexie is manipulative in these stories, so what? All writers are tricksters. The magic either works or it does not.

WAR DANCES

Although *War Dances*, a collection of poems, vignettes, and stories, won the 2010 PEN/Faulkner Award for Fiction, to many it may seem to be something of a mix tape made up of a few full-length short stories and a lot of detritus that just happened to be lying around in Alexie's file cabinet. The title story, told in first-person numbered fragments alternating between the narrator's problems with his hearing loss and with his father's foot amputation, replays the comic Native American persona who has appeared in previous Alexie collections. When the narrator tries to get a blanket for his hospitalized father, he encounters another Native American with whom he trades Indian jokes and barbs, which seems to be the main purpose of the encounter, although he does manage to borrow a nice heavy Pendleton blanket. The narrator's ailment is a tumor on the brain, but one that his doctor tells him many people live with their whole lives with no problem. After the father dies from alcoholism, the rest of the story evolves into various narrative diversions. First, the narrator does research on his family history, reprinting his interview with a man who had served with his grandfather when he was killed in action on Okinawa during World War II. The story also includes what is termed an "exit interview," in which Alexie, citing his father, has the opportunity to come up with more one-liners at the expense of both whites and Native Americans. The story ends with a poem about the father slicing his knee with a chain saw, followed by the father's itemized list of contradictions to the details in the poem. It's a compilation of Alexie cleverness and one-liners strung together loosely with the narrator's fear of dying and his father's death.

"The Ballad of Paul Nonetheless" is another Alexie riff (much ado about very little), this time about a man who sees a beautiful woman at an airport and starts pursuing her, running into her at various times, having fantasies about her, and divorcing his wife. In "A Senator's Son," a man becomes involved in a drunken gay bashing that threatens the career of his father, who is running for U.S. Senate. In "Fearful Symmetry," Alexie revives his familiar persona, the sound-alike Sherwin Polatkin. When this Hollywood screenwriter tries his hand at competing in a crossword puzzle competition, the result is embarrassing. "Breaking and Entering" is a simplistic exemplum on race about a Native American man who hits, with a child's aluminum bat, and accidentally kills an African American teenager who has broken into the Native American's house. The story ends with an obvious and predictable soul-searching encounter, in which the man finds himself uncomfortable in the presence of African Americans. The PEN/Faulkner award cited *War Dances* as a collection of "structurally inventive pieces," but the poems are ordinary and the stories are often excuses for Alexie's self-indulgent one-liners and jokes. After the seriousness of *Ten Little Indians*, it is disappointing to see Alexie reverting to his adolescent ways.

OTHER MAJOR WORKS

LONG FICTION: *Reservation Blues*, 1995; *Indian Killer*, 1996; *Flight*, 2007.

SCREENPLAYS: *Smoke Signals*, 1998; *The Business of Fancydancing*, 2002.

POETRY: *I Would Steal Horses*, 1992; *Old Shirts and New Skins*, 1993; *The Man Who Loves Salmon*, 1998; *One Stick Song*, 2000; *Dangerous Astronomy*, 2005; *Face*, 2009.

CHILDREN'S LITERATURE: *The Absolutely True Diary of a Part-Time Indian*, 2007.

MISCELLANEOUS: *The Business of Fancydancing: Stories and Poems*, 1992; *First Indian on the Moon*, 1993; *The Summer of Black Widows*, 1996 (poems and short prose).

BIBLIOGRAPHY

Baxter, Andrea-Bess. "Review of *Old Shirts and New Skins*, *First Indian on the Moon*, and *The Lone Ranger and Tonto Fistfight in Heaven*." *Western American Literature* 29, no. 3 (November, 1994): 277-280. A review of the three works with commentary on the appeals of Alexie's writing and its strengths.

Low, Denise. *The American Indian Quarterly* 20, no. 1 (Winter, 1996): 123-125. In examining Alexie's work through a postmodern lens, Low discusses his characters and rhetorical strategies in *The Lone Ranger and Tonto Fistfight in Heaven* and *The Business of Fancydancing*.

McFarland, Ron. "'Another Kind of Violence': Sherman Alexie's Poems." *American Indian Quarterly* 21, no. 2 (Spring, 1997): 251-264. Reviews various anthologies and types of Native American writing and writers with a focus on Alexie and his work.

Niatum, Duane, ed. *Harper's Anthology of Twentieth Century Native American Poetry*. San Francisco: Harper and Row, 1988. Features thirty-six contributors and attempts to address what makes Native American poetry unique.

Silko, Leslie Marmon. "Bingo Man--*Reservation Blues* by Sherman Alexie." *Nation* 260, no. 23 (June 12, 1995): 856-860. A review by a celebrated Native American writer of Alexie's short stories and poems, with special focus on Alexie's first novel, *Reservation Blues*.

Slethaug, Gordon E. "Hurricanes and Fires: Chaotics in Sherman Alexie's *Smoke Signals* and *The Lone Ranger and Tonto Fistfight in Heaven*." *Literature and Film Quarterly* 31 (2003): 130-140. Discusses the image of Native Americans presented in both the story and the film and compares and contrasts Alexie's techniques in both.

Tatonetti, Lisa. "Sex and Salmon: Queen Identities in Sherman Alexie's *The Toughest Indian in the World*." *Studies in American Fiction* 35 (Autumn, 2007): 201-219. Discusses human relationships, gay and otherwise, of the Native American.

West, Dennis. "Sending Cinematic Smoke Signals: An Interview with Sherman Alexie." *Cineaste* 23, no. 4 (1998): 28-32. Discusses the film *Smoke Signals* and short stories in *The Lone Ranger and Tonto Fistfight in Heaven*, followed by an in-depth interview with Alexie about his early influences and work.

Lisa-Anne Culp
Updated by Charles E. May-

NELSON ALGREN

Born: Detroit, Michigan; March 28, 1909
Died: Sag Harbor, New York; May 9, 1981
Also Known As: Nelson Algren Abraham

PRINCIPAL SHORT FICTION

The Neon Wilderness, 1947
The Last Carousel, 1973 (also includes sketches and poems)
The Texas Stories of Nelson Algren, 1995

OTHER LITERARY FORMS

Nelson Algren (AWL-gruhn) is probably best known for films made from his novels *The Man with the Golden Arm* (1949) and *A Walk on the Wild Side* (1956), but his work ranges from those violent novels and short stories to Hemingwayesque essays, verse, work on the avant-garde "little magazine" *Anvil,* sketches on life in major cities, travel sketches, journalistic reporting, and other factual and fictional pieces about places and people who have "a weakness."

ACHIEVEMENTS

Best known for his novels (*The Man with the Golden Arm* won the first National Book Award in 1950), Nelson Algren was both a popular and critical success with his short stories, which closely resemble his novels in character, setting, and theme. His stories have appeared regularly in both the *O. Henry Memorial Prize Stories* and *The Best American short Stories,* but his popularity waned as the American reading public lost interest in naturalistic fiction. For the most part, his stories are slices of life, packed with details and dialects, grotesques and losers, yet marked with a glimmer of idealism. Influenced by Ernest Hemingway and Stephen Crane, he has served as an influence on later naturalists such as John Rechy and Hubert Selby, Jr., who resemble him in their lower-class characters, urban settings, violent themes, and nightmarish vision.

BIOGRAPHY

Born in Detroit, the descendant of Nels Ahlgren, a Swedish Jew who changed his name to Isaac ben Abraham, Nelson Algren was brought up under the "El" on Chicago's poor West Side and was the "bard of the stumblebum" of the Polish community there in the Depression. He earned a degree in journalism at the University of Illinois but found it difficult to get a job after graduating. He drifted to the South and to Texas, where he wrote his first short story, "So Help Me," in an abandoned filling station outside Rio Hondo. This story led to his first novel, *Somebody in Boots* (1935). Algren's novel *The Man with the Golden Arm* reached the top of the best-seller list. He also received praise for his 1956 novel, *A Walk on the Wild Side.* Aside from some interviews, two travel books, and his collected stories, Algren wrote little after 1955. He traveled extensively, taught at various universities, and moved to New Jersey in 1975, finally settling in Sag Harbor, New York, where he died in 1981, shortly after having been elected to the American Academy of Arts and Letters. This belated recognition, for Algren's popularity had declined since the 1950's, was appreciated by Algren, who was having trouble publishing *The Devil's Stocking,* a fictionalized account of Rubin "Hurricane" Carter's life. The book was published posthumously in 1983.

ANALYSIS

Included in the collection *The Neon Wilderness,* the story "Design for Departure" contains the title phrase and sets the tone of the collection. The story contains some heavy-handed Christian symbolism, which can be seen in the names of the main characters, Mary and Christy. Mary closely resembles the protagonist of Stephen Crane's novel *Maggie: A Girl of the Streets* (1893); however, her world of "Kleenex, fifty-cent horse [betting] tickets and cigarette snipes" is more a collage than a slice of gutter life. Mary is a shell of a person in her job wrapping bacon and a passive victim of a rape by a deaf man named Christiano, which seems to affect her no more than the moral problems of engaging in a badger game with Ryan, the proprietor of The Jungle (a club), or the subsequent arrest and jail term of her boyfriend Christy. When Christy is released from jail, he finds Mary on the game and on drugs, and she warns him off: She is diseased. At her request, he gives her a fatal overdose. The character of Mary is so void of emotion or response to her life that it is difficult for the reader to feel anything for her. Although there are some bright passages of real-life dialogue in the story, they tend to contribute to the self-conscious tone of the story rather than elevate its quality.

"THE FACE ON THE BARROOM FLOOR"

A less self-conscious and more successful story is "The Face on the Barroom Floor," a sketch that introduces one of the prototypes of *A Walk on the Wild Side*. Algren renders the bloody, senseless fight in the story marvelously. Although he does not seem to understand the psychology of the prizefighter, he effectively describes the brutal poundings of the fight. He creates a

Nelson Algren (Library of Congress)

similar appeal through vivid description in "He Swung and He Missed." The little guy beaten to a pulp in the ring stands for the victim of "The System"; however, Algren occasionally succeeds in making him more than a symbol.

"HOW THE DEVIL CAME DOWN DIVISION STREET"

Algren's material is most successful when he records in journalistic manner, rather than manipulates as a writer of fiction, the real-life language and insights of his characters. Where "Design for Departure" is ambitious and basically fails, "How the Devil Came down Division Street" succeeds because Algren has taken the gothic and grotesque elements of an experience and set it down quickly and skillfully. Roman Orlov, trying to "drown the worm" that gnaws at his vitals, sits in the Polonia bar and stumblingly relates his bizarre and drunken tale of how his family's apartment was haunted. By the end of his story his character is clearly revealed: what the lack of hope and even the lack of a bed have made of him; how the consolations of religion are to the very poor only impediments to survival; and how that survival involves the acceptance of extraordinary circumstances that would be farcical if they were not so painful. The reader is moved to understand that for some people "there is no place to go but the taverns." With astonishment, one finds the answer to the question on which the whole story is built: "Does the devil live in a double-shot? Or is he the one who gnaws, all night, within?" In this story Algren has realized his ideal--to identify himself with his subjects.

"A BOTTLE OF MILK FOR MOTHER"

There is even more power of sympathy and understanding in "A Bottle of Milk for Mother," the tale of the "final difficulty" of Bruno "Lefty" Bicek. When a street-smart but doomed Polish boxer is charged with the robbery and murder of an old man in a shabby tenement hallway, fierce and unrelenting police interrogation leaves him in despair: "I knew I'd never get to be twenty-one." Kojaz, the wily cop, is also sensitively handled--the story should be read in connection with "The Captain Has Bad Dreams" and "The Captain Is Impaled"--as he inexorably pries from Lefty's grip what still another story calls "Poor Man's Pennies," the transparent alibis and compulsive lies of the downtrodden.

Among the "essential innocents" in Algren's work are the "born incompetents" (such as Gladys and Rudy in "Poor Man's Pennies"), the cops and robbers, the stumblebums, and the prostitutes. In "Please Don't Talk About Me When I'm Gone," the crowd draws back to let Rose be pushed into a paddy wagon, and she reflects: "My whole life it's the first time anyone made room for me." In "Is Your Name Joe?"--all her johns are Joe--another prostitute delivers a raving monologue that has a certain garish and surreal quality, reflecting the details in the world of the former convict and former prostitutes described in the remarkable story entitled "Decline and Fall in Dingdong-Daddyland." It is this surreal quality that salvages the stereotypes of *The Man with the Golden Arm*, the stories in *The Neon Wilderness*, and the best of the later stories ("The Face on the Barroom Floor," "The Captain Is Impaled," "Home to Shawneetown," and "Decline and Fall in Dingdong-Daddyland").

There is in Algren a strain of the surreal and grotesque that links him with William Burroughs and the writers who moved from depictions of the weird world of drug addicts to a harsh and often horrifying view of the "real" world from which they are desperately trying to escape. That, and not his social realism (in which he is surpassed by Frank Norris, Theodore Dreiser, and many others) or his "poetic" prose (in which Thomas Wolfe, William Faulkner, and others leave him far behind), makes Algren's work more than a mere document of American social protest or a clear precursor of other writers and gives it its own value.

OTHER MAJOR WORKS

LONG FICTION: *Somebody in Boots*, 1935; *Never Come Morning*, 1942; *The Man with the Golden Arm*, 1949; *A Walk on the Wild Side*, 1956; *The Devil's Stocking*, 1983.

NONFICTION: *Chicago: City on the Make*, 1951; *Who Lost an American?*, 1963; *Conversations with Nelson Algren*, 1964 (with H. E. F. Donohue); *Notes from a Sea Diary: Hemingway All the Way*, 1965; *Nonconformity: Writing on Writing*, 1996.

EDITED TEXTS: *Nelson Algren's Own Book of Lonesome Monsters*, 1962.

MISCELLANEOUS: *Entrapment, and Other Writings*, 2009.

BIBLIOGRAPHY

Brevda, William. "The Rainbow Sign of Nelson Algren." *Texas Studies in Literature and Language* 44, no. 1 (Winter, 2002): 392. Analyzes the symbolism of neon and of rainbows in Algren's fiction.

Cappetti, Carla. *Writing Chicago: Modernism, Ethnography, and the Novel*. New York: Columbia University Press, 1993. Although Cappetti's chapter on Algren focuses primarily on his novel *Never Come Morning*, it is helpful in understanding his short stories, for it deals with Algren's combination of both the realistic/naturalist and the Symbolist/Surrealist traditions. Discusses how Algren's fiction interrupts historicity and factuality with poetic devices that prevent the reader from lapsing into simple referentiality.

Cox, Martha Heasley, and Wayne Chatterton. *Nelson Algren*. Boston: Twayne, 1975. The best overall assessment of Algren's life and work. Contains an early chapter on the short stories, which are analyzed in some detail. The authors provide a chronology, a biographical chapter, an annotated bibliography, and a helpful index that groups the short stories by theme.

Donohue, H. E. F. *Conversations with Nelson Algren*. New York: Hill & Wang, 1964. Donohue's book consists of conversations, arranged chronologically, about Algren's life and work and therefore serves a biographical function. The conversation "The Army and the Writing" concerns, in part, Algren's short-story collection *The Neon Wilderness*, but the book is more valuable for Algren's comments on writing, writers, and politics.

Drew, Bettina. *Nelson Algren: A Life on the Wild Side*. New York: G. P. Putnam's Sons, 1989. The only Algren biography, this volume, which is well researched and readable, mixes biographical material with publication details about Algren's work. One chapter is devoted to his short-story collection *The Neon Wilderness*. Supplemented by a bibliography of Algren's work.

Giles, James R. *Confronting the Horror: The Novels of Nelson Algren*. Kent, Ohio: Kent State University Press, 1989. Giles provides brief commentary on some of Algren's short stories, but his book is most helpful in relating Algren's naturalism to a literary tradition that extends to later writers, such as Hubert Selby, Jr., and John Rechy. For Giles, Algren's fiction reflects his despair over the absurd state of humankind and the obscenity of death.

Horvath, Brooke. *Understanding Nelson Algren.* Columbia: University of South Carolina Press, 2005. Features a brief introduction to Algren's life and work and provides detailed analysis of *The Neon Wilderness* and *The Last Carousel*, as well as his other writings. Examines Algren's literary style, including his lyricism and humor, as well as the social and political concerns expressed in his work.

Ray, David. "Housesitting the Wild Side." *Chicago Review* 41 (1995): 107-116. Anecdotal discussion of Ray's acquaintance with Algren in the 1950's and 1960's. Discusses Algren's connection with Chicago, his relationship with Simon de Beauvoir, and efforts to structure and organize Algren's manuscripts.

Ward, Robert, ed. *Nelson Algren: A Collection of Critical Essays.* Madison, N.J.: Fairleigh Dickinson University Press, 2007. Although many of the essays focus on Algren's novels, this collection provides information that pertains to his short stories, including discussions of Algren as an "American outsider," his life and work within the context of Chicago history, and the paperback revolution and how it affected his reputation.

Leonard R. N. Ashley
Updated by Thomas L. Erskine

WOODY ALLEN

Born: Brooklyn, New York; December 1, 1935
Also Known As: Allen Stewart Konigsberg

PRINCIPAL SHORT FICTION

Getting Even, 1971
Without Feathers, 1975
Side Effects, 1980
Mere Anarchy, 2007

OTHER LITERARY FORMS

Woody Allen is best known as a filmmaker, for which he provides his own screenplays. He has written extensively for the theater and television, has supplied stand-up comedians (including himself) with original jokes, and has published numerous comic essays.

ACHIEVEMENTS

Woody Allen is widely accepted as a talented American humorist and filmmaker. This assessment is reinforced by a considerable number of prestigious awards garnered by Allen over the years. These include a Sylvania Award in 1957 for a script he wrote for a television special of Sid Caesar, Academy Awards for Best Director and Best Original Screenplay in 1977 for *Annie Hall* (1977), British Academy and New York Film Critics Awards in 1979 for *Manhattan* (1979), and New York and Los Angeles Film Critics Awards in 1987 for *Hannah and Her Sisters* (1986). *Match Point* (2005) was nominated for an Academy Award for Best Original Screenplay, and Allen received directing and writing nominations for Golden Globes for the same picture.

Similar recognition for Allen's dramatic film efforts has been slow in coming. *Interiors* (1978) and *September* (1987) both were greeted unenthusiastically by critics. *Crimes and Misdemeanors* (1989), a more difficult film to categorize, may have been an important breakthrough in this regard. His later serious efforts, such as *Match Point* (2005), have been regarded positively by critics.

Though overshadowed by his film career, Allen's short fiction has been well appreciated by critics. His story "The Kugelmass Episode" won an O. Henry Award in 1977. His collections of short fiction have generally been reviewed favorably. In addition to its own considerable merit, Allen's short fiction has served as a breeding ground for themes, ideas, and images more fully developed later in his films. Thus, while Allen's short stories certainly lack the polish and perfectionism of his motion pictures, they have played an important role in helping Allen to excel as a screenwriter and a director. Given Allen's marvelous productivity during his career, they also have contributed to his reputation as an artist whose creative juices never seem to ebb.

BIOGRAPHY

Woody Allen was born Allen Stewart Konigsberg in Brooklyn, New York, on December 1, 1935. He graduated from Brooklyn's Midwood High School in 1953 and briefly attended New York University and City College of New York. While in the process of abandoning his formal education, Allen took on his soon-to-be-famous pseudonym and became a full-time comedy writer for the David O. Alber public relations firm. At age nineteen, he went to Hollywood as part of the National Broadcasting Company's (NBC) Writers Development Program, and he soon became a highly successful writer for nightclub acts, Broadway revues, and television shows. In 1960, Allen began to perform as a stand-up comedian; this led to acting opportunities. At the same time, Allen continued to write, turning out comic prose for sophisticated periodicals such as *The New Yorker*, plays good enough to be produced on Broadway, and screenplays that would be made into feature films. Ultimately, Allen's dual career as performer and author came together as Allen wrote, directed, and starred in a number of distinguished motion pictures. Allen has been a longtime resident of New York City and has continued to base much of his work there.

After a dozen years living with actor Mia Farrow (who starred in about a dozen of his films), Allen and Farrow in 1992 and 1993 had a very public custody battle and bitter separation after Farrow discovered Allen was having an affair with her adopted daughter, Soon-Yi Previn. Soon-Yi has been married to Allen since 1997. After this time, Allen's films began to falter, both critically and at the box office. However, later, his films became reinvigorated with new locales (London and Spain) and new actors (Scarlet Johansson,

Penélope Cruz, Ian McShane, Colin Farrell, Anthony Hopkins). Allen believed that his films might have wider appeal if he were not starring in them, and he has developed more serious dramas. *Match Point* and *Vicky Cristina Barcelona* (2008) were both critically and financially successful compared to the rest of his films.

ANALYSIS

The overall emphasis of Woody Allen's short fiction is summarized by the title of his second book-length collection, *Without Feathers*. The title alludes to an Emily Dickinson line: "Hope is the thing without feathers. . . ." The particular hopelessness with which Allen deals, in his mirthful way, is that described, defined, and passed down by such philosophers and literary figures as Friedrich Nietzsche, Søren Kierkegaard, Albert Camus, and Franz Kafka. It is one in which the death of God, existential meaninglessness, and surreal distortions of time and space are the norm. In this world, anxiety abounds, human reason is essentially flawed, and truth disappears into the twin vacuum of moral relativism and perceptual uncertainty.

While Allen demonstrates an instinctive grasp of the issues raised by such a worldview, his treatment is, as one might expect in a humorist, always tongue in cheek. Allen is no scholar, nor is he trying to be one. He accepts and believes in the more or less existentialist premises that inform his work, although he does not take them seriously enough to ponder systematically. In fact, he makes fun of people who do so, particularly those who do it for a living. Allen does not sink into despair; instead, he uses the philosophical and literary atmosphere of his time as a convenient springboard for laughter. In essence, his work transforms the uncertainty of a Godless universe into fertile ground for his free-flowing style of comedy.

One technique that enables Allen to accomplish this goal is parody, or comic imitation. Most of Allen's fiction contains parody--ranging from imitation of Plato's *Apologia Sōkratous* (399-390 b.c.e.; *Apology*, 1675) to variations on Kafka and Count Dracula--and some stories are multiple parodies. Any mode of thought, scholarship, literary expression, or lifestyle that people celebrate or venerate is fair game to Allen. Indeed, the more seriously a philosophy is taken, the more fun he seems to have tipping it over onto its humorous side. This is not to say that Allen's humor is limited to parody or that it is always subtle. Allen is too much the stand-up comedian to let any opportunity for a laugh--no matter how vulgar or easy--pass by unexploited. He tolerates no lulls in his comedic fiction. On the contrary, he shoots for a pace of humor so rapid that the reader never has time to wonder when the next joke is coming. Finally, Allen's work often reaches back to his roots. While his stories are less autobiographical than some of his films, they often involve--at least in passing--Jewish characters and issues of importance to Jews.

"MR. BIG"

The characteristics listed above are amply illustrated by Allen's story "Mr. Big." In the story, Kaiser Lupowitz, a New York private investigator, is between cases when a beautiful blond calling herself Heather Butkiss (as suggested above, no joke is too small for Allen) comes to his office and asks him to search for a missing person. The missing person is Mr. Big, that is to say, God. Lupowitz demands to have all the facts before he takes the case. The blond admits that Butkiss is an alias, claiming that her real name is Claire Rosensweig and that she is a Vassar College student working on an assignment for her philosophy class. Lupowitz takes the case for his usual daily fee of one hundred dollars plus expenses.

The investigation begins with a visit to a local rabbi for whom Lupowitz had worked previously. After some revealing pokes at the notion of what it means to be God's "chosen people" (Allen likens it to a "protection" racket), Lupowitz visits an informer, Chicago Phil the atheist, in a pool hall to find out more about his client. There, he is told that she is really a Radcliffe student and that she has been dating an empiricist philosopher who dabbles in logical positivism and pragmatism (somehow, Arthur Schopenhauer also is mentioned). That evening, Lupowitz dines with his client. After a bout of lovemaking, the two discuss Kierkegaard. A telephone call from the police interrupts them; it seems someone answering God's description has just shown up in the morgue, a homicide victim. The police suspect an existentialist, possibly even Lupowitz himself.

Lupowitz's next stop is an Italian restaurant in Newark, where he questions His Holiness the Pope, who claims to have an exclusive pipeline to God. Lupowitz learns that his lovely client is actually in the science department at Bryn Mawr College. He makes further inquiries and returns to confront her with what he has learned. Her real name, he tells her, is Dr. Ellen Shepherd, and she teaches physics at Bryn Mawr. In traditional private-eye fashion, Lupowitz reveals a highly tangled plot involving Socrates, Immanuel Kant, and Martin Buber, among others. With a melodramatic flair, he names Ellen Shepherd (and therefore, perhaps, science) as God's killer. The story concludes with an equal mixture of flying bullets and philosophic allusions as the intrepid private eye sees justice through to the end.

Here one can see all Allen's basic ingredients. Philosophy, religion, and the hard-boiled detective genre are all lampooned, the last through the medium of parody. The question of God's existence is explored with a completely earnest lack of earnestness. Truth is treated as something elusive and perhaps irredeemably ephemeral. The wisecracks come one on top of the other and at varying levels of intellectual sophistication.

"THE KUGELMASS EPISODE"

Allen builds on this formula in what some critics believe to be one of his best stories, "The Kugelmass Episode." Here themes are raised that foreshadow his later films. Kugelmass is a professor of humanities at City College of New York. Feeling smothered in his marriage, he seeks approval from his analyst for the adulterous affair he feels to be approaching. When his analyst refuses to condone such behavior, Kugelmass breaks off his therapy. Shortly afterward, he is telephoned by a magician named Persky, who believes he has something that will interest Kugelmass. This turns out to be a cabinet that allows one admittance into the book of one's choice. Though he is skeptical, Kugelmass decides to enter the contraption with a copy of Gustave Flaubert's *Madame Bovary* (1857; English translation, 1886). Quite astonishingly, he is transported to just the right part of the novel so that he can be alone with Emma Bovary, returning to the twentieth century in time to keep his wife from becoming suspicious. (However, literature teachers did begin to wonder when a balding, middle-aged Jew first appeared in the original novel.) After another visit, Emma asks to make the return trip to New York City with Kugelmass. This is arranged by Persky, and the two lovers have a delicious weekend in the city. Emma is particularly taken with the great shopping. (Literature professors now have to ponder why Emma does not appear in the novel at all.)

It is at this point that things begin to go wrong. Persky's cabinet breaks down, and Emma is stuck in New York. Soon she and Kugelmass become permanently soured on each other. Persky finally fixes the cabinet and returns Emma to her fictional time and place. Kugelmass proclaims that he has learned his lesson but three weeks later decides to try Persky's cabinet again. This time he plans to go for more sex and less romance with the "monkey" in Philip Roth's *Portnoy's Complaint* (1969). Something goes wrong, and he is stranded, presumably forever, in a book on remedial Spanish.

Here the emptiness of the universe is merely the backdrop for a story that is about infatuation, magic, and the relation between different kinds of reality. Many of Allen's films involve the finer nuances of infidelity between lovers (or "hanky-panky," as it were), apparently one of the common ways people deal with the universe's meaninglessness. Magic--perhaps as an alternative manifestation of the miraculous or supernatural--has played a pivotal role in at least two of Allen's films, *Alice* (1990) and *Oedipus Wrecks* (1989). Interestingly, the magic goes wrong, just as God might have gone wrong somewhere along the line. Strikingly, the interaction between "real" and fictional characters serves as the central theme of his film *The Purple Rose of Cairo* (1985). In all these instances, Allen has moved from mirthful commentary on the dead end to which humanity has arrived to a more serious look at how people try to cope. Thus "Mr. Big" and "The Kugelmass Episode" illustrate different transitional points in Allen's development as an artist. Taken together, they indicate the general philosophy of life underlying Allen's work and point out the ways in which his stories have provided a foundation for his more elaborate efforts on film.

"THE CONDEMNED"

As is evident in "The Kugelmass Episode," Allen has an abiding interest in the foibles of moral conduct, particularly as it relates to love, sex, infatuation, and fidelity. He also writes quite often about some of the more grave moral-political questions of modern time. In "The Condemned," Allen parodies works by the French existentialists Albert Camus, Jean-Paul Sartre, and André Malraux in order to examine the propriety of political violence. The story begins with a ruthless informer named Brisseau, asleep in his bedroom. Cloquet, who has been assigned to assassinate Brisseau, stands over the bed, wrestling with his conscience. Cloquet has never before killed a human being. He did kill a mad dog once, but only after it had been certified insane by a board of qualified psychiatrists. Gathering his resolve, Cloquet puts his gun to Brisseau's head and is about to pull the trigger. Just then, Madame Brisseau enters the room, failing to notice the gun sticking out of her husband's ear as Cloquet takes cover behind a dresser. After Madame Brisseau exits the room, Cloquet regains consciousness (he had fainted) and resumes his internal dialogue. He wonders whether he is Cloquet the murderer or Cloquet who teaches the Psychology of Fowl at the Sorbonne. He reminisces about his first meeting with Brisseau and finally comes to the conclusion that he cannot possibly shoot anyone, even this man who clearly deserves it.

Dropping his gun, Cloquet flees, stopping off for a brandy before going to Juliet's house. Juliet asks Cloquet if he has killed Brisseau. Yes, he says. Juliet applauds. The two make love. The following morning, Cloquet is arrested for Brisseau's murder. He is subsequently tried and convicted. Awaiting execution, he tries to convert but finds that all the usual faiths are filled. On the eve of his death, Cloquet longs for freedom, relishing the opportunities he has missed to become a ventriloquist or to show up at the Louvre in bikini underwear and a false nose. Just before his execution, as he is about to faint from fear, Cloquet is released. The real murderer has confessed. Overjoyed, Cloquet rushes out to enjoy the life and freedom he had come so close to losing. Three days later he is arrested again, this time for showing up at the Louvre in bikini underwear and a false nose.

Not surprisingly, the issue of whether it is morally acceptable to commit murder for society's greater good is also central to at least two of Allen's films, *Love and Death* (1975) and *Crimes and Misdemeanors*. While the former is an unmitigated comedy, the latter film treats the issue with grim seriousness. This is not to say that Allen offers a sermon. He simply lays the issue out in all its complexity for the audience to ponder. Allen's comic treatment of moral and epistemological questions is not meant to disparage the importance of distinguishing right from wrong, truth from falsehood. Rather, Allen offers an alternative to simplistic solutions and, at the other extreme, pretentious intellectualizing as antidotes for modern despair. That alternative is laughter at oneself and at one's predicament. Perhaps, ultimately, this sort of self-recognition will lead to the answers all people seek.

MERE ANARCHY

Mere Anarchy is Allen's first collection of prose pieces in more than twenty-five years. It continues Allen's typical preoccupations with God, death, philosophy, psychoanalysis, and art, but it also reflects the cultural changes since the last collection in 1980. The first eight pieces are new, and the last ten were originally published in *The New Yorker*; more than a third of the eighteen are in some way about film, television, agents, or Broadway shows. Despite the title's allusion to William Butler Yeats's poem "The Second Coming," the age of media and mass entertainment is far more represented than in Allen's previous prose collections, with references to print media and academic literature dwindling, though ironically several pieces were inspired his work for *The New York Times*.

As the best pieces from *The New Yorker* show, Allen in his mid-seventies is still master of the comic sketch and funny story, extending the trail blazed by his idols S. J. Perelman, George S. Kaufmann, and Robert Benchley. Allen satirizes and parodies intellectual pretension and jargon by using absurd incongruities to highlight his precipitous descent from the sublime to the ridiculous. From the ideal, high-sounding, and ephemeral, he will abruptly crash to the banal, mundane, and material. For example, in his mockery of scientific theories and language "Strung Out," inspired by the science section of *The New York Times*, he

contemplates that if our sun exploded "this planet would fly out of orbit and hurtle through infinity forever--another reason to always carry a cell phone." He also muses on "little things the size of 'Planck length' in the universe, which are a millionth of a billionth of a billionth of a billionth of a centimeter" and asks the reader "[i]magine if you dropped one in a dark theater how hard it would be to find."

Sometimes, as the reader goes through the pieces, the names (E. Coli Biggs, Mike Umlaut, Hal Roachpaste), places (Camp Melanoma), and titles ("Behold a Pale Endocrinologist," "The Reluctant Embalmer," and "Gerbils and Gypsies") are enough to create a laugh, in the same way that Benchley, Perelman, and W. C. Fields could coin hilarious appellations and titles. The narrative situations also thrive on absurd incongruities and non sequiturs, an aspect of his comic prose that Allen has been developing. A narrator learns from a New Age spiritual "goddess" how to levitate and ends up nearly stuck in the air in "To Err Is Human--To Float, Divine." A shady film producer tries to hire an out-of-work literary writer to do a novelization based on a Three Stooges short feature in "This Nub for Hire." A schlockmeister tries to put on *Fun de Siècle*, a musical set in old Vienna with twelve-tone-scale music, Gustav and Alma Mahler as part of a love triangle, and Kafka doing a soft shoe in "Sing, You Sacher Tortes." A narrator on a trip to Heidelberg discovers philosopher *Friedrich Nietzsche's Diet Book* in "Thus Ate Zarathustra." Perhaps one of the best pieces gives a court transcript of the Walt Disney-Michael Ovitz suit about Ovitz's enormous severance package in "Surprise Rocks Disney Trial," which begins:

COUNSEL Will the witness please state his name.
WITNESS Mickey Mouse.
C Please tell the court your occupation.
W Animated rodent.

OTHER MAJOR WORKS

PLAYS: *Don't Drink the Water*, pb. 1966; *Play It Again Sam*, pb. 1969; *The Floating Lightbulb*, pb. 1981; *Central Park West*, pb. 1995 (one-act); *Three One Act Plays*, pb. 2003.

SCREENPLAYS: *What's New, Pussycat?*, 1965; *What's Up, Tiger Lily?*, 1966 (with others); *Take the Money and Run*, 1969 (with Mickey Rose); *Bananas*, 1971; *Everything You Wanted to Know About Sex but Were Afraid to Ask*, 1972 (partly based on David Ruben's book); *Play It Again Sam*, 1972 (screen version of his play); *Sleeper*, 1973 (with Marshall Brickman); *Love and Death*, 1975; *Annie Hall*, 1977; *Interiors*, 1978; *Manhattan*, 1979; *Stardust Memories*, 1980; *A Midsummer Night's Sex Comedy*, 1982; *Zelig*, 1983; *Broadway Danny Rose*, 1984; *The Purple Rose of Cairo*, 1985; *Hannah and Her Sisters*, 1986; *Radio Days*, 1987; *September*, 1987; *Crimes and Misdemeanors*, 1989; *Oedipus Wrecks*, 1989 (released as part of the *New York Stories* trilogy); *Alice*, 1990; *Husbands and Wives*, 1992; *Shadows and Fog*, 1992; *Manhattan Murder Mystery*, 1993; *Bullets over Broadway*, 1994; *Mighty Aphrodite*, 1995; *Everyone Says I Love You*, 1996; *Deconstructing Harry*, 1997; *Celebrity*, 1998; *Sweet and Lowdown*, 1999; *Small Time Crooks*, 2000; *The Curse of the Jade Scorpion*, 2001; *Hollywood Ending*, 2002; *Anything Else*, 2003; *Melinda and Melinda*, 2004; *Match Point*, 2005; *Scoop*, 2006; *Cassandra's Dream*, 2007; *Vicky Cristina Barcelona*, 2008; *Whatever Works*, 2009.

NONFICTION: *The Insanity Defense: The Complete Prose*, 2007.

BIBLIOGRAPHY

Allen, Woody. "Woody Allen on George S. Kaufman." *The New York Times Book Review*, October 24, 2004, p. 1. Allen talks about discovering the plays of Kaufman and trying to imitate his style of humor.

Baxter, John. *Woody Allen: A Biography*. London: HarperCollins, 1998. Offers insight into the life of the author-filmmaker.

Björkman, Stig. *Woody Allen on Woody Allen: In Conversation with Stig Björkman*. Revised ed. New York: Grove Press, 1993. Interviews conducted over several years starting in 1986, emphasizing Allen's filmmaking, early career in television and theater, writing, and acting.

Davis, Robert Murray. "A Stand-Up Guy Sits Down: Woody Allen's Prose." *Short Story* 2 (Fall, 1994): 61-68. Compares Allen's stories with those of Donald Barthelme; provides a reading of Allen's best-known story, "The Kugelmass Episode," in terms of its comic techniques.

De Navacelle, Thierry, *Woody Allen on Location*. New York: William Morrow, 1987. Presents an interesting portrait of Allen at work on the film *Radio Days*. Amply demonstrates both Allen's seriousness as an artist and the lengthy process by which his written work is transferred to the medium of film. Indicates the importance of revision as Allen brings his films to fruition (in contrast to the apparent spontaneity of his short fiction).

Galef, David. "Getting Even: Literary Posterity and the Case for Woody Allen." *South Atlantic Review* 64, no. 2 (Spring, 1999): 146-160. Examines Allen comic writing in his first three collections with a view toward his literary posterity.

Hirsch, Foster. *Love, Sex, Death, and the Meaning of Life*. New York: McGraw-Hill, 1984. Explores the philosophical themes that appear consistently throughout Allen's work. Helps to establish a continuous thread in Allen's prolific career and shows how some of the disturbing questions raised in his short fiction are dealt with in his more fully developed film efforts.

Kakutani, Michiko. "The Art of Humor I: Woody Allen." *The Paris Review* 136 (Fall, 1995): 200-222. In this special issue on humor, Allen is interviewed and discusses how humorists perceive reality, which writers most influenced his writing, which filmmakers most influenced his directing, and how he sees his development since his stand-up comedy days.

Lax, Eric. *Conversations with Woody Allen: His Films, the Movies, and Moviemaking*. New York: Alfred A. Knopf, 2009. Based on firsthand conversations, this book presents a detailed account of Allen's active professional career and some of his more interesting recreational endeavors (such as participation in jazz sessions).

_____. *Woody Allen: A Biography*. New York: Da Capo, 2000. In this updated edition, Lax covers Allen's formative years and provides detailed discussion of Allen's career. Offers insight into Allen's many influences, ranging from Ingmar Bergman to the Marx brothers.

Pinsker, Sanford. "Comedy and Cultural Timing: The Lessons of Robert Benchley and Woody Allen." *The Georgia Review* 42 (Winter, 1988): 822-837. Illuminating comparison of Allen with an early master of the one-liner. (Like Allen, Benchley doubled as a performer and writer.)

_____. "Woody Allen's Lovable Anxious Schlemiels." *Studies in American Humor* 5 (Summer/ Fall, 1986): 177-189. Examines Allen's most common character type, particularly in his early films. Provides an interesting contrast with Allen's stories, where the characters often are not nearly so lovable.

Reisch, Marc S. "Woody Allen: American Prose Humorist." *Journal of Popular Culture* 17 (Winter, 1983): 68-74. Focuses on Allen's talent as a comic writer, sorting out his place in a long line of American humorists.

Ira Smolensky
Updated by Joseph Francavilla

DOROTHY ALLISON

Born: Greenville, South Carolina; April 11, 1949

PRINCIPAL SHORT FICTION

Trash, 1988

OTHER LITERARY FORMS

Dorothy Allison's body of work is diverse. In addition to her short fiction, she has written poetry, novels, a memoir, and nonfiction. *The Women Who Hate Me* (1983), a collection of poetry, was written in response to negative relationships between women as a result of feminist ideals and included poems about her own problematic relations with her sisters. *Two or Three Things I Know for Sure* (1995) is a brief memoir that provides only a superficial overview of her life. She also has written two award-winning novels, *Bastard out of Carolina* (1992) and *Cavedweller* (1998), both of which were made into films. Her nonfiction is prolific and appears in varied publications. *Skin: Talking About Sex, Class, and Culture* (1994) contains a number of autobiographical essays and pieces about class status and literary connections.

ACHIEVEMENTS

Dorothy Allison has won significant recognition for her writing. Among her numerous awards, the short-story collection *Trash* won two Lambda Literary Awards: one for Best Lesbian Small Press Book and one for Best Lesbian Fiction. "Compassion," a story she added to the second publication of this collection, was chosen as one of the *Best American Short Stories, 2003* and was included in *Best New Stories from the South, 2003*. *Bastard out of Carolina*, her first novel, was a finalist for the 1992 National Book Award and won the Ferro-Grumley Award and the Bay Area Book Reviewers Award. In 1995, Allison won the American Library Association's Gay and Lesbian Book Award for her nonfiction book *Skin*, and her memoir *Two or Three Things I Know for Sure* was a *New York Times Book Review* notable book of the year. *Cavedweller*, her second novel, won the 1998 Lambda Literary Award for Best Lesbian Fiction and was a finalist for the Lillian Smith Prize. In 2007, Allison won the Robert Penn Warren Award for Fiction.

BIOGRAPHY

Three days after giving birth to Dorothy Allison, fifteen-year-old Ruth Gibson regained consciousness to find that her daughter had been named by her mother's sisters, who did not know the baby's father's identity, thus leading to the designation of "bastard" on Allison's birth certificate. This label would devastate both Gibson and Allison for much of their lives. A year after Allison's birth, her mother married and had a second daughter. Unfortunately, that husband was killed within another year.

Gibson married again when Allison was five years old. The abuse her stepfather visited on Allison is documented throughout her works. The physical abuse was so devastating that she suffered numerous broken bones, including her coccyx, and two hospitalizations. The molestations intensified to rape, and Allison contracted gonorrhea, which would lead to her inability to have children.

Though Gibson was a hardworking waitress, Allison's stepfather worked only sporadically. The continuing poverty and social ostracism reinforced Gibson's admonitions that the abuse be kept hidden. The abuse was so bad that twice extended family helped Allison's mother leave her husband, but each time Gibson and the girls returned. Allison found escape in reading and writing, which her mother encouraged. Until Allison was in her mid-twenties, she burned her stories, realizing that the words she had recorded were dangerous.

After she graduated from high school, Allison attended Florida Presbyterian College on a full scholarship. However, she did not fit in and struggled to

Dorothy Allison (Getty Images)

survive. During her stint in higher education, Allison discovered feminism and embraced her lesbianism. In 1971, she completed her bachelor's degree and began graduate courses at Florida State University.

Her writing career began in the mid-1970's. She helped begin the magazine that published her first poem, taught writing workshops, and aided in the promotion of feminism. She lived in both Washington, D.C., and New York City for a time, continuing in journalistic work and feminist activities. She completed a master's degree in the New School for Social Research in New York in 1981. She has taught at numerous colleges and universities and has continued to present her essays and stories at conferences across the country.

In the late 1980's, Allison moved to California after she fell down a staircase and had problems healing properly. When she finally began to get well, she met and fell in love with Alix Layman, with whom she has maintained a long-term relationship. The two adopted a son in the early 1990's.

ANALYSIS

Dorothy Allison's fiction stands out for its unrelenting topic matter. Her stories reveal the reality of broken lives, and she does this without sentimentalizing the events she thrusts upon her audience. As she reveals the tales of women who know suffering, her tone varies: self-deprecating humor, straightforward bluntness, and debilitating grief or anger,. In the introduction to the second edition of *Trash*, Allison says, "We were the bad poor. . . . We were not noble, not grateful, not even hopeful. We knew ourselves despised." In these statements and the stories that follow, she reveals her struggle with understanding and accepting the poverty that overwhelmed her childhood and the lives of her mother, aunts, and grandmothers.

Allison's dominant themes include poverty, incest, and abuse. She talks about children who die, about daughters who are molested, about wives who long for peace, and about lovers who cannot comprehend. Her narrators, always first person, are women, variations of herself. The speakers have mothers who are helpless in the face of physically strong and psychologically vicious men, or they are involved in lesbian relationships with lovers who cannot relate to the speakers' pasts.

Throughout the stories, however, there is a sense of what Allison calls "forgiveness" for herself and for those who did not or could not protect her. Despite content that Allison's mother once called "mean," positive themes of "love and compassion" become central ideas as the stories are read and reread. Another common thread seen in the short stories is lesbianism.

Influences on Allison's work are varied. Allison gives Toni Morrison credit for allowing her to write about incest. However, more often than not, she uses her own emotional situations to inspire the stories: feelings of wrath, the need to comprehend, the question of forgiveness, and the hope offered through feminism.

"RIVER OF NAMES"

The first story in *Trash*, "River of Names," is poetic prose that transforms brief narratives into snapshots of family members who died, were disfigured, or disappeared. However, these portraits are broken up with glimpses into the narrator's relationship with a lover whose background has provided her "the fairy tale she thinks is everyone else's life" and who cannot comprehend the "mysteries" of family that no one misses. The first image is a young child hanging in a barn; another is a homespun abortion. These are followed by stories of tortures inflicted by those who should be trusted. Though the accounts could be sentimental, their telling is so blunt that the traces of lives affected by poverty and abuse become almost nonchalant, and the narrator reveals that she shares them with her friends as if they are comic. However, the narrator's awareness of her own dishonesty in making light of the stories and her struggle over her own infertility as a result of abuse bring out the tragedy of these lost children.

"DEMON LOVER"

Katy, who craved complete control over her lovers, died of a drug overdose, but she still haunts the narrator. Late at night, the narrator remembers Katy, keeping the ghost alive and giving her the control she wanted during life. The overwhelming grief the narrator experiences is counterbalanced by both the anger and the sexual desire she still feels as the ghost tortures her with gentle caresses. As an example of the lesbian stories, this piece showcases the narrator's confusion, anger, and fear over a relationship that was not resolved before Katy's death.

"A LESBIAN APPETITE"

This story explores the idea of physical appetites for food, for sex, and for belonging. Thematic ideas of poverty, power, and lesbianism dominate the short sketches Allison offers like appetizers. The narrator begins with a description of food choices that provide comfort and security and then gives snippets of relationships as they connect to food. There is the lover who does not like to eat and as a result does not last, the one who admonishes about the unhealthy Southern food choices, and the one who thinks her mother's canned delicatessen items are the best. Food also sparks family memories and either forges connections or separates the narrator from those around her. When a supervisor takes the narrator out to eat, she cannot appreciate what he calls "the best in the world," but she does find joy in the simple offerings of a local diner.

However, food turns on the narrator. As a child, she is told by a teacher that poor children's brains do not develop because they lack the appropriate nutrients. As an adult, she is told by a doctor that her favorite foods have caused the burning in her stomach.

The story ends as the narrator dreams of a dinner party for all of the women with whom she has been involved. In the dream, she sees all of her former lovers, her mother, her aunts, her sisters, and her cousins. Her hunger is finally satisfied, because there is love where the food is shared with these important characters in her life.

"COMPASSION"

This story was completed in 2002 and has been included in the second publication of *Trash* and in numerous anthologies. Allison admits to having started "Compassion" shortly after her mother's death, and, like much of Allison's work, the story has autobiographical aspects. There are three sisters in the story: the unnamed narrator, Jo, and Arlene. The women are dealing with their mother's slow descent into death from cancer and their bitter feelings toward each other and their abusive stepfather. Jo, the oldest, seems to be the strongest. She has two daughters and a likable lover who keep her grounded, and her sisters believe that Jo has managed to work through much of the anger from her childhood. The narrator, like Allison, is a lesbian. She is the most financially stable of the three girls, and she covers her mother's excess expenses. Though the narrator has rotated among her mother's home, Arlene's apartment, and Jo's house during the early outbreaks of her mother's cancer, the narrator is staying with Jo while their mother dies. Arlene, the youngest, just wants peace. She has never been able to handle the violence from their past and refuses to admit that their mother is dying. Jack, their stepfather, is a recovering alcoholic, and their mother brags that he has done it on his own without any help from a program. Her daughters see this as his excuse to continue denying the violence he visited upon them as children.

As the women share the experience of their mother's illness, they begin to understand each other's motivations and pain. The narrator begins to recognize that Jo is not the rock that the narrator had always considered Jo to be, and the narrator acknowledges that Arlene's pain over their childhood is just as damaging as her own. Though they will probably never be extremely close, the sisters find a way to admit what their mother needs the most: a willingness on their parts to let her slip into the rest that she desires. The compassion they show their mother stretches to each other and extends into beginning a healing of their sibling relationships. The story ends simply with their mother's death.

Allison's ability to present a story with a straightforward honesty is again revealed. The story resonates with themes of forgiveness where it can be given and bitterness where it will not be offered. Understanding other people's pain and recognizing that individuals deal with life's horrors differently are important ideas as well.

OTHER MAJOR WORKS

LONG FICTION: *Bastard out of Carolina*, 1992; *Cavedweller*, 1998

POETRY: *The Women Who Hate Me*, 1983

NONFICTION: *Skin: Talking About Sex, Class, and Literature*, 1994; *Two or Three Things I Know for Sure*, 1995

BIBLIOGRAPHY

Blouch, Christine, and Laurie Vickroy, eds. *Critical Essays on the Works of American Author Dorothy Allison.* Lewiston, N.Y.: Edwin Mellen Press, 2004. This is the first collection of essays on Allison's work. Most essays focus on her first novel, but there are shared issues, so the collection is important to understanding her whole body of work.

Henninger, Katherine. "Claiming Access: Controlling Images in Dorothy Allison." *Arizona Quarterly: A Journal of American Literature, Culture, and Theory* 60, no. 3 (Autumn, 2004): 83-108. This article analyzes the use of photographs and treatment of poverty among whites in *Bastard Out of Carolina*, *Two or Three Things I Know for Sure*, and *Trash*.

Jarvis, Christina. "Gendered Appetites: Feminisms, Dorothy Allison, and the Body." *Women's Studies* 29, no. 6 (December, 2000): 763. This journal article considers the themes of sexuality and gender issues in Allison's short stories.

Jones, Stephanie. "Lessons from Dorothy Allison: Teacher Education, Social Class, and Critical Literacy." *Changing English: Studies in Culture and Education* 13, no. 3 (December, 2006): 293-305. This journal article considers the issues of social class, whiteness, and critical literacy in Allison's *Trash*.

Marsh, Janet Z. "Dorothy Allison." In *Twenty-First Century American Novelists*, edited by Wanda H. Giles and James R. Giles. Detroit, Mich.: Gale, 2009. Part of the *Dictionary of Literary Biographies* series, this article provides a brief biography of Allison.

Megan, Carolyn E. "Moving Toward Truth: An Interview with Dorothy Allison." *The Kenyon Review* 16, no. 4 (Fall, 1994): 71. This candid interview with Allison discusses her revelations about the incest and abuse that destroyed her childhood. Allison also reveals some of the life changes she made as result of her past.

Tokarczyk, Michelle M. *Class Definitions: On the Lives and Writings of Maxine Hong Kingston, Sandra Cisneros, and Dorothy Allison.* Selinsgrove, Pa.: Susquehanna University Press, 2008. This book explores the ways in which social status has affected the lives and writings of three outstanding feminist authors. The chapter on Allison provides biographical information as it pertains to her novels and her memoir.

Theresa L. Stowell

STEVE ALMOND

Born: Palo Alto, California; October 27, 1966

PRINCIPAL SHORT FICTION

My Life in Heavy Metal, 2002
The Evil B. B. Chow, and Other Short Stories, 2005
This Won't Take But a Minute, Honey, 2010 (includes essays and short stories)

OTHER LITERARY FORMS

In addition to his short fiction, Steve Almond (AH-muhnd) is widely known for detailing his personal obsessions and failings in nonfiction essays and books, including *Candyfreak: A Journey Through the Chocolate Underbelly of America* (2004), *(Not That You Asked): Rants, Exploits, and Obsessions* (2007), *Letters from People Who Hate Me* (2010), and *Rock and Roll Will Save Your Life* (2010). In 2006, he cowrote *Which Brings Me to You: A Novel in Confessions* with poet and novelist Julianna Baggott. Almond is also a regular contributor to therumpus.net, salon.com, and thehuffingtonpost.com, three online literary and contemporary culture sites.

ACHIEVEMENTS

Steve Almond's nonfiction book *Candyfreak* was a *New York Times* best seller, was featured on Food Network, and almost made him an episode on VH-1's reality show *Totally Obsessed* (a process detailed in the essay "How Reality TV Ate My Life" in *(Not That You Asked)*. He is the author of two collections of short stories, *My Life in Heavy Metal* and *The Evil B. B. Chow,* and has been awarded Pushcart Prizes for his stories "The Pass" (2003) and "The Darkness Together" (2006). His stories also have appeared in Best American Erotica in 2004 and 2005.

BIOGRAPHY

Steve Almond was born October 27, 1966, to an upper-middle-class Jewish family in Palo Alto, California, where he grew up, the grandson of political scientist Gabriel Almond and child of two psychiatrists, Richard and Barbara Almond. After high school, Steve Almond earned an undergraduate degree from Wesleyan University. He then spent more than seven years as a newspaper reporter, mainly covering rock music and criticism for weeklies in El Paso, Texas, and Greensboro, North Carolina, and for the *Miami New Times*. He received an M.F.A. in fiction writing from the University of North Carolina at Greensboro in 1996. Almond served as an adjunct professor, teaching creative writing at Boston College for five years, until he resigned in protest of the college's invitation to U.S. secretary of state Condoleezza Rice to speak at commencement. His resignation was published as an open letter in *The Boston Globe* on May 12, 2006, and the story was picked up and covered by Cable News Network (CNN) as well as by Fox News, where Almond later sparred with political talk-show host Sean Hannity. This incident is covered in "Demagogue Days" in *(Not That You Asked)* and in *Letters from People Who Hate Me* (2010). Since his resignation, Almond also has taken on the publishing industry, criticizing its system of agents and marketing decisions, a position that has led him to eschew having an agent himself and to self-publish some of his work, including *This Won't Take But a Minute, Honey* (2010), and promoting these practices in writing forums such as *The Associated Writing Programs Chronicle* and *Poets and Writers*. He continues to write and publish widely, including blog posts at salon.com and therumpus.net and book reviews for *The Boston Globe* and the *Los Angeles Times*, in addition to his literary fiction and essays. Almond also teaches at numerous prestigious literary conferences, festivals, and workshops. He lives outside Boston with his wife, Erin, and his two children, Josephine and Judah.

ANALYSIS

Steve Almond's stories are largely character-driven, written mainly in either first or limited third person, and they look at his characters during life transitions (a move to a new city, the end of a college semester) and sexual transitions (adolescence, adulthood, a new relationship). He has written a great deal about sexuality, from both male and female protagonists' positions, which has earned Almond both admiration and criticism. In response to this issue, Almond said during an interview, "People are so fearful of their own desires that it becomes prurient, that sex doesn't feel very emotional to me. . . . There's also an aesthetic thing at play. I lean heavily on physicality and emotion. . . . I write a lot of female protagonists [because it] feels more natural for a woman to be talking about her feelings in the way my characters do than for a man. I don't know if you've noticed, but men kind of check out when things get emotional." By examining his characters at their most vulnerable, their souls are revealed at their most honest, with the potential for either salvation or damnation. Almond's stories are written in the same terse, humorous, self-deprecating style and with the obsessive attention to detail for which he is known in his nonfiction writings. In a large sense, Almond's writings, whether fictional or not, are ruled by desire and the thwarting of those desires. He explains in *Candyfreak* that "we don't choose our freaks, they choose us. . . . We may have no conscious control over our allegiances. But they arise from our most sacred fears and desires and, as such, they represent the truest expression of our selves." Whether the obsession is with candy, a sports team, a rock band, politics, or reality television, "to be a fan is to live in a condition of willed helplessness."

MY LIFE IN HEAVY METAL

Almond's first collection deals with the various ways people grapple with each other, emotionally, violently, and sexually. Notably, the book contains three stories written from the perspective of the same protagonist, David, at different points in his life: The title story, published in *Playboy*, follows David at his first job after his college graduation; "Run Away, My Pale Love" looks at David when he returns to graduate school just before his thirtieth birthday; and "The Body

Steve Almond (Katy Winn/Corbis)

in Extremis" takes place during David's mid-thirties. Almond describes David as "this guy, who couldn't really keep his dick in order, or his life, and who sinned and was punished for his sins." As David himself puts it, "I am certain that you, too, have some . . . mad period of transgression in which your body, your foolish foolish body, led you toward tender ruin." In "My Life in Heavy Metal," David reviews rock bands for a paper in El Paso (much as the author did) and tries to live the rock-and-roll lifestyle by dividing his time between his live-in girlfriend Jo and a lifeguard named Claudia, who has the fascinating ability to ejaculate a copious volume of liquid. Inevitably, the situation comes to a head with Jo walking in on David and Claudia, a motif that is mirrored in the last story, "The Body in Extremis," where after a sexual affair with the adventurous Ling, David is surprised to find himself hurt when he walks in on her and her boyfriend. In a sense, the two stories provide a balanced morality, in which David both sins and is sinned against. The connection between the motifs of heavy-metal music and sex is perhaps obvious, but Almond explains it well in his essay "Tesla Matters (Dude)": "heavy metal was essentially tribal in nature and . . . had everything to do with rhythm and aggression and desire and conquest and physical release and death, which is to say, with sex."

THE EVIL B. B. CHOW

The stories of Almond's second collection cast a wider net, covering such far-flung topics as alien abduction, Michael Jackson's genitals, and Abraham Lincoln's interracial homoerotic fetish. Nonetheless, Almond's hallmark humor and sexual intimacy are still evident. In the title story, Almond does a clever inversion of "chick-lit" stereotypes by writing from the perspective of the female editor of a women's magazine, complete with obsequious gay underling, but who narrates without a whiff of sentimentality. She starts a relationship with an odd, short doctor to whom she inexplicably is attracted, despite his neediness and shortcomings in the bedroom. A few of the stories engage with the frustrations of evaluating creative writing in a way that manages to avoid metafictional pretension. "Appropriate Sex" involves a fiction teacher with nubile, oversexed students of questionable talent, and he attempts to navigate professionally the students' hormones and bad writing. Likewise, in "Larsen's Novel," a dentist is pushed relentlessly to read and comment on the six-hundred-page cliché-ridden novel of his best friend. In two stories that stray from Almond's adult themes, "I Am as I Am" and "The Problem of Human Consumption," he examines two adolescents at a difficult moment between childhood and the confusing world of grown-ups. "I Am as I Am" focuses on an accident that occurs during a kids' neighborhood baseball game: When one boy falls into a coma after he gets in the way of a swinging bat, the batter wants to apologize: "Eric wanted to tell [his mother] that he was scared, that he *needed* to say he was sorry." However, the situation is micromanaged by his parents, who are focused only on mitigating legal blame: "The feeling reminded him of having the chicken pox, a kind of quarantine." In "The Problem of Human Consumption," which switches between the points of view of a father and his teenage daughter, both characters are surprised into a brief moment of shared grief when the father discovers his deceased wife's wedding band while in his daughter's room. The

point of view zooms out to an omniscient narrator who tells the reader, "It is important to remember that this is only a single moment, this tentative caress, nothing they will speak of again. . . . . They are prisoners of this moment and wonderfully, terribly alive." Whether the relationships of his characters are sexual or not, Almond constantly reminds the reader that intimacy is awkward and messy, yet consoling.

"THE DARKNESS TOGETHER"

This story, which appeared in *Pushcart Prize XXX*, creates an interesting comparison with "The Problem of Human Consumption." Whereas the father and daughter of the latter are held apart by their grief over the absent mother, the mother and teenage son of "The Darkness Together" share a disturbingly erotic relationship in the absence of the father. As the narrator describes it, their overly familiar way of touching has "a practiced intimacy." However, during a train trip (a story strategy employed to great effect by Flannery O'Connor), they encounter a coarse stranger whose blunt observations provide a bright foil to the pair, pointing out the desires and fears that bind them. About the boy, Michael, the stranger says, "a boy of your son's age has certain thoughts, certain preoccupations. Pretending otherwise is really no solution. That creates all kinds of pressure." To the mother, the stranger says, "Mike can't stay around forever, after all, dressing and undressing in that room next to yours . . . both of you struggling to lift that large, unnameable need onto the other." When the stranger leaves, the final image of the mother and son is overtly sexual, but more confused than before, with the mother slipping between age and youth and with Michael asserting himself as a man.

THIS WON'T TAKE BUT A MINUTE, HONEY

This Won't Take But a Minute, Honey is a small self-published volume that consists of thirty flash-fiction stories, most a page or less; if flipped over head-to-tail, the book contains thirty mini-essays on the craft of writing, which Almond invites readers to apply to the fiction. The relatively new but popular genre of flash fiction incorporates many of the elements of a full-length story (plot, character, conflict), but compresses them into a narrative of less than five hundred words. Almond presents a range of styles--fantasies, potboilers, meditations, remembrances, and social commentaries--arranged into six sections of five stories each, moving from the backward gazing "i. An Imperfect Command of History" in an arc that becomes nearly circular with "vi. Major American Cities of Sadness," which makes a history of the present. On one page Almond inhabits the mind of a young soldier deciding the fate of his captives; on the next Almond is the avalanche that covers the survivors of a plane crash; after that Almond may be a girl in a brown smock punching the register at Roy Rogers or an adult remembering how, as an eight-year-old-boy, he loved his grandparents but did not realize they were old and that time would take them.

One of the book's central themes is how the individual perseveres against the context and flow of events. This theme of persistence, combined with the direct and careful crafting of Almond's prose, gives the narratives a sense of inevitability, which allows them to at times encompass dissonant and strange elements and still create the illusion that the story could never come out any other way.

OTHER MAJOR WORKS

LONG FICTION: *Which Brings Me to You: A Novel in Confessions*, 2006 (with Julianna Baggott).

NONFICTION: *Candyfreak: A Journey Through the Chocolate Underbelly of America*, 2004; *(Not That You Asked): Rants, Exploits, and Obsessions*, 2007; *Letters from People Who Hate Me*, 2010; *Rock and Roll Will Save Your Life*, 2010.

BIBLIOGRAPHY

Almond, Steve. "Are Agents Necessary?" *Poets and Writers* (January/February, 2004): 55-59. An argument against the pressure on fiction writers to submit to agents.

_____. "Author Economics." *Poets and Writers* (May/June, 2009): 67-70. Article in which Almond discusses the publishing industry and the effect of economic cycles on independent authors and bookstores.

_____. "Self-Publishing 101." *Poets and Writers* (May/June, 2010): 62-63. Guides authors through the process of self-publishing, including how to navigate vanity and private presses, marketing, and distribution.

Schillinger, Liesl. "Books of Style." *The New York Times*, September 23, 2007. Review of Almond's *(Not That You Asked)*, citing the writer's humor and references to sexuality.

Williamson, Eric Miles. "The Future of American Fiction." *Southern Review* (Summer, 2002): 666-675. An overview of debuting writers that identifies Almond as a promising short-fiction writer after the publication of his collection *My Life in Heavy Metal*.

Heidi K. Czerwiec

SHERWOOD ANDERSON

Born: Camden, Ohio; September 13, 1876
Died: Colón, Panama Canal Zone; March 8, 1941

PRINCIPAL SHORT FICTION

*Winesburg, Ohio: A Group of Tales of Ohio Small
    Town Life,* 1919
The Triumph of the Egg, 1921
Horses and Men, 1923
Death in the Woods, and Other Stories, 1933
The Sherwood Anderson Reader, 1947
*Certain Things Last: The Selected Short Stories of
    Sherwood Anderson,* 1992

OTHER LITERARY FORMS

Sherwood Anderson published seven novels, collections of essays, memoirs, poetry, and dramatizations of *Winesburg, Ohio: A Group of Tales of Ohio Small Town Life,* as well as other stories. He was a prolific article writer and for a time owned and edited both the Republican and Democratic newspapers in Marion, Virginia. In 1921, he received a two-thousand-dollar literary prize from *The Dial* magazine. While employed as a copywriter, Anderson wrote many successful advertisements.

ACHIEVEMENTS

Sherwood Anderson, a protomodernist, is generally accepted as an innovator in the field of the short story despite having produced only one masterpiece, *Winesburg, Ohio.* In his work, he not only revolutionized the structure of short fiction by resisting the literary slickness of the contrived plot but also encouraged a simple and direct prose style, one that reflects the spare poetry of ordinary American speech. Anderson's thematic concerns were also innovative. He was one of the first writers to dramatize the artistic repudiation of the business world

and to give the craft of the short story a decided push toward presenting a slice of life as a significant moment. His concern with the "grotesques" in society--the neurotics and eccentrics--is also innovative, as is the straightforward attention he pays to his characters' sexuality. Anderson's contemporaries Ernest Hemingway, William Faulkner, and John Steinbeck were influenced by his work, as were several later writers: Carson McCullers, Flannery O'Connor, Saul Bellow, Bobbie Ann Mason, and Raymond Carver.

BIOGRAPHY

Sherwood Anderson was the third of seven children of a father who was an itinerant harness maker and house painter and a mother of either German or Italian descent. His father was a Civil War veteran (a Southerner who fought with the Union), locally famed as a storyteller. His elder brother, Karl, became a prominent painter who later introduced Sherwood to Chicago's Bohemia, which gained him access to the literary world. Declining fortunes caused the family to move repeatedly until they settled in Clyde, Ohio (the model for Winesburg), a village just south of Lake Erie. The young Anderson experienced a desultory schooling and worked at several jobs: as a newsboy, a housepainter, a stableboy, a farmhand, and a laborer in a bicycle factory.

After serving in Cuba during the Spanish-American War (he saw no combat), Anderson acquired a further year of schooling at Wittenberg Academy in Springfield, Ohio, but remained undereducated throughout his life. Jobs as advertising copywriter gave him a first taste of writing, and he went on to a successful business career. In 1912, the central psychological event of his life occurred. He suffered a nervous breakdown, which led him to walk out of his paint factory in Elyria, Ohio. He moved to Chicago, where he began to meet writers such as Floyd Dell, Carl Sandburg, and Ben Hecht, a group collectively known as the Chicago Renaissance. A significant nonliterary contact was Dr. Trigant Burrow of Baltimore, who operated a Freudian therapeutic camp in Lake Chateaugay, New York, during the summers of 1915 and 1916. It should be noted, however, that Anderson ultimately rejected scientific probing of the psyche, for he typically believed that the human mind is static and incapable of meaningful change for the better. Publication of *Winesburg, Ohio* catapulted him into prominence, and he traveled to Europe in 1921, where he became acquainted with Gertrude Stein, Ernest Hemingway, and James Joyce. In 1923, while living in New Orleans, he shared an apartment with William Faulkner.

Anderson married and divorced four times. He and his first wife had three children. His second wife, Tennessee Mitchell, had been a lover to Edgar Lee Masters, author of the *Spoon River Anthology* (1915). His last wife, Eleanor Copenhaver, had an interest in the southern labor movement, which drew Anderson somewhat out of his social primitivism, and for a time in the 1930's he became a favorite of communists and socialists. His death, in Colón, Panama Canal Zone, while on a voyage to South America, was notable for its unique circumstances: He died of peritonitis caused by a toothpick accidentally swallowed while eating hors d'œuvres.

ANALYSIS

Sherwood Anderson's best-known and most important work is the American classic, *Winesburg, Ohio*. It is a collection of associated short stories set in the mythical town of Winesburg in the latter part of the nineteenth century. The stories catalog Anderson's negative reaction to the transformation of Ohio from a largely agricultural to an industrial society, which culminated about the time he was growing up in the village of Clyde in the 1880's. Its twenty-five stories are vignettes of the town doctor; the voluble baseball coach; the still attractive but aging-with-loneliness high school teacher; the prosperous and harsh farmer-turned-religious fanatic; the dirt laborer; the hotel keeper; the banker's daughter and her adolescent suitors; the Presbyterian minister struggling with temptation; the town drunk; the town rough; the town

homosexual; and the town "half-wit." The comparison to Masters's *Spoon River Anthology* is obvious: Both works purport to reveal the secret lives of small-town Americans living in the Midwest, and ironically both owe their popular success to the elegiac recording of this era, which most Americans insist on viewing idyllically. Anderson's work, however, differs by more directly relating sexuality to the bizarre behavior of many of his characters and by employing a coherent theme.

That theme is an exploration of psychological "grotesques"--the casualties of economic progress--and how these grotesques participate in the maturing of George Willard, the teenage reporter for the *Winesburg Eagle*, who at the end of the book departs for a bigger city to become a journalist. By then his sometimes callous ambition to get ahead has been tempered by a sense of what Anderson chooses to call "sophistication," the title of the penultimate story. The achievement of George's sophistication gives *Winesburg, Ohio* its artistic movement but makes it problematic for many critics and thoughtful Americans.

Sherwood Anderson (Library of Congress)

"THE BOOK OF THE GROTESQUE"

The prefacing story defines grotesques. A dying old writer hires a carpenter to build up his bed so that he can observe the trees outside without getting out of it. (While living in Chicago in 1915, Anderson had his own bed similarly raised so that he could observe the Loop.) After the carpenter leaves, the writer returns to his project--the writing of "The Book of the Grotesque," which grieves over the notion that in the beginning of the world there were a great many thoughts but no such thing as a "truth." People turned these thoughts into many beautiful truths, such as the truth of passion, wealth, poverty, profligacy, carelessness, and others; a person could then appropriate a single one of these truths and try to live by it. It was thus that he or she would become a grotesque--a personality dominated by an overriding concern that in time squeezed out other facets of life.

This epistemological fable, which involves a triple reduction, raises at least two invalidating questions: First, can there be "thoughts" without the truth to establish the self-differentiating process which generates thought? Second, if universals are denied and all truths have equal value (they are *all* beautiful), then why should a person be condemned for choosing only one of these pluralistic "truths"?

"HANDS"

The stories in *Winesburg, Ohio* nevertheless do grapple with Anderson's intended theme, and a story such as "Hands" clearly illustrates what he means by a grotesque. The hands belong to Wing Biddlebaum, formerly Adolph Myers, a teacher in a Pennsylvania village who was beaten and run out of town for caressing boys. Anderson is delicately oblique about Wing's homosexuality, for the story focuses on how a single traumatic event can forever after rule a person's life--Wing is now a fretful recluse whose only human contact occurs when George Willard visits him occasionally. George puzzles over Wing's expressive hands but never fathoms the reason for his suffering diffidence. "Hands," besides giving first flesh to the word grotesque, makes the reader understand that a character's volition is not necessarily the factor that traps him into such an ideological straightjacket; sympathy can therefore be more readily extended.

"THE PHILOSOPHER"

"The Philosopher" provides a more subtle illustration of a grotesque and introduces the idea that a grotesque need not be pitiable or tragic; in fact, he can be wildly humorous, as demonstrated at the beginning of the story with the philosopher's description:

> Doctor Parcival, the philosopher, was a large man with a drooping mouth covered by a yellow moustache . . . he wore a dirty white waistcoat out of whose pocket protruded a number of black cigars . . . there was something strange about his eyes: the lid of his left eye twitched; it fell down and it snapped up; it was exactly as though the lid of the eye were a window shade and someone stood inside playing with the cord.

It is George Willard's misfortune that Dr. Parcival likes him and uses him as a sounding board for his wacky pomposity. He wishes to convince the boy of the advisability of adopting a line of conduct that he himself is unable to define but amply illustrates with many "parables" that add up to the belief (as George begins to suspect) that all men are despicable. He tells George that his father died in an insane asylum, and then he continues on about a Dr. Cronin from Chicago who may have been murdered by several men, one of whom could have been yours truly, Dr. Parcival. He announces that he actually arrived in Winesburg to write a book. About to launch into the subject of the book, he is sidetracked into the story of his brother who worked for the railroad as part of a roving paint crew (which painted everything orange); on payday the brother would place his money on the kitchen table, daring any member of the family to touch it. The brother, while drunk, is run over by the rail car housing the other members of his crew.

One day George drops into Dr. Parcival's office for his customary morning visit and discovers him quaking with fear. Earlier a little girl had been thrown from her buggy, and the doctor had inexplicably refused to heed a passerby's call, perhaps because he is not a medical doctor. Other doctors, however, arrived on the scene, and no one noticed Dr. Parcival's absence. Not realizing this, the doctor shouts to George that he knows human nature and that soon a hanging party will be formed to hang him from a lamppost as punishment for his callous refusal to attend to the dying child. When his certainty dissipates, he whimpers to George, "If not now, sometime." He begs George to take him seriously and asks him to finish his book if something should happen to him; to this end he informs George of the subject of the book, which is: Everyone in the world is Christ, and they are all crucified.

Many critics have singled out one or another story as the best in *Winesburg, Ohio*; frequently mentioned are "The Untold Lie," "Hands," and "Sophistication." However, aside from the fact that this may be an unfair exercise because the stories in *Winesburg, Ohio* were written to stand together, these choices bring out the accusation that much of Anderson's work has a "setup" quality--a facile solemnity that makes his fictions manifest. "The Philosopher" may be the best story because Dr. Parcival's grotesqueness eludes overt labeling; its finely timed humor reveals Anderson's ability to spoof his literary weaknesses, and the story captures one of those character types who, like Joe Welling of "A Man of Ideas," is readily observable and remembered but proves irritatingly elusive when set down.

"Godliness"

Anderson exhibits a particular interest in the distorting effect that religious mania has on the personality, and several stories in *Winesburg, Ohio* attack or ridicule examples of conspicuous religiosity. "Godliness," a tetralogy with a gothic flavor, follows the life of Jesse Bentley, a wealthy, progressive farmer who poisons the life of several generations of his relatives with his relentless harshness until he becomes inflamed by Old Testament stories and conceives the idea of replicating an act of animal sacrifice. Because of this behavior, he succeeds in terrifying his fifteen-year-old grandson, the only person he loves, who flees from him never to be heard from again, thus breaking the grandfather's spirit.

"The Strength of God"

Two stories, "The Strength of God" and "The Teacher," are juxtaposed to mock cleverly a less extravagant example of piety. The Reverend Curtis Hartman espies Kate Swift, the worldly high school teacher, reading in bed and smoking a cigarette. The sight affronts and preoccupies him and plunges him into a prolonged moral struggle that is resolved when one night he observes her kneeling naked by her bed praying. He smashes the window through which he has been watching her and runs into George Willard's office shouting that Kate Swift is an instrument of God bearing a message of truth. Kate remains entirely oblivious of the reverend, for she is preoccupied with George, in whom she has detected a spark of literary genius worthy of her cultivation. Her praying episode--an act of desperation that the reverend mistook for a return to faith--was the result of her realization, while in George's arms, that her altruism had turned physical.

"Sophistication"

It is exposure to these disparate egoisms, the death of his mother, and a poignant evening with Helen White, the banker's daughter, that are gathered into the components of George's "sophistication," the achievement of which causes him to leave town. George's departure, however, has a decidedly ambivalent meaning. Anderson and other writers before and after him have shown that American small-town life can be less than idyllic, but *Winesburg, Ohio* is problematic because it is not simply another example of "the revolt from the village." In the story "Paper Pills," the narrator states that apples picked from Winesburg orchards will be eaten in city apartments that are filled with books, magazines, furniture, and people. A few rejected apples, however, which have gathered all their sweetness in one corner and are delicious to eat, remain on the trees and are eaten by those who are not discouraged by their lack of cosmetic appeal. Thus the neuroses of Anderson's grotesques are sentimentalized and become part of his increasingly strident polemic against rationality, the idea of progress, mechanization, scientific innovation, urban culture, and other expressions of social potency. Anderson never wonders why pastorals are not written by pastors but rather by metropolitans whose consciousnesses are heightened by the advantages of urban life; his own version of a pastoral, *Winesburg, Ohio*, was itself written in Chicago.

Anderson published three other collections of short stories in his lifetime, and other stories that had appeared in various magazines were posthumously gathered by Paul Rosenfeld in *The Sherwood Anderson Reader*. These are anthologies with no common theme or recurring characters, although some, such as *Horses and Men*, portray a particular milieu, such as the racing world or rustic life. Many of the stories, and nearly all those singled out by the critics for their high quality, are first-person narratives. They are told in a rambling, reminiscent vein and are often preferred to those in *Winesburg, Ohio* because they lack a staged gravity. The grotesques are there, but less as syndromes than as atmospheric effects.

"DEATH IN THE WOODS"

The gothic nature of the later stories becomes more pronounced, and violence, desolation, and decay gain ascendancy in Anderson's best story, "Death in the Woods," from the collection of the same name. This work also has another dimension: It is considered "to be among that wide and interesting mass of creative literature written about literature," for, as the narrator tells the story of the elderly drudge who freezes to death while taking a shortcut through the snowy woods, he explains that as a young man he worked on the farm of a German who kept a bound servant like the young Mrs. Grimes. He recalls the circular track that her dogs made about her body while growing bold enough to get at her bag of meat when he himself has an encounter with dogs on a moonlit winter night. When the woman's body is found and identified, the townspeople turn against her ruffian husband and son and force them out of town, and their dwelling is visited by the narrator after it becomes an abandoned and vandalized hulk.

Because Mrs. Grimes is such an unobtrusive and inarticulate character, the narrator is forced to tell her story, as well as how he gained each aspect of the story, until the reader's interest is awakened by the uncovering of the narrator's mental operations. This process leads the narrator to ponder further how literature itself is written and guides him to the final expansion: consciousness of his own creative processes. The transfer of interest from the uncanny circumstances of Mrs. Grimes's death to this awareness of human creativity lends some credibility to Sherwood Anderson's epitaph, "Life, Not Death, Is the Great Adventure."

"THE MAN WHO BECAME A WOMAN"

"The Man Who Became a Woman," from *Horses and Men*, is another critic's choice. A young horse groom is sneaking a drink at a bar and imagines that his image on the counter mirror is that of a young girl. He becomes involved in an appalling barroom brawl (its horror contradicts the popular image of brawls in Westerns), and later, while sleeping nude on top of a pile of horse blankets, he is nearly raped by two drunken black grooms who mistake him for a slim young woman. The several strong foci in this long story tend to cancel one another out, and the built-in narrative devices for explaining the reason for the telling of the story succeed only in giving it a disconnected feel, although it is the equal of "Death in the Woods" in gothic details.

"I AM A FOOL"

"I Am a Fool," also from *Horses and Men*, is Anderson's most popular story. Here a young horse groom describes a humiliation caused less by his own gaucheness with the opposite sex than by the gulf of social class and education that separates him from the girl. The story re-creates the universe of adolescent romance so well presented in *Winesburg, Ohio* and brings a knowing smile from all manner of readers.

"THE EGG"

In "The Egg" (from *The Triumph of the Egg*), a husband-and-wife team of entrepreneurs try their hand at chicken-raising and running a restaurant. They fail at both, and the cause in both instances is an egg. This is a mildly humorous spoof on the American penchant for quick-success schemes, which nevertheless does not explain the praise the story has been given.

"THE CORN PLANTING"

"The Corn Planting" (from *The Sherwood Anderson Reader*) is Anderson without histrionics. An elderly farm couple are told that their city-dwelling son has been killed in an automobile accident. In response, the pair rig a planting machine and set about planting corn in the middle of the night while still in their nightgowns. At this concluding point, a generous reader would marvel at this poignant and internally opportune description of a rite of rejuvenation. An obdurate one would mutter Karl Marx's dictum on the idiocy of rural life (not quite apropos since Marx was referring to European peasants, not technologically advanced American farmers); but this reader shall remark that the story itself functions within its confines and breezily add that Anderson's favorite appellation (and the title of one of his short stories) was An Ohio Pagan.

OTHER MAJOR WORKS

LONG FICTION: *Windy McPherson's Son*, 1916; *Marching Men*, 1917; *Poor White*, 1920; *Many Marriages*, 1923; *Dark Laughter*, 1925; *Beyond Desire*, 1932; *Kit Brandon*, 1936.

PLAY: *Plays: Winesburg and Others*, pb. 1937.

POETRY: *Mid-American Chants*, 1918; *A New Testament*, 1927.

NONFICTION: *A Story Teller's Story*, 1924; *The Modern Writer*, 1925; *Sherwood Anderson's Notebook*, 1926; *Tar: A Midwest Childhood*, 1926; *Hello Towns!*, 1929; *Perhaps Women*, 1931; *No Swank*, 1934; *Puzzled America*, 1935; *Home Town*, 1940; *Sherwood Anderson's Memoirs*, 1942; *The Letters of Sherwood Anderson*, 1953; *Selected Letters*, 1984; *Letters to Bab: Sherwood Anderson to Marietta D. Finley, 1916-1933*, 1985; *Southern Odyssey: Selected Writings by Sherwood Anderson*, 1997.

MISCELLANEOUS: *Sherwood Anderson: Early Writings*, 1989 (Ray Lewis White, editor).

BIBLIOGRAPHY

Appel, Paul P. *Homage to Sherwood Anderson: 1876-1941*. Mamaroneck, N.Y.: Paul P. Appel, 1970. A collection of essays originally published in homage to Anderson after his death in 1941. Among the contributors are Theodore Dreiser, Gertrude Stein, Thomas Wolfe, Henry Miller, and William Saroyan. Also includes Anderson's previously unpublished letters and his essay "The Modern Writer," which had been issued as a limited edition in 1925.

Bassett, John E. *Sherwood Anderson: An American Career*. Selinsgrove, Pa.: Susquehanna University Press, 2006. Reevaluates *Winesburg, Ohio* and Anderson's other short fiction and novels, but unlike previous studies, Bassett focuses more on Anderson's nonfiction, autobiographical, and journalistic writing. Also discusses how Anderson coped with the cultural changes of his time.

Campbell, Hilbert H. "The 'Shadow People': Feodor Sologub and Sherwood" Anderson's *Winesburg, Ohio*." *Studies in Short Fiction* 33 (Winter, 1996): 51-58. Discusses parallels between some of Sologub's stories in *The Old House, and Other Tales* and the stories in *Winesburg, Ohio*. Suggests that the Sologub stories influenced Anderson. Cites parallels to Sologub's tales in such Anderson stories as "Tandy," "Loneliness," and "The Book of the Grotesque."

Campbell, Hilbert H., and Charles E. Modlin, eds. *Sherwood Anderson: Centennial Studies*. Troy, N.Y.: Whitston, 1976. Written for Anderson's centenary, these eleven previously unpublished essays were solicited by the editors. Some of the essays explore Anderson's relationship with other artists, including Edgar Lee Masters, Henry Adams, Alfred Stieglitz, and J. J. Lankes.

Dunne, Robert. *A New Book of the Grotesques: Contemporary Approaches to Sherwood Anderson's Early Fiction*. Kent, Ohio: Kent State University Press, 2005. Offers a new interpretation of Anderson's early fiction by looking at it from a postmodern theoretical perspective, especially from poststructuralist approaches. Describes how his early fiction laid the groundwork for *Winesburg, Ohio* before it examines that book.

Ellis, James. "Sherwood Anderson's Fear of Sexuality: Horses, Men, and Homosexuality." *Studies in Short Fiction* 30 (Fall, 1993): 595-601. On the basis of biographer Kim Townsend's suggestion that Anderson sought out male spiritual friendships because he felt that sexuality would debase the beauty of woman, Ellis examines Anderson's treatment of sexuality as a threat in male relationships in the short stories "I Want to Know Why" and "The Man Who Became a Woman."

Gelfant, Blanche H., ed. *The Columbia Companion to the Twentieth-Century American Short Story*. New York: Columbia University Press, 2000. Includes a chapter in which Anderson's short stories are analyzed.

Hansen, Tom. "Who's a Fool? A Rereading of Sherwood" Anderson's 'I'm a Fool.'" *The Midwest Quarterly* 38 (Summer, 1997): 372-379. Argues that the narrator is the victim of his own self-importance and is thus played for a fool. Discusses class consciousness and conflict in the story.

Howe, Irving. *Sherwood Anderson*. Toronto: William Sloane Associates, 1951. This highly biographical work explores why Anderson, a writer with only one crucial book, remains an outstanding artist in American literature. The chapters on *Winesburg, Ohio* and the short stories are noteworthy; both were later published in collections of essays on Anderson. Includes a useful bibliography.

Lindsay, Clarence B. *Such a Rare Thing: The Art of Sherwood Anderson's "Winesburg, Ohio."* Kent, Ohio: Kent State University Press, 2009. Argues that *Winesburg, Ohio*, is a thoroughly modernist work that examines the aesthetic nature of romantic identity. Each of the small town's grotesque characters is in effect writing a romantic narrative about himself or herself, and each is trying to live his or her life according to that narrative.

Papinchak, Robert Allen. *Sherwood Anderson: A Study of the Short Fiction*. New York: Twayne, 1992. An introduction to Anderson's short stories that examines his search for an appropriate form and his experimentations with form in the stories in *Winesburg, Ohio*, as well as those that appeared before and after that highly influential book. Deals with Anderson's belief that the most authentic history of life is a history of moments when people truly live, as well as his creation of the grotesque as an American type that also reflects a new social reality. Includes comments from Anderson's essays, letters, and notebooks, as well as brief commentaries by five other critics.

Rideout, Walter B. *Sherwood Anderson: A Writer in America*. 2 vols. Madison: University of Wisconsin, 2007. A thoroughly researched biography that draws on existing biographies of Anderson, as well as on interviews with his friends and family members.

Small, Judy Jo. *A Reader's Guide to the Short Stories of Sherwood Anderson*. New York: G. K. Hall, 1994. Provides commentary on every story in *Winesburg, Ohio*, *The Triumph of the Egg*, *Horses and Men*, and *Death in the Woods*. Small summarizes the interpretations of other critics and supplies historical and biographical background, accounts of how the stories were written, the period in which they were published, and their reception.

Townsend, Kim. *Sherwood Anderson*. Boston: Houghton Mifflin, 1987. In this biography of Anderson, Townsend focuses, in part, on how Anderson's life appears in his writing. Supplemented by twenty-six photographs and a useful bibliography of Anderson's work.

Whalan, Mark. *Race, Manhood, and Modernism in America: The Short Story Cycles of Sherwood Anderson and Jean Toomer*. Knoxville: University of Tennessee Press, 2007. Examines narrative, gender, and history in *Winesburg, Ohio* and elements of primitivism in Anderson's work. Compares Anderson, Toomer, and Waldo Frank's depiction of the South.

Julian Grajewski
Updated by Cassandra Kircher Grajewsk

MAYA ANGELOU

Born: St. Louis, Missouri; April 4, 1928
Also Known As: Marguerite Annie Johnson

PRINCIPAL SHORT FICTION

"Steady Going Up," 1972
"The Reunion," 1983

OTHER LITERARY FORMS

Maya Angelou (MI-uh AN-juh-lew) is known primarily as a poet and autobiographer. She has produced half a dozen volumes of poetry, and *The Complete Collected Poems of Maya Angelou* was published in 1994. She has also written five volumes of autobiography, starting with *I Know Why the Caged Bird Sings* in 1969. In addition, she has written plays, screenplays, and children's stories.

ACHIEVEMENTS

I Know Why the Caged Bird Sings was nominated for the National Book Award in 1970, and Maya Angelou's first volume of poetry (*Just Give Me a Cool Drink of Water 'fore I Diiie*, 1971) was nominated for the Pulitzer Prize in 1972. Angelou was also nominated for Tony Awards for her performances in *Look Away* in 1973 and *Roots* in 1977, and won three Grammy Awards, including one for best spoken word or nontraditional album for "On the Pulse of Morning," the poem she read at the first inauguration of President Bill Clinton in 1993. Angelou received the Presidential Medal of Arts in 2000 and the Lincoln Medal in 2008. She holds more than thirty honorary doctorates.

BIOGRAPHY

Maya Angelou was born Marguerite Annie Johnson in St. Louis, Missouri, and spent time as a young girl in Stamps, Arkansas (near Hope, where Clinton grew up), and California. She was raped at the age of eight by her mother's boyfriend, a story that is retold in *I Know Why the Caged Bird Sings*, had a son by the time she was sixteen, and worked at a number of jobs before she became an artist. In her early career, she was a singer and actress, appearing in plays and musicals around the world through the 1950's and 1960's. She has since directed plays and films, recorded music and spoken word, and appeared on television as both a narrator and a series host. She has also taught at various American universities since the 1960's and at Wake Forest University since 1982. She has been an outspoken advocate of civil and human rights most of her adult life, and she has lectured and written widely about these issues for decades.

ANALYSIS

Maya Angelou has produced only a few short stories, but those stories, like her multiple volumes of autobiography, deal directly and poignantly with issues of African American life in America. Since her early years, Angelou has been a political activist and educator, and she is knowledgeable and articulate about civil rights and related issues. Her fiction, like her poetry and her nonfiction, reflects social issues and conditions in the second half of the twentieth century, when racial barriers were falling, but the problems behind them continued. In this sense, Angelou must be considered a social realist, for her stories demonstrate the difficulties of growing up an African American woman in an America still riven by racism and sexism. Dozens of anthologies and other collections of contemporary literature have excerpted pieces from one or another of Angelou's autobiographies because they raise so many important issues about modern America--about identity, education, gender, and race. Her short stories are only marginally more fictional and raise many of the same issues.

"STEADY GOING UP"

"Steady Going Up" was first published in the collection *Ten Times Black* in 1972 and has since been reprinted several times, including in Gloria Naylor's *Children of the Night: The Best Short Stories by Black Writers, 1967 to the Present* (1995). The story seems more dated than "The Reunion" but raises several important questions nonetheless. As the story opens, a young black man, Robert, is traveling by bus from his home in Memphis to Cincinnati. He has never before been out of Tennessee, but this is hardly a pleasure trip, for he is rushing to pick up his younger sister at the nursing school where she has suddenly become ill, possibly from kidney trouble. Robert has raised Baby Sister since their parents died within six months of each other: "He was three years older than she when, at fifteen, he took over as head of the family." Getting a job as a mechanic at a local garage, he has been able to support Baby Sister, see her through high school, and send her to nursing school. He has had to put his own life on hold (he plans to marry Barbara Kendrick when Baby Sister is finished with school), and now her illness may further complicate his life. The bus ride is full of understandable anxiety for Robert.

When the bus makes its last stop before Cincinnati, Robert gets off to relieve himself but is cornered in the "colored" bathroom by two white men, who have also been traveling on the bus. An older black woman, who was sitting across the aisle from Robert during the trip, has already warned him about the two men, who have been drinking and staring at him. Now they confront him, accusing him of going north to find white women. Robert cannot "stand the intention of meanness" in the two men, and he decides to act so that he will not miss the bus: "He wasn't going to get left with these two crazy men." When one tries to force him to drink the bourbon that has made them both drunk, Robert kicks him in the groin and then hits the other man over the head with the bottle. Robert manages to get back on the bus, hiding the blood on his hands and shirt, and the bus pulls away with the two men still sprawled in the bathroom. There is no resolution to the story except this escape. Robert has left "those crazy men"--at least for now--but the reader wonders what will happen to him. He may be free of them for the moment, but the hatred and violence they represent will continue to follow him. The story ends with a neutral description of

Maya Angelou (WireImage)

the continuing bus trip: "Then he felt the big motor turn and the lights darkened and that old big baby pulled away from the sidewalk and on its way to Cincinnati." Robert's problems--as for so many African Americans at this time--still lie before him.

"THE REUNION"

"The Reunion" has been collected several times, first in the Amina and Amiri Baraka collection *Confirmation: An Anthology of African American Women*. The story is short (only five pages) but is a much more positive short fiction than the earlier "Steady Going Up," with its lack of resolution. The story is set in 1958 and is narrated by a jazz pianist named Philomena Jenkins, who is playing the Sunday matinee at the Blue Palm Café on the South Side of Chicago with the Cal Callen band. It is a club filled with other African Americans, but suddenly on this day Philomena spots Miss Beth Ann Baker, a white woman sitting with Willard, a large black man. The sight sends Philomena back in memory to her painful childhood growing up in Baker, Georgia, where her parents worked for the Bakers, and she lived in the servants' quarters behind the Baker main house.

The memories are painful because these were "years of loneliness," when Philomena was called "the Baker Nigger" by other children, and she has moved a long way from "the hurt Georgia put on me" to her present success in jazz music. She fantasizes about what she will say to Beth Ann when she meets her, but when they finally face each other at the bar a little later in the story, it is Beth Ann who does all the talking. She is going to marry Willard, who is a South Side school teacher, she tells Philomena, and she claims she is very happy. However, her parents have disowned her and even forbidden her to return to Baker. It is clear that she is with Willard to spite her parents, for she sounds to Philomena like "a ten-year-old just before a tantrum," "white and rich and spoiled." When Beth Ann invites "Mena" to their wedding, the narrator replies simply, "Good-bye Beth. Tell your parents I said go to hell and take you with them, just for company." When she returns to her piano after this break, she realizes that Beth Ann

> had the money, but I had the music. She and her parents had had the power to hurt me when I was young, but look, the stuff in me lifted me up above them. No matter how bad times became, I would always be the song struggling to be heard.

Through her tears, Philomena has had an epiphany and experienced a form of reconciliation with her true self, in the recognition that art can transcend social inequity. In the story's last lines, "The piano keys were slippery with tears. I know, I sure as hell wasn't crying for myself." Like a number of other artists (James Baldwin and Amiri Baraka, among them), Maya Angelou posits art--and thus literature--as one way of getting above and beyond the social injustices that her society has created. Philomena cannot erase the painful childhood memories, but her music can lift her and others above them to another, healthier human plane. The hurt may remain, but the "song struggling to be heard" is stronger.

OTHER MAJOR WORKS

PLAYS: *Cabaret for Freedom*, pr. 1960 (with Godfrey Cambridge; musical); *The Least of These*, pr. 1966; *Encounters*, pr. 1973; *Ajax*, pr. 1974 (adaptation of Sophocles' play); *And Still I Rise*, pr. 1976; *King*, pr. 1990 (musical; lyrics with Alistair Beaton, book by Lonne Elder III; music by Richard Blackford).

SCREENPLAYS: *Georgia, Georgia*, 1972; *All Day Long*, 1974.

TELEPLAYS: *Black, Blues, Black*, 1968 (10 episodes); *The Inheritors*, 1976; *The Legacy*, 1976; *I Know Why the Caged Bird Sings*, 1979 (with Leonora Thuna and Ralph B. Woolsey); *Sister, Sister*, 1982; *Brewster Place*, 1990.

POETRY: *Just Give Me a Cool Drink of Water 'fore I Diiie*, 1971; *Oh Pray My Wings Are Gonna Fit Me Well*, 1975; *And Still I Rise*, 1978; *Shaker, Why Don't You Sing?*, 1983; *Poems: Maya Angelou*, 1986; *Now Sheba Sings the Song*, 1987 (Tom Feelings, illustrator); *I Shall Not Be Moved*, 1990; *On the Pulse of Morning*, 1993; *Phenomenal Woman: Four Poems Celebrating Women*, 1994; *The Complete Collected Poems of Maya Angelou*, 1994; *A Brave and Startling Truth*, 1995; *Amazing Peace: A Christmas Poem*, 2005; *Mother: A Cradle to Hold Me*, 2006.

NONFICTION: *I Know Why the Caged Bird Sings*, 1969 (autobiography); *Gather Together in My Name*, 1974 (autobiography); *Singin' and Swingin' and Gettin' Merry Like Christmas*, 1976 (autobiography); *The Heart of a Woman*, 1981 (autobiography); *All God's Children Need Traveling Shoes*, 1986 (autobiography); *Wouldn't Take Nothing for My Journey Now*, 1993 (autobiographical essays); *Even the Stars Look Lonesome*, 1997; *A Song Flung Up to Heaven*, 2002 (autobiographical essays); *Hallelujah! The Welcome Table: A Lifetime of Memories with Recipes*, 2004 (memoir and cookbook).

CHILDREN'S LITERATURE: *Mrs. Flowers: A Moment of Friendship*, 1986 (illustrated by Etienne Delessert); *Life Doesn't Frighten Me*, 1993 (poetry; illustrated by Jean-Michel Basquiat); *Soul Looks Back in Wonder*, 1993; *My Painted House, My Friendly Chicken, and Me*, 1994; *Kofi and His Magic*, 1996; *Angelina of Italy*, 2004; *Izak of Lapland*, 2004; *Mikale of Hawaii*, 2004; *Renie Marie of France*, 2004.

MISCELLANEOUS: *Letter to My Daughter*, 2008.

BIBLIOGRAPHY

Bloom, Harold. *Maya Angelou*. Philadelphia, Pa.: Chelsea House Publishers, 1998. The essays in this volume focus mainly on the autobiographies and the poetry, but there are several pieces on larger issues, such as Angelou's audience and the southern literary tradition.

Hagen, Lynn B. *Heart of a Woman, Mind of a Writer, and Soul of a Poet: A Critical Analysis of the Writings of Maya Angelou.* Lanham, Md.: University Press of America, 1996. While there have been a number of scholarly works addressing the different literary forms Angelou has undertaken (most devoted to autobiography), few critical volumes have appeared that survey her entire opus, and Hagen's is one of the best. Chapters include "Wit and Wisdom/ Mirth and Mischief," "Abstracts in Ethics," and "Overview."

King, Sarah E. *Maya Angelou: Greeting the Morning.* Brookfield, Conn.: Millbrook Press, 1994. Includes biographical references and an index. Examines Angelou's life, from her childhood in the segregated South to her rise to prominence as a writer.

Lupton, Mary Jane. *Maya Angelou: A Critical Companion.* Westport, Conn.: Greenwood Press, 1998. While focusing mainly on the autobiographies, Lupton's study is still useful as a balanced assessment of Angelou's writings. The volume also contains an excellent bibliography, particularly of Angelou's autobiographical works.

Moore, Lucinda. "A Conversation with Maya Angelou at Seventy-five." *Smithsonian* 34, no. 1 (April, 2003): 96. An interview with Angelou on the occasion of her seventy-fifth birthday. She discusses her views of herself, why she has never been bored, her advice for having a diverse career, the environment in which she writers, and her relationships with her mother and grandmother.

Pettit, Jayne. *Maya Angelou: Journey of the Heart.* New York: Lodestar Books, 1996. Includes bibliographical references and an index. Traces Angelou's journey from childhood through her life as entertainer, activist, writer, and university professor.

David Peck

MAX APPLE

Born: Grand Rapids, Michigan; October 22, 1941

PRINCIPAL SHORT FICTION

The Oranging in America, and Other Stories, 1976
Zip: A Novel of the Left and the Right, 1978
Three Stories, 1983
Free Agents, 1984
The Propheteers: A Novel, 1987
The Jew of Home Depot, and Other Stories, 2007

OTHER LITERARY FORMS

In addition to writing some critical articles and to editing a book on the fiction of the Southwest, Max Apple has written two novels, *Zip: A Novel of the Left and the Right* (1978) and *The Propheteers: A Novel* (1987), and two memoirs, *Roommates: My Grandfather's Story* (1994) and *I Love Gootie: My*

Grandmother's Story (1998). He was a contributor to *Liquid City: Houston Writers on Houston* (1987), a nonfiction work celebrating the Houston International Festival. In addition to writing novels and short stories, Apple has written three screenplays: *Smokey Bites the Dust* (1981), *The Air Up There* (1994), and *Roommates* (1995; an adaptation of his 1994 memoir).

ACHIEVEMENTS

In 1971, Max Apple received the National Endowment for the Humanities younger humanist's fellowship; he has also received grants from the National Endowment for the Arts and the Guggenheim Foundation. *The Oranging of America, and Other Stories* earned him the Jesse H. Jones Award from the Texas Institute of Letters in 1976, as did *Free Agents* in 1985. He won *Hadassah* magazine's Ribalous Award for the best Jewish fiction of 1985. Apple has also contributed stories to a number of periodicals. Five of his books have been recognized as *New York Times* Notable Books. Apple's essay "The American Bakery" was selected by *The New York Times* as one of the best to appear in the first one hundred years of the *Book Review*. In 2010, he won a Pew Fellowship in the Arts.

BIOGRAPHY

Max Isaac Apple was born October 22, 1941, in Grand Rapids, Michigan, to Samuel Apple and Betty Goodstein. Max Apple married Talya Fishman, and together they reared four children (two from a previous marriage): Jessica, Sam, Elisheva, and Leah. Apple received a B.A. in 1963 and a Ph.D. in 1970 from the University of Michigan. He did postgraduate study at Stanford University.

Following his graduation, Apple worked as an assistant professor of literature and humanities at Reed College in Portland, Oregon. In 1972, he accepted an appointment at Rice University in Houston, Texas, where he was assistant professor from 1972 to 1976, associate professor from 1976 to 1980, and professor of English beginning in 1980. After teaching at Rice University for twenty-nine years he retired briefly, but he later resumed teaching at the University of Pennsylvania, where he served on the faculty with his son, Sam.

Growing up in a three-generation Jewish household, in which a respect for language and an appreciation of humor and style in language were the norm, Apple naturally gravitated toward the idea of telling stories. During the early 1970's, Apple contributed to a study of Nathanael West edited by David Madden, *Nathanael West: The Cheaters and the Cheated* (1972), and to the journal *Studies in English*. In 1976, Apple gained recognition as a writer with *The Oranging of America, and Other Stories*.

ANALYSIS

Max Apple's early background no doubt helped to shape his literary career. Acquiring English as a second language after growing up in a Yiddish-speaking home contributed to his viewing mainstream American life as an outsider before becoming a part of that current; thus, he could recast his American life experience in terms that are simultaneously realistic and fantastic. By taking the perspective of the perpetual outsider, Apple has remained amazed at daily life in a way that he believes most people cannot.

Throughout his work, Apple develops at least four major themes or issues. He explores the intensity with which Americans expend their energy on pursuing the new, the hitherto unheard of; his writing traces how this restless yearning for the untried is connected to a basic need for safety and for immortality. He also searches for some middle ground between the ideal of the American Dream and the reality of it, aware all along of the impossibility of fulfilling that dream. Likewise, Apple addresses the ambiguity inherent in American enterprise. He perceives it partly as the pitch of a con artist to a gullible client and partly as a dreamer's response to genuine human need and desire. It is the mythic impulse of Americans to enlarge, improve, and keep moving, as opposed to the results of this impulse, that Apple sees as the focus for most Americans.

Whether developed consciously or not, a number of techniques characterize his work. Many of his stories are peopled with well-known public figures, such as Howard Johnson and J. Edgar Hoover. This technique serves as a shortcut by calling up an image of the person in the reader's mind, making long, detailed descriptions unnecessary and leaving Apple free to make the figure into something that is all his own. He deals with what he believes is more real about them than their physical reality: their status in readers' collective imagination. Another shortcut employed is compression. Apple has cited a line from the story "Inside Norman Mailer" as an example: Following a description of prizefighting, he simply says, "You've all seen it-- imagine it yourself!" He is thus spared the task of writing pages of description, when it is only the metaphor in which he is interested.

Apple sometimes recalls an early, minor event or thing from his childhood--for example, a gasoline station--and merges that memory with other, more fantastic material. Rhythm is a basic stylistic feature of his work. Whether a sentence is accurate is not nearly as important as whether the sentence sounds right, and, unlike many other writers, he is not concerned with a formal unity in his stories.

Though not all of Apple's stories deal with the Jewish experience, elements of Judaism and Jewish culture appear commonly in his writings. Apple frequently appeals to both the Jewish and the immigrant experience in constructing stories of social outsiders and those who somehow feel out of place among the rhythm of a lifestyle that seems to be occurring around them but separate from them. While many of his stories contain hints of social satire or cultural criticism, these themes are muted against Apple's deep compassion for characters who struggle to navigate the current of a slightly mystifying lifestyle, one in which they do not feel wholly included.

There is no thread of anger running through Apple's stories; his wit is tender and soft-edged. In his voice is almost an affection, as if he were admonishing a beloved family member with a gentle patience or even amusement. He welcomes diversity and tension for their own sake. Cultural clichés are transformed into shining gems. By polishing the cultural rubble of American life, he rejuvenates our spirits. His stories are basically optimistic.

"THE ORANGING OF AMERICA"

This title story of his 1976 collection demonstrates Apple's overtly fictive strategy. The oranging is that of the rooftops of Howard Johnson motels; he credits the poet Robert Frost as the source of inspiration for making them orange. Johnson, his secretary Millie, and Otis, a former busboy, feel a tingling when they come to a spot where people need to stop and rest; this is how Johnson chooses building sites for new motels. Combining his startling imagination with originality, wit, and economy, Johnson does most of his business in a Cadillac limousine equipped with an ice-cream freezer that produces twenty-eight flavors, though Johnson eats only vanilla. Years later, when Millie becomes ill, she investigates having her body frozen after death, and in order to make it possible for Millie to continue traveling with him, Johnson has the steel capsule from the Cryonic Society installed in a U-Haul trailer attached to the Cadillac.

"SELLING OUT"

Although the fantastic element is present, this story is basically plausible. The narrator inherits some money, and when his stockbroker cousin is unsuccessful in turning a satisfactory profit from it, he studies the market himself, sells what he has, and successfully reinvests the money based on his own studies. Like all the stories in *The Oranging of America, and Other Stories*, "Selling Out" is concerned with big-money action in the capitalist system. Apple lives up to his reputation for comic intelligence as he mimics American economics with a tender, insidious wit.

"WALT AND WILL"

Taking the two well-known Disney brothers of cartoon and amusement park fame, Apple uses them for his own purposes. Walt is fixated on motion, which later becomes the principle behind his genius for animation. He is as intensely absorbed in studying the way ants move as any scientist would be in history-making research, for he wants to duplicate the mechanics of animation that he sees in the natural world. His imagination opens to the possibilities of animating great works of art. After the animated Mickey Mouse is born, it is Will, the practical but visionary brother, who goads Walt into developing Walt Disney World in Florida; with the California Disneyland, their enterprise would be "like a belt around the country," and America would have her own national monuments, as Europe has. Walt, however, is entranced not with buildings and huge business deals but with movement, with films. Fantasy, reality, absurdity, and seriousness often merge in Apple's version of the making of the Mickey Mouse Empire.

"FREE AGENTS"

This hilarious fantasy features Apple's internal organs striking for autonomy, insisting that they should have the right to decide where, if ever, they are to be transplanted. His stomach is the narrator of the story. The organs go before a judge, the pituitary gland, who rules that, after a May 11 deadline, all organs, muscles, and tissues, whether Apple's original organs or some added after his birth, will become free agents. As such, they will be able to negotiate with any available bodies. In mock seriousness, the sentence is declared a fair one, made in the spirit of democratic fairness that has characterized the history of collective bargaining. Again, in typical fashion, Apple targets economic, social, and moral issues behind the mask of fantasy and malice-free humor.

"The Jew of Home Depot"

The title story of Apple's first collection in more than two decades tells the story of eighty-year-old Jerome Baumgarten, who is dying surrounded by gentiles and who is looking for a family of "real Jews" to accompany him as he moves toward death. The Chabad Lubavitcher family of Reb Avram Hirsch, with his son and daughters, comes to Marshall, Texas, to live in Baumgarten's home and guide him into Jewish living, just as he is preparing to depart from the world. As Baumgarten enters the lives of the Hirsch family, so, too, does the influence of the gentiles' lifestyle. Separated from the insulated Crown Heights community to which they are accustomed, the Hirsch family must grapple with matters of faith and self-sufficiency, as they struggle to fill a dying man's final wish without compromising their own lives. Apple treats the resulting cultural clashes with sympathy and without judgment, as his characters open literal and metaphorical doors to discourse and new experiences.

Other major works

SCREENPLAYS: *Smokey Bites the Dust* (1981), *The Air Up There* (1994), and *Roommates* (1995; an adaptation of his 1994 memoir).

NONFICTION: *Roommates: My Grandfather's Story*, 1994; *I Love Gootie: My Grandmother's Story*, 1998.

EDITED TEXT: *Southwest Fiction*, 1980

Bibliography

Bellamy, Joe David. *Literary Luxuries: American Writing at the End of the Millennium*. Columbia: University of Missouri Press, 1995. A record of Bellamy's search for a literary life, this book examines various facets of the literary scene in the late twentieth century. A section called "Contemporaries" provides brief overviews of sixteen writers, including Max Apple, whom Bellamy admires for the way he shows that "the spirit that made America what it is today is still operative" in such fictionalized figures as Howard Johnson in "The Oranging of America" and for his mellowness, which is described as an unusual quality of affection and a certain nostalgia that he generates while at the same time making his characters the butts of his ridicule.

While Apple creates fabulous fantasies, few laws of nature are suspended, making his stories strangely plausible. The book lauds Apple's formal economy, balance, and purposefulness of action and plot and concludes that his whimsicality and imaginative bravado are rarely forced.

Bennett, Patrick. *Talking with Texas Writers: Twelve Interviews*. College Station: Texas A and M University Press, 1980. In this interview with Apple, which is included along with those of eleven other Texas writers, he shares how he became a writer and describes some of his writing habits: writing in longhand, not preparing an outline, not devoting a set number of hours or words per day to writing. In the interview, Apple explains that his use of real names of fictionalized characters helps to bring his voice into the real world and identifies himself as a comic writer who looks for irony but who does not strive for a "punch line."

Chénetier, Marc. *Beyond Suspicion: New American Fiction Since 1960*. Philadelphia: University of Pennsylvania Press, 1996. While relevant references to Apple are made throughout the book, Chénetier focuses extensively on Apple in two chapters. "Cultural Tradition and the Present" finds that Apple devotes the core of his work to using glaring symbols, such as the orange roofs of Howard Johnson motels, to draw a line between the powers of myth and its "puny incarnations." The article also identifies Apple's ability to recycle materials, which some might deem unusable in literary writing, and to approach them in a fresh way. Another chapter deals with voice in writing. The author uses one of Apple's analogies, the ventriloquist who has a dummy: for Apple, the dummy is the fiction, the part of himself that gets the best lines, while he is the straight man who provides the tension that he desires in his sentences.

Hume, Kathryn. "Diffused Satire in Contemporary American Fiction." *Modern Philology* 105, no. 2 (2007): 300-325. Hume's article addresses Apple's use of literary tone in his novel *The Propheteers*. Drawing comparisons between Apple's novel and other contemporary works, including Thomas Pynchon's *Mason and Dixon* (1997) and Robert

Coover's *The Adventures of Lucky Pierre: Directors' Cut* (2002), Hume addresses samples of vastly differing modern American fiction in the context of general theories of satire and specifically of diffused satire. Though the article does not delve into Apple's short fiction, the themes and literary devices explored within offer insight into Apple's broader body of work.

McCaffrey, Larry, and Linda Gregory. *Alive and Writing: Interviews with American Authors of the 1990's*. Urbana: University of Illinois Press, 1987. Apple is one of thirteen writers interviewed. Apple explains his sense of realism as being "the way the world is," and cites Gabriel García Márquez's writing as an example of realistic fiction. He prefers fantasy, parody, and myth to more conventional forms. Choosing the short story over the novel as a means of expression is a matter of not having time for the longer genre. Other characteristics of his work that are discussed include his interest in what his characters' names represent, not in the persons themselves; in fact, he does not research these characters--Howard Johnson or Walt Disney, for example. He admits a decided preference for story writing to writing academic papers.

Rubin, Derek. *Who We Are: On Being (and Not Being) a Jewish American Writer*. New York: Schocken Books, 2005. This lively collection includes Apple's essay "Max and Mottele," in which the author addresses his struggles with identity and how these personal struggles have paved the way for his characters' existence in the space between two cultures. This essay also provides insight into the writer and his career, as well as his choices to employ or depart from his own background in crafting his stories.

Shatzky, Joel, and Michael Taub. *Contemporary Jewish American Novelists: A Bio-Critical Sourcebook*. Westport, Conn.: Greenwood Press, 1997. Apple is one of sixty-three Jewish American writers discussed; each entry includes biographical data as well as major works and themes. A final section traces each writer's development and emerging critical reception. Primary and secondary bibliographies are provided for each writer.

Wilde, Alan. "Dayanu: Max Apple and the Ethics of Sufficiency." *Contemporary Literature* 26, no. 3 (1985): 254. This article critiques Apple's literary writings, with particular attention to the stories of *Free Agents* and the writer's approach to concepts of the aesthetic and of psychological order. Themes of adaptation of the ethics of sufficiency, as addressed in this article, pertain more broadly to many of Apple's short stories and other literary works.

Victoria Price
Updated by Rachel E. Frier Price

ISAAC ASIMOV

Born: Petrovichi, Soviet Union (now in Russia);
   January 2, 1920
Died: New York, New York; April 6, 1992
Also known as: Paul French

PRINCIPAL SHORT FICTION

I, Robot, 1950
The Martian Way, 1955
Earth Is Room Enough, 1957
Nine Tomorrows, 1959
The Rest of the Robots, 1964
Asimov's Mysteries, 1968
Nightfall, and Other Stories, 1969
The Early Asimov, 1972
Tales of the Black Widowers, 1974
Buy Jupiter, and Other Stories, 1975
More Tales of the Black Widowers, 1976
The Bicentennial Man, and Other Stories, 1976
Good Taste, 1977
The Key Word, and Other Mysteries, 1977
Casebook of the Black Widowers, 1980
Computer Crimes and Capers, 1983
The Union Club Mysteries, 1983
The Winds of Change, and Other Stories, 1983
Banquets of the Black Widowers, 1984
The Disappearing Man, and Other Mysteries, 1985
Alternative Asimovs, 1986
Isaac Asimov: The Complete Stories, 1990-1992 (2
   volumes)
The Return of the Black Widowers, 2003

OTHER LITERARY FORMS

Isaac Asimov (AZ-eh-mof) was well known as a polymath and workaholic. His principal works are in the fields of science popularization and science fiction, where both his short stories and novels have been influential, but he also wrote extensively in history and literature, composed books for children and adolescents, as well as mystery and detective books for adults, and published books in such areas as mythology, humor, and biblical studies.

ACHIEVEMENTS

Capitalizing on what he called his "lucky break in the genetic sweepstakes," Isaac Asimov used his exceptionally lucid mind and vivid imagination to explain the past and possible future developments of science and technology through his fiction and nonfiction to a large audience of nonscientists. He was a successful communicator of ideas not only in science but also in a wide variety of literary, historical, even theological topics, but it is as a science-fiction writer that he will be best remembered. His ability to generate and extrapolate ideas on the development of science and technology and his creative visions of the human consequences of these developments helped found "social science fiction," which made this formerly pulp genre acceptable to many literary critics.

Asimov was honored for his work in both science fiction and science popularization. The Science-Fiction Writers of America voted his "Nightfall" the best science-fiction story of all time, and his Foundation trilogy won a Hugo Award in 1966 as "The Best All-Time Series." His novel *The Gods Themselves*, published in 1972, won both the Hugo and Nebula Awards, and his *Foundation's Edge* (1982) won a Hugo Award as the best novel in 1982. As a science popularizer, he received the James T. Grady Award of the American Chemical Society in 1965 and the American Association for the Advancement of Science-Westinghouse Science Writing Award in 1967.

BIOGRAPHY

Brought to the United States when he was three, Isaac Asimov was reared in New York by his Jewish parents and was taught to take education seriously, especially science. A child prodigy, he graduated from high school at fifteen and went on to earn his B.S., M.A., and Ph.D. in chemistry at Columbia University, with a brief interruption for noncombatant military service at the end of World War II. Although he failed to achieve his dream, and that of his parents, to become a doctor, Asimov did join the faculty of the medical school at Boston University, where he became an associate professor of biochemistry before turning to full-time writing. A science-fiction fan since his early teens, he published his first story at eighteen. After nineteen books of fiction in the 1950's, however, he concentrated much more heavily on nonfiction. He was married twice, to Gertrude Blugerman from 1942 to 1973, with whom he had two children, and to psychiatrist Janet Jeppson in 1973. In the early 1980's, Asimov endured a thyroid cancer operation, a heart attack, triple bypass surgery, and his second wife's mastectomy. He treated all these sufferings as temporary setbacks in the "game of immortality" that he played, writing as much as he could with the hope that at least some of his works would live beyond his death. Asimov died of kidney failure on April 6, 1992, in a New York hospital. He was seventy-two.

ANALYSIS

A naïve, untutored writer by his own admission, Isaac Asimov learned the art of commercial fiction by observing the ways of other science-fiction writers before him, with considerable assistance from John W. Campbell, Jr., editor of *Astounding Science Fiction*. Although the diction of pulp writers, for whom every action, however mundane, must have a powerful thrust, colored much of his earlier work, he soon developed a lucid style of his own, spare by comparison with the verbosity of others, which was spawned by the meager word rates for which they worked. Melodramatic action is not absent from his fiction, but confrontations are more commonly conversational than physical. Characters are seldom memorable, and there are few purple passages of description for their own sake; everything is subordinated to the story, itself often an excuse for problem solving to show scientific thinking in action.

Isaac Asimov (Library of Congress)

Although his first popularity came in the 1930's and 1940's, Asimov's best work was published in the 1950's. In addition to most of his novels, many of his best stories were written then, including "The Ugly Little Boy" (1958), which concerns a Neanderthal child snatched into the present and the consequences of his nonscientific governess's forming an attachment to him. This is one of several stories in which the results of science and technology and devotion to them are cast in a negative or at least ambivalent light, contrary to the view Asimov usually maintains.

Other stories from this period include "Franchise," in which a single voter decides those few issues computers cannot handle; "What If?," in which a newly married couple catches a glimpse of how their lives might have been; and "Profession," in which trends in accelerated education are taken to an extreme. Three stories concern societies so technologically sophisticated that what the reader takes for granted must be rediscovered: writing in "Someday," mathematics in "The Feeling of Power," and walking outdoors in "It's Such a Beautiful Day."

"The Last Question" extrapolates computer capabilities in the far future to a new Creation in the face of the heat death of the universe, while "Dreaming Is a Private Thing" concerns a new entertainment form which bears a certain resemblance to traditional storytelling.

Spanning his career, Asimov's robot stories generally involve an apparent violation of one or more of the "Three Laws of Robotics," which Campbell derived from Asimov's earliest variations on the theme. Their classical formulation is as follows:

1. A robot may not injure a human being or, through inaction, allow a human being to come to harm.

2. A robot must obey orders given it by human beings except where such orders would conflict with the First Law.

3. A robot must protect its own existence as long as such protection does not conflict with the First or Second Laws.

"Liar!"

While this formulation was an attempt to dispel what Asimov called the "Frankenstein complex," it was also a set of orders to be tested by dozens of stories. The best of the robot stories may well be "Liar!," in which a confrontation between robot and human produces an unusually emotional tale, in which the fear of machines is not trivialized away. "Liar!" introduces one of Asimov's few memorable characters, Susan Calvin, chief robopsychologist for U.S. Robots, whose presence between "chapters" of *I, Robot* unifies to some extent that first collection of Asimov's short fiction. Usually placid, preferring robots to men, Calvin is shown here in an uncharacteristic early lapse from the type of the dispassionate spinster into that of "the woman scorned."

The story begins with a puzzle, an attempt to discover why an experimental robot, RB-34 (Herbie), is equipped with telepathy. Trying to solve this puzzle, however, Calvin and her colleagues are sidetracked into the age-old problem of human vanity, which ultimately relegates the original puzzle and the robot to the scrap heap. Aware of the threat of harming them psychologically if he tells the truth, Herbie feeds the pride of the administrator, Alfred Lanning, in his

mathematics, along with the ambition of Peter Bogert to replace his superior, and the desire of Calvin to believe that another colleague, Milton Ashe, returns her affection, when he is in fact engaged to another.

As the conflict between Bogert and Lanning escalates, each trying to solve the original puzzle, Herbie is asked to choose between them. Present at the confrontation, Calvin vindictively convinces the robot that whatever it answers will be injurious to a human being, forcing it to break down. Since Herbie is a conscious being, more interested in romantic novels than in technical treatises, Calvin's act is not simply the shutting down of a machine but also an act of some malevolence, particularly satisfying to her, and the whole story underlines the human fear of being harmed, or at least superseded, by machines.

"Nightfall"

Asimov's next published story, "Nightfall," is still his best in the opinion of many readers, who have frequently voted it the best science-fiction story of all time, although it shows its age and the author's, since he was barely twenty-one when he wrote it. Written to order for Campbell, it begins with a quote from Ralph Waldo Emerson's *Nature* (1836) which Campbell and Asimov in turn have reinterpreted: "If the stars should appear one night in a thousand years, how would men believe and adore, and preserve for many generations the remembrance of the city of God." Asimov fulfilled Campbell's demand that the event, taken as an astronomical possibility, would drive men mad, but this conclusion is partly counterbalanced by the author's faith in the power of science to explain, without completely succumbing to, awe and superstition.

With the Emerson quote as an epigraph, "Nightfall" was committed to an inevitable, rather than a surprise, ending. From the start, the catastrophe is imminent, predicted by astronomers who have no idea of what is really in store. Aton 77, director of the university observatory where the action takes place, reluctantly permits a newspaper columnist, Theremon 762, to stay and observe, thus setting the stage for a story which is almost all exposition. Sheerin 501, a psychologist, becomes Theremon's major interlocutor, explaining both the physical and behavioral theory behind the predictions which the media and the populace have ridiculed.

Astronomical observation, gravitational theory, and archaeological findings have confirmed the garbled scriptural account of the Cultists' *Book of Revelations* that civilization on the planet Lagash must fall and rise every two millennia. Lit by six suns, Lagash is never in darkness, never aware of a larger universe, except when another world, a normally invisible "moon," eclipses the only sun then in the sky, an event which happens every 2049 years. In hopes of overcoming the anticipated mass insanity, the scientists have prepared a Hideout in which some three hundred people may be able to ride out the half-day of darkness and preserve some vestige of scientific civilization.

While Sheerin is explaining all this and glibly countering commonsense objections, a Cultist breaks in to threaten the "solarscopes," a mob sets out from the city to attack the observatory, and the eclipse indeed begins. Amid flickering torches, the scientists withstand the vandals' charge that they have desecrated the scriptures by "proving" them only natural phenomena. They then speculate ironically about a larger universe, even an Earthlike situation presumed inimical to life, but neither they nor the Cultists are prepared for the truth of "thirty thousand mighty suns" or the gibbering madness that demands light, even if everything must be burned down in order to obtain it.

Other than the astronomical configuration--a highly unlikely and inherently unstable situation and its consequences, there is nothing "alien" in the story, which is about potential human reactions. The diction is heavily influenced by 1930's pulp style, some pieces of the puzzle are not rationally convincing, and the story leaves loose ends untied, but it is dramatically convincing, like H. G. Wells's inversion of a similar dictum in "The Country of the Blind." Although Asimov's moral survives-- that people can, through scientific observations and reasoning, do something to improve their state-- it is largely overshadowed by the effectiveness of the ending. However well prepared for and rationalized away, the concluding vision of "Nightfall" evokes exactly that quasimystical awe and wonder Asimov is usually constrained to avoid.

"THE MARTIAN WAY"

Relying more on single "impossibilities," correlated extrapolation, and reasoning from present-day knowledge, Asimov's best fiction generally stems from the 1950's. The best example of his positive attitude toward future expansion by human beings and their knowledge, "The Martian Way" illustrates the conviction expressed by most of his novels and much of science fiction that the future lies "out there" in space beyond the "cradle" for human beings provided by Earth, its history and prehistory. A "space story" to be sure, "The Martian Way" also concerns political conflict, which is resolved not by drawn blasters at fifty paces but rather by reason and ingenuity, based on a setting and assumptions alien to Earthmen both at the time of writing and in the time period in which the novella is set.

A puzzle and a solution are presented, but they are an excuse on which to hang the story. The rise of a demagogic Earth politician, Hilder (modeled on Senator Joseph McCarthy, but echoing Hitler by name), threatens the human colony on Mars that depends on Earth for water, not only for drinking, washing, and industry but also as reaction mass for its spaceships. Among those who will be affected, Marlo Esteban Rioz and Ted Long are Scavengers, who snag empty shells of ships blasting off from Earth and guide them to Martian smelters. Although Rioz is the experienced "Spacer," the "Grounder" Long has a better grasp of "the Martian way," which means not tying one's future to Earth, but rather facing outward to the rest of the solar system and beyond.

Campaigning against "Wasters," Hilder draws parallels between past profligacy with oil and other resources with the present Martian use of water from Earth's oceans. The Martian colonists recognize the spuriousness of that charge, but they also recognize its emotional impact on Earth. The solution is a marriage of scientific elegance and technological brute force, breathtaking in context even to the Spacers themselves, who set off on a year's journey to bring back an asteroid-sized fragment of ice from Saturn's rings. How they do it is chronicled by the story, along with the euphoria of floating in space, the political wrangling with Earth, and the challenges of colonizing the new frontier.

Throughout the narrative resonates the claim by Long that Martians, not Earthmen, will colonize the universe. The fundamental difference lies less with the planet of one's birth than with the direction in which one looks to the future. Scientifically more astute and less burdened by racial prejudices, Martians work in teams rather than as individual heroes. Although there are distinct echoes of the legendary American West, the situation on Mars is more radically discontinuous with its predecessors on Earth. The arrival of an independent water supply is just the excuse they need to cut at last the umbilical cord to Earth and the past.

"THE DEAD PAST"

If "The Martian Way" points toward Asimov's novels, most of which take place off Earth, even beyond the solar system, "The Dead Past" is more typical of the extrapolation Asimov defends in his critical writings as "social science fiction." The novella begins harmlessly enough with a professor of ancient history being denied access to government-controlled chronoscopy, which would let him see firsthand the ancient city of Carthage. Although time-viewing is the central science fiction, the focus of the story switches to "the closed society," as Professor Potterly seeks to subvert governmental controls. Scientists in this near-future society have bartered their freedom of inquiry for recognition, security, and financial support. This position is defended by a young physics professor named Foster, whose future depends on his staying within the bounds of his discipline and of the controls that have evolved from governmental support of research.

The point is exaggerated, as is the conspiracy of silence surrounding chronoscopy, but the satirical edge is honed by the subsequent activity of the two academics and Foster's cooperative Uncle Ralph, a degreeless, prestigeless, but well-paid science writer. With his help and the shortcut supplied by his specialty, "neutrinics," Foster reinvents the chronoscope at a fraction of its earlier cost and difficulty, and the conspirators give out the secret to the world. In contrast to Foster's newly gained fanaticism, Potterly has begun to have doubts, in part because of his own wife's nostalgic obsessions. In a melodramatic confrontation with the Federal Bureau of Investigation (FBI), they discover that the chronoscope's

operating limits are between one hundred and twenty-five years and one second ago, making privacy in the present a thing of the past. Either a whole new utopian society will have to evolve, a doubtful supposition, or the government's suppression of information will turn out, in retrospect, to have been for the good. Although the story has flaws and its fantasy is almost certainly unrealizable, the satire is engaging, and the ending is a thoughtful variation on the theme that there may indeed be some knowledge not worth pursuing.

Asimov's fiction usually has a makeshift quality about it, his characterizations are often featureless, and his propensity for surprise endings and melodramatic diction and situations may irritate some readers. Nevertheless, his exploitation of scientific thought and rationality, his emphasis on the puzzle solving that makes up much of science, and his generally good-humored lucidity have made him, along with Robert A. Heinlein and Arthur C. Clarke, one of the cornerstones of modern science fiction.

OTHER MAJOR WORKS

LONG FICTION: *Pebble in the Sky*, 1950; *Foundation*, 1951; *The Stars Like Dust*, 1951; *Foundation and Empire*, 1952; *The Currents of Space*, 1952; *Second Foundation*, 1953; *The Caves of Steel*, 1954; *The End of Eternity*, 1955; *The Naked Sun*, 1957; *The Death-Dealers*, 1958 (also known as *A Whiff of Death*); *The Foundation Trilogy*, 1963 (includes *Foundation*, *Foundation and Empire*, and *Second Foundation*); *Fantastic Voyage*, 1966; *The Gods Themselves*, 1972; *Murder at the ABA: A Puzzle in Four Days and Sixty Scenes*, 1976; *Foundation's Edge*, 1982; *The Robots of Dawn*, 1983; *Foundation and Earth*, 1985; *Robots and Empire*, 1985; *Fantastic Voyage II: Destination Brain*, 1987; *Azazel*, 1988; *Prelude to Foundation*, 1988; *Nemesis*, 1989; *Robot Dreams*, 1989; *Robot Visions*, 1990; *Nightfall*, 1991 (with Robert Silverberg); *The Ugly Little Boy*, 1992 (with Silverberg); *Forward the Foundation*, 1993; *The Positronic Man*, 1993 (with Silverberg).

NONFICTION: *The Chemicals of Life: Enzymes, Vitamins, Hormones*, 1954; *Inside the Atom*, 1956; *The World of Carbon*, 1958; *The World of Nitrogen*, 1958; *Realm of Numbers*, 1959; *Words of Science and the History Behind Them*, 1959; *The Intelligent Man's Guide to Science*, 1960; *The Wellsprings of Life*, 1960; *Life and Energy*, 1962; *The Search for the Elements*, 1962; *The Genetic Code*, 1963; *A Short History of Biology*, 1964; *Asimov's Biographical Encyclopedia of Science and Technology*, 1964; *Planets for Man*, 1964 (with Stephen H. Dole); *The Human Body: Its Structures and Operation*, 1964; *The Human Brain: Its Capacities and Functions*, 1964; *A Short History of Chemistry*, 1965; *The Greeks: A Great Adventure*, 1965; *The New Intelligent Man's Guide to Science*, 1965; *The Genetic Effects of Radiation*, 1966; *The Neutrino: Ghost Particle of the Atom*, 1966; *The Roman Republic*, 1966; *The Universe: From Flat Earth to Quasar*, 1966; *Understanding Physics*, 1966; *The Egyptians*, 1967; *The Roman Empire*, 1967; *Science, Numbers, and I*, 1968; *The Dark Ages*, 1968; *Asimov's Guide to the Bible*, 1968-1969 (2 volumes); *The Shaping of England*, 1969; *Asimov's Guide to Shakespeare*, 1970 (2 volumes); *Constantinople: The Forgotten Empire*, 1970; *Electricity and Man*, 1972; *The Shaping of France*, 1972; *Worlds Within Worlds: The Story of Nuclear Energy*, 1972; *The Shaping of North America from Earliest Times to 1763*, 1973; *Today, Tomorrow, and . . .* , 1973; *Before the Golden Age*, 1974 (autobiography); *Earth: Our Crowded Spaceship*, 1974; *Our World in Space*, 1974; *The Birth of the United States, 1763-1816*, 1974; *Our Federal Union: The United States from 1816 to 1865*, 1975; *Science Past--Science Future*, 1975; *The Collapsing Universe*, 1977; *The Golden Door: The United States from 1865 to 1918*, 1977; *A Choice of Catastrophes: The Disasters That Threaten Our World*, 1979; *Extraterrestrial Civilizations*, 1979; *In Memory Yet Green: The Autobiography of Isaac Asimov, 1920-1954*, 1979; *Asimov on Science Fiction*, 1980; *In Joy Still Felt: The Autobiography of Isaac Asimov, 1954-1978*, 1980; *The Annotated "Gulliver's Travels*,*"* 1980; *In the Beginning*, 1981; *Visions of the Universe*, 1981; *Exploring the Earth and the Cosmos: The Growth and Future of Human Knowledge*, 1982; *The Roving Mind*, 1983;

The History of Physics, 1984; *Asimov's Guide to Halley's Comet*, 1985; *Exploding Suns*, 1985; *Robots: Machines in Man's Image*, 1985 (with Karen A. Frenkel); *The Edge of Tomorrow*, 1985; *The Dangers of Intelligence, and Other Science Essays*, 1986; *Beginnings: The Story of Origins--of Mankind, Life, the Earth, the Universe*, 1987; *Past, Present, and Future*, 1987; *Asimov's Annotated Gilbert and Sullivan*, 1988; *The Relativity of Wrong*, 1988; *Asimov on Science*, 1989; *Asimov's Chronology of Science and Discovery*, 1989; *Asimov's Galaxy*, 1989; *Frontiers*, 1990; *Asimov's Chronology of the World: The History of the World from the Big Bang to Modern Times*, 1991; *Atom: Journey Across the Subatomic Cosmos*, 1991; *I. Asimov: A Memoir*, 1994; *Yours, Isaac Asimov: A Lifetime of Letters*, 1995 (Stanley Asimov, editor); *It's Been a Good Life*, 2002 (Janet Jeppson Asimov, editor; condensed version of his 3 volumes of autobiography); *Conversations with Isaac Asimov*, 2005 (Carl Freedman, editor).

CHILDREN'S LITERATURE: *David Starr: Space Ranger*, 1952; *Lucky Starr and the Pirates of the Asteroids*, 1953; *Lucky Starr and the Oceans of Venus*, 1954; *Lucky Starr and the Big Sun of Mercury*, 1956; *Lucky Starr and the Moons of Jupiter*, 1957; *Lucky Starr and the Rings of Saturn*, 1958.

BIBLIOGRAPHY

"A Celebration of Isaac Asimov: A Man for the Universe." *Skeptical Inquirer* 17 (Fall, 1992): 30-47. Asimov is praised as a master science educator, perhaps the greatest of all time; he was responsible for teaching science to millions of people. Tributes are made by Arthur C. Clarke, Frederik Pohl, Harlan Ellison, L. Sprague de Camp, Carl Sagan, Stephen Jay Gould, Martin Gardner, Paul Kurtz, Donald Goldsmith, James Randi, and E. C. Krupp.

Asimov, Isaac. *Asimov's Galaxy: Reflections on Science Fiction*. Garden City, N. Y.: Doubleday, 1989. This compilation of sixty-six essays presents readers with Asimov's unique perspective on a genre to which he made many important contributions for fifty years. The topics deal with religion and science fiction, women and science fiction, time travel, science-fiction editors, and magazine covers. Particularly interesting are the items in the final section, "Science Fiction and I," in which Asimov writes frankly about his life and work.

Chambers, Bette. "Isaac Asimov: A One-Man Renaissance." *The Humanist* 53 (March/April, 1993): 6-8. Discusses Asimov's stature as a humanist and his presidency of the American Humanist Association. Addresses Asimov's support of the Committee for the Scientific Investigation of Claims of the Paranormal and his thoughts on censorship and creationism, pseudoscience, and scientific orthodoxy.

Fiedler, Jean, and Jim Mele. *Isaac Asimov*. New York: Frederick Ungar, 1982. This brief book is a primer on Asimov's work as a science-fiction writer. The authors give descriptions of most of Asimov's writings in the genre, including the Foundation trilogy, the robot stories, and the juvenile books. Some critics found this book too long on plot summaries and too short on analyses, but others thought the authors provided a clear and nonacademic treatment of Asimov's major works, besides giving some of his less well-known works long-overdue recognition. Contains notes, a bibliography, and an index.

Freedman, Carl, ed. *Conversations with Isaac Asimov*. Jackson: University Press of Mississippi, 2005. This collection of interviews with Asimov spans the period from 1968 to 1990. Asimov discusses such topics as the state of science-fiction writing and his own opinions about his classic work. Includes chronology, list of Asimov's books, and index.

Goble, Neil. *Asimov Analyzed*. Baltimore: Mirage, 1972. This unusual study of Asimov's work concentrates on his style in his science fiction and nonfiction. The critical analyses are detailed, with Goble going so far as to perform word-frequency counts to make some of his points.

Gunn, James. *Isaac Asimov: The Foundations of Science Fiction*. New York: Oxford University Press, 1982. Rev. ed. Lanham, Md.: Scarecrow Press, 1996. Gunn, a professor of English at the University of Kansas in Lawrence, is a science-fiction writer and a historian and critic of the genre. He has used his long personal friendship with Asimov to show how science fiction shaped Asimov's life and how he in turn shaped the field. The bulk of Gunn's book

is devoted to painstaking analyses of Asimov's entire science-fiction corpus. The book concludes with a chronology, a checklist of works by Asimov, a select list of works about him, and an index.

Hutcheon, Pat Duffy. "The Legacy of Isaac Asimov." *The Humanist* 53 (March/April, 1993): 3-5. A biographical account, noting Asimov's efforts to bring scientific understanding to people and to make people realize that to study humanity is to study the universe, and vice versa. Claims that Asimov saw the possibility of an eventual organization of a world government, warned against the abandonment of technology in humankind's search for solutions, and predicted the end of sexism, racism, and war.

Olander, Joseph D., and Martin H. Greenberg, eds. *Isaac Asimov*. New York: Taplinger, 1977. This collection of essays, which reviewers found useful and illuminating, includes analyses of Asimov's social science fiction, his science-fiction mysteries, and his Foundation trilogy. In an afterword, Asimov himself comments, amusingly and enlighteningly, on the essays, asserting that "no purposeful patterns or smooth subtleties can possibly be below the clear surface" of what he has written in his science-fiction stories. The book includes a select bibliography of Asimov's major science-fiction writings through 1976.

Palumbo, Donald. *Chaos Theory, Asimov's Foundations and Robots, and Herbert's "Dune": The Fractal Aesthetic of Epic Science Fiction*. Westport, Conn.: Greenwood Press, 2002. Looks at the history of epic science fiction through its two most outstanding examples. Includes bibliographical references and index.

Patrouch, Joseph F., Jr. *The Science Fiction of Isaac Asimov*. Garden City, N.Y.: Doubleday, 1974. Patrouch, a teacher of English literature at the University of Dayton, published science-fiction stories, and many reviewers found his critical survey of Asimov's writings in science fiction the best book-length study yet to appear. Patrouch discusses Asimov's style, his narrative skills, and his themes; he also provides detailed analyses of the principal short stories and novels.

Touponce, William F. *Isaac Asimov*. Boston: Twayne, 1991. Part of Twayne's United States Authors series, this volume is a good introduction to the life and works of Asimov. Includes bibliographical references and an index.

David N. Samuelson
Updated by Robert J. Paradowski

LOUIS AUCHINCLOSS

Born: Lawrence, New York; September 27, 1917
Died: New York, New York; January 26, 2010
Also known as: Andrew Lee

PRINCIPAL SHORT FICTION

The Injustice Collectors, 1950
The Romantic Egoists, 1954
Powers of Attorney, 1963
Tales of Manhattan, 1967
Second Chance: Tales of Two Generations, 1970
The Winthrop Covenant, 1976
Narcissa, and Other Fables, 1983
Skinny Island: More Tales of Manhattan, 1987
Fellow Passengers: A Novel in Portraits, 1989
False Gods, 1992 (fables)
Tales of Yesteryear, 1994
The Collected Stories of Louis Auchincloss, 1994
The Atonement, and Other Stories, 1997
The Anniversary, and Other Stories, 1999
Manhattan Monologues, 2002
The Young Apollo, and Other Stories, 2006
The Friend of Women, and Other Stories, 2007

OTHER LITERARY FORMS

A practicing attorney on New York's Wall Street for more than forty years, Louis Auchincloss (AW-kihn-clahs) first drew critical attention as a novelist, reaching his peak with such memorable social chronicles as *The House of Five Talents* (1960), *Portrait in Brownstone* (1962), *The Rector of Justin* (1964), and *The Embezzler* (1966); some of his strongest short fiction dates from around the same time. The novel *The Education*

of Oscar Fairfax (1995) was well received. Auchincloss also published several volumes of essays and criticism, notably *Reflections of a Jacobite* (1961), *Reading Henry James* (1975), *False Dawn: Women in the Age of the Sun King* (1984), and *The Man Behind the Book: Literary Profiles* (1996). *A Writer's Capital,* a selective autobiographical essay dealing with Auchincloss's inspirations and early evolution as a novelist, appeared in 1974.

ACHIEVEMENTS

Although Louis Auchincloss never won any literary awards, his greatest single achievement as a writer of prose fiction may well be his continued questioning of the distinction between short and long narrative forms. Many of his collections may, in fact, be read with satisfaction either piecemeal or from start to finish, affording the reader an enviable glimpse behind the scenes of power.

BIOGRAPHY

A second-generation Wall Street lawyer, Louis Stanton Auchincloss was born September 27, 1917, at Lawrence, Long Island, the summer home of his parents, J. Howland Auchincloss and Priscilla Stanton. Educated at Groton School and at Yale University, Louis Auchincloss began writing as a teenager and submitted his first finished novel as an undergraduate. Although the publisher Charles Scribner's Sons expressed interest in his planned second novel even as the firm rejected his first, young Auchincloss saw fit to take the rejection as an omen and embark on a law career with all deliberate speed. Actively seeking the best law school that would accept him without a bachelor's degree, he left Yale University after three years and enrolled in 1938 at the University of Virginia Law School, presumably having renounced literature for life.

In retrospect, Auchincloss's impulsive decision to leave Yale University prior to graduation turned out to have been a timely one; after receiving his law degree in 1941, he was hired by the well-known Wall Street firm of Sullivan and Cromwell and practiced his profession for several months before the United States went to war, with a job awaiting him upon his return from military service.

Commissioned in the Navy, Auchincloss served in both the Atlantic and the Pacific war theaters after an initial posting to an area little touched by the war, the Canal Zone, where he began to reconsider the option of creative writing. The young officer kept his eyes and ears open throughout the war, also reading voraciously to pass the long, idle hours at sea. At Groton School and at Yale University he had read mainly for academic success, but during the war he began to read for pleasure, steeping himself in the British, American, and Continental narrative traditions. By the time he was mustered out in 1945, Auchincloss had begun plotting a novel, *The Indifferent Children* (1947), combining his wartime observations with characters recalled from his early attempts at long fiction. Back in New York, he took an extended furlough to finish the novel before returning to legal practice at Sullivan and Cromwell in 1946.

Published the next year under the pseudonym Andrew Lee and over the objections of Auchincloss's parents (with whom he still lived), *The Indifferent Children* received enough good reviews to encourage the young lawyer to pursue his writing, particularly the short fiction later assembled in *The Injustice Collectors*. Following the publication of the novel *Sybil* in 1951, Auchincloss began to question his "double life" as attorney and author; with the moral and financial support of his parents, he resigned from Sullivan and Cromwell to work full time at his writing, only to conclude that the result--the novel *A Law for the Lion* (1953) and the stories collected in *The Romantic Egoists*--differed little in quality or quantity from what he had done before. By 1954, he was back on Wall Street

in search of a job, resigned to juggling dual careers but barred by company policy from returning to his old firm once he had resigned. Hired by the firm of Hawkins, Delafield, and Wood, Auchincloss rose to full partnership by 1958, the year following his marriage to Adèle Lawrence, a Vanderbilt descendant some thirteen years his junior with whom he would have three sons. His literary career, meanwhile, continued to flourish along with--and to survive--his legal practice, from which he retired at the end of 1986, in his seventieth year.

Along with his legal and literary work, Auchincloss was active in cultural and civic affairs. A life fellow of the Pierpont Morgan Library, he served as president of the Museum of the City of New York and as a member of the advisory board of the *Dictionary of Literary Biography*. Auchincloss died on January 26, 2010. He was ninety-two.

ANALYSIS

A keen and informed observer of American manners and morals, Louis Auchincloss established himself rather early in his career as the peer, if not the superior, of such social chroniclers as John P. Marquand and John O'Hara, with a particular insider's gift for exposing the well-concealed inner workings of society and politics. Writing in a clear, spare, even classical prose style, Auchincloss credibly "demystifies" for his readers the behavior of those in positions of privilege and power, persons whose actions and decisions help to make the rules by which all Americans should live.

A willing and grateful heir to the "novel of manners" tradition exemplified in the United States by Henry James and perpetuated by Edith Wharton, Auchincloss is first and foremost a writer of "chronicles," long or short, recording observations either topical or historical; well versed in the rules and patterns of Western civilization, Auchincloss tends to perceive historical value even in the topical, giving to his observations a stamp of scholarly authority often lacking in the work of other would-be social satirists. During the 1940's, at the start of his career, Auchincloss tended to deal with the historical present, in the aftermath of World War II; later, in fiction both long and short, Auchincloss focused primarily on the 1930's, the period of his adolescence and

Louis Auchincloss (FilmMagic)

young manhood, much as O'Hara in middle age returned to his own adolescent years, the 1920's, in search of clues to what had happened since that time in American society and politics.

Almost from the start, Auchincloss's narratives tended to blur the traditional boundaries separating long fiction from short fiction. In most of his collections, the stories are linked by theme and/or recurrent characters, and in certain volumes the tales are told by a single unifying narrator.

THE INJUSTICE COLLECTORS

Auchincloss's early short fiction, assembled in *The Injustice Collectors* in 1950 after being published separately in periodicals such as *Harper's* and *The New Yorker*, is unified by a theme suggested in the title, a nagging suspicion that most people, even those born to privilege, are frequently the authors of their own misfortunes. In his preface to the volume, Auchincloss relates that he has borrowed the title from a popular book by the psychiatrist Edmund Bergler, modifying its meaning to suit his own aspirations as a writer of short stories. A psychiatrist or even a novelist, he explains, may well probe the causes of the behavior described, while writers of short fiction must content themselves with recording the symptoms. Indeed, the evolution of Auchincloss's approach to narrative over the next four decades would frequently test and even cross the boundaries between long and short fiction, with assembled symptoms leading to a rather conclusive diagnosis. In his first volume of stories, however, Auchincloss had yet to unravel the tangled threads implicit in his chosen subject matter, let alone to follow them.

On balance, *The Injustice Collectors* is a rather traditional collection of stories in the manner of James or Wharton, with occasional flashes of originality and even brilliance. One of the tales, "Maud," clearly adumbrates the type of restless, thoughtful heroine who would populate Auchincloss's early novels, a woman whose expectations of life differ sharply from those of her parents. Feeling herself "imprisoned" in her attorney father's household, Maud Spreddon refuses to accept even her own potential capacity for love; engaged to marry her father's junior partner, Halsted Nicholas, who admires her rebellious streak and who has, in fact, waited for her to grow to marriageable age, Maud breaks the engagement abruptly, presumably doubting her fitness for marriage. Several years later, the two meet during World War II in London, where Maud is serving with the Red Cross and Halsted with the Army Air Corps. After a rather stormy reconciliation, Maud accepts Halsted's second proposal; when Halsted's plane is shot down over France two days later, a week before the Normandy invasion, Maud, unwilling to be pitied, resolves to keep the reconciliation a secret for life.

In "Fall of a Sparrow," Auchincloss points the way toward a theme that will loom large in his second collection: the social dynamics between reserve officers and careerists during wartime. Narrated by an officer known only as Ted, "Fall of a Sparrow" shows the shortcomings and eventual disgrace of Victor Harden, Ted's prep-school classmate whose outward success in school and service hides a deep-seated insecurity that proves in time to be his undoing. In *The Romantic Egoists*, Auchincloss would go even further in his delineation of military rivalries and factions, often raising serious questions in the reader's mind as to how the United States and its allies managed to win the war.

THE ROMANTIC EGOISTS

Unified by the narration of Peter Westcott, whose legal and naval experiences run roughly parallel to those of the author, *The Romantic Egoists* shows Auchincloss hitting his stride as a master of prose fiction, as do the novels published around the same time. "Loyalty Up and Loyalty Down," the fictional account of an incident later recalled in *A Writer's Capital*, pits Westcott and his fellow reservists against Harry Ellis, a career officer risen from the ranks, who happens to serve as their skipper. Although perhaps traditional as well as predictable, the tension between the college graduates and their commanding officer is here presented from a somewhat different perspective. What the reservists resent deeply about their skipper is his apparent willingness to let the rest of the Navy sink, if need be, in order to save his own ship; he repeatedly turns down authorized requests from other vessels for food and supplies, and when obliged to rescue surviving marines from a battle station he treats them with contempt, calling them names as he parades before them in a Chinese dressing grown. Westcott, willing but finally unable to serve as peacemaker, eventually allows Ellis to hang himself, observing the skipper's orders to the letter while preserving his own integrity; Westcott watches with combined amusement and consternation as the vessel, lead ship in a convoy, runs over a buoy, followed by all the ships in its wake. Only later will Westcott reflect on the possible danger to the other ships and on the depths to which the running feud with Ellis has finally reduced him.

Written in a similar vein, "Wally" contrasts the ambitions of the title character, one Ensign Wallingford, with those of Lieutenant Sherwood Lane, an Ivy Leaguer and "aristocrat" who, after more than a year of shuffling papers in the Canal Zone, believes that his background and training more than qualify him for a desk job in Washington, D.C. Of all the officers stationed in the Canal Zone and seeking a transfer, only Wallingford and Lane actively seek further shore duty; the others, motivated either by patriotism or by the spirit of adventure, expect to see action at sea. Wallingford, a native of Omaha and a graduate of the hotel school at Cornell University, wants nothing more or less than to serve as he has been trained, managing a hotel for the Navy somewhere in the United States. Whenever possible, Lane will block Wallingford's repeated requests for a transfer, uneasily seeing in the midwesterner's "ridiculous" ambitions a discomfiting and disquieting reflection of his own. In the end, with Westcott's covert assistance, Wally will finish out the war in Florida, helping to run a hotel for the Navy with one of his former Cornell professors as his commanding officer; Lane, surpassing either his or Westcott's wildest speculations, will end the war as a surviving hero, soon tiring of the Washington job and serving with high distinction as a line officer. "None of us, least of all Sherwood," concludes Westcott ruefully, "could really stand to live for any length of time with that part of ourselves we recognized in Wally."

"The Great World and Timothy Colt," the longest and arguably the strongest of the tales collected in *The Romantic Egoists*, began the author's detailed exploration of his own working environment as a lawyer on Wall Street and is as painstaking as his examination of social and professional dynamics in the Navy. A prototypical "workaholic" married to a former law-school classmate at Columbia University, Timothy Colt personifies the rising postwar "meritocracy," for whom ambition and hard work might well compensate for perceived disadvantages of "background." Seen from the perspective of his slightly younger associate Peter Westcott, "Timmy" Colt is hard-driving and meticulous, yet not without his personable side--at least at first. If Timmy works best under pressure, however, the pressure soon begins to exact its toll, leaving him particularly vulnerable to the gibes and taunts of Sam Liendecker, a rich, influential client to whose case Timmy and Westcott have been assigned by the managing partner. As Flora Colt will explain to Westcott, Liendecker instinctively senses Timmy's fundamental weakness--a nearly total lack of self-esteem that keeps him striving even harder to please those in need of his services. In time, Timmy, pushed beyond his limits, will insult the aging Liendecker in public, a breach of etiquette for which both his wife and his superiors expect him to apologize. Thus goaded, Timmy in fact will apologize--with Westcott as witness--and it is at that point that Timmy "sells out," in his own mind, to forces that he feels have conspired against him. Thereafter, he quite deliberately and consciously behaves as the antithesis of his former self, incidentally blaming his uncomprehending wife, as well as himself, for the direction that his career has taken. Timmy thus emerges as the ultimate "Romantic Egoist"--not an "egotist" but a self-absorbed dreamer for whom even the best of life will prove a disappointment.

As Auchincloss noted in his preface to the earlier collection, writers of short stories must content themselves with "symptoms." In time, however, the author of "The Great World and Timothy Colt" saw fit to broaden and deepen his analysis of Timmy with a full-fledged novel published under the same title in 1956. In the novel, several of the names are changed and some of the characters are changed or others added, but the central argument of the narrative remains quite the same: the quixotic Timmy, risking disbarment, willingly testifies in court to an offense that he did not, in fact, commit--except in his own mind.

Before long, Auchincloss would all but abandon short fiction for the better part of a decade, devoting his increasingly prodigious energies to "Wall Street" novels in the vein of *The Great World and Timothy Colt*. By the time his next collection appeared in 1963, Auchincloss would in turn have deserted the Wall Street novels in favor of the historically dimensional social chronicles, beginning with *The House of Five Talents*.

POWERS OF ATTORNEY

Arguably, Auchincloss by the early 1960's had "relegated" his Wall Street material to the shorter fictional form; the stories collected in *Powers of Attorney* indeed hark back to the themes and settings of novels written before 1960. The narrator Peter Westcott is gone for good, not to reappear--and then as Dan Ruggles--until *Fellow Passengers: A Novel in Portraits*, published as late as 1989. In place of a unifying narrator, however, Auchincloss presents a cast of recurrent characters who move throughout the stories, perhaps serving as the focal point in one tale and as part of the background in others. Perhaps predictably, the main "character" of *Powers of Attorney* is a Wall Street law firm, whose members often grapple with problems and decisions similar to those that beset Timothy Colt in the short story and later novel bearing his name. "The Deductible Yacht" tells the tale of a hereditary New York "aristocrat," born to high moral principles, for whom the elevation to partnership at Tower, Tilney, and Webb is inextricably linked to his professional relationship with the Armenian-born Inka Dahduh, a self-made tycoon who makes no secret of having the law "shaved" in his favor; in the end, Bayard Kip will accept both partnership and client as the price for maintaining his wife and family in the style toward which his background has pointed him.

"The Single Reader," among the more Jamesian of the stories in the collection, portrays the "secret life" of Morris Madison, the firm's senior tax specialist. Deserted early in life by an unfaithful spouse, Madison has devoted decades of his free time to a diary that he imagines as the modern-day equivalent of writer Saint-Simon's *Mémoires du duc de Saint-Simon: Ou, L'Observateur véridique sur le règne de Louis XIV* (1788; *The Memoirs of the Duke of Saint Simon on the Reign of Louis XIV*, 1857); when at last he contemplates remarriage to an eligible widow, Madison makes the mistake of asking the lady to read his multivolume journal, in which she no doubt correctly recognizes an indomitable rival for the aging lawyer's love.

TALES OF MANHATTAN

Tales of Manhattan, published in 1967 with a sequel, *Skinny Island: More Tales of Manhattan*, to follow twenty years later, is somewhat less unified--and less novelistic--in its construction than *Powers of Attorney*; nevertheless, groups of stories are internally linked, more or less demanding that they be read in sequence within each section. The opening sequence, "Memories of an Auctioneer," is narrated by Roger Jordan, an art dealer with the instincts of a sleuth, a keen eye for beauty, and a sharp nose for sniffing out fraud in life as in art. Persuaded that possessions, especially collections, offer psychological clues about their owners, Jordan manages to unearth more than a few juicy secrets; his observations, however, are not limited to artifacts. In "The Question of the Existence of Waring Stohl," Jordan at first suspects the title character, an obnoxious dilettante and would-be novelist, of "sponging off" his and Jordan's former professor, the eminent literary critic Nathaniel Streebe. Unknown to Jordan, however, Stohl is mortally ill; not long after

Stohl's early death, Streebe will reveal himself as the true parasite of the pair, having encouraged the young man's literary ambitions in order to write his posthumous biography, published to good reviews under the same title as the Auchincloss story.

SECOND CHANCE

Second Chance, published as a collection in 1970, contains some of Auchincloss's strongest short fiction, particularly "The Prince and the Pauper," ironically sharing its title with a tale by Mark Twain. "The Prince and the Pauper" in many respects summarizes the entire Auchincloss canon, showing the mobility and true pragmatism that lie beneath the apparent structure of "society." Balancing the fortunes of the "aristocratic" attorney Brooks Clarkson against those of Benny Galenti, a former office boy and law-school dropout (owing to the pregnancy of Teresa, now his wife) whom Brooks singled out for special treatment and in time elevated to office manager with appropriate raises in pay, Auchincloss portrays with enviable skill the social dynamics at work in American society. Benny, the son of immigrants, believes that he can never shake off his debt to Brooks, who provided him not only with a decent salary but also with investment advice and, on occasion, a loan with which that advice might be followed. At the time of the story, Brooks has lost his position with the law firm, continuing a long slide into alcoholism and general disrepair that he seems to have wished upon himself, together with his wife Fanny; the implication is that Brooks felt somehow undeserving of, and threatened by, his elevated status, both professional and social, and finding in the Galentis a vitality and drive somehow lacking in himself and Fanny. The story ends with Benny somewhat reluctantly accepting for the sake of his family a membership in the Glenville Club, from which the Clarksons have long since been expelled for drunken misbehavior and nonpayment of dues. Society, implies Auchincloss, will continue to make and to break its own rules.

THE PARTNERS

The Partners, published in 1974, differs little in form or concept from the earlier *Powers of Attorney*. Once again, the "life" described is that of a Wall Street law firm in transition. Perhaps the strongest story in the collection is "The Novelist of Manners," in which a

best-selling, scandal-mongering novelist is defended successfully against a libel charge by Leslie Carter, a junior partner in the firm, who is stationed in Paris to handle European business. As the case proceeds, Carter, who harbors some literary aspirations of his own, persuades the middle-aged Dana Clyde to try his hand at a "serious" novel, taking a respite from the "good life" of parties and sports cars in order to do so. Clyde does as he is told, but when the novel finally appears it is little different from what he has produced before. Carter, meanwhile, is stunned to find himself portrayed in the novel as a character who commits suicide at the end, having discovered his own impotence on his honeymoon with the novel's heroine. As Clyde's wife Xenia explains to Carter, Clyde can never forgive Carter for pushing him beyond his limits and has taken his revenge. Reminiscent of the author's own conclusions after leaving from the law in favor of his writing, the destiny of Clyde and Carter also allows Auchincloss to make his own wry comments on the fate of the "novel of manners," of which he may well be the last traditional, nonsensational practitioner.

FELLOW PASSENGERS

Fellow Passengers, subtitled *A Novel in Portraits*, represents one of Auchincloss's more intriguing experiments in blending long and short fiction. Unlike the vignettes in *The Book Class*, the "portraits" presented here can be read profitably as individual stories, each evoking memorable characters. For the first time since *The Romantic Egoists*, all the tales are told by a semi-autobiographical narrator, in the present case a gracefully aging lawyer known as Dan Ruggles. Like Peter Westcott in the earlier collections, Ruggles tends to stand aside from the action that he recalls, revealing relatively little of himself save for his reactions. If anything, the details of Ruggles's life are drawn even closer to Auchincloss's own than those of Westcott; a case in point, "Leonard Armster" recounts in barely fictionalized form the short, troubled, but somehow exuberant life of the author's friend Jack Woods, recalled in *A Writer's Capital* as a major influence on Auchincloss's aspirations and development as a writer. One cannot help but suspect that the other portraits are drawn equally true to life now that their models are dead, yet in each case Auchincloss moves away from illustration or photography toward archetype and art, portraying the characters against the background of their time, usually the 1930's.

THE ATONEMENT, AND OTHER STORIES

Auchincloss's attention to short fiction did not stop with publication of *The Collected Stories of Louis Auchincloss* in 1994. *The Atonement, and Other Stories*, issued on Auchincloss's eightieth birthday, presents twelve new selections. It portrays characters and situations similar to those in early works. These later stories display no major innovations in theme or technique, but they reveal no diminishing of Auchincloss's narrative powers. As the title suggests, a persistent theme in this collection is the attempt to make amends for past misconduct.

The title story, described by one reviewer as a miniature *Bonfire of the Vanities* (alluding to the 1987 novel by Tom Wolfe), portrays Sandy Tremain, a wealthy Wall Street investment banker whose partner is arrested for illegal insider trading. Equally guilty but able to elude prosecution, Sandy consults his father, a retired teacher who has devoted his entire life to the preparatory school where he was first a student and then a beloved master. Sandy considers confession, divorce, and solitary exile to a foreign country as a possible response to his dilemma. His father, however, describes such a course as a "bath of self-pity" and affirms that Sandy's real and more difficult obligation is to stand with his wife and family.

In "The Hidden Muse" Auchincloss develops a character much like himself and dramatizes once more the tug of war between law and literature. The protagonist, David Hallowell, is a young World War II veteran and promising associate at a Wall Street law firm. In this case the misdeed that demands atonement is a sin against himself. David's lawyer father dies prematurely, and his mother desperately wants her only son to achieve glory in the same profession. Throughout his school years David indulges his talent for writing fiction, but, in acceding to his mother's demands, he later abandons his secret muse. When his friend and mentor at the law firm rises to a full partnership, David has an epiphany. He realizes that his major concern is not what the firm can do for him, but what he can do with it. He resolves to resign his position and ends the story

with plans for transforming his coworkers into characters in a novel.

In "The Last Great Divorce" Clarinda Eberling presents a first-person apology for her life. On the occasion of her daughter's divorce in 1961, Clarinda looks back at the very public breakup of her own marriage in 1938. Joe Eliot and Howard Eberling were best friends and partners in a law firm. Clarinda married Joe but loved the more assertive Howard. After sixteen years with Joe, she engineers an affair with Howard that ultimately terminates two marriages, a long friendship, and a business partnership. To Clarinda's dismay, however, Howard attempts "a kind of atonement" by retiring from public life and becoming an academic. Clarinda accepts her exile but can never completely atone for the pain she has inflicted on her two lovers and her drug-abusing son.

MANHATTAN MONOLOGUES

The first eight stories fulfill the promise of the title of the book; the last two are told by an omniscient narrator who moves from the consciousness of one character to another. In the first section, "Old New York," the narrator of "All That May Become a Man" can never feel the equal of his father, who charged up San Juan Hill with Theodore Roosevelt. In "The Heiress," Aggie Wheelock, granddaughter of a tycoon, cannot dismiss the thought that she may have married the wrong man. The title "Harry's Brother" suggests the plight of the upright narrator, whose good-for-nothing brother, Harry, is everybody's favorite. The first three stories in part 2, "Entre Deux Guerres," are set mainly in the era of the Great Depression, and the overall theme is one of disillusion. In "The Marriage Broker," Aunt Kate, the title character, attempts unsuccessfully to make a good marriage for her son, Damon. In "Collaboration," the narrator is dismayed when his idol is accused of collaborating with the Nazis. The narrator of "The Justice Clerk" discovers that the admired Supreme Court justice for whom he clerks has a vindictive nature and racist attitudes. The last four stories (including three in the section "Nearer Today")-- "He Knew He Was Right," "The Treacherous Age," "The Merger," and "The Scarlet Letters"--deal with betrayal, emotional, financial, or sexual.

The themes and characters are recognizably this author's--the problems of the rich, the once rich, and the near rich. The dialogue of the mostly Yale- and Harvard-educated characters is always sophisticated. The narration and often the dialogue are sprinkled with literary allusions and French phrases. The central characters are always found among the advantaged, but *Manhattan Monologues* reminds the reader that the lives of the rich can be just as unpredictable, unrewarding, and unhappy as those of the poor.

THE YOUNG APOLLO, AND OTHER STORIES

In 2006, *The Young Apollo, and Other Stories* appeared; the twelve stories form a cumulative examination of the changing values experienced by the well-born and the moneyed class in America during the first half of the twentieth century. Several stories feature elderly characters who look back wistfully, sometimes sadly, to the old New York of the nineteenth century. In "Other Times, Other Ways," eighty-year-old Camilla Hunter compares the Wall Street scandal that disgraced her husband in 1937 with the indictment for inside trading suffered by Bronson Newton, husband of her favorite niece, in 1981. Backs had been turned on Camilla and her husband, whereas Bronson is thought only to be playing the Wall Street game--this time, unfortunately, losing. Nobody thinks any the worse of him. In "Lady Kate," the narrator looks back from 1933 to the Mauve Decade, when she was young and associated with Mrs. Astor and Henry Adams. At one point, her husband tells her that she has the dubious honor of presiding over the decline and fall of Newport society. Mrs. Chanler in "The Attributions," serves as an audience for Leonardo Luchesi's account of his biography. She is past eighty in the early 1950's, and he is an Italian who has raised himself from poverty, largely by affixing himself to an American tycoon. She was intimate with Adams and Edith Wharton; he becomes a not completely trustworthy art expert. In "Due Process," the eighty-one-year-old narrator, born in Blue Hill, Virginia, despite having been for many years a successful New York lawyer, is an unreconstructed southerner who, to the dismay of all who know him, lends his expertise to those who are opposing racial integration in 1954. Perhaps the most imaginative treatment of the longing for a lost world is "The Grandeur

That Was Byzantium." In the year 330, Caius Lentulus Desideratus, lover of the old Roman gods, ways, and traditions, understands that, now that the emperor Constantine has converted to Christianity, everything will change.

Other themes are developed. In the title story, Lionel Manning, the young Apollo, inspires an historian, a novelist, and a sculptor to do their finest work, while he can write only mediocre poetry himself. In "Pandora's Box," Amos Herrick, an upright tax lawyer, is finally cajoled into socializing with a disreputable client. The story's title is predictive of Amos's career thereafter. In "Pa's Darling," Kate, the eldest and favorite daughter, writes an assessment of her relationship with her father. In chronicling the great man's weaknesses, Kate reveals much about herself. In "A Case History," Marvin Daly, born in 1918, feels isolated in a society not yet receptive to homosexuality.

THE FRIEND OF WOMEN, AND OTHER STORIES

The Friend of Women, and Other Stories, published in 2007, comprises five stories and a one-act play. The title story, rendered "L'Ami des Femmes" in the text, examines the lives of Alfreda Belknap, a member of an old but undistinguished New York clan; Cora King, daughter of a famous salon hostess; and Letitia "Letty" Bernard, a Jewish heiress. The narrator is Hubert Hazelton, head of the English department at a girls' private Manhattan day school. He becomes and remains the "ami" of the title. In 1945, Letty marries Eliot Amory, a charming young lawyer whose family has lost its fortune. Alfreda marries Tommy Newbold, an unimaginative lawyer, and Cora marries Ralph Larkin, older than she and heir to a Pittsburgh steel fortune. Tommy proves to have a low sperm count. He believes his son is the product of artificial insemination but, in truth, Eliot is the natural father. Eliot also has an affair with Cora. Hazelton confronts the already guilt-ridden Eliot, who then commits suicide. In "The Devil and Rufus Lockwood," the narrator, Percy Goodheart, an Anglican priest, is chaplain of Averhill. The Reverend Rufus Lockwood is the charismatic headmaster, a clergyman of a more worldly than a spiritual disposition. At the conclusion, the narrator betrays Lockwood. The story poses but does not answer the question: Was he right in doing so? "The Call of the Wild" is the story of bland, dependable Harry Phelps, whose nasty wife drives him into the arms of a woman whose reputation is rather tarnished. The thoroughly unwise alliance fails, as everyone predicted, but Harry has found it a liberating experience. In "The Conversion of Fred Coates," the title character has always done the right thing for the wrong reason. When he does the wrong thing for the right reason, his wife, Anita, loves him all the more. "The Omelet and the Egg," is the story of Kate Rand, a housewife who becomes a famous novelist and produces consternation in her husband's family.

The final piece, "The Country Cousin," is a one-act comedy in three scenes. The dialogue, as in the rest of the book, is urbane, witty, and often literary in nature. The conclusion is completely satisfying. Elida Rodman, the poor relation from Augusta, Maine, completely outmaneuvers her demanding Park Avenue relations--her aunt, her cousin, and his wife--and marries a rich and charming man.

OTHER MAJOR WORKS

LONG FICTION: *The Indifferent Children*, 1947 (as Andrew Lee); *Sybil*, 1951; *A Law for the Lion*, 1953; *The Great World and Timothy Colt*, 1956; *Venus in Sparta*, 1958; *Pursuit of the Prodigal*, 1959; *The House of Five Talents*, 1960; *Portrait in Brownstone*, 1962; *The Rector of Justin*, 1964; *The Embezzler*, 1966; *A World of Profit*, 1968; *I Come as a Thief*, 1972; *The Partners*, 1974; *The Dark Lady*, 1977; *The Country Cousin*, 1978; *The House of the Prophet*, 1980; *The Cat and the King*, 1981; *Watchfires*, 1982; *Exit Lady Masham*, 1983; *The Book Class*, 1984; *Honorable Men*, 1985; *Diary of a Yuppie*, 1986; *The Golden Calves*, 1988; *Fellow Passengers*, 1989; *The Lady of Situations*, 1990; *Three Lives*, 1993 (novellas); *The Education of Oscar Fairfax*, 1995; *Her Infinite Variety*, 2001; *The Scarlet Letters*, 2003; *East Side Story*, 2004; *The Headmaster's Dilemma*, 2007; *Last of the Old Guard*, 2008.

NONFICTION: *Reflections of a Jacobite*, 1961; *Pioneers and Caretakers: A Study of Nine American Women Novelists*, 1965; *Motiveless Malignity*, 1969; *Edith Wharton: A Woman in Her Time*, 1971; *Richelieu*, 1972; *A Writer's Capital*, 1974; *Reading Henry James*, 1975; *Life, Law, and Letters: Essays and Sketches*, 1979; *Persons of Consequence: Queen Victoria and Her Circle*, 1979; *False Dawn: Women in the Age of the Sun King*, 1984; *The Vanderbilt Era: Profiles of a Gilded Age*, 1989; *J. P. Morgan: The Financier as Collector*, 1990; *Love Without Wings: Some Friendships in Literature and Politics*, 1991; *The Style's the Man: Reflections on Proust, Fitzgerald, Wharton, Vidal, and Others*, 1994; *La Gloire: The Roman Empire of Corneille and Racine*, 1996; *The Man Behind the Book: Literary Profiles*, 1996; *Woodrow Wilson*, 2000; *Theodore Roosevelt*, 2001; *Writers and Personality*, 2005.

BIBLIOGRAPHY

Cornwell, Rupert. "Louis Auchincloss: Writer Who Chronicled the Lives and Times of America's WASP Elite." *The Independent*, February 2, 2010. A long obituary heavily focused on literary criticism.

Gelderman, Carol W. *Louis Auchincloss: A Writer's Life*. Columbia: University of South Carolina Press, 2007. A good biography of the writer, updated from the 1993 edition published by Crown. Includes bibliographical references and an index.

"Louis Auchincloss." *Daily Telegraph*, February 1, 2010. A long unsigned obituary featuring specific discussion of twelve of the author's works.

Parsell, David B. *Louis Auchincloss*. Boston: Twayne, 1988. Parsell's sixth chapter, entitled "The Novel as Omnibus: Auchincloss's Collected Short Fiction," is recommended for those seeking to explore Auchincloss's singular approach to short and long fiction.

Piket, Vincent. *Louis Auchincloss: The Growth of a Novelist*. Basingstoke, England: Macmillan, 1991. Part of the New Directions in American Studies series, this critical look at Auchincloss's career includes bibliographical references and an index.

Plimpton, George. "The Art of Fiction CXXXVIII: Louis Auchincloss." *The Paris Review* 36 (Fall, 1994): 72-94. In this interview, Auchincloss discusses his fiction and nonfiction, commenting on his relationship with editors, how important plot and character are in his fiction, and his notion of literary style as a reflection of the personality of the writer.

Tintner, Adeline R. "Louis Auchincloss Reinvents Edith Wharton's, 'After Holbein.'" *Studies in Short Fiction* 33 (Spring, 1996): 275-277. Argues that Auchincloss uses a section of Wharton's "After Holbein" in the episode "The Dinner Out," in his novelistic collection *The Partners*. Suggests that in these two stories the fear of death lingers over royal feasts.

David B. Parsell; Albert Wilhelm
Updated by Patrick Adcock

B

James Baldwin

Born: Harlem, New York; August 2, 1924
Died: St. Paul de Vence, France; December 1, 1987

PRINCIPAL SHORT FICTION
Going to Meet the Man, 1965

OTHER LITERARY FORMS

In addition to one edition of short stories, James Baldwin published more than twenty other works, including novels, essays, plays, a screenplay on Malcolm X, a play adaptation, a children's book, two series of dialogues, and a collection of poetry, as well as numerous shorter pieces embracing interviews, articles, and recordings.

ACHIEVEMENTS

James Baldwin received numerous awards and fellowships during his life, including the Rosenwald, John Simon Guggenheim Memorial Foundation, and *Partisan Review* Fellowships, a Ford Foundation grant, and the George Polk Memorial Award. In 1986, shortly before his death, the French government made him a Commander of the Legion of Honor.

BIOGRAPHY

James Arthur Baldwin grew up in Harlem. While he was still attending DeWitt Clinton High School in the Bronx he was a Holy Roller preacher. After high school, he did odd jobs and wrote for *The Nation* and *The New Leader.* A turning point for him was meeting Richard Wright, who encouraged him to write and helped him obtain a fellowship that provided income while he was finishing an early novel. After moving to Paris in 1948, Baldwin became acquainted with Norman Mailer and other writers. His first major work, *Go Tell It on the Mountain,* appeared in 1953 and was followed by a long list of books. He moved back to New York in 1957, and during the 1960's his writing and speeches made him an important force in the Civil Rights movement. Following the assassination of Martin Luther King, Jr., Baldwin returned to Europe several times and again settled in France in 1974, where he lived until his death. He continued his productivity in the 1980's. He died in 1987 of stomach cancer and is buried near Paul Robeson's grave at Ferncliff Cemetery in Ardsley, New York.

ANALYSIS

James Baldwin is widely regarded as one of the United States' most important writers in the latter part of the twentieth century. Baldwin's writing career spanned more than four decades and is remarkable for its wide diversity of literary expression, encompassing fiction, nonfiction, poetry, and plays. He was considered the most important American writer during the 1950's, 1960's, and 1970's on the issue of racial inequality. The repeated thrust of his message, centered on being black in a white America, touched a responsive chord. Disgusted with American bigotry, social discrimination, and inequality, he exiled himself in France, where he poured out his eloquent and passionate criticism. Baldwin also wrote with compelling candor about the church, Harlem, and homosexuality. He often fused the themes of sex and race in his work. Today, Baldwin's essays are considered his most important contribution to literature.

"THE MAN CHILD"

Baldwin's "The Man Child," the only story in *Going to Meet the Man* that has no black characters, scathingly describes whites, especially their violent propensities. The central character is Eric, an eight-year-old. The story opens as he, his mother, and his father are giving a birthday party for Jamie, his father's best friend. In the next scene Eric and his father walk together and then return to the party. After a brief summary of intervening events, the story moves forward in time to a day when Jamie meets Eric, entices him into a barn, and breaks his neck. The story described thus, its ending seems to be a surprise, and it certainly is a surprise to Eric. In fact, his sudden realization that he is in grave danger is an epiphany. "The Man Child" is thus a coming-of-age story, an account of a young person's realization of the dark side of adult existence. Eric, however, has little time to think about his realization or even to generalize very much on the basis of his intimation of danger before he is badly, perhaps mortally, injured.

The story, however, contains many hints that violent action will be forthcoming. A reader can see them even though Eric cannot because Eric is the center of consciousness, a device perfected, if not invented, by Henry James. That is, Eric does not narrate the story so the story does not present his viewpoint, but he is always the focus of the action, and the story is in essence an account of his responses to that action. The difference between his perception of the events he witnesses (which is sometimes described and sometimes can be inferred from his actions) and the perception that can be had by attending carefully to the story encourages a reader to make a moral analysis and finally to make a moral judgment, just as the difference between Huck Finn's perception and the perception that one can have while reading Mark Twain's *Adventures of Huckleberry Finn* (1884) at first stimulates laughter and then moral evaluation. Eric's lack of perception is a function of his innocence, a quality that he has to an even larger extent than has Huck Finn, and thus he is less able to cope in a threatening world and his injury is even more execrable. If the measure of a society is its solicitude for the powerless, the miniature society formed by the three adults in this story, and perhaps by implication the larger society of which they are a part, is sorely wanting.

To be more specific about the flaws in this society and in these persons, they enslave themselves and others, as is suggested very early in the story: "Eric lived with his father . . . and his mother, who had been captured by his father on some faroff unblessed, unbelievable night, who had never since burst her chains."

James Baldwin (Getty Images)

Her husband intimidates and frightens her, and his conversation about relations between men and women indicates that he believes she exists at his sufferance only for sex and procreation. Her role becomes questionable because in the summary of events that happen between the first and last parts of the story one learns that she has lost the child she had been carrying and cannot conceive anymore. The two men enslave themselves with their notions about women, their drunkenness (which they misinterpret as male companionship), their mutual hostility, their overbearing expansiveness, in short, with their machismo. Eric's father is convinced that he is more successful in these terms. He has fathered a son, an accomplishment the significance of which to him is indicated by his "some day all this will be yours" talk with Eric between the two party scenes. Jamie's wife, showing more sense than Eric's mother, left her husband before he could sire a son. Jamie's violent act with Eric is his psychotic imitation of the relation of Eric's father to Eric, just as his whistling at the very end of the story is his imitation of the music he hears coming from a tavern. Eric is thus considered by the two men to be alive merely for their self-expression. His father's kind of self-expression is potentially debilitating, although somewhat benign; Jamie's version is nearly fatal.

"GOING TO MEET THE MAN"

"Going to Meet the Man" is a companion to "The Man Child," both stories having been published for the first time in *Going to Meet the Man*. Whereas the latter story isolates whites from blacks in order to analyze their psychology, the former story is about whites in relation to blacks, even though blacks make only brief appearances in it. The whites in these stories have many of the same characteristics, but in "Going to Meet the Man" those characteristics are more obviously dangerous. These stories were written during the height of the Civil Rights movement, and Baldwin, by means of his rhetorical power and his exclusion of more human white types, helped polarize that movement.

The main characters in "Going to Meet the Man" are a family composed of a southern deputy sheriff, his wife, and his son Jesse. At the beginning of the story they are skittish because of racial unrest. Demonstrations by blacks have alternated with police brutality by whites, each response escalating the conflict, which began when a black man knocked down an elderly white woman. The family is awakened late at night by a crowd of whites who have learned that the black man has been caught. They all set off in a festive, although somewhat tense, mood to the place where the black man is being held. After they arrive the black man is burned, castrated, and mutilated--atrocities that Baldwin describes very vividly. This story, however, is not merely sensationalism or social and political rhetoric. It rises above those kinds of writing because of its psychological insights into the causes of racism and particularly of racial violence.

Baldwin's focus at first is on the deputy sheriff. As the story opens he is trying and failing to have sexual relations with his wife. He thinks that he would have an easier time with a black, and "the image of a black girl caused a distant excitement in him." Thus, his conception of blacks is immediately mixed with sexuality, especially with his fear of impotence. In contrast, he thinks of his wife as a "frail sanctuary." At the approach

of a car he reaches for the gun beside his bed, thereby adding a propensity for violence to his complex of psychological motives. Most of his behavior results from this amalgam of racial attitudes, sexual drives, fear of impotence, and attraction to violence. He recalls torturing a black prisoner by applying a cattle prod to his testicles, and on the way to see the black captive he takes pride in his wife's attractiveness. He also frequently associates blacks with sexual vigor and fecundity. The castration scene is the most powerful rendition of this psychological syndrome.

The deputy sheriff, however, is more than a mere brute; he tries to think of his relation to blacks in moral terms. Their singing of spirituals disconcerts him because he has difficulty understanding how they can be Christians like himself. He tries to reconcile this problem by believing that blacks have decided "to fight against God and go against the rules laid down in the Bible for everyone to read!" To allay the guilt that threatens to complicate his life he also believes that there are a lot of good blacks who need his protection from bad blacks. These strategies for achieving inner peace do not work, and Baldwin brilliantly describes the moral confusion of such whites:

> They had never dreamed that their privacy could contain any element of terror, could threaten, that is, to reveal itself, to the scrutiny of a judgment day, while remaining unreadable and inaccessible to themselves; nor had they dreamed that the past, while certainly refusing to be forgotten, could yet so stubbornly refuse to be remembered. They felt themselves mysteriously set at naught.

In the absence of a satisfying moral vision, violence seems the only way to achieve inner peace, and the sheriff's participation in violence allows him to have sex with his wife as the story ends. Even then, however, he has to think that he is having it as blacks would. He is their psychic prisoner, just as the black who was murdered was the white mob's physical prisoner.

Late in this story one can see that Jesse, the sheriff's eight-year-old son, is also an important character. At first he is confused by the turmoil and thinks of blacks in human terms. He wonders why he has not seen his black friend Otis for several days. The mob violence, however, changes him; he undergoes a coming-of-age, the perversity of which is disturbing. He is the center of consciousness in the mob scene. His first reaction is the normal one for a boy: "Jesse clung to his father's neck in terror as the cry rolled over the crowd." Then he loses his innocence and it becomes clear that he will be a victim of the same psychological syndrome that afflicts his father: "He watched his mother's face . . . she was more beautiful than he had ever seen her. . . . He began to feel a joy he had never felt before." He wishes that he were the man with the knife who is about to castrate the black man, whom Jesse considers "the most beautiful and terrible object he had ever seen." Then he identifies totally with his father: "At that moment Jesse loved his father more than he had ever loved him. He felt that his father had carried him through a mighty test, had revealed to him a great secret which would be the key to his life forever." Thus for Jesse this brutality is a kind of initiation into adulthood, and its effect is to ensure that there will be at least one more generation capable of the kind of violence that he has just seen.

"Sonny's Blues"

Whereas "The Man Child" has only white characters and "Going to Meet the Man" is about a conflict between whites and blacks, "Sonny's Blues" has only black characters. Although the chronology of "Sonny's Blues" is scrambled, its plot is simple. It tells the story of two brothers, one, the narrator, a respectable teacher and the other, Sonny, a former user of heroin who is jailed for that reason and then becomes a jazz musician. The story ends in a jazz nightclub, where the older brother hears Sonny play and finally understands the meaning of jazz for him. The real heart of this story is the contrast between the values of the two brothers, a contrast that becomes much less dramatic at the end.

The two brothers have similar social backgrounds, especially their status as blacks and, more specifically, as Harlem blacks. Of Harlem as a place in which to mature the narrator says, "boys exactly like the boys we once had been found themselves encircled by disaster. Some escaped the trap, most didn't. Those who got out always left something of themselves behind, as some animals amputate a leg and leave it in a trap." Even when he was very young the narrator had a sense of the danger and despair surrounding him:

When lights fill the room, the child is filled with darkness. He knows that every time this happens he's moved just a little closer to that darkness outside. The darkness outside is what the old folks have been talking about. It's what they've come from. It's what they endure.

The narrator learns after his father's death that his father, though seemingly a hardened and stoical man, had hidden the grief caused by the killing of his brother.

At first the narrator believes that Sonny's two means for coping with the darkness, heroin and music, are inextricably connected to that darkness and thus are not survival mechanisms at all. He believes that heroin "filled everything, the people, the houses, the music, the dark, quicksilver barmaid, with menace; and this menace was their reality." Later, however, he realizes that jazz is a way to escape: He senses that "Sonny was at that time piano playing for his life." The narrator also has a few premonitions of the epiphany he experiences in the jazz nightclub. One occurs when he observes a group of street singers and understands that their "music seemed to soothe a poison out of them." Even with these premonitions, he does not realize that he uses the same strategy. After an argument with Sonny, during which their differences seem to be irreconcilable, his first reaction is to begin "whistling to keep from crying," and the tune is a blues. Finally the epiphany occurs, tying together all the major strands of this story. As he listens to Sonny playing jazz the narrator thinks that

freedom lurked around us and I understood, at last, that he could help us be free if we would listen, that he would never be free until we did. Yet, there was no battle in his face now. I heard what he had gone through, and would continue to go through.

The idea in that passage is essentially what Baldwin is about. Like Sonny, he has forged an instrument of freedom by means of the fire of his troubles, and he has made that instrument available to all, white and black. His is the old story of suffering and art; his fiction is an account of trouble, but by producing it he has shown others the way to rise above suffering.

OTHER MAJOR WORKS

LONG FICTION: *Go Tell It on the Mountain*, 1953; *Giovanni's Room*, 1956; *Another Country*, 1962; *Tell Me How Long the Train's Been Gone*, 1968; *If Beale Street Could Talk*, 1974; *Just Above My Head*, 1979.

PLAYS: *The Amen Corner*, pr. 1954, pb. 1968; *Blues for Mister Charlie*, pr., pb. 1964; *A Deed from the King of Spain*, pr. 1974.

SCREENPLAY: *One Day, When I Was Lost: A Scenario Based on "The Autobiography of Malcolm X,"* 1972.

POETRY: *Jimmy's Blues: Selected Poems*, 1983.

NONFICTION: *Notes of a Native Son*, 1955; *Nobody Knows My Name: More Notes of a Native Son*, 1961; *The Fire Next Time*, 1963; *Nothing Personal*, 1964 (with Richard Avedon); *A Rap on Race*, 1971 (with Margaret Mead); *No Name in the Street*, 1971; *A Dialogue*, 1973 (with Nikki Giovanni); *The Devil Finds Work*, 1976; *The Evidence of Things Not Seen*, 1985; *The Price of the Ticket*, 1985; *Conversations with James Baldwin*, 1989; *Collected Essays*, 1998; *Native Sons: A Friendship That Created One of the Greatest Works of the Twentieth Century-- "Notes of a Native Son,"* 2004 (with Sol Stein).

CHILDREN'S LITERATURE: *Little Man, Little Man: A Story of Childhood*, 1976.

BIBLIOGRAPHY

Bloom, Harold, ed. *James Baldwin*. Updated ed. New York: Chelsea House, 2007. This collection includes three previously published essays about Baldwin's short fiction: "'Sonny's Blues,' James Baldwin's "Image of Black Community," by John M. Reilly; "The Jazz-Blues Motif in James Baldwin's 'Sonny's Blues,'" by Richard N. Albert, and "Fire as the Symbol of a Leadening Existence in 'Going to Meet the Man,'" by Arthenia Bates Millican.

DeGout, Yasmin Y. "'Masculinity' and (Im)maturity: 'The Man Child' and Other Stories in Baldwin's "Gender Studies Enterprise." In *Re-Viewing James Baldwin: Things Not Seen*, edited by D. Quentin Miller. Philadelphia: Temple University Press, 2000. Examines how Baldwin's work deconstructs traditional concepts of manhood and gender.

de Romanet, Jerome. "Revisiting Madeleine and 'The Outing': James Baldwin's "Revision of Gide's Sexual Politics." *MELUS* 22 (Spring, 1997): 3-14. A discussion of Baldwin's story "The Outing" in terms of its contrast with André Gide's Calvinist guilt. Discusses sexual identity in this story and other Baldwin fictions. Argues that Baldwin's exile in France was as concerned with racial identity as with sexual emancipation.

Dickstein, Morris, ed. *Critical Insights: James Baldwin*. Pasadena, Calif.: Salem Press, 2011. Collection of original and reprinted essays providing critical readings of the key themes and contexts of Baldwin's work, including an analysis of "Going to Meet the Man." Also includes a biography, a chronology of major events in Baldwin's life, a complete list of his works, and a bibliography listing resources for further research.

Field, Douglas, ed. *A Historical Guide to James Baldwin*. New York: Oxford University Press, 2009. Provides a brief biography and several critical essays examining Baldwin's work, including discussions of his use of the blues, Baldwin and sexuality, Baldwin and the Civil Rights movement, and Baldwin criticism in perspective.

Gelfant, Blanche H., ed. *The Columbia Companion to the Twentieth-Century American Short Story*. New York: Columbia University Press, 2000. Includes a chapter in which Baldwin's short stories are analyzed.

Kinnamon, Kenneth, ed. *James Baldwin: A Collection of Critical Essays*. Englewood Cliffs, N.J.: Prentice-Hall, 1974. A good introduction to Baldwin's early work featuring a collection of diverse essays by such well-known figures as Irving Howe, Langston Hughes, and Eldridge Cleaver. Includes a chronology of important dates, notes on the contributors, and a select bibliography.

Leming, David. *James Baldwin: A Biography*. New York: Alfred A. Knopf, 1994. A biography of Baldwin written by one who knew him and worked with him for the last quarter-century of his life. Provides extensive literary analysis of Baldwin's work and relates his work to his life.

Porter, Horace A. *Stealing the Fire: The Art and Protest of James Baldwin*. Middletown, Conn.: Wesleyan University Press, 1989. Originally a doctoral dissertation, Porter later expanded his material and published it after Baldwin's death. Porter attempts to relate Baldwin to the larger African American tradition of social protest.

Sanderson, Jim. "Grace in 'Sonny's Blues.'" *Short Story*, n.s. 6 (Fall, 1998): 85-95. Argues that Baldwin's story illustrates his integration of the personal with the social in terms of his residual evangelical Christianity. Maintains that at the end of the story, when the narrator offers Sonny a drink, he puts himself in the role of Lord, and Sonny accepts the cup of wrath; the two brothers thus regain grace by means of the power of love.

Sherard, Tracey. "Sonny's Bebop: Baldwin's 'Blues Text' as Intracultural Critique." *African American Review* 32 (Winter, 1998): 691-705. A discussion of Houston Baker's notion of the "blues matrix" in Baldwin's story "Sonny's Blues." Examines the story's treatment of black culture in America as reflected by jazz and the blues. Discusses how the "blues text" of the story represents how intracultural narratives have influenced the destinies of African Americans.

Standley, Fred L., and Nancy V. Burt, eds. *Critical Essays on James Baldwin*. Boston: G. K. Hall, 1988. An attempt to anthologize the important criticism on Baldwin in one definitive volume. More than thirty-five articles focus on Baldwin's essays, fiction, nonfiction, and drama.

Sylvander, Carolyn Wedin. *James Baldwin*. New York: Frederick Ungar, 1980. This good overview of Baldwin's work provides an aesthetic perspective, a bibliographical summary, and an analysis of individual works, with greater emphasis given to Baldwin's plays, novels, and short stories.

Tomlinson, Robert. "'Payin One's Dues': Expatriation as Personal Experience and Paradigm in the Works of James Baldwin." *African American Review* 33 (Spring, 1999): 135-148. A discussion of how Baldwin was affected by his exile in Paris. Argues that the experience internalized the conflicts he experienced in America. Suggests that Baldwin used his homosexuality and exile as a metaphor for the experience of the African American.

Tsomondo, Thorell. "No Other Tale to Tell: 'Sonny's Blues' and 'Waiting for the Rain.'" "*Critique* 36 (Spring, 1995)": 195-209. Examines how art and history are related in "Sonny's Blues." Discusses the story as one in which a young musician replays tribal history in music. Argues that the story represents how African American writers try to reconstruct an invalidated tradition.

Weatherby, W. J. *James Baldwin: Artist on Fire*. New York: Donald I. Fine, 1989. A lengthy personal reminiscence of Baldwin by a close friend who calls his memoir a portrait. Rich in intimate detail and based on conversations with more than one hundred people who knew Baldwin. Reveals the man behind the words.

John Stark
Updated by Terry Theodore

TONI CADE BAMBARA

Born: New York, New York; March 25, 1939
Died: Philadelphia, Pennsylvania; December 9, 1995
Also known as: Miltona Mirkin Cade

PRINCIPAL SHORT FICTION

Gorilla, My Love, 1972
The Sea Birds Are Still Alive: Collected Stories, 1977
Raymond's Run: Stories for Young Adults, 1989
Deep Sightings and Rescue Missions: Fiction, Essays, and Conversations, 1996.

OTHER LITERARY FORMS

Before Toni Cade Bambara (bam-BAHR-ah) published her first collection of stories, *Gorilla, My Love,* she edited two anthologies, *The Black Woman: An Anthology* (1970) and *Tales and Stories for Black Folks* (1971), under the name Toni Cade. Her 1980 novel, *The Salt Eaters,* was well received and won many awards. She was also an active screenwriter whose credits included Louis Massiah's *The Bombing of Osage Avenue* (1986), about the bombing of the Movement (MOVE) Organization's headquarters in Philadelphia, and Massiah's *W. E. B. Du Bois--A Biography in Four Voices* (1995). Her friend and editor, Toni Morrison, edited a collection of her previously uncollected stories and essays called *Deep Sightings and Rescue Missions: Fiction, Essays, and Conversations* (1966), and her final novel, *Those Bones Are Not My Child,* was published in 1999.

ACHIEVEMENTS

The Salt Eaters won numerous awards, including the American Book Award, the Langston Hughes Society Award, and an award from the Zora Neale Hurston Society. Toni Cade Bambara's work on *The Bombing of Osage Avenue* led to an Academy Award for Best Documentary and awards from the Pennsylvania Association of Broadcasters and the Black Hall of Fame. Her other honors include the Peter Pauper Press Award (1958), the John Golden Award for Fiction from Queens College (1959), a Rutgers University research fellowship (1972), a Black Child Development Institute service award (1973), a Black Rose Award from *Encore Magazine* (1973), a Black Community Award from Livingston College, Rutgers University (1974), an award from the National Association of Negro Business and Professional Women's Club League, a George Washington Carver Distinguished African American Lecturer Award from Simpson College, *Ebony* magazine's Achievement in the Arts Award, a Black Arts Award from the University of Missouri (1981), a Documentary Award from the National Black Programming Consortium (1986), and a nomination for the Black Caucus of the American Library Association Literary Award (1997).

BIOGRAPHY

Toni Cade Bambara was born Miltona Mirkin Cade in New York City in 1939 and grew up in Harlem, Bedford-Stuyvesant, and Queens, New York, and in Jersey City, New Jersey. She attended Queens College in New York and received a B.A. degree in theater arts in 1959, the same year she published her first short story, "Sweet Town." From 1960 to 1965, she worked on an M.A. degree in American literature at City College of New York, while also working as a caseworker at the Department of Welfare, and later as program director of the Colony Settlement House. Starting in 1965, she taught at City College for four years before moving on to Livingston College at Rutgers University in 1969. She also taught at Emory University, Spelman College (where she was a writer-in-residence during the 1970's), and Atlanta University, at various times teaching writing, theater, and social work.

Her publication of *The Black Woman*, an anthology of poetry, fiction, and nonfiction by established writers (such as Nikki Giovanni, Alice Walker, and Paule Marshall) and students demonstrated her commitment to both the women's movement and the Civil Rights movement. By the time she had published her first collection of short stories, *Gorilla, My Love*, in 1972, she had adopted the last name of Bambara from a signature she found on a sketch pad in a trunk of her grandmother's belongings.

Bambara's belief in the connection between social activism and art was strengthened by a trip to Cuba in 1973, when she met with women's organizations there. The increased urgency of concern for social activism appears in her second collection of short stories, *The Sea Birds Are Still Alive*. After her first novel, *The Salt Eaters*, was published in 1980 and received numerous awards, she increasingly turned her attention to her work in the arts, becoming an important writer of independent films, though she never stopped working on fiction. She died of cancer on December 9, 1995.

ANALYSIS

Toni Cade Bambara's short fiction is especially notable for its creativity with language and its ability to capture the poetry of black speech. In a conversation that was printed in her posthumous collection *Deep Sightings and Rescue Missions* as "How She Came by Her Name," she claimed that in the stories from *Gorilla, My Love* about childhood, she was trying to capture the voice of childhood, and she was surprised that readers received these efforts to use black dialect as a political act. Nonetheless, her writing (like her work as a teacher, social worker, and filmmaker) was always informed by her sense of social activism and social justice in the broadest sense. In her later work outside the field of short fiction (in films and in her last novel), she focused on the bombing of the black neighborhood in Philadelphia where the MOVE Organization was headquartered, the life of W. E. B. Du Bois, and the Atlanta child murders of the 1980's, all topics that were rife with political meaning.

Nonetheless, what enlivens her writing is her originality with language and a playful sense of form that aims more to share than to tell directly. Another essay

from *Deep Sightings and Rescue Missions*, "The Education of a Storyteller" tells of Grandma Dorothy teaching her that she could not really know anything that she could not share with her girlfriends, and her stories seem to grow out of the central wish to share things with this target audience of black women peers. Her stories are usually digressive, seldom following a linear plot. Most of them are structured in an oral form that allows for meaningful side issues with the aim of bringing clear the central point to her audience. Though this technique can be daunting when used in the novel-length *The Salt Eaters*, it allows her to make her short stories into charming, witty, and lively artistic performances in which social messages emerge organically.

GORILLA, MY LOVE

Gorilla, My Love was Toni Cade Bambara's first collection of her original work, and it remains her most popular book. The stories in it were written between 1959 and 1970, and as she explains in her essay, "How She Came by Her Name," she was trying to capture the language system in which people she knew lived and moved. She originally conceived it as a collection of the voices of young, bright, and tough girls of the city, but she did not want it to be packaged as a children's book, so she added some of the adult material to it. "My Man Bovane," for instance, features a matronly black woman seducing a blind man at a neighborhood political rally, while her children look on in disapproval. Similarly, among the fifteen stories (most of which are written in the first person) that make up this book is "Talkin Bout Sonny," in which Betty and Delauney discuss their friend Sonny's recent breakdown and assault on his wife. Delauney claims he understands exactly how such a thing could happen, and it is left unclear how this unstable relationship between Betty and Delauney (who is married) will resolve itself.

Most of the stories, however, focus on young girls determined to make their place in the world and the neighborhood. "The Hammer Man," for instance, tells of a young girl who first hides from a mentally disturbed older boy she has humiliated in public but later futilely attempts to defend against two policemen who try to arrest him. The adult themes and the childhood themes come together best in "The Johnson Girls," in which a young girl listens in as a group of women try to console Inez, whose boyfriend has left with no promise of return. As the young narrator listens in the hope that she will not have to endure "all this torture crap" when she becomes a woman, it becomes clear that the intimate conversation between women is a form of revitalization for Inez.

A delightful preface to *Gorilla, My Love* assures the reader that the material in the book is entirely fictional, not at all autobiographical, but it is hard for a reader not to feel that the voices that populate the work speak for Bambara and the neighborhood of her youth.

"GORILLA, MY LOVE"

The title story of Bambara's first book-length collection of her own work, "Gorilla, My Love" is also her most irresistible work. The narrator is a young girl named Hazel who has just learned that her "Hunca Bubba" is about to be married. She is clearly upset about both this news and the fact that he is now going by his full name, Jefferson Winston Vale. The story proceeds in anything but a linear manner, as Hazel sees a motion-picture theater in the background of Hunca Bubba's photos, and starts to tell about going to the films on Easter with her brothers, Big Brood and Little Jason. When the motion picture turns out to be a film about Jesus instead of "Gorilla, My Love," as was advertised, Hazel gets angry and demands her money back, and not getting it, starts a fire in the lobby-- "Cause if you say Gorilla My Love you supposed to mean it."

What is really on her mind is that when Hunca Bubba was babysitting her, he promised he was going to marry her when she grew up, and she believed him. Hazel's attempt to keep her dignity but make her feeling of betrayal known by confronting Hunca Bubba is at once both a surprise and a completely natural outgrowth of her character. Her grandfather's explanation, that it was Hunca Bubba who promised to marry her but it is Jefferson Winston Vale who is marrying someone else, is at once both compassionate and an example of the type of hypocrisy that Hazel associates with the adult world. The example she gives in her story about going to the film makes it clear that she has always seen her family as better than most, but she sees hypocrisy as a universal adult epidemic.

"RAYMOND'S RUN"

"Raymond's Run," a short story that was published in a collection of stories for young adults, is about the relationship between the narrator, Hazel (not the same girl from "Gorilla, My Love," but about the same age), her retarded brother, Raymond, and Gretchen, another girl on the block. Hazel's reputation is as the fastest thing on two feet in the neighborhood, but coming up to the annual May Day run, she knows that her new rival, Gretchen, will challenge her and could win. Mr. Pearson, a teacher at the school, suggests it would be a nice gesture to the new girl, Gretchen, to let her win, which Hazel dismisses out of hand. Thinking about a Hansel and Gretel pageant in which she played a strawberry, Hazel thinks, "I am not a strawberry . . . I run. That is what I'm all about." As a runner, she has no intention of letting someone else win.

In fact, when the race is run, she does win, but it is very close, and for all her bravado she is not sure who won until her name is announced. More important, she sees her brother Raymond running along with her on the other side of the fence, keeping his hands down in an awkward running posture that she accepts as all his own. In her excitement about her brother's accomplishment, she imagines that her rival Gretchen might want to help her train Raymond as a runner, and the two girls share a moment of genuine warmth.

The central point of the story is captured by Hazel when she says of the smile she shared with Gretchen that it was the type of smile girls can share only when they are not too busy being "flowers of fairies or strawberries instead of something honest and worthy of respect . . . you know . . . like being people." The honest competition that brought out their best efforts and enticed Raymond to join them in his way brought them all together as people, not as social competitors trying to outmaneuver one another but as allies.

"THE LESSON"

"The Lesson" is a story about a child's first realization of the true depth of economic inequity in society. The main characters are Miss Moore, an educated black woman who has decided to take the responsibility for the education of neighborhood children upon herself, and Sylvia, the narrator, a young girl. Though it is summer, Miss Moore has organized an educational field trip. This annoys Sylvia and her friend, Sugar, but since their parents have all agreed to the trip, the children have little choice but to cooperate. The trip is actually an excursion to a high-priced toy store, F. A. O. Schwartz.

The children look with astonishment at a toy clown that costs $35, a paperweight that sells for $480, and a toy sailboat that is priced at $1,195. The children are discouraged by the clear signs of economic inequality. When Miss Moore asks what they have learned from this trip, only Sugar will reply with what she knows Miss Moore wants them to say: "This is not much of a democracy." Sylvia feels betrayed but mostly because she sees that Sugar is playing up to Miss Moore, while Sylvia has been genuinely shaken by this trip. At the end, Sugar is plotting to split the money she knows Sylvia saved from the cab fare Miss Moore gave her, but Sylvia's response as Sugar runs ahead to their favorite ice cream shop, "ain't nobody gonna beat me at nothin'," indicates she has been shaken and is not planning to play the same old games. However, Sylvia cannot so easily slough it off.

"MEDLEY"

The most popular story from *The Sea Birds Are Still Alive*, "Medley" is the story of Sweet Pea and Larry, a romantic couple who go through a poignant breakup in the course of the story. Though neither of them is a musician, both are music fans, and their showers together are erotic encounters in which they improvise songs together, pretending to be playing musical instruments with each other's body. Sweet Pea is a manicurist with her own shop, and her best customer is a gambler named Moody, who likes to keep his nails impeccable. Because he goes on a winning streak after she starts doing his nails, he offers to take her on a gambling trip as his personal manicurist, for which he pays her two thousand dollars. Sweet Pea takes the offer, though Larry objects, and when she gets back, he seems to have disappeared from her life. Nonetheless, she remembers their last night in the shower together, as they sang different tunes, keeping each other off balance, but harmonizing a medley together until the hot water ran out.

Though Sweet Pea is faced with the choice of losing two thousand dollars or her boyfriend and chooses the money, the story does not attempt to say that she made the wrong choice. Rather, it is a snapshot of the impermanence of shared lives in Sweet Pea's modern, urban environment. This transience is painful, but is also the basis for the enjoyment of life's beauty.

OTHER MAJOR WORKS

LONG FICTION: *The Salt Eaters*, 1980; *Those Bones Are Not My Child*, 1999.

SCREENPLAYS: *The Bombing of Osage Avenue*, 1986 (documentary); *W. E. B. Du Bois--A Biography in Four Voices*, 1995 (with Amiri Baraka, Wesley Brown, and Thulani Davis).

NONFICTION: "What It Is I Think I'm Doing Anyhow," in *The Writer on Her Work*, 1981 (Janet Sternburg, editor).

EDITED TEXTS: *The Black Woman: An Anthology*, 1970; *Tales and Stories for Black Folks*, 1971; *Southern Exposure*, 1976 (periodical; Bambara edited volume 3).

BIBLIOGRAPHY

Ashe, Bertram D. "From Within the Frame: Narrative Negotiations with the Black Aesthetic in Toni Cade Bambara's 'My Man Bovanne.'" In *From Within the Frame: Storytelling in African-American Fiction*. New York: Routledge, 2002. Examines the use of the "narrative frame" in Bambara's short story and other fiction written by African Americans. Ashe maintains that African American fiction traditionally features an "inside the text listener" who situates the story for its readers. He describes how Bambara in "My Man Bovanne" dispenses with the frame as a narrative device. Ashe also analyzes the story in terms of the Black Power and Black Aesthetic movements of the 1960's.

Butler-Evans, Elliott. *Race, Gender, and Desire: Narrative Strategies in the Fiction of Toni Cade Bambara, Toni Morrison, Alice Walker*. Philadelphia: Temple University Press, 1989. The first book-length study to treat Bambara's fiction to any extent, this study uses narratology and feminism to explore Bambara's works.

Franko, Carol. "Toni Cade Bambara." In *A Reader's Companion to the Short Story in English*, edited by Erin Fallon, et al., under the auspices of the Society for the Study of the Short Story. Westport, Conn.: Greenwood Press, 2001. Aimed at the general reader, this essay provides a brief biography of Bambara followed by an analysis of her short fiction.

Graves, Roy Neil. "Bambara's 'The Lesson.'" *The Explicator* 66, no. 4 (Summer, 2008): 214-217. An analysis of Bambara's short story.

Hargrove, Nancy. "Youth in Toni Cade Bambara's *Gorilla, My Love*." In *Women Writers of the Contemporary South*, edited by Peggy Whitman Prenshaw. Jackson: University Press of Mississippi, 1984. A thorough examination of an important feature of Bambara's most successful collection of short fiction--namely, that most of the best stories center on young girls.

Holmes, Linda J., and Cheryl A. Wall, eds. *Savoring the Salt: The Legacy of Toni Cade Bambara*. Philadelphia: Temple University Press, 2007. Collection of essays commemorating Bambara's life, discussing her writings, and describing the importance of her contributions to African American literature. In one esssay Salamishah Tillett analyzes *Gorilla, My Love*; some of the other essays are written by Toni Morrison, Amiri Baraka, Ruby Dee, Nikki Giovanni, and Audre Lorde.

Muther, Elizabeth. "Bambara's Feisty Girls: Resistance Narratives in *Gorilla, My Love*." *African American Review* 36, no. 3 (Fall, 2002): 447. A lengthy examination of this short-story collection that focuses on its depiction of relationships between adults and their betrayed children.

Sklar, Howard. "Narrative Structuring of Sympathetic Response: Theoretical and Empirical Approaches to Toni Cade Bambara's 'The Hammer Man.'" *Poetics Today* 30, no. 3 (Fall, 2009): 561-607. Examines how narratives produce sympathy in their readers, providing a detailed analysis of Bambara's short story to demonstrate how she "systematically moves readers from dislike to sympathy for the story's protagonist."

Vertreace, Martha M. *Toni Cade Bambara*. New York: Macmillan Library Reference, 1998. The first full-length work devoted to the entirety of Bambara's career. A part of the successful Twayne series of criticism, this book will be quite helpful for students interested in Bambara's career.

Willis, Susan. "Problematizing the Individual: Toni Cade Bambara's Stories for the Revolution." In *Specifying: Black Women Writing the American Experience*. Madison: University of Wisconsin Press, 1987. Though largely centered on an analysis of *The Salt Eaters*, this essay also has clear and informative analysis of Bambara's most important short fiction.

Thomas J. Cassidy

MELISSA BANK

Born: Boston, Massachusetts; October 11, 1960

PRINCIPAL SHORT FICTION

The Girls' Guide to Hunting and Fishing, 1999

OTHER LITERARY FORMS

Melissa Bank's story collection, *The Girls' Guide to Hunting and Fishing*, was her first book. She completed a screenplay based on the book's title story in 1999, which was adapted as the film *Suburban Girl*, released in 2007. Her first novel, *The Wonder Spot*, was published in 2005.

ACHIEVEMENTS

Melissa Bank won the Nelson Algren award in 1993 for her story "My Old Man." *The Girls' Guide to Hunting and Fishing* was on *The New York Times* bestseller list for more than two months. On her reading tours, she drew standing-room only crowds. Her work has been broadcast on National Public Radio's "Selected Shorts." The bidding war that ended with a $275,000 advance for her first book, a collection of short stories that obviously struck a chord with many young women, created the biggest publishing story of 1999. The book was reviewed by every major newspaper in the English-speaking world, and Bank has been interviewed by numerous papers, magazines, television shows, and Internet sites.

Biography

Melissa Bank was born in Boston in 1960 and grew up in a suburb of Philadelphia. Her father was a neurologist, who died of leukemia in his late fifties. She studied art at Hobart College in upstate New York, but she did not do well in that subject, changing her major and graduating in 1982 with a degree in American Studies. She moved to New York City, where she worked for two years as an editorial assistant in a publishing house. She then entered graduate school at Cornell University in 1985 and earned an M.F.A., after which she taught English at Cornell for three years.

Bank moved back to New York City in 1989, where she worked as a copywriter at the McCann-Erickson advertising agency. During the nine years she worked in advertising, she took some creative writing classes at Columbia University and spent all her free time after work and on weekends writing stories. However, she had little luck in publishing them except in small-circulation journals; her first story, "Lucky You," appeared in 1989 in *The North American Review*.

Bank's big break came in 1997, when Francis Ford Coppola commissioned her to write a story in reaction to the popular book *The Rules: Time Tested Secrets for Capturing the Heart of Mr. Right* (1996), a how-to guide for getting a man, for his *Zoetrope* magazine. As a result, she sent the story and others to an agent who in turn sent them out to ten publishers, nine of whom wanted to publish them in a book. Viking Press won a bidding war for the manuscript, giving Bank an unusually large advance for a first book of short stories. She was later commissioned to write a screenplay based on the title story for a film for Coppola's studio. Bank settled in New York City with her Labrador retriever, Maybelline.

Analysis

Although it may be primarily a case of "being at the right place at the right time," few collections of short stories, particularly collections by a new author, receive the kind of media attention that Melissa Bank's *The Girls' Guide to Hunting and Fishing* received during the summer of 1999. Billed by publishers as "fiction" on the book jacket, hoping readers would take it as a novel rather than the less popular short-story form, these seven loosely connected stories became one of the most popular "take-to-the-beach books" of the year.

Much of the ballyhoo resulted from Bank being commissioned by the prestigious filmmaker Francis Ford Coppola to write the title story; however, part of the fuss was also due to the popularity of the British single-girl novel, *Bridget Jones's Diary: A Novel* (1999; a successful motion picture of which was released in 2001), and the negative reaction of many feminists to the retrograde book *The Rules*, which instructed women how to attract men by playing manipulative games.

Melissa Bank (AP Photo/Kathy Willens)

The central character of most of Bank's stories is Jane Rosenthal, the classic wise-cracking young Jewish working girl, who "comes of age." With the exception of the longest story in the collection, "The Worst Thing a Suburban Girl Could Imagine," which deals with Jane's ways of coping with the death of her father, most depend primarily on clever one-liners typical of stand-up comedy routines. Bank's witticisms put her in the camp of similar 1990's writers, such as Amy Hempel and Lorrie Moore.

"ADVANCED BEGINNERS"

This is probably the most conventional, creative-writing-class story in the collection, and because it is so well made, it is in some ways the most satisfying. The story focuses on young Jane Rosenthal's reaction to her brother's first serious girlfriend, Julia--a reaction that combines jealousy, because she feels Julia is the "kind, helpful, articulate daughter" her parents really wanted and deserved, and sisterly affection, because she can talk to her about such things as love and sex about which she cannot talk to her parents.

Even this story, however, gets much of its energy from the smart talk of the young protagonist, which has made some reviewers call her a kind of female Holden Caulfield. For example, when she tells her friend that breasts are to sex what pillows are to sleep, she adds, "Guys might think they want a pillow, but they'll sleep just as well without one." The most effective parts of the story are the conversations and camaraderie between Jane and the older Julia, who gives her a copy of *The Great Gatsby*.

Overall, the story has more depth than most stories in the collection because of Jane's gradual coming-of-age understanding of the difficulty of loving and having a relationship. At the end, after her brother breaks up with Julia, Jane goes out on her dock looking for the green light that Gatsby looked for, feeling scared that her brother has failed at loving someone, for, she says, "I had no idea myself how to do it." The story's treatment of this theme is a promising introit to the book that is not always fulfilled by later stories.

"THE WORST THING A SUBURBAN GIRL COULD IMAGINE"

Bank has told interviewers that this is her favorite story in the collection. Either because it deals with a subject so central to the collection--Jane's relationship with her father and her resulting relationship with an older man--or because it is the longest, most serious and most ambitious story in the collection, this is the story that best determines if Bank can write a sustained and serious fiction.

Almost as important to this story as her father, who is dying of leukemia, is Archie Knox, an older man with whom Jane has had an affair in the earlier story "My Old Man," but with whom she has broken up. Here, Archie, an editor, returns to further complicate her life, which is already complicated by her father's illness and a new editor, Mimi, who treats Jane as a menial assistant on whom she foists most of her own work.

"The Worst Thing a Suburban Girl Could Imagine" reads much more like an abbreviated novel than the tightly built short story that opens the book. The emphasis in this story is a young professional woman's dilemma of coping with paternalistic older men and exploitative professional women. At the climax of the story, Jane's lover Archie is hospitalized with a disease of the pancreas as a result of his alcoholism, and her father dies. As a result, she is able to see her life "in scale" and understand that it is just her life, not momentous as she had always thought. Putting things in perspective, she stands up to her dominating female superior, who then delivers what is probably the central thematic line of the story, "We are all children until our fathers die." At the end of the story, Jane's realization about her life after her father's death also gives her the courage to say no to Archie's proposal of marriage.

"THE GIRLS' GUIDE TO HUNTING AND FISHING"

The title story of Bank's collection, a title that made some booksellers stock it in the sports section, is the story that began Bank's phenomenal career with its publication by Francis Ford Coppola. It is not a profound story by any means, rather more like a story typical of the old-fashioned sophistication of *Cosmopolitan* magazine. In this story, Jane Rosenthal is the young working woman often depicted in slick magazines, television situation comedies, and films. She is smart, witty, and attractive, but for some reason, in spite of dating often, she faces that age-old "girl problem": men who cannot commit.

The story is based on the premise that Jane meets a man at a friend's wedding and carries on a courtship, against her better judgment, according to a book entitled *How to Meet and Marry Mr. Right*. Throughout the story, she imagines the faces of the two authors of the book, Faith Kurtz-Abromowitz and Bonnie Merrill, giving her advice every time she is tempted to follow her intuition and be herself. In an obvious parody of the popular advice book *The Rules*, Bank peppers the story with one-line advice in boldface type, of which the most important for Jane is to suppress her one-liners; the rule is: "Don't be funny . . . Funny is the opposite of sexy."

As Jane follows such advice as "don't accept a date less than four days in advance," "don't say 'I love you first'," and "don't bring up marriage," the manipulation tactics seem to be working. She continues to "keep him guessing," to "let him pay," and to "be mysterious," even though she tries to rebel against the advice, for she wants this relationship to "be real." The story advances in predictable situation comedy fashion when Robert, tiring of the games Jane plays, stops calling her, and Jane decides in a final bit of fantasy dialogue with Faith and Bonnie, that she will be herself. "No more hunting or fishing," Jane says. At the end of the story, Robert tells her that he was interested in her at first but became less interested when she began the manipulative games. Jane saves all by being her irresistibly clever self. When Robert says he is a "goofball in search of truth," she replies, "I'm a truthball in search of goof," and, naturally, he falls in love with her all over again. The story ends with the feel-good line "There is no stopping us now. Both of us are hunters and prey, fishers and fish."

OTHER MAJOR WORKS

LONG FICTION: *The Wonder Spot*, 2005.

SCREENPLAY: *The Girls' Guide to Hunting and Fishing*, wr.1999.

BIBLIOGRAPHY

Caldwell, Gail. "Bright Girl, Big City." *Boston Globe*. May 30, 1999, p. D1. Says *The Girls' Guide to Hunting and Fishing* is the American book industry's answer to *Bridget Jones's Diary*, with the hope that a well-timed trend may constitute "a Zeitgeist, or at least a barrelful of profits." Argues that the experiences in the book are predictable and the over-the-top one-liners "stick out like drugstore jewelry on a little girl."

Carey, Lynn. "Hunting and Fishing Frenzy." *Buffalo News*, August 21, 1999, p. 7C. In this interview article, Bank says the father in the stories is mostly autobiographical, but she refuses to discuss the origins of the story about breast cancer. Bank argues against the frequent comparison of her book to British author Helen Fielding's *Bridget Jones's Diary*.

Chonin, Neva. "A Guide Women Can Identify with." *San Francisco Chronicle*, June 22, 1999, p. E1. An interview story that discusses the buzz that developed around Bank's *Zoetrope* story months before it was printed. Bank says she is "flattered but flummoxed" by her sudden popularity; she says her goal was just to get published so she could get a decent university teaching job but that she now both loves and hates her new celebrity status.

Iovine, Julie V. "At Home with Melissa Bank." *The New York Times*, July 22, 1999, p. F1. This interview story provides biographical notes, discusses the media attention Bank has received, and quotes Bank on her reaction to being in the literary limelight after years of writing alone.

Klinghoffer, David. "Female Trouble." *National Review* 51 (July 12, 1999): 55. Puts Bank's collection in the context of the social problems faced by single women in their thirties in the United States, particularly the problem of finding a husband. Reports on a panel discussion featuring Bank and Helen Fielding, author of *Bridget Jones's Diary*, and comments on the humor in both of their books.

Lanham, Fritz. "Love, Happiness Are Trophies Melissa Bank's Heroine Seeks." *Houston Chronicle*, August 1, 1999, p. 18. An interview story with biographical background. Bank discusses her relationship to Jane Rosenthal, the heroine of her stories, as well as Rosenthal's development throughout the stories.

Lehmann-Haupt, Christopher. "She Lives to Tell About Growing Up." *The New York Times*, June 17, 1999, p. E9. In this review, Lehmann-Haupt calls *The*

Girls' Guide to Hunting and Fishing a charming, funny collection of seven linked fictions. Argues that all the humor of the stories turns on Jane's "wonderfully clear sense of the trickiness of language."

Vnuk, Rebecca. "Hip Lit for Hip Chicks." *Library Journal* 130, no. 12 (July 1, 2005): 42-45. *The Girls' Guide to Hunting and Fishing* is one of the books referenced in this discussion of the "chick lit" genre. Analyzes chick lit's appeal to young women, its use

of humor and popular culture references, and how it differs from "women's literature."

Weaver, Courtney. "Jane's Addiction." *The New York Times*, May 30, 1999, p. 23. Relates the stories to themes and types from women's magazines. Argues there is no real character development in the stories and no unified structure; says it feels like an unfinished novel, divided up into stories.

Charles E. May

RUSSELL BANKS

Born: Newton, Massachusetts; March 28, 1940

PRINCIPAL SHORT FICTION

Searching for Survivors, 1975
The New World, 1978
Trailerpark, 1981
Success Stories, 1986
The Angel on the Roof: The Stories of Russell Banks, 2000

OTHER LITERARY FORMS

Russell Banks has published several collections of poetry and many novels. His novels *Continental Drift* (1985) and *Cloudsplitter* (1998) were finalists for the Pulitzer Prize, *Affliction* (1989) was nominated for both the PEN/Faulkner Award for Fiction and the Irish International Prize, and Cloudsplitter was a PEN/Faulkner Award finalist. Other major works include *Family Life* (1975, revised 1988), *Hamilton Stark* (1978), *The Sweet Hereafter* (1991), and *Rule of the Bone* (1995).His poems, stories, and essays have appeared in the Boston Globe Magazine, *Vanity Fair, The New York Times Book Review, Esquire,* and *Harper's.*

ACHIEVEMENTS

Russell Banks has been awarded a Woodrow Wilson Foundation Award, a John Simon Guggenheim Memorial Fellowship, a National Endowment for the Arts

grant, the Ingram Merril Award, the Fels Award, the John Dos Passos Award, the St. Lawrence Prize for Fiction from St. Lawrence University and *Fiction International*, the American Academy of Arts and Letters Award for work of distinction, and the Laure Battalion Prize for best work of fiction translated into French for the French edition of *The Darling* (2004). His work has been anthologized in *Prize Stories: The O. Henry Awards* and *The Best American Short Stories*.

BIOGRAPHY

Russell Earl Banks was born in Newton, Massachusetts, on March 28, 1940, and raised in New Hampshire. The first in his family to attend college, Banks found the atmosphere at Colgate University incompatible with his working-class background and relinquished his scholarship after eight weeks. He headed for Florida, fully intending to align himself with rebel Cuban leader Fidel Castro, but lacking enough incentive and money he worked at odd jobs until his career path became clear. He was at various times a plumber (like his father), a shoe salesman, a department store window dresser, and an editor.

In 1964 he enrolled at the University of North Carolina at Chapel Hill and graduated Phi Beta Kappa in 1967. His sense of political and social injustice became more finely honed in this city, which is touted as the most northern of the southern states, the most dramatic incident being the disruption of an integrated party by gun-wielding members of the local Ku Klux Klan.

A John Simon Guggenheim Memorial Foundation Fellowship in 1976 allowed him to move to Jamaica, where he immersed himself in the culture, trying to live as a native rather than as a tourist. The experience of living in an impoverished nation helped him professionally, as well as personally, and gave him a broad perspective on issues of race. Married four times and the father of four grown daughters, Banks has taught at major universities, including Columbia University, Sarah Lawrence College, New York University, and Princeton University. Critic Fred Pfeil called Banks

> the most important living white male American on the official literary map, a writer we, as readers *and* writers, can actually learn from, whose books help and urge us to change.

ANALYSIS

Russell Banks's work is largely autobiographical, growing out of the chaos of his childhood: the shouting and hitting, physical and emotional abuse inflicted on

Russell Banks (Christopher Felver/CORBIS)

the family by an alcoholic father, who abandoned them in 1953. Being forced at age twelve to assume the role of the man in the family and always living on the edge of poverty greatly influenced Banks's worldview and consequently his writing. Banks's struggle to understand the tight hold that the past has on the present and the future led him to create a world in which people come face to face with similar dilemmas. Banks's characters struggle to get out from under, to free themselves from the tethers of race, class, and gender. He writes of working people, those who by virtue of social status are always apart, marginalized, often desperate, inarticulate, silenced by circumstances. He aims to be their voice, to give expression to their pain, their aspirations, their angst. Their emotional makeup can be as complex as those more favored by birth or power. In an interview in *The New York Times Book Review*, Banks noted that

> part of the challenge . . . is uncovering the resiliency of that kind of life, and part is in demonstrating that even the quietest lives can be as complex and rich, as joyous, conflicted and anguished, as other seemingly more dramatic lives.

Banks's main strength, besides his graceful style, keen powers of observation, intelligence, and humanity, is his ability to write feelingly of often unlovable people. He never condescends or belittles. He does not judge. He always attempts to show, rather than tell, why a person is as he or she is, and it is in the telling that Banks is able to understand himself and exorcize the devils of his own past. He did not necessarily set out on self-discovery, but he learned, through writing, who he was and what he thought. He grew to understand himself through understanding the elements of his past that shaped him.

Banks is sometimes grouped with Raymond Carver, Richard Ford, and Andre Dubus as writers in a "Trailer-Park Fiction" genre, which, according to critic Denis M. Hennessy,

> examine[s] American working-class people living their lives one step up from the lowest rung on the socioeconomic ladder and doing battle every day with the despair that comes from violence, alcohol, and self-destructive relationships.

Some of Banks's plots and themes are derivative, with heavy borrowings from Mark Twain and E. L. Doctorow, but his unique touch sets them apart. Banks is both a chronicler and a critic of contemporary society.

Influenced by the point of view of a member of a lynch mob, Banks attempts to elicit an understanding of the perpetrators as well as of the victims of crimes, cruelties, and injustices. He believes that understanding a situation depends on knowing how the players who created it were created themselves. His characters all search for transformation, for something that will redeem them, lift them above their present circumstances. Their searches lead them to greater desolation and very seldom to contentment. The lower echelon is forever pitted against and at the mercy of the middle class. Hennessy has called Banks's short fiction the "testing ground of his most innovative ideas and techniques." The major themes revolve around disharmony, both in the family and in society, and the eternal search for the lost family. Banks admits that much of his fiction centers on "Russell Banks searching for his father. . . . I spent a great deal of my youth running away from him and obsessively returning to him."

SEARCHING FOR SURVIVORS

Banks's first collection combines reality and fantasy, with the fourteen stories divided into three general groups: five moral and political parables, a trilogy of stories that feature Latin American revolutionary Che Guevara, and six substantially autobiographical tales set in New England. Banks's experiments with narrative style, structure, and point of view met with mixed response. He was credited for trying but faulted for lacking a unifying thread. Critic Robert Niemi says of the parables that if the

theme . . . is the modern divorce between cognition and feeling [they] stylistically enact that schism with a vengeance . . . almost all [being] solemn in tone, and written in a detached, clinically descriptive style that tends toward the cryptic.

Each story ends on a note of either defeat or disillusionment. Survival is highly unlikely. The American Dream has failed.

The opening tale deals with a man driving along the Henry Hudson Parkway, thinking about his childhood friend's car, a Hudson, and about the explorer, who was set adrift in 1611 in the waters that eventually bore his name. The narrator imagines going to the shores of Hudson Bay to look for evidence of the explorer's fate. Therein is an attempt to understand the past. Banks often deals with

the Old World and the early exploration of North America, and he shows the connections between those who set out from their comfortable but unjust homelands to settle the unknown, and modern Americans who have been shunted out of their safe cocoons of fixed values and family security into the relativistic reality of the latter half of the twentieth century.

In a story confirming Thomas Wolfe's thesis that one "can't go home again," a young man returns from adventures with guerrilla leader Che Guevara, only to find his hometown irrevocably changed and himself so different that no one recognizes him. In another story, "With Che at Kitty Hawk," a newly divorced woman and her two daughters visit the Wright Brothers Memorial. An almost-happy ending has the woman feeling somewhat liberated after being trapped in marriage, but that optimism is fleeting. In yet another story, "Blizzard," Banks shifts the narrator, first having him be omniscient, then having him speak through a man who is losing touch with reality, succumbing to guilt and bleak wintery surroundings.

THE NEW WORLD

Banks's search for a comfortable voice caused him to continue to experiment with narrative voice, switching from first to second-person, and sometimes to third person, at times unsettling readers and critics who deemed his shifts haphazard rather than intentional. Never fully at ease with an omniscient, all-knowing narrator, yet not wanting his storyteller to be a character, an integral player, and hence subject to the vagaries of plot, Banks tries to approach his writing as the telling of a story to a partner, perhaps in a darkened room while lying comfortably in bed. He wants to share his story, yet not to tell it from a position of privilege. This approach gives the reader the immediacy needed for involvement in the story, but, at the same time, enough detachment on the part of the narrator to trust him.

Banks called his second collection, which was far more positively received,

> a carefully structured gathering of ten tales that dramatize and explore the process and progress of self-transcendence, tales that . . . embrace the spiritual limits and possibilities of life in the New World.

The collection is divided into two parts: "Renunciation" and "Transformation." The opening story, "The Custodian," deals with a forty-three-year-old man whose father's death finally frees him "to move to a new village . . . to drink and smoke and sing bawdy songs." As he is now also free to marry, he, "reasoning carefully . . . conclude[s] that he would have good luck in seeking a wife if he started with women who were already married." Fortuitously, he has many married male friends and thus begins his series of conquests. He proposes to a few likely prospects; they succumb; he changes his mind; they return to their husbands, never to know satisfaction again.

In another story, "The Conversion," a young boy is wracked by guilt at not being a good person, at engaging in excessive masturbation, and always falling short of what he thought he should be. Alvin wants to change. He wants to be good, decent, and chaste. He fails miserably until one day he sees an angel in a parking lot and decides to become a preacher. His conversion, the reader realizes, is not so much religious as it is a hope to start anew. His new religious life starts as a dishwasher in a religious camp. Robert Niemi observes that, "much like Banks in his youth, Alvin is torn between the promise of upward mobility and loyalty to his father's proletarian ethos." Alvin's father suspects him of "selling out his working-class identity by associating himself with a bourgeois profession," reflecting Banks's own social background in which attempts to move upward were considered a criticism of what was left behind.

Historical figures are featured in some of the stories: Simón Bolívar, Jane Hogarth (wife of the eccentric painter William), Edgar Allan Poe, and others. In the Hogarth tale, "Indisposed," the wife is sadly used by the husband, who treats her as a sexual convenience

and housekeeper. She is overwhelmed by the nothingness of her existence. She is fat and self-loathing until she experiences a sickbed transformation that allows her to move beyond "pitying [her large, slow] body to understanding it." She is then, according to Niemi, able to "inhabit her body fully and without shame, thus reclaiming herself." Then, when her husband is caught in the upstairs bed with the young domestic helper, Jane is able to exact swift punishment and completely change the tenor of the home. Niemi observes that Banks's history

> shades into fiction and fiction melds into history. [His] central theme, though, is the enduring human need to reinvent the self in order to escape or transcend the constrictions of one's actual circumstances. This means creating a "new world" out of the imagination, just as the "discovery" of the Americas opened up vast horizons for a culturally exhausted Old World Europe.

Banks believes that "the dream of a new life, the dream of starting over" is the quintessential American Dream, the ideological keystone of American civilization from its inception to the present day.

TRAILERPARK

In this collection, perhaps his most structurally satisfying, Russell Banks takes the reader into the very heart of a community of people who, while not having lowered expectations, do have less grandiose or unrealistic ambitions than those in the mainstream. They go through life earning enough to meet basic needs, never going far beyond their environs. Some work full time, some seasonally; some leave for a while and then return. Most seem to find the day-to-day process of getting by nearly enough. Heartaches, anger, depression, and just plain weirdness are often eased with marijuana and alcohol.

This collection's twelve stories are interrelated because they all deal with the residents of the Granite State Trailerpark in Catamount, New Hampshire. The resident have little in common other than the circumstances of their housing. They are detached physically, as well as emotionally, yet they do form a community with at least some common concerns. One of the residents notes that when you are "a long way from where you think you belong, you will attach yourself to people you would otherwise ignore or even dislike." Each story deals with one of the dozen or so denizens, all of whom are "generally alone in the world."

Trailer #1 is the heartbeat of the park, where French Canadian manager Marcelle Chagnon oversees operations. She lost a child when an unscrupulous doctor found her more interesting than her illness. Bank teller Leon LaRoche lives in #2 next to Bruce Severance, in #3, a college student who is an afficionado of home-grown cannabis. Divorcée Doreen Tiede and her five-year-old daughter are in #4 next to the burned remains of #5, where Ginnie and Claudel Bing lived until Ginnie left the stove burner on. Retired army captain Dewey Knox is in #6; Noni Hubner and her mother Nancy are in #7. Merl Ring, in #8, enjoys self-imposed isolation, eagerly awaiting the blasting winters when he can set up his equipment in the middle of frozen Skitters Lake and spend months of solitary ice fishing. The former resident of #9, Tom Smith, killed himself, and the place remains empty. The only black resident, Carol Constant, sometimes shares #10 with her brother Terry. Number 11 houses Flora Pease and more than 115 guinea pigs, which threaten to overtake the trailer and the whole park. The opening story, "The Guinea Pig Lady," introduces all the residents as they share their concerns about the situation. Most notable is the trailer and occupant not mentioned at all--#12, probably the narrator's place. Banks's park people have offbeat but understandable pathologies. Some are just achingly lonely. Critic Johnathan Yardley credits Banks with drawing together a "small but vibrant cast of characters, a human comedy in microcosm" made up of "utterly unconnected people [who] find themselves drawn together by the accident of living in the same place; the trailer park, grim and dreary as it may be, is a neighborhood."

SUCCESS STORIES

This 1986 collection of twelve stories--six autobiographical--six parabolic, has more to do with failed attempts to change the course of lives than it does with acquisition of fame and fortune. The characters in the collection have been called "dreamers, nourished on giddy expectations, but disenfranchised by accidents of class, economy, looks or simple luck." They think that life holds all sorts of possibilities but learn quickly that

fate has not cast a favorable eye on them. Banks sets out to show that success is more elusive for the disenfranchised.

Four stories revolve around Earl Painter, a young child in the story "Queen for a Day," who writes to the host of the popular television show of the same name numerous times hoping that his mother's plight will land her a place as a contestant. In subsequent stories, Earl attempts to come to grips with his parents and their lies and imaginings. His search for fulfillment leads him to Florida, where he experiences short-lived success. He toys with the idea of marrying into a new life but instead engages in adultery with a neighbor's wife, learning from her husband that he is just one of her many dalliances.

These stories are interspersed with ones that are either fabular or close to surreal. Three deal with situations possibly slated to show a similarity between Third World exploitation and an American tendency to disenfranchise the working class. All deal with the terrible consequences of false promises of success.

One story, "Sarah Cole: A Type of Love Story," shows the impermeability of the walls separating the classes. The hero, exceptionally handsome, develops an unlikely relationship with his antithesis, an alarmingly ugly barroom pickup named Sarah. His initial curiosity about lovemaking with someone so badly put together turns into a kind of commitment but not one strong enough to be made public. The contrast in their appearances proves too great for him. He is indeed superficial and acts hatefully. Years later, the truth of his love dawns on him, but Sarah is long gone, and he is left with his shame.

Critic Trish Reeves notes in an interview that "the irony of finally becoming a literary success by writing about the failure of the American Dream was not lost on Banks." He said:

I still view myself in the larger world the way I did when I was an adolescent. . . . [as a member of] a working class family: powerless people who look from below up. I'm unable to escape that--how one views oneself in the larger structure is determined at an extremely early age. The great delusion is that if you only can get success then you will shift your view of yourself . . . you will become a different person. That's the longing, for success is really not material goods, but in fact to become a whole new person.

OTHER MAJOR WORKS

LONG FICTION: *Family Life*, 1975 (revised 1988); *Hamilton Stark*, 1978; *The Book of Jamaica*, 1980; *The Relation of My Imprisonment*, 1983; *Continental Drift*, 1985; *Affliction*, 1989; *The Sweet Hereafter*, 1991; *Rule of the Bone*, 1995; *Cloudsplitter*, 1998; *The Darling*, 2004; *The Reserve*, 2008.

POETRY: *Fifteen Poems*, 1967 (with William Matthews and Newton Smith); *30/6*, 1969; *Waiting to Freeze*, 1969; *Snow: Meditations of a Cautious Man in Winter*, 1974.

NONFICTION: *The Autobiographical Eye*, 1982 (David Halpern, editor); *The Invisible Stranger: The Patten, Maine Photographs of Arturo Patten*, 1999; *Dreaming Up America*, 2008.

EDITED TEXT: *Brushes with Greatness: An Anthology of Chance Encounters with Greatness*, 1989 (with Michael Ondaatje and David Young).

BIBLIOGRAPHY

Chapman, Jeff, and Pamela S. Dean. *Contemporary Authors* 52 (1996). A short but information-packed study under the headings "Personal," "Career," "Memberships," "Awards and Honors," "Writings," and "Sidelights" (containing author quotes and discussions, mostly of longer fiction but also touching on *Trailerpark*) followed by an invaluable list of biographical and critical sources.

Contemporary Literary Criticism 37, 1986. Provides a good overview of Banks's life up to 1985 and gives a substantial sampling of literary criticism.

Contemporary Literary Criticism 72, 1992. A strong biographical overview of Banks's life and influences, followed by critical analyses of work published between 1986 and 1991. Included is a valuable interview conducted by writer Trish Reeves that provides a good understanding of the author. Top literary critics provide illuminating commentary.

McEneaney, Kevin T. *Russell Banks: In Search of Freedom*. Santa Barbara, Calif.: Praeger/ABC-CLIO, 2010. Analyzes all of Banks's works, arguing that he is a leader in the "postmodern, neorealist tradition of American fiction." Provides a brief biography, describing how Banks's life experiences influenced his philosophy, plots, themes, and settings; discusses his works' examination of race, communication, sexual and family relations, religion, popular culture, and other topics; explicates his vision of American history and liberty. Devotes one chapter to his early stories, another to his early novellas, and a chapter each to *Trailerpark* and *Angel on the Roof*.

Meanor, Patrick, ed. *American Short Story Writers Since World War II*. Vol. 130 in *Dictionary of Literary Biography*. Detroit: Gale Research, 1993. Good background material on Banks's life and the general content of his fiction with some discussion of thematic and narrative approaches.

Niemi, Robert. *Russell Banks*. New York: Twayne, 1997. A comprehensive biography that includes critical analyses of all Banks's major literary works. It is rife with charming and telling details that convey the essence of the author, but it maintains the objectivity necessary to present a fair portrait.

Trucks, Rob. *The Pleasure of Influence: Conversations with American Male Fiction Writers*. West Lafayette, Ind.: NotaBell Books, 2002. A collection of comprehensive interviews with American male writers of fiction, including Banks, who discuss their literary influences and their own works.

Gay Annette Zieger

KEITH BANNER

Born: Anderson, Indiana; April 18, 1965

PRINCIPAL SHORT FICTION
The Smallest People Alive, 2004

OTHER LITERARY FORMS

Keith Banner (keeth BA-nur) is well known for his debut novel, *The Life I Lead* (1999).

ACHIEVEMENTS

Keith Banner's short story "The Smallest People Alive," first published in *The Kenyon Review*, was honored as an O. Henry Prize Story in 2000, and it was published subsequently in the *O. Henry Prize Stories* volume of the same year. Following *The Smallest People Alive*, Banner's stories have been anthologized in *Everything I Have Is Blue* (2005) and *Keeping the Wolves at Bay* (2010), and they have been published in *Third Coast, Other Voices, Lodestar Quarterly, Oxford Magazine*, and *Nerve*.

BIOGRAPHY

Keith Banner was born in Anderson, Indiana, and grew up nearby, spending his summers in Elizabethton, Tennessee, where his mother and father were from originally. Banner graduated from Pendleton Heights High School in Indiana in 1983 and attended Indiana University-Purdue University at Indianapolis, receiving a B.A. in English in 1991. After finishing his undergraduate degree, Banner attended Miami University in Oxford, Ohio, and finished an M.A. in creative writing in 1993. Beginning at age thirteen and continuing through college, Banner worked a variety of odd jobs. His work life began at a local drive-in restaurant, and after that he moved on to other fast-food restaurants, telemarketing firms, libraries, and group homes. He worked as a janitor and

a convenience-store cashier. After finishing his degrees, however, in 1993 Banner began doing social work, helping people with developmental disabilities have their voices heard through home visits and reporting on their living conditions. He also has assisted the developmentally disabled in forming "self-advocacy" groups and meetings to represent themselves on important issues and concerns. This is Banner's main vocation, what he considers "his real job." This calling has led him to create two nonprofit arts organizations in Cleveland, Ohio, where he has continued to live and work. In 2003, Banner founded Visionaries and Voices, whose mission is to provide artistic and cultural opportunities for artists with disabilities. In 2009, he founded Thunder-Sky, Inc., in honor of artist Raymond Thunder-Sky, which archives his works and supports other unconventional artists in the community. Banner divides his time among social work, serving as president of the board of Thunder-Sky, Inc., and teaching creative writing at Miami University.

ANALYSIS

Keith Banner's short fiction features characters living in the same Midwest where Banner was born and raised. Although the "Smallest People Alive," in the collection's title story, refers to premature infants at a hospital, it is applicable to Banner's characters and subject matter in general, the "smallest people" being those who do not make much of a blip on the radar of modern culture or cultural consciousness. The "smallest people" in Banner's stories are unlovely people often overlooked in fiction as in life: They are the rural, uneducated, poor, obese, homosexual, bisexual, developmentally and physically disabled. In short, they are the "invisible" ones, forgotten by society, shoved into institutions, backwater towns, trailer parks, halfway houses; they are often untreated or mistreated in serious literature. Though the "smallest people" are portrayed occasionally in contemporary fiction, they are seldom brought to light with the honesty and tenderness with which Banner paints them. In Banner's fiction, these outsiders struggle within the constraints of their lives and try to find a way to make life work for them. Banner dramatizes his marginalized characters' struggle to find love and an outlet for their desire. A central theme in Banner's stories is how characters, denied "traditional" or "accepted" forms of expression for their love and desire, find a way to express themselves and make life bearable; in other words, his stories depict the conflict between the force of love and the pressure to conform to "normalcy." Furthermore, Banner bucks the trend in much of contemporary gay fiction to depict his characters heroically casting off the shackles of living in secret, hiding their identity from themselves, their families, and society; instead, Banner's characters often choose to make a home of their secret and live in it, coming to terms with the life they lead, reconciling and navigating their constraints and working within them rather than breaking out of them. The result is a complex, nuanced portrait of strange, uncomfortable slices of life, in which the characters themselves may not come to radical epiphanies. Readers of Banner's fiction, however, emerge with a fuller picture of American life and the hidden alcoves in which Banner's characters live their lives.

"THE WEDDING OF TOM TO TOM"

The narrator describes arriving as a new hire to a group home for the developmentally disabled, where among other residents live two middle-aged mentally retarded persons called Tom A. and Tom B. Already filled with trepidation about her new situation, the narrator finds her misgivings are intensified on the first night when she accidentally walks in on the Toms blatantly engaged in a sexual act. She ponders quitting on the spot but decides not to: She has enough problems. She is broke, her crack-addict ex-boyfriend Archie will not stop calling and professing his love for her, and her father thinks he's a psychic. In spite of these pressures on the narrator, Tom A. and Tom B. are at the center of the story. Tom B. can talk and reason, while Tom A. can manage only a few words; he basically follows the other Tom around like a lovesick puppy. They have lived in the same group homes all of their lives and

have developed a strong bond and sexual attraction for each other; they are in love. Their cohabitation is in jeopardy; because they constantly sneak off, their group-home manager is threatening to send them to separate facilities. Although at first the narrator tries to discourage Tom and Tom's sexual activities, it soon becomes clear to her that they truly love each other, and they give each other the only fulfillment each has access to in his life; she ends up basically letting them do whatever they want together, as long as they are discreet. Shortly before their separation seems imminent, the narrator and her alcoholic friend Rachel--who works at the home as well--take the two Toms off in a minivan to the narrator's home, where they are to be "married" by the narrator's father. The Toms are joined in mock matrimony and seem happy, and the narrator takes them to a hotel, where she stays in an adjoining room to keep an eye on the Toms while they celebrate their nuptials. Archie is waiting for her at the hotel, and the narrator finally agrees to see him again.

"The Wedding of Tom to Tom" represents many of Banner's themes. The narrator, down on her luck--marginalized herself--puts herself in a strange situation to try to make ends meet and to get her life back on track. There, she discovers love in a doubly unlikely situation for the "normal" world: between two mentally challenged people, between two men. Their physical relationship, described in rather explicit detail, illustrates another common theme for Banner: that sex and intimacy can take place anywhere, between anyone, not just between beautiful people, as American popular culture seems to preach. Dubious of these observations at first, the narrator soon enough allows herself to let go of her expectations and traditional notions of love and recognizes the Toms' love as real and valid. This same realization, in different forms, takes place for everyone involved in the wedding: the narrator's friend, her father, the bystanders gathered there. This newfound acceptance and understanding allow the narrator to give Archie another chance; though he is not a good bet by society's standards, it becomes clear that he really cares for her. Although the situation is not perfect, she decides that allowing love and desire a chance is better than cutting them off.

"HOLDING HANDS FOR SAFETY"

"Holding Hands for Safety" is narrated by Brian, a slightly overweight sixteen-year-old who works part time at Burger King and lives in the same run-down apartment complex in a bad neighborhood as his eighteen-year-old cousin Trent. Trent has a developmentally disabled younger half-sister named Courtney (her exact diagnosis is never revealed). Although Trent lives his life as straight, and probably perceives himself as straight, he and Brian (whom Trent calls Clyde) engage in sexual acts often. Even though Brian has a significant infatuation with Trent, their relationship is complex; Brian never allows himself to voice his feelings for Trent because of the homosexual taboo in their community and because of the incest taboo. In spite of everything stacked against their relationship, those stolen, intimate moments with Trent still make Brian feel comfortable and fulfilled. Brian has come to terms with his lot in life at a young age: He is often called "fag" at school and is aware of how others see him, but he is neither angry nor bitter, in large part because of his relationship with his cousin.

One day, Trent shows up at Brian's apartment and announces that he killed Courtney and hid her body in a nearby dumpster. This seems unbelievable at first--a teenage prank--but after Trent leaves that day, Courtney turns up missing, and Trent disappears. The police and local media are involved, and the guilt and fear grow to such an unbearable level inside Brian that he eventually searches the dumpster where Courtney's body is supposed to be and finds her there, dead. A morning not long after that, Trent shows up in Brian's room as he awakens. Trent tells Brian the story of what happened--her death was unintentional--and afterward, Brian and Trent kiss before he sneaks out the window again. The story ends with Brian watching a crowd gather around a makeshift memorial erected in Courtney's honor; he has to decide whether to turn in Trent or not, and as the story closes, it is not clear what Brian will do.

In "Holding Hands for Safety," Banner again exposes readers to plausible, all-too-real people in unfortunate circumstances outside the norms of American culture. The main character finds love and an outlet for desire in an unlikely--even illicit--place, in a relationship that is clearly outside the bounds of the acceptable in his community. Brian, however, has come to terms with his circumstances, and at one point in the story, he even relishes keeping his homosexuality a secret. He supposes someday he will not be able to, and he will have to move away, but for the time being he enjoys the secret life. He has found safety and comfort in hiding, as do many of Banner's characters. Trent, too, is typical of Banner's characters: Though he does not live a completely, outwardly, or admittedly homosexual lifestyle, he has those desires and neither questions them nor is ashamed to act on them. He, too, is at home in his brand of secrecy. The death of Courtney, in this story, is something of a sidebar to its main themes. She is characterized as a sweet innocent (though her annoying habits lead to her death when Trent loses his patience and overreacts, a testament to the high level of patience and tolerance living with the developmentally disabled can demand), and she acts as a reminder to Brian of the cruelty of the world, a cruelty to which he risks exposure by coming out and declaring his sexuality, or even his relationship to Trent, to the community at large.

"THE SMALLEST PEOPLE ALIVE"

"The Smallest People Alive" is narrated by Mike, a twenty-two-year-old homosexual, self-described as on the verge of obesity. He lives with Adam, a homosexual hairdresser, upon whom Mike has an unrequited crush. The story opens as he goes to visit a high school friend, Ben, at Ben's parents' house in rural McCordsville, Ohio, near Mike's hometown of Dayton. Two years before, Ben had tried to poison himself with carbon monoxide in his parents' car in their garage. Though he was unsuccessful and found before he died, he sustained brain damage that resulted in Ben having to use a walker to get around and having a severe speech impediment. Mike is spending a week of "vacation" with Ben to help lift his spirits and because the two had been close before the "accident." As the story progresses, it is revealed that Ben is homosexual and that Ben's inability to cope with his homosexuality had prompted his suicide attempt. In contrast, during the aftermath of Ben's attempt, Mike was presented to Ben as a "homosexual that doesn't hate himself," a model to show how Ben could live the rest of his life and "make the best of it."

Mike tells Ben's parents he plans to take Ben to a film in town about an hour away. The real plan, however, is to go to a gay bar where the two of them used to hang out. Ben drinks a bottle of peach Schnapps on the way, which reacts badly with some prescription drugs he is taking and causes him to have a seizure in the parking lot of the bar. Mike gets Ben back in the car and immediately drives him home. Back at Ben's house, Mike cleans Ben up and bandages a wound on his head. Ben takes Mike in his room and shows him several photo albums of clippings of attractive men: from catalogs, celebrity magazines, anything he can find; Ben is clearly tortured by his isolating lack of speech. As the story closes, Ben instructs Mike to lock the door and turn out the lights; they make love, and Mike describes feeling as if he is going back in time to when they were just two young, stupid boys, while looking forward to the week ahead.

As with the previous two stories, "The Smallest People Alive" illustrates a character trying to make the best of living under crushing constraint. In this case, Ben's constraints are literal and manifold: his inability to get around physically of his own volition, his capacity for expression limited by his language problems, his homosexuality being taboo in his community, his isolation living in a small town and with his parents. Even so, as becomes clear the night of his seizure, Ben still feels desire, as shown by his secret notebooks. Though Ben has a strong impulse to escape into the oblivion of alcohol, at his core are human desire and need, even though he has limited means of expressing them. Mike sees this and reaches out to Ben in the only way Mike knows how, simultaneously assuaging his own loneliness and desire. Another interesting aspect of "Smallest People" is Mike being forced into the limelight as the "perfect" gay male, a model for survival. For Mike, this mantle is uncomfortable because he feels pressured to make his life look tidier than it is. The story illustrates how neither side of the "equation"--between "model homosexual" and "self-hating homosexual"--can be entirely accurate. Real people live in the gray area between, a treacherous human territory.

OTHER MAJOR WORKS
LONG FICTION: *The Life I Lead*, 1999.

BIBLIOGRAPHY

Bergman, David. "Banner Year." *Kenyon Review* 21, no 1 (Winter, 1999): 182-184. Bergman's introduction to and critical overview of Banner's short fiction locates Banner's work as fiction that blurs and breaks down the barrier that separates gay literature from excellent fiction.

Blaustein, David. "Just Folks." *Lambda Book Report* 13, nos.1-2 (August/September, 2004): 25. Blaustein discusses prominent themes of *The Smallest People Alive* in this favorable review.

Bouldrey, Brian. "In Flannery O'Connor's Footsteps." *Lambda Book Report* 7, no. 8 (March, 1999): 6. Although focusing on the novel *The Life I Lead*, this interview contains insights into Banner's themes and purposes applicable to his short fiction.

Alan C. Haslam

AMIRI BARAKA

Born: Newark, New Jersey; October 7, 1934
Also known as: Everett LeRoi Jones

PRINCIPAL SHORT FICTION

Tales, 1967
The Fiction of LeRoi Jones/Amiri Baraka, 2000
Tales of the Out and the Gone, 2007

OTHER LITERARY FORMS

Amiri Baraka (ah-MIH-ree bah-RAH-kah) has been a cultural activist and professional writer since the early 1960's, and in that time he has produced a wide range of works, including plays, essays, stories, and poems. Best known for dramas produced in the 1960's (*Dutchman*, 1964; *The Baptism*, 1964; *The Toilet*, 1964), he has also written a novel (*The System of Dante's Hell*, 1965), collections of poetry (*Preface to a Twenty Volume Suicide Note*, 1961), *The Autobiography of LeRoi Jones/Amiri Baraka* (1984), and several books on African American music (*Blues People: Negro Music in White America*, 1963; *The Music: Reflections on Jazz and Blues*, 1987).

ACHIEVEMENTS

Amiri Baraka has won a number of awards and fellowships, particularly for his poetry and drama (such as the Playwright's Award at North Carolina's Black Drama Festival in 1997). *Dutchman* won an Obie Award for Best American Off-Broadway Play, and the following year Jones was granted a John Simon Guggenheim Memorial Foundation Fellowship. In 1984 and again in 2010, he received an American Book Award; in 1989, he won a PEN/Faulkner Award for Fiction. He has also founded or supported numerous journals (such as *Yugen* magazine, with his first wife, Hettie Cohen), theater groups (such as the Black Arts Repertory Theatre), and other cultural organizations,

especially in the African American community, and he has edited several important books on black culture (such as *Home: Social Essays*, 1966). In 1989, Baraka was given the Langston Hughes Medal for outstanding contribution to literature. He received the James Weldon Johnson medal in 2001 and the Lifetime Achievement Award from the Los Angeles Pan African Festival in 2003. His work has been translated into and published in a number of other languages and countries.

BIOGRAPHY

Amiri Baraka was born Everett LeRoi Jones in 1934 in Newark, New Jersey. He was raised there and has lived for most of his life in or near New York City, where many of his plays were first staged. He served in the U.S. Air Force from 1954 to 1957, mainly in Puerto Rico. He attended Rutgers and Howard Universities and did graduate work at the New School for Social Research and Columbia University. He has been a faculty member at a number of American universities, including the New School (1962-1964) and Yale University (1977-1978). Baraka accepted a teaching position at the State University of New York at Stony Brook in 1980 and retired from there in 2000; he is now professor emeritus. Baraka was married twice: first to Cohen and then to his current wife, Amina Baraka (born Sylvia Robinson), with whom he has five children. Both wives, artists in their own right, have been collaborators with Baraka. He founded *Yugen* magazine with Cohen in the 1960's. He and Amina Baraka founded the music group Blue Ark: The Word Shop and codirect Kimaka's Blues People, an "art space." In July, 2002, Baraka became Poet Laureate of New Jersey. After his poem about the attack on the World Trade Center on 9/11, *Somebody Blew Up America* (2003), was published, New Jersey governor Jim McGreevey wanted to remove Baraka from the post but was unable to do so legally, so the New Jersey legislature passed legislation in 2003 that allowed McGreevey to abolish the position. In response, Baraka was named Poet Laureate of Newark Public Schools. He continues to read his poetry and write in his retirement.

ANALYSIS

Amiri Baraka's literary career has had three distinct periods. In the first period (1957-1964), he was influenced by, and became a part of, the predominantly white avant-garde Beat movement in the arts. From 1965 to 1974, Baraka became a black nationalist (indicated by his rejection of the name LeRoi Jones), and many of his better-known plays, such as *The Slave* (1964) and *The Toilet* (1964), reflect his confrontational racial views from this period. Since 1974, Baraka has continued working as a political activist and writer, but his writing has increasingly encompassed a Marxist Third World view. Many of Baraka's short stories--although they have continued to be reprinted--first appeared in his earlier black nationalist period in the 1960's and reflected both the literary experiments of

Amiri Baraka (WireImage)

his Beat period and the increasingly political attitudes of his black nationalism. While many of these stories hold mainly historical interest today, the best are still compelling examples of how radical political views and experimental prose styles could be fused in the 1960's, when a number of writers, both white and African American, were trying to merge their art and their politics.

TALES

This collection of fiction was published in 1967 and contains sixteen short prose pieces written during the previous decade and published in various small literary magazines. Most of these stories are distinguished by an experimental prose style wedded to a strong political analysis. The first nine in the collection have a fairly traditional narrative line. "Uncle Tom's Cabin: Alternate Ending," for example, is a six-page story that centers on the interaction between a fifth-grader and his racist teacher, but the brief story also includes multiple points of view and a surprise ending. The last seven stories in the collection, however, reject traditional storytelling for a poetic prose style closer to the rhythms of jazz. "Words" is prose poetry written in "the alien language of another tribe" and dated "Harlem 1965." "Answers in Progress"--reprinted along with "Words" in Baraka's 1979 *Selected Plays and Prose*--features spaceships and the musical group Art Blakey and the Jazz Messengers. So, while the prose content can often be combative and challenging, Baraka's style became increasingly fragmentary in structure, poetic in style, and cryptic in meaning, particularly in the last stories collected in *Tales*. Put another way, readers can see Baraka in this collection moving away from traditional fiction and toward poetry and essays.

"A CHASE (ALIGHIERI'S DREAM)"

The story that opens *Tales* is only a few pages in length, but into it Baraka has packed a great deal of meaning. The title is the first clue, leading readers back through his novel (*The System of Dante's Hell*, 1965) to the Italian Dante Alighieri, whose *La divina commedia* (c. 1320; *The Divine Comedy*, 1802) contains one of the most powerful descriptions of hell in all of literature. Baraka's hell is the modern ghetto and in particular Newark, New Jersey, where he grew up. As critic Lloyd Brown describes "A Chase," "The story as a whole is a nightmarish series of images through which the writer presents an overview of life in the black ghetto." The story's narration is a surreal and staccato stream of consciousness through which the young protagonist links together a number of disparate images:

> Faces broke. Charts of age. Worn thru, to see black years. Bones in iron faces. Steel bones. Cages of decay. Cobblestones are wet near the army stores. Beer smells, Saturday. To now, they have passed so few lovely things.

Like the protagonist in "The Screamers," the narrator here is in a nightmarish flight through the streets of the inner city. Hell, Baraka shows, is here and now, and there seems to be no escape from it.

"THE SCREAMERS"

Reprinted at least half a dozen times since its appearance in *Tales*, generally in collections of African American fiction, "The Screamers" is Baraka's best-known short story. The narrative covers one night in a black jazz nightclub in Newark (probably in the early 1950's) from the perspective of a young man listening to "Harlem Nocturne" and other popular dance tunes. What makes this night unique is the performance of saxophonist Lynn Hope, who in an inspired moment leads the musicians through the crowd and out into the streets. "It would be the form of the sweetest revolution, to hucklebuck into the fallen capital, and let the oppressors lindy hop out." The police arrive and attack the crowd, a riot ensues, and the marchers "all broke our different ways, to save whatever it was each of us thought we loved." The story has a number of elements common to Baraka's fiction: the positive depiction of African American cultural forms (including a kind of "bop" jazz language), the conflict between this culture and white oppressors, and the metaphor of African American art--here music, but it could stand as easily for writing--as an inspirational cultural form, which, while it cannot finally overcome white oppression, at least achieves a moment of heightened consciousness for the people (here called "Biggers," in reference to the central character, Bigger Thomas, of Richard Wright's 1940 novel *Native Son*, listening to the music and being moved by it.

"THE DEATH OF HORATIO ALGER"

The titles of Baraka's stories--such as "Uncle Tom's Cabin: Alternate Ending" or "A Chase (Alighieri's Dream)"--often carry the larger meaning of the work, even when the story makes no further reference to it. In the case of "The Death of Horatio Alger," the tale seems a fairly simple description of a childhood fight. The narrator of the tale, Mickey, is playing dozens--an African American word game of insults aimed at participants' parents--with his best friend, J. D., and in front of three white friends. J. D. misunderstands one of the insults and attacks Mickey, and then they both attack the three white boys (who do not understand the African American word game to begin with). The story is thus about communication and its failure, about the Alger myths of equality and freedom, and about the alienation Baraka's protagonists often experience. As Brown accurately writes of the story, "In stripping himself of insensitive white friends and Horatio Alger images of American society, Mickey is putting an end to his alienation from his black identity."

"THE ALTERNATIVE"

Plot line in "The Alternative" has been replaced by multiple images substituting for short-story narrative. The setting is an African American university, and the story reverberates with references from that environment (such as Thomas Hobbes, Albert Camus, Federico García Lorca, and Nat King Cole), and the piece is thus the most allusive in the *Tales* collection. It is clear that this setting is also part of the cause of the alienation of the central character, Ray McGhee, in this surreal depiction of college dormitory life. Like many of Baraka's plays (such as *Dutchman*), "The Alternative" describes the tension between an individual outsider and the group. In Brown's interpretation of the story, he says,

> The erudition that is the key to middle-class success and future leadership also sets him apart from other blacks, even from those who, like himself, have chosen the middle-class "alternative."

The lack of a linear plotline and its replacement by lines of dialogue and images may explain why in later decades Baraka has dropped attempts at prose fiction to write nonfiction prose, poetry, and drama.

TALES OF THE OUT AND THE GONE

This collection of short fiction was published in 2007 but written over an almost thirty-year span, from 1974 to 2003. Most of these tales have not been published before. The collection is presented chronologically, which allows the reader to see how Baraka's short fiction has developed over time. The twenty-five pieces in the book are divided into two sections. The first, "War Stories," comprises six stories written between 1974 and 1985. Two of these were previously published: "Norman's Date" in the July, 1983, issue of *Playboy*, and "Blank" in *Callaloo* in 1985.

In his introduction, Baraka riffs about having chosen to call his stories "tales." He likes the "old" sound of the word, and it reminds him of his mother's labeling of his own "frequent absences from the literal." He reminds his readers of the many possible meanings of "out" and of his literary influences, from Alexander Pushkin and Edgar Allan Poe to Franz Kafka and Ray Bradbury, plus the musical rhythms of Thelonious Monk and John Coltrane. If his attitude toward the war he has waged is not clear enough, he signs the introduction "The Last Poet Laureate of New Jersey."

"War Stories" was written during Baraka's second period of creativity, when he was shifting from black nationalism to a Third World Marxist perspective. These tales are comparatively long and traditional in structure, though there is some experimentation--for example, "Blank" presents the reader with three alternative endings--but the Marxist analysis is foregrounded. "Neo-American" demonstrates Baraka's break with black nationalism as it pictures political infighting among African Americans and presents an ugly portrait of Mayor Ken Goodson, who strongly resembles Newark's first African American mayor, Kenneth Gibson. The war Baraka depicts in this series of stories is clearly a class war.

The second section, also titled "Tales of the Out and the Gone," is introduced by a short reflection, "Northern Iowa: Short Story and Poetry," in which Baraka examines the relationship between the short story ("short enough & pointed enough to make your teeth curl") and poetry ("a turn . . . evolution, in a sense). These musings prepare the reader for the changes in style found in the eighteen tales that follow. These are short,

fragmented, musical, and poetic in style--more poetry than prose--with regular references to popular culture and popular genres, including comics and science fiction. They clearly connect to postmodern writers such as Thomas Pynchon, but also they echo Baraka's roots in Beat poetry. One of the more developed stories, "Conrad Loomis and the Clothes Ray," combines science fiction with fairy tale. Loomis, a friend of the narrator, is a chemist and would-be entrepreneur whose latest invention, the clothes ray, allows him to "wear" clothes of his own design. However, when the narrator touches Loomis, he realizes that, like the emperor in the fairy tale, his friend has no clothes. This does not curb Loomis's enthusiasm about the ray and its potential to make him rich. He will beat the system because, rather than being intelligent, he is "outtelligent."

Baraka, who has guarded his own outsider status, makes "out" a mantra in these stories. In "Dig This! Out?"--a tale that contains a poem--the speaker says, "Out/ is/ my/ castle./ Gone/ is my/ name/ who leaves/ burnt lies/ beyond the moon."

OTHER MAJOR WORKS

LONG FICTION: *The System of Dante's Hell*, 1965.

PLAYS: *Dutchman*, pr., pb. 1964; *The Slave*, pr., pb. 1964; *The Toilet*, pr., pb. 1964; *The Baptism*, pr. 1964, pb. 1966; *Experimental Death Unit No. 1*, pr. 1965, pb. 1969; *Jello*, pr. 1965, pb. 1970; *A Black Mass*, pr. 1966, pb. 1969; *Arm Yourself, or Harm Yourself*, pr., pb. 1967; *Slave Ship: A Historical Pageant*, pr., pb. 1967; *Great Goodness of Life (A Coon Show)*, pr. 1967, pb. 1969; *Madheart*, pr. 1967, pb. 1969; *The Death of Malcolm X*, pb. 1969; *Bloodrites*, pr. 1970, pb. 1971; *Junkies Are Full of (SHHH...)*, pr. 1970, pb. 1971; *A Recent Killing*, pr. 1973, pb. 1978; *S-1*, pr. 1976, pb. 1978; *The Motion of History*, pr. 1977, pb. 1978; *The Sidney Poet Heroical*, pb. 1979 (originally as *Sidnee Poet Heroical*, pr. 1975); *What Was the Relationship of the Lone Ranger to the Means of Production?*, pr., pb. 1979; *At the Dim'cracker Convention*, pr. 1980; *Weimar*, pr. 1981; *Money: A Jazz Opera*, pr. 1982; *Primitive World: An Anti-Nuclear Jazz Musical*, pr. 1984, pb. 1997; *The Life and Life of Bumpy Johnson*, pr. 1991; *General Hag's Skeezag*, pb. 1992; *Meeting Lillie*, pr. 1993; *The Election Machine Warehouse*, pr. 1996, pb. 1997.

POETRY: *Spring and Soforth*, 1960; *Preface to a Twenty Volume Suicide Note*, 1961; *The Dead Lecturer*, 1964; *Black Art*, 1966; *A Poem for Black Hearts*, 1967; *Black Magic: Sabotage, Target Study, Black Art--Collected Poetry, 1961-1967*, 1969; *In Our Terribleness: Some Elements and Meaning in Black Style*, 1970 (with Fundi [Billy Abernathy]); *It's Nation Time*, 1970; *Spirit Reach*, 1972; *Afrikan Revolution*, 1973; *Hard Facts*, 1975; *AM/TRAK*, 1979; *Selected Poetry of Amiri Baraka/LeRoi Jones*, 1979; *Reggae or Not!*, 1981; *Transbluesency: The Selected Poems of Amiri Baraka*, 1995; *Wise, Why's, Y's*, 1995; *Funk Lore: New Poems, 1984-1995*, 1996; *Somebody Blew Up America, and Other Poems*, 2003; *Un Poco Low Coup*, 2004; *Mixed Blood: Number One*, 2005.

NONFICTION: *"Cuba Libre,"* 1961; *The New Nationalism*, 1962; *Blues People: Negro Music in White America*, 1963; *Home: Social Essays*, 1966; *Black Music*, 1968; *A Black Value System*, 1970; *Kawaida Studies: The New Nationalism*, 1971; *Raise Race Rays Raze: Essays Since 1965*, 1971; *Strategy and Tactics of a Pan-African Nationalist Party*, 1971; *Crisis in Boston!*, 1974; *The Creation of the New Ark*, 1975; *Daggers and Javelins: Essays*, 1984; *The Autobiography of LeRoi Jones/Amiri Baraka*, 1984; *The Artist and Social Responsibility*, 1986; *The Music: Reflections on Jazz and Blues*, 1987 (with Amina Baraka); *Conversations with Amiri Baraka*, 1994 (Charlie Reilly, editor); *Jesse Jackson and Black People*, 1994; *Eulogies*, 1996; *Digging: Afro American Be/At American Classical Music*, 1999; *Bushwacked! A Counterfeit President for a Fake Democracy: A Collection of Essays on the 2000 National Elections*, 2001; *National Elections*, 2001; *Jubilee: The Emergence of African-American Culture*, 2003 (with others); *The Essence of Reparations*, 2003; *Digging: The Afro-American Soul of American Classical Music*, 2009; *Home: Social Essays*, 2009.

EDITED TEXTS: *The Moderns: New Fiction in America*, 1963; *Black Fire: An Anthology of Afro-American Writing*, 1968 (with Larry Neal); *African Congress: A Documentary of the First Modern Pan-African Congress*, 1972; *Confirmation: An Anthology of African-American Women*, 1983 (with Amina Baraka).

MISCELLANEOUS: *Selected Plays and Prose*, 1979; *The LeRoi Jones/Amiri Baraka Reader*, 1991; *Insomniacathon: Voices Without Restraint*, 1999 (audiocassette).

BIBLIOGRAPHY

Brown, Lloyd W. *Amiri Baraka*. Boston: Twayne, 1980. Chapter 4 focuses on the short stories and includes the sections "The Writer as Divided Self" and "Toward Black Nationalism." Brown's is clearly the best analysis of individual Baraka short stories, and, like Werner Sollors, Brown identifies both the formal and thematic elements that tie these different stories together.

Fox, Robert Eliot. *Conscientious Sorcerers: The Black Post-Modernist Fiction of LeRoi Jones/Baraka, Ishmael Reed, and Samuel R. Delaney*. New York: Greenwood Press, 1987. Chapter 2 is a discussion of Baraka's novel and the stories collected in *Tales*, in a comparative study of "three of the most important and gifted American authors to have emerged in the tumultuous period of the 1960's."

Gwynne, James B., ed. *Amiri Baraka: The Kaleidoscopic Torch*. Harlem, N.Y.: Steppingstones Press, 1985. This collection of poems and essays for and about Baraka includes Richard Oyama's analysis of "The Screamers," titled "A Secret Communal Expression," as well as essays by Clyde Taylor and E. San Juan, Jr.

Lacey, Henry C. *To Raise, Destroy, and Create: The Poetry, Drama, and Fiction of Imamu Amiri Baraka (LeRoi Jones)*. Troy, N.Y.: Whitston, 1981. In the last chapter, "Recapitulation," Lacey traces the autobiographical origins of many of Baraka's short stories. While he recognizes Baraka's faults-- "extreme privacy of reference, frequent experimental failure, and racist dogma, to name only a few"--he also identifies Baraka's main merits: "daring and frequently successful verbal approximations of jazz music, vibrant recreation of black speech, and a consummate portrayal of the black middle-class psyche."

Sollors, Werner. *Amiri Baraka/LeRoi Jones: The Quest for a "Populist Modernism."* New York: Columbia University Press, 1978. In chapter 7 of this early study, Sollors examines the themes and forms of Baraka's lone novel and his short stories. The stories in *Tales* "may be considered the logbook of a fiction writer who under the social pressures of the 1960's, catapulted himself out of writing fictions while writing a swan-song to telling tales."

Watts, Jerry Gaffio. *Amiri Baraka: The Politics and Art of a Black Intellectual.* New York: New York University Press, 2001.Watts looks behind the public

image of Baraka, who is widely acknowledged to be one of the most controversial figures of the last fifty years. Watts refers to his book as a commentary rather a biography or intellectual history; he focuses on both Baraka's writing and personal life, including his effort to sustain his image as a outsider.

David Peck
Updated by Elsie Galbreath Haley

ANDREA BARRETT

Born: Cape Cod, Massachusetts; July 17, 1955

PRINCIPAL SHORT FICTION

Ship Fever, and Other Stories, 1996
Servants of the Map: Stories, 2002

OTHER LITERARY FORMS

Andrea Barrett (BEHR-eht) published four moderately successful novels before *Ship Fever, and Other Stories* catapulted her to fame. Since then, her ambitious historical novel *The Voyage of the Narwhal* was published to excellent reviews in 1998, although it did not receive the critical attention her collection of stories did. Her novel *The Air We Breathe* was published in 2007.

ACHIEVEMENTS

In 1992, Andrea Barrett won a National Endowment for the Humanities Fellowship, using the time that award provided to write the pieces in *Ship Fever, and Other Stories*, which won the 1996 National Book Award. She has received a John Simon Guggenheim Memorial Foundation Fellowship and an honorary degree from Union College. In 2001, she won a MacArthur Fellowship. *Servants of the Map* was a finalist for the 2003 Pulitzer Prize for fiction.

BIOGRAPHY

Andrea Barrett grew up on Cape Cod; her father was a ski racer and later a ski patrolman. Uncertain about a career, she was in and out of graduate school in the late 1970's and early 1980's, doing advanced study first in zoology and then in medieval and Reformation history. She held a number of low-paying jobs--receptionist, billing clerk, customer service representative, greenhouse technician, clerk, secretary, and research assistant--and in the late 1980's, she did freelance medical editing, book reviewing, and teaching. She said she learned a great deal of biology and medicine from several of these jobs, which she has used in her fiction.

Barrett said that she shifted from science to writing because she realized while in graduate school that what she had was a passion for the passion of science; it took her many years to realize that what she mistook for her own obsessions with science were, in fact, other people's obsessions. Although she has devoted most of her time to research and writing, she has been a faculty member at the Bread Loaf Writers' Conference and has taught regularly in the M.F.A. program at Warren Wilson College in North Carolina, where she was living in 2000 with her husband, a biologist. In 2004, she began teaching writing at Williams College in Williamstown, Massachusetts.

ANALYSIS

Although the stories in Andrea Barrett's National Book Award-winning *Ship Fever, and Other Stories* focus on characters caught up in pursuits in the natural sciences, her real emphasis is on the vulnerable human element behind the scientific impulse. Many of the stories are historical fictions in the classic sense: They involve real people from the past, often famous scientists, such as Gregor Mendel and Carl Linnaeus, and the stories present the past as it impinges upon and informs the present. All of Barrett's stories use scientific fact and historical events to throw light on basic human impulses and conflicts.

Barrett is a consummate stylist, a writer who chooses words carefully and never wastes a single one. In "The Behavior of the Hawkweeds," Mendel's paper on the hybridization of edible peas is held up by his present-day admirer as a "model of clarity. . . . It represented everything that science should be." Indeed, Barrett's stories are similarly models of clarity, representing everything that narrative art should be.

"THE BEHAVIOR OF THE HAWKWEEDS"

"The Behavior of the Hawkweeds," which was selected for *The Best American Short Stories* in 1995, is typical of Barrett's short fiction. Told by the wife of a mediocre twentieth century science professor, who greatly admires the geneticist Gregor Mendel, it includes the historical account of how Mendel allowed himself to be misdirected from his valuable studies of the hybridization of the edible pea to a dead-end study of the hawkweed by the botanist Carl Nageli, until Mendel finally gave up in despair.

"The Behavior of the Hawkweeds" also contains the more personal story of how the narrator's grandfather accidentally killed a man he thought was trying to abuse her as a child. These stories from the past parallel stories in the present, in which the narrator finds herself leading a meaningless life at middle age and in which her husband, having achieved nothing of scientific value, spends his retirement continually retelling the Mendel stories his wife told him.

"BIRDS WITH NO FEET"

"Birds with No Feet" is about the difference between the impulse that drives the true scientist and that which compels the mere collector and observer. It is the story of contrasting parallels between Alec Carriere, a young man who gathers specimens in the Amazon in the 1850's, and Alfred Wallace, an established scientist, who is also a collector of biological specimens. The basic difference

Andrea Barrett (AP Photo/Gino Domenico)

between the two men is that Wallace is interested in the method whereby species mutate into new species, and Carriere has no concept of "method" and no time to theorize.

Obsessed by the urgency to capture and name everything he sees, "caught like a fly in the richness around him, drowning in detail," Carriere wonders why all he has observed has not crystallized into some "shimmering structure." Even his capture of the great Bird of Paradise, which lacks wings or feet, is superseded by Wallace's return to London with the same bird. The story ends with Carriere's fear he has never been a true scientist.

"THE LITTORAL ZONE"

One of the most compact stories in the collection, "The Littoral Zone" centers on Jonathan and Ruby, teachers of zoology and botany, who met fifteen years earlier while doing summer research on an island off New Hampshire. The story is about the inexplicable puzzle of what draws two people together and what holds them together. At the time of the story, Jonathan and Ruby are near fifty and their children cannot imagine them young and strong and wrung by passion.

The title of the story refers to the space between high and low watermarks, where organisms struggle to adapt to the daily rhythm of immersion and exposure. When the two meet and realize their mutual attraction, Barrett describes it in terms of the littoral zone metaphor: "They swam in that odd, indefinite zone where they were more than friends, not yet lovers, still able to deny to themselves that they were headed where they were headed." The littoral zone, Barrett seems to suggest, is that time in a relationship between the high point of passion and the low point of everyday life. Neither of the two could now, if pressed, explain what drew them together.

"Ship Fever"

The longest story in the collection, long enough to be designated a novella, is "Ship Fever," another name for typhus in the nineteenth century, when it was particularly prevalent among poor immigrants and refugees who left Europe for North America. The story takes place in the 1840's when thousands fled the great famine in Ireland. The central focus is on a fictional doctor, the young Lauchlin Grant of Quebec, who volunteers for the public health service on Grosse Isle, a quarantine station for Irish immigrants.

The plot of the story is driven by the doctor's initial motivation to volunteer for this seemingly hopeless effort because of his love for the young Susannah Rowley, whose husband is a journalist in Ireland sending back stories and letters about the famine. Stung by her accusation that he is doing nothing to help the suffering Irish immigrants, the doctor goes to Grosse Isle and is so affected by the horrors he sees there that he becomes obsessed with caring for the sick and dying and trying to prevent the spread of the disease.

Barrett's fondness for parallel actions is manifested in this story when the doctor rescues Nora Kynd, who looks much like Susannah, a young woman who has been given up for dead. Separated from her two brothers, who are sent into the central part of Canada because they have not been infected by the disease, Nora is nursed back to health by the doctor. Because of her fine nursing skills, she stays on and helps others. When the doctor becomes ill himself, she tries unsuccessfully to bring him back to health.

The story ends when Nora leaves Grosse Isle and goes to the city to tell Susannah about the doctor's death, only to discover that she, too, is ill. Finally, Nora goes to look for her brothers, saying she will travel to the United States if she cannot find them. Thematically, the idea of starting fresh, that which brought the many immigrants to North America in the first place, is the story's final emphasis.

Servants of the Map

Barrett explores connections among science, history, and storytelling in the six new stories in *Servants of the Map*. Like the scientists and historians described in her work, Barrett says she is highly obsessive; all of her stories and novels are the result of painstaking research and scrupulous writing and rewriting. However, for all her attention to detail and focus on fact and the puzzles of science, the real mystery in her stories is that of human motivation, particularly the drive to "see" and to "know."

The title story is a carefully constructed novella about Max Vigne, a nineteenth century surveyor who is part of an exploration party to the Himalayas. In a series of letters to his wife, Clara, back in England, Vigne discovers writing's power to construct reality by going beyond mapping and recording a higher level of perception, thereby creating a map not only of the physical world but also of the human mind. The story was selected for *The Best American Short Stories: 2001* and *Prize Stories 2001: The O. Henry Awards*.

Characters in *Servants of the Map* rematerialize in different stories. Rose and Bianca, competitive siblings in "The Marburg Sisters," reappear in "The Forest" and "The Mysteries of Ubiquitin." In the former, Bianca, doomed to languish in the shadows of the bright light of her successful scientist sister, takes an elderly visiting scientist to a magical sighting of deer in a forest clearing, in the process establishing a sense of conjunction among cultures, individuals, and the past and present. The latter is a traditional story of how Rose idolized a young zoologist when she was eight years old. Later, when she is thirty-one and he is fifty-one, she has a brief affair with him, and she discovers to be an aging man whose scientific approach is old fashioned and who is unable to understand her own complex study of the mysteries of ubiquitin, a protein that binds to other molecules and marks them for degradation.

Barrett also returns to one of the central characters in the title novella of her earlier collection, Irish immigrant Nora Kynd, who at the end of "Ship Fever" leaves the horrors of the typhus epidemic in Quebec at the age of twenty-three and goes to the United States. In "The Cure," Nora, twenty years later, finds one of her long-lost brothers, Ned, who runs an inn. Barrett reveals that Ned had sailed on the *Narwhal* in her novel of ideas, *The Voyage of the Narwhal*, where he had been befriended by the novel's hero, the naturalist Erasmus Wells.

Although these character reappearances create pleasurable little shocks of recognition for the reader, they are more than narrative gimmicks; they are indications of Barrett's conviction that science, history, and storytelling construct narratives--whether they are called scientific theories, historical accounts, or fiction--to reveal connections, relationships, and the interdependence of all things.

OTHER MAJOR WORKS

LONG FICTION: *Lucid Stars*, 1988; *Secret Harmonies*, 1989; *The Middle Kingdom*, 1991; *The Forms of Water*, 1993; *The Voyage of the Narwhal*, 1998; *The Air We Breathe*, 2007.

EDITED TEXT: *The Story Behind the Story: Twenty-Six Writers and How They Work*, 2004 (with Peter Turchi).

BIBLIOGRAPHY

Barrett, Andrea. "An Interview with Andrea Barrett." Interview by Marian Ryan. *The Writer's Chronicle* 32 (December, 1999): 4-9. An extensive interview in which Barrett talks candidly about a wide variety of concerns important to her. She talks about how stories are a way of knowledge, about how the lens of historical fiction allows her to express her deepest feelings, and about the technical experimentation that gave rise to many of the stories in *Ship Fever, and Other Stories*.

Basbanes, Nicholas A. "Author's 'Private Passion' Goes Public." *The Memphis Commercial Appeal*, March 16, 1997, p. G4. An article about Barrett's publicity tour after winning the National Book Award. Barrett describes the origin of *Ship Fever, and Other Stories* and how she taught herself to write short fiction for the book.

Gaffney, Elizabeth. "Andrea Barrett, the Art of Fiction No. 180." *The Paris Review* 168 (Winter, 2003). Compelling interview with Barrett about the writers who profoundly affected her as she was growing up.

Greene, Janice. "Science as a Metaphor for Longing." *The San Francisco Chronicle*, January 28, 1996, p. 5. This review of *Ship Fever, and Other Stories* claims Barrett's stories of the past have more vitality than those of the present. Singles out the title story as one that is rich with contrasts; says it sums up the focus of all her stories--that the pursuit of fulfillment, like the pursuit of science, is a quest for truth.

Lanham, Fritz. "Keeping Success in Perspective." *The Houston Chronicle*, November 1, 1998, p. Z26. An interview-based story about Barrett on the publication of *The Voyage of the Narwhal*. Provides biographical information about Barrett's education and research methods. She describes her decision to shift from history to fiction and her first disappointing efforts to write a novel.

Lippman, Laura. "The Very Humble Andrea Barrett." *St. Louis Post Dispatch*, March 9, 1997, p. 1D. An interview story that includes biographical information and quotes Barrett on the writing life: "If people knew how happy it can make you, we would all be writing all the time. It's the greatest secret of the world."

Mallon, Thomas. "Under the Microscope." *The New York Times*, January 28, 1996, p. 24. This review of *Ship Fever, and Other Stories* suggests that Barrett's scientific bent is rare among fiction writers; praises her ability to weave together science and fiction; argues that the charge that Barrett works too hard to make her connections is out of place.

Martelle, Scott. "Lost in the Pursuit of Love and Science." *The Buffalo News*, February 4, 1996, p. 5E. Says that Barrett has found a nexus in the schism in American culture between art and science. Says the title story of *Ship Fever, and Other Stories* is the weakest work in the collection, for the real history never gets integrated into the fiction the way it does in her other stories.

Streitfeld, David. "A Literary Write of Passage." *The Washington Post*, November 23, 1996. P. G1. An interview-based story on the occasion of Barrett's winning the National Book Award. Streitfeld describes Barrett's reaction to receiving the award and speculates on its influence on her writing career.

Van den Berg, Laura. "About Andrea Barrett." *Ploughshares* 33 (Fall, 2007): 207-12. An interview-profile that summarizes the major events in Barrett's life and comments briefly on her fiction.

Written and updated by Charles E. May

JOHN BARTH

Born: Cambridge, Maryland; May 27, 1930

PRINCIPAL SHORT FICTION

Lost in the Funhouse, 1968

On with the Story, 1996

The Book of Ten Nights and a Night: Eleven Stories, 2004

Where Three Roads Meet, 2005

OTHER LITERARY FORMS

The majority of John Barth's fiction is in the novel form. He has also written critical articles and essays on the nature of fiction and the state of the art. Some of his material has been recorded, since several of his stories require an auditory medium to achieve their original purposes and effects.

ACHIEVEMENTS

Honors accorded to John Barth and to his work include a Brandeis University Creative Arts Award in 1965, a Rockefeller Foundation grant for 1965-1966, a National Institute of Arts and Letters grant in 1966, the National Book Award for *Chimera* (1972) in 1973, and the F. Scott Fitzgerald Award for outstanding achievement in American literature in 1997. In 1974, he was elected to both the National Institute of Arts and Letters and the American Academy of Arts and Sciences.

BIOGRAPHY

John Simmons Barth's first artistic interest was in music, and he studied briefly at the Juilliard School of Music before entering The Johns Hopkins University in Baltimore, Maryland, in the fall of 1947. He married Harriette Anne Strickland in January, 1950. In 1951, he received his B.A. in creative writing, and his first child, Christine, was born. Barth completed his M.A. in 1952 and began work on his Ph.D. in the aesthetics of literature. His second child, John, was born in 1952, and with his wife expecting a third child (Daniel, born in 1954), Barth abandoned work on his Ph.D. and took a teaching job at Pennsylvania State University in 1953. In 1965, he left Pennsylvania State to teach at the State University of New York at Buffalo. Divorced from his first wife in 1969, Barth married Shelly Rosenberg on December 27, 1970. Barth was Alumni Centennial Professor of English and Creative Writing at The Johns Hopkins University from 1973 to 1990, when he became professor emeritus.

ANALYSIS

As a leading developer and writer of metafiction, John Barth wrote a body of work that, through the use of the fantastic and the absurd as well as the realistic and the romantic, portrays the human experience in the second half of the twentieth century. He is considered a leading writer in the field of postmodernist fiction.

Barth, who always hoped to bring alive philosophical alternatives in his stories, reviving old themes of literature and life--literature's because they *are* life's--is able to make a progression through these short fictions, retackling the problems, not by repetition but by constantly distilling the possibilities of technique. He has clearly opened the narrative consciousness, the academic ear, and the imagination of readers and writers alike. While he never presumes to answer one of his posed questions, his inventiveness and sincerity make his stories experiences of real substance and of words. Throughout the collection, words and stories help to ease human pain and serve as a source of curious investigation and delight.

LOST IN THE FUNHOUSE

Although John Barth is best known for his novels, his stories "Night-Sea Journey," "Lost in the Funhouse," "Title," and "Life-Story" from his collection of short fiction *Lost in the Funhouse* are frequently anthologized. The book is a sequence of related stories that operate in a cycle, beginning with the anonymity of origins and concluding, like the serpent with its tail in its mouth, with the anonymity of a life's conclusion and the narrator's exhaustion of his art. Some of Barth's characters are nameless, having both a personal and a universal dimension. Others, such as those in "Echo" and "Menelaiad," take their names from mythology. Three stories, "Ambrose His Mark," "Water Message," and "Lost in the Funhouse," reveal three turning points in the life of a developing character, Ambrose: his naming as an infant; his first consciousness of *fact*, in both conflict and alliance with a romanticized truth; and a larger apprehension of life suffused with his first sexual consciousness. Barth's characters, or voices, are all natural storytellers compelled to make sense of what they experience; they become living metaphors for states of love, art, and civilization. As they quest, the author joins them, so that Barth's technique often conforms with his subject matter. Only the first two Ambrose stories could be considered conventional in structure; the remaining stories are fictions that investigate each individual's experience through voice shift, idea, and the self-evident play of language.

In these stories Barth questions the meaning of love, love in relation to art, and the artist's and lover's place within civilization--not merely time-bounded culture, but art's progress through history, its aspirations, and its failures. Barth's characters face the revelation that the individual facts of their lives are painful, that self-knowledge hurts and is in conflict with their original visions of the world. The characters turn to storytelling, not only to comprehend the complexities of their personal lives, but also to preserve their sanity as they encounter knowledge. The creation of artifice literally kills time, and by virtue of narrative organization, even

John Barth (Oscar White/CORBIS)

when suffering cannot be explained, life may become bearable. In "Life-Story," which spans only part of a day, the narrator speaks of himself:

> Even as she left he reached for the sleeping pills cached conveniently in his writing desk and was restrained from their administration only by his being in the process of completing a sentence. . . . There was always another sentence to worry about.

In "Autobiography," a story written for monophonic tape, the speaker says, "Being me's no joke," and later, "I'm not what either parent or I had in mind."

The tradition underlying Barth's stories is the language itself, the very process of storytelling, not merely the genre of story. In this sense his work has much in common with experimental films and some contemporary poetry, as his characters transform their personal worlds of fact into worlds of fiction. For Barth, that is one solution of the fact of existence. The question remains: Does one then become nothing more than one's story? If the body does not live, does it matter that the words might, even if they can solve nothing? The very playfulness and intrigue of Barth's language, along with its intellectual complexity, suggests that romantic disillusion may be at least temporarily combated through the vehicle of self-examining narrative. The underlying fear is that the story might exhaust itself, that fiction might become worn out and the words have nowhere to go but back into the narrator's mind.

"Night-Sea Journey," which opens the collection, is the story of the life of a single sperm cell as it travels toward the possibility of linkage and conception upon the shores of a mythic Her. The narrator is the sperm and is quoted throughout by the authorial voice, yet the narrator addresses himself and finally the being he may become, not an audience, so the story reads as a first-person interior monologue. Being "spoken inwardly," "Night-Sea Journey" is similar to later stories in the collection, which are first-person accounts by the author. This similarity effects a parallel between the struggles of the sperm cell and later struggles by the author, which, in turn, parallel the struggles everyone faces in the journey through life.

At first, the narrator shares the determination of the other "swimmers" to "reach the shore" and "transmit the Heritage." His enthusiasm, however, wanes as he considers the philosophy of a friend, who has since "drowned." The friend claimed that since their ultimate destiny is to perish, the noble thing to do is to commit suicide. He considered the hero of heroes to be he who reached the shore and refused "Her." Pondering this and such questions as whether the journey is real or illusory, who or what causes the difficult passage, and whether arrival will mean anything at all, the narrator considers various possible explanations of the meaning, if any, of the journey. Barth parodies philosophical and religious positions familiar to the sophisticated reader. He also parodies common adolescent ramblings about the meaning of life: "Love is how we call our ignorance of what whips us." The whipping results from the sperm's tail, causing movement toward an unknown destiny. Barth makes deliberate use of clichés and puns to ease the reader into identification with the narrator's voice, which speaks phrases the reader undoubtedly has spoken in baffling or despairing moments. The humor is as adolescent as the state of the speaker's anxieties: "I have seen the best swimmers of my generation go under."

Constantly suspicious that the journey is meaningless, the speaker is finally swayed to accept his pessimistic friend's advice: He gives up and ceases to swim. However, his decision has come too late. By continuing to live he has been drawn ever nearer to the "shore" and is pulled by the force of the female element. He reaches "a motionless or hugely gliding sphere" and is about to become a link in another cycle of life and death. Before joining with Her, however, he expresses his "single hope" that he might transmit to the being he is becoming "a private legacy of awful recollection and negative resolve." The speaker declares: "You to whom, through whom I speak, do what I cannot: terminate this aimless, brutal business! Stop your hearing against her song! Hate Love!" In spite of the speaker's desire to end all night-sea journeys, all life-- "Make no more"--he cannot resist biological fate and plunges "into Her who summons, singing . . . 'Love! Love! Love!'" This conclusion and Barth's parody throughout the story of attempts to understand life suggest that the meaning of life may be nothing more than life itself. To borrow a statement from *Chimera*, "the key to the treasure is the treasure."

"Lost in the Funhouse" appears midway in the collection. It opens with young Ambrose, perhaps the being formed through the union of the sperm with Her in "Night-Sea Journey," traveling to Ocean City, Maryland, to celebrate Independence Day. Accompanying him through this eventual initiation are his parents, an uncle, his older brother Peter, and Magda, a thirteen-year-old neighbor who is well developed for her age. Ambrose is "at that awkward age" when his voice and everything else is unpredictable. Magda is the object of his first sexual consciousness, and he experiences the need to do something about it, if only barely to touch her. The story moves from painful innocence and aspects of puppy love to the stunned realization of the pain of self-knowledge. Barth uses printed devices, italics, and dashes to draw attention to the storytelling technique throughout the presentation of conventional material: a sensitive boy's first encounters with the world, the mysterious "funhouse" of sexuality, illusion, and consciously realized pain.

As the story develops, Barth incorporates comments about the art of fiction into the narrative:

He even permitted the single hair, fold, on the second joint of his thumb to brush the fabric of her skirt. Should she have sat back at that instant, his hand would have been caught under her. Plush upholstery prickles uncomfortably through gabardine slacks in the July sun. The function of the *beginning* of a story is to introduce the principal characters, establish their initial relationship, set the scene for the main action . . . and initiate the first complication or whatever of the "rising action."

Such moments, when the voice seems to shift outside Ambrose's consciousness, actually serve to unite the teller with the tale, Barth with his protagonist, and life with art. Among other things, "Lost in the Funhouse" is a portrait of the artist as an adolescent. The developing artist, "Ambrose . . . seemed unable to forget the least detail of his life" and tries to fit everything together. Most of all, he needs to know himself, to experience his inner being, before he will have something to express.

Ambrose develops this knowledge when he becomes lost in the carnival funhouse, which, on one level, represents the mind. Just before emerging from the funhouse, he strays into an old, forgotten part of it and loses his way. Separated from the mainstream--the funhouse representing the world for lovers--he has fantasies of death and suicide, recalling the "negative resolve" of the sperm cell from "Night-Sea Journey." He also finds himself reliving incidents with Magda in the past and imagining alternative futures. He begins to suffer the experience of illusion and disillusion: "Nothing was what it looked like." He finds a coin with his name on it and imagines possible lives for himself as an adult.

These experiences lead to a new fantasy: Ambrose dreams of reciting stories in the dark until he dies, while a young girl behind the plyboard panel he leans against takes down his every word but does not speak, for she knows his genius can only bloom in isolation. This fantasy is the artistic parallel to the sperm's union with "Her" in "Night-Sea Journey." Barth thus suggests that the artist's creative force is a product of a rechanneled sexual drive. Although Ambrose "would rather be among the lovers for whom funhouses are designed," he will construct, maybe operate, his own

funhouse in the world of art. His identity as an artist derives from the knowledge he has gained of his isolation, the isolation of the artist, who is not "a person," but who must create a self and a world, or, rather, selves and worlds. The difference between lovers and artists, however, may not be as definitive as it seems, for Barth's fiction implies that Ambrose's predicament may be universal.

The final story in *Lost in the Funhouse* is "Anonymiad," the life story of a minstrel who becomes an artist, perhaps an Ambrose grown up, as well as an alter ego for Barth. If translated into realistic terms, the life of the minstrel would parallel Barth's literary career. The minstrel grows up singing in a rural setting with the most lovely goatherd maiden as his mistress. Dreaming of fame, he takes his song to the city, where he meets Queen Clytemnestra and becomes a court minstrel. As he becomes more musically adept, he spends more time in court intrigues than with his maiden, Merope. When King Agamemnon goes off to war, an interloper, Aegisthus, steals the Queen's love, woos Merope, and casts the minstrel on a deserted island with nine casks of wine. To each of these the minstrel gives the name and properties of one of the nine muses. For the remainder of his life the minstrel, without his lyre, composes something new, literature, which he casts adrift in the empty wine bottles. These bottles parallel the sperm cell of "Night-Sea Journey," transmitting the Heritage.

Isolated on his island, like Ambrose in the funhouse, the minstrel is unhappy. His life has not worked out, his work has been mediocre and unacclaimed, love has failed, and later he says that his "long prose fictions of the realistical, the romantical and fantastical" are not what he meant them to be. He writes these fictions on the island to structure his life; he tans the hides of native goats and sends his manuscripts out to sea in the large urns after drinking up all the wine. Urn by urn, he writes his way through the panorama of fiction's possibilities. Then he loses interest and decides that all he has written is useless. There is one amphora left, and one goat, hard to catch, whom he names Helen. Rousing himself, he decides to write one final, brilliant piece, his "Anonymiad," which he hopes will be filled with the "pain of insight, wise and smiling in the terror of our life." Everything must be deliberated to get all this on a single skin. This is vital, as an earlier work had come floating back to shore in its urn, drenched and unreadable. After painstakingly writing this final piece, the writer sees it only as a "chronicle of minstrel misery." No more living creatures exist on the island; the writer is totally alone. In spite of these facts, however, the minstrel is content. He has sent his "strange love letter" to Merope, his muse. He knows that "somewhere outside myself, my enciphered spirit drifted, realer than the gods, its significance as objective and undecoded as the stars." He imagines his tale "drifting age after age, while generations fight, sing, love, expire." Sadly, he thinks: "Now it passes a hairsbreadth from the unknown man or woman to whose heart, of all hearts in the world, it could speak fluentest, most balmly--but they're too preoccupied to reach out to it, and it can't reach out to them." Like the minstrel, his tale will drift and perish, but as the story ends, "No matter." A noontime sun "beautiful enough to break the heart" shines on the island, where "a nameless minstrel wrote it." The collection of stories ends, turning back toward its tabula rasa of origin.

On with the Story

On with the Story gathers together twelve short pieces that Barth had previously published separately in periodicals. He insisted that *Lost in the Funhouse*, many pieces of which had similarly been published separately, was "neither a collection nor a selection, but a series . . . meant to be received 'all at once' and as here arranged." Reviewers of *On with the Story* were quick to see that it also constituted a work with its own unity and integrity. Ron Loewinsohn, for example, found a clear structural arrangement: "a dozen stories arranged in three groups of four, concerning beginnings, middles, and endings." D. Quentin Miller noted the focus provided by Barth's device of "concluding the book with continuations of the eleven stories that precede the conclusion, in reverse order" and the coherence provided by "the series of interchapters depicting a vacationing husband and wife who exchange stories in bed"--a recycling of the dramatic situation of Shahriar and Scheherazade in *Alf layla wa-layla* (fifteenth century; *The Arabian Nights' Entertainments*, (1706-1708) which he links to Barth's frequent

reliance on the device of the frame tale in his novels. Several stories suggest parallels with this framing story of the couple, who appear to be at the end of or at least at a turning point in their relationship, though these connections are left open for the reader's speculation rather than filled out in detail.

A thematic principle of coherence is suggested by the book's two epigraphs, one from the physicist Werner Heisenberg and one from a standard textbook on narrative (cowritten by Barth's early critical champion Robert Scholes), and several of the stories explicitly parallel the laws of physics with those of narrative. In "Ad Infinitum: A Short Story" and "On with the Story," for example, Barth takes two of ancient philosopher Zeno of Citium's paradoxes--Achilles's inability to catch the tortoise and the arrow that can never hit its target--as the core of stories designed to demonstrate the range of narrative techniques available for the depiction of temporal and spatial relations in fiction.

Barth also forges links between *On with the Story* and his first book of short stories, *Lost in the Funhouse*. The narrator of the final story in *On with the Story*, "Countdown: Once Upon a Time," was himself, "once briefly lost in a funhouse, and a quarter-century later found a story in that loss," suggesting his identity with Ambrose, the author-figure from the earlier work. Even the title connects the two works, as the phrase "on with the story" appeared at the end of the author's note to *Lost in the Funhouse*. As Loewinsohn stipulates, however, the connection is to be thought of not as a return, the closing of a circle, but rather as the typical Barthian spiral, a near-repetition with a difference: "There it signified a beginning, meaning 'Let's get the story started.' Here it is a plea for continuity: 'Let's not allow the story to end.'"

The Book of Ten Nights and a Night

The Book of Ten Nights and a Night: Eleven Stories includes stories the earlier versions of which had appeared in various periodicals during the period 1960 through 2001. As important to the book as the stories, perhaps more important, is the framed narrative that encompasses them. At the outset, the reader is introduced to three recurring characters. Author is Barth or some persona he has invented for himself. Graybard is the narrator, who is smitten with Wysiwyg, the Muse of Story. Her name is an acronym for a term to be revealed later, Author explains, but it never is. She is a beautiful, seductive water nymph, and she and Graybard are soon lovers (metaphorically, he explains). Wysiwyg's pet name for him is Geeb. After each story is told, she critiques it and guides his further efforts. Author remains in his Scriptorium while dispatching Graybard nightly to the Imaginarium, where the stories are created. The eleven nights of the framed narrative are Tuesday, September 11, through Friday, September 21, 2001, and the terrorist attacks upon New York and Washington are a constant backdrop. Author wonders if it is appropriate at all to be writing stories under the circumstances.

The first story, "Help!" is a schematic, using that single word in every possible sense--declarative, exclamatory, interrogatory--and set to musical notes. Wysiwyg declines to accept it, so "Landscape: The Eastern Shore" becomes the true first night's story (Maryland's Eastern Shore is the setting for most of the stories) and recounts the final hours of Claude Morgan, old captain of a dredge-boat. Stories for nights two and three, "The Ring" and "Dead Cat, Floating Boy," are described by the narrator as creative nonfiction. The first deals with the complications arising from the narrator-protagonist's discovery of a man's wedding band while snorkeling off Grand Cayman Island, the other with an attractive woman who seeks his help in aiding a cat who has been run over in the street. Wysiwyg wants no more fact-based fiction, so night four features a sleeping Charles P. Mason, who hears the words "A Detective and a Turtle" as if from a soundtrack, and spends the following eighteen pages searching for a story that will accommodate them both. In "The Rest of Your Life," the calendar function on the computer of George Fischer breaks, displaying the date as August 27, 1956, leading to ruminations about that particular date and later about the passage of time itself. In "The Big Shrink," the wealthy host of a party offers his theory that the universe is neither expanding nor collapsing but shrinking. Later, in playing a dangerous word game, the college professor protagonist is trapped into saying that if there were no stigma, guilt, or shame attached, he might well be unfaithful. His wife is disappointed with this purely theoretical response, and,

sixteen months later, he senses his marriage, though not unhappy, is shrinking. "Extension," the story for the seventh night, points up the irony of an aging couple's desire to expand their rural hideaway at the same time that their lives are contracting. In "And Then There's the One," the protagonist Adam's concern when his seventeen-year-old granddaughter, Donna, blithely announces that she will never have babies leads him to thoughts about the generations of the human race and eventually to the mind-numbing conclusion that, at the least, every person is every other person's cousin. The story for the ninth night, "9999," is a numerical extravaganza, recounting Frank and Pam Parker's near obsession with isodigitals, alternating digiters, sequentials, and the European-style palindromes. "Click" is a study of where and with what results following the links of computer commands will lead. "Wysiwyg" is the story for the eleventh night. Is she another Scheherazade or, as Graybard tells her story, a girl born illegitimate to a Jewish graduate student, adopted by a kindly couple of lapsed Lutherans, and brought up as their own? At thirteen, she learns the truth, and a turbulent, rebellious life follows--or, perhaps, Graybard's entire tale is fanciful, just as Wysiwyg has been fanciful from the outset.

WHERE THREE ROADS MEET

Where Three Roads Meet: Novellas is a study in threes. The first story is "Tell Me"; the second, "I've Been Told: A Story's Story," is a response to the first; the third and final, "As I Was Saying," seems to posit that no story ever ends. "Tell Me" features three Freds as main characters: Al*fred* Baumann (budding scholar), Wil*fred* Chase (writer with raw but obvious talent), and Wini*fred* Stark (free-spirited fiancé of one and lover of both). They are collegians during the post-World War II period, and not only are they involved in a ménage à trois, but they also form a musical trio performing at a venue called the Trivium. Their world is shattered by Al's acute myeloblastic leukemia and Winnie's abortion of Will's baby. The second novella is a story told by a story. It erratically follows the activities of one Philip Norman Blank, the resemblance of whose name to the phrase "fill in the blank" has been a lifelong irritant to him. Meanwhile, in the framed story, Fred (the story himself), Isidore or "Izzy" (the narrator), and

Hitherto Unmentioned Female Third Person (the reader) vie for ascendency in telling Blank's story. He is left on the side of a highway, out of gas, and with no idea where he was going, while these three key elements of his tale argue among themselves. "As I Was Saying" is primarily an audiotape made by three sisters--Thelma, Grace, and Aggie Mason--on New Year's Eve, 1999. When the girls, now in their seventies, were undergraduates, they worked their way through college as campus prostitutes. A book written years before by a former customer and friend has recently excited new interest in the subject--especially on the part of the author's scholar-son. The tape is the sisters' response. However, in typical Barthian fashion, a narrative voice is heard, supposedly at the end, reminding that all are figments and the end is not really the end.

THE DEVELOPMENT

The Development is the Heron Bay Estates, a gated community on Maryland's Eastern Shore, and nine interconnected stories about its residents: primarily retired or late middle-aged, upper-middle-class Anglo-Saxons. Versions of the first eight appeared earlier in various literary magazines; the ninth, "Rebeginning," acts as a summing up. Barth occasionally plays with the narrative point of view, but, on the whole, these are more conventional stories than those in his previous two collections. A recurring theme is the decline into old age, sickness, and death. Ethel Bailey dies of cervical cancer in "Peeping Tom." Her distraught widower, Sam, later stabs himself with a borrowed machete (but survives). In the same story, "Toga Party," Dick and Susan Felton, seeing nothing ahead but the ravages of old age, succeed in committing suicide in their garage after the party. Pete and Debbie Simpson's much-prized daughter, Julie, is killed by a drunken driver on the Baltimore Beltway. Her death is alluded to in multiple stories. Finally, George and Carol Walsh are crushed beneath the rubble of their house when a freak tornado strikes the Heron Bay Estates in "The End" (which in typical Barth fashion turns out not to be the end). Religion is mentioned in virtually every story but always as a counterpoint to the protagonists' invariable agnosticism and thorough secularism. The author seems at pains to be saying that, as these characters face the vicissitudes of their stories, they have only their own devices to rely upon.

OTHER MAJOR WORKS

LONG FICTION: *The Floating Opera*, 1956, revised 1967; *The End of the Road*, 1958; *The Sot-Weed Factor*, 1960; *Giles Goat-Boy: Or, The Rev. New Syllabus*, 1966; *Chimera*, 1972 (three novellas); *Letters*, 1979; *Sabbatical: A Romance*, 1982; *The Tidewater Tales: A Novel*, 1987; *The Last Voyage of Somebody the Sailor*, 1991; *Once upon a Time: A Floating Opera*, 1994; *Coming Soon !*, 2001; *The Development*, 2008.

NONFICTION: *The Friday Book: Essays, and Other Nonfiction*, 1984; *Further Fridays: Essays, Lectures, and Other Nonfiction*, 1995.

BIBLIOGRAPHY

Barth, John. "Interview." *Short Story*, n.s. 1 (Spring, 1993): 110-118. Discusses Barth's love for the short story and why he does not write more of them. Talks about minimalism and self-reflexivity; examines the nature of the story in *The Arabian Nights' Entertainments* and Edgar Allan Poe; explains why he tries to stay as non-ideological as possible; surveys the changes in short fiction from the mid-1970's to the early 1990's.

Birkerts, Sven. "Lost in the Rest Home (*The Development*)." *The New York Times Book Review*, October 5, 2008, p. 13. Addresses the theme of old age and its indignities, which is pervasive throughout the book. The title of the review, of course, plays off the earlier *Lost in the Funhouse*.

Bowen, Zack. *A Reader's Guide to John Barth*. Westport, Conn.: Greenwood Press, 1994. A concise overview of Barth's first ten books of fiction (through *The Last Voyage of Somebody the Sailor*), with a short but thoughtful chapter on *Lost in the Funhouse*. Contains good bibliographies (including one of articles and book chapters on *Lost in the Funhouse*), a brief biographical sketch, and an interesting appendix: "Selected List of Recurrent Themes, Patterns, and Techniques."

_____. "Barth and Joyce." *Critique* 37 (Summer, 1996): 261-269. Discusses how Barth followed James Joyce in the grandness of his narrative scheme, his ironic focus on a region, and his personal overtones in his fiction. Explores Barth's anxiety about this influence.

Fogel, Stan, and Gordon Slethaug. *Understanding John Barth*. Columbia: University of South Carolina Press, 1990. In this text, the authors present a comprehensive interpretation of Barth's works, from *The Floating Opera* to *The Tidewater Tales*. Chapter 6 is devoted entirely to *Lost in the Funhouse*, with discussion of how Barth's short fiction fits into his oeuvre. Each chapter includes notes at its end. Fogel and Slethaug have included both a primary and a secondary bibliography. The primary bibliography is especially useful for its list of uncollected short stories, and it includes the stories' date and place of publication. An index divided by work and a general index conclude the book.

Friedell, Deborah. "If This Were a Headline (*Where Three Roads Meet: Novellas*)." *The New York Times Book Review*, December 25, 2005, p. 15. A Christmas Day review of the book, ironically timed, perhaps, because of the dark character of the stories.

Harris, Charles B. *Passionate Virtuosity: The Fiction of John Barth*. Urbana: University of Illinois Press, 1983. This work has a chapter entitled "'A Continuing, Strange Love Letter': Sex and Language in *Lost in the Funhouse*," which concentrates on Barth's stories from the aspect of the reader and writer relationship. Exhaustive notes at the end of the chapter direct the reader to further sources, as does the secondary bibliography at the end of the book. Includes an index.

Kiernan, Robert F. "John Barth's Artist in the Fun House." *Studies in Short Fiction* 10 (Fall, 1973): 373-380. Calls "Autobiography" a tour de force, capturing a fiction in the process of composing its own autobiography. Fiction tends necessarily to a life of its own and to an inordinate degree of self-reflection.

McLaughlin, Robert L. "Review of *The Book of Ten Nights and a Night*." *Review of Contemporary Fiction* 72, no. 5 (March 1, 2004): 191. One of the early reviews of the book, appearing almost immediately after its publication.

Schulz, Max F. *The Muses of John Barth: Tradition and Metafiction from "Lost in the Funhouse" to "The Tidewater Tales."* Baltimore: The Johns Hopkins University Press, 1990. Schulz concentrates on the themes of "romantic passion and commonsense love" in Barth's work, with an emphasis on "the textual domestication of classical myths." In the chapter entitled "Old Muses and New: Epic Reprises, Self-Reflexive Bedtime Stories, and Intertextual Pillow Talk," Schulz discusses what he calls the "Thalian design" of *Lost in the Funhouse*. Notes to the chapters are included at the end of the text, as is an index.

Waldmeir, Joseph J., ed. *Critical Essays on John Barth*. Boston: G. K. Hall, 1980. Although an early critical work, this text does contain four essays specifically on *Lost in the Funhouse*. Each essay includes notes, and a general index can be found at the end of the book.

Walkiewicz, E. P. *John Barth*. Boston: Twayne, 1986. This book is useful for biographical details: It includes a chronology of Barth's life and work. Contains also considerable discussion of *Lost in the Funhouse*, which makes this a good all-around reference. Supplemented by primary and secondary bibliographies, notes, and an index.

Zhang, Benzi. "Paradox of Origin(ality): John Barth's 'Menelaiad.'" *Studies in Short Fiction* 32 (Spring, 1995): 199-208. Argues that in the story "Menelaiad" Barth transforms a mythological story into a postmodern "trans-tale" about the tension between past and the present and between originality and repetition.

James L. Green; Jo-Ellen Lipman Boon
and William Nelles
Updated by Patrick Adcock Nelles

DONALD BARTHELME

Born: Philadelphia, Pennsylvania; April 7, 1931
Died: Houston, Texas; July 23, 1989

PRINCIPAL SHORT FICTION

Come Back, Dr. Caligari, 1964
Unspeakable Practices, Unnatural Acts, 1968
City Life, 1970
Sadness, 1972
Amateurs, 1976
Great Days, 1979
Sixty Stories, 1981
Overnight to Many Distant Cities, 1983
Forty Stories, 1987
Flying to America: Forty-five More Stories, 2007
   (Kim Herzinger, editor)

OTHER LITERARY FORMS

In addition to his 150 or so short stories, Donald Barthelme (BAR-thehl-mee) published four novels, a children's volume that won a National Book Award, a number of film reviews and unsigned "Comment" pieces for *The New Yorker,* a small but interesting body of art criticism, and a handful of book reviews and literary essays, two of which deserve special notice: "After Joyce" and "Not Knowing."

ACHIEVEMENTS

For nearly three decades, Donald Barthelme served as American literature's most imitated and imitative yet inimitable writer. One of a small but influential group of innovative American fictionists that included maximalists John Barth, Robert Coover, and Thomas Pynchon, Barthelme evidenced an even greater affinity to the international minimalists Samuel Beckett and Jorge Luis Borges. What distinguishes Barthelme's fiction is not only his unique "zero degree" writing style but also, thanks to his long association with the mass-circulation magazine *The New Yorker,* his reaching a larger and more diversified audience than most of the experimentalists, whose readership has chiefly been limited to the ranks of college professors and their students. The oddity of a fiction based largely upon "the odd linguistic trip, stutter, and fall" (*Snow White,* 1967) has led some critics to compare Barthelme's work with that of Anthony Trollope. Although antirealistic in form, Barthelme's fictions are in fact densely packed time capsules--not the "slices of life" of nineteenth century realists such as Émile Zola but "the thin edge of the wedge" of postmodernism's version of Charles Dickens's hard times and Charles Chaplin's modern ones. Despite their seeming sameness, his stories cover a remarkable range of styles, subjects, linguistic idioms, and historical periods (often in the same work, sometimes in the same sentence). Despite their referential density, Barthelme's stories do not attempt to reproduce mimetically external reality but instead offer a playful meditation on it (or alternately the materials for such a meditation). Such an art makes Barthelme in many respects the most representative American writer of the 1960's and of the two decades that followed: postmodern, postmodernist, post-Freudian, poststructuralist, postindustrial, even (to borrow Jerome Klinkowitz's apt term) postcontemporary.

BIOGRAPHY

Often praised and sometimes disparaged as one of *The New Yorker* writers, a narrative innovator, and a moral relativist whose only advice (John Gardner claimed) is that it is better to be disillusioned than deluded, Donald Barthelme was born in Philadelphia on April 7, 1931, and moved to Houston two years later. He grew up in Texas, attended Catholic diocesan schools, and began his writing career as a journalist in Ernest Hemingway's footsteps. His father, an architect who favored the modernist style of Ludwig Mies van der Rohe and Le Corbusier, taught at the University of Houston and designed the family's house, which became as much an object of surprise and wonder on the flat Texas landscape as his son's oddly shaped fictions were to become on the equally flat narrative landscape of postwar American fiction. While majoring in journalism, Barthelme wrote for the university newspaper as well as the *Houston Post*. He was drafted in 1953 and arrived in Korea on the day the truce was signed--the kind of coincidence one comes to expect in Barthelme's stories of strange juxtapositions and incongruous couplings.

After his military service, during which he also edited an army newspaper, Barthelme returned to Houston, where he worked in the university's public relations department ("writing poppycock for the President," as he put it in one story), and where he founded *Forum*, a literary and intellectual quarterly that published early works by Walker Percy, William H. Gass, Alain Robbe-Grillet, Leslie Fiedler, and others. He published his first story in 1961, the same year that he became director of the Contemporary Arts Museum of Houston. The following year, Thomas Hess and Harold Rosenberg offered him the position of managing editor of their new arts journal, *Location*. The journal was short-lived (only two issues ever appeared), but Barthelme's move to New York was not. Taking up residence in Greenwich Village, he published his first story in *The New Yorker* in 1963, his first collection of stories, *Come Back, Dr. Caligari*, in 1964, and his first novel, *Snow White* (among other things an updating of the Grimm Brothers' fairy tale and the Walt Disney feature-length animated cartoon), in 1967.

Although he left occasionally for brief periods abroad or to teach writing at Buffalo, Houston, and elsewhere, Barthelme spent the rest of his life chiefly in Greenwich Village, with his fourth wife, Marion Knox. He lived as a writer, registering and remaking the "exquisite mysterious muck" of contemporary urban American existence, as witnessed from his corner of the global (Greenwich) village.

ANALYSIS

Donald Barthelme's fiction exhausts and ultimately defeats conventional approaches (including character, plot, setting, theme-- "the enemies of the novel" as fellow writer John Hawkes once called them) and defeats too all attempts at generic classification. His stories are not conventional, nor are they Borgesian *ficciones* or Beckettian "texts for nothing." Thematic studies of his writing have proved utterly inadequate, yet purely formalist critiques have seemed almost as unsatisfying. To approach a Barthelme story, the reader must proceed circuitously via various, indeed at times simultaneous, extraliterary forms: collage, caricature, Calder mobile, action painting, jazz, atonality, the chance music of John Cage, architecture, information theory, magazine editing and layout, ventriloquism, even Legos (with all their permutational possibilities, in contrast with the High Moderns' love of cubist jigsaw puzzles). In Barthelme's case, comparisons with twentieth century painters and sculptors seem especially apropos: comical like Jean Dubuffet, whimsical and sad like Amedeo Modigliani, chaste like Piet Mondrian, attenuated like Alberto Giacometti, composite like Kurt Schwitters, improvisational like Jackson Pollock, and whimsical like Marc Chagall and Paul Klee. Like theirs, his is an art of surfaces, dense

Donald Barthelme (Time & Life Pictures/Getty Images)

rather than deep, textured rather than symbolic, an intersection of forces rather than a rendered meaning. Adjusting to the shift in perspective that reading Barthelme entails--and adjusting as well to Barthelme's (like the poet John Ashbery's) unwillingness to distinguish between foreground and background, message and noise--is difficult, sometimes impossible, and perhaps always fruitless.

However attenuated and elliptical the stories may be, they commit a kind of "sensory assault" on a frequently distracted reader, who experiences immediate gratification in dealing with parts but epistemological frustration in considering the stories as wholes, a frustration which mirrors that of the characters. Not surprisingly, one finds Barthelme's characters and the fictions themselves engaged in a process of scaling back even as they and their readers yearn for that "more" to which Beckett's figures despairingly and clownishly give voice. Entering "the complicated city" and singing their "song of great expectations," they nevertheless--or also--discover that theirs is a world not of romantic possibilities (as in F. Scott Fitzgerald's fiction) but of postmodern permutations, a world of words and undecidability, where "our Song of Songs is the Uncertainty Principle" and where "double-mindedness makes for mixtures." These are stories that, like the red snow in Barthelme's favorite and most Borgesian work, "Paraguay," invite "contemplation" of a mystery that there is "no point solving--an ongoing low-grade mystery." Expressed despondently, the answer to the question, "Why do I live this way?"--or why does Barthelme write this way?--is, as the character Bishop says, "Best I can do." This, however, sums up only one side of Barthelme's double-mindedness; the other is the pleasure, however fleeting, to be taken "in the sweet of the here and the now."

"ME AND MISS MANDIBLE"

Originally published as "The Darling Duckling at School" in 1961, "Me and Miss Mandible" is one of Barthelme's earliest stories and one of his best. Written in the form of twenty-six journal entries (dated September 13 to December 9), the story evidences Barthelme's genius for rendering even the most fantastic, dreamlike events in the most matter-of-fact manner possible. The thirty-five-year-old narrator, Joseph,

finds himself sitting in a too-small desk in Miss Mandible's classroom, having been declared "officially a child of eleven," either by mistake or, more likely, as punishment for having himself made a mistake in his former life as claims adjuster (a mistake for justice but against his company's interests). Having spent ten years "amid the debris of our civilization," he has come "to see the world as a vast junkyard" that includes the failure of his marriage and the absurdity of his military duty. At once a biblical Joseph in a foreign land and a Swiftian Gulliver among the Lilliputians, he will spend his time observing others and especially observing the widening gap between word and world, signifier and signified, the ideals expressed in teachers' manuals and the passions of a class of prepubescents fueled by film magazine stories about the Eddie Fisher/Debbie Reynolds/Elizabeth Taylor love triangle. Unlike his biblical namesake, Joseph will fail at reeducation as he has failed at marriage and other forms of social adjustment, caught by a jealous classmate making love to the freakishly named Miss Mandible.

"A SHOWER OF GOLD"

The coming together of unlike possibilities and the seeming affirmation of failure (maladjustment) takes a slightly different and more varied form in "A Shower of Gold." The former claims adjuster, Joseph, becomes the impoverished artist, Peterson, who specializes in large junk sculptures that no one buys and that even his dealer will not display. Desperate for money, he volunteers to appear on *Who Am I?*, the odd offspring of the game show craze on American television and of existentialism transformed into pop culture commodity. (There is also a barber who doubles as an analyst and triples as the author of four books all titled *The Decision to Be*.) Peterson convinces the show's Miss Arbor that he is both interesting enough and sufficiently de trop to appear on *Who Am I?*, only to feel guilty about selling out for two hundred dollars. Watching the other panelists be subjected to a humiliating barrage of questions designed to expose their bad faith, Peterson, accepting his position as a minor artist, short-circuits the host's existential script by out-absurding the absurd (his mother, he says, was a royal virgin and his father, a shower of gold). Peterson's situation parallels Barthelme's, or indeed any American writing at a time when, as Philip Roth pointed out in 1961, American reality had begun to outstrip the writer's imagination, offering a steady diet of actual people and events far more fantastic than any that the writer could hope to offer. What, Roth wondered, was left for the writer to do? "A Shower of Gold" offers one possibility.

"THE INDIAN UPRISING"

"The Indian Uprising" and "The Balloon" represent another possibility, in which in two quite different ways Barthelme directs the reader away from story and toward the act of interpretation itself (interpretation as story). As Brian McHale and Ron Moshe have demonstrated, "The Indian Uprising" comprises three overlapping yet divergent and even internally inconsistent narratives: an attack by Comanche on an unidentified but clearly modern American city; the narrator's (one of the city's defenders) unsatisfying love life; and the conflict between modern and postmodern sensibilities manifesting itself in a variety of allusions to modernist texts, including T. S. Eliot's *The Waste Land* (1922). Near the end of his poem, Eliot writes, "These fragments I have shored against my ruins." "The Indian Uprising" presents a very different approach, transforming Eliot's shoring up of high culture into a "barricade" that recycles Eliot and Thomas Mann, along with ashtrays, doors, bottles of Fad #6 sherry, "and other items." Behind Eliot's poem lies the possibility of psychic, spiritual, and sociocultural wholeness implied by Eliot's use of the "mythic method." Behind Barthelme's story one finds recycling rather than redemption and instead of the mythic method what Ronald Sukenick has called "the Mosaic Law," or "the law of mosaics, a way of dealing with parts in the absence of wholes." Short but beyond summary, filled with non sequiturs, ill-logic, self-doubts, and anti-explanations, "The Indian Uprising" rises against readers in their efforts to know it by reducing the story to some manageable whole. At once inviting and frustrating the reader's interpretive maneuvers, "The Indian Uprising" follows the "plan" outlined in "Paraguay" insofar as it proves "a way of allowing a very wide range of tendencies to interact."

Attacking and defending are two operant principles at play here, but just who is attacking and what is being defended are never made clear. Sides change, shapes shift in a story in which American Westerns, the Civil Rights movement, and American involvement in Vietnam all seem to have their parts to play, but never to the point where any one can be said to dominate the others. Small but indomitable, the story resists the linearity of an interpretive domino theory in favor of a semiotic quagmire (more evidence of Barthelme's interest in current affairs--Vietnam, in this case--and "mysterious muck"). In "The Indian Uprising," there is no final authority to come like the cavalry to the rescue and so no release from the anxiety evident in this and so many other Barthelme stories. While there may be no permanent release, however, there is some temporary relief to be had in the "aesthetic excitement" of "the hard, brown, nutlike word" and in the fact that "Strings of language extend in every direction to bind the world into a rushing ribald whole."

"THE BALLOON"

"The Balloon" is a more compact exploration and a more relentless exploitation of interpretation as a semiotic process rather than a narrowly coded act. Covering only a few pages (or alternately an area forty-five city blocks long by up to six blocks wide), "The Balloon" is Barthelme's American tall-tale version of the short French film *The Red Balloon* and an *hommage* to Frederick Law Olmsted (who designed New York's Central Park) and environmental artist Christo (one of his huge sculptural wrappings). Analogies such as these help readers situate themselves in relation to the inexplicable but unavoidable oddity of "The Balloon" in much the same way that the viewers in the story attempt to situate themselves in relation to the sudden appearance of a balloon which, even if it cannot be understood ("We had learned not to insist on meanings"), can at least be used (for graffiti, for example) and appreciated despite, or perhaps because, of its apparent uselessness. Ultimately the narrator will explain the balloon, thus adding his interpretive graffiti to its blank surface. The balloon, he says, was "a spontaneous autobiographical disclosure" occasioned by his lover's departure; when, after twenty-two days, she returns, he deflates the balloon, folds it, and ships it to West Virginia to be stored for future use. His explanation is doubly deflating, for while the balloon's "apparent purposelessness" may be vexing, in a world of "complex machinery," "specialized training," and pseudoscientific theories that make people marginal and passive, the balloon has come to exist as the "prototype" or "rough draft" of the kind of solution to which people will increasingly turn, to what the Balloon Man calls his best balloon, the Balloon of Perhaps. Until the narrator's closing comments, the balloon is not a scripted text but a blank page, not an object but an event, not a ready-made product, a prefab, but a performance that invites response and participation. It is a performance that the narrator's explanation concludes, assigning both an origin (cause) and a destination (result, function, use, addressee). Even as the explanation brings a measure of relief, it also adds a new level of anxiety insofar as the reader perceives its inadequacy and feels perhaps a twinge of guilty pleasure over having made so much of so little. In a way, however, the balloon was always doomed to extinction, for it exists in a consumer culture in which even the most remarkable objects (including "The Balloon") quickly become all too familiar, and it exists too in a therapeutic society in thrall to the illusion of authoritative explanations.

"ROBERT KENNEDY SAVED FROM DROWNING"

Appearing only two months before the real Robert F. Kennedy's assassination, "Robert Kennedy Saved from Drowning" explores epistemological uncertainty by exploiting the contemporary media and its audience's claims to know public figures, whether politicians or celebrities (a distinction that began to blur during the eponymous Kennedy years). The story exists at the intersection of two narrative styles. One is journalistic: twenty-four sections of what appear to be notes, each with its own subject heading and for the most part arranged in random order (the last section being a conspicuous exception) and presumably to be used in the writing of a profile or essay "about" Kennedy. The other is Kafkaesque fantasy and is evoked solely by means of the reporter's use of journalistic shorthand, the initial "K," which "refers" to Kennedy but alludes to the main characters of the enigmatic novels *Der Prozess* (1925; *The Trial*, 1937) and *Das Schloss* (1926; *The Castle*, 1930) and ultimately to their equally enigmatic author, Franz Kafka himself.

The narrator of "See the Moon?" claims that fragments are the only forms he trusts; in "Robert Kennedy Saved from Drowning," fragments are the only forms the reader gets. The conflicting mass of seemingly raw material--quotes, impressions, even fragments of orders to waiters--saves Kennedy from drowning in a media-produced narcissistic image that turns even the most inane remarks into orphic sayings. Kennedy cannot drown; he can only float on the postmodern surface. Instead of the Kennedy image, Barthelme turns Kennedy into a series of images, the last being the most ludicrous and yet also the most revealing: Kennedy as Zorro, masked and floundering in the sea, his hat, cape, and sword safely on the beach. Saved from drowning (by the narrator), Kennedy is unmasked as a masked image, a free-floating signifier, a chameleon in superhero's clothing who proves most revealing when most chameleon-like, offering a summary of Georges Poulet's analysis of the eighteenth century writer Pierre Marivaux. Only here, at this third or even fourth remove, will many readers feel that they have gotten close to the "real" Kennedy:

> The Marivaudian being is, according to Poulet, a pastless, futureless man, born anew at every instant. The instants are points which organize themselves into a line, but what is important is the instant, not the line. The Marivaudian being has in a sense no history. Nothing follows from what has gone before. He is constantly surprised. He cannot predict his own reaction to events. He is constantly being *overtaken* by events. A condition of breathlessness and dazzlement surrounds him. In consequence he exists in a certain freshness which seems, if I may say so, very desirable. This freshness Poulet, quoting Marivaux, describes very well.

"VIEWS OF MY FATHER WEEPING"

"Views of My Father Weeping" combines epistemological uncertainty with typically postmodern problematizing of the relationship between past and present (hinted at in the above quotation). Several days after his father has died under the wheels of an aristocrat's carriage, the narrator sets out to investigate whether the death was accidental, as the police reported, or an example of the aristocracy's (and the police's) indifference to the poor. Spurred on less by a desire for truth and justice than a vague sense of filial obligation and even more by the slight possibility of financial gain, but fearful that he may be beaten for making inquiries, perhaps (like his father) even killed, the narrator-son proceeds, more hesitant than Hamlet. Hamlet had his father's ghost appear to remind him of his duty to avenge a murder most foul. Barthelme's story also has a ghost (of sorts), a weeping father who sits on his son's bed acting in decidedly untragic fashion like a spoiled, sulky child whose very identity as father the son quietly questions. Complicating matters still further, this father seems to appear in a second story within "Views of My Father Weeping," which takes place in a more contemporary and clearly, although fantastically, American setting. These important if often blurred differences aside, the two narrators suffer from the same twin diseases that are pandemic in Barthelme's fiction: abulia (loss of the ability to decide or act) and acedia (spiritual torpor). They certainly would benefit from a reading of a slightly later story, "A Manual for Sons," a self-contained part of Barthelme's second novel, *The Dead Father* (1975), which concludes with this advice:

> You must become your father, but a paler, weaker version of him. The enormities go with the job, but close study will allow you to perform the job less well than it previously has been done, thus moving toward a golden age of decency, quiet, and calmed fever. Your contribution will not be a small one, but "small" is one of the concepts that you should shoot for. . . . *Fatherhood can be, if not conquered, at least "turned down" in this generation*--by the combined efforts of all of us together.

The extreme brevity of his densely allusive and highly elliptical stories suggests that Barthelme sides with the smallness of sons in their comic struggle with their various fathers (biological, historical, cultural). Against the authoritative word of the All Father, Barthelme offers a range of ventriloquized voices. "Here I differ from Kierkegaard," says one of the characters in "The Leap." "Purity of heart is not," as Kierkegaard claimed, to will one thing; it is, rather, "to will several things, and not know which is the better, truer thing, and to worry about this forever." Barthelme's own double-mindedness and preference for mixtures and

the guilty pleasures of the son's uncertainty and anxiety of influence become especially apparent in his collages of verbal and visual materials in which he puts the magazine editor's skills--layout in particular--to the fiction writer's use in order to achieve for fiction the kind of "immediate impact" generally available only to those working in the visual arts. "At the Tolstoy Museum," one of the best of these collages, literalizes, chiefly through visual means, the canonization of Leo Tolstoy as a metaphorical giant of literature, a cultural institution, an object of public veneration. Visitors to the "Tolstoy Museum" must gaze at the prescribed distances and times and in the proper attitude of awe and submission. Readers of "At the Tolstoy Museum," on the other hand, find all the rules broken, temporal and spatial boundaries transgressed, and distances subject to a new and fantastic geometry. Against the museum as a repository of cult(ural) memorabilia, the story serves a narrative riposte in the form of a study in perspective. Barthelme whittles Tolstoy down to manageable size by exaggerating his proportions (much as he does with another dead father in his second novel): the thirty thousand photographs, the 640,086 pages of the Jubilee edition of Tolstoy's works, the coat that measures at least twenty feet high, the head so large it has a hall of its own (closed Mondays, Barthelme parenthetically adds), even a page-long summary of one of Tolstoy's shortest stories, "The Three Hermits." There are also the two huge Soviet-style portraits on facing pages, identical in all but one feature: the tiny figure of Napoleon I (The Little Emperor), from Tolstoy's *Voyna i mir* (1865-1869; *War and Peace*, 1886), playing the part of viewer/reader. Best of all is Barthelme's rendering of The Anna-Vronsky Pavilion devoted to the adulterous pair from *Anna Karenina* (1875-1877; English translation, 1886), a cut-out of a nineteenth century man and woman superimposed on an early (and now adulterated) study in perspective dating from 1603. "At the Tolstoy Museum" does more than merely mix and match, cut and paste. It makes hilariously clear the artifice of art and of what the passive consumer of culture may naïvely assume is both natural and eternal.

"SENTENCE"

"Sentence" makes a similar point, but it does so by exploring the literal in a quite different way. As its title suggests, the story takes the form of a single sentence of approximately twenty-five hundred words and manages to combine the brevity, open-endedness, and formal innovation that together serve as the hallmarks of Barthelme's idiosyncratic art. The subject of "Sentence" is the sentence itself: its progress and process. Beginning with one of Barthelme's favorite words, "or" ("etc." and "amid" are others), it proceeds by means of accretion and ends (if a work without any terminal punctuation can be said to end) as much an "anxious object" as any of those works of modern art to which Harold Rosenberg applied that phrase. Even as it pursues its own meandering, self-regarding, seemingly nonreferential way down the page, "Sentence" remains mindful of its reader, no less susceptible to distraction than the sentence itself and lured on by whatever promise the sentence holds out yet also feeling threatened by the sentence's failure to play by the rules. As the narrator sums up, "Sentence" is "a human-made object, not the one we wanted of course, but still a construction of man, a structure to be treasured for its weakness, as opposed to the strength of stones."

Earlier in "Sentence," Barthelme alludes to the Rosetta Stone that Jean François Champollion used to decipher the ancient Egyptian hieroglyphs. Barthelme's fiction, although written in a familiar language, proves more resistant to decoding. Barthelme uses the past as he uses the present, but neither offers anything approaching an interpretive touchstone, only the raw material, the bits and bytes out of which he constructs his oddly shaped but nevertheless aesthetically crafted "archaeological slices." Built upon the cultural ruins of an ancient Norse tale entitled "The Princess and the Glass Hill," "The Glass Mountain" resembles "Sentence" and "The Balloon" more than it does its nominal source in that it too is largely about one's reading of it. "I was trying to climb the glass mountain," the narrator declares in the first of the story's one hundred numbered sections (most only one sentence long). Like the reader, the narrator is "new to the neighborhood," persistent, comically methodical, and methodologically absurd; the plumber's friends he uses to scale the glass mountain at the corner of Thirteenth Street and Eighth Avenue seem no less inappropriate than his by-the-book how-to approach drawn from medieval romance--or

the reader's efforts to climb (surmount, master) Barthelme's see-through metafiction by means of equally outdated reading strategies. Once atop the glass mountain the narrator finds exactly what he hoped to, "a beautiful enchanted symbol" to disenchant. Once kissed (like the frog of fairy tales), the symbol proves disenchanting in a quite different sense of the word, changed "into only a beautiful princess" whom the narrator (now himself disenchanted) hurls down in disappointment. Having staked his life on the eternal symbol of medieval romance, the narrator finds the temporary and the merely human (princess) disappointing.

Making a postmodern something, however small and self-consuming, out of the existential nothing became Barthelme's stock-in-trade, most noticeably in "Nothing: A Preliminary Account." His art of the nearly negligible works itself out comically but almost always against a sympathetic understanding for the permanence for which the climber in "The Glass Mountain" and the characters in so many of his other stories, such as "The New Music," yearn. A fusion of two stories published earlier the same year, one with the same title, the other entitled "Momma," "The New Music" takes the dialogue form that Barthelme often used to new and dizzying heights of nearly musical abstraction, akin to what Philip Roth would accomplish more than a decade later in his novel, *Deception* (1990). The subject here is slight (even for Barthelme), as the story's two unidentified, no-longer-young speakers go through (or are put through) a number of routines analogous to vaudeville comedy and improvisational jazz. After a few opening bars, one speaker suggests that they go to Pool, "the city of new hope. One of those new towns. Where everyone would be happier." They then segue into an exchange on, or consideration of, the new music done as a version of the familiar song "Momma Don' 'Low." Among the many things that Momma (now dead) did not allow was the new music. "The new music burns things together, like a welder," or like the sculptor Peterson from "A Shower of Gold," or like Barthelme, who along with his two speakers understands what the new music always has been and always will be: ever changing, ever ephemeral, ever new, and forever beyond momma's prohibitions and the reader's explanations.

OTHER MAJOR WORKS

LONG FICTION: *Snow White*, 1967; *The Dead Father*, 1975; *Paradise*, 1986; *The King*, 1990.

CHILDREN'S LITERATURE: *The Slightly Irregular Fire Engine: Or, The Hithering Thithering Djinn*, 1971.

BIBLIOGRAPHY

Barthelme, Helen Moore. *Donald Barthelme: The Genesis of a Cool Sound*. College Station: Texas A&M University Press, 2001. The author, a senior university lecturer, was married to Barthelme for a decade in the 1950's and 1960's. She traces his life from his childhood in Houston to his development as a writer.

Couturier, Maurice, and Regis Durand. *Donald Barthelme*. London: Methuen, 1982. This brief study focuses on the performance aspect of Barthelme's stories and considers them in relation to the multiplicity of varied responses that they elicit from readers. Readings are few in number but highly suggestive.

Daugherty, Tracy. *Hiding Man: A Biography of Donald Barthelme*. New York: St. Martin's Press, 2009. Argues that Barthleme was writing in the modernist tradition of Samuel Beckett and James Joyce, and that he used advertisements, sentences from newspaper articles, instruction guides, and popular and commercial elements in order to make literature, not to subvert it.

Gelfant, Blanche H., ed. *The Columbia Companion to the Twentieth-Century American Short Story*. New York: Columbia University Press, 2000. Includes a chapter in which Barthelme's short stories are analyzed.

Gordon, Lois. *Donald Barthelme*. Boston: Twayne, 1981. This volume, in Twayne's United States Authors series, makes up in breadth what it lacks in depth. Although the book has no particular point to make about Barthelme and his work, it does provide useful and accurate summaries of most of his work. A comprehensive introduction for undergraduates unfamiliar with the fiction, as is Stanley Trachtenberg's Understanding Donald Barthelme(1990).

Hudgens, Michael Thomas. *Donald Barthelme, Postmodernist American Writer*. Lewiston, N.Y.: Edwin Mellen Press, 2001. Analyzes a cross section of Barthleme's work, viewing him within the context of upscale New York City, the art circuit, and *The New Yorker*, where he made his reputation. Describes the influence of painting on his writing.

Klinkowitz, Jerome. "Donald Barthelme." In *A Reader's Companion to the Short Story in English*, edited by Erin Fallon, et al., under the auspices of the Society for the Study of the Short Story. Westport, Conn.: Greenwood Press, 2001. Klinkowitz, who has written extensively and perceptively on Barthelme, provides a brief biography followed by an analysis of his short fiction.

_____. *Donald Barthelme: An Exhibition*. Durham, N.C.: Duke University Press, 1991. Klinkowitz is easily the best informed and most judicious scholar and critic of contemporary American fiction in general and Barthelme in particular. Building on his Barthelme chapter in *Literary Disruptions*, he emphasizes the ways in which Barthelme reinvented narrative in the postmodern age and places Barthelme's fiction in the larger aesthetic, cultural, and historical contexts. The single most important study of Barthelme.

_____. *Literary Disruptions: The Making of a Post-Contemporary American Fiction*. 2d ed. Urbana: University of Illinois Press, 1980. Informed, accurate, and intelligent, Klinkowitz's book is the necessary starting point for any serious discussion of Barthelme and his work. The emphasis is on Barthelme's interest in structure, his revitalizing of exhausted forms, his words as objects in space rather than mimetic mirrors, and the imagination as a valid way of knowing the world.

Molesworth, Charles. *Donald Barthelme's Fiction: The Ironist Saved from Drowning*. Columbia: University of Missouri Press, 1982. Objecting to those who emphasize the experimental nature of Barthelme's fiction, Molesworth views Barthelme as essentially a parodist and satirist whose ironic stance saves him from drowning in mere innovation.

Olsen, Lance, ed. *Review of Contemporary Fiction* 11 (Summer, 1991). In addition to the editor's excellent bio-critical introduction and Steven Weisenburger's bibliography of works by and about Barthelme, this special issue on Barthelme reprints an early story and offers seven new essays, including especially noteworthy ones by Jerome Klinkowitz on the uses to which Barthelme put his unsigned "Comment" pieces from *The New Yorker* and Brian McHale and Ron Moshe on "The Indian Uprising." Also contains shorter appreciations of and critical commentary on Barthelme from twenty critics and fiction writers.

Patteson, Richard, ed. *Critical Essays on Donald Barthelme*. New York: G. K. Hall, 1992. A collection of critical essays on Barthelme from book reviews and academic journals. Provides an overview of critical reaction to Barthelme in the introduction. Essays deal with Barthelme's use of language, his fragmentation of reality, his montage technique, and his place in the postmodernist tradition.

Roe, Barbara L. *Donald Barthelme: A Study of the Short Fiction*. New York: Twayne, 1992. An introduction to Barthelme's short stories, with discussion of the major stories arranged in chronological order. Also includes several interviews with Barthelme, as well as previously published essays by other critics.

Stengel, Wayne B. *The Shape of Art in the Stories of Donald Barthelme*. Baton Rouge: Louisiana State University Press, 1985. Discusses such themes as play, futility, stasis, affirmation, and education in four types of stories: identity stories, dialogue stories, social fabric stories, and art-object stories. Focuses on Barthelme's emphasis on art in his self-reflexive stories.

Waxman, Robert. "Apollo and Dionysus: Donald Barthelme's Dance of Life." *Studies in Short Fiction* 33 (Spring, 1996): 229-243. Examines how the interplay between the Apollonian search for order and the Dionysian longing for freedom from convention informs much of Barthelme's work and is often embodied in the metaphor of music.

Robert A. Morace A. Morace

FREDERICK BARTHELME

Born: Houston, Texas; October 10, 1943

PRINCIPAL SHORT FICTION

Rangoon, 1970
Moon Deluxe, 1983
Chroma, 1987
The Law of Averages: New and Selected Stories,
   2000

OTHER LITERARY FORMS

Frederick Barthelme (BAR-thehl-mee) has written several novels, including *Second Marriage* (1984), *Tracer* (1985), *Natural Selection* (1990), *The Brothers* (1993), *Painted Desert* (1995), *Bob the Gambler* (1997), *Elroy Nights* (2003), and *Waveland* (2009). An essay, "On Being Wrong: Convicted Minimalist Spills Bean," was published in 1988.

ACHIEVEMENTS

Also a visual artist, Frederick Barthelme has exhibited in the Seattle Art Museum (1969) and the Museum of Modern Art in New York (1970). He won the Eliot Coleman Award for prose from The Johns Hopkins University for his story "Storyteller" in 1976-1977. He also received grants from the National Endowment for the Arts in 1979 and 1980. In 2004, his novel *Elroy Nights* was nominated for the PEN/Faulkner Award for Fiction.

BIOGRAPHY

Frederick Barthelme was born in Houston, Texas, on October 10, 1943. Two of his brothers, Donald and Steven, have also published fiction. Initially desiring to be a painter, he studied at Tulane University (1961-1962), and the University of Houston (1962-1965, 1966-1967). He briefly attended the Museum of Fine Arts in Houston in 1965-1966. After working on his visual arts career for a few years, he started writing fiction. In 1976-1977, Barthelme received the Eliot Coleman Award for Prose from The Johns Hopkins University. He also received grants from the National Endowment for the Arts and the University of Southern Mississippi. Receiving his M.A. from Johns Hopkins University in 1977, he was then appointed professor at the University of Southern Mississippi, where he also edits the *Mississippi Review* and directs the Center for Writers.

ANALYSIS

Frederick Barthelme's short stories are frequently offered as examples of "minimalism." Focusing on the surface of events, minimalism generally refuses to delve into a character's psychological motivations and avoids overt narratorial commentary. Because this style is often attacked for its supposed moral defeatism and lack of historical sensibility, it is especially useful to consider Barthelme's essay "On Being Wrong: Convicted Minimalist Spills Bean" (1988) when examining his writing. In this playful manifesto, Barthelme maintains that minimalist stories deliberately react against the postmodernist obsession with language, while simultaneously rejecting conventional realism. Human experience, according to Barthelme, "is so enigmatic that only the barest suspicion of it can be got on the page with any assurance."

Barthelme usually sets his stories in malls, restaurants, and apartment complexes, rendering a vision of contemporary America that fastens upon the subdued sublimities of day-to-day existence. Suggesting that most people overlook or repress the weird peculiarity of the objects and situations they face in their daily lives, Barthelme augments the uncanny dimensions of suburban experience through stylistic experimentation. Narrators startle the reader by using the second-person

Frederick Barthelme (Time & Life Pictures/Getty Images)

form of address ("you"); everyday objects take on qualities independent from their common uses, creating an atmosphere that is both disturbing and quietly celebratory. Usefully locating this fiction within the literary mode of the"grotesque," Robert H. Brinkmeyer maintains that Barthelme's fiction "knots together the alien with the familiar and challenges the beholder to resolve the ambivalence that this intermingling evokes."

Uncomfortable in their lives and with each other, yet at ease with incongruity, Barthelme's characters find little to distinguish public from private experience. Although they are keen observers of their environments' particularities, popular culture often forms the basis of their relationship with each other and the world. Desiring change while suspecting that attempts at personal transformation will be only cosmetic or, worse, result in self-deception, these characters face the confusions of late twentieth century life with integrity and an appreciable curiosity. Critic Timothy Peters detects a modest heroism in their unwillingness "to look back, to be nostalgic, or even to scheme for a more aesthetically or materially rewarding future."

"SHOPGIRLS"

"Shopgirls," from the collection *Moon Deluxe*, encapsulates one of the central themes of Barthelme's work: how a consumer- and media-based culture influences the men and women who live within it. Initially set in a mall, "Shopgirls" follows a chronic voyeur who scrutinizes the female clerks in a department store. Andrea, who oversees purses, forces an encounter with the narrator, surprisingly inviting him to have lunch with the various women he has been observing. They tease and fawn over him, then bicker among themselves, after which Andrea invites him to spend the night. In her apartment, she relates a bizarre story about her hurricane-obsessed father, who once attempted suicide when a storm failed to arrive, leaving him crippled. The couple does not sleep together; instead, the narrator fantasizes about further voyeuristic meanderings on another floor of the department store. When, during lunch, one of the women confesses that their cultural obligation is to "make the women feel envious and . . . men feel cheated," the reader sees voyeurism's frustrating disconnections extending to social relations as a whole. Barthelme's innovative point of view. Although Barthelme often uses this stylistic maneuver, his particular application of it in "Shopgirls" heightens the story's emphasis on voyeurism, foregrounding the degree to which media technology and the image have influenced contemporary American culture.

"SAFEWAY"

"Safeway," from *Moon Deluxe*, employs one of Barthelme's favorite plot devices: A man and woman negotiate the unpredictable waters of initiating a sexual relationship. "Safeway" also adopts the second-person, but on this occasion, "you" are directed through the viewpoint of a man shopping for waffles. Waiting in the checkout line with Sarah, a woman he has just met, the narrator becomes embroiled in the unexplained anger of two men. These men add a peculiar twist to the story when one of them refers to a photograph of the other's wife. She is standing in front of a Confederate painting with a cast on one leg, supported by a cane from World War I, presumably in a pornographic pose. Barthelme passes quickly over this startling image, devoting the remainder of the story to Sarah and the narrator flirting in a restaurant, making plans for a tryst.

No affair begins because the narrator gives Sarah a false address to his apartment, the story offering no rationale for his deception. Inundating the story with brand names, Barthelme shows individuals being evaluated on the basis of their consumer choices. When someone glances at the narrator after noticing his waffles, he recognizes that "his opinion of your entire life is instantly communicated." Brand names also provide the only reliability in a life controlled by chance.

Because the narrator is keenly observant of the "random data" his day presents to him, Barthelme implies that one's understanding of the world is thoroughly shaped by the incidental. Although the narrator is acutely sensitive to the nuances of his environment--the grocery store's "parking lot [has] a close, magical look"--he seems oblivious to the workings of his mind, as his playing football with the cream cartons in the restaurant demonstrates. This equivocation of significance affects interpretation. The nuns in their "brilliant blue habits" would ordinarily suggest a religious symbol; here, however, such a moment is a visual tableau rather than a sign of potential redemption. Similarly, the historically ironic photograph contributes to the story's atmosphere without offering a readily understandable meaning. This commitment to unrooted images connects Barthelme to postmodernism.

"DRIVER"

This story from *Chroma* fulfills Brinkmeyer's comment that almost all "of Barthelme's protagonists are haunted by the fear that their lives are . . . ordered but repetitious, without worry but without wonder." While the narrator's wife, Rita, sleeps, he watches a television program on customized low-riding cars. The next morning he trades in his Toyota for a low-rider airbrushed with a painting showing the Virgin Mary surrounded by salivating wolves. If the narrator is going through a mid-life crisis, it is not the usual kind. Going out for a drive with Rita, he finds her delightful. Discovering kids roller skating in a parking lot, Rita comments on the scene's "amazing" charm. Later, the narrator channel surfs almost until dawn, when he decides to take the car out again. The deserted downtown looks "like one of those end-of-the-world movies." Once again, he stops in a parking lot, convincing two dogs that had been chasing a bird to get into the car. Heading home, he tells the dogs about his dissatisfactory old life. The narrator's admiration of the dogs' single-minded pursuit coincides with his own gratification in having followed a series of impulses. His astonished perception that a larger reality has been going on outside his previously confined, egocentric existence leads to a classic epiphany. Whether Barthelme undercuts this private revelation by having the narrator recount it to the uncomprehending dogs depends on the reader. The diverse references scattered throughout "Driver" complicate its emotional range. Hollywood's generic films are juxtaposed uneasily with the untapped story that the man who painted the discomfiting image on the car died in Vietnam. Should the reader be suspicious when the narrator drives around his secretary's apartment? Why are the dogs identical twins and what of their owner or owners? By hinting at but not resolving these narrative dilemmas, Barthelme dramatizes the claim in "On Being Wrong: Convicted Minimalist Spills Bean" that an empty parking lot "might as well be an ancient temple."

"CHROMA"

The title story from this collection reveals an intricate network of sexual politics. The narrator's wife, Alicia, spends alternate weekends with her young lover, George. Next door live Juliet and Heather, a lesbian couple, although Juliet offers to sleep with the narrator to offset Alicia's infidelity. On a weekend when Alicia is supposed to be with George, she returns home early, the story concluding with the narrator sitting beside the bathtub, overcome by Alicia's loveliness while he watches her bathe. Barthelme does not judge this unusual sexual dynamic, but neither does he gloss over the pain, anger, and confused tenderness shared by these people. The word "chroma" refers to a pure color, suggesting the subtle but distinctly rendered portrayals of the four major characters. Like many of Barthelme's stories, "Chroma" is written in the present tense; in this instance, the effect is to magnify the inherent perplexities of time. Early in the story, Juliet and the narrator have a late breakfast in a section of town that has been subject to urban renewal. After rejecting many of the restaurants, they choose an old restaurant that also has its faults, but it has "been there for thirty years, so all the things wrong with that are deeply wrong." Age

confers authenticity over fashion. The narrator worries over saying things to Juliet that will be true in the present moment but will seem false at a later time. The notion that the passing of events reconfigures, even mitigates, their original importance becomes clear when Juliet plays Nat King Cole on a tape--not the original record, Barthelme notes--and the narrator suddenly remembers what it was like to hear the music for the first time decades earlier. To the narrator, people float along the surface of time without truly living within it, a condition that undermines communication and self-knowledge. Alicia's remarks when the narrator queries her on a seemingly meaningful gesture--"If I thought something I only thought it for a second and I don't remember what it was, so leave me alone"--typify the isolation and bewilderment caused by temporal experience. If the couple's relationship is erratic, it provides the narrator with a complex understanding of time.

OTHER MAJOR WORKS

LONG FICTION: *War and War*, 1971; *Second Marriage*, 1984; *Tracer*, 1985; *Two Against One*, 1988; *Natural Selection*, 1990; *The Brothers*, 1993; *Painted Desert*, 1995; *Bob the Gambler*, 1997; *Elroy Nights*, 2003; *Waveland*, 2009.

NONFICTION: *Double Down: Reflections on Gambling and Loss*, 1999 (with Steven Barthelme).

MISCELLANEOUS: *Guilty Pleasures*, 1974; *The Teachings of Don B.: Satires, Parodies, Fables, Illustrated Stories and Plays of Donald Barthelme*, 1992 (Kim Herzinger, editor); *Not-knowing: The Essays and Interviews of Donald Barthelme*, 1997 (Kim Herzinger, editor)

BIBLIOGRAPHY

Bing, Jonathan, ed. "Frederick Barthelme." In *Writing for Your Life #4.*Wainscott, N.Y.: Pushcart Press, 2000. Includes a brief interview in which Barthelme discusses his writing.

Brinkmeyer, Robert H., Jr. "Suburban Culture, Imaginative Wonder: The Fiction of Frederick Barthelme." *Studies in the Literary Imagination* 27 (Fall, 1994). Discusses Barthelme's fiction in terms of the southern tradition and its examination of place. Ties Barthelme's evocation of suburban mystery to the grotesque, concluding that Barthelme's fiction celebrates wonder.

Hughes, John C. *The Novels and Short Stories of Frederick Barthelme: A Literary Critical Analysis.* Lewiston, N.Y.: Edwin Mellen Press, 2005. Reviews previous criticism of Barthelme's fiction and focuses on close readings of his texts. Hughes argues that Barthelme is best read as a "contemporary moralist," but one who describes how modern people actually live, instead of someone who prescribes a code of ethics. Devotes one chapter to analysis of *Moon Deluxe* and *Chroma.*

Peters, Timothy. "The Eighties Pastoral: Frederick Barthelme's *Moon Deluxe* Ten Years On." *Studies in Short Fiction* 31 (Spring, 1994): 175-195. Begins by comparing Vladimir Nabokov's *Lolita* (1955) to Barthelme's fiction. Engages critics who disparage Barthelme's writing by arguing that it confronts the dreamscape of contemporary suburban America.

Michael Trussler

RICK BASS

Born: Fort Worth, Texas; March 7, 1958

PRINCIPAL SHORT FICTION

The Watch, 1989
Platte River, 1994
In the Loyal Mountains, 1995
The Sky, the Stars, the Wilderness, 1997
The Hermit's Story, 2002
The Lives of Rocks, 2006

OTHER LITERARY FORMS

Rick Bass's first two collections of essays, *The Deer Pasture* (1985) and *Wild to the Heart* (1987), revealed both his active concerns as an environmentalist and his passion for hunting and fishing. His 1989 book, *Oil Notes,* revealed his wealth of specialized knowledge as a petroleum geologist. Bass's nonfiction books on wildlife and the West--*Caribou Rising: Defending the Porcupine Herd, Gwich-'in Culture, and the Arctic National Wildlife Refuge* (2004), *Why I Came West* (2008), and *The Wild Marsh: Four Seasons at Home in Montana* (2009)--are as well known as his fiction. He is also the author of three novels: *Where the Sea Used to Be* (1998), *The Diezmo* (2009), and *Nashville Chrome* (2010).

ACHIEVEMENTS

Many of Rick Bass's short stories have been selected for the annual collection *The Best American Short Stories,* the O. Henry Award, and the Pushcart Prize. In 1987, he received the General Electric Younger Writers Award, and in 1988 he was awarded a PEN/Nelson Algren Award special citation. Bass's memoir, *Why I Came West,* was short-listed for the National Book Critics Circle Award for Memoir/Autobiography in 2008. His collection of stories, *The Lives of Rocks,* was short-listed for the Story Prize in 2006.

BIOGRAPHY

Rick Bass was born in Fort Worth, Texas, on March 7, 1958. While growing up in south Texas, he often went deer hunting with his grandfather; during these hunting trips his grandfather told him stories about his family. These stories and Bass's personal experiences on the hunting trips formed the basis of his first book, *The Deer Pasture,* and many of his subsequent works. In 1976 he enrolled at Utah State University and in 1979, following in his father's footsteps, received a degree in geology. After college he took a job as a petroleum geologist in Jackson, Mississippi, and, while prospecting for oil, he wrote *Oil Notes,* a journal of his work and meditations.

In 1987, Bass decided to write full time. He gave up his job as a petroleum geologist and moved to a remote ranch in Yaak, Montana, near the Canadian border.

Within his first two years in Montana he had stories published in several prestigious magazines, *The Paris Review*, *The Southern Review*, *Cimarron Review*, *Antaeus*, and *The Quarterly*. In 1988, he published his first collection of short stories, *The Watch*. He has written and published several novellas, some illustrated by his wife Elizabeth Hughes Bass, and he published his first full-length novel, *Where the Sea Used to Be*, in 1998.

ANALYSIS

Rick Bass is a writer preoccupied with the connections between the human animal and the wilderness. His characters work with and against the wilderness in which he places them and are defined by this struggle. The physical environment in a Bass story is as alive and intricate as any of the human characters. He is a minimalist whose narrators are usually first-person, rarely named, and seem often to have inherited their fated behaviors from other family members. Many of these first-person narratives have as one of their major themes the maturation of the narrator. The narrator of

Rick Bass (AP Photo/Independent Record, Jason Mohr)

"In the Loyal Mountains" is greatly influenced by an uncle, a bizarre and strong-willed man, whose devotion to hunting and fishing make him sound like Bass's descriptions of his own grandfather, and by a girl from "the wrong side of the tracks," one of society's more "civilized" wildernesses. Bass's female characters, both major and minor, seem always to function as satellites of male characters, even in "The Myths of Bears," where he gives the woman a role as large as that of her male counterpart. At times this makes the women of Bass's stories seem secondary, sometimes even superfluous. Consequently, the men often seem immature or incomplete.

In his review of *The Watch*, Bass's first collection of short stories, Joseph Coates writes about other critics' use of the term "Magical Realism" in regard to Bass's stories,

> that quality, if it exists in his work, appears not in the kind of surreal events or atmosphere that we see in García Márquez but in the arbitrary strangeness of Bass' situations, which he somehow makes plausible.

Coates compares Bass's voice to those "particularly American" voices of Mark Twain, F. Scott Fitzgerald, and Ernest Hemingway.

"THE WATCH"

This title story from the collection *The Watch* was reprinted in *New Stories from the South 1988*. The dominant theme of the story is the power of loneliness and feelings of alienation to warp an individual's senses of reality and morality. Hollingsworth and his seventy-seven-year-old father Buzbee are the only inhabitants of a town whose inhabitants were nearly all killed long ago. Because Buzbee is only fourteen years older than his son, their relationship has, at times, been more like that of brothers. When Buzbee runs off to the swamps and establishes a commune with women from a local town who have been abused by husbands and lovers, Jesse, an aging cyclist who can never quite keep up with the pack that daily rides past Hollingsworth's general store, stops to drink his usual half a Coke and offers to help catch Buzbee for the thousand-dollar reward Hollingsworth has posted. When they catch Buzbee, Hollingsworth chains him to the store porch. The great irony here is that Hollingsworth risks life and limb to bring his father back so he will have someone to talk to, but Buzbee grieves like a caged animal and refuses to talk or listen. Jesse, who became fat and out of shape during the hunt, buys a new bike and goes into intensive training to keep up with the pack of cyclists who pass by Hollingsworth without ever stopping or speaking.

"IN THE LOYAL MOUNTAINS"

This title story from the book *In the Loyal Mountains* was reprinted in *New Stories from the South 1991*. The first-person narrator, a man born with one leg noticeably shorter than the other, tells the story of how he was raised by his father, a minor professional golfer, and his mother, a housewife who often traveled with her husband. Whenever they traveled the boy stayed with his uncle Zorey and, for one summer, with a girl "from the wrong side of the tracks" named Spanda, who was the boy's companion, lover, and the only one he ever knew who was "attracted" to his shorter leg. Most of the story concentrates on the adventures the boy experienced that one summer in the Loyal Mountains with his uncle Zorey, a very rich and eccentric man who had a passion for eating wild game and fish that he had killed himself, and with Spanda, his first lover but a person he never believed did or could love him. In his adult life he seems to have lost his adoration for Zorey; he refers to him as a crook. When his three-year-old son becomes moody and distant or has temper tantrums, he fears that the boy may be destined to become like Zorey. His greatest fear seems to be that everyone is helplessly fated to become what they become.

"FIRES"

"Fires" appears in *In the Loyal Mountains* and was reprinted in *The Best American Short Stories 1996*. As in most of Bass's stories, two of the driving themes of "Fires" are isolation and the fear of being trapped. An unusual element of this story is that the protagonist's fear is not of being trapped; he is afraid of being a trapper, of somehow emotionally holding someone against his or her will: "I haven't lived with a woman for a long time. Whenever one does move in with me, it feels as if I've tricked her, caught her in a trap, as if the gate has been closed behind her. . . . " This fear has become so strong that when Glenda, a competitive runner,

comes to the remote area where the protagonist lives for high-altitude training, he fails to recognize her offerings of love. In a final act of seeming madness, she starts a grass fire, and they have to take refuge together in a pond. When the heat of the burning world around them becomes so hot they have to move to the center of the pond and keep ducking under to protect their faces, she tries to make her feelings known: "'Please, love' Glenda was saying, and I did not understand at first that she was speaking to me. 'Please.'" At the end she runs away.

"WEJUMPKA"

"Wejumpka" won a Pushcart Prize in 1996. On a camping trip with boys his age, eight-year-old Montrose drew the name "Wejumpka" while pulling Indian names out of a wooden box. When the camping trip ended, the rest of the boys, who had also taken Indian names, went back to their real names, but Montrose liked his new name so much that he insisted from then on that everyone call him Wejumpka. When he was eleven the unnamed narrator of the story lost a game of liar's poker to Wejumpka's father, Vern, and thus became Wejumpka's godfather. Vern and the narrator decided that before entering junior high school, Wejumpka had to change his name. From a wooden bowl he drew the name Vern, Jr. His behavior is unusual for a boy his age. His first response to people is to grab and hug them, a habit he is forced to break while in junior high school, and in the final scene of the story he demonstrates a remarkable ability to endure physical stress. There is virtually no plot to this story. It is a character study and a gentle reminder that fate can be the quirkiest of characters.

"THE MYTHS OF BEARS"

An O. Henry Award winner in 1998, "The Myths of Bears" is a wild and gruesome story of escape, pursuit, freedom, and survival. Trapper, a hunter of virtually anything with fur, has been going through some dramatic changes. At night "he imagines that he is a wolf, and that the other wolves in his pack have suddenly turned against him . . . he's roused in bed to snarl and snap at everything in sight." His wife Judith, a six-foot-tall woman with curved feet so large she does not need snowshoes, becomes so afraid of him that she breaks through a window of their cabin and flees into the night during a blizzard. Trapper feels "Betrayed; abandoned. He'd thought she was tame. He'd not understood she was the wildest, most fluttering thing in the woods." It takes him almost a year to track her, trap her, and bring her back. Judith often thinks of allowing him to catch her. She misses his attentions, but her view of their relationship has changed. "It is not that he is a bad man, or that I am a bad woman, she thought. It's just that he is a predator, and I am prey." Both characters evolve as products of the wilderness in which this story is set.

"THE HERMIT'S STORY"

A magical metaphor initiates and energizes Bass's short stories in his collection *The Hermit's Story*. In the contributors' notes to the *Best American Short Stories 1999*, Bass said that as soon as he heard about a frozen lake with no water in it, he knew he wanted to write a story about that. When a female dog trainer and the Canadian man who has hired her get caught in a freezing storm, they fall into a fairy-tale wonderland created when a shallow lake freezes over and the water under the ice percolates down into the soil. The result, says Bass, is a realm in which the air is a thing of its own and reality takes on the feeling of dream--a zone in which appearances disappear and the essence of things is revealed.

"THE FIREMAN"

Metaphors for alternate realities fascinate Bass. He has said that "The Fireman," which appeared in the *Best American Short Stories 2001*, began with the image of a lost fireman puncturing a tiny hole in a hose to create an umbrella-like protective mist, a temporary "tiny refuge or brief harbor from duress." "The Fireman" is a kind of awe-inspired paean to the passion of a fireman, a passion that Bass says takes on a rhythm of its own, like a living thing. Indeed, it is not plot but poetry that makes this story fascinating. The trick of such stories is to catch the reader up in the poetry of place or the magic of the moment in which ordinary people are miraculously transformed and mere things are illuminated with significance.

"THE CAVE"

"The Cave," is perhaps the purest example of Bass's fascination with creating magical worlds. A former coal miner goes naked into a narrow mineshaft with his equally naked girlfriend. They get separated,

find each other, make love, board a small boxcar for an underground rail ride, make love, get lost, make love, come full circle around the little mountain under which they have wandered, then come out into the light and are ready to "rejoin the unaltered flow of things." Summarized, the story sounds absurd, but by the sheer power of imaginative projection and narrative drive, Bass makes it work.

"HER FIRST ELK"

The two most powerful stories in Bass's collection *The Lives of Rocks*-- "Her First Elk" and the title story--focus on a woman named Jyl. In the first story, she is just out of college. During the first hour of the first day of a hunt she has gone on alone, she shoots a giant elk, her first. However, the story is not about the hunt but rather the obligations of the hunter after the kill. When Jyl finds the body of the elk, she encounters two brothers in their sixties who agree to help her. Most of the story deals with Jyl's introduction to field dressing the animal--a process that is performed by the two men with such precision and respect that the animal takes on a mythic aura, bigger than life, something deified. Jyl marvels at a privileged glimpse of these two lives of "cautious competence" and is surprised at how mythic the animal and the act seem. The story is reminiscent of William Faulkner's "The Bear" for its mythic elevation of the hunt and its celebration of the hunter's responsibility to the sacred animal.

"THE LIVES OF ROCKS"

In the title story, the longest in the book, Jyl is an older woman with cancer, living alone in a cabin in the wilderness. Her nearest neighbors are an industrious fundamentalist Christian family named the Workmans. In order to provide a little magic for the work-hardened lives of the two children in the family--a fifteen-year-old boy and a seven-year-old girl-- she carves small boats and sends them downstream with little messages. The two children visit her throughout the winter, bringing food and keeping her supplied with firewood. Jyl introduces them to the work of her dead father, who was an archeologist, and the boy finds the mysteries of the lives of rocks fascinating, in spite of the fact that they challenge his fundamentalist beliefs. The bond between the ill woman and the children, as she tells them stories and reads them books and they tend to her needs, is the core of the story. When the children stop coming, Jyl worries about them and undertakes the arduous journey to their house on the other side of the mountain, only to find it deserted. At the end of the story, she sits outside the lonely cabin in the snow, crying in her loneliness. Told with sympathy and restraint, "The Lives of Rocks" is an elegiac symphony of loneliness and love.

OTHER MAJOR WORKS

LONG FICTION: *Fiber*, 1998 (novella); *Where the Sea Used to Be*, 1998; *The Diezmo*, 2005; *Nashville Chrome*, 2010.

NONFICTION: *The Deer Pasture*, 1985; *Wild to the Heart*, 1987; *Oil Notes*, 1989; *Winter: Notes from Montana*, 1991; *The Ninemile Wolves: An Essay*, 1992; *The Book of Yaak*, 1996; *The Lost Grizzlies: A Search for Survivors in the Wilderness of Colorado*, 1998; *The New Wolves*, 1998; *Brown Dog of the Yaak: Essays on Act and Activism*, 1999; *Colter: The True Story of the Best Dog I Ever Had*, 2000; *Caribou Rising: Defending the Porcupine Herd, Gwich-'in Culture, and the Arctic National Wildlife Refuge*, 2004; *Why I Came West*, 2008; *The Wild Marsh: Four Seasons at Home in Montana*, 2009.

EDITED TEXTS: *The Roadless Yaak: Reflections and Observations About One of Our Last Great Wild Places*, 2002; *Falling from Grace in Texas: A Literary Response to the Demise of Paradise*, 2004 (with Paul Christensen).

BIBLIOGRAPHY

Bass, Rick. "Rick Bass: Lessons from the Wilderness." Interview by David Long. *Publishers Weekly* 242 (June 26, 1995): 82-83. Discussion of Bass's daily writing schedule, how he began writing while working as a geologist, and his passion for the environment.

Dixon, Terrell F. *American Nature Writers* 1. New York: Charles Scribner's Sons, 1996. A lengthy discussion of Bass's love of nature and the wilderness essays of *Wild to the Heart*. Emphasizes the importance of natural settings in his writing and includes some biographical information.

Gelfant, Blanche H., ed. *The Columbia Companion to the Twentieth-Century American Short Story*. New York: Columbia University Press, 2000. Includes a chapter in which Bass's short stories are analyzed.

Gorra, Michael. "Outside: Rick Bass's Novellas Offer Meticulous Observations of the Natural World." *The New York Times Book Review*, December 14, 1997, 13. In this review of the three novellas in Bass's *The Sky, the Stars, the Wilderness*, Gorra praises Bass for his ability to bring the wilderness alive, to pin it to the page for all to experience. Gorra explains why he believes the first two novellas, "The Myths of Bears" and "Where the Sea Used to Be," are not as successful as the final novella, "The Sky, the Stars, the Wilderness."

O'Grady, Brian, and Rob Sumner. "A Conversation with Rick Bass." October 4, 2003. http://willow-springs.ewu.edu/interviews/bass.pdf. An extensive interview in which Bass talks about why he writes, how he writes, the importance of fiction, and the relationship of fiction to social issues.

Weltzian, O. Alan, ed. *The Literary Art and Activism of Rick Bass*. Salt Lake City: University of Utah Press, 2001. In this collection of critical essays on Bass's work, fifteen scholars discuss social, political, and personal issues in his fiction and nonfiction.

Edmund August
Updated by Charles E. May

RICHARD BAUSCH

Born: Fort Benning, Georgia; April 18, 1945

PRINCIPAL SHORT FICTION

Spirits, and Other Stories, 1987
The Fireman's Wife, and Other Stories, 1990
Rare and Endangered Species, 1994
Aren't You Happy for Me?, and Other Stories, 1995
The Selected Stories of Richard Bausch, 1996
Someone to Watch over Me: Stories, 1999
The Stories of Richard Bausch, 2003
Wives and Lovers, 2004
Something Is Out There, 2010

OTHER LITERARY FORMS

Richard Bausch (bowsch) has published more than a dozen novels, including *Take Me Back* (1981), which was nominated for a PEN/Faulkner Award. *The Last Good Time* (1984) was adapted for film in 1994. Bausch's other activities include editing *The Cry of an Occasion: Fiction from the Fellowship of Southern Writers* (2001) and coediting, with R. V. Cassill, the seventh edition of *The Norton Anthology of Short Fiction* (2006).

ACHIEVEMENTS

Richard Bausch's collection *Spirits, and Other Stories* was nominated for a PEN/Faulkner Award. His stories frequently appear in *New Stories from the South: The Year's Best* and in *The Best American Short Stories* series. Bausch received a National Endowment for the Arts grant in 1982 and a John Simon Guggenheim Memorial Foundation Fellowship in 1984. In 1992, he won the Lila Wallace-*Reader's Digest* Writers Award and in 1993 an American Academy of Arts and Letters Award in Literature. His collection *The Stories of Richard Bausch* won a PEN/Malamud Award in 2004.

BIOGRAPHY

Richard Carl Bausch was born April 18, 1945, in Fort Benning, Georgia, and he grew up in rural Virginia, outside Washington, D.C. After high school, he worked as a rock singer, songwriter, and comedian. From 1966 to 1969, he was a survival instructor in the United States Air Force. In 1969, he married Karen Miller, a photographer, and started a family. When he was twenty-five, Bausch entered George Mason University; he received his B.A. in 1974. With his wife and a new baby, he moved to Iowa, where he enrolled in the prestigious University of Iowa Writers' Workshop and in 1975 was awarded an M.F.A. When his works did not sell, Bausch began looking for a job. First he took a temporary position at George Mason University, and then he taught for two years at Northern Virginia Community College. Returning to George Mason, he eventually became a full professor of English and the holder of the Heritage Chair of Creative Writing. He then moved to the University of Memphis, where he held the Lillian and Morrie A. Moss Chair of Excellence. Bausch has also been a visiting professor at the University of Virginia-Charlottesville and at Wesleyan University.

ANALYSIS

The fact that Richard Ford wrote the introduction to Richard Bausch's first British collection of short stories indicates how closely Bausch is allied to such contemporary realists as Ford, Bobbie Ann Mason, and Raymond Carver. As critic Paul Elie explains in *Commonweal* (November 9, 1990), these writers have been nicknamed the "Dirty Realists" because they write about ordinary people whose lives have taken a turn for the worse and are not likely to get any better. The fiction of the Dirty Realists is all the more poignant because the characters are perceptive enough to see how little the future holds for them.

However, Bausch's Catholicism sets him apart from the other Dirty Realists. Where they see heartbreak and despair as simply a part of life, Bausch often views them as the product of sinful human nature. Over and over again, his characters distance themselves from one another. As a result, marriages end, families disintegrate, and individuals are left alone and desolate. "Wedlock," from *The Fireman's Wife, and Other Stories*, is about a relationship that dies after a day and a half. Once the new bride begins to view her husband objectively, rather than with the eyes of love, she first finds him ridiculous and then repulsive.

Some of Bausch's stories may be read as showing the operation of divine grace in human life, whether by prompting someone to plead the case for forgiveness, as Tom does in "The Brace," or by bringing people together in a new relationship, as in "The Billboard" from *Rare and Endangered Species*. Admittedly, in his short fiction Bausch seems much more certain about sin than he is about grace. In "Fatality," which appears in *The Stories of Richard Bausch*, a father kills his abusive son-in-law not in a fit of rage but after what he believes is a totally reasonable calculation. It is only after returning home that he realizes that he has put out of his reach all that makes his own life meaningful. Obviously, Bausch clearly believes that only by forgiving others can people make their own lives bearable.

"AREN'T YOU HAPPY FOR ME?"

The title work in Bausch's first British collection, which previously appeared in *Rare and Endangered Species*, is one of the author's most admired short stories. "Aren't You Happy for Me?" begins with a telephone call from Melanie Ballinger in Chicago to her parents in Charlottesville, Virginia, informing them that she is pregnant and that she plans to marry the man responsible, William Coombs, who was her college literature professor. Coombs is forty years older than Melanie and, as her father John points out rather nastily, old enough to be his father, rather than his son-in-law. While Melanie is talking to her mother Mary, John realizes that if he does not pretend to accept Melanie's decision, he will lose her, and he promises Melanie that he will work on his feelings. He never does tell her his own news: that Mary and he are getting a divorce. When out of habit John turns to Mary for comfort, he

discovers that he can no longer reach her. All John and Mary have left is the past; the best they can do is to remember how happy they were when Melanie was a toddler and they were as sure of their love as Melanie and William are of theirs. "Aren't You Happy for Me?" is typical of Bausch's short fiction both in its subject, the erosion of relationships, and in its bleak ending. While John may now have new insights about time, love, and loss, he is still left uncomforted.

"NOT QUITE FINAL"

In "Not Quite Final" from *Someone to Watch over Me*, the Ballingers get another chance. Evidently Melanie has forgiven her parents for not approving of her marriage. She has even persuaded William to move to Charlottesville because, as she puts it, their baby needs to become acquainted with her grandparents. On moving day, while Mary keeps the baby, John is helping Melanie haul furniture into her new apartment. William just watches; he is too arthritic to help. When she discovers that he also forgot to get the water turned on, Melanie becomes irritated. However, she insists that she knew what William was like when she married him, and their affection toward each other is no different from that of any other newlyweds. John is trying very hard to be tactful about his son-in-law. He slips only once, when he rebukes two young telephone installers for staring at Melanie. After they leave, William makes it clear that he did not need John's aid, and John feels impelled to apologize to William. Oddly, that incident seems to bring the two men closer to an understanding. Mary also appears to soften toward John. While taking care of her granddaughter, she admits, she thinks of how much she misses her husband, and the two embrace. Thus Bausch indicates that people who care enough can transcend their differences. If divine grace truly operates in this world, it may be by inspiring them to try.

"THE HARP DEPARTMENT IN LOVE"

From *Something Is Out There*, "The Harp Department in Love" also involves a young woman married to a much older man. The story is told from the perspective of Josephine Stanislowski, whose husband is John Stanislowski, or "Stan," a retired music professor. Stan is thirty years older than Josephine, who was once his student. The two have a close relationship, based on their mutual interests, their respect for each other as professionals, and their shared sense of humor, which is illustrated by his once introducing Josephine to campus visitors as "The Harp Department," a phrase that became his affectionate nickname for her. At the beginning of the story, however, Josephine is in tears because Stan has moved out. She had been foolish enough to become involved in a flirtation with Bradford Smith, a young man her age, and though the affair went no further than a single kiss, Bradford misinterpreted her feelings and informed John that Josephine had fallen in love with him. John hit Bradford, went home, packed up, and left. Alone in their house, Josephine realizes that Stan has given her the first emotional security she has ever known. Her life with him has been a stark contrast to her early years when, without a father, she trailed after her mother, a dancer, from one seedy nightclub to another. However, though Stan was recognized early as a musical genius, he has not been fortunate in his relationships with women. His first three marriages ended in divorce. That fact, along with his consciousness that he is no longer young, sent him into his marriage to Josephine fearing the worst, even though she did share his passion for music.

By the time Stan telephones her, Josephine is ready to tell him that she loves him and to beg him to come home. This time, the fates do seem to be against them, for when Stan arrives, Josephine is busy warding off the advances of a friend's husband, whom she had promised to delay until the preparations for his surprise party were complete. After she kicks out her would-be suitor, Josephine plays one of her songs, and Stan praises her. They have both expressed their love for each other, and they are back together, but as is customary in a Bausch story about marital love, even reconciliation does not guarantee the restoration of innocence.

"THE BRACE"

"The Brace," from *The Fireman's Wife, and Other Stories*, is narrated in the first person by a young wife and mother. She is worried because her father, a famous playwright, is on his way to visit them, and she fears a confrontation between him and her brother James, who is staying with them. James has hated his father ever since he portrayed their mother as a useful

but trivial woman in a play called "The Brace." The narrator, too, dislikes their father. Though she has spent her life trying to please him, she can never do so. He does not bother to hide his contempt for her husband Tom, a good but unsophisticated man, and their mundane life together. During this visit, however, it is the narrator who is inflexible. When her father attempts some explanation of his past conduct, she will not listen to him. Left alone, she suddenly imagines a time when her own son will treat her in the same way. She also realizes that when her father, her husband, and her brother spend the evening together, they will ignore their differences and connect in a way that excludes her. She now knows that there is no one to "brace" her, not even Tom. She is quite alone. In a *Publishers Weekly* interview that coincided with the publication of *The Fireman's Wife, and Other Stories*, Bausch identified "The Brace" as his favorite story in the collection, primarily, he says, because the narrator is so brave. It is not easy to face isolation or to anticipate the loss of love.

"VALOR"

Next to compassion for others, Bausch admires courage. The protagonist of "Valor," from *Someone to Watch over Me*, has both. A middle-aged shoe salesman with a domineering wife and a parasitical brother-in-law, Gabriel Aldenburg has come to Sam's bar for a little peace and quiet. Standing by the door, Aldenburg sees a Cadillac ram into a school bus. Immediately he rushes out, gets the driver to safety, then pulls the children out of the burning bus. When he gets home, no one wants to hear his story. His wife has her own announcement to make: She is moving out. When she refuses to watch the news report, Aldenburg becomes so angry that she feels a bit frightened. Realizing that he cannot reach her, he slips back into his usual insignificance. Though Aldenburg cannot impress his family, whether or not he will now have a higher opinion of himself is left an open question. Bausch's habit of ending his stories with some issue still unresolved is evidence of his commitment to realism. Life is rarely as neat as one would like it to be.

"TWO ALTERCATIONS"

"Two Altercations," from *The Stories of Richard Bausch*, is another story in which Bausch leaves the future to the reader's imagination. It begins at night, with a newly married woman lying awake, brooding about her husband and their future. Although the two of them seem to be living together in harmony, Ivy cannot help believing that Michael has a secret self, which he will not reveal even to his wife. She has begun to wonder about his feelings for her; she has even considered the possibility of his leaving her, perhaps for another woman. The next morning, Ivy tries to dismiss these anxieties from her consciousness. That evening, while Michael and Ivy are driving home from the university where both work, the traffic comes to a standstill, they see people fighting and hear gunshots, and a blood-covered man brushes against the passenger side window. Ivy takes cover on the seat and screams for Michael. When a policeman appears and helps her out of the car, she realizes that Michael had fled without her. After he reappears, he insists that he thought his wife was behind him, but the fact that he is still having trouble breathing makes it clear that he had panicked. Ivy now has an important decision to make. On one hand, she can accept his version of events, thus making it possible for Michael to remember the incident in the way that is most flattering to him; on the other hand, she can insist on the truth. She chooses the latter course. As a result, Michael is enraged, while Ivy, triumphant, foolishly assumes that the incident will be forgotten.

WIVES AND LOVERS

Wives and Lovers consists of three novellas. Two of them appeared in earlier collections of short stories; only "Requisite Kindness" had not been published previously. In an interview in *The Carolina Quarterly*, Bausch explained that he had meant originally to include the three works in his 2003 collection, but because of space considerations, it was decided to bring them out as a separate volume. The title "Requisite Kindness" is particularly appropriate. Although it begins with the bickering of a family gathered for a funeral, it ends as a moving statement of the redemptive power of simple kindness. The person who best illustrates this quality is Elena Townsend Hutton, who takes care of her grandsons when her son Henry leaves them to get drunk or to chase women or when his wife Lorraine takes to the bottle or perhaps takes her revenge by having a fling with another man. Ironically, after

thirty-five years of forgiving Henry and taking him back, Lorraine has finally left her husband. However, their sons are living out the pattern they learned from their parents. After the funeral, Elena's grandson Brian, who has lost four wives by cheating on them, is rejected for the same reason by a girl he had hoped to marry. As the section ends, he is weeping for himself and for his loss of the grandmother who always inspired him with hope.

The second section of "Requisite Kindness" is set six days earlier. After Lorraine walks out, Henry feels so lost that he leaves his own house and moves in with his mother and his sister Natalie. Elena is delighted to be taking care of her boy again, and Henry feels more secure than he has since he was a child. However, the day after Natalie has left on a vacation trip to California, Elena falls and breaks her shoulder. When she begs Henry to take her home from the hospital, he does so. Now for the first time in his life, Henry has to devote himself to someone else. As his mother approaches death, Henry tends to her with unfailing patience and consideration; his becomes almost a religious mission, and when Brian appears, his presence seems like an intrusion, a violation of a sacred trust. At the end of the novel, when Henry realizes that Elena is dead, it is as if a spell has broken. Now it becomes clear that the man who seemed so unpleasant in the first part of the novel honored his mother during her final days, exhibiting the selfless kindness that she had always insisted was the secret of a redemptive life.

OTHER MAJOR WORKS

LONG FICTION: *Real Presence*, 1980; *Take Me Back*, 1981; *The Last Good Time*, 1984; *Mr. Field's Daughter*, 1989; *Violence*, 1992; *Rebel Powers*, 1993; *Good Evening Mr. and Mrs. America, and All the Ships at Sea*, 1996; *In the Night Season*, 1998; *The Putt at the End of the World*, 2000 (with Lee K. Abbott, Dave Barry, Tim O'Brien, and others); *Hello to the Cannibals*, 2002; *Thanksgiving Night*, 2006; *Peace*, 2008.

POETRY: *Three Extremes: Poems and Prose*, 2009.

EDITED TEXTS: *The Cry of an Occasion: Fiction from the Fellowship of Southern Writers*, 2001; *The Norton Anthology of Short Fiction*, 2006 (with R. V. Cassill).

BIBLIOGRAPHY

Bausch, Richard. Interview with Art Taylor. *The Carolina Quarterly* 57, no. 1 (Winter, 2005): 69-76. The author comments at length on such matters as his approach to his craft, his thematic preoccupations, and his experiences both as a student and as a teacher in an M.F.A. program. An invaluable source.

Cahill, Thomas. "Fireworks Hidden and Deep." *Commonweal* 114 (October 9, 1987): 568-569. In this review of *Spirits, and Other Stories*, it is argued that Bausch's superb style and well-drawn characters will cause him to be remembered when more fashionable writers are forgotten. His preoccupation with fatherhood and "caring" is linked to the Catholic doctrine of the Real Presence.

Desmond, John F. "Catholicism in Contemporary American Fiction." *America* 170 (May 14, 1994): 7-11. Bausch is one of a number of fine Catholic writers who, avoiding "sentimentality and easy dogmatism," show their characters facing very real evils, which they can survive only with the aid of divine grace.

Greenya, John. "Tales of Virginia and Winter Dread." *The Washington Times*, March 12, 2010, p. B07. A review of *Something Is Out There*, praising the author for the "deceptively simple" style in which he dramatizes the unhappiness of his characters but nevertheless suggests that, like those of William Faulkner, they will "endure."

Pesetsky, Bette. "Quarrels over Who Said What and When." *The New York Times Book Review*, August 19, 1990, p. 9. Insists that though Bausch's characters are often called ordinary, they are unusual in their intelligence and in their yearning for meaning. Seven of the stories in *The Fireman's Wife, and Other Stories* are discussed in terms of a common theme, "redemption through understanding."

Russo, Maria. "In Richard Bausch's Stories, Peril and Temptation." *The New York Times Book Review*, February 28, 2010, p. 5. The stories in *Something Is Out There"* reflect the dangers of free will. "The Harp Department in Love" and "Sixty-Five Million Years" are discussed at length.

Shields, Carol. "The Life You Lead May Be Your Own." *The New York Times Book Review*, August 14, 1994, p. 6. Ignoring the literary fashions of the 1970's and the 1980's, Bausch has continued to write realistic domestic fiction. Again in *Rare and Endangered Species*, various relationships, including marriages, are threatened by change, betrayal, and sheer boredom, and yet his characters try valiantly to remain true to each other and to their own best selves.

Written and updated by
Rosemary M. Canfield Reisman

Charles Baxter

Born: Minneapolis, Minnesota; May 13, 1947

Principal short fiction

Harmony of the World, 1984
Through the Safety Net, 1985
A Relative Stranger, 1990
Believers: A Novella and Stories, 1997
Gryphon: New and Selected Stories, 2011

Other literary forms

Charles Baxter has written the novels *First Light* (1987), *Shadow Play* (1993), *The Feast of Love* (2000), *Saul and Patsy* (2003), and *The Soul Thief* (2008), as well as the collection of poetry *Imaginary Paintings, and Other Poems* (1989). In addition, Baxter writes fine literary nonfiction, including his essays on imagination and daily life collected in *Burning Down the House: Essays on Fiction* (1997) and in *The Art of Subtext: Beyond Plot* (2007). He has also edited a number of volumes, such as a collection of essays by creative writers, *The Business of Memory: The Art of Remembering in an Age of Forgetting* (1999), and the fiction collection *Best New American Voices 2001* (2001).

Achievements

Editors consistently select Charles Baxter's stories for the annual *The Best American Short Stories,* *The Pushcart Prize,* and *Prize Stories: The O. Henry Awards.* He won the Associated Writing Programs Award in 1984 for his first collection of fiction and has been awarded National Endowment for the Arts and Lila Wallace-*Reader's Digest* Fund grants, as well as a John Simon Guggenheim Memorial Fellowship. In 1997, the American Academy of Arts and Letters bestowed the Award in Literature on him, and in 2000 his novel *The Feast of Love* was a finalist for the National Book Award. His list of honors also includes a Lawrence Foundation Award, Michigan Author of the Year Award, and a *Harvard Review* award.

Biography

Charles Morley Baxter was born in Minneapolis, Minnesota, on May 13, 1947. He attended Macalester College in St. Paul, Minnesota, earning his bachelor's degree in 1969. Baxter published his first book of poetry in 1970. After teaching high school English in the small town of Pinconning, Michigan, during 1969-1970, he began graduate work at the State University of New York at Buffalo, completing a Ph.D. in 1974, the same year he published his poetry collection *The South Dakota Guidebook.* He returned to Michigan to teach at Wayne State University in Detroit in 1974. In July, 1976, he married Martha Ann Hauser, a teacher. At Wayne State, Baxter moved through the ranks, achieving full professorship in 1985.

In 1984, Baxter published his first collection of short stories, *Harmony of the World,* for which he received both the Associated Writing Programs Award and the Lawrence Foundation Award. The following year, he published his second collection of short stories, *Through the Safety Net,* followed by his novel *First Light* in 1987. In 1989, Baxter left Wayne State to begin teaching at the University of Michigan at Ann Arbor. He also began teaching in the Warren Wilson writing program in 1986.

During the 1990's, Baxter continued to regularly contribute literary criticism and short stories to a host of literary journals of the highest quality, including *Prairie Schooner, Michigan Quarterly,* and *Minnesota Review,* a journal he had edited in 1967-1969. During the same decade, he published two collections of short fiction (*A Relative Stranger* and *Believers*) and the novel *Shadow Play.* His short story "Gryphon" was adapted as a television special for middle-schoolers, with the usual significant changes to plot and setting, in 1998; the program was broadcast as a part of the Public Television Service's (PBS) *Wonderworks* series.

Although Baxter's fiction had won plaudits and readers from his earliest works, his novel *The Feast of Love* was his breakout book. A recasting of *A Midsummer Night's Dream*, the intricate story weaves together various people's experiences in love and life. The book was nominated for a National Book Award and adapted for a film released in 2007, directed by Robert Benton and starring Morgan Freeman and Greg Kinnear.

In 2003, Baxter published *Saul and Patsy*, a novel-length expansion of his short-story chronicles of a bemused married couple in a small Michigan town. Like *The Feast of Love*, critics observed that the novel has a patchwork feel, like a series of short stories packed together, less linear than a novel, but perhaps more true to life than a more straightforward plot. In the same year, Baxter was appointed the Edelstein-Keller Chair in Creative Writing at the University of Minnesota. Baxter returned to the short-fiction form in a group of stories collected in *Gryphon: New and Selected Stories*.

ANALYSIS

The stories in Charles Baxter's collections are internally linked by theme, image, and motif. The title story in each collection suggests thematic ties to other stories in the collection. As a musician composes a symphony, building variations around an initial theme, Baxter works and reworks, connecting ideas in multiple ways. While some stories seem more closely linked than others, taken as a whole, each collection says something different about the human experience.

For example, in *Harmony of the World*, a number of stories concern music, musicians, or artists. Thematically, Baxter plays with notions of harmony and discord and the way these notions play out in human relationships. Likewise, in *A Relative Stranger*, Baxter explores both the relatedness of strangers and the strangeness of relatives. In these stories he seems to tell the reader that no matter how different or far apart people are, they are nonetheless connected. Conversely, he also demonstrates in these stories that no

matter how closely related people may be, they still have to live their lives alone in their skins. Finally, in *Believers*, an especially fine collection, Baxter meditates on the relationship between belief and truth. He demonstrates in these stories both how belief can change the perception of truth and how truth can impact belief.

Baxter accomplishes these sophisticated linkages through the invention of characters who are both varied and individual, rich and self-contradictory. Baxter develops these characters by offering snapshots of their lives, brief still shots revealing where each is located in the moment of the story. Like real people, they are not all one way or another; rather, they are a complicated stew of thoroughly human qualities.

HARMONY OF THE WORLD

Baxter's first collection of short stories, published in 1984, met with strong and favorable reviews. The title of the collection is ironic; the ten stories focus not on harmony but on discord and tricks of fate. The characters in the stories (many of them musicians, a further irony) fail to establish harmonious relationships with

Charles Baxter (AP Photo/Hannah Foslien)

other people. Moreover, they do not realize that they are out of harmony with themselves and the culture. Although often mediocre in talent and intellect, they demand perfection in others, as if the harmony they seek can be found outside themselves. For example, the title story, "Harmony of the World," is taken from an opera by Paul Hindemith, a composition that music critics generally consider a failure. Likewise, the main character is a music reviewer, a failed concert pianist who has settled for passing judgment on the music of others rather than on creating music himself. He breaks off a relationship with a singer because she, too, is mediocre. The story, included in *The Best American Short Stories 1982*, reveals Baxter's strong sense of character, dialogue, and detail.

A RELATIVE STRANGER

Critics often cite "Fensted's Mother" as one of Baxter's best stories. It first appeared in *The Atlantic Monthly*, and noted writer Margaret Atwood chose it for inclusion in *The Best American Short Stories 1989*. The opening story in Baxter's collection, it takes as its subject Fensted, a publicist for a computer company, and his aging mother, a socially progressive atheist. Fensted, who attends church regularly, invites his mother to attend the English composition class he teaches at night school. She is a great hit, siding with Fensted's students in a discussion of the logical inconsistency of the sentence "I, like most people, have a unique problem." Fensted wants to talk about logic; the students, egged on by his mother, want to talk about problems. Although closely related, Fensted and his mother seem unable to speak the same language. In spite of their obvious love for each other, they remain relative strangers.

The title story of the collection, "A Relative Stranger," expands the theme explored in "Fensted's Mother." Baxter seems to be asking: What does it mean to be related to someone else? In this story, a middle-aged man, Oliver, suddenly discovers that he has a brother, Kurt. Although Oliver knew that he had been adopted as an infant, he did not realize that he had a sibling. Kurt chooses to contact Oliver at a time when Oliver's wife has left him and his life is a mess. Kurt, on the other hand, is a successful businessman. The meeting between the brothers does not go as planned.

Although related, the two are strangers to each other. Baxter carefully reveals the odd sense of familiarity and strangeness Oliver feels. After Oliver punches Kurt in a bar, the two establish a relationship that is, while not close, brotherly. Through this story, Baxter once again demonstrates that fraternity does not guarantee compatibility. Although the two brothers struggle to understand each other, like Fensted and his mother, they speak different languages.

BELIEVERS

Baxter's 1997 collection contains seven stories and a novella and represents some of his finest work. The characters in *Believers* struggle with issues of truth and belief and the conflict such issues often produce. The range of characters in this collection seems wider than in his earlier work, and the believers in the stories include a young woman who believes she is in love, a man who believes that his former wife waves to him to cross a flooded river, a group of friends who believe they know one another well, and a former priest who loses his belief on a trip to Nazi Germany. Although the stories in *Believers* are about faith and truth, and although the stories carry religious imagery and theological undertones, they do not close with epiphanies. In his book of essays on fiction, *Burning Down the House*, Baxter includes a whole chapter, "Against Epiphanies," in which he argues that too much contemporary fiction depends on the epiphanic ending. Baxter's stories do not provide characters who arrive at some important insight in the closing paragraphs. Rather, the stories end as they have grown, moving toward inevitable yet complicated and ambiguous endings, endings that seem to point to some truth hidden somewhere just under the surface.

Believers is the novella that gives the collection its name and establishes a number of important thematic concerns. Jack Pielke narrates the story, trying to piece together the fragments of his father's life in order to arrive at the truth. Issues of belief are strong in the story. Jack's father Franz, the son of German immigrants, was a former Catholic priest, a man who believed profoundly in God and God's creation until a trip to Nazi Germany with a jaded American couple irreversibly changed him. Jack is the quintessential researcher, supplying genealogical background, interviewing everyone who knew his father, hounding his mother for details about their union. The one person who could perhaps help him the most is mute: Franz Pielke, a stroke victim, has not spoken for more than two years. Jack's struggle, then, is to give voice to his father's life. He believes a careful reconstruction of that life will reveal some sort of truth. Jack wants to understand his father, his rejection of the priesthood, his marriage to his mother, and his fatherhood. Most of all, he wants to know what happened to his father's faith and what both the gift and the loss of that faith have cost him. What Jack discovers, however, is that like all lives, his father's is more than the sum of its parts, and that all he, Jack, can render is a textual reconstruction of lived experience, not the truth at all.

GRYPHON

Gryphon is a collection of twenty-three stories, a number of which have been published before, such as "Harmony of the World" and the much-anthologized "Fensted's Mother." The popular title story, "Gryphon," first appeared in Baxter's collection *Through the Safety Net*. It concerns a fourth-grade substitute teacher in Baxter's legendary town of Five Oaks, Michigan. Miss Ferenczi has a different relationship to truth than most fourth-grade teachers, telling her students that six times eleven is sixty-eight "when I am in the room," explaining that pyramids focus cosmic energy, and informing them that she has seen a gryphon in a cage. She may be making facts up, she may be expanding her students' imaginations, or the story may be a complex amalgam of both these things. Baxter has said that the story is based on his own experience teaching in Michigan.

Other stories in the collection bear relationship to classic works of short fiction. "Horace and Margaret's Fifty-Second," for instance, features a couple and a story line with strong resemblances to Vladimir Nabokov's famous story "Signs and Symbols." In Baxter's telling, the couple, now in old age, are losing their memories and their grip on meaning. As is usual with Baxter's fiction, even the material that might be depressing in the hands of other writers is presented with gentleness and insight, making his stories a meditation on rather than a condemnation of the human condition.

OTHER MAJOR WORKS

LONG FICTION: *First Light*, 1987; *Shadow Play: A Novel*, 1993; *The Feast of Love*, 2000; *Saul and Patsy*, 2003; *The Soul Thief*, 2008.

POETRY: *Chameleon*, 1970; *The South Dakota Guidebook*, 1974; *Imaginary Paintings, and Other Poems*, 1989.

NONFICTION: *Burning Down the House: Essays on Fiction*, 1997; *The Art of Subtext: Beyond Plot*, 2007.

EDITED TEXTS: *The Business of Memory: The Art of Remembering in an Age of Forgetting*, 1999; *Best New American Voices 2001*, 2001(with John Kukla and Natalie Danford); *Bringing the Devil to His Knees: The Craft of Fiction and the Writing Life*, 2001 (with Peter Turchi); *A William Maxwell Portrait: Memories and Appreciations*, 2004 (with Michael Collier and Edward Hirsch).

BIBLIOGRAPHY

_____. "An Interview with Charles Baxter." Interview by Kevin Breen. *Poets and Writers* 22 (September, 1994): 60. An interview focusing on Baxter's creation of characters. Especially useful for fiction writers trying to refine their craft.

Baxter, Charles. *Burning Down the House: Essays on Fiction*. St. Paul, Minn.: Graywolf Press, 1997. In nine essays, written with humor, insight, and care, Baxter explores the relationship between imagination and daily life, the way characters develop, and his ideas about fiction. An important collection for anyone who wants to know more about Baxter and his art.

Gelfant, Blanche H., ed. *The Columbia Companion to the Twentieth-Century American Short Story*. New York: Columbia University Press, 2000. Includes a chapter in which Baxter's short stories are analyzed.

Griffiths, Sarah, and Kevin J. Kehrwald. *Delicious Imaginations: Conversations with Contemporary Writers*. West Lafayette, Ind.: NotaBell Books, 1998. Provides a chapter-length interview with Baxter, who shares his ideas about the writing of fiction. Other chapters include interviews with such important contemporary writers as Larry Brown, Rick Bass, and Robert Olen Butler.

Lee, Don. "About Charles Baxter." *Ploughshares* 25, nos. 2/3 (1999), 210-217. Baxter discusses his life, difficulty writing novels, *Saul and Patsy*, and the enchantments of the ordinary. Online at http://www.pshares.org/read/article-detail.cfm?intArticleID=4709.

McSpadden, Marsha, and Trevor Gore. "A Conversation with Charles Baxter." *Missouri Review* 31, no. 1 (2008): 100-110. An interview about *The Soul Thief*, the current state of the short story, and Baxter's views on fiction.

Reinsmith, William A., "'Gryphon': Taming the Fabulous Beast." *Eureka Studies in Teaching Short Fiction* 5 (2004): 140-146. Provides approaches to and analysis of one of Baxter's most popular stories.

Van Wert, William F. "Charles Baxter and the Rites of Fiction." *Michigan Quarterly Review* 38 (Winter, 1999): 135-143. A review of *Believers* and *Burning Down the House* offering close and convincing analyses of "Flood Show," "Kiss Away," "Reincarnation," and "Saul and Patsy Are in Labor," as well as examining some of the features of fiction Baxter explores in his book of essays.

Winans, Molly. "Bigger Than We Think: The World Revealed in Charles Baxter's Fiction." *Commonweal* 124 (November 7, 1997): 12-16. Argues that Baxter's best work is his short fiction, a genre that allows him to develop interesting characters and small truths in the exploration of the ordinary. Compares Baxter to other short-story writers, such as Frank O'Connor and Flannery O'Connor. Suggests that Baxter's stories can be discussed in "theological terms," including forgiveness, sin, and faith.

Diane Andrews Henningfeld
Updated by Martha Bayless

ANN BEATTIE

Born: Washington, D.C.; September 8, 1947

PRINCIPAL SHORT FICTION

Distortions, 1976
Secrets and Surprises, 1978
Jacklighting, 1981
The Burning House, 1982
Where You'll Find Me, and Other Stories, 1986
What Was Mine, and Other Stories, 1991
Park City: New and Selected Stories, 1998
Perfect Recall: New Stories, 2001
Follies: New Stories, 2005

OTHER LITERARY FORMS

Ann Beattie (BEE-tee) is best known for her short stories, particularly those that first appeared in *The New Yorker*, but she has also written several novels. The first, *Chilly Scenes of Winter* (1976), appeared simultaneously with *Distortions*, a rare occurrence in the publishing world, especially for a first-time author. Her second novel, *Falling in Place* (1980), is her most ambitious and her best. In *Love Always* (1985), she uses an approach that is close to that of her short stories. The subject matter is narrower, and the characters are distanced from the narrative voice. Her novel *Picturing Will* was published in 1989. In 1986 and 1987, she worked on her first nonfiction project, the text to accompany a monograph containing twenty-six color plates of the paintings of Alex Katz. *My Life, Starring Dara Falcon* (1997) has been criticized as weak; *The New York Times* called it an "ill-conceived experiment" that "must surely mark a low point" in her career.

ACHIEVEMENTS

Ann Beattie has been called the most imitated short-story writer in the United States, an amazing claim for a woman whose publishing career began in the 1970's. Along with such writers as Raymond Carver, she is a premier practitioner of minimalism, the school of fiction writing that John Barth has characterized as "less is more." In 1977, she was named Briggs-Copeland Lecturer in English at Harvard University, where she apparently was uncomfortable. She used a John Simon Guggenheim Memorial Foundation grant to leave Harvard and move back to Connecticut, where she had attended graduate school. In 1980, she received an award of excellence from the American Academy of Arts and Letters and a Distinguished Alumnae Award from American University. In 1992, she was elected to the American Academy and Institute of Arts and Letters.

BIOGRAPHY

Born on September 8, 1947, Ann Beattie grew up with television, rock music, and the other accouterments of the baby boomers. The child of a retired U.S. Health, Education, and Welfare Department administrator, Beattie took a B.A. in English at American University in 1969 and completed her M.A. at the University of Connecticut in 1970. She began, but did not complete, work on her Ph.D. In 1972, she married David Gates, a writer for *Newsweek* and a singer. Together they had one son. Later, they divorced. Before her appointment at Harvard, Beattie taught at the University of Virginia, Charlottesville. After living in the Connecticut suburbs and in New York City, she returned to Charlottesville and the university in 1985. She appeared as a waitress in the film version of *Chilly Scenes of Winter* (1979) and, after her divorce, was named one of the most eligible single women in America. In 1985, Beattie met painter Lincoln Perry, whom she later married. The couple lived for a time in Charlottesville. Later, Beattie and Perry settled in a turn-of-the-century farmhouse in York, Maine, one of America's oldest cities. Beattie says she does not go to book-publishing parties, does not know many writers, has an unlisted phone number, and shies away from writers' colonies.

ANALYSIS

Ann Beattie has been called the spokesperson for a new lost generation, an Ernest Hemingway for those who came of age during the 1960's and 1970's. Many of her themes and much about her style support the assertion that she, like Hemingway, voices a pervasive and universal feeling of despair and alienation, a lament for lost values and fading chances for constructive action. However, to limit one's understanding of Beattie's work to this narrow interpretation is a mistake.

Beattie shares much with writers such as Jane Austen, who portrayed ironically the manners and social customs of her era, and with psychological realists such as Henry James, who delved into the meanings behind the subtle nuances of character and conflict. Beattie's primary themes are loneliness and friendship, family life, love and death, materialism, art, and, for want of a better term, the contemporary scene. Her short fiction tends to be spare and straightforward. Her vocabulary and her sentence structure are quite accessible, or minimalist, to use a literary label. Even when the stories contain symbols, their use is most often direct and self-reflexive.

Beattie's combination of subject matter and style leads to a rather flat rendering of the world, and Beattie is sometimes criticized for that flatness. Because her narrators usually maintain a significant distance from the stories and their characters, critics and readers sometimes assume that Beattie is advocating such remove and reserve as the most feasible posture in contemporary life. Even her most ironic characters and narrative voices, however, experience a profound longing for a different world. Despite the ennui that dominates the texture of their lives, Beattie's characters hold on to the hope of renewal and redemption, often with great fierceness, which frequently suggests that these people, clutching at hope so hard, are white-knuckling their way through life. If members of the generation about which she writes are indeed lost, they have not accepted their condition, even though they recognize it. They are still searching for the way out, for a place in which to find themselves or to be found.

"DWARF HOUSE"

"Dwarf House," the first story in *Distortions*, establishes an interest in the grotesque, the bizarre, and the slightly askew that surfaces several times in this first of Beattie's collections. The main characters of the story are James and MacDonald, brothers who struggle to find understanding and respect for each other and to deal with their possessive and intrusive mother. Because James, the older of the two, is a dwarf, Beattie immediately plays upon the collection's title and places the story beyond the plane of realism.

The irony of the story develops as the reader realizes that MacDonald's supposedly normal life is as distorted as the life of his sibling. When MacDonald goes to visit James in the dwarf house where James lives, along with several other dwarfs and one giant, MacDonald finds himself repulsed by the foreign environment. However, when he gets home, he cannot face his own "normal" world without his martinis. He is as alienated and isolated at home and at work as he would be if he were a dwarf. Beattie uses the ludicrous--the exaggerated scenario of James's life, complete with his wedding to a fellow dwarf, conducted by a hippie minister and culminating in the releasing of a caged parrot as a symbol of hope and the new freedom of married life--to bring into focus the less obvious distortions of regular American life.

MacDonald is typical of many Beattie characters. He is relatively young--in his late twenties--and well educated. He works, but his work provides little challenge or stimulation. He has enough money to live as he wants, but he struggles to define what it is he does want. His wife is his equal--young, well educated, hip--but they have little to talk about.

Ann Beattie (The Washington Times /Landov)

MacDonald wants to make his brother's life more normal--that is, get him out of the dwarf house, the one place where James always has been happy, and back into their mother's home, where James and MacDonald will both be miserable. MacDonald is motivated not by malice toward James but by an overdeveloped sense of guilt and responsibility toward his mother, a trait he shares with many of Beattie's young male characters. By the story's end, the reader cannot say who is better off: James, whose life is distorted but productive and satisfying to him, or MacDonald, who has everything a man could want but still lacks an understanding of what it is he should do with what he has.

"THE LIFEGUARD"

In "The Lifeguard," the final story in *Distortions*, Beattie portrays the offbeat and grotesque elements that permeate the collection in a sharply realistic setting, where their humor and irony disappear. The impact of these elements is, then, all the more forceful for the reader's sense of sudden dislocation. Without warning, the book becomes too real for comfort, and at the same time it continues to use shades of the unreal to make its point.

"The Lifeguard" tells the story of the Warner family and their summer vacation. The mother, Toby, finds herself fantasizing about the young college student who is the lifeguard on the beach. However, when her children Penelope and Andrew die in a boat deliberately set afire by their playmate Duncan Collins, the incapacity of the lifeguard and the inappropriateness of her infatuation are too vividly brought home to Toby. The monstrousness of Collins's action is but another kind of distortion; there are no simple lives in a distorted world.

"A VINTAGE THUNDERBIRD"

If *Distortions* emphasizes the outward manifestations of the disordered contemporary world, *Secrets and Surprises*, the second collection, turns inward, as its title suggests. "A Vintage Thunderbird" features a woman who comes to New York to have an abortion against the wishes of her husband. The friends to whom she turns, Karen and Nick, have their own problems in love. By mirroring the sense of loss that follows the abortion with the sense of loss felt by Karen and Nick when she sells the vintage car of the title,

Beattie addresses the connection between spiritual and emotional needs and material needs.

Very few of the people in Beattie's fiction suffer for want of material goods; almost all suffer from lack of spiritual and emotional fulfillment. The interesting aspect of this dichotomy is that the characters do not, as a rule, actively pursue material well-being. Their money is often inherited, as are their houses and many of their other possessions. The main character in "Shifting," for example, inherits an old Volvo from an uncle with whom she was never very close. The money earned by these characters is almost always earned halfheartedly, without conspicuous ambition or enthusiasm. They are not yuppies, who have substituted acquisition for all human emotion. They are people who, by accident of birth or circumstance, have not had to acquire material wealth; for whatever reason, wealth comes to them.

What does not come is peace, satisfaction, and contentment. When a material object does provide emotional pleasure, as the Thunderbird does for Karen and Nick, Beattie's characters tend to confuse the emotion with the symbol and to conclude, erroneously, that ridding themselves of the object will also rid them of the gnawing doubts that seem to accompany contentment and satisfaction. It is sometimes as frightening, Beattie seems to suggest, to be attached to things as to people.

"THE CINDERELLA WALTZ"

In *The Burning House*, Beattie's third collection, she turns to the dark, richly textured veins of her standard subject matter to produce stories that are less humorous but more humane, less ironic but wiser than those in the earlier collections. Infidelity, divorce, love gone bad--all standard Beattie themes--are connected to parenthood and its attendant responsibilities, to homosexuality, to death, and to birth defects. The affairs and the abortions that were entered into, if not concluded, with a "me-generation" bravado suddenly collide with more traditional values and goals.

Many of Beattie's characters, both married and single, have lovers. In fact, having a lover or having had one at some time during a marriage is almost standard. In "The Cinderella Waltz," Beattie adds a further complication to the de rigueur extramarital affair by making the husband's lover a male. However, in much the same way that she makes the unusual work in a

story such as "Dwarf House," Beattie manages to make this story more about the pain and suffering of the people involved than about the nontraditional quality of the love relationship.

The wife in "The Cinderella Waltz," left to understand what has happened to her marriage and to help her young daughter to reach her own understanding, finds herself drawn into a quiet, resigned acceptance of her husband's relationship with his lover. She laments the loss of innocence in the world, for her child and for them all, but she chooses to go forward with the two men as part of her life and the child's. She rejects--really never even considers--the negative, destructive responses that many women would have.

"The Cinderella Waltz" ends with images of enormous fragility--glass elevators and glass slippers. They are images that her characters embrace and cling to, recognizing that fragile hope is better than none. The cautious nature of such optimism is often mistaken for pessimism in Beattie's work, but her intention is clearly as affirmative as it is tentative.

"WINTER: 1978"

Another story from *The Burning House*, "Winter: 1978," offers a glimpse of most of Beattie's concerns and techniques. An unusually long story for Beattie, "Winter: 1978" features a selfish mother who is hosting a wake for her younger son, who has drowned in a mid-winter boating accident. His death is mystifying, for there were life preservers floating easily within his reach, a fact that suggests the ultimate despair and surrender often present in Beattie's characters. An older son blames the mother for placing too much guilt and responsibility on the dead son, but the older son has done nothing to assume some of that burden. The older son's former wife, their child, his current girlfriend, and his best friend are all present at the wake. The best friend's girlfriend is alone back in California, having her uterus cauterized. His former wife seems inordinately grief-stricken until it is revealed that the dead man was her lover. During the course of the wake, which lasts several days, she becomes the lover of her former husband's best friend.

This extremely baroque and convoluted situation contains much that is ironically humorous, but also it reflects deep pain on the part of all the characters, not only the pain of having lost a loved one but also the pain of reexamining their own lives and measuring them against the idea of death. That sort of existential questioning, rarely overt but frequently suggested, contributes to the idea of a lost generation brought to life on the pages of Beattie's fiction.

However, Beattie rarely leaves her characters in perpetual existential angst, as is the case in a Hemingway story, such as "A Clean, Well-Lighted Place," an embodiment of the existential despair and the longing for some minute, self-created order and refuge typical of the original literary lost generation. Instead, Beattie often opts for a neo-Romantic, minimalist version of hope and redemption, of continued searching as opposed to acquiescence.

"Winter: 1978" concludes with the absentee father, the surviving son, taking his child upstairs for a bedtime story. The little boy, like the daughter in "The Cinderella Waltz," is far too wise to take comfort from the imaginary world of the story; he has been exposed to far too much of the confused adult world of his parents. On this occasion, however, he pretends to believe, and he encourages his father's tale about the evolution of deer. According to the story, deer have such sad eyes because they were once dinosaurs and cannot escape the sadness that comes with having once been something else.

This story serves as a metaphor for the melancholy cast of characters in this and Beattie's other collections of short fiction. Almost all of her characters have a Keatsian longing to connect with a better, more sublime existence that seems to be part of their generational collective consciousness. Far too aware and too ironic to follow the feeling and thereby to transcend reality, they linger in their unsatisfactory lesser world and struggle to accommodate their longing to their reality.

"Snow"

More than her other collections, *Where You'll Find Me* displays Beattie's awareness of her reputation as a writer. In particular, in a story called "Snow," she appears to write a definition of the kind of story her work has come to define. Less than three pages long, the story takes a single

image, that of snow, and uses it not only as a symbol of the lost love the narrator is contemplating but also as a metaphor for storytelling as practiced by the author.

The remembered lover explained to the narrator at one point that "any life will seem dramatic if you omit mention of most of it." The narrator then tells a story, actually one paragraph within this story, about her return to the place where the lovers had lived in order to be with a dying friend. She offers her story-within-the-story as an example of the way in which her lover said stories should be told.

The narrator goes on to say that such efforts are futile, bare bones without a pattern to establish meaning. For her, the single image--snow, in this case--does more to evoke the experience of her life with the man than does the dramatized story with the details omitted. In the story's final paragraph, the narrator concludes that even the single image is too complex for complete comprehension. The mind, let alone the narratives it creates, is incapable of fully rendering human experience and emotion. The best a writer, a storyteller, can do is to present the essence of the experience in the concrete terms in which his or her consciousness has recorded it.

What the reader inevitably receives, then, is minimal, to return to John Barth's theory. It is equally important, however, that Barth argues that the minimal can be more than enough. The characters in this collection are generally older and wiser than their predecessors. They have, as a rule, survived an enormous loss and are still hoping for a richer, more rewarding life or at least one in which they feel less out of place and alone.

"Janus"

Andrea, the real-estate agent who is the main character of "Janus," is typical. Safely married to a husband who is interesting and financially secure, she is also successful in her career. The two of them take great pleasure in the things that they have accumulated. However, Andrea takes most pleasure in a relatively inexpensive and quite ordinary-looking ceramic bowl, a gift from a former lover who had asked her to change her life, to live with him.

Although she has long since turned him down, Andrea finds herself growing increasingly obsessed with the bowl. She begins to believe that all of her career success comes from the bowl's being precisely placed in the homes that she shows to her clients. A mystery to her, the bowl seems to be connected to the most real, the most private parts of herself. She loves the bowl as she loves nothing else.

She fears for its safety. She is terrified at the thought that it might disappear. She has lost the chance that the lover represented, choosing instead stasis and comfort, remaining intransigent about honoring her previous commitments. Sometimes she goes into her living room late at night and sits alone, contemplating the bowl. She thinks, "In its way, it was perfect; the world cut in half, deep and smoothly empty."

Such is the world that Beattie observes, but Beattie is, after all, an artist, not a real-estate agent. All that Andrea can do is contemplate. Beattie can fill the bowl, to use a metaphor, with whatever she chooses. She can capture, again and again, the story behind the "one small flash of blue, a vanishing point on the horizon," that Andrea can only watch disappear.

Barth's description of the impulse behind minimalism, the desire "to strip away the superfluous in order to reveal the necessary, the essential," is a fair assessment of Beattie's work. However, it is equally important to recall what necessary and essential elements remain after the superfluous has been stripped away. They are love, friendship, family, children, music, and creativity. Beattie fills the bowl of her fiction with much the same fruits that other writers have used.

"WINDY DAY AT THE RESERVOIR"

In contrast to her earlier, so-called minimalist stories, Beattie's later short fictions seem to be moving toward length and elaboration, making more use of novelistic techniques of character exploration and realistic detail. "Windy Day at the Reservoir," the longest story in her collection *What Was Mine*, focuses on two people who, while house-sitting for another couple, make a number of discoveries both about the homeowners and about themselves--for example, about the vacationing couple's impending breakup because of the wife's mastectomy and their own inability to have

children. The point of view moves from the house-sitting husband, to the wife, to the mentally disabled son of the housekeeper, who walks into the reservoir and drowns. The final section focuses on the housekeeper, who provides a novelistic resolution to the two couples, who both break up. Ending with a realistic resolution rather than a metaphoric embodiment of conflict, the story reflects Beattie's moving away from short-story techniques to novelistic devices.

"GOING HOME WITH UCCELLO" AND "PARK CITY"

A clear contrast between short-story and novelistic technique can be seen in the difference between two of the eight stories in Beattie's collection of selected stories, *Park City*: "Going Home with Uccello" and the title story "Park City." In the former, a woman on a trip to Italy with her boyfriend has a realization about why he has taken her there when he flirts with a Frenchwoman about an Paolo Uccello painting. The woman understands that he has taken her to Italy not to persuade her to join him in London forever but to persuade himself that he loves her so much that no other woman can come between them. The story ends in a typical Beattie ambiguity about whether the man in the story can commit himself to a relationship or whether he is continuing, as so many of Beattie's male characters do, to look for some ineffable dream.

In "Park City," the central character spends a week at a Utah ski resort during the off-season looking after her half-sister's daughter, Nell, who is three, and her half-sister's boyfriend's daughter, Lyric, who is fourteen. The story is filled with dialogue among the three females in which it seems increasingly clear that the woman is more naïve than the precocious fourteen-year-old. In one particular encounter, the girl spins out a long invented tale to a stranger about having had breast implants. The story ends when the central character tries to get on a ski lift with the child Nell and the two almost fall off. They are saved by a man who, significantly, tells her, "the one thing you've got to remember next time is to request a slow start."

FOLLIES: NEW STORIES

Follies: New Stories is made up of nine short and one much longer story, that being the book's first, "Fléchette Follies." As is so often the case with Beattie, the title comes directly from the text of the story.

George Wissone, an operative of the Central Intelligence Agency, or some secret government agency, is thinking about the land mines he had to avoid on one of his missions. When stepped on, they send out fléchettes, shrapnel fragments, causing a chain reaction. "Fléchette Follies" is a story of a chain reaction. George (his real name is Lawrence Krebs, and he is known also by several other aliases) is involved in a minor automobile accident with Nancy Gregerson, employee of a Charlottesville, Virginia, nursing home. Her drug-addicted son, Nicky, has gone missing in London. George's job has been, along with his friend and associate, Rich O'Malley, snatching children who are in miserable situations in uncooperative foreign countries and spiriting them back to the United States. George's lover, Paula, is living in Los Angeles and has decided to break off their relationship. George agrees, for reasons unclear even to himself, to find Nicky for Nancy. Ironies abound. In London, George, who has survived many dangerous missions during his career, is run over and killed by a minicab outside the Chinese restaurant where he has found Nicky working. This accident is the distorted mirror image of the one that opens the story. Paula decides that she wants George back but does not know where he is. Rich and his wife, Linda, are desperately searching for the searcher, who has disappeared. Rich cannot believe Nancy's story that she has no idea where George has gone, but she hires another private investigator to find Nicky. The story has no denouement. The chain reaction goes on beyond the last sentence, just as in real life.

The narrative point of view is first person in half the stories, a limited, and sometimes shifting, third person in the other half. Relationships--filial, romantic, and professional--are often strained or ambiguous. In "Find and Replace," the daughter-protagonist cannot dissuade her mother from marrying an unsuitable man. In "Duchais," the student-protagonist learns that his job as Professor Duchais's assistant is really that of a body servant to the eccentric professor, his drunken mother, and her religious-fanatic driver. "Tending Something" is the story of an unsatisfactory surprise birthday party and its even worse aftermath. "Mostre" is the twin stories of an American man and woman in Rome, linked by only two chance meetings. A counterpoint to their activities is an essay on the Fontana di Trevi by the woman's thirteen-year-old

nephew, left behind at boarding school. In "The Rabbit Hole as Likely Explanation," an addled elderly mother believes her son and daughter to be the minor children of her husband's second family. This delusion gives their conversations a nonsensical Alice in Wonderland tone. At one point, when the son has disappeared for a time, the mother even suggests that he has decided to fall down a rabbit hole and have an adventure. In "That Last Odd Day in L.A.," a wisecracking professor, who cannot prevent himself from alienating even those he loves, has a curious, almost mystical, experience encountering a deer in the Hollywood Hills. The other stories are marked by the same biting, often sardonic, humor and disarming plot construction.

THE NEW YORKER STORIES

The New Yorker Stories are forty-eight in number. Each is accompanied by the date of its original publication. The collection covers Beattie's work, ranging from April 8, 1974, to November 27, 2006. The 1960's and 1970's are well represented by twenty stories. They present the era's recognizable figures from the demimonde (although Beattie's skill prevents their becoming stereotypes): graduate students, living hand to mouth, drinking too much, smoking marijuana, and taking one lover after another; college dropouts; worn-out and cynical professors, especially those who have lost tenure; failed artists; rootless young couples, married or living together, deeply dissatisfied with their relationships but lacking the insight to understand why. Three of the later stories-- "That Last Odd Day in L.A." (April 15, 2001), "Find and Replace" (November 5, 2001), and "The Rabbit Hole as Likely Explanation" (April 12, 2004)--previously appeared in *Follies: New Stories*. The stories in between deal with familiar Beattie themes: disappointment, disillusionment, the death of love, the random nature of physical and emotional disasters.

The comparison to Hemingway is apt in the earlier stories, wherein Beattie's prose is more spare than in her later work. The stories are set primarily in urban areas (the majority of these in New York City), university communities, and popular vacation sites. Even without the furnished dates of publication, the reader would be aware of the contemporaneous nature of the action. The stories are filled with references to the politics of the day (the Nixon-McGovern presidential campaign, the Lyndon

Johnson administration), references to the popular culture, especially music (Bob Dylan's latest song, Stevie Wonder, Cyndi Lauper), and, in the latest, to the Iraq War. There is scarcely a successful nuclear family to be found. Divorce is a common condition, and the stories are filled with stepparents. Parents find it difficult to communicate with their children and children with their parents. In marriages which have been sustained, the husband or the wife--or both--may find that habit has long since replaced love. Many titles are illustrative: "Downhill," "Secrets and Surprises," "The Burning House," "Gravity," "Skeletons," "Coping Stones," "The Confidence Decoy." The characters are, of course, of all ages, but most of the central characters in the later stories are either approaching or have reached middle age, old enough to be firmly entangled in family relations. Their dialogue is frequently elliptical, inviting the listener (and the reader) to read between the lines. The narrator often switches abruptly from past to present tense, presumably to better reflect the immediacy of the scene. The overarching theme appears to be the impermanence of all things, at least in the last quarter of the twentieth century and the first decade of the twenty-first in America. Society no longer has, if it ever did, values that can sustain individuals and their relationships. However, the characters soldier on, some heroically and others because there is simply nothing else to do.

In the thirty-odd years that Beattie has been publishing short stories, mostly in *The New Yorker*, her milieu and her method have changed little, which has led some to complain that she has nothing new to say about the era she has evoked so sharply. However, Beattie has said, "My test was not did I get it right about the sixties, but is it literature. I am not a sociologist."

OTHER MAJOR WORKS

LONG FICTION: *Chilly Scenes of Winter*, 1976; *Falling in Place*, 1980; *Love Always*, 1985; *Picturing Will*, 1989; *Another You*, 1995; *My Life, Starring Dara Falcon*, 1997; *The Doctor's House*, 2002; *Walks with Men*, 2010.

NONFICTION: *Alex Katz*, 1987.

CHILDREN'S LITERATURE: *Goblin Tales*, 1975; *Spectacle*, 1985.

EDITED TEXT: *The Best American Short Stories 1987*, 1987.

BIBLIOGRAPHY

Atwood, Margaret. "Stories from the American Front." *The New York Times Book Review*, September 26, 1982, p. 1. Discusses *The Burning House* as it represents the loss of the American Dream for the children of the 1960's. For Beattie, freedom equals the chance to take off, run away, split. Beattie's stories chronicle domesticity gone awry, where there are dangers and threats lurking beneath the surface of even the most mundane events. Observes that most of the stories in this collection concern couples in the process of separating.

Barth, John. "A Few Words About Minimalism." *The New York Times Book Review*, December 28, 1986, p. 1. Explores Beattie's spare style and considers her fiction as it represents a stylistic trend in the American short story. Spends a considerable amount of space describing the origins of the contemporary minimalist movement in American short fiction. Sees this form as a nonverbal statement about theme: the spareness of life in America. Places Beattie's work among that of other minimalists, including Raymond Carver, Bobbie Ann Mason, James Robison, Mary Robison, and Tobias Wolff. Discusses Edgar Allan Poe as an early proponent of minimalism. Says that Beattie's fiction is clearly shaped by the events surrounding the Vietnam War. A helpful essay for gaining an understanding of Beattie as a minimalist.

Beattie, Ann. "An Interview with Ann Beattie." Interview by Steven R. Centola. *Contemporary Literature* 31 (Winter, 1990): 405-422. Contains a photograph of Beattie. This article is useful to the general reader, providing information about Beattie's biography. Beattie discusses herself as a feminist writer and talks about how she goes about creating credible male protagonists. Asserts that most of her fiction centers on exploring human relationships. Discusses *Falling in Place, Love Always, Chilly Scenes of Winter*, and *Picturing Will*. Talks about F. Scott Fitzgerald and his novel, *The Great Gatsby* (1925). Says that she is not interested in capturing American society but in capturing human nature.

_____. "Summer Visitors." *The American Scholar* 74, no. 3 (Summer, 2005): 76-83. Beattie discusses her work in the fourth decade of her career.

Berman, Jaye, ed. *The Critical Response to Ann Beattie*. Westport, Conn.: Greenwood Press, 1993. Includes contemporary reaction to Beattie's novels and short-story collections and presents as scholarly and academic analyses of her work by various critics.

Gelfant, Blanche H. "Ann Beattie's Magic Slate: Or, The End of the Sixties." *New England Review* 1 (1979): 374-384. Examines Beattie's short stories as reflecting the concerns of adults who came of age during the hippie years. Discusses Beattie's desolate landscapes and the pervading sense of doom found in much of her fiction. Focuses on *Secrets and Surprises* and *Distortions*, saying that they are a requiem for the freedom and wildness of the United States of the 1960's. Beattie concentrates on what amounts to the trivia of the everyday in order to make her points about the minutiae of the average person's life. Also compares Beattie's fiction with that of Joan Didion. Sees Beattie as a writer who explores the violence, inertia, futility, and helplessness of contemporary American culture.

Hansen, Ron. "Just Sitting There Scared to Death." *The New York Times Book Review*, May 26, 1991, p. 3. Discusses Beattie's collection *What Was Mine, and Other Stories*. Hansen says that Beattie's fiction provides insightful portraits of people in their thirties and forties who experience broken marriages and shattered dreams. Comments on Beattie's ability to portray a realistic male point of view. Says that her females in this book are ill-defined and hard to understand. Hansen is critical of Beattie's style as being too elliptical and relying too much on inference rather than on direct commentary. Despite this shortcoming, he says that the collection is a success, describing it as an almost photojournalistic chronicle of the disjunctions in the contemporary world. Categorizes *What Was Mine, and Other Stories* as being more introspective than Beattie's earlier collections of short fiction.

McKinstry, Susan Jaret. "The Speaking Silence of Ann Beattie's Voice." *Studies in Short Fiction* 24 (Spring, 1987): 111-117. Asserts that Beattie's female speakers puzzle readers because they tell two stories at once: an open story of the objective, detailed present juxtaposed against a closed story of the subjective past, which the speaker tries hard not to tell.

Murphy, Christina. *Ann Beattie*. Boston: Twayne, 1986. Good general introduction to Beattie's work. Discusses her major stories, illustrating her central themes and basic techniques. Discusses the relationship between her stories and her novels and her place in the development of the contemporary American short story.

Opperman, Harry, and Christina Murphy. "Ann Beattie (1947-   ): A Checklist." *Bulletin of Bibliography* 44 (June, 1987): 111-118. A useful guide to Beattie's work. Contains a helpful but brief introductory essay that identifies Beattie as an important authorial voice who came of age during the 1960's. Views her as a literary descendant of Hemingway. Her characters are refugees from the Woodstock generation, idealistic dreamers caught by ennui, drifters, and people who are emotional burnouts. Says that her characters resemble those of F. Scott Fitzgerald: They have outlived their youthful romanticism and are materialistic rather than idealistic. Also compares her to John Cheever and John Updike. Provides primary and secondary bibliographies through 1986.

Porter, Carolyn. "The Art of the Missing." In *Contemporary American Women Writers: Narrative Strategies*, edited by Catherine Rainwater and William J. Scheick. Lexington: University Press of Kentucky, 1985. Argues that Beattie economizes not by developing a symbolic context, as James Joyce and Sherwood Anderson did, but rather by using the present tense and thus removing any temptation to lapse into exposition, forcing the background to emerge from dialogue of character consciousness.

Schwartz, Christina. "A Close Read: What Makes Good Writing Good." *Atlantic Monthly* 295, no. 3 (April, 2005): 104. As the title suggests, Beattie's method in this story is closely examined in an unsigned article. Illustrated.

Shulevitz, Judith. "Ann Beattie: Distilling Her Generation." *The New York Times Book Review*, November 21, 2010, p. 14. Illustrated. A long review of *The New Yorker Stories*, commenting specifically on "A Platonic Relationship," "Fancy Flights," "Wolf Dreams," "Snakes' Shoes," "The Lawn Party," "Colorado," "Afloat," "That Last Odd Day in L.A.,"

and "The Rabbit Hole as Likely Explanation." Shulevitz suggests that much of Beattie's humor, so prevalent in her early work, has diminished over time.

Jane Hill; Melissa E. Barth and Charles E. May
Updated by Patrick Adcock

MADISON SMARTT BELL

Born: Franklin, Tennessee; August 1, 1957

PRINCIPAL SHORT FICTION
Zero db, and Other Stories, 1987
Barking Man, and Other Stories, 1990

OTHER LITERARY FORMS

Madison Smartt Bell's essays on literary topics have appeared in such publications as *Harper's* and *The Review of Contemporary Fiction*. His historical novel *All Souls' Rising* (1995) was a finalist both for a National Book Award and for a PEN/Faulkner Award. It won a Maryland Library Association Award and an Annisfield-Wolf Award. In 1996, Bell was included in *Granta* magazine's list of "Best American Novelists Under Forty."

ACHIEVEMENTS

Madison Smartt Bell's short stories have been selected for such series as *The Best American Short Stories* and *New Stories from the South: The Year's Best*, as well as for various anthologies, including *That's What I Like (About the South) and Other New Southern Stories for the Nineties*. In 1980, Bell was awarded Hollins College's Andrew James Purdy Fiction Award. Bell received a Lillian Smith Award in 1989, a John Simon Guggenheim Memorial Foundation Fellowship in 1991, and both a Maryland State Arts Council Individual Artist Award and a George A. and Eliza Gardner Howard Foundation Award in 1991-1992. He was awarded a National Endowment for the Arts

Fellowship in 1992. In 2008, the American Academy of Arts and Letters named Bell one of the recipients of the Strauss Livings Award, an annual stipend of $50,000 for five years.

BIOGRAPHY

Madison Smartt Bell was born on August 1, 1957, in Franklin, Tennessee. He was educated at the Montgomery Bell Academy in Nashville and at Princeton University, where he won awards for fiction writing and was elected to Phi Beta Kappa. In 1979, he graduated summa cum laude. He then spent a year in New York working at various jobs and doing research and writing for the Franklin Library. From 1979 to 1984, Bell was a director of a film production company, the 185 Corporation.

After a year's study at Hollins College, Bell received his master's degree in English and creative writing in 1981. Back in New York, he continued working for the Franklin Library and also for the Berkeley Publishing Corporation. His first novel, *The Washington Square Ensemble*, was published in 1983.

The following year, Bell moved to Baltimore, Maryland, and became an assistant professor of English at Goucher College, a position he held until 1986. In 1985, he married the poet Elizabeth Spires. After a year as a lecturer at the University of Iowa Writers' Workshop, Bell returned to Goucher as writer-in-residence in 1988, eventually becoming a professor of English; from 1999 to 2008, he directed Goucher's Kratz Center for Creative Writing. He has also taught graduate writing seminars at Johns Hopkins University.

ANALYSIS

In his essay "Less Is Less: The Dwindling American Short Story," Madison Smartt Bell classifies himself as a traditional writer, one who believes that only by observing the most minute details can one arrive at universal truths. Although Bell's methods are traditional, his characters are the products of contemporary society. Whether they live in the rural South or in the urban Northeast, they are lonely, alienated figures without a clear sense of purpose. Their world is marked by cruelty, violence, and death, all of which Bell describes in harrowing detail. In "Triptych I," from *Zero db, and Other Stories*, gruesome descriptions of hog butchering frame the central incident, a human death in which the victim's arm is charred on a hot stove burner. Here and elsewhere, Bell uses structure to remind his readers that they are animals, too, not much different from the hogs, rats, and cockroaches that they kill.

However, human beings can rise above their animal nature. Some of Bell's characters act on principle. The dog trainer in "Black and Tan," from *Barking Man, and Other Stories*, stops working with boys because he has doubts about his methods; the waitress in "Monkey Park," from *Zero db, and Other Stories*, will not leave her husband even though she loves another man. Other characters are compassionate. In "Move on Up," from *Barking Man, and Other Stories*, homeless people display a touching generosity toward one another. One also has to admire the semiliterate narrator of one of Bell's funniest stories, "The Naked Lady," from *Zero db, and Other Stories*. Although he enjoys shooting rats and watching barroom brawls, this character is essentially a kindly soul, who worries about his roommate's career as a sculptor and even lets their rat-eating snake warm itself in his bed. Even if individuals have lost their faith in the myths that once sustained them, Bell believes that they can still find meaning in their willingness to connect with one another.

"IRENE"

In "Irene," from *Zero db, and Other Stories*, a young girl becomes the central reality in the narrator's life. After experiencing some personal disappointments, the narrator moves into a Puerto Rican neighborhood in Newark, New Jersey, hoping that in isolation he will turn into a creative genius. In fact, however, he sinks into apathy. One night his neighbors invite him to join them on their steps, and he is so struck by the beauty of a twelve-year-old girl named Irene that he cannot get her out of his mind. He even fantasizes about marrying her. On one occasion, when he sees her crying, he takes her into his apartment until she calms down. The narrator finally pulls himself together, gets a job, and moves away, but he can never forget Irene. He only hopes that she has some recollection of him. Though he now knows that his fantasies of instantaneous success and marriage to Irene will never be realized, the narrator has found himself by connecting with another human being.

"TODAY IS A GOOD DAY TO DIE"

"Today Is a Good Day to Die," from *Zero db, and Other Stories*, is an initiation story. The protagonist is a young army lieutenant, who in 1875 has been assigned to General George A. Custer's unit at Fort Robinson as an observer. That is also his function in terms of the story. Though he is a West Point graduate, the lieutenant has a great deal to learn about war and even more to learn about this conflict. His initiation begins when a whiskey trader tries to sell him a leatherlike object that was once a squaw's breast. The falsity of the trader's justification, that Native Americans are not human beings, becomes clear to the lieutenant when one saves him from death in the snow. While they sit together beside the fire, the Native American draws a sketch to show the lieutenant how Custer's men massacred unarmed Native American women and children. Though he does fight at the Little Bighorn, the lieutenant later deserts and starts walking toward the mountains, discarding his uniform and then destroying his watch. His final words, which urge a buzzard to eat of his body, echo the Eucharist, suggesting that he sees his death as expiation for the sins of his race. The lieutenant is no longer an observer; he has become a participant in the eternal battle between good and evil.

"CUSTOMS OF THE COUNTRY"

One of Bell's major themes is that one can find goodness and heroism at even the lowest levels of society. The first-person narrator of "Customs of the Country," from *Barking Man, and Other Stories*, is a reformed drug addict. While she was in the throes of withdrawal, she became irritated with her little boy

Davey and threw him across the room, breaking his leg. As a result, he was taken away from her. Ever since, her one goal has been to get Davey back. She is now free of drugs, visits Davey whenever she can, and with her earnings as a waitress has hired a lawyer and fixed up her apartment for a social worker's approval. However, the authorities' supposed "evaluation" is a fraud; they have long since decided to give Davey to foster parents. In the end, the narrator shows herself to be far more compassionate than the bureaucrats. When she hears the man next door beating his wife even more viciously than usual, she incapacitates him with a skillet and then offers to take the wife along with her. The wife does not leave; as the narrator says, she is stuck in her rut. Ironically, in her refusal to take chances, the wife is no different from the bureaucrats. By contrast, in the narrator the reader sees true heroism.

"DRAGON'S SEED"

Unlike most of Bell's short fiction, "Dragon's Seed," from *Barking Man, and Other Stories*, ends in poetic justice. Mackie Loudon, an elderly sculptor, lives in a decaying house, alone except for her demons. After she discovers that a boy she has befriended, who stays next door with a man called Gil, is a kidnap victim in the hands of a child pornographer, Mackie informs the police. However, Gil has no difficulty convincing them that Mackie is crazy. Later, he tells her that he has disposed of the boy and then pushes her off an embankment. Mackie ends up in the hospital. After she is released the following spring, Mackie breaks into Gil's place, sets him on fire, and burns down the house. Bell's use of mythology makes the story even more effective. The reader first sees Mackie carving a head of Medusa, the Gorgon who turned men to stone; later she shapes that head into her own likeness, and as Medusa, kills Gil. The dragon's teeth sowed by the Greek hero Jason emerged as fighting men; similarly, when Mackie returns, her memories of the boy, whose name was Jason, give her the strength to effect retribution.

OTHER MAJOR WORKS

LONG FICTION: *The Washington Square Ensemble*, 1983; *Waiting for the End of the World*, 1985; *Straight Cut*, 1986; *The Year of Silence*, 1987; *Soldier's Joy*,

1989; *Doctor Sleep*, 1991; *Save Me, Joe Louis*, 1993; *All Souls' Rising*, 1995; *Ten Indians*, 1996; *Anything Goes*, 2002; *The Stone That the Builder Refused*, 2004; *Devil's Dream*, 2009.

NONFICTION: *History of the Owen Graduate School of Management*, 1985; *George Garrett: An Interview*, 1988; *Narrative Design: A Writer's Guide to Structure*, 1997; *Master of the Crossroads* (2000): *Lavoisier in the Year One: The Birth of a New Science in an Age of Revolution*, 2005; *Charm City: A Walk Through Baltimore*, 2007; *Toussaint Louverture: A Biography*, 2007.

EDITED TEXT: *New Stories from the South: The Year's Best, 2009*, 2009.

BIBLIOGRAPHY

Bell, Madison Smartt. "An Essay Introducing His Work in a Rather Lunatic Fashion." *Chattahoochee Review* 12 (Fall, 1991): 1-13. Bell explains how he came to share the southern Agrarians' distrust of technology. His own spiritual pilgrimage led him to Giordano Bruno and animism, a faith that Bell believes could save the world from environmental disaster.

_____. Interview by Bob Summer. *Publishers Weekly* 232 (December 11, 1987): 45-46. A lengthy biographical essay, supported by extensive quotations. Bell says he will always consider himself a southerner; he went to New York only because he had to move outside the South in order to find his own voice. Comments on "Triptych II," his first published story.

_____. "An Interview with Madison Smartt Bell." Interview by Mary Louise Weaks. *The Southern Review* 30 (Winter, 1994): 1-12. In this 1992 interview, Bell explains how he came to know Andrew Lytle and Allen Tate and why he still holds Agrarian views. He comments at length on "Today Is a Good Day to Die."

_____. "Less Is Less: The Dwindling American Short Story." *Harpers* 272 (April, 1986): 64-69. Bell criticizes the minimalists, arguing that their fiction merely reflects the sameness and emptiness of contemporary life; traditional writers, like Ellen Gilchrist, George Garrett, Peter Taylor, and Bell himself, know that one must observe the most minute details before attempting generalizations about people or society.

_____. "Time and Tide in the Southern Short Story." In *That's What I Like (About the South) and Other New Southern Stories for the Nineties*, edited by George Garrett and Paul Ruffin. Columbia: University of South Carolina Press, 1993. Bell insists that short stories by the newer southern writers lack the historical perspective that has defined southern literature. Fortunately, he maintains, a few writers, such as Fred Chappell, Richard Bausch, and Mary Hood, remain true to their roots; however, southern literature may be less distinctive now because so many writers from other regions are expressing their sense of alienation.

Bernays, Anne. "Heartbreak in the Monkey Park." *The New York Times Book Review*, February 15, 1987, 15. In her review of *Zero db, and Other Stories*, Bernays states that the collection displays an amazing variety of voice and tone, and she discusses five of the stories. She comments that Bell combines affection for his characters just as they are with anger because they are not better people.

Chappell, Fred. "The Helplessness of Compassion." *The Washington Post Book World* (February 1, 1987): 7. Chappell maintains that in *Zero db, and Other Stories*, Bell shows his characters responding in different ways to the cruelty around them; some retreat into despair, while others find that by empathizing with those around them, they can make their own lives better.

DeMarinis, Rick. "The Hero Is a Mouse." *The New York Times Book Review*, April 8, 1990, 11. A thoughtful analysis of *Barking Man, and Other Stories*. Sums up Bell's world as a perilous place in which ordinary people are often extraordinarily heroic. Though Bell is no sentimentalist, he can find good in seemingly worthless characters.

Gathman, Roger. "*PW* Talks with Madison Smartt Bell." *Publishers Weekly* 247, no. 35 (August 28, 2000): 52. Bell discusses his novel *Master of the Crossroads*, a fictionalized account of the Haitian slave revolt of the 1790's. This is the second novel in his trilogy about the Haitian revolutionary Toussaint-Louverture, which also includes *All Souls' Rising* and *The Stone That the Builder Refused*.

McCarthy, Paul D. "Pounding Out the Dents." *Los Angeles Times Book Review*, September 30, 1990, 12. Points out how the two parts of *Barking Man, and Other Stories* differ in tone and theme. Notes also how recurring motifs unify the collection.

Rosemary M. Canfield Reisman

SAUL BELLOW

Born: Lachine, Quebec, Canada; June 10, 1915
Died: Brookline, Massachusetts; April 5, 2005
Also known as: Solomon Bellows

PRINCIPAL SHORT FICTION

Mosby's Memoirs, and Other Stories, 1968
Him with His Foot in His Mouth,
    and Other Stories, 1984
Something to Remember Me By: Three Tales, 1991
The Actual, 1997 (novella)
Collected Stories, 2001

OTHER LITERARY FORMS

Saul Bellow is known primarily for his novels, which include *The Adventures of Augie March* (1953), *Herzog* (1964), *Mr. Sammler's Planet* (1970), and *Ravelstein* (2000). He also published plays, a book of nonfiction prose about a trip to Jerusalem, and a number of essays.

ACHIEVEMENTS

Few would deny Saul Bellow's place in contemporary American literature. Any assessment of his contributions would have to account for his realistic yet inventive style, the rich Jewish heritage upon which he draws, the centrality of Chicago in his fictional world, the role of the intellectual, and a fundamental wit, rare in contemporary American fiction. In 1976, Bellow's achievement was internationally recognized when he was awarded the Pulitzer Prize and the Nobel Prize in Literature. He also won the 1988 National Medal of Arts and three National Book Awards--for *The Adventures of Augie March* in 1954, for *Herzog* in 1965, and for *Mr. Sammler's Planet* in 1971. In 1997, *The Actual* won the National Jewish Book Award, given by the Jewish Book Council.

BIOGRAPHY

Saul Bellow was born in Canada, spent his first nine years in the Montreal area, then moved to Chicago and graduated from high school there. He spent his first two years of college at the University of Chicago and the last two at Northwestern University, graduating in 1937. That same year he began a brief interlude of graduate work in anthropology at the University of Wisconsin. A few years later he started his writing career. He also taught at the University of Chicago from 1962 to 1993, moving to Boston University thereafter. He was married five times and had four children. In 1996, he became coeditor of a new literary journal, *The Republic of Letters*. Bellow died in 2005 at his home in Massachusetts.

ANALYSIS

Saul Bellow's stature in large measure owes something to the depths to which he plumbed the modern condition. He addressed the disorder of the modern age, with all its horror and darkness, as well as its great hope. Though intensely identified with the United States, his heroes are preoccupied with dilemmas arising out of European intellectual and cultural history. Bellow's fictional world is at once cerebral and sensual. His concern is with the interconnections between art, politics, business, personal sexual proclivities and passions, the intellectual, and the making of culture in modern times. He is heady, like German writer Thomas Mann, revealing the limitations and powers of the self. Few contemporary American writers deal with such weighty issues as masterfully as does Bellow.

Bellow's honors and reputation document but do not explain his importance, although it will be more clearly seen in the future when some of the main tendencies of American fiction of his era have been fully developed. He is important because he both preserved and enhanced qualities that are present in the great fictional works of the eighteenth and nineteenth centuries yet he fully participated in the tumult and uncertainty of the modern era. Though he often opposed the political left and espoused "traditional" cultural positions, Bellow was not primarily a polemical writer. His main concern was not with maintaining social or cultural order but was more spiritual and philosophical in nature. In this, he differed from the group of "New York intellectuals" who centered in the 1940's and 1950's on the journal *Partisan Review*. Although Bellow was for a time friendly with members of this group, he took pains to distance himself from it and to stress his essential independence of any creed or ideology, as his paramount concern was for the individual. This theme is especially prominent in his short fiction, whose smaller canvas gives heightened emphasis to Bellow's stress on the struggle of the individual for self-definition and development against the background of the sundry obstacles the world has in store.

Bellow's characters have selves and interact with a society and a culture that Bellow created in detail after careful observation. In some of his works, especially *Mr. Sammler's Planet*, Bellow's attitude toward that society and that culture borders on scorn, but his attitude has been earned, not merely stated in response to limitations on his own sensibility. The interaction between self and society in his work occurs against the backdrop of moral ideas. This is not to say that Bellow was didactic; rather, his work is infused with his sophisticated understanding of moral, social, and intellectual issues. In addition to preserving a rich but increasingly neglected tradition, Bellow enriched that tradition. After the exuberant opening words of *The Adventures of Augie March*, he also added new possibilities to the prose style of American fiction. In short, his work offers some of the benefits that readers in previous centuries sought in fiction--most notably, some ideas about how to be a person in the world--yet it also provides a technical brilliance that Bellow keeps in rein instead of letting it control his work.

MOSBY'S MEMOIRS, AND OTHER STORIES

The stories collected in *Mosby's Memoirs, and Other Stories* explore characteristic Bellow themes and clearly demonstrate the writer's moral and aesthetic vision. "Looking for Mr. Green" is set in Chicago during the Depression and recounts the efforts of a civil servant, George Grebe, to deliver relief checks to black residents of the south side. This is the stuff of social protest literature, and Bellow's story does dramatize the suffering that was endemic at that time, but it is much more than didactic. Bellow avoids a single-minded attack on economic injustice and the resulting inartistic story by, among other things, using a number of contrasts and ironies. For example, two scenes set on the streets and in the tenements of Chicago are separated by a scene at Grebe's office, and in that scene a philosophical discussion between Grebe and his boss, Raynor, is interrupted by a welfare mother's tirade. The basic situation of the story is ironic, because it seems odd that anyone would have trouble delivering checks to persons who desperately need them. These persons, however, are difficult to ferret out, and their neighbors will not reveal their whereabouts because they fear that Grebe is a bill collector, process-server, or other source of trouble, and because he is white. This irony vividly illustrates the degree to which the Depression has exaggerated the instinct of self-preservation and widened the gulf between blacks and whites.

Saul Bellow (©The Nobel Foundation)

Grebe's name points out several of the contrasts in "Looking for Mr. Green." Grebes are birds known for their elaborate courtship dances, but George Grebe is a bachelor. More important for the story, grebes live in pairs rather than in flocks and remain in their own territories, but George, because of his job, is forced into society and into territory where he is an alien, not only because he is white but also because he is the son of the last English butler in Chicago and was a professor of classics. This is not to say that he is a stranger to trouble: He "had had more than an average seasoning in hardship." Despite his troubles, Grebe is shocked by suffering, distrust, and decrepit physical settings.

Oddly enough, these conditions are for him not only a moral problem but also an epistemological one. Raynor, his supervisor, brings up this problem by asserting that "nothing looks to be real, and everything stands for something else, and that thing for another thing." In contrast, Grebe later concludes that objects "stood for themselves by agreement, . . . and when the things collapsed the agreement became visible." The physical setting and the social and economic structure in this story are rapidly deteriorating, if not collapsing. Grebe complicates his analysis by asking "but what about need?" thereby suggesting that because of the Depression the agreement itself is collapsing and perhaps with it reality. Some of the persons he meets want to hasten that collapse. The welfare mother "expressed the war of flesh and blood, perhaps turned a little crazy and certainly ugly, on the place and condition," and another person advocates an alternate agreement, a plan whereby blacks would contribute a dollar apiece every month to produce black millionaires. Grebe's finding Mr. Green indicates that he can do something about this obscure world in which appearance and reality are mixed. Near the end of the story he asserts that it "was important that there was a real Mr. Green whom they could not keep him from reaching because he seemed to come as an emissary from hostile appearances."

"The Gonzaga Manuscripts" is a subtle story that traces changes in a young man, Clarence Feiler, and puts those changes in the context of important issues pertinent to the proper functions of literature and to its relation to everyday reality. Bellow carefully delineates the psychological state of Feiler, to whom literature makes an

enormous difference, and shows the impingement upon him of Spanish society, which also was the environment of the writer about whom he cares passionately, Manuel Gonzaga. These themes are developed in the context of Feiler's search in Madrid and Seville for the unpublished manuscripts of poems written by Gonzaga. Feiler learns finally that the poems are lost forever, buried with Gonzaga's patron.

When Feiler arrives in Spain he is a confirmed Gonzagan, and while searching for the manuscripts he immerses himself in Spanish society and even in Gonzaga's former milieu. Bellow meticulously paints in the Spanish background by describing the cities, religious processions, political climate, and a representative group of Spaniards. As a result of his immersion Feiler begins virtually to relive Gonzaga's poems. For example, early in the story Feiler quotes part of a poem:

I used to welcome all
And now I fear all.
If it rained it was comforting
And if it shone, comforting,
But now my very weight is dreadful.

The story ends thus: "as the train left the mountains, the heavens seemed to split. Rain began to fall, heavy and sudden, boiling on the wide plain. He knew what to expect from the redheaded Miss Walsh at dinner." That is, the rain is not comforting, and he fears that Miss Walsh will continue to torment him.

Feiler maintains his allegiance to Gonzaga, but there is considerable evidence in the story indicating that his allegiance is misplaced. For example, Gonzaga's friends are unimpressive. His best friend, del Nido, is a babbling mediocrity who sees little need for more poetry, and Gonzaga's patron has had the poems buried with her, thus denying them to the world. Another acquaintance misunderstands Feiler's search, thinking that he is after mining stock. One of Gonzaga's main beliefs is that one needs to take a dim view of human potential; he advocates being little more than a creature and avoiding the loss of everything by not trying to become everything. Even though Feiler himself has few aspirations besides finding the lost poems, he ends in despair. In fact, Gonzaga resembles the writers whom Bellow castigates in "Some Notes on Recent American Fiction" because of their minimal conception of human potential and their concomitant solicitousness for their own sensibility. Bellow's essay is a defense of a view of literature that Feiler unflatteringly contrasts to Gonzaga's.

"Mosby's Memoirs" was published in 1968, two years before *Mr. Sammler's Planet*, and, like that novel, is a study in world weariness. Mosby is writing his memoirs in Oaxaca, Mexico, where the fecund land and the earthy existence of the people stand in contrast to his own dryness. His mind ranges back through his life, particularly to recall two friends: Ruskin, a poet who has a theoretical bend of mind, and Lustgarden, who alternates between endlessly elaborated Marxism and piratical capitalism. At the end of the story Mosby is in a tomb that, along with his inability to get enough air to breathe, suggests that he is moribund. Although *Mr. Sammler's Planet* depicts a sympathetic character fending off as best he can the horrors of contemporary life, "Mosby's Memoirs" shows the danger of rejecting one's era.

Mosby's critique is conservative: He had worked for Hearst, had shaken Franco's hand, had agreed with Burnham's emphasis on managing, even to the point of admiring Nazi Germany's skill at it. Partly because Lustgarden's Marxism is not made to appear attractive either, Mosby's politics are not as unattractive as his attitude toward other persons. He is intolerant and is characterized by "acid elegance, logical tightness, factual punctiliousness, and merciless laceration in debate." Even more damaging to him is a scene at a concert in which he is described as "stone-hearted Mosby, making fun of flesh and blood, of those little humanities with their short inventories of bad and good." His attitude is also obvious in his treatment of Lustgarden in his memoirs. Rather than using his friend's disastrous attempts to make money as a political parable or as an occasion to demonstrate pity, Mosby plans to use them for comic relief, in the process eschewing his "factual punctiliousness" in order to make Lustgarden more laughable.

HIM WITH HIS FOOT IN HIS MOUTH, AND OTHER STORIES

The stories brought together in *Him with His Foot in His Mouth, and Other Stories* can be divided into two types: The title story and *What Kind of Day Did You Have?* (both novella-length pieces) feature powerful,

aging Jewish intellectuals trying to come to grips with the course their lives have taken and bridge the world of ideas with the sensate, real world around them; the other three stories in the volume-- "Zetland: By a Character Witness," "A Silver Dish," and "Cousins"--are cut from the same fabric as is "Looking for Mr. Green." They vividly, almost nostalgically, evoke a past, between the world wars and after, and portray the assimilation of Jews in the United States. What is impressive in all of these stories is the wide historical swath they cut; Bellow's concern here, as elsewhere, is no less than the human condition in the twentieth century.

Herschel Shawmut, the narrator of *Him with His Foot in His Mouth*, a man in his sixties, is a successful Jewish musicologist. His story, a sort of confession, is addressed to a "Miss Rose" whom he evidently mortally offended with an inadvertent verbal barb years ago. Shawmut also confesses to other slips of the tongue. As he writes about all the incidents, revealing a certain pattern of personality, he attributes them simply to fate. His confession also reveals that he has been swindled by his own brother Philip, a materialist living a sumptuous bourgeois life in Texas. Philip convinces his naïve brother to hand over all of his hard-earned money (made from his musicological ventures) and form a partnership in a company rife with fraud and other illegal activities. After Philip's untimely death, Shawmut, hounded by creditors, seeks exile. He is, in the end, living a lonely life in Canada. Through his confessions, Shawmut seems to find some kind of order and the satisfaction of having articulated the nature of his fate, for better or worse.

Victor Wulpy, the older Jewish intellectual in *What Kind of Day Did You Have?* is a charismatic figure who sweeps a much younger Katrina Goliger, mother of two, off her feet. On the day in question, Wulpy calls Katrina to ask her to come to Buffalo and fly back to Chicago with him for a speaking engagement. Not daring to question this cultural giant, she takes off immediately, cancelling an appointment with a psychiatrist for an evaluation of her psychiatric condition in a fierce battle with her former husband for custody of her children. In the climactic scene of the story, the small Cessna plane they are in seems, in the thick of a winter storm, to be in a fatal dive toward Lake Michigan. In the face of possible death Katrina wants Wulpy to say he loves her, but he refuses. "If we don't love each other," she then wonders aloud, "What are we doing? How did we get here?" In the end, Wulpy makes his speaking engagement and Trina makes it home, to find her children gone. Soon they return, escorted by Krieggstein, a police officer and a suitor waiting for the passing of the Wulpy phase.

Bellow's Jewish wit, evident in all these stories, sparkles in "A Silver Dish" and "Cousins," both cleverly conceived. In "A Silver Dish," sixty-year-old Woody Selbst mourns his father's death and recalls an incident in his youth. Woody's mother and father had split up, leaving Woody's upbringing in the hands of his mother and a Protestant evangelical minister. Woody's father, "Pop," returns one day to ask his son a favor. Would he introduce his father to a certain wealthy Protestant, Mrs. Skoglund, who had made money in the dairy business? Woody reluctantly agrees and takes his father to the woman's home. While she and her suspicious maid leave the room to pray and decide whether or not to comply with Pop's request for money, Pop steals a silver dish from a locked cabinet. Woody and his father get into a scuffle, and his father promises to put the dish back if Mrs. Skoglund coughs up the money. She does, but Pop, unbeknownst to his son, keeps the dish. When the dish is missed, Woody gets the blame and falls from grace in the eyes of the evangelical crowd--which is exactly the effect his father desired.

In "Cousins," the narrator, Ijah Brodsky, an international banker, tells the story of his contact with three cousins. The first, Tanky Metzger, is connected to mobs and wants Ijah to use his influence with a certain judge and gain a lighter sentence. The second cousin is Mordecai, or "Cousin Motty," whom Ijah goes to visit in the hospital after he has been hurt in an automobile crash. Cousin Motty has letters to deliver to Ijah from another cousin, Scholem Stavis. The intellectual in the family, Stavis has ended up, however, driving a cab. All through the narrative are reminiscences, a calling up of the past, a restitching of old relationships. Ijah's existence seems somehow to be tied to, and defined by, his connection to these cousins.

THE ACTUAL

The Actual, a short, self-contained novella, has many of the traits and characteristics associated with Bellow's earlier work. In fact, for these reasons it is an excellent introduction to Bellow's fictional world. However, strikingly for a work published in its author's eighty-second year, it also breaks new ground for Bellow. The hero of *The Actual* is a man named Harry Trellman, who is at the time of the action semiretired and living in Chicago. Trellman has always been perceived by those he encounters as a bit different from everyone else, standing out from the rest of the crowd. Trellman worked as a businessman in Asia and later served as an adviser to Siggy Adletsky, a tycoon and racketeer who controls a huge financial empire and who is now ninety-two years old. Adletsky finds Trellman valuable because of his wide-ranging knowledge. This is a situation often found in Bellow's work: the alliance between the shady millionaire and the intellectual.

As a teenager, Trellman had been in love with Amy Wustrin, who had eventually chosen as her second husband Trellman's best friend in high school, Jay Wustrin. Throughout the years, Harry Trellman had kept firm to the inner image of Amy in his mind even as he went through his varied career and activities. After Jay Wustrin dies prematurely, he is buried in the cemetery plot originally reserved for Amy's father, who had sold it to him years earlier. Now Amy wants to remove Jay's body to the burial plot of his own family so that her father, who is still alive at an advanced age, can eventually be buried there. In a limousine provided by Adletsky, Amy and Trellman disinter and rebury the body. Moved by this scene of death and renewal, Trellman confesses to Amy that he has always loved her, that he has what he terms an "actual affinity" for her (hence the title of the story). He then asks her to marry him.

This declaration of love is striking as Trellman, for most of his life, has remained uncommitted and rather inscrutable, not exposing his inner secrets to others. Harry's privacy is contrasted with the willful self-exposure of men such as Jay Wustrin, who love making a spectacle of themselves. This dichotomy between the public and private man is mirrored by the tensions in Trellman's relationship with Adletsky, who is concerned only with money and profit-making, yet needs the intellectual-minded, knowledgeable Trellman in order to succeed; equally, Trellman becomes dependent on the financial largesse of Adletsky. Trellman stands slightly outside the world's network of relationships yet cannot do entirely without them.

In most of his fictions, Bellow's male protagonists tend to have troubled relationships with women and are often suffering in the aftermath of divorce. The serenity of Trellman's love for Amy stands in vivid contrast, especially to earlier short fictions of Bellow's, such as *What Kind of Day Did You Have?* and sounds a note of romantic celebration that is basically unprecedented in Bellow's work.

OTHER MAJOR WORKS

LONG FICTION: *Dangling Man*, 1944; *The Victim*, 1947; *The Adventures of Augie March*, 1953; *Seize the Day*, 1956; *Henderson the Rain King*, 1959; *Herzog*, 1964; *Mr. Sammler's Planet*, 1970; *Humboldt's Gift*, 1975; *The Dean's December*, 1982; *More Die of Heartbreak*, 1987; *A Theft*, 1989; *The Bellarosa Connection*, 1989; *Ravelstein*, 2000; *Novels, 1944-1953*, 2003 (includes *Dangling Man*, *The Victim*, and *The Adventures of Augie March*); *Novels, 1956-1964*, 2007 (includes *Seize the Day*, *Henderson the Rain King*, and *Herzog*).

PLAYS: *The Wrecker*, pb. 1954; *The Last Analysis*, pr. 1964; *Under the Weather*, pr. 1966 (also known as *The Bellow Plays*; includes *Out from Under*, *A Wen*, and *Orange Soufflé*).

NONFICTION: *To Jerusalem and Back: A Personal Account*, 1976; *Conversations with Saul Bellow*, 1994 (Gloria L. Cronin and Ben Siegel, editors); *It All Adds Up: From the Dim Past to the Uncertain Future*, 1994.

EDITED TEXT: *Great Jewish Short Stories*, 1963.

BIBLIOGRAPHY

American Studies International 35 (February, 1997). A special issue on Bellow, in which a number of distinguished contributors discuss the importance of his work as a symbol of the civilization of the United States. The issue contains tributes, critiques, and analyses of Bellow's thought and art.

Bach, Gerhard, and Gloria L. Cronin, eds. *Small Planets: Saul Bellow and the Art of Short Fiction*. East Lansing: Michigan State University Press, 2000. Collection of essays focusing on the short stories, including discussions of "Looking for Mr. Green," "A Father-to-Be," "Leaving the Yellow House," "The Old System, "Mosby's Memoirs," "What Kind of Day Did You Have?" "A Silver Dish," and "Him with His Foot in His Mouth." Other essays examine his novellas, including *Seize the Day*, *The Actual*, and *The Bellarosa Connection*. Also includes a selected bibliography of Bellow's short fiction.

Bellow, Saul. "Moving Quickly: An Interview with Saul Bellow." *Salmagundi* (Spring/Summer, 1995): 32-53. In this special section, Bellow discusses the relationship between authors and characters, writer John Updike, intellectuals, gender differences, Sigmund Freud, and kitsch versus avant-garde art.

Bloom, Harold, ed. *Saul Bellow*. New York: Chelsea House, 1986. This volume, with an introduction by Bloom, is an omnibus of reviews and essays on Bellow. Collected here are comments on Bellow by writers such as Robert Penn Warren, Malcolm Bradbury, Tony Tanner, Richard Chase, and Cynthia Ozick. Gives the reader a good sense of early critical responses to Bellow.

Boyers, Robert. "Captains of Intellect." *Salmagundi* (Spring/Summer, 1995): 100-108. Part of a special section on Bellow. A discussion of characters in stories from the collection *Him with His Foot in His Mouth, and Other Stories* as captains of intellect who pronounce authoritatively on issues of the modern. Discusses Bellow as an intellectual leader with a multifaceted perspective.

Chavkin, Allan, ed. *Critical Insights: Saul Bellow*. Pasadena, Calif.: Salem Press, 2012. Collection of original and reprinted essays providing critical readings of Bellow's work. Also includes a biography, a chronology of major events in Bellow's life, a complete list of his works, and a bibliography listing resources for further research.

Cronin, Gloria L. "Small Planets: The Short Fiction of Saul Bellow." In *A Companion to the American Short Story*, edited by Alfred Bendixen and James Nagel. Malden, Mass.: Wiley-Blackwell, 2010. A comprehensive, chronological analysis of Bellow's short stories and novellas, placing these works within biographical and literary contexts.

Cronin, Gloria L., and L. H. Goldman, eds. *Saul Bellow in the 1980's: A Collection of Critical Essays*. East Lansing: Michigan State University Press, 1989. This anthology brings together a sampling of a wave of criticism that focuses variously on Bellow's women, his debts to Judaism, connections to theories of history, and modernism.

Freedman, William. "Hanging for Pleasure and Profit: Truth as Necessary Illusion in Bellow's Fiction." *Papers on Language and Literature* 35 (Winter, 1999): 3-27. Argues that Bellow's realism is a search for truth, not the discovery of it. Discusses how Bellow deals with the question of whether a man is isolated or a member of a human community. Contends that for Bellow the value of literature is the ceaseless search for truth in a world that promises truth but seldom provides it.

Friedrich, Marianne M. *Character and Narration in the Short Fiction of Saul Bellow*. New York: Peter Lang, 1995. Friedrich argues that Bellow's short fiction goes "against the grain of postmodernism" by his use of mimesis (imitiation), which in his later short fiction moves toward parable, romance, fairy tale and myth. Some of the stories analyzed include "Looking for Mr. Green," "Leaving the Yellow House," "A Silver Dish," "What Kind of Day Did You Have?" and "Cousins."

Gelfant, Blanche H., ed. *The Columbia Companion to the Twentieth-Century American Short Story*. New York: Columbia University Press, 2000. Includes a chapter in which Bellow's short stories are analyzed.

The Georgia Review 49 (Spring, 1995). A special issue on Bellow in which a number of contributors discuss his life and art, his contribution to American thought and culture, and the wide range of his works.

Kiernan, Robert. *Saul Bellow*. New York: Continuum, 1989. Provides a useful chronology of Bellow's life and production. Traces the writer's development from *Dangling Man* to *More Die of Heartbreak*. The best book on Bellow for the general reader.

Miller, Ruth. *Saul Bellow: A Biography of the Imagination*. New York: St. Martin's Press, 1991. Traces Bellow's travels, linking the author's life to his work. Contains useful appendices, a bibliography, a listing of interviews, and a table of contents from *The Noble Savage*, a journal edited by Bellow.

Pifer, Ellen. *Saul Bellow Against the Grain*. Philadelphia: University of Pennsylvania Press, 1990. In a study that deals comprehensively with the writer's oeuvre, Pifer's central observation is that Bellow's heroes are divided against themselves and conduct an inner strife that dooms and paralyzes them. Their struggle, like Bellow's, is a search for language to articulate the modern condition.

John Stark
Updated by Allen Hibbard and Nicholas Birns

AIMEE BENDER

Born: Los Angeles, California; June 28, 1969

PRINCIPAL SHORT FICTION
The Girl in the Flammable Skirt, 1998
Willful Creatures, 2005

OTHER LITERARY FORMS

The first novel of Aimee Bender (AY-mee BEHN-dur), *An Invisible Sign of My Own*, was published in 2000. Her second novel, *The Particular Sadness of Lemon Cake*, appeared in 2010.

ACHIEVEMENTS

Aimee Bender won Pushcart Prizes for "Jinx" in 2003 and for "End of the Line" in 2005. Both of these short stories appear in her second collection.

BIOGRAPHY

Aimee Bender grew up in Santa Monica, California, in the early 1980's. Her father was a psychiatrist, and her mother was a dancer. As a child, Bender was a budding writer, but she let writing fall by the wayside after elementary school. At Palisades High School, Bender followed her mother's artistic bent in choir and drama, but she did no further writing until college. Her instructors at the University of California, San Diego, where she received a bachelor's degree in 1991, encouraged her writing. She moved to San Francisco and taught reading at an elementary school dominated by children of Russian immigrants. In the fall of 1995, the University of California, Irvine (UCI), accepted Bender into its graduate writing workshop program, one of only eleven students. She received a master of fine arts degree in 1997 and was awarded a one-year fellowship to teach composition and creative writing and edit the campus literary journal, *Faultline*. During her graduate studies, Bender lived on Balboa Island, but she moved to West Hollywood after attaining her degree. She joined the faculty at the prestigious University of Southern California creative writing program in 2001.

Bender's works have appeared in numerous literary periodicals. Her first published work was "Dreaming in Polish," which appeared in the *Santa Monica Review* in spring of 1995. Over the years, her stories have appeared in the *Colorado Review*, *Cream City Review*, *Missouri Review*, *The Antioch Review*, *Faultline*, *North American Review*, *GQ*, *Story*, *Granta*, *Paris Review*, *Harper's*, and *Electric Literature*.

ANALYSIS

When she was at UCI, Aimee Bender was the only one in her class to concentrate on the short-story form. While she claims to admire both this format and that of the novel, perhaps she chose the former because it fit her mythic, didactic style. Bender admits to feeling more comfortable in this form. Her early influences included the tales and fables of Jacob and Wilhelm, the Brothers Grimm, Hans Christian Andersen, and others, and her work certainly mimics these children's stories but in an adult manner. Although many of her classmates wrote their first novels in the custom of the young--set in seedy, angst-ridden apartments--Bender "did try to write more traditional things, but . . . didn't enjoy it as much." In fact, she found mythic tales "liberating."

Bender's characters live in a never-never land somewhere between life and the pages of a story by Sir James Barrie, who created Peter Pan, but their problems and conflicts are real, the ones that people try to avoid at all costs. They are the unconscionable burdens of life that make humanity wake up in the middle of the night, sweaty and frightened. Her characters feel incredibly isolated and yearn for human contact, to the point of sacrificing their moral beliefs. They suffer loss and deformity, yet they must cope with these losses and the results (sometimes offspring) of these deformities. Just as Hansel and Gretel were abandoned in the forest, so Bender's characters must adapt to their tragedies with humor, compassion, and creativity.

Rebecca Meacham's review of *Willful Creatures* characterizes Bender's stories as "at once comic, sad, witty, and wondrous," featuring writing that "draws our sympathy for characters of all shapes and sizes, be they animal, vegetable, or appliance." Justin Taylor notes that Bender's tendency to use unnamed narrators might frustrate some readers, but that Bender is "simply cutting away the fat," further noting that she's also "willing to part with a lot of the musculature." Although pared-down in some ways, the characters in *Willful Creatures* are better developed and carry powerful, passionate messages.

However, sometimes they fail. As Hugh Garvey pointed out in *The Village Voice*, "the tales in *Flammable* are also unified by the characters' disturbing inability to resolve the conflicting desires for obliteration and connection." While this conflict may seem to be a paradox, it parallels the human choice of fight or flight when faced with distasteful dilemmas. Bender's characters cannot decide (as many people cannot) whether to accede to the incomprehensible, and sometimes fatal, vagaries of life or to do battle with the unknown and unloved. Through them, she suggests that the solution is that there is no solution at all. Everyone must simply cope as best as he or she can with the afflictions of life.

Aimee Bender (Getty Images)

"CALL MY NAME"

The speaker in this first-person narrative is decked out like a bird of prey in a dress the color of dried blood. Like many single women, she seeks a mate for a sex-driven relationship, but he must be someone nonthreatening, someone she can dominate--or can she? Spreading her spoor around the subway, she spots a likely target. At first he ignores her slithery advances, but then she senses "he's getting the sexual vibe which makes me feel . . . alive." The speaker follows him home, trying to make her lust transform him, but he remains steadfast in his refusal of her. He has no wish to make the connection. Finally, he lets her into his apartment, after which she finds herself naked and tied to a chair. Has she won? Has she failed? She hears the sound of winning, but the reader has to wonder if this tale of power and its fatal links is not also an anti-Edenic refutation of the irrefutable attraction of sex.

"WHAT YOU LEFT IN THE DITCH"

A young woman's husband returns home from the war without lips. Like many of Bender's stories focusing on the recurring theme of mutilation and loss, this very bizarre image must be viewed in the context of loss of communication and contact that may occur after a debilitating rift in a relationship. The wife cannot cope with the return of only a partial husband, in fact hardly a husband at all, as he must wear a pacifier-like prosthesis until his lips can be restored. He becomes her child, someone who must be fed and nurtured, even if this chore is distasteful. She buries her loyalty to him as she buries in the backyard the "dead sweaters" she has knitted and sets off to seduce the checker at the grocery store. However, he is too perfect to "save" her and restore her loss. In the end, she returns to her husband, covering her ears in an imitation of his disability, equalizing their losses so that they may recover their lost relationship.

"SKINLESS"

Superficially, this story is about the naïve notion that love and trust will overcome racial and ethnic hatred. Beneath it all, there are undertones of frustration, loss, and contempt. Renny, a neo-Nazi inmate of a halfway house, and Jill, the activities director of the facility, are in conflict but not necessarily with each other. In fact, each is looking for a mother. For Renny, this madonna figure takes the form of the mothers of his brother's amours; for Jill, this figure is herself. The found object must also be destroyed, and Renny finds himself scratching out the images of women in photos, while Jill wonders what lies, literally, beneath the skins of her lover and her rabbi. She needs to find "what exactly they were made of." In an odd replication of the death of the philosopher Hypatia, she needs to do more than scratch the surface of their beings. However, this story is not about the connection between Jew and neo-Nazi but rather a look at forced coexistence between enemies. The ending is ambiguous, as Renny has the opportunity to either make love to Jill or push her off a cliff. The only clue offered is the sexual connection they appear to make, which may or may not salvage a relationship forged in hell.

"Dreaming in Polish"

"There was an old man and an old woman and they dreamed the same dreams." In a small town, prophets are easily believed and often revered, and so it is in this tale of two Holocaust victims, who repeat their visions, in fragments, to the villagers. When the dreams begin to come true, the town is thrown into a frenzy of obedience. Whatever is augured must be fulfilled, even to the covering of a statue of a vaguely Greek figure. The caretaker of the statue is a young woman who works in a store during the day but must care for her invalid father at night. Her mother, who is inclined to walking excursions and visiting Holocaust museums, decides to abandon them for a short trip to a nearby display. Her absence causes an undue share of responsibilities to fall on the daughter, which is the theme of the story. She is overwhelmed by her love for her father and by the burden his illness has placed on her. The statue, strong and silent, becomes an icon of hope and recovery, a regeneration of their family unit. The old couple? They begin to speak only in Polish, and even in their glossolalia they are revered and upheld as New World Isaiahs.

"The Ring"

Two robbers break into kitchens and find precious jewels in canisters of dry goods. They steal diamond, ruby, and emerald rings, but the ruby turns out to be cursed. It starts to turn everything red, and in a frenzy they return it, but the wife of the robber cannot live without it, so her husband resteals it to make her happy. They fly to

Tahiti, but the ring turns the sea red for a mile, so they destroy it "in [the] red wet mouth of the ocean." This is the most fablelike of the stories in its simplistic rhetoric; however, the magic lies not in the extraordinary jewels-- which are amazingly easy to come by, being guarded only by a large white cat--but in the ordinary items. The sugar in the ruby's canister is the only essence in the world, it seems, not affected by its crimson taint. The robber's wife characterizes her husband as a "baker," and they delight in flour-coated sex. A celebration of the commonplace, this is a venue where thieves are safe.

Willful Creatures

Willful Creatures comprises fifteen stories, separated into three sections. While many of Bender's stories address similar concerns, the three sections have specific themes.

The first section deals with the ways humans can be cruel to others. "End of the Line" hinges on Bender's penchant for magical realism or fantasy elements. The story tells of a man, called the big man, who goes to a pet store and purchases not a dog or cat but a little man who is kept in a cage. At first he buys things for the little man that will make his cage comfortable, and the little man helps the big man with his accounts, but soon the big man begins to torture and abuse his pet. After weeks of horrible treatment, the big man realizes that he cannot break the little man and begins treating him humanely again, promising to let him go home, if he can come along and see where the little people live. The story concludes with the big man begging to be allowed into their community and the little people hiding in terror, waiting for him to leave. The first section concludes with "Debbieland," in which an unnamed narrator, who refers to herself in first person plural, recounts a series of abusive actions against a high school classmate named Debbie. During college, they have a romantic relationship. Years later, the two meet by chance and have an awkward conversation, which includes Debbie having to correct the narrator on a key point: that her name is Anne. This is somehow worse than any of the other indignities she has suffered, yet the narrator comments that Debbie now has "more fodder for her insulted self."

The second part examines various failed relationships. In "Motherf----," a conceited man who pursues sexual relationships with single moms falls in love with a woman whom he cannot have. The opening of "Fruit and Words" introduces a couple who are having a familiar argument, and just when the woman thinks that the relationship might finally be over, the man suggests they drive to Vegas to get married. Once there, he has second thoughts and leaves her to get home on her own. A sudden obsessive craving for mango leads her on a road trip and to a store called Fruit and Words. Along with ripe delicious fruits, the store sells words, made of solids, liquids, and gases. For example, pieces of nuts spell out NUT. Accused of breaking one of the words, she flees the store with her mangoes, but she finds they are completely rotten when she arrives home. In "Jinx," a miscommunication about a boy ruins the friendship of two teenage girls. "I Will Pick Out Your Ribs (From My Teeth)" is a sad portrait of a dysfunctional relationship between a man and his girlfriend, Janie, who is depressed and suicidal. In his poignant description of the too-familiar emergency room, he notes that when he looks for the crossword puzzles in the magazines, they're always already filled in, and "worse: they're filled in by me. And I can't even correct myself because I still don't know the same answers I didn't know last time I was here."

The third section could be described as Bender's exploration of faith and redemption. The opening story, "Job's Jobs," depicts a writer who is threatened with death if he continues writing. God is the one doing the threatening, so the writer agrees. He then begins painting, but God makes him stop, and the same thing happens when the writer tries acting, gourmet cooking, and a dozen other activities. In the end, the man is completely isolated by God, unable to speak or see, but he continues to think creatively and remember beautiful things that he made or saw. In "The Case of the Salt and Pepper Shakers," a detective solves an unusual double murder: the husband poisons his wife at lunch, but later that afternoon, before she dies, she stabs him to death. The detective is obsessed with the number of salt-and-pepper shaker sets the couple has, and, as he investigates, he learns their significance to the couple and the history of their relationship, once positive and strong. "The Leading Man" recounts the life of a boy born with nine of his ten fingers shaped like keys. As he grows up, he finds the doors that the keys fit, and as he opens them, his fingers become normal. Some of the doors he opens are

important, some are of less consequence, but the ninth, which takes him many years to find, allows him to save the life of a child.

OTHER MAJOR WORKS
    LONG FICTION: *An Invisible Sign of My Own*, 2000; *The Particular Sadness of Lemon Cake*, 2010.

BIBLIOGRAPHY
Garvey, Hugh. "Writers on the Verge: Aimee Bender." *The Village Voice* 43 (June 2, 1998): 79-80. This is a profile of Bender with helpful insights into her overall themes and influences.
Lewis, William Henry. "Tales of Sexual Zealots." *The Washington Post*, October 18, 1998, p. X10. Bender's initial offering defies expectations of the typical first novel/anthology. This collection describes what fables can do when used as social tools. Several narrative methods are displayed, and the author concentrates on the conflict between the modern and the old-fashioned, between nonsectarian and Jew. In addition, she concentrates on the trade-off of power and sex between men and women.
Meacham, Rebecca. "The Stuff of Wonder." *Women's Review of Books* 25, no. 4 (July/August, 2006): 12-13. Meacham reviews *Willful Creatures*, paying particular attention to "Fruit and Words."
Taylor, Justin. "Willful Creatures." *American Book Review* 27, no. 2 (January/February, 2006): 28. Taylor compares and contrasts Bender's two short-story collections, making interesting points about the writer's style and impact.
Tillman, Aaron. "Dreaming with the Dead: Convergent Spaces in Leslie Marmon Silko's *Ceremony* and Aimee Bender's, 'Dreaming in Polish.'" In *The Intersection of Fantasy and Native America: From H. P. Lovecraft to Leslie Marmon Silko*, edited by David D. Oberhelman and Amy H. Sturgis. Altadena, Calif.: Mythopoetic, 2009. Tillman compares and contrasts the use of and description of dream and dreamlike states in Silko's novel and Bender's first published short story, "Dreaming in Polish," which later appeared in her first collection.

Jennifer L. Wyatt
Updated by Elizabeth Blakesley

PINCKNEY BENEDICT

Born: Lewisburg, West Virginia; April 12, 1964

PRINCIPAL SHORT FICTION
Town Smokes, 1987
The Wrecking Yard, 1992
Miracle Boy, and Other Stories, 2010

OTHER LITERARY FORMS

The first novel of Pinckney Benedict (PIHNK-nee BEHN-ih-dihkt), *Dogs of God,* was published in 1994. He edited, with his wife Laura Benedict, two anthology volumes of poetry and prose, *Surreal South,* in 2007 and 2009. He also wrote the screenplay for the film *Four Days* (1999).

ACHIEVEMENTS

Pinckney Benedict has received literary fellowships from the National Endowment for the Arts, the Illinois Arts Council, and the West Virginia Commission on the Arts. He also was awarded a Michener Fellowship from the Writers Workshop at the University of Iowa, as well as the *Chicago Tribune's* Nelson Algren Award and the John Steinbeck Award. His story "Miracle Boy" was included in the *O. Henry Prize Stories, 1999,* and his story "Zog-Nineteen: A Scientific Romance" was selected for the *O. Henry Prize Stories, 2001.* Several of his stories have won the Pushcart Prize and have appeared in *Stories from the South: The Year's Best.*

BIOGRAPHY

Arthur Pinckney Benedict was born on a dairy farm near Lewisburg, West Virginia, on April 12, 1964. He went to high school at the Hill School in Pottstown, Pennsylvania, where he studied Latin and Greek, and he was delighted to discover that classical literature was full of the same kinds of heroes and monsters as the "Weird War" comic series he enjoyed as a child.

While attending college at Princeton, he became a fan of the stories of his fellow West Virginia writer Breece D'J Pancake; after Benedict read Pancake, Benedict knew not only that he wanted to write but also what he wanted to write. While at Princeton, Benedict became a protégé of his teacher, Joyce Carol Oates, who supervised his undergraduate thesis, which became the basis of his first book, *Town Smokes.*

After graduating from Princeton in 1986, Benedict attended the Iowa Writers' Workshop at the University of Iowa, from which he received an M.F.A. in 1988. During his attendance at Iowa, *Town Smokes* was published and won several awards, all of which helped launch his teaching career at Oberlin College in Ohio. While teaching at the summer Appalachian Writers' Workshop in Hindman, Kentucky, Benedict met Laura Philpot, who became his wife in 1990. He and his wife moved back to his birthplace in Greenbrier County, West Virginia, where they lived in the early 1990's while he held various short-term writer-in-residence positions at several different universities. During this time, he published his second short-story collection, *The Wrecking Yard* and his first novel *Dogs of God.* Benedict accepted a tenure-track position at Hope College in Michigan in 1996 and a position in the creative-writing program at Hollins University in Virginia in 1998. He left Hollins to accept a full professor position at Southern Illinois University in Carbondale in 2006, His third collection of short stories, *Miracle Boy, and Other Stories,* was published in 2010.

ANALYSIS

Perhaps the best advice Pinckney Benedict ever received was from Oates, his undergraduate teacher at Princeton, who urged him to write about his own region and to use his own idiom. However, because Benedict's characters often are said to reflect negative regional stereotypes, she also told him after the publication of his novel *Dogs of God* that he was going to "set the tourist industry in West Virginia back by one hundred years." Benedict's rural West Virginia world is often filled with violent car wrecks, cruelty to animals, human viciousness, and what a sheriff in his story "Odom" calls "crazy backward ridge-running mountain rats." However, Benedict's milieu is less the realistic world of Erskine Caldwell than it is the mythic world of William Faulkner. Although Benedict's stories are firmly rooted in the physical world of the Appalachian Mountains, like those of Eudora Welty, he endows his characters with universal significance by compelling them to confront primal forces. With the early death of Pancake and the departure of Jayne Anne Phillips from the state, Benedict became the voice of rural West Virginia.

"THE SUTTON PIE SAFE"

This is a classic father-son story about a ten-year-old boy named Cates, whose father shoots a large black snake, promising to make the boy a belt like the one his own father made for him when he was a child. However, this plan is spoiled when the well-to-do wife of a local judge comes to the farm to buy a Sutton Pie Safe, or bread box, that belonged to the boy's grandfather. The boy's father, who refuses to be treated like a common merchant, confronts his wife, who wants to sell the bread box, with the accusation: "You're not going to leave me anything, are you?" Although the judge's wife is successful in buying the pie safe, the father is reconciled to the loss until he cuts open the snake and finds a dead mouse inside. When the boy, upset by the sight of the dead mouse (which somehow seems to symbolize his father's loss of status), fails to confirm to his father than he wants the belt, the father slices the body of the snake into pieces and tells his son to think about this the next time he wants something. The lesson the boy learns, of course, has to do with the importance of maintaining pride in spite of material need.

"TOWN SMOKES"

The title story of Benedict's debut collection of stories is a mountain-style coming-of-age piece about a fourteen-year-old boy, whose father has just died under a fallen tree. The boy goes through his father's possessions, which become his, finding a gun, a knife, clothes, and an old Gideon Bible, the pages of which the father used to roll his cigarettes. The boy tells his uncle, his only surviving relative, that he is going down the mountain to town to get some cigarettes, but the uncle knows that the boy is not coming back. The boy believes he is ready to leave the mountain but is not sure why; the most he can say is that he is tired of smoking dried old tobacco rolled in Bible pages and wants to smoke a real cigarette for a change. On the journey down the mountainside, the boy faces one more coming-of-age trial: a confrontation with two boys who rob him of the few dollars left by the father. When the boy reaches town, he discovers that many people have lost everything in a flood caused by incessant rain and the break of an earthen dam. The owner of a drugstore, feeling sorry for the boy, gives him a pack of cigarettes. Enjoying his "town smokes," the boy knows he will not go back up the mountain and decides he will go up the river to look at where the earth dam broke, to see a real river, not mere creeks like those up the mountain, with nothing to hold it back. "Yessir, that would be something to see." In this simple story of poignant irony, a pack of store-bought cigarettes comes to stand for the promise of a better life for a mountain boy.

"THE WRECKING YARD"

The central metaphor of the title story of Benedict's second collection is the wrecking yard: a graveyard for what's left of the iconic mountain cars after accidents, often caused by fast, reckless driving. The two central characters, who drive the wreckers that follow after accidents, are what the state police at an accident scene call parasites, swarming about the place where the blood collects.

The story opens with the irresistible appeal that fast and fancy cars have for young mountain men. When the owner of Papaduke's Auto Salvage and Wrecking Yard drives into the yard with a 1966 Chevrolet Impala on his flatbed, Perry, who runs the crusher at the yard, decides he must have it. Weasel, the other man who works at the yard, is slowly stealing parts to rebuild a 1970 GTO. The story focuses on two accidents the men go to: one involving a cattle truck, with dead steers strewn about, and the other involving a car driven by a reckless young man that goes over a cliff, throwing a young woman passenger into the branches of a large tree. As the rescuers bring the body of the girl over the edge of the cliff, Perry is shaken by what he sees. When the ambulance takes the body away and he is left alone at the accident site, he picks up a hubcap from the crashed car and tosses it over the edge of the cliff, watching the wind catch it and send it into the bushes below him in a tangled wooded place that he cannot see. The value that fast cars hold for mountain boys and the frequent horrific result of that fascination form the heart of this story.

"MIRACLE BOY"

When three boys want to see the scars of someone named Miracle Boy, it seems obvious that the title story of Benedict's third collection will be about sin and redemption. Jesus, after all, is the most significant "miracle boy" in Western culture, and if one is a doubting Thomas, one wants to see the stigmata. Benedict makes his Miracle Boy a soft and jiggly kid, who, after having lost his feet in a farm accident, walks with a limp when they are sewed back on. When beaten down, the boy says, "It's miracles around us every day . . . Jesus made the lame to walk . . . and Jesus, he made me to walk too."

After three boys--Geronimo, Eskimo, and Lizard--mercilessly bully the lame child and throw his specially made shoes up on a high-powered wire, Lizard is the only one who seems nagged by guilt for what they have done. When he climbs up the pole, his driving of nails just below his body to step up on creates a powerful image of the cross, as Lizard, trying to atone, pulls himself up higher and higher by his own bootstraps, as it were, to reach the holy grail of those grimy shoes. When he reaches the top and frees the shoes, he can see the whole world around him. He knows he is in the palm of the hand of something; he just does not know what.

In the final scene, Miracle Boy's father tells Lizard, "Your Mommy may not know what you are. . . . But I do." The reader knows, too--for Lizard is suffering man, trying to atone for his sins. It is inevitable that he looks at Miracle Boy with "curious eyes, seeing him small, like a bird or a butterfly." As Lizard holds out the shoes like a gift, Benedict ends the story with echoes of his Southern short-story masters: Welty and Flannery O'Connor.

"BRIDGE OF SIGHS"

In "Bridge of Sighs," Benedict uses the vehicle of a cattle epidemic to explore a universal human reality, the "sickness unto death" that befalls all. Lord Byron called the bridge spanning one of the canals in Venice the Bridge of Sighs, because when prisoners were taken across it, they looked out one of the small windows and sighed at their last view of the world before being placed in a dungeon. Benedict does not emphasize this allusion, but the fact that the name is given to the walkway over which animals and workers cross in an abattoir, or slaughterhouse, combined with a suit named "The Exterminator" and an instrument named Humane Cattle Killer, urges a universal reading of the story.

Frightened by a man in an Exterminator suit, the boy finally sees his father's loving eyes through the eyeholes--an effective image of the kind of make-believe monster that frightens children in fairy tales. Similarly, at the end of the story, a two-headed monster turns out to be two spring calves. The real problem, according to the boy, is telling the difference between what's happening and what one thinks is happening. His father helps him with that. At the end of the story, it comes down to the powerful desire to deny death, to insist that nothing is wrong, "Nothing wrong at all."

OTHER MAJOR WORKS

LONG FICTION: *Dogs of God*, 1994.

SCREENPLAY: *Four Days*, 1999 (adaptation of John Buell's novel)

EDITED TEXT: *Surreal South*, 2007 (with Laura Benedict); *Surreal South '09*, 2009 (with Benedict).

BIBLIOGRAPHY

Brosi, George. "Pinckney Benedict, a Gleeful Writer." *Appalachian Heritage* 38 (Winter, 2010): 18-23. A biographical sketch and appreciation of Benedict, emphasizing his love of writing and his boyish pride in his work. Discusses Benedict's early love of comic books, science fiction, and horror stories.

Douglas, Thomas E. "Interview with Pinckney Benedict." In *Interviewing Appalachia: The Appalachian Journal Interviews, 1978-1992*, edited by Jerry Wayne Williams and Edwin T. Arnold. Knoxville:

University of Tennessee Press, 1994. Benedict talks about the influence and inspiration of Pancake on his early stories but argues that the stories in *Town Smokes* have more comic aspects than Pancake's tales.

Egerton, Katherine. "'When You Were a Man': Pinckney Benedict's Fathers and Sons." *Appalachian Heritage* 38 (Winter, 2010): 44-48. Discusses how Benedict's style has evolved from the spare prose of *Town Smokes* to the lush style of *Miracle Boy*. Argues that the central theme throughout his career is boyhood and how far a father will go to keep a son safe and then send him out to be a man in the world. Discusses the stories "Odom," "Sutton Pie Safe," and "Bridge of Sighs."

Leebron, Fred. "All the Darkness and All the Light: The Work of Pinckney Benedict." *Appalachian Heritage* 38 (Winter, 2010): 13-16. Argues that Benedict's central theme is that while people do each other harm, there is both realism and a "shocking grace and humor" in that reality. Says that Benedict investigates regions of darkness, within which he finds a kind of energy with its own intense light

McWhorter, Diane. "Cigarettes Rolled from the Bible." *The New York Times Book Review*, July 12, 1987, p. 13. This is an important early review of Benedict's *Town Smokes*. McWhorter praises Benedict's writing but raises the hackles of Kentucky writer Jim Wayne Miller for emphasizing the "otherness" of Appalachian hill folk. Noting that Benedict's characters are maimed by the machinery of the huge coal trucks that menace the region, McWhorter argues that his border country misfits lead barbarous lives that seem tragically sweet when they cling to the Deep South notion of redemption--a joyous sensitivity to the mechanical world of guns and automobiles.

Charles E. May

STEPHEN VINCENT BENÉT

Born: Bethlehem, Pennsylvania; July 22, 1898
Died: New York, New York; March 13, 1943

PRINCIPAL SHORT FICTION
Thirteen O'Clock, 1937
Tales Before Midnight, 1939
Twenty-five Short Stories, 1943

OTHER LITERARY FORMS

Stephen Vincent Benét (beh-NAY) created a sensation when his long epic poem *John Brown's Body* (1928) was published, and despite his many volumes of poems, including *Western Star* (1943), *John Brown's Body* remains his best-known and most popular work. He also wrote Hollywood screenplays, librettos, and an opera, and he composed radio addresses and scripts used for patriotic propaganda during World War II. In addition, Benét published five novels.

ACHIEVEMENTS

American history, especially that of the Civil War, is integral to the fiction of Stephen Vincent Benét. Whether folklore, fantasy, or parable, his writing reverberates with history, not only American but also European, since he lived in France for several years. His characters range from European immigrants to expatriates from America, from slaves to frontiersmen, from the World War I lost generation eccentrics to religionists. His fictional modes include irony, satire, sentimentality, and romanticism. Benét imbues his fiction with themes of national pride, freedom with responsibility, the cardinal virtues, and the fair play of living the good life.

His honors and prizes include a John Simon Guggenheim Memorial Foundation Fellowship (1926), which was extended for six months (1927), a Pulitzer Prize (1929) for *John Brown's Body*, election to the National Institute of Arts and Letters (1929), an O. Henry Memorial Prize for the short story (1936), an honorary degree from Yale University (1937), election to the American Academy of Arts and Sciences (1938), and a Pulitzer Prize, awarded posthumously, for *Western Star*.

BIOGRAPHY

Descendant of a grandfather and father who were both West Point graduates and Army men, Stephen Vincent Benét traveled and lived with his family on military posts throughout the United States. This familiarity with the locales and terrains of the United States provided a rich background for his short stories and poems. Colonel James Walker Benét, an omnivorous reader with a deep love of country and history, inflamed his younger son with these same passions. Like his older brother William Rose Benét, a well-known writer, editor, and magazine founder, Stephen Vincent Benét was graduated from Yale University in 1919. He was given a Yale travel award and a John Simon Guggenheim Memorial Foundation grant, permitting him to spend initially eighteen months in France and to attend the Sorbonne in Paris. He lived in France several years and attributed his particular love for the United States to having gained perspective on his native land from his European travels. On his return to the United States in 1923, he published a volume of poetry, *King David*, a broadside edition of his poem "The Ballad of William Sycamore, 1790-1880," and *Jean Huguenot*, a novel. In 1926, he returned with a John Simon Guggenheim Memorial Foundation Fellowship to France, where he worked on *John Brown's Body*, a poem about the Civil War, which won the Pulitzer Prize in 1929. He was also elected to the National Institute of Arts and Letters the same year. In 1933 he became editor of the Yale Series of Younger Poets Competition and two years later began reviewing for the New York *Herald Tribune* and *Saturday Review of Literature*. In 1936 his short story "The Devil and Daniel Webster" was awarded the O. Henry Memorial Prize for the best American short story of the year. His stories "Johnny Pye and the Fool-Killer" and "Freedom's a Hard-Bought Thing" won similar honors in 1937 and 1940, respectively.

ANALYSIS

Stephen Vincent Benét achieved mastery of the short-fiction form only after laborious and persistent efforts. His preference was for poetry and the freedom it offered as opposed to the restrictions of the short story. Perhaps because of this, he never experimented with the short-story form and unflinchingly favored traditionally structured stories with a definite beginning, middle, and end. He also skillfully employed the traditional device of the narrator to bring about a sense of immediacy and the interesting possibility of self-revelation and concealment which this perspective offered; he was not, however, an innovator of any new form of the short story.

Early in his career, Benét reconciled his conscience with his economic needs by writing original short stories designed to elicit popular appeal. He achieved this self-appeasement by basing his stories on material from American history and folklore and transfusing it with his vivid imagination. The reconciliation resulted in such stories as "The Devil and Daniel Webster," "Daniel Webster and the Sea Serpent," "Daniel

Stephen Vincent Benét (Library of Congress)

Webster and the Ides of March," "Jacob and the Indians," "A Tooth for Paul Revere," "Freedom's a Hard-Bought Thing," and "Johnny Pye and the Fool-Killer."

"THE DEVIL AND DANIEL WEBSTER"

The first Webster story, "The Devil and Daniel Webster," was published in 1936 in *The Saturday Evening Post*, and its tremendous success gave Benét immediate national recognition and fame. The cause of its success was deeply rooted; it sparked the latent historic and cultural feelings in the American mind. Moreover, in Webster, Benét found an ideal folk hero who had all the myth surrounding his character to provide ample material for productive characterization. The basis for the conflict in the story is extremely interesting. Webster was renowned for his superb oratorical powers, and consequently he was the perfect protagonist to meet the Devil in an oratorical contest and defeat him. This symbolic contest between the representatives of good and evil had wide appeal and was complemented not only by Benét's use of local humor but also by the story's inherent universal significance. These elements of the story, combined with the tones of pathos and human nobility, make it more than a simple humorous fantasy--it is a classic American fable. The New England dialect of the narrator forms a striking blend with the rhythm and visual imagery drawn from several literary sources. In addition, Benét's use of little-known historical characters on the jury--Simon Girty, the renegade, and the Reverend John Smeet, the strangler--adds novelty and helps give the story a sustained interest. The narrator's final comment that the Devil "hasn't been seen in the state of New Hampshire from that day to this" and "I'm not talking about Massachusetts or Vermont" redeems the story from heavy didacticism.

The story, however, has a moral derived from the grass roots of American tradition. It is, from one perspective, an American version of the story of Job and the Faust legend. Although the name Jabez Stone is implicitly suggestive, Stone is initially unlike Job. He is a poor man plagued by bad luck. When his troubles multiply, he sells his soul to the Devil, not for power like Faust, but for the typically American goal of material prosperity. Unlike with Faust, the tug-of-war for Jabez's soul is not between God and the Devil but between the

epitome of Americanism, Daniel Webster, and Mr. Scratch. Jabez, however, is not damned like Faust, for the American virtues embedded in Webster make him use his capacity to reason, to awaken pity from a biased jury. Webster points out that since the Devil is a foreign prince, he has no authority over an American citizen. The Devil's line of argument is clever and logical. He dates his citizenship back to the day when the first injustice was done to the Indians and when the first slave ship set sail from Africa; and when Webster permits the Devil to choose any judge and jury as long as they are American citizens, the Devil selects Judge Hathorne of the Salem witch trials and a dozen wicked men from hell. Webster uses his powers of elocution to awaken pity from the jury by reviving their sense of manhood. He recalls the simple pleasures of life that can be enjoyed only in freedom. He concedes that although errors and discrimination have taken place in America, something new has been born out of all this--a freer, more vital way of life built by everybody's efforts. Although Jabez is a mean man, he is a man and thus has some good in him. Webster then stresses the fact that being a man is a matter of pride because even in Hell a man's mettle can be recognized.

In his concluding statements Webster makes, through his plea for Jabez, a plea for himself and for humankind. Webster observes that the jurors were out to get Jabez, as well as condemn him, if he fought them with their own weapons. He evokes their sympathy by recalling the symbolic journeying of all men, which is filled with failures and deceptions. Only real men, he stresses, can see the inherent greatness of the journey. This triggers the latent chords of manhood in the jury and their spokesman declares: "The jury has considered its verdict. We find for the defendant, Jabez Stone." The verdict is tempered by the spirit rather than the letter of the law, for the spokesman adds: "but even the damned may salute the eloquence of Mr. Webster." Resorting to a similar spirit Webster also lets the Devil go. The Devil will be back, but his evil has been conquered in some of the United States by humanity, justice, and the representative of a country who symbolizes all of humankind's positive hopes. These layers of symbolic connotations give Benét's story a depth that equals its humor.

Benét's other two Webster tales cannot measure up to the quality of "The Devil and Daniel Webster." In "Daniel Webster and the Sea Serpent," for example, Benét weaves another humorous myth, but the story has little, if any, national significance. Nevertheless, he often channeled this penchant for history into realism and achieved aesthetically laudable results.

In stories such as "The Die-Hard," "Jacob and the Indians," and "Freedom's a Hard-Bought Thing," Benét uses the historical base to portray realism. His technique in these stories is to focus on a protagonist who represents a given historical period and to make his experiences reflect the essence of that period. This type of story obviously requires a strong central character who has to be typical and yet distinct and plausible enough to sustain the reader's interest. Probably the best story of this genre is "Freedom's a Hard-Bought Thing," which won the O. Henry Memorial Award for the best short story of 1940. The story, which derives its effect from its realism and its moral, is equally notable for depicting faithfully the colorful dialect and point of view of specific ethnic groups. The story has a strong narrative core with the narrator, a black woman, telling the children the story of Cue, a plantation slave. Benét's faithful depiction of her speech patterns, rhythms, and diction helps to individualize her but does not obstruct the flow of the plot.

"FREEDOM'S A HARD-BOUGHT THING"

Cue, the protagonist of "Freedom's a Hard-Bought Thing," grows up to be a proud, strong, and affable young man. He likes his work at the plantation blacksmith shop and has no complaints about his life until his parents die in an epidemic. Soon after this, their cabin is given to new slaves, and all that remains is their burial ground. The tragedy changes Cue's complacent outlook on life, and he begins to ask himself questions. This state leads him to Aunt Rachel, a conjure woman, who diagnoses his problem as freedom sickness:

> It's sickness in your blood. . . . It's a sickness in your liver and veins. Your daddy never had it that I know of--he took after his mommy's side. His daddy was a corromante and they is bold and free, and you takes after him. It is the freedom sickness, son Cue.

Aunt Rachel then tells Cue about the underground road and how to find it. Cue then runs away but is caught and whipped. Because of his good record, however, his owners are easy on him. The failure of his attempted escape makes him ponder Aunt Rachel's advice about learning the wisdom of nature by observing her creatures. He even channels his effort toward learning to read so he may acquire some of the wisdom of the white people.

Eventually he meets a white man who tells him of freedom and the underground railroad. Cue again fails to escape because he gives the last place on a boat to his girlfriend Sukey. Cue is branded a runaway and all his bitterness is diverted toward Aunt Rachel because the burden of gaining freedom literally drains him. She then reassures him by reminding him of the ancient freedom of her people and the long tedious road ahead for him. Her words of wisdom solidify Cue's faith, and he feels that he is bound to be a witness to freedom. Soon after this, Cue is sold to new owners and he confronts deliberate cruelty and suffering for the first time. Finally he manages to escape and through the underground railroad arrives in Canada--a free man finally. Unable at first to grasp totally the ramifications of his new state, he ultimately gives himself a full name--John H. Cue--to symbolize his nascent freedom.

One of the reasons for the overwhelming impact of the story is its resemblance to biblical parables. Cue's dual strength of body and mind make him a symbol for all slaves who have struggled to attain freedom, and the dialect of his narrator, as well as the direct invocations of God, remind the reader of the King James Bible. The storyteller's name, "Aunt Rachel," recalls the Old Testament, and her specific memory of her past juxtaposed with the symbolic connotations of Cue's story makes "Freedom's a Hard-Bought Thing" a narrative of a whole people. In addition, Benét's portrayal of Cue is specific and select enough to individualize him and make the overall effect of the story extremely realistic. Details in setting, such as the bubbling pot in Aunt Rachel's cabin and her advice to Cue to study the wisdom embedded in the creatures of nature add both realism and a dash of local color. Finally Benét's sentimentalism in rewarding Cue with another Sukey at the end has a thematic justification; it represents the reevolution and continuity of the race under its newly acquired freedom.

"JOHNNY PYE AND THE FOOL-KILLER"

Benét was not always an optimist and did not always stress fulfillment of hopes in his tales. Through "Johnny Pye and the Fool-Killer" Benét vented a subdued preoccupation to illustrate the dismal aspect of folklore. This story deals with the failure of people who do not follow the rudiments of common sense. Johnny Pye, the protagonist, is the typical naïve youth who is initiated to the ways of the world through hard experience. Johnny, an orphan in a small town, has foster parents, a miller and his wife, who treat him like a fool because they think that is the proper way to bring up a child. When the miller tells him that he is the most foolish boy he has ever seen, Johnny, already fearful of the legendary Fool-Killer, runs away. Johnny's life after this is a series of apprenticeships with a quack doctor, who makes the mistake of returning to a town he had previously visited, and a merchant, who is totally obsessed with making money. These follies make Johnny run away again to avoid entrapment in similar situations. He then meets an inventor of a perpetual motion machine, a drunken fiddler, impetuous soldiers and Indians, a Republican Congressman, a Democratic Congressman, and finally a president of the United States; the last three barrage Johnny with the notion of the omniscience of their respective parties.

On the night he wins the hand of the girl he loves, Johnny hears the dogged steps of the Fool-Killer, but he marries her anyway and accepts the president's appointment to be the postmaster in his hometown. Soon after this, Johnny encounters the Fool-Killer, an old scissors-grinder, putting an edge on a scythe. The Fool-Killer tells Johnny that it is his time. The old man, however, gives Johnny a deferral when he protests. He even agrees to give Johnny the first reprieve in history if he can answer one question: How can a person be a human being and not be a fool?

When Johnny is forty he faces the first major tragedy in his own family--his eldest son drowns. Obsessed with grief, Johnny confronts the Fool-Killer. The Fool-Killer evades him and reminds him that even though his grief cannot be healed, time will pass by, and that

his present responsibilities lie in taking care of his wife and the other children. Time passes and Johnny becomes a grandfather, although his wife dies.

When Johnny is ninety-two years old, he meets the Fool-Killer for the final time. Since the last meeting, Johnny has gone through a great deal and has an answer to the Fool-Killer's question: All humans are basically fools, although the wise and the brave account for the occasional progress. Humanity is a conglomerate of different types and qualities of humans, and only a creature foolish by nature could have been ejected from the Garden of Eden or chosen to come out of the sea onto dry land. Johnny realizes that he has no use for a man who has not been labeled a fool by any of his acquaintances. This answer satisfies the Fool-Killer, who offers Johnny eternal life. Johnny, after pondering the problem, declines on the grounds that his physical decay will continue with the progression of years. In addition, Johnny realizes that with his wife and friends gone, he would have no one to talk to if he decided to accept the Fool-Killer's offer. He questions the Fool-Killer to find out if he would see his friends eventually on the Day of Judgment if he decided to stay around. The Fool-Killer answers: "I can't tell you that . . . I only go so far." Johnny leaves with him, content to go that distance.

In "Johnny Pye and the Fool-Killer," Benét varies his style to suit his material. Although the story begins with a direct address to the reader-- "You don't hear much about the Fool-Killer these days"--the narrator has no symbolic identity other than that specific function. He remains anonymous and blends the elements of humor, folklore, and native wisdom to enhance the total impact. He narrates the tale without serious moralizing and integrates a subtle, refined humor directed to underline the pretensions and eccentricities of the American character. The shift in tone implicit in Johnny's discovery that the "Fool-Killer" is a manifestation of time is achieved smoothly and without any abrupt recourse to philosophical discourse. The theme of the story finally comes into focus when Johnny realizes that folly is an essential and humanizing frailty. His recognition is a reflection of the vision of the "New American Adam" as a creature with distinct possibilities and human flaws. Benét's larger focus, however, is on human morality. The pathos in the final scene, tempered with hope, seems to be a fitting epitaph for Johnny and a fitting ending to an American Fable.

Benét's forte was not the short story, yet his tales will always be popular because of their typically American grassroots. Although his stories were written during a period of national and world upheavals, their patriotic blend of American history, wisdom, and folklore has a timeless quality because it captures the essence of the American spirit--freedom, justice, equality, opportunity, and plain common sense.

OTHER MAJOR WORKS

LONG FICTION: *The Beginning of Wisdom*, 1921; *Young People's Pride*, 1922; *Jean Huguenot*, 1923; *Spanish Bayonet*, 1926; *James Shore's Daughter*, 1934.

PLAY: *Nerves*, pr. 1924 (with John Chipman Farrar); *That Awful Mrs. Eaton*, pr. 1924 (with Farrar); *The Headless Horseman*, pr., pb. 1937; *The Devil and Daniel Webster*, pr. 1938.

RADIO PLAY: *We Stand United, and Other Radio Scripts*, 1945.

POETRY: *Five Men and Pompey*, 1915; *Young Adventure*, 1918; *Heavens and Earth*, 1920; *King David*, 1923; *Tiger Joy*, 1925; *John Brown's Body*, 1928; *Ballads and Poems, 1915-1930*, 1931; *A Book of Americans*, 1933 (with Rosemary Carr Benét); *Burning City*, 1936; *The Ballad of the Duke's Mercy*, 1939; *Western Star*, 1943.

NONFICTION: *America*, 1944; *Stephen Vincent Benét on Writing: A Great Writer's Letters of Advice to a Young Beginner*, 1946; *Selected Letters of Stephen Vincent Benét*, 1960.

MISCELLANEOUS: *Selected Works of Stephen Vincent Benét*, 1942 (Basil Davenport, editor); *Stephen Vincent Benét: Selected Poetry and Prose*, 1942 (Davenport, editor); *The Last Circle: Stories and Poems*, 1946.

BIBLIOGRAPHY

Benét, Stephen Vincent. *Selected Letters of Stephen Vincent Benét*. Edited by Charles A. Fenton. New Haven, Conn.: Yale University Press, 1960. A broad selection of letters reflecting Benét's moods and perceptions about places in the United States and Europe, the people and the literary and social scenes, especially during the 1920's, 1930's, and the few years that he lived in the 1940's.

Bleiler, Everett Franklin. *The Guide to Supernatural Fiction*. Kent, Ohio: Kent State University Press, 1983. Includes a list and commentary on several stories by Benét that deal with themes of fantasy and extrasensory perceptions and hallucinations.

Bunge, Nancy. "American History in the Short Stories of Stephen Vincent Benét and Nathaniel Hawthorne." In *Stephen Vincent Benét: Essays on His Life and Work*, edited by David Garrett Izzo and Lincoln Konkle. Jefferson, N.C.: McFarland, 2003. Comparison of the two writers includes discussion of Benét's stories "Johnny Pye and the Fool-Killer," "A Town for Paul Revere," and "The Devil and Daniel Webster." Maintains that in his historical short stories, Benét affirms that "despite human frailty, the human race as a whole progresses."

Fenton, Charles A. *Stephen Vincent Benét: The Life and Times of an American Man of Letters*. New Haven, Conn.: Yale University Press, 1958. A definitive biography that not only presents the well-documented life of Benét but also comments on the works. Fenton had the cooperation of Rosemary Carr (Mrs. Benét) and access to Benét's diaries.

Partenheimer, David. "Benét's 'The Devil and Daniel Webster.'" *The Explicator* 55 (Fall, 1996): 37-39. Discusses how Benét makes a legend out of Webster, the great American politician and orator, and at the same time paradoxically damns him for his willingness to sell his soul for fame.

Roache, Joel. "Stephen Vincent Benét." In *American Short-Story Writers, 1910-1945*. Vol. 102 in *Dictionary of Literary Biography*. Detroit: Gale Research, 1991. Delineates the writings of Benét and provides a short biography and a commentary on the subject matter and themes of representative short stories. A straightforward and readable article, succinctly written.

Singer, Robert. "One Against All: The New England Past and Present Responsibilities in 'The Devil and Daniel Webster.'" *Literature/Film Quarterly* 22 (1994): 265-271. Discusses the 1941 film version of Benét's story. Argues that the Faust theme in the story and the screenplay that he coauthored uniquely dramatize the conflict between Satan and the American statesman. Argues that the film is a perceptive political treatment of the Depression and the coming of war in the late 1930's.

Snow, Richard F. "Benet's Birthday." *American Heritage* 49 (October, 1998): 6-7. A biographical sketch that comments on Benét's winning the Pulitzer Prize and his attempts to forge a clear American language that was large enough for poetry but also idiomatic and spare.

Stroud, Parry. *Stephen Vincent Benét*. New York: Twayne, 1962. A critique that focuses on Benét's liberalism, reflected in his writings. Stroud places the writer in a historical and cultural frame in an interpretation of Benét's themes. The analysis is clear in its literary perspective and its biographical framework.

Zia Hasan
Updated by Julia B. Boken

GINA BERRIAULT

Born: Long Beach, California; January 1, 1926
Died: Greenbrae, California; July 15, 1999

PRINCIPAL SHORT FICTION

The Mistress, and Other Stories, 1965
The Infinite Passion of Expectation, 1982
Women in Their Beds: New and Selected Stories, 1996
The Great Petrowski: A Fable, 2000
The Tea Ceremony: The Uncollected Writings, 2003 (includes short stories, essays, speeches, and a fragment of a novel)

OTHER LITERARY FORMS

Gina Berriault (behr-ee-OH) authored five novels, *The Descent* (1960), *Conference of Victims* (1962), *The Son* (1966), *The Lights of Earth* (1984), and *Afterwards* (1998). She also wrote a screenplay, adapted from her story of the same title, *The Stone Boy* (1984). The film version was directed by Christopher Cain.

ACHIEVEMENTS

Gina Berriault received numerous awards, including a fellowship from Centro Mexicano de Escritores, Mexico City, Mexico (1963), the National Book Critics Circle Award (1996), the Commonwealth Club Gold Medal and the Bay Area Book Reviewers Award (1997), and the PEN/Faulkner Award for Fiction and

the Rea Award (1997). She also received awards from *The Paris Review*, including the Aga Khan Prize for Fiction, and her work has appeared in *Prize Stories: The O. Henry Awards*.

BIOGRAPHY

Gina Berriault was born in Long Beach, California, to Russian-Jewish immigrants. Her father, who worked as a marble cutter and later as a writer, was not always able to secure employment. Her mother went blind when Berriault was fourteen years old, which, Berriault suggested, influenced her writing. An avid reader, Berriault started to write her own stories in grammar school. Although a drama teacher in high school offered to pay her tuition at a prestigious drama school, the death of Berriault's father prevented her from taking the offer, and she received no further formal education or any formal training as a writer. Instead, Berriault worked various jobs, including clerk, waitress, and news reporter in order to support her mother, brother, and sister.

Berriault was married to J. V. Berriault, a musician, whom she later divorced. Supporting herself and her daughter through her writing, her first success came in 1958 when seven of her stories were collected in Scribners's *Short Story I*. In the 1960's, Berriault lived and wrote in Mexico for a time and wrote articles for *Esquire*, eventually gaining recognition as a writer of serious fiction. She taught creative writing at San Francisco University and at Ohio State University, and she received an appointment as a scholar at the Radcliffe Institute for Independent Study. She died in 1999 at the age of seventy-three.

ANALYSIS

Although Gina Berriault wrote short stories for three decades, she is still considered an undervalued writer who does not receive the critical or commercial attention she deserves. She is often described as a "writer's writer," that is, someone with an enthusiastic following within the literary community but who is unknown outside of it. It is as a writer of short stories that she is best known and admired, and many of her stories have appeared in anthologies. These often brief stories deploy a detached economical prose style to empathically but unsentimentally portray a wide variety of characters in crisis situations. Unable to change their lives or to fully identify or express their feelings of loss, despair, and loneliness, Berriault's characters often suffer in silence and isolation. Particularly important is the theme of unrealized expectations, which contrast with the hard realities in which her characters actually live.

Another virtue of Berriault's work was that she could write convincingly from both male and female perspectives and from the vantage point of both youth and age. Her characters also come from a variety of social, ethnic, and economic backgrounds. Using California, especially the Bay Area, as the setting for many of her stories, her picture of modern California is a far cry from its image as a land of milk and honey. Many of her West Coast denizens lead bleak lives in diminished circumstances, having ended up in dead-end marriages or dead-end jobs.

Berriault's brevity and her pessimistic vision of life have much in common with the minimalist writers of the 1980's, such as Raymond Carver. Her unsentimental depiction of hardship has given her a reputation as a writer of gritty realism, but her work also has an intellectual and poetic side, which gives complexity and mystery to her otherwise often very short stories.

"THE BYSTANDER"

Although this is a very short story, Berriault is able to imply a larger social world, depicting the marginal side of American life and featuring people who are

down on their luck, living out their years in inexpensive boarding houses and state institutions. Told from the perspective of eighteen-year-old Arty, the "bystander" of the title, the story reveals that Arty's father, Lewis, has become an embittered and disappointed man, who has worked all his life and feels he has nothing to show for it. An irrational assault on his girlfriend has landed him in a mental ward, where Arty, whom he has raised since his wife's death, has come to visit him. Much of the story is taken up by the disjointed conversation between father and son, so that it appears to be more of a vignette in which inconsequential details dominate--the two talk in a desultory way about where to eat, how to treat a cold, tool boxes, and travel directions. The underlying point, however, is that Lewis has become weak and dependent and that Arty has assumed a more parental role. When Arty departs, it dawns on him that the strong man he once saw as a good father and provider no longer exists and that he must stand by helplessly as his father utterly loses his old, heroic identity and becomes simply another inmate warehoused in a bleak asylum.

"DEATH OF A LESSER MAN"

"Death of a Lesser Man" is a stream-of-consciousness story, which mixes memory, fantasy, and reality. When Claudia's husband Gerald suddenly faints at a party, they both fear he has a terminal illness. While they wait for him to undergo a series of tests, Claudia experiences a psychological crisis in which she guiltily realizes that Gerald's death would constitute a liberation for her, the possibility of another existence filled with new chances for passion, adventure, and intellectual stimulation. Claudia is also haunted by an imagined stalker, a nightmarish figure, who seems be stealing away the dreams that have sustained her in her daily life. These dreams are fueled by memories of a special time in her past, a brief visit to Paris, where she prowled the streets looking for the French writer Albert Camus. Instead of finding Camus, however, the menacing dolt of her previous dreams and fears seems to invade her bed at the end of the story, cropping her hair with large, cold scissors and leaving her in a state of utter desolation.

"THE INFINITE PASSION OF EXPECTATION"

"The Infinite Passion of Expectation" is told from the perspective of a young waitress who has been paying a small fee for therapy from an elderly English psychiatrist. The old man tells the waitress that he still allows himself great expectations of love and other pleasures and has advised her to do the same. In fact, at age seventy-nine, the ever-youthful psychiatrist is actually considering marriage to, or at least a love affair with, the young waitress, beginning a tentative if somewhat manipulative courtship of her. Learning from the lessons of the psychiatrist, however, she rejects him, realizing a love affair with the old man would cut off many other possibilities for her, virtually ending her life. Because of her diminished circumstances, the waitress had always thought that to dream was to delude herself, but inspired by the old man's advice and example she gives herself over to "the infinite passion of expectation."

"DIARY OF K. W."

"Diary of K. W." is told through a series of entries in the diary of an old woman known only by her initials, K. W. She is undergoing a psychological crisis, which begins when she is fired from a job as a substitute helper in a grammar school cafeteria. Reasoning that if the children eat their food they will only grow up to suffer as she has, she refuses to serve them their hot lunches. She also begins deliberately to starve herself, even while trying to reach out to the neighbors in her apartment building, notably a new tenant, a self-involved Dutch architect. She occasionally leaves in his mailbox samples of her artwork, which she signs, semi-anonymously, "K. W." The reader begins to realize that, although her last job was a poorly paid and unglamourous one, K. W. is actually an artist and an intellectual, and that she had once been valedictorian of her class, been married, and had a promising life. It all ended, however, in poverty and isolation. Although she is scrupulous about feeding the architect's neglected cats, she allows herself to starve to death without seeking help, and her neighbors never realize that she is dying. More than the hungry body, however, this is a story about the hungry soul. Her diaries tell readers that she wishes to be judged not by her body or by her external circumstances but by her soul, which she describes as a Janus-like entity, which can simultaneously look at who she is and who she might have been.

"THE STONE BOY"

This story, set on a family farm, concerns the tragic accidental shooting of the family's older brother Eugie by his younger brother Arnold. The nine-year-old Arnold seems to show no remorse for accidentally shooting and killing Eugie while they were on their way to do their morning chores. Shunned by his community and family, Arnold begins to live within himself, unable to articulate his grief and denied the comfort he needs from others. Although Arnold tries to reach out to his parents, and they, in spite of their grief and anger, try to reach out to him, there is never a reconciliation. Arnold is left permanently estranged from his family, presenting an unreadable, unreachable "stone face" to the world that does not reveal his inner world of anguish and loneliness.

OTHER MAJOR WORKS

LONG FICTION: *The Descent*, 1960; *Conference of Victims*, 1962; *The Son*, 1966; *The Lights of Earth*, 1984; *Afterwards*, 1998.

SCREENPLAY: *The Stone Boy*, 1984.

MISCELLANEOUS: *The Tea Ceremony: The Uncollected Writings*, 2003 (includes short stories, essays, speeches, and a fragment of a novel).

BIBLIOGRAPHY

Amdahl, Gary. "Making Literature." *The Nation* 262, no. 25 (June 24, 1996): 31-32. Important review of *Women in Their Beds*, which suggests that Berriault ought to be as familiar to readers as Toni Morrison or John Updike. Laments her lack of recognition, praises her as a writer who has written magnificently and consistently for forty years, and singles out the depth of understanding she brings to the creation of her characters.

Berriault, Gina. "'Don't I Know You?': An Interview with Gina Berriault." Interview by Bonnie Lyons and Bill Oliver. *Literary Review* 37, no. 4 (Summer, 1994): 714-723. Discusses Berriault's childhood, her father, her favorite authors, her opinions of contemporary fiction, and the pressures on contemporary writers to evade or falsify the truth. Describing the purpose of her fiction as compassion and comprehension,

Berriault also notes that, like all serious writers of fiction, she is a political writer.

_____. *The Tea Ceremony: The Uncollected Writings*. Washington, D.C.: Shoemaker, Hoard, 2003. This posthumously issued collection features five previously unpublished short stories, an excerpt from a novel, and nonfiction works. It also contains an essay by Richard Yates in which he measures "The Achievement of Gina Berriault."

Dubus, Andre. "The Infinite Passion of Expectation." *America* 151 (September 8, 1984). This important review by one of the finest contemporary American short-story writers praises this collection as the best book of short stories by a living American author.

Gelfant, Blanche H., ed. *The Columbia Companion to the Twentieth-Century American Short Story*. New York: Columbia University Press, 2000. Includes a chapter in which Berriault's short stories are analyzed.

Harshaw, Tobin. "*Women in Their Beds*." *New York Times Book Review*, May 5, 1990, 22. Praises Berriault's gift for language, the complexity of her characterization, and her ability to engage the reader sympathetically in the crises her characters face. Faults Berriault's stories for being too low-key.

Milton, Edith. "Lives That Touch Without Intimacy." *The New York Times Book Review*, January 8, 1983. Positive review of *The Infinite Passion of Expectation*, describing the stories as flawless miniatures presenting paralyzed characters whose shattered expectations have led them to live in dreams or in the past rather than the present world.

Poore, Charles. "Books of the Times: The Moment of Truth Doesn't Need Stretching." *The New York Times*, September, 1965. Praises Berriault for finding originality in what otherwise might be seen as predictable subjects. Draws attention to her economy and her minimalist, open endings, her sympathetic picture of the down-and-out, and her satiric look at intellectual bohemia in the Bay Area.

Shelnutt, Eve, ed. "Almost Impossible." In *The Confidence Woman: Twenty-six Woman Writers at Work*. Atlanta, Ga.: Longstreet Press, 1991. Insightful interview with Berriault in which she discusses the nature of writing, her own creative process, her identity as a woman writer, and her students' reactions to her short stories.

Margaret Boe Birns

Wendell Berry

Born: Henry County, Kentucky; August 5, 1934

Principal short fiction

The Wild Birds: Six Stories of the Port William Membership, 1986

Fidelity: Five Stories, 1992

Watch with Me: And Six Other Stories of the Yet Remembered Ptolemy Proudfoot and His Wife, Miss Minnie, Née Quinch, 1994

Two More Stories of the Port William Membership, 1997

That Distant Land: The Collected Stories, 2004

Three Short Novels, 2002

Other literary forms

A prolific writer, Wendell Berry has published more than forty books in all of the major genres, including novels, novellas, short-story collections, essays, nonfiction, and poetry volumes. Wallace Stegner remarked, "It is hard to say whether I like this writer better as a poet, an essayist, or a novelist. He is all three, at a high level."

Achievements

A master of poetry, fiction, and the essay, prolific in all these genres, Wendell Berry is considered one of America's foremost progressive agrarian writers and spokesmen for small farming and traditional rural life. Berry has received a Guggenheim

Foundation Fellowship (1961), the Vachel Lindsay Prize (1962), a Rockefeller Foundation Fellowship (1965), a National Endowment of the Arts grant (1969), a National Institute of Arts and Letters award (1971), the Jean Stein Award from the American Academy and Institute of Arts and Letters (1987), the Milner Award (1987), a Lannan Foundation Award for Nonfiction (1989), the Orion Society's John Hay Award (1993), the T. S. Eliot Award for Creative Writing (1994), the Aiken Taylor Award for Poetry (1994), the Thomas Merton Award (1999), the Poet's Prize (2000), the Premio Artusi Award (2008), and the Cleanth Brooks Medal for Lifetime Achievement from the Fellowship of Southern Writers (2009).

BIOGRAPHY

The eldest of four children in a fifth-generation farming family, Wendell Erdman Berry was born in Henry County, Kentucky, on August 5, 1934. His father, John Marshall Berry, was a prominent local attorney and aide to a congressman, Virgil Chapman. Wendell Berry attended Millersburg Military Institute (MMI) and the University of Kentucky, Lexington, earning a B.A. in 1956. After earning an M.A. in English at the University of Kentucky in 1957, he married Tanya Amyx in 1957, and their daughter, Mary Dee, was born in 1958. Berry studied creative writing with Stegner at Stanford University in 1958 and 1959.

When Berry returned to Kentucky in 1960 to farm for a year, he published his first novel, *Nathan Coulter*. A Guggenheim Fellowship in creative writing took him to France and Italy in 1961 and 1962, and he subsequently taught at New York University for two years before returning to the University of Kentucky English Department. His son, Pryor Clifford, was born in 1962. Berry published his poetry volume *The Broken Ground* in 1964, and a Rockefeller Foundation Fellowship followed in 1965. In 1964, Berry bought the 125-acre Lane's Landing Farm in Port Royal, Kentucky, and settled with his family there to raise sheep. A prolific writer, he published his first essay collection, *The Long-Legged House*, in 1969, and many additional novels, poetry volumes, and essay collections earned him growing recognition and awards as a leading cultural critic and defender of rural America.

ANALYSIS

Though Wendell Berry has published four small editions of short stories and two novellas, *That Distant Land*, a collection of his short stories, is the primary source for study. Of Berry's thirty-two short stories, all but nine are included in *That Distant Land*. His short stories incorporate themes related to farming, good husbandry, community, a concern for land and place; to social justice and the rule of law, marriage, neighborliness, and aging; and to love, suffering, forgiveness, and redemption.

In his short stories, Berry offers an idealized vision of an agrarian moral and social order grounded in a small rural community of self-supporting but interconnected family farms marked for the most part by stable marriages, hard work, thrift, good husbandry, friendship, supportive communities of farmers and townspeople, living traditions, and intergenerational memory. The stories' time span is from about 1888 through the present, though most stories are set in the Great Depression era. Many of Berry's stories deal with testing the limits of or reaffirming the moral and

Wendell Berry (AP Photo/Ed Reinke)

social order of his fictional "Port William Membership." In these stories, Berry constantly retells fictional versions of his own life. If the work of Berry's fiction is to imagine local culture, then "The Work of Local Culture" is to create the fertile soil for the creative imagination to know the conditions and possibilities of its particular place.

His characters discipline their lives and create order through thrift, hard work, honesty, charity, forbearance, and love. Men and women are esteemed according to the content of their characters: their probity, rectitude, and responsibility. The Port William Membership is a living community, remembered as it existed before World War II. In this region, burley tobacco is the major crop, along with livestock and garden produce. The mark of a successful farmer is a full barn, smokehouse, pantry, and larder at the end of the season. Some fail through shiftlessness or alcoholism, but more often through greed or discontent with the possibilities of rural life; when they leave, they disrupt the community.

In the postwar years, discontent with farm life, greed, heedless expansion, expensive machinery, debt, agribusiness, and the incursion of suburbs all eroded Berry's agrarian ideal. However idealized, Port William is in decline, along with the rest of rural America, and its prospects are uncertain.

Berry's short stories tend to be moralistic or didactic, emphasizing character development, setting, description, and theme more than dramatic development, suspense, or action. Whatever dramatic conflict exists is subtle and grows out of self-awareness, conflicts, or deficiencies in character, while other stories are primarily tall tales or humorous sketches. In large part, the story is built around the narrator-protagonist's insights or awareness of lessons of life. Berry's stories often illustrate agrarian themes introduced in his essays.

PORT WILLIAM MEMBERSHIP

Consisting of insiders and outsiders, the Port William Membership is Berry's fictional community, located in rural north-central Kentucky. It is composed of five major families--the Beechums, Feltners, Coulters, Wheelers, and Catletts--and some notable outsiders, such as town barber Jayber Crow and truck driver Sam Hanks. Another notable outsider who defies social conventions, is the "wayward" Burley Coulter, bachelor, farmer, and hunter. Often Berry's stories involve the narrator's recollection of a major family event, retold for its moral or ethical significance. Elders such as Ben Feltner, Elton Penn, Tol Proudfoot, and attorney Wheeler Catlett often serve as teachers and moral exemplars.

The membership is held together by collective memory, intergenerational generosity, and neighborly assistance in times of need. As the repository of those memories, narrator Andy Catlett looks back to the wisdom and behavior of his parents and grandparents. Gender roles are traditional in Berry's fiction, with women remaining in the background as farm wives and mothers, with the exception of Hannah Coulter. African American farm families are occasionally mentioned, notably in *The Hidden Wound* (1970). Some of Berry's comic sketches recall the Southwestern, tall-tale humor of Mark Twain and William Faulkner.

THE WILD BIRDS

In the title story of the *The Wild Birds,* lawyer Wheeler Catlett must untangle a land-inheritance dilemma when Burley Coulter wants to will his land to his illegitimate son, Danny Branch, rather than sell it to Nathan and Hannah Coulter, who are farming it. When Burley refuses to legally affirm his paternity, appealing to local awareness of his common-law relationship with Kate Branch, Wheeler must deal with the legal and moral implications of Burley's unconventional decision.

"The Boundary" and "That Distant Land" recount Matt Feltner's last days as an elderly farmer who had an incapacitating stroke while checking his livestock fences in a steep, inaccessible part of his farm. Lying paralyzed on the ground and waiting to be rescued, he is still able to appreciate the beauty of nature and feel gratitude for the land and life he has been given. The elegiac tone of the story is conveyed through Matt's loving appreciation of the beauty of his farm's rolling hills and pastoral landscape. "That Distant Land" shifts to grandson Andy Catlett's memories of sitting with his grandfather, Matt, bedridden after that stroke. Berry presents the dignity of age and dying within the circle of family after a life well lived.

FIDELITY

This volume contains the powerful story "Pray Without Ceasing," in which the narrator, Andy Catlett, is given an old newspaper clipping describing his great-grandfather's murder and its aftermath. Distraught Thad Coulter shoots his best friend, Ben Feltner, over a financial misunderstanding, and Ben's family forgoes revenge for forgiveness, resulting in eventual reconciliation through marriage between the families. "A Jonquil for Mary Penn" recalls how a struggling young farm couple is welcomed into the community through small acts of kindness and generosity.

The title story, "Fidelity," deals with the legal and moral consequences of Danny Branch's decision to rescue his dying father, Burley Coulter, from life-support machinery in a Louisville hospital so that he can die with dignity at home in Port William surrounded by his family. The conventions of the modern legal and medical world collide with an older set of rural customs that value human dignity and respect for the dying. Danny must answer to the law for bringing his father home to die outdoors under a tree at his favorite campsite, but Danny has been faithful to Burley's wishes. "Making It Home" describes bachelor farmer Art Rowanberry's discharge from the Army and return to Port William and civilian life after serving on the front in World War II.

WATCH WITH ME

This collection of seven often whimsical and comic stories is about Ptolemy (Tol) Proudfoot and his wife, Miss Minnie Quinch, a childless, odd, but devoted farmer-schoolteacher couple. A large man, Tol is a skillful and industrious farmer who much admires and often defers to his better-educated, petite wife, Miss Minnie. The stories of their courtship and marriage recall their humorous attempts to drive their new Model A Ford, their misadventures in going to the state fair, Miss Minnie's disapproval of hard liquor, Tol's outwitting a Louisville grocer, and how, in the manner of Twain's humor, Tol and his cousins' mischief resulted in a dog and cat chase disrupting a family Sabbath dinner. "The Solemn Boy" recalls the Proudfoots' generosity to a homeless man and boy during the Great Depression years. On a serious note, in "Watch with Me," Tol and his neighbors struggle long and hard to disarm a mentally deranged neighbor, Nightlife, who has walked off with Tol's loaded shotgun and is in danger of harming himself or others.

THAT DISTANT LAND

This edition includes twenty-three stories arranged chronologically and interlinked with Berry's six Port William novels to create a sustained narrative of the lives of five generations of rural life from 1888 to the present. The collected volume also includes a map of Port William and a genealogy of Berry's four major families--the Beechums, Feltners, Coulters, and Wheelers--although others, such as the Proudfoots and Catletts, are not included. It combines all of the stories in *The Wild Birds*, *Fidelity*, and *Watch with Me*, plus four never-before-collected stories.

In "The Hurt Man," Matt Feltner recalls the moral lessons learned from his mother's sheltering and protecting a wounded man from a mob. "Don't Send a Boy to Do a Man's Work" has a folktale quality, in which Athey Keith recalls from his youth the chaos that ensued at a fall pig-killing when his father's unexpected trip to Louisville left him alone to supervise it. Everyone got drunk on moonshine, the local Ku Klux Klansmen raided, and only the timely return of his father saved the year's meat. "It Wasn't Me" describes Jack Beecham's generosity to a struggling young farmer, Elton Penn, an act that can never be repaid except with gratitude. "The Discovery of Kentucky" humorously recounts Burley Coulter's attempts to disrupt the governor's inaugural parade with some too-authentic scenes from Kentucky frontier life. In the last story, "The Inheritors," Danny Branch survives a drive home from the Louisville stockyards with the elderly and confused but imperturbable Wheeler Catlett, who drives on the wrong side of the interstate facing oncoming traffic.

OTHER MAJOR WORKS

LONG FICTION: *Nathan Coulter*, 1960 (revised 1985); *A Place on Earth*, 1967 (revised 1983); *The Memory of Old Jack*, 1974; *Remembering*, 1988; *A World Lost*, 1996; *Jayber Crow*, 2000; *Hannah Coulter*, 2004; *Andy Catlett:Early Travels*, 2006.

POETRY: *November Twenty-six, Nineteen Hundred Sixty-Three*, 1963; *The Broken Ground*, 1964; *Openings*, 1968; *Findings*, 1969; *Farming: A Hand Book*, 1970; *The Country of Marriage*, 1973; *An Eastward Look*, 1974; *Horses*, 1975; *Sayings and Doings*, 1975; *To What Listens*, 1975; *The Kentucky River: Two Poems*, 1976; *There Is Singing Around Me*, 1976; *Three Memorial Poems*, 1976; *Clearing*, 1977; *The Gift of Gravity*, 1979; *A Part*, 1980; *The Wheel*, 1982; *Collected Poems, 1957-1982*, 1985; *Sabbaths*, 1987; *Traveling at Home*, 1989; *Sabbaths, 1987-1990*, 1992; *Entries*, 1994; *The Farm*, 1995; *A Timbered Choir: The Sabbath Poems, 1979-1997*, 1998; *The Selected Poems of Wendell Berry*, 1998; *Given: New Poems*, 2005; *The Mad Farmer Poems*, 2008; *Leavings*, 2010

NONFICTION: *The Long-Legged House*, 1969; *The Hidden Wound*, 1970; *The Unforeseen Wilderness*, 1971; *A Continuous Harmony*, 1972; *The Unsettling of America: Culture and Agriculture*, 1977; *Recollected Essays, 1965-1980*, 1981; *The Gift of Good Land*, 1981; *Standing by Words*, 1983; *Home Economics*, 1987; *Harland Hubbard: Life and Work*, 1990; *What Are People For?*, 1990; *Standing on Earth*, 1991; *The Discovery of Kentucky*, 1991; *Sex, Economy, Freedom, and Community*, 1993; *Another Turn of the Crank*, 1995; *Life Is a Miracle: An Essay Against Modern Superstition*, 2000; *In the Presence of Fear: Three Essays for a Changed World*, 2002; *The Art of the Commonplace: The Agrarian Essays of Wendell Berry*, 2002 (Norman Wirzba, editor); *Citizenship Papers: Essays*, 2003; *Standing by Words: Essays*, 2005; *The Way of Ignorance, and Other Essays*, 2005; *Conversations with Wendell Berry*, 2007 (Morris Allen Grubbs, editor); *Bringing It to the Table: On Farming and Food*, 2009; *Imagination in Place: Essays*, 2010.

BIBLIOGRAPHY

Angyal, Andrew J. *Wendell Berry*. New York: Twayne, 1995. An introductory critical biography of Berry's life and career through the mid-1990's, including a selected primary and secondary bibliography.

Bonzo, J. Matthew, and Michael R. Stevens. *Wendell Berry and the Cultivation of Life: A Reader's Guide*. Grand Rapids, Mich.: Brazos Press, 2008. A critical overview and thematic introduction to Berry's writings.

Goodrich, Jane. *The Unforeseen Self in the Works of Wendell Berry*. Columbia: University of Missouri Press, 2001. A book-length critical study that views Berry primarily as an autobiographical writer using five different points of view to reimagine his life from various perspectives.

Merchant, Paul, ed. *Wendell Berry*. Lewiston, Ida.: Confluence Press, 1991. A collection of interviews, letters, poems, reminiscences, and appreciative and interpretive essays about Berry's work.

Peters, Jason, ed. *Wendell Berry: Life and Work*. Lexington: University Press of Kentucky, 2007. A collection of biographical sketches, personal accounts, literary criticism, and social commentary about Berry's life and work.

Shuman, Joel James, and L. Roger Owens, eds. *Wendell Berry and Religion: Heaven's Earthly Life*. Lexington: University of Kentucky Press, 2009. A collection of essays on the Christian ideals of stewardship, reverence, and fellowship in Berry's writings, with topics including medicine, law, ministry, and education.

Smith, Kimberly K. *Wendell Berry and the Agrarian Tradition*. Lawrence: University Press of Kansas, 2003. A book-length study of Berry's agrarian social and political philosophy, moral vision, and agrarian democracy in terms of the American agrarian and environmental traditions.

Andrew J. Angyal

DORIS BETTS

Born: Statesville, North Carolina; June 4, 1932
Also known as: Doris June Waugh Betts

PRINCIPAL SHORT FICTION

The Gentle Insurrection, and Other Stories, 1954
The Astronomer, and Other Stories, 1965
Beasts of the Southern Wild, and Other Stories, 1973

OTHER LITERARY FORMS

Doris Betts is the author of several novels: *Tall Houses in Winter* (1957), *The Scarlet Thread* (1964), *The River to Pickle Beach* (1972), *Heading West* (1981), a February, 1982, Book-of-the-Month Club selection, *Souls Raised from the Dead* (1994), and *The Sharp Teeth of Love* (1997).

ACHIEVEMENTS

Doris Betts won the 1954 University of North Carolina G. P. Putnam Award for her first short-story collection, *The Gentle Insurrection, and Other Stories*, and her third collection, *Beasts of the Southern Wild, and Other Stories*, was a National Book Award finalist. The state of North Carolina presented her with its Medal for Literature in 1975. She won a John Dos Passos Award in 1983 and a Medal of Merit from the Academy of Arts and Letters in 1989.

BIOGRAPHY

Doris June Waugh Betts is the daughter of William Elmore and Mary Ellen Freeze Waugh. She was educated in the public schools of Statesville, North Carolina, and at the University of North Carolina at Greensboro (1950-1953) and later at Chapel Hill (1954). On July 5, 1952, she married Lowry Matthew Betts, a lawyer. They had three children. Betts claimed that her childhood experiences as an Associate Reform Presbyterian have stayed with her:

"The Bible is a strong source in my writing because I grew up in a strict religious family, strongly fundamentalist. . . . Bible stories themselves are marvelous, really marvelous, background for a writer--a lot of the rhythms, to begin with, in the Bible are good for writers. And secondly, all these stories are very physical, very specific and concrete."

Betts taught English, including writing, at the University of North Carolina at Chapel Hill. She received a Tanner Award for excellence in undergraduate teaching in 1973, the same year that *Beasts of the Southern Wild, and Other Stories* was nominated for a National Book Award. She and her husband bought a farm near Chapel Hill. Betts declined a nomination for chancellorship of the University of North Carolina but continued to teach for many years. When she retired, an endowed chair at the university was named in her honor, The Doris Betts Distinguished Professor in Creative Writing.

ANALYSIS

Doris Betts's fiction is strongly rooted in the landscape and experiences of North Carolina. Her first collections were solidly realistic stories about her own part of that state, the Piedmont Upper South, and they focus on everyday concerns, such as growing up, growing old, racial tensions, family relationships, and death as it is perceived by the dying and the living left behind. Her later work, although still centered on everyday experiences and characters, time, and mortality, also moved into fantasy and passed through a concern with death into a consideration of the afterlife. Her later stories, as always rich in diction and image, operate on several levels simultaneously.

THE GENTLE INSURRECTION, AND OTHER STORIES

Betts's earliest collection, *The Gentle Insurrection, and Other Stories*, presents twelve tales, each involving a paradox or oxymoron. In all of them, characters who would cause an insurrection by breaking out of their situations or typical lifestyles go no further than contemplating changes or making plans for them. The plots concern race relations in a small southern town in the 1950's, mothers deserting children, children coming of age, love, illness, and death. The characters face the burdens of ordinary life as they struggle against serious odds, especially loneliness. Betts's universal theme is the difficulty of achieving real understanding between people.

In this collection, then, there is at least momentary defiance by individuals toward their situations and their discovery that life is not a matter of finding happiness on some climactic day. While the characters seek self-identity, independence, and, often, love, the issue of morality usually lurks in the background. These threads remained central to Betts's fiction, long and short, throughout her writing career. Her style is suggestive, metaphysical, economical, flexible, and religiously allusive; her sobriety and humor are also in evidence. The setting is characteristically southern, in terms of both geography and mind frames.

An example of someone involved in a "gentle insurrection" by attempting to break out of her mold is Agnes Parker in "Miss Parker Possessed." Here a fortyish public librarian tries to jettison her persona of an unloved old maid who focuses on her library duties completely and efficiently. Her "other self" longing to emerge reveals an inner being that presses her to declare her love for Lewis Harvey, a widower and the head teller at the Merchants' and Industrial Bank in her town.

At a meeting of the Committee of Councilmen Supervising Library Management, Miss Parker evidences her state of mind when she suggests that the library acquire a competent textbook on sex. Previously, her "second personality" had shocked some prudish women at the Ladies Bi-Monthly Book Club, which Agnes Parker has attended regularly. Overhearing Mr. Harvey and another council member discussing the possibility of first hiring a library assistant and then pensioning off the apparently sickly Miss Parker, she enters the meeting room and resumes her former demeanor. She can now meet Mr. Harvey's glance and let out a long breath without the earlier fluttering in her chest. Rather, she sees the longed-for lover of her timid desires as a balding individual with protruding front

teeth, an unpleasant-looking scar on his left index finger, and a similarly unattractive mole behind his ear.

The resumption of her former routines, responsibilities, and persona suggest the sorrow of a lost opportunity to love and communicate--elements so crucial in Betts's thinking--and thus the return to her earlier empty life. That is how the author achieves the oxymoron promised in the collection title.

THE ASTRONOMER, AND OTHER STORIES

In the first movement of Betts's *The Astronomer, and Other Stories*, the eponymous hero (his real name is Horton Beam) retires from the huge, noisy textile mill in North Carolina where he has spent most of his adult life. It is his last day, and his coworkers give him a gold watch as he collects his last paycheck. At last, after a lifetime of subservience to the machine, he crosses a patch of grass outside the plant in defiance of a Keep Off the Grass sign and mutters (under his breath), "They can all go to hell." It is important for the tone of the story and for Beam's ultimate position in life that he does not have the courage to yell it out loud or to commit any major infraction of the rules. He tells his coworkers on that last day that he is going to do nothing. At the house where he has lived alone since his wife died years ago, his watch off, he begins looking at the books left in the house and comes across his dead son's copy of Walt Whitman's *Leaves of Grass* (1855) and sees the line ". . . heard the learned astronomer." Beam decides on impulse to become a Learned Astronomer. This is a novel (or novella) of ideas, a short allegory set in prose form, a multileveled symbolic novel in the tradition of Nathaniel Hawthorne, and, as it turns out, a consummate exercise in mythopoetic fiction--for Betts's artistry is such that it can be all these things, and in such a short space.

The next day, a young man, Fred Ridge, appears on Horton Beam's doorstep, wanting to rent a room. The Astronomer ignores him and studies his star charts all day, but the young man is still there at nightfall, so Beam rents him a room. The next morning Ridge presents The Astronomer with his paramour--and the representative of the labyrinth--Eva, who has abandoned her husband and children and run off with Ridge, one of her husband's used-car salesmen. These characters are not merely people but the allegorical embodiments of ideas or forces or human options and choices. Eva reminds one of Eve by her name, but she is more like Lilith, the first (and evil) wife of Adam. Lilith, according to legend, objected to the recumbent position in sexual intercourse, preferring the superior one; when Adam tried to compel her obedience, she uttered the name of God and left. Lilith became the destroyer of the newborn (just as, later in the short story, Eva aborts the love child she conceived during her affair with Ridge). God is supposed to have sent three angels, Senoy, Sansenoy, and Semangelof, to fetch Lilith back; she would not go but agreed to spare newborn children if the names of the three or their likenesses on an amulet appeared above the infants. This led to the apotropaic rite formerly practiced by devout Jews in which a message in charcoal was written inside a charcoal circle on the wall of the newborn's room: "ADAM AND EVE. OUT, LILITH!" Jewish children who laughed in their sleep were supposed to have been caressed by Lilith.

The other Hebrew legend about Lilith is that she ruled as queen in Zmargad and in Sheba; in another, because she left Adam before the Fall, she was immortal, and she not only strangled sleeping infants but also seduced men in their sleep. In this novella, The Astronomer, at the height of his infatuation for Eva, feels that he has for a moment seen through sheet and mattress and boards and earth right down to hell, which is certainly congruent to Eva's representing Lilith. If Lilith is a demon, then The Astronomer represents Judeo-Christian spiritual history against the forces of darkness, another reading of the allegorical content of this novella. The Astronomer at another point claims identification with Adam in that he gives names to stars. It might also be noted, however, that this allegory is not merely religious, but also aesthetic; its conflict is between the artists and those involved in the quotidian burdens of life. To give the story a "middle reading," these are real people, too, in a real workaday North Carolina. The car lot where Fred Ridge used to work for Eva's husband was depressing, Eva says. The progress of life annoys her; for her, the momentary pleasures of life, the feeling of slight removal from things rushing to their conclusions, are part and parcel of living. She fears final things, and so, from the beginning, her

adventure with Ridge and her abandonment of the children can only be a momentary loop in the straight road to death through alienation and despair. She is not, perhaps, a good example of those who live recklessly by improvisation, dedicated to survival by their wits, but here, as in so many Betts stories, there are no final winners.

Eva is a sensualist. She has, like her little girl, chewed tar from the telephone poles, and she asks The Astronomer if he has ever chewed peach-tree gum or eaten wild locusts (this reference is almost biblical). Eva is pregnant with Fred's child, however, and she goes to an abortionist on the street running between the black and white communities. He makes her prostitute herself as the price of the abortion. Eva's troubles, her new sordid life, and his going down into Nighttown to find her force a conversion upon The Astronomer (and it might be remembered that in Hebrew legend, Lilith goes East, beyond Eden, to live by the Red Sea, home of the lascivious demons). It is not quite a religious experience; Betts's control does not leave her for an instant. The Astronomer begins to think of Ridge, and he begins to feel sexual desire for Eva as she recovers from her abortion; desire is something he has not felt for a long, long time. He comes alive; he thinks he can hear the grass growing. His telescope becomes covered with dust. After Eva recovers, both of them disappear, an ending that shocks the reader but provides a perfect conclusion to the story.

"THE SPIES IN THE HERB HOUSE"

"The Spies in the Herb House," in *The Astronomer, and Other Stories*, is a beautiful evocation through unobtrusive prose of a happy childhood; it is based on a wickedly funny conceit: that two innocent young girls growing up in Piedmont, North Carolina, during World War II could believe that a popular graffito could stand for Fight Until Children Killed. There is not much motion in the story, in the great tradition of stories of childhood remembered, and it is rather closely autobiographical (one little girl's name is Doris), but the diction, the timing of the joke (and it is timed as expertly as any stand-up comedian's), and the characterization of the girls all make the story more than worthwhile. The Herb House of the story is a large, ugly wooden building in the Herb Capital of the World (Statesville,

North Carolina), where elder flowers, true love, wild cherry bark, blackberry and pokeweed roots, sumac berries, ginseng, sassafras bark, catnip, balm of Gilead buds, and other herbs were stored until a few years before the story opened; the warehouse is no longer in use. It is the sort of place two tomboys like Doris and Betty Sue would break into, and they do.

Once inside, they discover an "X" on a box, which they mistake for a swastika (this story takes place during World War II, and Doris's playmate has boyfriends in the service who write her letters). Later, the girls, who believe that they have discovered a German spy hideout, have "other dreadful discoveries to make." They see "two long glass counters against one wall. They were about as high as the glass counters which held candy at the dime store. By taking turns, by twisting our necks, we could see they were lined with velvet." Doris immediately deduces the German spies are engaged in diamond smuggling. "Why would the Germans do that?" Betty Sue asks. "Submarines cost money!" Doris says. Then they see the graffito written on the wall and deduce its meaning too and feel utterly powerless and alone. "There was so much I understood that day--valor, and patriotism, and the nature of the enemy. Even my fear was specific. The war had come to me and I did not have to go to it. I was one with all the innocent victims of history." This is not a bad discovery, however frightening, to make at any age.

"BENSON WATTS IS DEAD AND IN VIRGINIA"

Betts said about the story "Benson Watts Is Dead and in Virginia" that it "is a logical extension of the things that interest me most in fiction, which, as I say, are mortality and time. . . . " The premise is intriguing. It is in fact the one question that has tormented every human culture since time began: Where do we go when we die? In this first-person narrative, Benson Watts, a sometime schoolteacher, dies and wakes up in Virginia. He is sixty-five and survived by grandchildren, "none of whom I liked very much." He looks like John L. Lewis and teaches United States and world history in high schools all over Texas.

When he wakes up one day, he is bald, younger, forty again, dressed in Dacron trousers and a pair of shoes he has never owned. Around his neck hangs a medallion that says:

1. Dwell, then travel
2. Join forces
3. Disremember

He finds a house he immediately recognizes as the one Henry David Thoreau built by Walden Pond. Shortly thereafter, Olena, a pregnant red-headed woman in a hairdresser's white uniform, appears; she is in her late twenties and has stayed alive eating persimmons. Next, as throughout the story, animals from medieval bestiaries once read by Benson Watts begin to follow them everywhere, coming almost close enough to be seen in detail. Then the two are joined by Melvin Drum, a connoisseur of religions and a street-corner preacher, who is beaten to death in an alley by men who mistake his identity. There is, at this point, a welter of religious ideas, allusions, references, symbols, and speculations entering the story. Betts is writing here of Everyman Dead, not just a meditation on the Christian heaven or purgatory, limbo or paradise.

The three have been following, at first separately and then together, the first injunction written on Watts's disc: "Travel." All three begin to travel through endless virgin forests, over pure limpid streams, deeper and deeper into a world that none of them recognizes. Now, with the exception perhaps of Watts, they begin to obey the third injunction: "Disremember." Watts begins to make love to Olena. Drum disappears. They continue to drift across an empty planet thick with forests. The baby in Olena's body disappears, the first disconcerting sign: Perhaps their time in this limbo is keyed to the number of years each has lived. Finally Olena dies, leaving Watts alone. The tale ends with Watts closing his journal (the story has been a sort of epistle intended for dispatch to the Void, or perhaps for the next one to come along) and waiting for an end he cannot imagine. The novella is built around a powerful idea, which accounts for most of its thrust, but its execution and the expert blending of philosophy with realistic rendering of the human beings involved make it almost unique in American letters. Betts breaks new ground in her first fantasy short story and dramatizes many beliefs and attitudes toward death. The most important thing about the story, however, is that it reads almost like a biblical tale: It is authentic, human, and cathartic.

OTHER MAJOR WORKS

LONG FICTION: *Tall Houses in Winter*, 1957; *The Scarlet Thread*, 1964; *The River to Pickle Beach*, 1972; *Heading West*, 1981; *Souls Raised from the Dead*, 1994; *The Sharp Teeth of Love*, 1997.

BIBLIOGRAPHY

Betts, Doris. "Whispering Hope." In *Shouts and Whispers: Twenty-one Writers Speak About Their Writing and Their Faith*, edited by Jennifer L. Holberg. Grand Rapids, Mich.: W. B. Eerdmans, 2006. Betts and the other writers describe what it means to be a writer working in the context of their Christian faith.

Brown, W. Dale. "Interview with Doris Betts." *The Southern Quarterly* 34 (Winter, 1996): 91-104. In this detailed interview, Betts discusses her Christian faith and how it relates to her fiction.

Evans, Elizabeth. "Another Mule in the Yard: Doris Betts's Durable Humor." *Notes on Contemporary Literature* 11 (March, 1981): 5-6. Evans's thesis is that "Doris Betts produces durable humor which often turns funny lines and situations into dark melancholy where humor remains, but overrun with pessimism and despair." This creates an incongruity that "frequently emphasizes the bitterness that undergirds the characters' lives." The article focuses on the story "The Dead Mule."

_____. *Doris Betts*. New York: Twayne, 1997. An authoritative critical interpretation of Betts's long and short fiction.

Gelfant, Blanche H., ed. *The Columbia Companion to the Twentieth-Century American Short Story*. New York: Columbia University Press, 2000. Includes a chapter in which Betts's short stories are analyzed.

Holman, David Marion. "Faith and the Unanswerable Questions: The Fiction of Doris Betts." *The Southern Literary Journal* 15 (Fall, 1982): 15-22. This article contains analyses of Betts's characterization, treatment of faith, and use of the grotesque in her short fiction. The discussion centers on three short stories: "The Ugliest Pilgrim," "The Astronomer," and "The Mandarin," although the longer fiction is also discussed briefly.

Lang, John. "Mapping the Heart's Home: Doris Betts's 'The Astronomer.'" *The Southern Literary Journal* 31 (Fall, 1998): 70-77. Examines themes of love, forgiveness, and the search for order in "The Astronomer." Shows that as the protagonist moves spatially through the story, he also moves socially from isolation to a sense of family and community and morally from complacency to active questioning.

Ragan, Sam, et al. "A Tribute to Doris Betts." *Pembroke Magazine* 18 (1986): 275-284. Included in the transcript of the 1985 North Carolina Writer's Conference is this tribute to and analysis of Betts's fiction by Sam Ragan, Robert Mason, Lee Smith, and William Friday. Contains both personal and critical appraisal of Betts's career, concerns, and short and long fiction, as well as anecdotes and fond remembrances.

Scura, Dorothy M. "Doris Betts at Mid-Century: Her Voice and Her Art." In *Southern Women Writers: The New Generation*, edited by Tonette Bond Inge. Tuscaloosa: University of Alabama Press, 1990. A general discussion of Betts's themes and techniques, focusing particularly on the short stories, which Scura contends are her natural forte. Summarizes the critical reception of Betts's stories and her themes of love and death, relationships between the sexes, and growing up.

Walsh, William. "An Interview with Doris Betts." *High Plains Literary Review* 4 (Winter, 1989-1990): 82-102. The most extensive of the interviews Betts has granted, this article allows the reader to hear her views on her work, past and present, and her thoughts on the future. Also contains examples of her wit and humor.

Wolfe, George. "The Unique Voice: Doris Betts." In *Kite-Flying and Other Irrational Acts: Conversations with Twelve Southern Writers*, edited by John Carr. Baton Rouge: Louisiana State University Press, 1972. This article provides an introduction to Betts's philosophy, her critical approach to writing, anecdotes about her early experiences in writing and publishing, and sources for some of her works. Betts also discusses biblical and other religious influences in her work and talks about the South, where she grew up. The introduction includes a brief biographical summary and a physical description of Betts.

John Carr
Updated by Mary LeDonne Cassidy and Peter B. Heller

AMBROSE BIERCE

Born: Horse Cave Creek, Ohio; June 24, 1842
Died: Mexico(?); January, 1914(?)

PRINCIPAL SHORT FICTION

Cobwebs: Being the Fables of Zambri the Parse,
1884
Tales of Soldiers and Civilians, 1891 (also known as
In the Midst of Life, 1898)
Can Such Things Be?, 1893
Fantastic Fables, 1899
My Favourite Murder, 1916
Ghost and Horror Stories of Ambrose Bierce, 1964
The Collected Fables of Ambrose Bierce, 2000 (S. T.
Joshi, editor)
*The Short Fiction of Ambrose Bierce: A Comprehen-
sive Edition,* 2006 (3 volumes; S. T. Joshi,
Lawrence I. Berkove, and David E. Schultz,
editors)

OTHER LITERARY FORMS

As a lifelong journalist and commentator, Ambrose
Bierce (AM-brohz bihrs) wrote prodigiously. He was
fond of vitriolic epigrams and sketches, together with
miscellaneous works of literary criticism, epigrams,
and both prose and verse aphorisms.

ACHIEVEMENT

Ambrose Bierce for many years was labeled a misanthrope or pessimist, and his dark short stories of
murder and violence were understood as the work of a
man who, obsessed with the idea of death, showed
himself incapable of compassion. A less moralistic and
biographical reevaluation of Bierce's work, however,
reveals his intellectual fascination with the effect of the
supernatural on the human imagination. Many of his
morally outrageous stories are "tall tales," which certainly cannot be taken at face value. Their black humor,
combined with the coolly understated voices of their
criminal or psychopathic narrators, reflects a society
gone to seed and pokes fun at the murderous dangers of
American life in the West during the Gilded Age.

BIOGRAPHY

Ambrose Gwinett Bierce was brought up on the farm
in Horse Cave Creek, Ohio, where he was born in 1842.
Although information about his early life is sparse, the
evidence of his stories and the fact that he quarreled with
and repudiated his large family with the exception of one
brother indicate an unhappy childhood and an abnormal
hatred of parental figures. His only formal education con-
sisted of one year at a military academy. He fought with
the Indiana infantry in the American Civil War, was
wounded at the battle of Kennesaw Mountain, and ended
the conflict as a brevet major. After the war, he settled in
California, where, following a brief stint as a watchman
at the San Francisco mint, he drifted into literary work.
He wrote for the San Francisco *Argonaut* and *News Letter*
and published his first story, "The Haunted Valley"
(1871), in the *Overland Monthly.* He married and, on
money received as a gift from his father-in-law, traveled
abroad to England in 1872, returning to California in
1876 because of bad health. Upon his return he again became associated with the *Argonaut.* From 1879 to 1881
he took part in the Black Hills gold rush, returning in
1881 to San Francisco, having found no success as a
miner. There he began, in association with the San Francisco *Wasp,* his famous column "The Prattler," transferred to William Randolph Hearst's San Francisco *Examiner* upon the *Wasp*'s failure, and continued at the
Examiner until 1896, when Hearst sent him to Washington as a correspondent for the New York *American.*
Much of Bierce's subsequently collected work appeared
first in "The Prattler." Divorced in 1904, Bierce resigned
from the Hearst organization in 1909 and, in a final quixotic gesture, disappeared into Mexico in the thick of the
Mexican Revolution. He was never heard from again.

ANALYSIS

Perhaps the most rewarding way to approach Ambrose Bierce's writing is to note that it was in many respects the product of two intertwined biographical factors, inseparable for purposes of analysis. The first of these reflects Bierce's thorny and irascible personality, which made him, on the one hand, quarrel with practically everyone he ever knew, and on the other, follow romantic and often impossible causes, the last of which led to his death. The second reflects his lifelong employment as a journalist, more specifically as a writer of short columns, generally aphoristic in nature, for various newspapers. The interaction of these two often contradictory strands explains, as well as any single factor can, both the strengths and the weaknesses of Bierce's writing.

Philosophically, Bierce's work is almost completely uncompromising in its iconoclasm; his view of existence is despairing, revealing only the bitterness of life within a totally fallen world promising neither present happiness nor future redemption. This "bitterness," which almost every critic has remarked in Bierce's work, is not completely fortunate. It can, and in Bierce's case often does, lead to that kind of adolescent cynicism which delights in discovering clouds in every silver lining. Too many of the insights that once seemed sterling are now fairly obviously only tinfoil. The definition of "economy" in *The Devil's Dictionary* (1911) is a case in point: "Purchasing the barrel of whiskey that you do not need for the price of the cow that you cannot afford"--an arresting idea, certainly, succinctly expressed, but by no means a profound one. In fact, it is precisely the kind of item one would expect to find on the editorial page of the morning newspaper and perhaps remember long enough to repeat at the office. Indeed, this particular aphorism did first appear in a newspaper, with most of the other contents of *The Devil's Dictionary* and, predictably, did not really survive the transformation into book form. *The Devil's Dictionary*, like much of Bierce's work, is now much more generally read about than actually read.

"AN OCCURRENCE AT OWL CREEK BRIDGE"

At its best, however, Bierce's cynicism is transformed into often-passionate statements of the tragedy of existence in a world in which present joys are unreal and future hopes vain, as a glance at one of Bierce's best-known stories, "An Occurrence at Owl Creek Bridge," will show.

This story, for all its apparent simplicity, has attracted uniform critical admiration and has been complimented not only by being extensively anthologized but also by having been made into an award-winning film. Purporting to be an incident from the American Civil War, the story opens with the execution by hanging of a Confederate civilian. His name, Peyton Farquhar, is revealed later, as is his apparent crime: He was apprehended by Union soldiers in an attempt to destroy the railroad bridge at Owl Creek, from which he is about to be hanged. The hangman's rope breaks, however, precipitating Farquhar into the current below. He frees his bound hands and, by swimming, manages to escape both the fire of the Union riflemen who have been assembled to witness the execution and, more miraculously, the fire of their cannon. Reaching shore, Farquhar sets out for home along an unfamiliar road, and after a night-long journey in a semidelirious condition arrives at his plantation some thirty miles away.

Ambrose Bierce (Library of Congress)

His wife greets him at the entrance, but as he reaches to clasp her in his arms he suffers what is apparently a stroke and loses his senses. He has not, it develops, suffered a stroke; the last sentence of the story tells readers what has really happened. The rope had not broken at all: "Peyton Farquhar was dead; his body, with a broken neck, swung gently from side to side beneath the timbers of the Owl Creek bridge."

"An Occurrence at Owl Creek Bridge" sounds, in summary, contrived. What is it, after all, more than a tired descant on the familiar theme of the dying man whose life passes before his eyes, coupled with the familiar trick of the unexpected happy ending put in negative terms? The answer, from the perspective of one who has read the story rather than its summary, is that it is much more. For one thing, careful readers are not left totally unprepared for the final revelation; they have been alerted to the fact that something may be amiss by Bierce's remark that Farquhar had, before his apparent death, fixed "his last thoughts upon his wife and children." Moreover, Farquhar's journey home is described in terms that become constantly less real. The unreality of the details of his homeward journey not only expresses Farquhar's growing estrangement from the world of reality, his "doom," perhaps, or--for those more at home in modern Freudianism--his "death wish," but also subtly indicates that what *seems* to be happening in the story may not in fact actually *be* happening, at least in the real world. In any event, Bierce's point is clear and reinforced within the story by a consistent movement in grammatical usage from the actual, "he was still sinking" (speaking of Farquhar's fall from the bridge into the water), toward the hypothetical, such as "doubtless," the word Bierce uses to describe Farquhar's apparent return to his plantation.

What, then, makes this story more than the predictable reverse of the typical tricky story with the illogical happy ending? The difference is to be found simply in Bierce's uncompromisingly negative view of the world. Readers begin in a world where everyone is symbolically sentenced to death, from which his or her reprieve is only temporary, and readers wander with Farquhar through a field of illusions that become more attractive as they escape the confines of reality. Readers end reaching for a beauty and love that was sought but was unobtainable, dead under Owl Creek Bridge. The symbolism of Owl Creek is not gratuitous: Wise old owls discover that every road leads only to death.

"Chickamauga"

The master image of "An Occurrence at Owl Creek Bridge" of a delusory journey leading to an ultimately horrible and horrifying revelation is central to many of Bierce's stories, one more of which is worth brief mention here. "Chickamauga," though not as well known as the former story, is equally chilling and equally cunning in its artistry. It tells of a nameless young boy, "aged about six years," who with toy sword in hand wanders away from his home one day into the adjacent woods, where he successfully plays soldier until, unexpectedly frightened by a rabbit, he runs away and becomes lost. He falls asleep, and when he awakens it is nearly dusk. Still lost, his directionless night journey through the forest brings him upon a column of retreating soldiers, all horribly wounded and unable to walk, who are trying to withdraw from a battle (presumably the 1863 Battle of Chickamauga in the American Civil War, although this is never specifically stated) that has been fought in the neighborhood and of which the child, whom readers later discover to be both deaf and mute, has been unaware. In a ghastly parody of military splendor, the child takes command of these horribly wounded soldiers and leads them on, waving his wooden sword. As the ghastly cavalcade limps forward, the wood mysteriously begins to brighten. The brightness is not the sun, however, but the light from a burning house, and when the little boy sees the blazing dwelling he deserts his troops and, fascinated by the flames, approaches the conflagration. Suddenly he recognizes the house as his own, and at its doorway he finds the corpse of his mother.

Again, the magic of this story vanishes in paraphrase, in which the masterfully controlled feeling of horror inevitably sounds contrived, the revelation slick rather than profound. The compelling quality of "Chickamauga" is largely a function of Bierce's style, which at once conceals and reveals what is going on. The story of a small boy who wanders off into the woods with a toy sword and who is frightened by a rabbit scarcely seems to be the kind of fictional world in which such uncompromising horrors should logically take place. On a symbolic level, however, the story has a curiously compelling logic. The first reading of the tale leaves one with a slightly false impression of its meaning. The story does not tell us, as it seems to, and as so many fairy tales do, that it is better not to leave home and venture into the wild wood; the story's meaning is darker than this. In the world of "Chickamauga," safety is to be found neither at home nor abroad. By wandering away into the woods the boy perhaps escaped the fate of those who remained at home, and yet his symbolic journey has only brought him back to a world where death is everywhere supreme. To emphasize this point more strongly, in 1898 Bierce retitled the book of short stories in which both the above tales appeared *In the Midst of Life*. Readers are expected to complete the quotation themselves: " . . . we are in death."

Although most of Bierce's stories that are widely remembered today deal with military themes, many of his other stories are quite frankly supernatural. By and large these supernatural stories seem less likely to survive than his military ones, if only because Bierce has less sense for the implicit thematic structure of supernatural tales than he does for macabre stories about the military. His ghost stories are avowedly "shockers," without the psychological depth to be found in the works of true masters of the supernatural. They do not have the profundity, for example, of Mary Shelley's *Frankenstein* (1818) or Bram Stoker's *Dracula* (1897). Nevertheless, the best of them do have a certain compelling quality simply because of the bizarre nature of the revelation of what lies at the heart of the supernatural event which Bierce relates.

"THE DAMNED THING"

"The Damned Thing" offers a convenient case in point. This is, quite simply, the story of a man who is hunted down and finally killed by some kind of animal, apparently a wildcat. The reader never knows precisely what kind of animal it is, however, since it has one peculiar quality: It is invisible. The story is told with the last scene first. This last scene, entitled "One Does Not Always Eat What Is on the Table," takes place at the coroner's inquest over the body of one Hugh Morgan, who has met a violent death. His friend, William Harker, explains how Morgan had acted inexplicably on a hunting trip, apparently falling into a fit. The coroner's jury agrees, at least to an extent. Their ungrammatical verdict is "We, the jury, do find that the remains come to their death at the hands of a mountain lion, but some of us thinks, all the same, they had fits." In the closing scene of the story, Morgan's diary is introduced as explanation, and in the diary there is his growing awareness that he is being stalked by some kind of invisible animal. A pseudoscientific rationale is given for this invisibility. The animal is "actinic," at least according to Morgan. "Actinic" colors, readers are informed, are colors that exist at either end of the spectrum and that cannot be perceived by the human eye. Readers have, in other words, either an infrared or an ultraviolet mountain lion. Neither choice is particularly satisfactory, and the difficulty with the willing suspension of disbelief in the tale is indicated by precisely this: The science is bad, yet it pretends not to be. The notion of an ultraviolet mountain lion is basically more silly than chilling, and since the story has no fiber to it other than the revelation of what the mountain lion actually consists of, readers cannot take it seriously. In fact, readers feel vaguely victimized and resentful, as though having been set up as the butt of some kind of pointless joke.

Even in this story, relatively unsuccessful as it is, readers see at work the underlying preoccupations that make some of Bierce's other stories unforgettable. The attempt in a Bierce story is always to shock someone by removing him from a commonplace world and placing him--like the little boy in "Chickamauga"--in another world in which laws are recognizable, though strange. The logic of a Bierce story is often very like the logic of a nightmare, in which the reader is placed in the position of the dreamer. When trapped in a nightmare, the reader feels the presence of a certain inexorable logic, even though one may not, at the moment, be able to define exactly how that logic operates or of what precisely it consists. It is the feeling for the presence of this hostile and malevolent order that gives the best of Bierce's stories their perennial fascination.

OTHER MAJOR WORKS

POETRY: *Vision of Doom*, 1890; *Black Beetles in Amber*, 1892; *How Blind Is He?*, 1896; *Shapes of Clay*, 1903; *Poems of Ambrose Bierce*, 1995.

NONFICTION: *Nuggets and Dust Panned in California*, 1873; *The Fiend's Delight*, 1873; *Cobwebs from an Empty Skull*, 1874; *The Dance of Death*, 1877; *The Dance of Life: An Answer to the Dance of Death*, 1877 (with Mrs. J. Milton Bowers); *The Cynic's Word Book*, 1906; *The Shadow on the Dial, and Other Essays*, 1909; *Write It Right: A Little Blacklist of Literary Faults*, 1909; *The Devil's Dictionary*, 1911; *The Letters of Ambrose Bierce*, 1922; *Twenty-one Letters of Ambrose Bierce*, 1922; *Selections from Prattle*, 1936; *Ambrose Bierce on Richard Realf by Wm. McDevitt*, 1948; *A Sole Survivor: Bits of Autobiography*, 1998 (S. T. Joshi and David E. Schultz, editors); *The Fall of the Republic, and Other Political Satires*, 2000 (S. T. Joshi and David E. Schultz, editors); *A Much Misunderstood Man: Selected Letters of Ambrose Bierce*, 2003 (S. T. Joshi and David E. Schultz, editors).

TRANSLATION: *The Monk and the Hangman's Daughter*, 1892 (with Gustav Adolph Danziger; of Richard Voss's novel).

MISCELLANEOUS: *The Collected Works of Ambrose Bierce*, 1909-1912; *Shadows of Blue and Gray: The Civil War Writings of Ambrose Bierce*, 2002 (Brian M. Thomsen, editor).

BIBLIOGRAPHY

Berkove, Lawrence. *A Prescription for Adversity: The Moral Art of Ambrose Bierce*. Columbus: Ohio State University Press, 2002. Focuses on Bierce's short fiction to argue that Bierce was not a misanthrope but was a moral and compassionate writer. Among the short stories analyzed are "A Son of the Gods," "A Horseman in the Sky," and "An Occurrence at Owl Creek Bridge."

Bierce, Ambrose. *A Much Misunderstood Man: Selected Letters of Ambrose Bierce*. Edited by S. T. Joshi and David E. Schutz. Columbus: Ohio State University Press, 2003. A collection of the author's correspondence that aims to create a more sympathetic portrait than is usually presented of Bierce.

_____. *Phantoms of a Blood-Stained Period: The Complete Civil War Writings of Ambrose Bierce*. Edited by Russell Duncan and David J. Klooster. Amherst: University of Massachusetts, 2002. This volume collects all of Bierce's Civil War writings and places each piece in the historical context of the war. The lengthy introduction describes Bierce's battlefield experiences and discusses their effect on his psyche and literary expression.

_____. *The Short Fiction of Ambrose Bierce: A Comprehensive Edition*. Edited by S. T. Joshi, Lawrence I. Berkove, and David E. Schultz. Knoxville: University of Tennessee Press, 2007. This comprehensive collection of Bierce's short fiction is covered in three volumes spanning 1868-1910. The general introduction, as well as the introductions to the sections, are lucidly written, drawing attention to the themes and literary devices that appear in many of Bierce's stories. The editors provide a wealth of information on Bierce's short fiction and give readers the tools to critically examine the works.

Butterfield, Herbie. "'Our Bedfellow Death': The Short Stories of Ambrose Bierce." In *The Nineteenth Century American Short Story*, edited by A. Robert Lee. Totowa, N.J.: Barnes & Noble, 1985. A brief, general introduction to the themes and techniques of some of Bierce's most representative short stories.

Conlogue, William. "A Haunting Memory: Ambrose Bierce and the Ravine of the Dead." *Studies in Short Fiction* 28 (Winter, 1991): 21-29. Discusses Bierce's symbolic use of the topographical feature of the ravine as a major symbol of death in five stories, including "Killed at Resaca," "Coulter's Notch," and "The Coup de Grace." Shows how the ravine symbolizes the grave, the underworld, and lost love for Bierce, all derived from his Civil War memories and the death of his first love.

Davidson, Cathy N., ed. *Critical Essays on Ambrose Bierce*. Boston: G. K. Hall, 1982. A comprehensive compilation of thirty essays and reviews of Bierce's work, this collection is an essential tool for any serious study of Bierce. Davidson's introduction locates the essays in relation to the ongoing process of reevaluating Bierce's work, and her thoroughly researched bibliography contains more than eighty further critical references.

_____. *The Experimental Fictions of Ambrose Bierce: Structuring the Ineffable*. Lincoln: University of Nebraska Press, 1984. Discusses how Bierce intentionally blurs distinctions between such categories as knowledge, emotion, language, and behavior. Examines how Bierce blurs distinctions between external reality and imaginative reality in many of his most important short stories.

Grenander, Mary Elizabeth. *Ambrose Bierce*. New York: Twayne, 1971. This volume is well researched, balanced, and readable, and it is perhaps the single most accessible study of Bierce's work and life. Contains a valuable, annotated bibliography and a list of primary sources.

Hoppenstand, Gary. "Ambrose Bierce and the Transformation of the Gothic Tale in the Nineteenth-Century American Periodical." In *Periodical Literature in Nineteenth-Century America*, edited by Kenneth M. Price and Susan Belasco Smith. Charlottesville: University Press of Virginia, 1995. Examines Bierce's relationship to the San Francisco periodicals, focusing on the influence he had in bringing the gothic tale into the twentieth century. Discusses themes and conventions in "The Damned Thing" and "Moxon's Master."

McWilliams, Carey. *Ambrose Bierce: A Biography*. Hamden, Conn.: Archon Books, 1967. A reprint of the 1929 edition, with a new introduction that tells of the book's origin in McWilliams's collaboration with Bierce's surviving daughter Helen. Based on oral interviews of people who knew Bierce, this is the first scholarly study of his life.

O'Connor, Richard. *Ambrose Bierce*. Boston: Little, Brown, 1967. A popular biography by a prolific writer on the American West. Very readable, the book interprets Bierce's work as that of a despairing moralist. Complemented by a select bibliography.

Talley, Sharon. *Ambrose Bierce and the Dance of Death*. Knoxville: University of Tennessee Press, 2009. Uses psychoanalytical theory to examine the motif of death in Bierce's works, including the short stories in *In the Midst of Life* and his Civil War writings.

Woodruff, Stuart C. *The Short Stories of Ambrose Bierce: A Study in Polarity*. Pittsburgh, Pa.: University of Pittsburgh Press, 1964. Argues that Bierce's fiction derives from a series of violent oscillations between art and life and idealism and cynicism. Maintains that Bierce's major theme is the inscrutable universe that blocks man's every effort to live his dreams. Discusses the polarity between the true and permanent art Bierce hungered for and the popular journalism he took up.

James K. Folsom
Updated by R. C. Lutz

AMY BLOOM

Born: New York, New York; June 18, 1953

PRINCIPAL SHORT FICTION

Come to Me, 1993
A Blind Man Can See How Much I Love You, 2000
Where the God of Love Hangs Out, 2009

OTHER LITERARY FORMS

Amy Bloom is primarily known for her collections of short stories, but she has written two novels, *Love Invents Us* (1997) and *Away* (2007). Both have received critical acclaim. Her nonfiction work, *Normal: Transsexual CEOs, Cross-dressing Cops, and Hermaphrodites with Attitude* (2002), demonstrates her capacities in the field of psychology and nontraditional gender roles. This interest in psychoanalysis is also found in her creation of the screenplay for and participation in the production of *State of Mind* (2007), a television series for Lifetime Television.

ACHIEVEMENTS

In addition to three collections of short stories, Amy Bloom has written two acclaimed novels. She has been nominated for the National Book Award and the National Book Critics Circle Award. Her works have appeared in *The O. Henry Prize Stories* and *The Best American Short Stories*. She also has written for *The Atlantic Monthly*, *The New York Times*, *The New Yorker*, and *Vogue*. Her novel *Away* was listed as Best Fiction of 2007 by *The Washington Post*, the *Los Angeles Times*, and *The Denver Post*. This work also received the distinction of Notable Book by the American Library Association.

BIOGRAPHY

Amy Bloom was born in 1953 and grew up in what she has described as a privileged part of Long Island,

outside New York. Both of her parents earned their living as journalists; her mother wrote for magazines, and her father was a financial journalist. She was encouraged to read from an early age. She received her B.A. in theater and political science from Wesleyan University, and she went on to become an actor. However, after several parts in productions, Bloom decided to obtain a graduate degree in social work. She received an M.S.W. from Smith College. This led to her work as a clinical therapist for ten years. She started writing in her mid-thirties and remembers taking care of her children during the day and writing at night.

Bloom started her writing career by penning mysteries, but soon she moved on to short stories. Her first story was published by a little-known Canadian feminist magazine. Shortly afterward, her stories appeared in *The Best American Short Stories* and *The New Yorker*. Her work as a clinical therapist and writer led to her participation in the screenplay for the Lifetime Television network show *State of Mind*, which examined the professional lives of psychiatrists.

Bloom has worked as a part-time lecturer of creative writing in the Department of English at Yale University. She also has been named the Kim-Frank Family University Writer in Residence at Wesleyan University. Bloom, who describes herself as bisexual, is divorced and has two daughters and a son. She lives in Connecticut.

ANALYSIS

Amy Bloom's stories are saturated with the unusual realities that life inevitably brings. The reader is encouraged, with wit and compassion, to embark on a journey into an often unmentioned, or at least seldom brought up, realm of humanity. In particular, she creates characters in situations that most readers would not define as normal. With extraordinary care, wisdom, and humor, Bloom links people caught up in emotional and physical impairments with underlying desires of love and longing. Impossible pasts and improbable futures cannot be satisfied. Many stories involve illnesses that cannot be survived. Numerous characters are ruled by their wants. The outcomes of these played-out psychologies are often tragic. Nonetheless, Bloom, with linguistic wit and surprising imagery, turns these sad tales into sagas of endurance and survival.

The author's ability to show how people think may be related to her years of work as a clinical psychoanalyst. Readers encounter odd compromises made by families and couples as they struggle to maintain fragile emotional relationships. These are people whose lives suffer various forms of psychological trauma, but who invariably endure by means of tolerance and acceptance. This will to endure is presented as a conquest of love that exceeds the boundaries of despair. Their present dilemmas are made bearable by remembered happiness. Using uncanny lyrical imagery combined with kitchen-counter colloquial speech, Bloom evokes the healing properties of love. Often, this love is unconventional and derived by means of unforeseen epiphanies, spontaneous forgiveness, and unreciprocated sacrifices.

Amy Bloom (Getty Images)

Bloom's first two collections, *Come to Me* and *A Blind Man Can See How Much I Love You*, comprise unrelated short stories. These stand-alone tales demonstrate Bloom's ability to create solid characters in few words. Her third collection, *Where the God of Love Hangs Out*, is divided into several vignettes of four chronological episodes. Each can be read as a separate short story. However, by examining the grouped stories in their entirety, the reader can encounter the true sense of tragedy overcome that is Bloom's emblematic message. The author also revisits some previous characters from her early novels. They reappear, many years later, with new and ongoing struggles in overcoming life's challenges. For example, in both *A Blind Man Can See How Much I Love You* and *Where the God of Love Hangs Out*, the Sampson family, first introduced in *Come to Me*, is revisited.

COME TO ME

Bloom brings the reader into her textual world without pity. Grief, sorrow, fear, misplaced faith, and love are rendered in a straightforward and unforgiving manner. Human dignity is present, but in a battered form that allows only eventual acceptance as its final answer. This collection of everyday tragedy is both disturbing and oddly comforting. The stories reveal a place that all readers have heard of, but where few have yet to venture. It is the realm of love, but love without preconceived consequences. The themes are perfectly penned, and in very few words, the reader enters the convoluted lives of the characters and then bids them farewell, after observing human nature run its flawed course.

The range of characters is vast. It includes women, men, old, young, African Americans, whites, Jews, Catholics, and more. In the twelve stories in this collection, the reader finds many who confront problems that have no specific resolution. In "Love Is Not a Pie," a daughter discovers at her mother's funeral that the mother has been involved in a sexual trio for many years. "Silver Water" exposes the depth of emotion that euthanasia brings to a family that consciously permits their mother and sister to die of an overdose. "Psychoanalysis Changed My Life" presents a humorous but warped situation in which a woman's psychoanalyst is being treated by another psychologist. "Sleepwalking" features a stepson who makes love to the wife of his deceased father in her bereavement.

Deviant human behavior is seldom appealing. In this collection of stories, it is not cleaned up for the reader. To the contrary, what the reader sees is life's ugly moments. However, true to her methodology, Bloom exposes her characters as they lose their grip on life. Regardless, they endure. Life goes on for everyone, and love endures even the most tragic and twisted circumstances.

A BLIND MAN CAN SEE HOW MUCH I LOVE YOU

Bloom presents these stories without judging the characters. The themes are from life's grimy regions, but the dialogue and narration are presented without negative connotation. Life simply appears as a series of negative events, with characters who carry on in spite of it all. The text reveals the underlying desire of all characters to live a normal life, yet it confirms that no such life exists. That is, all is normal, including the unspeakably bleak and terminally horrid events that appear without reason in some lives.

This collection of deviant tales shows Bloom's penchant for visiting the unseemly side of life. Lovers, families, coworkers, and others seem unable to stop their behaviors that damage others as well as themselves. The stories go from hope to hopelessness and then peter out, ending with an acceptance that all must simply go on. The author was involved in psychoanalysis for years and has stated that many people simply will not let go of past psychological baggage and carry on with their lives. Many of the stories present this same philosophy.

The themes in these eight stories range from incest and its inevitable Oedipal guilt to schizophrenia. The action of these stories is located in the psyches of the characters. The list of plots involves the almost unthinkable made real by the wit of Bloom's uncanny and simple dialogues and revelations of the characters' thoughts. In one, a woman endeavors to adopt a disturbed, one-armed child after her own baby dies. In another, a mother lovingly accompanies her daughter through a sex change to become a man. In the process, the mother discovers life is not what one expects, but often it is all that one will get.

Bloom's characters are real, at times too real. They all have problems that seem to come directly from the psychiatrist's couch. Their mental and verbal dialogues are full of cultural trivia that reveals Bloom's irreverent wit and wisdom. After finishing this collection of tales, the reader will leave with a concrete vision of what mental anguish can do to the many forms of love that life allows. Each story has an inevitable ending in which everything is more or less accepted without resolution. The frailty of the human condition simply carries on until death.

WHERE THE GOD OF LOVE HANGS OUT

In *Where the God of Love Hangs Out*, Bloom opens serious wounds in an area that most hold dear: love relationships. The reader takes an almost voyeuristic tour of the underbelly of some unseemly aspects of love in an all-too-real world of unconventional relationships between spouses, lovers, relatives, and friends. The reader witnesses middle-aged, pain-ridden lovers who are unfaithful to their marital partners, unexpected friendship brought on by senseless and cruel murder, emotional damage derived from semi-incestuous trysts, and all sorts of everyday tragedies that are seldom associated with love in literature.

This collection of short stories is divided into several sections. Each section, whether a single chapter or a vignette of several chapters, forms an individual tale. The two lengthy compilations follow a specific style that starts with the presentation of an unexpected and seemingly unbearable incident or development that slowly, across decades, is dealt with by the characters. This is not to say that all ends well. To the contrary, none of the tales has a truly happy conclusion; most end in death.

In "William and Clare," the reader encounters lovers who take in stride the brutal realities of the physical impairments of the elderly. In one example, they simply isolate William's gout-ridden and swollen foot during sex and other activities. Throughout the book, Bloom uses language that is surprisingly straightforward, as though the reader were listening to irreverent comments meant for friends and family. As with the other works of Bloom, each of the characters is somewhat dysfunctional, but each has something that others admire. A recurring style employed by the author in several of her stories is the presence of televised news in the background of scenes, as if to mirror the negative aspects of the characters' lives.

Most of the stories in this collection expose a stream of difficulties across several decades, including disapproving and self-absorbed children from previous marriages, aging and failing bodies, and the inevitable acceptance that life could have been better. Bloom does not leave the reader with an easy out. As opposed to many short stories, these works do not tie up loose ends and do not finish with everyone dead or happy. There is no solution to the dilemmas of nontraditional lives and marriages. Instead, there is an acceptance of the lack of fulfillment.

In "Between Here and Here," Bloom engages the reader's imagination by presenting lifelike images outside of the textual realm. The protagonist, Alison, draws weather maps that depict storms of hatred and other meteorological graphics that show her deep-seated abhorrence of her father. This is an example of the use of nature as a positive or a negative counterbalance in many of the stories in this work. Snow, light, cold, storms, and other elements of the natural world are injected into these works, as if nature itself mirrors the calamitous and unstoppable events that life presents. As in other stories in this book, the stark and cruel realities of Alison's early life become mitigated as time progresses.

Where the God of Love Hangs Out is a work that forces readers to confront their ideas of what love is. In a surprisingly fresh approach, Bloom's God of Love hangs out in a strange part of people's lives, where failure, illness, and the Grim Reaper are never far away.

OTHER MAJOR WORKS

LONG FICTION: *Love Invents Us*, 1997; *Away*, 2007.
SCREENPLAY: *State of Mind*, 2007.
NONFICTION: *Normal: Transsexual CEOs, Cross-dressing Cops, and Hermaphrodites with Attitude*, 2002.

BIBLIOGRAPHY

Ellis, Sherry. "Characters That Won't Go Away." In *Illuminating Fiction: A Collection of Author Interviews with Today's Best Writers of Fiction*. Los Angeles: Red Hen Press, 2009. Intriguing article that give readers insight into Bloom's methods of character development. Includes biographical information and bibliographical references.

Johnson, Sarah Anne. "Writing and Therapy Have Nothing in Common." In *Conversations with American Women Writers*. Hanover, N.H.: University Press of New England, 2004. Informative chapter on Bloom discusses how her background as a clinical psychologist has little to do with her writing. Includes bibliographical references.

Shwartz, Ronald B. *For the Love of Books: 115 Celebrated Writers on the Books They Love Most*. New York: Berkeley Books, 2000. Bloom speaks about what she finds valuable in collections of short stories and novels. Provides interesting attitudes that can be seen in many of her works. Includes bibliographical references.

Paul Siegris

ARNA BONTEMPS

Born: Alexandria, Louisiana; October 13, 1902
Died: Nashville, Tennessee; June 4, 1973

PRINCIPAL SHORT FICTION
The Old South, 1973

OTHER LITERARY FORMS

Arna Bontemps (bahn-TAHM) was a prolific writer of African American histories, biographies, and children's books, as well as an editor and anthologist. His best-known adult novel is *Black Thunder* (1936). He and Countée Cullen adapted Bontemps's first novel, *God Sends Sunday* (1931), as a Broadway musical, *St. Louis Woman* (pr. 1946). His poetry collection, *Personals*, appeared in 1963.

ACHIEVEMENTS

Arna Bontemps was awarded prizes by *Opportunity* (*Journal of Negro Life*) for poetry and for his story "A Summer Tragedy." He was also granted two Rosenwald grants and two John Simon Guggenheim Memorial Foundation Fellowships for creative writing. In 1956, he received the Jane Addams Children's Book Award and was a finalist for the Newbery Medal. He was named an honorary consultant to the Library of Congress in American cultural history in 1972.

BIOGRAPHY

Arnaud Wendell Bontemps descended from a prosperous, light-complexioned family of "Creoles of Color" (French and African American heritage) in Louisiana; when he was a small child, he and his nuclear family and almost all of his mother's extended family migrated to California. After his mother's death, he lived on his grandmother's farm near Los Angeles until his father sent him away to boarding school to complete his secondary education. As Bontemps was leaving to enroll at Pacific Union College, his father commanded him to renounce his African American past, about which the boy learned a great deal from his Louisiana relatives, who were living in California or were visiting there. His appreciation of his racial past continued to grow.

After receiving his B.A. in English, Bontemps moved to New York, where he became a part of the Harlem Renaissance, along with Zora Neale Hurston, Jean Toomer, and Langston Hughes, who became one of Bontemps's closest friends and his literary collaborator. In New York, Bontemps taught school and married Alberta Johnson in 1926. They had five children.

Bontemps taught for a year at Oakwood Academy in Huntsville, Alabama, and learned about racial oppression through the famous trials of the "Scottsboro Boys," which were being held nearby. He escaped to California, where he finished his second novel. Settling in Chicago, Bontemps received a master's degree in library science from the University of Chicago. He then returned to the South to accept a position as a full professor and head librarian at Fisk University in Nashville, where he remained until 1966, when he was named writer-in-residence at the University of Illinois at Chicago Circle. In 1969, he rejoined the Fisk faculty to serve as writer-in-residence. He died in Nashville in 1973.

ANALYSIS

The Old South, Arna Bontemps's collection of short stories, contains fourteen selections, the first of which is an important essay, "Why I Returned," an account of his early life in Louisiana and California and his later life in Alabama and Tennessee. All of the selections are set in the South of the 1930's, a time when this region was yet unchanged and thus "old," or concern characters from the South. Some of the stories are also autobiographical ("The Cure," "Three Pennies for Luck," and "Saturday Night"), and some are sharply satirical portraits of influential white women: a wealthy patron of young black musicians in "A Woman with a Mission" and a principal of a black boarding school in "Heathens at Home." The titles of these latter stories are self-explanatory.

Bontemps was brought up in the Seventh-Day Adventist Church, for which his father had abandoned the Creoles' traditional Catholicism. The boarding school and college Bontemps attended as well as the academy where he taught in Alabama were sponsored by the Adventists. Though Bontemps did not remain active in this church, he was deeply religious all his life. Several of his stories thus have religious settings and themes, including "Let the Church Roll On," a study of a black congregation's lively charismatic church service. Bontemps was influenced by music early on; his father and other relatives had been blues and jazz musicians in Louisiana. "Talk to the Music," "Lonesome Boy, Silver Trumpet," and "A Woman with a Mission" all concern young black musicians.

Arna Bontemps (Library of Congress)

Several selections concern black folk culture and folklore ("The Cure," "Lonesome Boy, Silver Trumpet," and "The Devil Is a Conjurer"); the last story reflects the human desire to invest nature with a sense of the mysterious, which unimaginative men find foolish and unprofitable. In addition, at least seven of Bontemps's stories, including the three named above, involve a young boy or man seeking or discovering meaning and worth in family and community, which some Bontemps scholars believe was a principal desire in the author's own life.

Bontemps's short stories treat sensitive political, economic, and social themes that are also employed in his two novels of slave revolts, *Black Thunder* and *Drums at Dusk* (1939).

"Blue Boy" in *The Old South* concerns an escaped black murderer who is hunted down and killed after he commits a second homicide. The action in this story is seen from two perspectives, that of a young child and of the criminal himself. Critic Robert Bone argues that the criminal named Blue is in fact "Bontemps's apotheosis that of the blues hero." In his best stories Bontemps achieves an aesthetic distance, mastery of literary form, and a belief in transcendence in spite of his characters' struggles in a world that often denies them human value. Though Bontemps's stories have been compared with those of Richard Wright, Bontemps's are less angry and acerbic.

"A SUMMER TRAGEDY"

"A Summer Tragedy," first published in *Opportunity* in 1935, is Bontemps's best-known, most frequently anthologized, and perhaps most successful short story because of its artistic interlacing of setting, symbolism, characterization, and folklore. As Bontemps's biographer, Kirkland C. Jones, has observed, this story is "to the Bontemps canon what 'Sonny's Blues' has become to [James] Baldwin's short fiction efforts--outstanding."

An elderly black couple, Jennie and Jeff Patton, have for decades been tenant farmers on Greenbrier Plantation in an unnamed southern state. The Pattons are ill, frail, and barely ambulatory; Jennie is nearly blind. Their five adult children have all died in violent situations, none of which is specified, suggesting that life for blacks, particularly the young, is dangerous and uncertain in the South.

The opening scene reveals the old couple dressing in their clean but threadbare black "Sunday-best." Their actions are described, slowly and painfully, as they prepare for some great, momentous occasion. The story is set in the fullness of the green, fecund early summer fields; all of nature--plants, animals, and birds--seems to be celebrating life, youth, warmth, and procreation, as contrasted with the aging, pinched, wintry, weary, and deathlike lives of Jennie and Jeff. Nevertheless, they affirm their love for each other and resolve to persevere in their plans, which are not clear to the reader until late in the story. At first, Bontemps's narrative seems almost naturalistic in the tradition of Theodore Dreiser as the Pattons reflect upon their lives of hard, monotonous, futile labor that has left them only more debt-ridden. Their existence seems to be a cruel trap, a vicious, meaningless struggle. They own an old, battered, hard-to-crank Model-T Ford that will later serve a vital but ominous purpose.

The story is not merely documentary with dreary details. Jeff and Jennie are presented as three-dimensional characters through a psychological point of view that allows the reader to share their thoughts, feelings, and memories. Bontemps had also skillfully used folk motifs to provide both verisimilitude and foreshadowing. The Pattons' sickly "frizzly" chickens, for example, which are supposed to protect the farm from evil spirits by devouring them, seem to be as death-doomed as their owners.

Jeff reflects on the many mules he has worn out in his years of plantation toil. His stingy employer has allowed him to have only one mule at a time; thus a long succession of mules has been killed by excessive and unremitting toil. Jeff is not aware that he is symbolically a mule for whom the callous old Major Stevenson has also had no sympathy. Moreover, Jeff himself has never felt pity for a man who is too weak to work.

Passing a neighbor's house on the journey through the countryside, Jennie is silently amused to think that their neighbor, Delia, who sees the Pattons' car drive past, is consumed with curiosity to know their destination. Delia, it seems, had once made passes at Jeff when he was a young married man. By refusing to supply Delia with any information, Jennie feels she is punishing her neighbor for her long-ago indiscretion. Such

details as these help humanize and individualize Bontemps's characters, making them psychologically credible. The reader gradually becomes aware that because of the couple's love for each other and their fear that one may grow too weak to help the other, they are determined to perish together.

As the Pattons near the high banks of the river levee, they can hear the rushing water. They drive over the levee and into the dark, swirling water. (Some readers contend that the stream is Louisiana's Red River, which flows near Bontemps's birthplace.) In death, Jeff and Jennie have preserved their independence and dignity. As the car sinks, one wheel sticks up out of the mud in a shallow place--fate's ironical monument to the lives and courageous deaths of Jeff and Jennie Patton. Free of histrionics and sentimentality, this well-handled story is, as critic Robert Bone contends, truly "compelling."

"TALK TO THE MUSIC"

In the years just prior to World War I, young Norman Taylor leaves his home in Rapides Parish (where Bontemps himself was born) and travels two hundred miles to attend college in New Orleans. However, instead of enrolling in college as his parents expect, Norman informally enrolls in a real-life course in blues music, which he studies in the notorious Storyville area, where the inimitable blues singer Mayme Dupree performs in a night club. Apparently Norman has not been able to "study" the blues in Rapides Parish, where it may have been considered "the Devil's music" by good churchgoing folk. Norman pretends to be a waiter at the club and is finally able to hear the fabulous Mayme sing her own style of blues. Her singing moves the audience to look into their hearts and individual and collective pasts and thus both figuratively and literally "talk to" (communicate with) the music as it is performed. Later Norman confesses to Mayme that her blues touched him like Adam and Eve's wail over their innocence lost in Eden, but Mayme comments that he is "crazy." Nevertheless, "Talk to the Music" richly evokes scenes and senses in New Orleans and convincingly dramatizes the young man's struggles to hear Mayme's blues and to learn from her lips about her loves and losses--which are shared not only by African Americans but also by all humanity.

OTHER MAJOR WORKS

LONG FICTION: *God Sends Sunday*, 1931; *Black Thunder*, 1936; *Drums at Dusk*, 1939.

PLAY: *St. Louis Woman*, pr. 1946 (with Countée Cullen).

POETRY: "Hope," 1924 (appeared in *The Crisis* magazine); *Personals*, 1963.

NONFICTION: *Father of the Blues*, 1941 (with W. C. Handy; biography); *They Seek a City*, 1945 (with Jack Conroy; revised as *Anyplace but Here*, 1966); *One Hundred Years of Negro Freedom*, 1961 (history); *Free at Last: The Life of Frederick Douglass*, 1971; *Arna Bontemps--Langston Hughes Letters: 1925-1967*, 1980.

CHILDREN'S LITERATURE: *Popo and Fifina: Children of Haiti*, 1932 (with Langston Hughes); *You Can't Pet a Possum*, 1934; *Sad-Faced Boy*, 1937; *The Fast Sooner Hound*, 1942 (with Jack Conroy); *We Have Tomorrow*, 1945; *Slappy Hooper: The Wonderful Sign Painter*, 1946 (with Conroy); *The Story of the Negro*, 1948; *Chariot in the Sky: A Story of the Jubilee Singers*, 1951; *Sam Patch*, 1951 (with Conroy); *The Story of George Washington Carver*, 1954; *Lonesome Boy*, 1955; *Frederick Douglass: Slave, Fighter, Freeman*, 1959; *Famous Negro Athletes*, 1964; *Mr. Kelso's Lion*, 1970; *Young Booker: Booker T. Washington's Early Days*, 1972; *The Pasteboard Bandit*, 1997 (with Hughes); *Bubber Goes to Heaven*, 1998.

EDITED TEXTS: *The Poetry of the Negro*, 1949 (revised 1971; with Langston Hughes); *The Book of Negro Folklore*, 1958 (with Hughes); *American Negro Poetry*, 1963; *Great Slave Narratives*, 1969; *Hold Fast to Dreams*, 1969; *The Harlem Renaissance Remembered*, 1972.

BIBLIOGRAPHY

Bone, Robert. "Arna Bontemps." In *Down Home: A History of Afro-American Short Fiction from Its Beginnings to the End of the Harlem Renaissance*. New York: G. P. Putnam's Sons, 1975. Provides brief but incisive analyses of four of the stories from *The Old South*: "Boy Blue," "A Summer Tragedy," "The Cure," and "Three Pennies for Luck." Notes the use of nature symbolism and folklore in Bontemps's short stories.

Canaday, Nicholas. "Arna Bontemps: The Louisiana Heritage." *Callaloo* 4 (October-February, 1981): 163-169. Traces the significant influence of Bontemps's Louisiana great-uncle, Buddy (Joe Ward), on the author's novel *God Sends Sunday* and on "The Cure" in *The Old South*.

Gable, Craig, ed. *Ebony Rising: Short Fiction of the Greater Harlem Renaissance Era*. Bloomington: Indiana University Press, 2004. Includes two short stories by Bontemps published in 1933 and 1934, respectively: "A Summer Tragedy" and "Barrel Staves." The lengthy introduction by Darryl Dickson-Carr provides an overview of the literature produced during the Harlem Renaissance that helps to place Bontemps's work in the context of this movement.

James, Charles L. "Arna Bontemps: Harlem Renaissance Writer, Librarian, and Family Man." *New Crisis* 109, no. 5 (September/October, 2002): 22-28. This profile of Bontemps describes his family and educational backgrounds, discusses the reasons his parents left Louisiana, and addresses the author's experience of racism. Includes photographs.

Jones, Kirkland C. "Bontemps and the Old South." *African American Review* 27, no. 2 (1993): 179-185. Argues that Bontemps's fiction makes greater use of the "Old South" than the works of any other Harlem Renaissance writer. Offers brief but perceptive critiques of five of *The Old South* selections: "Summer Tragedy," "The Cure," "Talk to the Music," "Boy Blue," and "Why I Returned."

_____. *Renaissance Man from Louisiana: A Biography of Arna Wendell Bontemps*. Westport, Conn.: Greenwood Press, 1992. The first full-scale biography of Bontemps. Treats the author's life and career in detail but only cursorily analyzes or evaluates the writings.

Yardley, Jonathan. Review of *The Old South*, by Arna Bontemps. *The New York Times Book Review*, December, 1973, 11. Comments on the impression of informality and chattiness the reader gets on a first reading of Bontemps's stories, but a second reading reveals his concern about race relations while avoiding bitterness.

Philip A. Tapley

ROBERT BOSWELL

Born: Sikeston, Missouri; December 8, 1953
Also Known As: Shale Aaron

PRINCIPAL SHORT FICTION
Dancing in the Movies, 1986
Living to Be a Hundred, 1994
The Heyday of the Insensitive Bastards, 2009

OTHER LITERARY FORMS

Robert Boswell (BAHZ-wehl) is the author of a number of novels, including *Century's Son* (2002), *American Owned Love* (1997), *Mystery Ride* (1993), *The Geography of Desire* (1989), and the science-fiction-genre *Virtual Death* (1995, under the pseudonym Shale Aaron). He also has written a nonfiction account of a treasure hunt, *What Men Call Treasure: The Search for Gold at Victorio Peak* (2008), with David Schweidel; a book on writing, *The Half-Known World: On Writing Fiction* (2008); and a play, *Tongues* (1999).

ACHIEVEMENTS

Robert Boswell has garnered many awards, including a Guggenheim Fellowship, the Iowa School of Letters Award for Fiction, the PEN West Award for Fiction, two National Endowment for the Arts Fellowships, and the Evil Companions Award for fiction associated with the American West. His science-fiction novel *Virtual Death* was a finalist for the Philip K. Dick Award for a distinguished work of science fiction, a rarity for an author who usually works out of the genre. His stories have been selected for *The Best American Short Stories, Prize Stories: The O. Henry Awards*, and *Pushcart Prize Stories* and have appeared in major periodicals, such as *The New Yorker, Esquire, Harvard Review*, and others. His play *Tongues* won the John Gassner Award, given by the New England Theatre Conference to new playwrights. In addition, Boswell

was a guest editor of the literary journal *Ploughshares* for winter 1996-1997. "Glissando," one of the stories from *Living to Be a Hundred*, was made into a film of the same name by Chip Hourihan in 2002 and screened at film festivals. The novel *Mystery Ride* formed the basis for *Twelve Mile Road* (2003), a made-for-television film shown on Columbia Broadcasting System (CBS). The novel *Crooked Hearts* (1987) was made into a 1991 feature film with Peter Berg and Jennifer Jason Leigh, directed by Michael Bortman.

BIOGRAPHY

Born in Missouri, Robert Boswell spent his early years on a tobacco farm in rural Kentucky, where his father was an elementary-school principal. Boswell's experiences during the integration of the schools helped form his continuing awareness of race and social relations. The family later moved to Arizona, where the teenage Boswell fell in with a rough crowd, giving rise to the experiences described in pieces such as 2009's "Rescued by Junkies." From there Boswell attended the University of Arizona, where in time he found a new focus and graduated with a double major in English and psychology. This was followed by an M.A. in rehabilitation counseling, which he practiced briefly before returning to earn an M.F.A. from the University of Arizona in 1984. His thesis, a collection of short stories, won the Iowa School of Letters Award for Fiction. The thesis later appeared, with slight revisions, as his first collection of short fiction, *Dancing in the Movies*. The Arizona M.F.A. program had another benefit: It was there that Boswell met Antonya Nelson, a fellow student; the two married in 1984. While in the M.F.A. program, he worked as a teaching assistant, and he subsequently taught at Northwestern University and after two years, starting in 1989, at New Mexico State University. His first novel, *Crooked Hearts*, appeared in 1987 and was followed by *The Geography of Desire* two years later. The 1990's were an especially prolific period, seeing publication of three more novels, *Mystery Ride*, *Virtual Death*, and *American Owned Love*, as well as the collection *Living to Be a Hundred*. In addition, his play *Tongues* was produced by the American Southwest Theatre Company in Las Cruces, New Mexico. His stories also appeared widely in the most selective periodicals and garnered a number of awards. Throughout the period Boswell also taught for the long-distance M.F.A. program at Warren Wilson College and at numerous writers' conferences. The next decade saw the publication of the novel *Century's Son* and the short-fiction collection *The Heyday of the Insensitive Bastards*. In addition, Boswell branched out, spending years working on a nonfiction account, *What Men Call Treasure: The Search for Gold at Victorio Peak*, and publishing a collection on writing, adapted from his renowned teaching lectures, *The Half-Known World*.

ANALYSIS

Robert Boswell's fiction tackles the tough, gritty realities of everyday lives, exposing the raw fears and naked needs that characters would like to hide from each other and from themselves. The protagonists--often people striving to achieve small dreams who are frequently disappointed--are observed with an eye that is wry and unflinching. As his fiction has progressed, his protagonists have become typically older and more outwardly jaded, their hopes and sorrows thrown into sharper relief, while the author's ways of depicting their situations have become more thoughtful and far reaching. The predicaments of the characters and their relation to outward reality illustrate Boswell's observation, stated in his nonfiction *The Half-Known World*, that "secrets function to the extent that their revelation creates an equal portion of mystery. The world then remains half known."

DANCING IN THE MOVIES

Boswell's first collection, comprising six stories, is unified by an interest in the nuances of the characters' inner lives and in the humanity of those who fail to live up to their own ideas of themselves. In "Flipflops," for instance, a man and woman, attempting a daring romantic escapade, instead find themselves witnesses to a drowning, and the man's failure to save the victim is punctuated by an unwitting squabble with the victim's widow over a pair of flipflops. The whole is set against the backdrop of a joke that the protagonist cannot remember correctly, and the story ends with a downhearted but humane acceptance of the many levels on which plans can fail. The collection as a whole illuminates the path characters take to small but important disappointments.

LIVING TO BE A HUNDRED

The eleven stories of *Living to Be a Hundred* tend to revolve around men at critical junctures in their lives, often moments of recognition rather than decision points. These men strive to find their way in relationships, whether in marriage or with other family members. Boswell is shrewd in portraying the way in which people are blind to the ways they contribute to their sorrows, while showing what it is like to retain hope in the crushing circumstances of dysfunction and grief. The title story was chosen by Margaret Atwood for inclusion in *The Best American Short Stories*, and the collection won the PEN West Award for Fiction.

THE HEYDAY OF THE INSENSITIVE BASTARDS

Boswell's third collection, published in 2009, shows the writer at the peak of his powers, attempting to portray his characters' efforts and frailties, sometimes through experimental means. The thirteen stories in the volume depict a variety of baffled people in heartland America, trying to live their lives without full acknowledgment of what drives them. Along the way Boswell employs devices to emphasize the elasticity of reality. "No River Wide," for instance, shuttles between times and settings in its depiction of the unresolved fates of two friends, showing that life may be lived forward but it is not linear. "A Sketch of Highway on the Nap of a Mountain" portrays a woman whose often comic difficulties with language underscore the difficulty of all communication and contribute an additional layer to her observations.

OTHER MAJOR WORKS

LONG FICTION: *Crooked Hearts*, 1987; *The Geography of Desire*, 1989; *Mystery Ride*, 1993; *Virtual Death*, 1995 (as Shale Aaron); *American Owned Love*,1997*; Century's Son*, 2002.

PLAY: *Tongues*, pr. 1999.

NONFICTION: *What Men Call Treasure: The Search for Gold at Victorio Peak*, 2008 (with David Schweidel); *The Half-Known World: On Writing Fiction*, 2008.

BIBLIOGRAPHY

Boswell, Robert. *The Half-Known World: On Writing Fiction*. Minneapolis, Minn.: Graywolf Press, 2008. A collection of pieces on fiction writing adapted from Boswell's popular talks. Boswell's essays have an emphasis, unusual in the world of craft, on the importance of fiction in helping readers engage with the world. Useful for those who want an insight into Boswell's philosophy and how fiction relates to wider social concerns.

Clark, William, and Sybil Steinberg. Interview with Robert Boswell. *Publishers Weekly* 240, no. 4 (January 25, 1993): 65. A profile of Boswell's career with a look at the authors who have most influenced him, notably Mark Twain.

Lee, Don. "About Robert Boswell: A Profile." *Ploughshares* 22 (Winter, 1996/1997). A revealing profile of Boswell's formative years, his turnaround from drug use, and details on his early career.

Martha Bayless

JANE BOWLES

Born: New York, New York; February 22, 1917
Died: Málaga, Spain; May 4, 1973
Also known as: Jane Auer, Jane Stajer Auer

PRINCIPAL SHORT FICTION

Plain Pleasures, 1966
My Sister's Hand in Mine, 1978 (includes short stories)

OTHER LITERARY FORMS

In addition to her short stories, Jane Bowles (bohlz) wrote a novel and a play. She began several other works of fiction, including another novel, in her notebooks, selections from which have been published in various collections of her work. Her letters have been collected by Millicent Dillon in *Out in the World: Selected Letters of Jane Bowles, 1935-1970* (1985).

ACHIEVEMENTS

Jane Bowles's literary output, though small in quantity, has received accolades for its originality and experimentation. Her unique use of language and nontraditional narrative techniques has led to stories that are as unsettling in their form as they are in their content. Her characters are often drawn as both grotesque and comic, yet Bowles maintains a compassionate stance toward them--a technique that is usually absent in more experimental contemporary writing. The characters themselves can be seen as experimental: They are mostly women, either strong-willed and assertive or curiously passive, yet they behave in ways that surprise and shock the reader. Her works operate on a series of contrasts or opposing tensions; like Bowles herself, her fiction is an enigma and a delight, challenging the reader with its puzzling obscurity and its compelling humanity.

BIOGRAPHY

Jane Auer Bowles was born in New York City in 1917, the only child of Sidney and Claire Auer. In 1927, her family moved to Woodmere, Long Island. Jane was thirteen years old and away at summer camp when her father died unexpectedly; she and her mother moved back to New York soon thereafter. As a child, Bowles had a French governess and learned to speak French before English. Later, she attended boarding school but left after less than a year, having fallen from a horse and broken her leg. She developed tuberculosis of the knee and went to Switzerland for treatment. She remained there for two years, studying with a French tutor and spending most of her convalescence confined to bed. From these early experiences, she learned to use her imagination to escape the physical pain and emotional isolation that she felt, developing a captivating wit and charm to deflect attention from her physical disabilities.

She left Switzerland in 1934 and met the writer Louis-Ferdinand Céline on board the ship to New York. They visited frequently during the voyage, and by the time Bowles returned to New York, she had decided to become a writer. In 1935, she began a novel in French, "Le Phaéton Hypocrite" (the hypocritical Phaëton), the manuscript of which has not survived. From 1935 on, Bowles began frequenting nightclubs in Greenwich Village and meeting other young people with literary and artistic interests. At this point, she set the pattern for years to come: frequent partying, relationships with both men and women, heavy drinking, and occasional depressions brought on, it seemed, by her inability to settle down to writing.

In 1937, she was introduced to Paul Bowles, who was at the time a composer and poet. They were married on February 21, 1938. Their marriage was unusual, in that they maintained very separate personal lives and

Jane Bowles (Time & Life Pictures/Getty Images)

often lived apart, yet they were devoted to each other. Paul Bowles was very encouraging of Jane's work, even when she went through long periods of writer's block. In fact, he credits her writing with his own beginning as a writer of fiction.

Bowles began her novel *Two Serious Ladies* (1943) in 1938. Like much of her fiction, it is partly autobiographical, although not in any traditional sense. She wrote most of her short stories and a play, *In the Summer House* (pr. 1953; pb. 1954), in the 1940's. Although most of her work was published in magazines during that decade, her collection of short stories, *Plain Pleasures*, did not appear until 1966. In 1948, she moved to Morocco, where Paul had been living since 1947. From the 1950's on, Bowles continued to live in Tangier and traveled often. Her complicated personal relationships with women and a busy social life often took precedence over her writing, a discipline that she found increasingly difficult. Writing had always been a struggle but also something that she felt compelled to do; she was envious of those who wrote easily. In 1957, she suffered a stroke, after which her health steadily declined. She spent the last years of her life in a hospital in Málaga, Spain, where she died in 1973.

ANALYSIS

Jane Bowles's short stories deal with personal relationships between characters who behave in bizarre and unpredictable ways. The stories contain an undercurrent of fear or foreboding, the cause of which is only sometimes revealed. Characters leave their usual environments and must then cope with new, often hostile ones. Portrayals of women predominate; family relationships--especially mothers and daughters, and sisters--form the core of ever-shifting narratives of emotional betrayal and psychological trauma. Despite the serious and even grim nature of the stories, they are also filled with humor and tenderness. Bowles's wit shines through in amusing dialogues (or, more often, monologues) and comic juxtapositions of characters' reactions to their situations. The settings for the stories are places Bowles knew from her travels: Central America, North Africa, and the northeast United States.

"A GUATEMALAN IDYLL"

"A Guatemalan Idyll" and "A Day in the Open" were Bowles's first published stories. They were originally conceived as part of her novel, *Two Serious Ladies*, but at the advice of her husband, Paul, these pieces were edited from the novel and published separately. "A Guatemalan Idyll" interweaves several plots. In one, an unnamed male traveler, in Guatemala on business, has an affair with Señora Ramirez, who is staying at the same pension. In another plot, Lilina Ramirez, her younger daughter, buys a snake from some boys on the street and then later lets it loose in the middle of town, where it is squashed by a bus. Accompanying Lilina at this moment is Enrique, a young boy whose head is bandaged as the result of falling on a rusty nail. Later in the story, Señora Ramirez takes a walk out of town, toward a volcano in the distance, and falls asleep in a little kiosk near a convent. A boy wakes her and then she seduces him. Consuelo Ramirez (Lilina's older sister) and Señorita Córdoba (a beautiful and well-bred young lady) are both secretly in love with the American traveler. The story ends with the traveler's departure.

The juxtaposition of these several plots, together with the strange events and their symbolic details, forms a richly compelling and multilayered narrative. The opposing tensions of sin and pleasure, guilt and justification, and remorse and indifference are common to Bowles's fiction. Another subplot involves Señora Ramirez's corset, which--like Lilina's snake and the half-ruined convent--symbolizes the oppression of religion, with its doctrine of original sin. Ultimately, the title of the story is ironic: What appears on the surface to be a pleasant vacation in the country for the various characters turns out to be fraught with guilt, disgust, and a lack of emotional tenderness.

"A Day in the Open" can be read as a companion piece to "A Guatemalan Idyll." Señor Ramirez, whose wife and two daughters are staying at a pension in a small town, hires two prostitutes to accompany him and a business associate on a picnic out in the country. Inez, one of the prostitutes, is straightforward and businesslike, more concerned with the financial aspects of their transaction. In contrast, her colleague, Julia, who is physically more delicate and suffering from an undiagnosed pain in her side, expresses genuine tenderness and love for Señor Ramirez. Alfredo, the business associate, remains aloof throughout the story, more interested in the numbers in a ledger than in the naked women at the picnic. Toward the end of the story, Señor Ramirez proves his physical strength by carrying Julia toward a waterfall (which, like the volcano in Señora Ramirez's landscape, seems to symbolize dangerous passion). He suddenly slips and drops Julia, who cuts her head on the rocks. They all leave the picnic site abruptly, Julia with her profusely bleeding head bandaged in a shawl.

A condensed and less complex version of "A Guatemalan Idyll," "A Day in the Open" deals similarly with sin and its effects: here, Julia's injury. The four characters suggest several combinations of opposites (strength and weakness, vitality and disinterest, cunning and stupidity), yet Bowles manages to transcend their being mere abstractions by giving them humane qualities, too. This story, like much of Bowles's work, casts the landscape in a vaguely sinister light, delightful in its natural beauty but also threatening in its power for destruction.

"CAMP CATARACT"

The physical setting of "Camp Cataract" involves such a contrast: The camp is located near a spectacular waterfall, which turns out to be the site of a character's death at the end of the story. Harriet, a self-described nature lover, has gone to Camp Cataract for her nerves. She enjoys being there and away from home, where she lives with her sister Sadie, who like Harriet is not married, and another sister, Evelyn, and her husband, Bert Hoffer. Sadie, who fears that Harriet might one day leave them for good, goes to Camp Cataract to convince Harriet to come home. Harriet, by no means pleased with Sadie's surprise visit (according to her doctor, Harriet is to have no family visitors), avoids her as much as possible.

"Camp Cataract" is the most elaborate and longest of Bowles's short stories, involving many of her recurrent thematic elements: troubled individuals trapped in troubling relationships, unattached middle-aged women, physical and psychological disabilities, emotionally upsetting incidents, and a violent, unexpected ending. The plot suddenly turns on itself: the reader believes that Sadie and Harriet have met for lunch and had a conversation in the woods, when in actuality, Sadie has imagined it all. Harriet later goes to meet her near the waterfall and finds that Sadie has disappeared; and although it is not explicitly stated, the reader can assume that Sadie has committed suicide by jumping off the bridge that goes behind the cataract. Bowles often wrote unsettling endings to her stories, endings that have both a grim finality and a troubling lack of closure.

"PLAIN PLEASURES"

"Plain Pleasures" differs from many of Bowles's stories in that its protagonists are a man and a woman, rather than two women. Alva Perry is a reserved widow in her early forties; her neighbor of many years, John Drake, is also middle-aged and painfully shy. One night, Mrs. Perry invites Mr. Drake (whom she barely knows) to a potato bake--one of life's "plain pleasures"--outside their tenement, and in turn, he invites her out to dinner the next night. She is angry and inimical throughout the meal. She has too much to drink and goes upstairs, looking for a rest room but ending up in what turns out to be the proprietor's bedroom. She passes out; the proprietor discovers her there and explains the situation to Mr. Drake, who leaves the restaurant, disconsolate.

The story ends with Mrs. Perry awakening in the strange room, then going down into the dining room, whispering "My sweet John Drake." Her comment is puzzling, given her harsh treatment of him during dinner the night before. Millicent Dillon, in her biography of Jane Bowles, explains that "In fact what has happened, but is not explicitly stated in the story, is that in the night she has been raped by the proprietor. Only after this violation is she able to feel tenderness for John Drake." "Plain Pleasures" is another ironic title, for although the story begins with a rather sweet encounter between two lonely people, it ends up with a typically Bowlesian undercurrent of violence--in this case, the leering and unsavory proprietor.

"EVERYTHING IS NICE"

"Everything Is Nice" was originally published as a nonfiction article entitled "East Side: North Africa." Paul Bowles later edited it, changed the narrator to third person, and included it in the collection *Plain Pleasures*. In the story, Jeanie, an American woman, and Zodelia, a Muslim woman, go together to a house where other Muslim women are gathered. They ask Jeanie questions about her life and her curious behavior: They want to know why she spends half her time with Muslims and half her time with Nazarenes (a term for Christians or Westerners in general). Jeanie soon tires of their questions and leaves abruptly, promising Zodelia that she will see her the next day.

Like Jeanie, Bowles divided her time in Tangier between her community of Moroccan friends and a group of expatriate Westerners. The tension that Bowles felt between the two cultures is evident in this story when the Muslim women ask Jeanie--partly out of polite interest but also with a tone of accusation--about her mother, her husband, and the Nazarene hotel where she lives part of the time. Jeanie's ambivalent position is symbolized at the end of the story by the powdery blue whitewash that rubs off on her finger when she touches a wall. It reminds her of a time when she once reached out to touch the face of a clown. While the Muslim women at the house insist that "everything is nice," Jeanie feels uncomfortable in her roles; she is caught between two different worlds, an anomaly in both, an amusing oddity to be observed but one who ultimately presents a false face to the outside world.

"A STICK OF GREEN CANDY"

The interior world of a solitary little girl predominates in "A Stick of Green Candy." Mary plays extensive imaginative games (she is the head of a regiment) in a clay pit near her house, avoiding the public playground full of other children. One day a boy from a house nearby infiltrates her hideout, and she follows him home. She meets his mother, who chats amiably with Mary, but Mary instead seeks "the dark gulf that always had separated her from the adult world." She leaves the house suddenly, taking with her a stick of green candy, which the boy's mother had offered her. After the boy's intrusion into her private space of imagination, however, Mary loses the ability to continue her games with the pretend regiment. Mary's abrupt entrance into a more sociable interaction creates an ambivalent ending, with Mary turning a "cold face" away from the clay pit and creeping back home.

The stories discussed above are all included in *Plain Pleasures*. In the expanded edition of Bowles's collected works, *My Sister's Hand in Mine*, several other stories appear that were not included in the 1966 collection. Three of these-- "Andrew," "Emmy Moore's Journal," and "Going to Massachusetts"-- were written as part of longer, unfinished works. They all deal with characters who are trying to escape their current existence for a new life in a new location: Andrew simply wants to get away and ends up being inducted into the Army; Emmy Moore leaves Paul, her husband of sixteen years, for the Hotel Henry, where she begins to write her journal; and Bozoe Flanner is supposed to go to Massachusetts but gets only as far as the next town up the road. A common thread in these and other stories by Bowles is the feeling of being trapped in a stagnating situation, with only partial success in getting away from it The three other pieces in *My Sister's Hand in Mine*-- "The Iron Table," "Lila and Frank," and "Friday"--were selected from Bowles's notebooks. These fragments involve Hemingwayesque conversations between couples, usually in restaurants, on topics ranging from the decline of Western civilization to a small-town stranger's lack of appetite.

The fiction of Bowles is by no means conventional or predictable. Her characters shift from one topic to another in a single sentence; they behave erratically and often suffer extreme mood changes; they remain in difficult and unproductive relationships. In Bowles's fiction, a sense of community--even a gathering of unpleasant eccentrics--seems preferable to isolation. Those characters who do choose to be alone engage in an alternative world of imagination. Whether deliberately and playfully obscure or rife with layers of symbols and intentional multiple meanings, the fiction of Jane Bowles always manages to captivate.

OTHER MAJOR WORKS

LONG FICTION: *Two Serious Ladies*, 1943.

PLAY: *In the Summer House*, pr. 1953, pb. 1954.

NONFICTION: *Out in the World: Selected Letters of Jane Bowles, 1935-1970*, 1985 (Millicent Dillon, editor).

MISCELLANEOUS: *The Collected Works of Jane Bowles*, 1966; *Feminine Wiles*, 1976.

BIBLIOGRAPHY

Adams, Don. "One Is Never Quite Totally in the World: Jane Bowles' Allegorical Realism." In *Alternative Paradigms of Literary Realism*. New York: Palgrave Macmillan, 2009. Adams's examination of little-known and underappreciated writers includes a chapter on Bowles in which he analyzes the short story "Camp Cataract" and some of her other works.

Ashbery, John. "Up from the Underground." Review of *The Collected Works of Jane Bowles*. *The New York Times Book Review*, February 29, 1967, p. 5. In this oft-quoted review, Ashbery calls Bowles "one of the finest modern writers of fiction, in any language." He observes that Bowles's work often involves a conflict between weak and strong characters. Ashbery also praises her use of local color in dialogue and details.

Dillon, Millicent. "Jane Bowles: Experiment as Character." In *Breaking the Sequence: Women's Experimental Fiction*, edited by Ellen G. Friedman and Miriam Fuchs. Princeton, N.J.: Princeton University Press, 1989. This essay revises Dillon's comments (in her 1981 biography) about Bowles's writer's block. Dillon asserts that the fragments that characterized Bowles's writing (which Bowles saw as artistic failures) can instead be seen as "a valid expression of her own narrative vision." She adds that the sudden shifts in plot and narrative voice, which marked Bowles's work as eccentric when it first appeared, can be appreciated in a critical climate forty years later, which takes a more accepting attitude toward experimental forms.

_____. "Keeper of the Flame." *The New Yorker* 72 (January 27, 1997): 27-28. Discusses the efforts of an eighteen-year-old Spanish high school student to have Bowles's remains exhumed from the cemetery of San Miguel in Málaga, in order to make way for a freeway, and reburied in Marbella.

_____. *A Little Original Sin: The Life and Work of Jane Bowles*. New York: Holt, Rinehart and Winston, 1981. This illuminating and thoroughly researched biography gives full coverage of Bowles's life and offers insightful commentary on her work. Dillon suggests that much of Bowles's work (and in turn, her life) was concerned with the notion of sin and its absolution, with imagination as another powerful force in her writing.

Edwards, Brian T. "Three Serious Writers, Two Serious Authors: Jane Bowles, Mohammed Mrabet, and the Erotics of Collaboration Politics of Translation." In *Morocco Bound: Disorienting America's Maghreb, from Casablanca to the Marrakech Express*. Durham, N.C.: Duke University Press, 2005. Examines American representations of the Maghreb during the period from 1942, when the United States entered the North African campaign in World War II, through 1973. The chapter on Jane Bowles includes a close reading of "Camp Cataract" that discusses her use of Arabic, bridge motifs, and the themes of speech and communication in the story.

Gentile, Kathy Justice. "'The Dreaded Voyage into the World': Jane Bowles and Her Serious Ladies." *Studies in American Fiction* 22 (Spring, 1994): 47-60. Discusses the concept of dread in Bowles's short fiction and her novel. Argues that her work has been neglected because of her avant-garde reputation and because of the subject of dread. Claims that her heroine in the story "Camp Cataract" confronts dread from a perspective of existential freedom.

Green, Michelle. *The Dream at the End of the World: Paul Bowles and the Literary Renegades in Tangier*. New York: HarperCollins, 1991. Green provides a fascinating portrait of the exotic "outpost" of Tangier in the decades after World War II. She gives additional biographical information about Jane and Paul Bowles, plus factual information about Jane Bowles's works and their publication history.

Lougy, Robert E. "The World and Art of Jane Bowles, 1917-1973." *CEA Critic*, no. 49 (1987): 157-173. Lougy explores the major themes and forms of Bowles's work: isolation, fragmentation, guilt, and eccentricity. He often provides biographical background for aspects of her fiction and labels her a much more contemporary author than many other writers of her time.

Skerl, Jennie, ed. *A Tawdry Place of Salvation: The Art of Jane Bowles*. Carbondale: Southern Illinois University Press, 1997. A good interpretation of Bowles's characters, settings, and themes. Includes bibliographical references and an index.

Whitaker, Rick. "Jane Bowles." In *The First Time I Met Frank O'Hara: Reading Gay American Writers*. New York: Four Walls Eight Windows, 2003. Whitaker analyzes the work of Bowles and other writers who demonstrate a "gay sensibility," which he describes as "original and fresh . . .clever, scornful of laws, introspective, energetic, and sexy . . . with a degree of irony, and wit; and . . . almost always a background of melancholy."

Ann A. Merrill

PAUL BOWLES

Born: New York, New York; December 30, 1910
Died: Tangier, Morocco; November 18, 1999

PRINCIPAL SHORT FICTION

A Little Stone: Stories, 1950
The Delicate Prey, and Other Stories, 1950
The Hours After Noon, 1959
A Hundred Camels in the Courtyard, 1962
The Time of Friendship, 1967
Pages from Cold Point, and Other Stories, 1968
Three Tales, 1975
Things Gone and Things Still Here, 1977
Collected Stories,1939-1976, 1979
Midnight Mass, 1981
In the Red Room, 1982
A Distant Episode: The Selected Stories, 1988
Call at Corazón, and Other Stories, 1988
Unwelcome Words, 1988
A Thousand Days for Mokhtar, and Other Stories,
    1989
*Too Far from Home: The Selected Writings of
    Paul Bowles,* 1993
The Stories of Paul Bowles, 2001

OTHER LITERARY FORMS

Though he began his literary career relatively late, Paul Bowles (bohlz) produced a significant body of work in a variety of forms, including the novel (his most famous is *The Sheltering Sky,* 1949), travel essays, poetry, and an autobiography (*Without Stopping,* 1972). Bowles also translated the work of some Moroccan writers and published the collection *Too Far from Home: The Selected Writings of Paul Bowles* in 1993. Before turning to writing, Bowles won fame as a composer.

ACHIEVEMENTS

Paul Bowles won the Rea Award in 1991, and his first novel, *The Sheltering Sky,* was widely acclaimed as an existential masterpiece. *Esquire* magazine called the creative nonfiction work *Points in Time* (1982) a "brilliant achievement, innovative in form."

BIOGRAPHY

Paul Frederic Bowles's life spans much of the twentieth century, but the events that dominated the lives of his contemporaries in the United States had little effect on him. After attending the University of Virginia, Bowles went to Europe, where his literary career began with the publication of some youthful poems in the journal *Transitions.* During the 1930's, Bowles drifted from New York to Berlin, Paris, and Mexico. In New York and Berlin, he studied music with Aaron Copland. His musical career was furthered in Paris, where he studied with Virgil Thomson. Also in Paris, Bowles met Gertrude Stein, to whom he attributed the initial impetus for his subsequent writing career. Stein criticized his poetry and suggested that he devote himself to music instead, but she also urged him to go to Morocco. He took her advice, and eventually Morocco became his permanent home.

In 1938, Bowles married Jane Auer (Jane Bowles), a playwright and novelist. They traveled to diverse places such as Mexico, Central America, and Ceylon (now Sri Lanka), journeys that Bowles recalls in his travel essays, collected in *Their Heads Are Green and Their Hands Are Blue* (1963). During the 1940's, Bowles composed music for ballet and opera (*The Wind Remains*), as well as incidental music for drama, including Tennessee Williams's *The Glass Menagerie* (pr. 1944). When Jane Bowles was working on her novel *Two Serious Ladies* (1943), Paul Bowles decided to try his hand at a novel as well. The result was *The Sheltering Sky,* published in 1949, a year after the Bowleses made Tangier their permanent residence.

The novel, with its stark existentialism, was a critical success and reached *The New York Times* best-seller list. While *The Sheltering Sky* would remain his most popular and critically acclaimed work, Bowles continued to produce a steady stream of highly crafted stories, novels, and works of nonfiction. He also translated the tales of Moroccan oral storytellers, as well as the published work of North African authors.

As Paul Bowles's literary output flourished, Jane Bowles, suffering a stroke, ended her writing career in 1957. Although she survived the illness, her health and emotional outlook declined so badly that she would never again compose fiction. In 1967 she was committed to a Spanish psychiatric hospital, and she died in 1973. Bowles, devastated by his wife's death, wrote little original material for nearly a decade. Then, in 1982, he broke his silence with *Points in Time*. This avant-garde work of creative nonfiction received strong critical praise and proved that Bowles's literary energies were still powerful.

Public interest in Bowles reached a new height with the 1990 release of Bernardo Bertolucci's film version of *The Sheltering Sky*, in which Bowles had a minor role, and with the 1995 Paul Bowles symposium and celebration at the Lincoln Center. A sharp increase in critical and biographical studies of Paul Bowles occurred in the 1990's as well. Bowles died of a heart attack in Tangier in 1999.

ANALYSIS

Paul Bowles is best placed in a category by himself. Though his work is tangentially related to that of other writers--the southern gothic of William Faulkner and Flannery O'Connor, the sexual primitivism of D. H. Lawrence, and the neocolonial meditations of Graham Greene and E. M. Forster, all of which suggest themselves as influences--Bowles occupies a unique place in literature. No other writer has produced a body of work that so consistently rejects the culture that has given birth to it. The intensity with which Bowles and his principal characters spurn the Western world and all it stands for distinguishes his stories even from other literature of exile.

Paul Bowles (Genevieve Naylor/Corbis)

Bowles's work has received only scattered critical acclaim. Perhaps because he lived most of his life in Morocco and because most of his work is set outside the United States, he remains outside the American literary scene and has not been the focus of considerable critical attention. Nevertheless, Bowles has been acclaimed by important writers, such as Gore Vidal and Tennessee Williams. Bowles's affinity for the grotesque and lurid has led some reviewers to dismiss his work as gratuitously violent. Indeed, the pessimism and nihilism that dominate his stories can be overwhelming. Beneath the surface violence, however, the reader finds a consistent, thoughtful, and chilling vision of life.

His clear style presents readers with a very real world, yet the reality readers so palpably experience in reading Bowles is ultimately a hallucination. His stories concentrate on the ambiguity of human morality. Order is only superficial in this world; readers sense its inevitable dissolution at every turn. The jungle and the desert reside within every human situation, and the rationality with which readers attempt to suppress them proves to be their greatest self-delusion.

Bowles's stories are generally set in exotic locations, North Africa and Latin America being his favorite landscapes. Physical setting is crucial in his work. It is more than backdrop; often it becomes a modulating force, regulating and tempering the characters who wander into its domain. These characters are often visiting Westerners, who, spiritually empty themselves, come with a superficial craving for new experiences. Beneath the surface, however, these lost ciphers have no truly purposeful quest. They are merely fleeing the vacuity of their Western world; they seek nothing except escape.

Many of Bowles's stories have no Western characters at all. Even then, the alienation inherent in the landscape is evident and, indeed, prominent. No facile primitivism surfaces in Bowles's world. The non-Westerners are not noble savages; they are isolated and displaced persons as well, brutalized by the landscape and compelled to see into the heart of darkness beating there. This is the world Bowles explores. It is a brutal world, both nightmarish and stark in its features. Bowles's style matches the landscape: He writes without adornment or prettiness. This clear and honest style is not without grace, but it is the grace of the desert about which he so often writes, a grace many find too austere.

"A DISTANT EPISODE"

One of Bowles's first stories, and one of his finest, is the macabre "A Distant Episode," which first appeared in *The Delicate Prey, and Other Stories*. Several writers and critics, including Williams, hailed this as one of the finest American short stories. A nameless American professor of linguistics visits a small town in the Sahara, where he tries to strike up a conversation with a surly waiter. The waiter reluctantly promises to help the professor purchase some boxes made from camel udders. They walk by moonlight through a dangerous part of town, encountering corpses and wild dogs, until the waiter abandons the professor on a cliff. The hostile nomadic group that makes the boxes is encamped somewhere beneath the cliff, and despite all foreboding, the professor descends to find them. There, he is robbed and beaten. In the morning, the nomads cut out his tongue and depart into the desert. The professor lives among

them for months; dressed in a rattling suit of smashed tin cans, he is brought out as a sort of clown and made to entertain the community. "A Distant Episode" is the quintessential Bowles story. All his principal themes are starkly set forth in the account of the professor's transformation from curiosity-seeker to curiosity. Something takes hold of him in this foreign setting, something over which he has no control, and the civilized veneer of the Westerner is easily wiped away. Significantly, the linguist loses his tongue, and thus the apparent gratuitousness of the violence becomes psychologically telling. He loses not only his tongue but also his mind and spirit.

"THE ECHO"

Another early story, "The Echo," also from *The Delicate Prey, and Other Stories*, extends Bowles's obsession with inhospitable landscapes. Aileen, a college-age woman from the United States, has come to live with her expatriate mother in Colombia. The mother lives in an impressive house perched near a cliff with a woman named Prue. Prue is an artist, quite masculine in both appearance and attitude, who seems to be the lover of Aileen's mother. The antagonism between lover and daughter builds to the point that Aileen's mother asks Aileen to leave. On the day of Aileen's departure, in a final encounter, Prue taunts Aileen until the girl explodes and viciously attacks her. In this story, the daughter's estrangement from her mother is reflected in the alien landscape, so that it is the place itself that first prompts Aileen's primal scream and then literally echoes it from the black walls of the gorge. Once again, Bowles's character is stripped of her superficial civility and forced to confront the dark stranger within.

"PAGES FROM COLD POINT"

Mr. Norton, in the story "Pages from Cold Point," is the Bowles character who most embodies the extremity of Western nihilism. A clever, if blighted, cynic, Norton undertakes the journey so typical of Bowles's characters--the journey from civilization (in this case, civilization at its most refined: the university campus) to a primitive land in the Third World where Western certainties have a way of dissolving. Norton leaves the university after the death of his wife (her name, Hope, is significant) and goes to a tropical island with his teenage son, Racky. Bit by bit, Norton learns that the attention his son is paying to the young boys of the island town has stirred up trouble. Shockingly, in the scene when father confronts son, an incestuous affair begins. Racky's hopelessness and corruption are the disturbing by-products of a society gone haywire. The seduction proves easy and even appears "natural" to Norton, who feels that nothing drastic has happened. His description is so understated as to be disturbing. Readers are reminded that in Bowles's world, corruption is insidious and pervasive.

"AT PASO ROJO"

Bowles is fascinated by what happens to people when their civilized notions are suddenly disturbed by some encounter with primitive people or a foreboding landscape. In the story "At Paso Rojo," first appearing in *The Delicate Prey, and Other Stories*, the drama is played out in the psychological terrain of sexual repression and maladjustment. The story is set in Central America. It concerns the visit of two sisters, both middle-aged spinsters, to the ranch of their brother following the death of their mother. One of the sisters, Chalia, disturbed and vulnerable after the loss of her mother, begins behaving oddly. There seems little doubt that the brutal landscape has some bearing on her crack-up. After a ride in the country, Chalia finds herself alone with one of the ranch hands, a young and virile mestizo. She makes advances but is rejected. Chalia exacts revenge by stealing money from her brother and then giving the money to the mestizo. Later, Chalia encounters the drunk boy on the road and pushes him over a small cliff. When he is found, still a bit drunk and with a large amount of money in his pocket, the theft is revealed. Chalia denies having given him the money, and the ranch hand is dismissed. This unpredictable eruption of violent, even sadistic, behavior in a normally "civilized" character is fascinating to Bowles. Again and again in his fiction, the characters fall prey to violent urges that they do not understand. Ultimately, these urges lead to a masochistic desire for annihilation.

"THE DELICATE PREY"

One of Bowles's most acclaimed stories is "The Delicate Prey," a stunning story of three Arab merchants who undertake a perilous journey across remote regions of the Sahara desert. Several days into the journey, the three merchants encounter a solitary traveler. Although wary, they allow the stranger to travel with them since he is alone and not of the barbaric nomadic group known as the Reguiba (the same bunch that captured the professor in "A Distant Episode"). The stranger claims to be a good shot and promises to supply the traveling party with gazelle meat. A few days later, the stranger goes off to shoot gazelles. Upon hearing gunshots, the elder merchant, hoping to join in the shooting, pursues the stranger. After more shots, a second merchant departs in pursuit, leaving the youngest of the party alone. Eventually, the stranger returns alone, and the boy is easily captured. The stranger mutilates, rapes, and murders the boy, all without the slightest compunction. The stranger later arrives at a trading town and tries to sell the merchants' leather, a type of leather that is unique to the merchants' band. Thus he is discovered, and some travelers from the merchants' town capture him and bury him in the sand of the desert, leaving only his head exposed.

"The Delicate Prey" is a demanding story. Bowles insists that readers look inside themselves and account for the cruelty that they find there. There is nothing noble about the characters, and certainly the story presents the reader with a world devoid of altruism. A first encounter with the story produces a feeling of strangeness and terror. To examine it more closely, however, is to uncover something familiar and haunting in this simple tale. The reader knows what is going to happen and yet is still horrified. The retribution exacted in the story's conclusion is severe and grotesque, and yet, in a strange way, gratifying. Bowles wants to direct readers' attention to the darkness present not only in their gratuitously violent actions but also in their sense of justice. The queasiness they experience is in part attributable to the fact that they recognize the ineluctable pattern of the action. The characters are not monsters. They are acting, if anything, all too humanly.

"TAPIAMA"

A predominant theme in Bowles's stories is the encounter of spiritually bankrupt Americans with alien cultures. In the story "Tapiama," which first appeared in *The Time of Friendship*, this theme is amply articulated. It is a story that reminds the reader of Samuel Beckett or Jean-Paul Sartre. Nothing seems to happen in the story, certainly nothing like the shocking events upon which Bowles's stories so often turn. Still, an unnerving suspense is created by the constant threat of such an event. In the end, though the conclusion is shadowy and uncertain, "Tapiama" is a story that resonates with revelation.

In the story, an American photographer in a Latin American country goes for a midnight walk along the beach. He is puzzled by a light on the water and, upon hailing it, is asked by a boatman if he wishes to go to Tapiama. It is all quite mysterious to him, yet he agrees to go on the boat. He has no idea why he goes. This is a typical moment in a Bowles story: The protagonist seems to suffer a sudden loss of will, a Westernized version of acedia. He recognizes the absurdity of it all, yet he feels compelled to let events run their course: He will not assert himself. The boat arrives in Tapiama, which appears to be a factory town run by a sugar concern. The protagonist drifts into a seedy bar. He is accosted by a prostitute and by a belligerent gendarme. Ants crawl on the beams, a dead snake hangs from the rafters, and a monkey dances. In this bizarre setting, the American gets drunk on the local brew. When he finally manages to escape, the effort exhausts him, and he lies in the bottom of a boat, content to drift where the current takes him. Finally, the boat is discovered by some men who begin poling it upriver into the jungle and some unknown fate.

The theme of "Tapiama"--and, in fact, of many of Bowles's stories--is neatly captured in the closing pages. The American, drunk and nearly unconscious, hears the sound of a bird calling from the jungle. When he imitates the call, the strangers in the boat with him explode with laughter. This is a bird, they explain to him, that tries to sit in the nests of other birds and fights with them until it is driven off. Its call means "Nobody wants me." This is the condition of the photographer and all Bowles's Westerners. Slumming their way through other cultures, they fight and are driven off by the "natives." Nobody likes them, and indeed there is little to like. Their homelessness is indicative of their spiritual emptiness.

TOO FAR FROM HOME

Another alienated American appears in *Too Far from Home*, set in the Niger River Valley, a Bowles novella appeared in the collection *Too Far from Home: The Selected Writings of Paul Bowles*. Anita, fleeing New York City and a painful divorce, arrives in North Africa to live with her brother Tom, an artist who revels in exotic desert landscapes. From the moment she arrives, Anita feels out of place in the vast, hot, African spaces, and she takes out her tensions on Tom and the household staff. She is particularly uncomfortable with Sekou, a local chieftain who acts as head of the household.

One morning, Tom asks Anita to purchase film from his friend Mme Massot, the French woman who owns the camera shop in the nearby village. Tom sends Sekou to act as Anita's guide. On the way, two young Americans on a motorcycle collide with Sekou, wounding him in the leg. Incensed, Anita shouts dire warnings at the motorcyclists. A few days later, Anita, walking amid the high dunes, discovers the Americans, their motorcycle wrecked, their bodies splattered with blood. She assumes they are dead and leaves the scene, telling no one. Soon after, she has nightmares about consuming a headless man's flesh, a dream she claims Sekou has willed upon her.

Just before she leaves Africa, Anita hears that the motorcyclists did not die from their injuries; they perished from exposure. Therefore, she may have been able to save their lives if she had reported the accident. She also learns that Sekou claims she cursed the motorcyclists when she screamed abuse at them, thus causing their death through magic. Sekou believes that his leg will not improve until Anita withdraws her curse and forgives the young men. He has dreamed of visiting her in her sleep to beg her to forgive the young men, but she has always refused. Anita, hearing this tale, forgives them out loud before Sekou, who approves. The next morning, when Anita leaves the Niger River, she feels healed and realizes she will miss the North African landscape, the adobe village, and most of all Sekou.

While this story possesses many key Bowles motifs, its conclusion possesses an ambivalence out of character for the usually uncompromisingly grim author. Like *The Sheltering Sky*, *Too Far from Home* portrays a dysfunctional artistic couple in a foreign country, although in this story they are brother and sister. Still, there are unconscious incestuous connections between Tom and Anita, who often act like a married couple. Anita even becomes jealous of Mme Massot's interest in Tom and his artwork. Also, *Too Far from Home* contains spiritually empty Westerners in an alien landscape, as well as sudden and brutal violence. However, while Anita's failure to understand the Niger River realm and its culture result in her passionately violent curse and the tragic death of two young men, the curse and Sekou's forgiveness lead Anita to reconcile with North Africa, its people, and her emotional being.

OTHER MAJOR WORKS

LONG FICTION: *The Sheltering Sky*, 1949; *Let It Come Down*, 1952; *The Spider's House*, 1955; *Up Above the World*, 1966.

POETRY: *Scenes*, 1968; *The Thicket of Spring: Poems, 1926-1969*, 1972; *Next to Nothing*, 1976; *Next to Nothing: Collected Poems, 1926-1977*, 1981.

NONFICTION: *Yallah*, 1957; *Their Heads Are Green and Their Hands Are Blue*, 1963; *Without Stopping*, 1972; *Points in Time*, 1982; *Days: Tangier Journal, 1987-1989*, 1991; *Conversations with Paul Bowles*, 1993 (Gena Dagel Caponi, editor); *In Touch: The Letters of Paul Bowles*, 1994 (Jeffrey Miller, editor).

TRANSLATIONS: *The Lost Trail of the Sahara*, 1952 (of R. Frison-Roche's novel); *No Exit*, 1958 (of Jean-Paul Sartre's play); *A Life Full of Holes*, 1964 (of Driss ben Hamed Charhadi's autobiography); *Love with a Few Hairs*, 1967 (of Mohammed Mrabet's fiction); *M'Hashish*, 1969 (of Mrabet's fiction); *The Lemon*, 1969 (of Mrabet's fiction); *The Boy Who Set the Fire*, 1974 (of Mrabet's fiction); *The Oblivion Seekers*, 1975 (of Isabelle Eberhardt's fiction); *Harmless Poisons, Blameless Sins*, 1976 (of Mrabet's fiction); *Look and Move On*, 1976 (of Mrabet's fiction); *The Big Mirror*, 1977 (of Mrabet's fiction); *The Beggar's Knife*, 1985 (of Rodrigo Rey Rosa's fiction); *Dust on Her Tongue*, 1989 (of Rey Rosa's fiction); *Chocolate Creams and Dollars*, 1992 (of Mrabet's fiction).

EDITED TEXT: *Claudio Bravo: Drawings and Paintings*, 1997 (revised 2005).

MISCELLANEOUS: *The Paul Bowles Reader*, 2000.

BIBLIOGRAPHY

Caponi, Gena Dagel, ed. *Conversations with Paul Bowles*. Jackson: University Press of Mississippi, 1993. In this collection of reprinted and unpublished interviews, Bowles talks about his life and art, even though he claims that the man who wrote his books does not exist except in the books. Bowles has a penchant for perverse responses to interview questions but still communicates a great deal about his relationship with his work.

_____. *Paul Bowles: Romantic Savage*. Carbondale: Southern Illinois University Press, 1994. A biographical and critical study of Bowles's life and art that examines the sources of his fiction, his major themes and techniques, and his methods of story composition.

Carr, Virginia Spencer. *Paul Bowles: A Life*. New York: Scribner, 2004. Carr was close friends with Bowles, and her biography is based upon her personal experiences with the writer, as well as ten years of research and interviews with about two hundred of Bowles's acquaintances.

Chandarlapaty, Raj. *The Beat Generation and Counterculture: Paul Bowles, William S. Burroughs, Jack Kerouac*. New York: Peter Lang, 2009. Examines the work of the three authors, including the relevance of their attempts to write about exotic non-Western cultures and repressed minority cultures in the United States. The first part of the book focuses on the work of Bowles, providing analyses of his novels and devoting one chapter to the short stories in *A Hundred Camels in the Courtyard*.

Dillon, Millicent. "Tracing Paul Bowles." *Raritan* 17 (Winter, 1998): 47-63. In these excerpts from her biography of Bowles, *You Are Not I*, Dillon traces the relationship between Bowles and his wife Jane Bowles, revaluates earlier views in her biography of Jane Bowles, and recounts her own speculations on Paul Bowles's life and work.

Ficociello, Robert. "Fish(ing) for Colonial Counter-Narratives in the Short Fiction of Paul Bowles." In *Paradoxical Citizenship: Edward Said*, edited by Silvia Nagy-Zekmi. Lanham, Md.: Lexington Books, 2006. Analyzes Bowles's short fiction to demonstrate how the writer was able to create a "tenacious, perceptive, and culturally confident native population" in his work.

Gelfant, Blanche H., ed. *The Columbia Companion to the Twentieth-Century American Short Story*. New York: Columbia University Press, 2000. Includes a chapter in which Bowles's short stories are analyzed.

Green, Michelle. *The Dream at the End of the World: Paul Bowles and the Literary Renegades in Tangier*. New York: HarperCollins, 1991. A lively account of the artistic and socialite sets that congregated in Tangier in the 1940's and 1950's. Investigates the life of Bowles and those who came to stay with him in Morocco. Offers interesting background details for readers of Bowles's fiction. Includes an index and photographs.

Hibbard, Allen. *Paul Bowles: Magic and Morocco*. San Francisco: Cadmus, 2004. Hibbard, a close friend of Bowles's, examines the influence of North African magic and Moroccan culture upon his friend's sensibilities and fiction.

_____. *Paul Bowles: A Study of the Short Fiction*. New York: Twayne, 1993. This introduction to Bowles's short fiction discusses his debt to Edgar Allan Poe's theories of formal unity and analyzes his short-story collections as carefully organized wholes. Includes material from Bowles's notebooks and previously published essays by other critics.

Patterson, Richard. *A World Outside: The Fiction of Paul Bowles*. Austin: University of Texas Press, 1987. This scholarly examination of Bowles's work is comprehensive in its analysis. *The Sheltering Sky* is given much attention. Patterson's notes and index are quite good.

Pounds, Wayne. *Paul Bowles: The Inner Geography*. New York: Peter Lang, 1985. A good introduction to Bowles and his use of landscape. Demonstrates the connection between setting and the spiritual states of Bowles's characters.

Sawyer-Laucanno, Christopher. *An Invisible Spectator: A Biography of Paul Bowles*. New York: Weidenfeld & Nicolson, 1989. Presents a readable account of Bowles's life and offers some intriguing speculation on the connection between the events of his life and the plots of his stories. The index and notes are useful, and a select bibliography lists Bowles's major works in literature and music.

Stephen Benz
Updated by John Nizalowski Benz

KAY BOYLE

Born: St. Paul, Minnesota; February 19, 1902
Died: Mill Valley, California; December 27, 1992

PRINCIPAL SHORT FICTION

Short Stories, 1929
Wedding Day, and Other Stories, 1930
The First Lover, and Other Stories, 1933
The White Horses of Vienna, and Other Stories, 1936
The Crazy Hunter, and Other Stories, 1940
Thirty Stories, 1946
The Smoking Mountain: Stories of Postwar Germany, 1951
Three Short Novels, 1958 (includes *The Crazy Hunter*, *The Bridegroom's Body*, and *Decision*)
Nothing Ever Breaks Except the Heart, 1966
Fifty Stories, 1980
Life Being the Best, and Other Stories, 1988

OTHER LITERARY FORMS

In addition to her short stories, Kay Boyle (boyl) published several novels, volumes of poetry, children's books, essay collections, and a book of memoirs. *Breaking the Silence: Why a Mother Tells Her Son About the Nazi Era* (1962) is her personal account, written for adolescents, of Europe during the Nazi regime. Boyle also ghostwrote, translated, and edited many other books. Hundreds of her stories, poems, and articles have appeared in periodicals ranging from the "little magazines" published in Paris in the 1920's to *The Saturday Evening Post* and *The New Yorker*, for which she was a correspondent from 1946 to 1953.

ACHIEVEMENTS

Both prolific and versatile, Kay Boyle has been respected during her long career for her exquisite technical style and her ardent political activism. She was very much a part of the expatriate group of writers living in Paris in the 1920's, and her work appeared in the avant-garde magazines alongside that of stream of consciousness and complex interior monologues. That her work was highly regarded is evidenced by her many awards: two John Simon Guggenheim Memorial Foundation Fellowships; O. Henry Awards in both 1935 and 1961; an honorary doctorate from Columbia College, Chicago; and membership in the National Institute of Arts and Letters. She taught at San Francisco State University and Eastern Washington University.

BIOGRAPHY

Born into an affluent family in St. Paul, Minnesota, in 1902, Kay Boyle moved and traveled frequently and extensively with her family during her childhood. After studying architecture for two years in Cincinnati, Boyle married Robert Brault, whose family never accepted her or the marriage. What was to have been a summer trip to France in 1923 became an eighteen-year expatriation, during which Boyle continued to write poetry and fiction. Boyle left her husband to live with editor Ernest Walsh until his death from tuberculosis in 1926. Boyle later returned to Brault with Walsh's child. They divorced in 1932, when she married Laurence Vail, a fellow American expatriate. After her marriage to Vail also ended in divorce, Boyle married Joseph von Franckenstein, an Austrian baron who had been forced out of his homeland during the Nazi invasion. She lived much of the time in Europe and was a correspondent for *The New Yorker*. She returned to the United States in 1953; Franckenstein died in 1963. Boyle taught at San Francisco State University from 1963 to 1979 and at Eastern Washington University in 1982. Her arrest and imprisonment following an anti-Vietnam War demonstration is the basis of her novel *The Underground Woman* (1975). She would remain actively involved in movements protesting social injustices and violations of human rights.

ANALYSIS

In a 1963 article Kay Boyle defines what she saw as the role of the serious writer: to be "the spokesman for those who remain inarticulate . . . an aeolian harp whose sensitive strings respond to the whispers of the concerned people of his time." The short-story writer, she believed, is "a moralist in the highest sense of the word"; the role of the short-story writer has always been "to speak briefly and clearly of the dignity and integrity of [the] individual." Perhaps it is through this definition that the reader may distinguish the central threads that run through the variegated fabric of Boyle's fiction and bind it into a single piece.

In the 1920's, when the young expatriate artists she knew in Paris were struggling to cast off the yokes of literary convention, Boyle championed the bold and experimental in language, and her own early stories are intensely individual explorations of private experiences. When the pressures of the social world came to bear so heavily on private lives in the twentieth century that they could not be ignored, Boyle began to expand the scope of her vision and vibrate to the note of the *new* times to affirm on a broader scale the same basic values--the "dignity and integrity" of the individual. Beginning in the 1930's, her subject matter encompassed the rise of Nazism, the French resistance, the Allied occupation of postwar Germany, and the civil rights and anti-Vietnam War movements in the United States, yet she never lost sight of the individual dramas acted out against these panoramic backdrops.

In the same article Boyle also quotes Albert Camus's statement that "a man's work is nothing but a long journey to recover through the detours of art, the two or three simple and great images which first gained access to his heart." In Boyle's journey of more than fifty years, a few central themes remained constant: a belief in the absolute essentiality of love to human well-being--whether on a personal or a global level; an awareness of the many obstacles to its attainment; and a tragic sense of loss when love fails and the gulfs between human beings stand unbridged.

"WEDDING DAY"

"Wedding Day," the title story of her first widely circulated volume of short stories, published in 1930, is typical of her early works. It is an intense exploration

Kay Boyle (Library of Congress)

of a unique private experience written in an experimental style. The action is primarily psychological, and outward events are described as they reflect states of consciousness. This story is representative of Boyle's best work for decades to come, both in its central concern with the failure of love and in its bold and brilliant use of language.

"The red carpet that was to spurt like a hemorrhage from pillar to post was stacked in the corner," the story begins. From the first sentence the reader senses that things are out of joint. The wedding cake is ignored as it is carried into the pantry "with its beard lying white as hoarfrost on its bosom." "This was the last lunch," Boyle writes, and the brother and sister "came in with their buttonholes drooping with violets and sat sadly down, sat down to eat." To the funereal atmosphere of this wedding day, Boyle injects tension and bitterness. The son and mother argue as to whether the daughter will be given the family's prized copper saucepans, and he mocks the decorum his mother cherishes when he commands her not to cry, pointing his finger directly at her nose "so that when she looked at him with dignity her eyes wavered and crossed" and "she sat looking proudly at him, erect as a needle staring through its one open eye." As the mother and son bicker over who wanted the wedding in the first place, the bride-to-be is conspicuously silent. Finally, as the son snatches away each slice of roast beef his mother carves until she whimpers her fear of getting none herself, he and his sister burst into laughter. He tosses his napkin over the chandelier, and she follows him out of the room, leaving their mother alone "praying that this occasion at least pass off with dignity, with her heart not in her mouth but beating away in peace in its own bosom."

With the tension between children and mother clearly delineated and the exclusive camaraderie between brother and sister suggested, Boyle shifts both mood and scene and describes in almost incantatory prose the pair's idyllic jaunt through the spring afternoon in the hours remaining before the wedding:

> The sun was an imposition, an imposition, for they were another race stamping an easy trail through the wilderness of Paris, possessed of the same people, but of themselves like another race. No one else could by lifting of the head only be starting life over again, and it was a wonder the whole city of Paris did not hold its breath for them, for if anyone could have begun a new race, it was these two.

The incestuous overtones are strong. "It isn't too late yet, you know," the brother repeatedly insists as they stride through the streets, take a train into the *bois*, and row to the middle of a pond. "Over them was the sky set like a tomb," and as tears flow down their cheeks, the slow rain begins to fall. There is perfect correspondence between landscape and emotion, external objects mirroring the characters' internal states. The rain underscores the pair's frustration and despair as they realize the intensity of their love and the impossibility of its fulfillment:

> Everywhere, everywhere there were other countries to go to. And how were they to get from the boat with the chains that were on them, how uproot the willowing trees from their hearts, how strike the irons of spring that shackled them? What shame and shame that scorched a burning pathway to their dressing rooms! Their hearts were mourning for every Paris night and its half-hours before lunch when

two straws crossed on the round table top on the marble anywhere meant I had a drink here and went on.

The inevitable wedding itself forms the final segment of the story, and the lyrical spell binding the pair is broken the instant they set foot in the house again to find their mother "tying white satin bows under the chins of the potted plants." The boy kicks down the hall the silver tray that will collect the guests' calling cards, and his mother is wearily certain "that this outburst presaged a thousand mishaps that were yet to come." The irony of the story lies not only in the reversal of expectations the title may have aroused in the reader but also in the discrepancy between different characters' perceptions of the same situation. The self-pitying matron worries only about the thousand little mishaps possible when a major disaster--the wedding itself--is imminent; but the guests arrive "in peace" and the brother delivers his sister to the altar. Boyle captures magnificently the enormous gulf between the placid surface appearance and the tumultuous inner reality of the situation as she takes the reader inside the bride's consciousness:

> This was the end, the end, they thought. She turned her face to her brother and suddenly their hearts fled together and sobbed like ringdoves in their bosoms. This was the end, the end, the end, this was the end.
>
> Down the room their feet fled in various ways, seeking an escape. To the edge of the carpet fled her feet, returned and followed reluctantly upon her brother's heels. Every piped note of the organ insisted that she go on. It isn't too late, he said. Too late, too late. The ring was given, the book was closed. The desolate, the barren sky continued to fling down dripping handfuls of fresh rain.

The mindless repetition of the phrase "the end" and the blind panic of the bride's imaginary flight have an intense psychological authenticity, and the recurrence of the brother's phrase "It isn't too late" and its perversion in "Too late, too late," along with the continuing rain, are evidence of the skill with which Boyle has woven motifs into the fabric of her story.

"Wedding Day" ends with dancing, but in an ironic counterpoint to the flight she had imagined at the altar, the bride's feet "were fleeing in a hundred ways throughout the rooms, fluttering from the punch bowl to her bedroom and back again." Through repetition and transformation of the image, Boyle underscores the fact that her path is now circumscribed. While the brother, limbered by the punch, dances about scattering calling cards, the mother, "in triumph on the arm of the General, danced lightly by" rejoicing that "no glass had yet been broken." "What a real success, what a *real* success," is her only thought as her feet float "Over the oriental prayer rugs, through the Persian forests of hemp, away and away" in another absurdly circumscribed "escape" that is yet another mockery of the escape to "other countries" that the pair had dreamed of that afternoon on the lake.

Ironies and incongruities are hallmarks of Kay Boyle's fiction. For Boyle, reality depends on perception, and the fact that different perceptions of the same situation result in disparate and often conflicting "realities" creates a disturbing world in which individuals badly in need of contact and connection collide and bounce off one another like atoms. In "Wedding Day" Boyle juxtaposes a *real* loss of love with the surface gaiety of a wedding that celebrates no love at all, but which the mother terms "a *real* success." She exposes the painful isolation of each individual and the tragedy that the only remedy--a bonding through love--is so often thwarted or destroyed.

The barriers to love are many, both natural and man-made. In some of Boyle's stories those who would love are severed by death. Sometimes, as in the case of the brother and sister in "Wedding Day," love's fulfillment is simply made impossible by the facts of life in this imperfect world, and although readers can mourn for what has been lost, they can hardly argue about the obstacle itself--the incest taboo is nearly universal. In many of her other works, Boyle presents a more assailable villain. In "Wedding Day" she treats unsympathetically the mother, who stands for all the petty proprieties that so often separate people. Boyle finds many barriers to human contact to be as arbitrary and immoral as the social conventions that cause Huck Finn's "conscience" to torment him as he helps his friend Jim to escape slavery, and in her fiction she quietly unleashes her fury against them. An obstacle she attacks repeatedly is a narrow-mindedness that blinds

individuals to the inherent dignity and integrity of others, an egotism that in the plural becomes bigotry and chauvinism.

"THE WHITE HORSES OF VIENNA"

While Boyle and her family were living in Austria in the 1930's, she was an eyewitness as the social world began to impose itself on private lives, and she began to widen the scope of her artistic vision; yet her "political" stories have as their central concern the ways in which external events affect the individual. In one of her best-known stories, "The White Horses of Vienna," which won the O. Henry Award for best story of 1935, Boyle exposes the artificial barricades to human understanding and connection. The story explores the relationship between a Tyrolean doctor, who has injured his leg coming down the mountain after lighting a swastika fire in rebellion against the current government, and Dr. Heine, the young assistant sent from Vienna to take over his patients while he recovers. The Tyrolean doctor and his wife see immediately that Dr. Heine is a Jew.

The Tyrolean doctor is a clean-living, respected man. He had been a prisoner of war in Siberia and had studied abroad, but the many places in which he had been "had never left an evil mark." Boyle writes: "His face was as strong as rock, but it had seen so much of suffering that it had the look of being scarred, it seemed to be split in two, with one side of it given to resolve and the other to compassion." In his personal dealings it is the compassionate side that dominates. When his wife asks in a desperate whisper what they will do with "*him*," the Tyrolean doctor replies simply that they will send for his bag at the station and give him some *Apfelsaft* if he is thirsty. "It's harder on him than us," he tells her. Neither has the wife's own humanity been extinguished entirely by institutionalized bigotry, for when Dr. Heine's coat catches fire from a sterilizing lamp on the table, she wraps a piece of rug around him immediately and holds him tightly to smother the flames. Almost instinctively, she offers to try patching the burned-out place, but then she suddenly bites her lip and stands back "as if she had remembered the evil thing that stood between them."

The situation of the Tyrolean doctor, described as a "great, golden, wounded bird," is counterpointed in a story Dr. Heine tells at dinner one evening about the famous Lipizzaner horses of the Spanish Riding School in Vienna, still royal, "without any royalty left to bow their heads to, still shouldering into the arena with spirits a man would give his soul for, bending their knees in homage to the empty, canopied loge where royalty no longer sat." He tells of a particular horse that the government, badly in need of money, had sold to an Indian maharaja. When the time had come for the horse to be taken away, a wound was discovered cut in his leg. After it had healed and it was again time for the horse to leave, another wound was found on its other leg. Finally the horse's blood was so poisoned that it had to be destroyed. No one knew who had caused the wounds until the horse's devoted little groom committed suicide that same day. When the after-dinner conversation is interrupted by the knocking of Heimwehr troops at the door, "men brought in from other parts of the country, billeted there to subdue the native people," the identification between the doctor and the steed is underscored. He cannot guide the troops up the mountain in search of those who have lit that evening's swastika fires because of his wounded leg.

Dr. Heine is relieved that the rest of the evening will be spent with family and friends watching one of the Tyrolean doctor's locally renowned marionette shows. After staring out the window at the burning swastikas, the "marvelously living flowers of fire springing out of the arid darkness," the "inexplicable signals given from one mountain to another in some secret gathering of power that cast him and his people out, forever out upon the waters of despair," Dr. Heine turns back, suddenly angry, and proclaims that the whole country is being ruined by politics, that it is impossible to have friends or even casual conversations on any other basis these days. "You're much wiser to make your puppets, *Herr Doktor*," he says.

Even the marionette show is political. The characters are a clown who explains he is carrying artificial flowers because he is on his way to his own funeral and wants them to be fresh when he gets there, and a handsome grasshopper, "a great, gleaming beauty" who prances about the stage with delicacy and wit to the music of Wolfgang Amadeus Mozart. "It's really marvellous! He's as graceful as the white horses at Vienna, *Herr Doktor*," Dr. Heine calls out in delight. As the conversation continues between the clown, called "Chancellor," and the grasshopper addressed as "The Leader," Dr. Heine is not laughing so loudly. The Chancellor has a "ludicrous faith in the power of the Church" to support him; the Leader proclaims that the cities are full of churches, but "the country is full of God." The Leader speaks with "a wild and stirring power that sent the cold of wonder up and down one's spine," and he seems "ready to waltz away at any moment with the power of stallion life that was leaping in his limbs." As the Chancellor proclaims, "I believe in the independence of the individual," he promptly trips over his own sword and falls flat among the daisies.

At the story's conclusion, Dr. Heine is standing alone on the cold mountainside, longing to be "indoors, with the warmth of his own people, and the intellect speaking." When he sees "a small necklace of men coming to him" up the mountain, the lights they bear "coming like little beacons of hope carried to him," Dr. Heine thinks, "Come to me . . . come to me. I am a young man alone on a mountain. I am a young man alone, as my race is alone, lost here amongst them all."

Ironically, what Dr. Heine views as "beacons of hope" are carried by the Heimwehr troops, the Tyrolean doctor's enemies. As in "Wedding Day," Boyle presents a single situation and plays off the characters' reactions to it against one another to illustrate the gaps between individuals and the relativity of truth and reality in the world.

His personal loyalties transcending his politics, Dr. Heine rushes to warn the family of the Heimwehr's approach. When the troops arrive they announce that the Austrian chancellor, Englebert Dollfuss, had been assassinated in Vienna that afternoon. They have come to arrest the doctor, whose rebel sympathies are known. "Ah, politics, politics again!" cries Dr. Heine, wringing his hands "like a woman about to cry." He runs outdoors and takes the doctor's hand as he is being carried away on a stretcher, asking what he can do to help. "You can throw me peaches and chocolate from the street," replies the Tyrolean doctor, smiling, "his cheeks scarred with the marks of laughter in the light from the hurricane lamps that the men were carrying down." His wife is not a good shot, he adds, and he missed all the oranges she had thrown him after the February slaughter. At this image of the Tyrolean doctor caged like an animal but still noble, with his spirit still unbroken, Dr. Heine is left "thinking in anguish of the snow-white horses, the Lipizzaners, the relics of pride, the still unbroken vestiges of beauty bending their knees to the empty loge of royalty where there was no royalty any more."

In "The White Horses of Vienna," Boyle expresses hope, if not faith, that even in the face of divisive social forces, the basic connections of compassion between individuals might survive. In a work that is a testament to her humanity, she presents the Tyrolean doctor's plight with such sensitivity that readers, like the Jewish assistant, are forced to view with understanding and empathy this proud man's search for a cause that will redeem the dignity and honor of his wounded people while at the same time abhorring the cause itself. Boyle sees and presents in all its human complexity what at first glance seems a black-and-white political issue. Boyle, however, was no Pollyanna. As the social conflict that motivates this story snowballed into world war and mass genocide, she saw with a cold, realistic eye how little survived of the goodwill among human beings she had hoped for. In many of her stories written in the 1940's and in subsequent years, she examined unflinchingly and sometimes bitterly the individual tragedies played out in the shadow of the global one.

"WINTER NIGHT"

In "Winter Night," published in 1946, Boyle draws a delicate portrait of a little girl named Felicia and a woman sent by a "sitting parent" agency to spend the evening with her in a New York apartment. The woman, in her strange accent, tells Felicia that today is an anniversary, that three years ago that night she had begun to care for another little girl who also studied ballet and whose mother, like Felicia's, had to go away. The difference was that the other girl's mother had been sent away on a train car in which there were no seats, and she never came back, but she was able to write a short letter on a smuggled scrap of paper and slip it through the cracks on the floor of the moving train in the hope that some kind stranger would send it to its destination.

The woman can only comfort herself with the thought that "They must be quietly asleep somewhere, and not crying all night because they are hungry and because they are cold."

"There is a time of apprehension which begins with the beginning of darkness, and to which only the speech of love can lend security," the story begins, as Boyle describes the dying light of a January afternoon in New York City. Felicia and the "sitting parent," both left alone, have found that security in each other. When, after midnight, Felicia's mother tiptoes in the front door, slipping the three blue foxskins from her shoulder and dropping the velvet bag on a chair, she hears only the sound of breathing in the dark living room, and no one speaks to her in greeting as she crosses to the bedroom: "And then, as startling as a slap across her delicately tinted face, she saw the woman lying sleeping on the divan, and Felicia, in her school dress still, asleep within the woman's arms." The story is not baldly didactic, but Boyle *is* moralizing. By juxtaposing the cases of the two little girls left alone by their mothers and cared for by a stranger, she shows that the failure of love is a tragic loss on an individual as well as on a global scale. Again, personal concerns merge with political and social ones, and readers find the failure of love on any level to be the fundamental tragedy of life.

Some of the stories Boyle has written about the war and its aftermath are less subtle, "artistic" explorations of individual struggles as they are frankly moralistic adventure stories written for commercial magazines, and they were more popular with the public than with the critics. One of her finest works was also a product of her war experiences. *The Smoking Mountain: Stories of Postwar Germany* consists of eleven stories, several originally published by *The New Yorker*, which had employed Boyle as a correspondent for the express purpose of sending "fiction out of Germany." It is prefaced by a seventy-seven-page nonfiction account of a de-Nazification trial Boyle witnessed in Frankfurt in 1948, which reveals her immense skill as a reporter as well. The book presents a painful vision. Any hope that a renewed understanding among peoples might result from the catastrophic "lesson" of the war is dashed, for the point of many of the stories and certainly of the introduction is how little difference the war has made in the fundamental attitudes of the defeated but silently defiant Germans who can still say of 1943 and 1944-- "the years when the gas chambers burned the brightest. . . . Those were the good years for everyone."

In 1929, Boyle, with writers Hart Crane, Vail, and others, signed Eugene Jolas's manifesto, "Revolution of the Word," condemning literary pretentiousness and outdated literary conventions. The goal, then, was to make literature at once fresh and experimental and at the same time accessible to the reader. Boyle would remain politically involved and productive as a writer, publishing collections of poetry, short stories, and essays into the 1980's. She would continue in her work to test the individual against events of historical significance, such as the threat of Nazism or the war in Vietnam. Although critics have accused her later works of selling out to popular taste and her style of losing its innovative edge, Boyle remained steadfast in defining her artistic purpose as a moral responsibility to defend the integrity of the individual and human rights. To do so, Boyle argued, she must be accessible to the public.

OTHER MAJOR WORKS

LONG FICTION: *Process*, wr. c. 1925, pb. 2001 (Sandra Spanier, editor); *Plagued by the Nightingale*, 1931; *Year Before Last*, 1932; *Gentlemen, I Address You Privately*, 1933; *My Next Bride*, 1934; *Death of a Man*, 1936; *Monday Night*, 1938; *Primer for Combat*, 1942; *Avalanche*, 1944; *A Frenchman Must Die*, 1946; *1939*, 1948; *His Human Majesty*, 1949; *The Seagull on the Step*, 1955; *Generation Without Farewell*, 1960; *The Underground Woman*, 1975.

POETRY: *A Glad Day*, 1938; *American Citizen Naturalized in Leadville, Colorado*, 1944; *Collected Poems*, 1962; *Testament for My Students, and Other Poems*, 1970; *This Is Not a Letter, and Other Poems*, 1985; *Collected Poems of Kay Boyle*, 1991.

NONFICTION: *Breaking the Silence: Why a Mother Tells Her Son About the Nazi Era*, 1962; *Being Geniuses Together, 1920-1930*, 1968 (with Robert McAlmon); *The Long Walk at San Francisco State, and Other Essays*, 1970; *Words That Must Somehow Be Said: The Selected Essays of Kay Boyle, 1927-1984*, 1985.

CHILDREN'S LITERATURE: *The Youngest Camel*, 1939, 1959; *Pinky, the Cat Who Liked to Sleep*, 1966; *Pinky in Persia*, 1968.

EDITED TEXTS: *365 Days*, 1936 (with others); *The Autobiography of Emanuel Carnevali*, 1967; *Enough of Dying! An Anthology of Peace Writings*, 1972 (with Justine van Gundy).

BIBLIOGRAPHY

Austenfeld, Thomas Carl. *American Women Writers and the Nazis: Ethics and Politics in Boyle, Porter, Stafford, and Hellman*. Charlottesville: University Press of Virginia, 2001. Analyzes the work of the four women writers, who were expatriates in Germany and Austria in the 1930's. Focuses on Boyle's novels and short stories describing the Nazi occupation.

Bell, Elizabeth S. *Kay Boyle: A Study of the Short Fiction*. New York: Twayne, 1992. An excellent introduction to Boyle's short stories. Includes bibliographical references and an index.

Boyle, Kay. "Kay Boyle: An Eightieth Birthday Interview." Interview by David R. Mesher. *The Malahat Review* 65 (July, 1983): 82-95. As the title suggests, this interview with Boyle was conducted on the occasion of her eightieth birthday. In it, she discusses her life and her work.

Carpenter, Richard C. "Kay Boyle." *English Journal* 42 (November, 1953): 425-430. Provides a helpful and general look at Boyle's early novels and short fiction.

_____. "Kay Boyle: The Figure in the Carpet." *Critique: Studies in Modern Fiction* 7 (Winter, 1964-1965): 65-78. Carpenter rejects the common complaint that Boyle is a mere "stylist," discussing her thematic depth, particularly in "The Bridegroom's Body" and "The Crazy Hunter."

Elkins, Marilyn, ed. *Critical Essays on Kay Boyle*. New York: G. K. Hall, 1997. A collection of reviews and critical essays on Boyle's work by various critics, reviewers, and commentators.

Gelfant, Blanche H., ed. *The Columbia Companion to the Twentieth-Century American Short Story*. New York: Columbia University Press, 2000. Includes a chapter in which Boyle's short stories are analyzed.

Hollenberg, Donna. "Abortion, Identity Formation, and the Expatriate Woman Writer: H. D. and Kay Boyle in the Twenties." *Twentieth Century Literature* 40 (Winter, 1994): 499-517. Discusses the theme of self-loss through the roles of marriage and motherhood in Boyle's early works. Shows how expatriation allowed some psychic space to explore the effect of gender roles on her aspirations. Examines the effect of inadequate maternal role models upon her identity as an artist.

Lesinska, Zofia P. *Perspectives of Four Women Writers on the Second World War: Gertrude Stein, Janet Flanner, Kay Boyle, and Rebecca West.* New York: Peter Lang, 2002. Examines the works that Boyle and three other women writers created during the 1930's and World War II. Maintains that these writers transcended the conventions of war writing, which had traditionally focused on diplomacy and military campaigns. Instead, their work emphasized the importance of social, cultural, and political histories, narrating these stories with a sense of empathy for the nonvictorious.

Mellen, Joan. *Kay Boyle: Author of Herself.* New York: Farrar, Straus and Giroux, 1994. Drawing on personal conversations with Boyle and her family, Mellen discusses the autobiographical nature of Boyle's writing and lays bare much of Boyle's own mythologizing of her life in her autobiographical writing.

Porter, Katherine Anne. "Kay Boyle: Example to the Young." In *The Critic as Artist: Essays on Books, 1920-1970,* edited by Gilbert A. Harrison. New York: Liveright, 1972. This essay examines Boyle as she fits in the literary movement of her time. Focuses on some of her stories, as well as on the novel *Plagued by the Nightingale.*

Spanier, Sandra Whipple. *Kay Boyle: Artist and Activist.* Carbondale: Southern Illinois University Press, 1986. Heavily annotated, thorough, and the first critical biography and major work on Boyle. Supplemented by select but extensive primary and secondary bibliographies. Illustrated.

Twentieth-Century Literature 34 (Fall, 1988). A special issue on Boyle, with personal reminiscences by Malcolm Cowley, Jessica Mitford, Howard Nemerov, and Studs Terkel, among others. Contains several critical essays on Boyle's work.

Sandra Whipple Spanier
Updated by Lou Thompson

T. CORAGHESSAN BOYLE

Born: Peekskill, New York; December 2, 1948
Also known as: T. C. Boyle, Thomas John Boyle,
  Tom Boyle

PRINCIPAL SHORT FICTION

Descent of Man, 1979
Greasy Lake, and Other Stories, 1985
If the River Was Whiskey, 1989
Without a Hero: Stories, 1994
T. C. Boyle Stories: The Collected Stories of T.
  Coraghessan Boyle, 1998
After the Plague: Stories, 2001
The Human Fly, and Other Stories, 2005
Tooth and Claw, 2005
Wild Child: Stories, 2010

OTHER LITERARY FORMS

The novels of T. Coraghessan (koh-RAG-ehs-ahn) Boyle (boyl), which explore many of the same subjects and themes as his short fiction, have received popular attention and critical praise. *The Road to Wellville* (1993) was adapted for a motion picture in 1994. Boyle is one of the most prolific literary/popular fiction writers in the United States. Since the turn of the twenty-first century, he has published not only four new collections of short stories, but also five novels: *Drop City* (2003), *The Inner Circle* (2004), *Talk, Talk* (2006), *The Women* (2009), and *When the Killing's Done* (2011).

ACHIEVEMENTS

T. Coraghessan Boyle received a National Endowment for the Arts Fellowship in 1977. *Descent of Man*, his first collection of stories, won the St. Lawrence Award for Short Fiction. His novel *Water Music* (1981) received the Aga Khan Award, and another novel, *World's End* (1987), was awarded the PEN/ Faulkner Award for Fiction. *Drop City* was a finalist for the National Book Award in 2003. Boyle's stories have been frequently chosen for inclusion in *Best American Short Stories* and *O. Henry Award Stories*. He won the National Magazine Award for "Wild Child" in 2007 and the Ross MacDonald Award for a body of work by a California writer in 2007. He was inducted into the American Academy of Arts and Sciences in 2009.

BIOGRAPHY

Born into a lower-middle-class family in Peekskill, New York, in 1948, Thomas John Boyle was a rebellious youth who performed in a rock-and-roll band, committed acts of vandalism, and drank heavily. He did not get along with his father, a school-bus driver whose alcoholism killed him at age fifty-four, in 1972. Boyle's mother, a secretary, was also an alcoholic and died of liver failure. Assuming the name T. Coraghessan Boyle at the State University of New York at Potsdam, he studied saxophone and clarinet until he realized that he lacked the necessary discipline for music. He then drifted into literature. After college, to avoid military service during the Vietnam War, he taught English for two years at his alma mater, Lakeland High School, in Shrub Oak, New York, while indulging in heroin on weekends.

In 1972, Boyle entered the creative writing program at the University of Iowa, where he studied under Vance Bourjaily, John Cheever, and John Irving, earning a Ph.D. in 1977, with a short-story collection, later published as *Descent of Man*, serving as his dissertation. Such academic achievement is ironic for someone placed in a class for slow learners in the second grade. Boyle became a teacher at the University of Southern California, where he founded an undergraduate creative writing program, and he settled in Woodland Hills with his wife, Karen Kvashay, and their children, Kerrie, Milo, and Spencer. One of the most public and flamboyant writers of his time, Boyle delights in performing public and recorded readings.

ANALYSIS

During a time when the majority of serious American writers have been concerned with the minutiae of everyday life, T. Coraghessan Boyle has stood out by exploring a wide range of subjects, locales, periods, and strata of society. Distinctive as a stylist, storyteller, and satirist, Boyle enthusiastically encompasses numerous literary conventions into his fiction, turning them into something fresh and often humorous. He examines both the detritus and the silliness of the world, exulting in its absurdities.

His short fiction is most notable for its extraordinary range of subjects, which include a chimpanzee who has translated Charles Darwin, Friedrich Nietzsche, and Noam Chomsky into Yerkish; the final performance of blues musician Robert Johnson; the importation of starlings into the United States; an attempt to improve the public image of the Ayatollah Khomeini; and a statue of the Virgin Mary that re-creates a man's sins

T. Coraghessan Boyle (Getty Images)

for all the world to see. Boyle's stories delve into such topics as violence, sexuality, paranoia, guilt, and the clichés of popular culture. While some of his stories are realistic, most exaggerate the world's absurdities for comic effect. His tone is predominantly satirical but rarely angry.

"BLOODFALL"

"Bloodfall" depicts the effects of an apparently endless rainfall of blood on seven young adults who live together. Although they smoke marijuana, burn incense, and listen to thunderously loud rock and roll, they are not hippies but well-to-do materialists who use electric toothbrushes and drive BMWs. They sleep together in a bed that they appropriately think of as "the nest," since they have attempted to withdraw from the often disconcerting realities of the outside world, seeking comfortable refuge in their home.

The inexplicable rain of blood cuts them off completely from the rest of the world by knocking out their telephone and television. They cannot drive to get food because they cannot see through a blood-smeared windshield. Their response to this terrifying situation is to ignore it: "Isabelle said it would be better if we all went to bed. She expressed a hope that after a long nap things would somehow come to their senses." The blood begins to stain everything about their antiseptic existence: their white clothing when they venture outside, their white carpet when the flood begins to seep under their door. They are confident that the bloodfall will stop, since logic demands that it will, and it does. Since such an event is illogical to begin with, however, "Bloodfall" ends with the start of a new downpour, this time consisting of "heavy, feculent, and wet" fecal matter.

Boyle often satirizes modern human beings' feeble efforts to protect themselves from outside forces, as in "Peace of Mind," an attack on home security systems, but the image of the blood invading the white world of these smug materialists is his strongest statement on this theme. Boyle's vividly contrasting images of red and white and his telling accumulation of the trite details of the lives of contemporary American consumers contribute to the story's effectiveness. As throughout his fiction, Boyle borrows from the conventions of popular culture, in this case horror fiction and films, to create a compelling vision of modern alienation.

"THE BIG GARAGE"

"The Big Garage" is an equally frightening but more comic horror story. When the Audi belonging to B. breaks down, a tow truck mysteriously appears and takes it to Tegeler's Big Garage, an enormous service center in the middle of nowhere. Because it is late at night and no mechanics are available, B. is forced to sleep on a cot in a storage closet where other customers are also waiting for their vehicles to be repaired. B. discovers that he must go through a complicated maze to the appointment office and fill out a seven-page application for an appointment to have his car serviced. Fed up with this nonsense, B. confronts a team of German mechanics who taunt him and throw him down a chute into the car wash, where he is washed and waxed. After trying and failing to escape by hitchhiking, B. gives in and goes across the street to Tegeler's Big Lot, where the owner of the Big Garage sells his broken customers Tegelers, his own inferior make.

B. is caught up in a bureaucratic nightmare out of a Franz Kafka novel, such as *Der Prozess* (1925; *The Trial*, 1937). Boyle takes a familiar situation and exaggerates it to show how everyday life can become an impersonal, nerve-racking, and humiliating experience. He makes a serious statement about alienation and the often vicious insensitivity of a consumer culture while also having fun through slapstick and literary parody.

"THE OVERCOAT II"

Boyle combines homage to a favorite work of literature with political satire in "The Overcoat II," an updating of Nikolai Gogol's "Shinel" ("The Overcoat") to the Moscow of the 1980's. Akaky Akakievich Bashmachkin, a devoted clerk in the Soviet bureaucracy, has no interests outside his work, no time for anything but waiting in endless queues for scarce goods. The only blemish on his party-line life is the cheap, tattered overcoat he has bought because a central department store clerk, attacking the quality of Soviet-made products, tried to sell him a black-market overcoat.

Akaky is ridiculed by his unpatriotic coworkers because he appears to use the coat to give himself the aura of a Marxist saint. Old Studniuk, one of the fourteen residents who share his apartment, tells Akaky he must use the black market to get everything he can: "There ain't no comrade commissioner going to come round and give it to you." Akaky sells his television set and exhausts his savings to spend three months' salary on a camel's hair overcoat with a fox collar. His fellow clerks are impressed, and one, Mishkin, invites Akaky to his home. After leaving Mishkin's house, where he had one of the best times of his life, Akaky is beaten and his coat stolen. The police recover the coat but keep it and fine Akaky for receiving stolen goods. Feeling betrayed by all he has believed in, Akaky develops pneumonia, dies, and is soon forgotten. The police inspector who has interrogated him wears the coat proudly.

Like "Ike and Nina," in which President Dwight D. Eisenhower and the wife of Premier Nikita S. Khrushchev have an affair in 1959, "The Overcoat II" satirizes Soviet life. Gogol's Akaky dies from the despair of losing his beloved coat, and Boyle's Akaky from losing his belief in the Soviet system, something even more irreplaceable. Gogol ends his story with Akaky's ghost seeking revenge against those who have wronged him; Boyle's story ends with an enemy profiting from the clerk's naïve belief in a system that exploits him. The happiness that Akaky experiences at Mishkin's party must be short-lived, for in Boyle's paranoid universe, some unexpected, uncontrollable force is out to get the individual. Only those as cynical as the society in which they live can survive.

"TWO SHIPS"

The uncontrollable force confronting the protagonist of "Two Ships" is his childhood best friend. The teenage Jack and Casper are rebels together, assaulting symbols of wealth and religion. They run away from home, but Jack gives up two weeks before Casper. During this experience, Jack recognizes the streak of madness in his friend and is both repelled by and attracted to it: "He was serious, he was committed, his was the rapture of saints and martyrs, both feet over the line." Casper's passion leads him to convert fervently to Marxism. When he is drafted during the Vietnam War, he deserts the Army.

Jack does not see Casper for several years after he goes into the Army, but he receives several packages containing lengthy, incoherent poems expressing Casper's political views. Jack then goes to law school, marries, and settles down. After he receives a telephone call from Casper asking him to stick up for his friend, Jack tells an agent at the Federal Bureau of Investigation (FBI) that Casper is "seriously impaired." Following eleven months in a mental institution, Casper returns to his hometown, and Jack is frightened. Casper finally visits him but terrifies Jack even further by saying little. Jack begins packing.

More than guilt about betraying his friend to the FBI, Jack experiences shame over how their lives have diverged: "I'd become what we'd reacted against together, what he'd devoted his mad, misguided life to subverting." Jack is disturbed by Casper's reminding him how he has failed himself through his willingness to play society's game by its rules, his becoming a corporate attorney who defends polluters, his lack of passion for and commitment to anything but his family, and his failure to accept any responsibility for the state of the world. "Two Ships" effectively blends such major Boyle subjects as paranoia, friendship, and betrayal. His characters are constantly betraying each other and themselves.

"The Hector Quesadilla Story"

While generally satirical and often condemnatory, Boyle's fiction is not always cynical and unforgiving. "The Hector Quesadilla Story," one of the best baseball stories ever written, demonstrates the possibility of getting a chance to overcome failure. The title character plays for the Los Angeles Dodgers but only pinch-hits because he is too old, too fat, and too slow to perform well in the field. (Boyle has loosely based this character on Manny Mota, the legendary pinch hitter for the Dodgers in the 1970's.) A grandfather whose official baseball age is several years short of actuality, Hector lives only to eat the spicy Mexican food that he passionately loves and to play the game that he loves even more. He keeps telling his wife he will play one more season but secretly has no intention of quitting. Meanwhile, he waits patiently at the end of the bench to prove himself again, to come alive in the only way he knows how.

Hector is convinced that something special will happen during a game with the Atlanta Braves, whom the Dodgers are battling for first place, because it falls on his birthday. With the score tied in the ninth inning,

he is denied his "moment of catharsis," his chance to win the game. As the contest drags on into extra innings, the manager refuses to let him bat because the Dodgers have run out of players and Hector would have to play in the field if the score remained tied. With his team trailing by one run in the bottom of the thirty-first inning in the longest game in major league history, Hector finally gets his chance but is foolishly thrown out trying to stretch a double into a triple. When the next batter hits a home run, Hector is forced to pitch for the first time because no one else is available. All seems lost when the Braves score four runs off him in the next inning, but Hector redeems himself with a bases-loaded home run to tie the score once again. The game then "goes on forever."

"The Hector Quesadilla Story" works on two levels. On one, it is about the most magical quality of baseball: "How can he get old?" Hector asks himself. "The grass is always green, the lights always shining, no clocks or periods or halves or quarters, no punch-in and punch-out: this is the game that never ends." Without the restraints of time seen in such games as football and basketball, a baseball game could theoretically last forever. On the second level, the story deals with how the individual feels the limitations that time imposes upon him and how he fights against them. Hector tries to ignore what his body, his family, and common sense tell him. Because a baseball game can go on forever, so can he. He appropriates the magic of the game for himself; "it's a game of infinite surprises." Boyle makes baseball a metaphor for life itself.

"Sorry Fugu"

The tone of most of Boyle's stories is primarily comic, and in one of the best, "Sorry Fugu," he also displays the gentler side of his satire. Albert D'Angelo, owner and chef of D'Angelo's, wants his new restaurant to be both good and successful. He wants it to meet the challenge of Willa Frank, the restaurant critic who always gives negative reviews, even to those places that Albert reveres. He fears and longs for the day when she and her companion, known only as "the Palate," will enter his establishment. Luckily, Albert knows when the great moment has arrived, since one of his employees knows Willa and her boyfriend, Jock McNamee. Unfortunately, she has come on one of those nights when all goes wrong, and Albert knows he has failed on the first of her three visits. They arrive the second time with an older couple. Albert is prepared this time, only to see each of them pass the dishes to Jock, who is not interested in any of them.

Albert understands what to do on the third visit after his employee tells him that what Jock really likes is the "shanty Irish" food his mother used to make. Albert then ignores what the couple orders and serves the Palate peas, boiled potatoes, a slab of cheap, over-cooked meat, and catsup. When the outraged Willa charges into the kitchen, Albert seduces her with squid rings in aioli sauce, lobster tortellini, *taglierini alla piz-zaiola*, Russian *coulibiac* of salmon, and fugu, a Japa-nese blowfish. Willa confesses that she relies on Jock's crude judgment, since at least he is consistent in dis-liking everything, and that she is afraid to risk a posi-tive review.

While other American writers of Boyle's generation fill their fiction with brand names and trendy antiques as a means of delineating their characters, Boyle uses food to explore their social status and individuality. What is most important about "Sorry Fugu," however, is its depiction of the roles of the critic and the artist. Boyle satirizes the superficiality of many critics through Willa's uncertainty about her tastes and dis-honesty in relying on Jock's lack of taste. Albert is an artist in the care he takes in creating his dishes: "Albert put his soul into each dish, arranged and garnished the plates with all the patient care and shimmering inspira-tion of a Toulouse-Lautrec bent over a canvas." Boyle takes the same care as a stylist, as when Albert contem-plates Willa's name: "It was a bony name, scant and lean, stripped of sensuality, the antithesis of the round, full-bodied Leonora. It spoke of a knotty Puritan tough-ness, a denying of the flesh, no compromise in the face of temptation." Since Boyle has said in interviews that he wants to be both popular and critically praised, Al-bert appears to be a self-portrait of an artist who needs to be judged by the highest standards.

WITHOUT A HERO

Boyle continued his eclectic exploration of the ab-surdities of the world in his short-story collection *Without a Hero*. "Filthy with Things" tells the hu-morous yet oddly disturbing story of a married couple suffocating in a world of suburban materialism that has advanced so far beyond their control that they must hire an organizing specialist to kick them out of their own house and take possession of their belongings. As the narrator watches the workers sort through and cat-alog everything he owns, he feels "as if he doesn't exist, as if he's already become an irrelevance in the face of the terrible weight of his possessions," or, more broadly, of a late twentieth century American culture in which materiality often defines the person.

One of the most prominent of Boyle's many recur-ring obsessions is his interest in the influence that ani-mals have on human behavior, and vice versa. The nar-rator of "Carnal Knowledge" gets involved with a group of animal-rights activists when he falls in love with Alena, a militant vegetarian whose crippled dog urinates on him at the beach. After quitting his job to take part in antifur demonstrations in Beverly Hills, the narrator is coerced into taking part in a plot to "lib-erate" thousands of turkeys from a poultry farm a few weeks before Thanksgiving. The raid does more harm than good, however, when large numbers of turkeys wander onto a fog-enshrouded freeway and cause a truck to jackknife. After being spurned by Alena, who travels north with another man to defend grizzly bears, the protagonist drives by the accident scene, where the road is "coated in feathers, turkey feathers" and where there is "a red pulp ground into the surface of road." He promptly returns to eating the Big Macs that he has been subconsciously craving for days. Beneath the humor of such stories lies a message to which Boyle often returns: The universe is an ambiguous, unpredict-able place, and each person must find his or her own solitary way to negotiate its absurdities.

T. C. BOYLE STORIES

T. C. Boyle Stories: The Collected Stories of T. Cor-aghessan Boyle is a 691-page volume that includes all of the tales from the author's previous short-story col-lections, plus four stories previously unpublished in book form and three previously unpublished anywhere, an impressive sixty-eight stories written over a twenty-five-year period. Although reading a complete collec-tion of an author's work often means plowing through the mediocre to get to the good (and this book is no exception), one benefit is the opportunity to see the development of the writer over time. In Boyle's case, there is a clear tendency for early stories to be driven more by premise than by character. In stories such as "Bloodfall," characterization tends to be subordinate to the idea. In subsequent stories, Boyle demonstrates a willingness to invest more time and effort in exploring the multiple dimensions of his characters, and by the 1980's, a clear preference for dwelling on the subtleties of the human condition has emerged.

In the midst of this development, several common threads tie most, if not all, of Boyle's stories together, most notably his use of humor of all types--parody, slapstick, satire, wit, and irony--and his dedication to keen observation rendered through bold, colorful language. This latter quality, which seems to be missing from a large portion of contemporary American fiction, is a clear reflection of Boyle's belief that it is possible for fiction to possess the same vitality as rock-and-roll music.

"AFTER THE PLAGUE"

The title story of Boyle's collection *After the Plague* is an apocalyptic story about a man who, because he has been on a wilderness writing retreat, has managed to escape a pandemic disease that has wiped out practically the entire human race. However, given Boyle's delight in making even the end of the world an excuse for a funny story, the man meets a girl, but he soon realizes that he cannot tolerate her even if she were the last woman on earth. When he meets another girl whom he likes much better, the first woman harasses him until, miracle of miracles, they discover the first woman's old boyfriend. Thus, according to Boyle, in spite of the "almost end of the world," everyone lives happily ever after.

"ALMOST SHOOTING AN ELEPHANT"

All of the stories in Boyle's *The Human Fly* anthology are aimed at the "young adult" market and have been published previously in other Boyle collections, with the exception of the comic take on George Orwell's famous essay "Shooting an Elephant," entitled "Almost Shooting an Elephant." The story is told in flippant first-person narration by a young man sent to rural India to put in a Verizon grid so the natives can have television and digital subscriber line (DSL) hookups in their huts. However, when an elephant escapes, the man finds himself stalking it with a very inadequate rifle.

"TOOTH AND CLAW"

The two themes of Boyle's collection *Tooth and Claw*--animals and losers--are united in the title story, which, Boyle says in the contributors' notes to the *Best American Short Stories 2004*, returns to the Darwinian conundrum of his first collection *Descent of Man*. Taking its title from Alfred, Lord Tennyson's *In Memoriam* (1850), which warns of "Nature, red in tooth and claw," the story is about a lonely loser who wins a wild cat, specifically an African serval, in a barroom dice roll. Although he hopes the cat will heat up a sexual relationship with the waitress who gives him advice on how to care for it, like all wild things--women, relationships, and sex--the creature cannot be tamed or controlled.

"SWEPT AWAY"

A classic example of Boyle's comic ability, "Swept Away" takes place on the Shetland Islands, on the north coast of Scotland. Here, the winds blow with such gale force that when visiting American Junie Ooley steps off the ferry, she gets hit by a flying twelve-pound tom cat. The result, irresistible enough to be included in the 2003 *O. Henry Prize Stories*, is a whimsical folktale with a love-struck hero and heroine doomed to be swept away from each other, like Pecos Bill and Calamity Jane.

WILD CHILD

Of the fourteen stories in the collection *Wild Child*, some, especially those dealing with children, such as "Balto," "Sin Dolor," and the title story, are wisely and carefully controlled and thus emotionally irresistible. Others, such as "Admiral," "Bulletproof," and "Ash Monday," exemplify a significant satiric point. Still others, such as "La Conchita," "The Unlucky Mother of Aquiles Maldonado," and "Thirteen Hundred Rats" are just clever excuses for stories.

"BALTO"

The focus of "Balto" is a twelve-year-old girl named Angelle, who is coached by her father's lawyer to lie on the witness stand about an automobile accident in which she and her father have been involved. The accident takes place when Angelle's father, who already has one driving-under-the-influence offense on his record, is too drunk to drive and asks the child to take the wheel. His lawyer has advised him to plead guilty to the charge of driving under the influence, but he wants Angelle to lie to avoid the more serious charge of child endangerment, which may mean that Angelle and her sister will be taken into foster care. At the crucial moment on the witness stand, Angelle, who is well aware of her father's lack of responsibility and resentful of his insistence that her mother will never return, tells the truth that she was driving and then looks defiantly into her father's face. "Balto" is a carefully controlled story in which Boyle resists any temptation to make light of the seriousness of what is at stake. It is not a very complex piece, but it is an affecting one. Stephen King chose it for *Best American Short Stories, 2007*.

"SIN DOLOR"

"Sin Dolor" (without pain), told by a Mexican doctor who delivers a baby to Francisco and Mercedes Tunes, two street vendors, is also a serious story involving a child. When the couple brings the boy back to the doctor a few years later with burns on his hands because he has picked up hot coals, and then again with broken legs from jumping off a shed roof, the doctor discovers that the child does not feel pain. Becoming both professionally and personally interested in the boy's miraculous ability, the doctor begins spending time with him and writing up his observations, sending them to a colleague who is a famous geneticist. However, the father angrily confronts the doctor and tells him to stay away, in spite of the fact that he is told his son has a great gift and may hold the key to helping humankind be free from pain. The boy disappears for a time until one day the doctor sees the father exhibiting him on a street corner, sticking steel skewers in his body and placing a red hot knife on his flesh. When the doctor tries to get the boy to leave his parents, he refuses, saying that his family will always come first. However, he says what they do not understand is that he does hurt, and he points to his heart. The boy dies a week later when, urged on by a group of children who follow him about as if he were a god, he jumps off a three-story building. "Sin Dolor" is a simple story of parental exploitation, ignorance, greed, and heartlessness.

"WILD CHILD"

The longest tale in the collection, and in many ways the most controlled, is the title story about the famous feral child, Victor of Aveyron, discovered living alone in the forests of southern France in 1797. When Victor, who modern commentators suggest was probably autistic, is turned over to the Institute for Deaf-Mutes in Paris so his behavior can be recorded, he is placed in the care of a twenty-five-year-old doctor named Jean-Marc Gaspard Itard and an older woman named Madame Guérin. Itard's Enlightenment ideals hold that since morality and language are what separate man from beast, when they are taught to an animal-like creature it will become fully human. However, in spite of Itard's attempts to educate the boy, Victor cannot learn. When he masturbates in sight of female inmates and a nun, the cry goes up that he is "incurable" and should be castrated and put away in prison or an insane asylum. Victor passes out of the public eye and is cared for by Madame Guérin until he dies at age forty. "Wild Child" is a straightforward, historical tale, well told by a storyteller who obviously could not resist its legendary simplicity.

OTHER MAJOR WORKS

LONG FICTION: *Water Music*, 1981; *Budding Prospects: A Pastoral*, 1984; *World's End*, 1987; *East Is East*, 1990; *The Road to Wellville*, 1993; *The Tortilla Curtain*, 1995; *Riven Rock*, 1998; *A Friend of the Earth*, 2000; *Drop City*, 2003; *The Inner Circle*, 2004; *Talk Talk*, 2006; *The Women*, 2009; *When the Killing's Done*, 2011.

EDITED TEXT: *Doubletakes: Pairs of Contemporary Short Stories*, 2003.

BIBLIOGRAPHY

Boyle, T. Coraghessan. Interview by David Stanton. *Poets & Writers* 18 (January/February, 1990): 29-34. Boyle explains his need to promote himself through readings and interviews, his strong self-confidence in his abilities, his doubts about creative writing programs, and the positive effect that writing novels has had on his short fiction. He believes that his earlier stories call too much attention to themselves.

_____. "The Maximalist Novelist." Interview by Helen Dudar. *The Wall Street Journal*, November 5, 1990, p. A13. This interview discusses Boyle's work habits; his attitudes toward his art, teaching, and success; and his fear of running out of material.

_____. "A Punk's Past Recaptured." Interview by Anthony DeCurtis. *Rolling Stone*, January 14, 1988, 54-57. In his most revealing interview, Boyle talks about his drug use, the importance of understanding history, and the autobiographical element in his fiction. He expresses the desire to be like Kurt Vonnegut, in showing that literature can be both serious and entertaining, and like John Updike, in constantly changing his approach to fiction and improving as an artist.

_____. "Rolling Boyle." Interview by Tad Friend. *The New York Times Magazine*, December 9, 1990, 50, 64, 66, 68. Boyle portrays himself as a missionary for literature who promotes himself to ensure that he is read. He comments on the new maturity and reality in some of his fiction but admits that the absurd and bizarre are more natural for him. Boyle also expresses pessimism about the future of the human race.

Chase, Brennan. "Like, Chill!" *Los Angeles* 38 (April, 1993): 80-82. A biographical sketch, focusing on Boyle's successful literary career and celebrity status in Hollywood. Boyle maintains that he is an academic whose purpose is to write.

Gleason, Paul William. *Understanding T. C. Boyle*. Columbia: University of South Carolina Press, 2009. Provides a general analysis of Boyle's works, as well as close readings of specific texts. Chapter 2 focuses on the short fiction from *Descent of Man* to *Tooth and Claw*.

Vaid, Krishna Baldev. "Franz Kafka Writes to T. Coraghessan Boyle." *Michigan Quarterly Review* 35 (Summer, 1996): 533-549. As if writing a letter from Kafka, Vaid discusses the work of Boyle, investigates the similarity between the two writers, and argues that the reader could grow as tired of Kafka's logic as of Boyle's broad panoramas.

Walker, Michael. "Boyle's 'Greasy Lake' and the Moral Failure of Postmodernism." *Studies in Short Fiction* 31 (Spring, 1994): 247-255. Argues that because postmodernism lacks moral standards, such exaggerations and self-absorption as can be seen in Boyle's story are but substitutes for a moral point of view. Claims that Boyle's story is a parody of the story of revelation. Compares the story to John Updike's "A & P," insisting that Boyle denies his protagonist any possibility of learning anything from his experience.

Michael Adams; Douglas Long
Updated by Charles E. May

RAY BRADBURY

Born: Waukegan, Illinois; August 22, 1920

PRINCIPAL SHORT FICTION

Dark Carnival, 1947

The Martian Chronicles, 1950, revised 1997

The Illustrated Man, 1951

The Golden Apples of the Sun, 1953

The October Country, 1955

A Medicine for Melancholy, 1959

Twice Twenty-two, 1959

The Machineries of Joy, 1964

Autumn People, 1965

Vintage Bradbury, 1965

Tomorrow Midnight, 1966

I Sing the Body Electric!, 1969

Long After Midnight, 1976

"The Last Circus," and "The Electrocution," 1980

The Stories of Ray Bradbury, 1980

Dinosaur Tales, 1983

A Memory of Murder, 1984

The Toynbee Convector, 1988

Quicker Than the Eye, 1996

Driving Blind, 1997

One More for the Road: A New Short Story Collection, 2002

Bradbury Stories: One Hundred of His Most Celebrated Tales, 2003

The Best of Ray Bradbury: The Graphic Novel, 2003

The Cat's Pajamas, 2004

Summer Morning, Summer Night, 2008

We'll Always Have Paris: Stories, 2009

The Stories of Ray Bradbury, 2010

OTHER LITERARY FORMS

Although Ray Bradbury (BRAD-bur-ee) has described himself as essentially a short-story writer, his contributions to a wide variety of other genres have

been substantial. Indeed, he has intentionally sought to compose successfully in virtually every literary form. His best-known novels are *Fahrenheit 451* (1953), *Dandelion Wine* (1957), and *Something Wicked This Way Comes* (1962), the last being his favorite of all of his works. Among his screenplays, the most successful have been *Moby Dick* (1956), written in collaboration with filmmaker John Huston, and *Icarus Montgolfier Wright* (1961) with George C. Johnson, which was nominated for an Academy Award. Bradbury had his stage plays produced in Los Angeles and New York City, and several of them have been published, representative samples of which are *The Anthem Sprinters and Other Antics* (1963) and *The Pedestrian* (1966). He also wrote many plays for radio and television. Some of the most important of the several volumes of poetry that he published were collected in *The Complete Poems of Ray Bradbury* (1982). He also wrote books for children and adolescents, including *Ahmed and the Oblivion Machines: A Fable* (1998); compiled anthologies of fantasy and science-fiction stories, such as *The Circus of Dr. Lao and Other Improbable Stories* (1956); and published nonfiction works dealing with his interests in creativity and the future, such as *Yestermorrow: Obvious Answers to Impossible Futures* (1991).

ACHIEVEMENTS

Despite Ray Bradbury's once being named the United States' best-known science-fiction writer in a poll, his actual literary accomplishments are based on an oeuvre whose vast variety and deeply humanistic themes transcend science fiction as it is commonly understood. His many stories, from gothic horror to social criticism, from playful fantasies to nostalgic accounts of midwestern American life, have been anthologized in several hundred collections, in English as well as in many foreign languages, and several of the stories that he published early in his career now occupy a distinguished niche in twentieth century American literature.

Some of his early tales were recognized with O. Henry Prizes in 1947 and 1948, and in 1949 he was voted Best Author by the National Fantasy Fan Federation. Bradbury's "Sun and Shadow" won the Benjamin Franklin Magazine Award as the best story of 1953-1954, and in 1954 he received a National Institute of Arts and Letters Award in Literature. His novel *Fahrenheit 451* won a gold medal from the Commonwealth Club of California, and his book *Switch on the Night* (1955) was honored with a Boys Club of America Junior Book Award in 1956. He received the Mrs. Ann Radcliffe Award of the Count Dracula Society in 1965 and 1971, the Writers Guild of America West Valentine Davies Award in 1974, and the World Fantasy Award for Life Achievement in 1977. Whittier College gave him an honorary doctor of literature degree in 1979. PEN, an international writers' organization of poets, playwrights, editors, essayists, and novelists, gave Bradbury its Body of Work Award in 1985. In 1988, Bradbury won the Nebula Award, and in 1995 he was named Los Angeles Citizen of the Year.

Bradbury's fame was bolstered in the first decade of the twenty-first century, when he received a string of highly prestigious honors, beginning with the Medal for Distinguished Contribution to American Letters bestowed upon him by the Board of Directors of the National Book Foundation in 2000. Two years later he received a star on the Hollywood Walk of Fame, and in 2004 the U.S. government awarded Bradbury the National Medal of the Arts. In 2007, the board responsible for awarding the Pulitzer Prizes presented Bradbury with a special citation, celebrating his career as a writer. That same year, the French Ordre des Arts et des Lettres gave him a medal of honor.

BIOGRAPHY

Ray Douglas Bradbury often makes use of his own life in his writings, and he has insisted that he has total recall of the myriad experiences of his life through his photographic--some would say eidetic--memory. He stated that he always had vivid recollections of the day of his birth, August 22, 1920, in Waukegan, Illinois. Leonard Spaulding Bradbury, his father, was a lineman with the Bureau of Power and Light (his distant ancestor Mary Bradbury was among those tried for witchcraft in Salem, Massachusetts); Esther Marie Moberg, his mother, immigrated to the United States from Sweden when she was very young. A child with an exceptionally lively imagination, Ray Bradbury amused himself with his fantasies but experienced anguish from his nightmares. His mother took him to his first film, *The Hunchback of Notre Dame* (1923), when he was three years old, and he was both frightened and entranced by Lon Chaney's performance. This experience began his lifelong love affair with motion pictures, and he wrote that he could remember the scenes and plots of all the films that he ever had attended.

As he grew up, Bradbury passed through a series of passions that included circuses, dinosaurs, and Mars (the last via the writings of Edgar Rice Burroughs). Neva Bradbury, an aunt, assisted his maturation as a person and a writer by introducing him to the joys of Edgar Allan Poe. In Bradbury's view, the most important event in his childhood occurred in 1932 when a carnival came to town. He attended the

Ray Bradbury (AP Photo)

performance of a magician, Mr. Electrico, whose spellbinding act involved electrifying himself to such an extent that sparks jumped between his teeth and every white hair on his head stood erect. Bradbury and the magician became friends, and their walks and talks along Lake Michigan behind the carnival so energized his imagination that, a few weeks after this encounter, he began to compose stories for several hours a day. One of his first efforts was a sequel to a Martian novel of Burroughs.

During the Great Depression, Bradbury's father had difficulty finding work, and in 1932 the family moved to Arizona, where they had previously spent some time in the mid-1920's. Still in search of steady work, his father moved the family to Los Angeles, which was where Bradbury attended high school and which became his permanent home. His formal education ended with his graduation from Los Angeles High School, but his education as a writer continued through his extensive reading and his participation in theater groups (one of which was sponsored by the actor Laraine Day). To support his writing, he worked as a newsboy in downtown Los Angeles for several years.

In World War II, Bradbury's poor eyesight prevented him from serving in the Army, but this disappointment gave him the freedom to pursue his career as a writer, and his stories began to be published in such pulp magazines as *Weird Tales* and Hugo Gernsback's *Amazing Stories*. The high quality of Bradbury's stories was quickly recognized, and he was able to get his new stories published in such mass-circulation magazines as *Collier's*, *The Saturday Evening Post*, *Harper's Magazine*, and *Mademoiselle*. Because of his success as a writer, he had the financial security to marry Marguerite Susan McClure in 1947 (they had met when she, a book clerk, had waited on him). The marriage produced four daughters.

By the early 1950's, Bradbury, recognized as an accomplished science-fiction and fantasy writer, began his involvement with Hollywood through an original screenplay that would eventually be released as *It Came from Outer Space* (1952). In the mid-1950's, he traveled to Ireland in connection with a screenplay of *Moby Dick* that he wrote with John Huston (he later drew on his experiences with the Irish for several

stories and plays that took his work in a new direction). Upon his return to the United States, Bradbury composed a large number of television scripts for such shows as *Alfred Hitchcock Presents*, *Suspense*, and *The Twilight Zone*.

During the late 1950's and early 1960's, Bradbury moved away from science fiction, and his stories and novels increasingly focused on humanistic themes and his midwestern childhood. In the late 1960's and throughout the 1970's and 1980's, Bradbury's output of short and long fiction decreased, and his ideas found outlets in such literary forms as poems, plays, and essays. He also participated in a number of projects, such as "A Journey Through United States History," the exhibit that occupied the upper floor of the United States Pavilion for the New York World's Fair in 1964. Because of this display's success, the Walt Disney organization hired him to help develop the exhibit Spaceship Earth for the Epcot Center at Disney World in Florida. Bradbury continued to diversify his activities during the 1980's by collaborating on projects to turn his novel *Fahrenheit 451* into an opera and his novel *Dandelion Wine* into a musical. In the late 1980's and early 1990's, he returned to some of the subjects and themes that had earlier established his reputation with the publication of short-story collections *The Toynbee Convector*, *Quicker Than the Eye*, and *Driving Blind*, and the novels *A Graveyard for Lunatics: Another Tale of Two Cities* (1990) and *Green Shadows, White Whale* (1992).

In the late twentieth and early twenty-first century, Bradbury remained active as a writer in a number of genres, including novels such as *From the Dust Returned* (2001), *Let's All Kill Constance* (2002), and a sequel to *Dandelion Wine* entitled *Farewell Summer* (2006). He also published several volumes of poetry, collected in 2002 in one volume, *They Have Not Seen the Stars*, and collections of essays and interviews. A massive compilation of his short fiction appeared as *Bradbury Stories: 100 of His Most Celebrated Tales* in 2003. Several new collections of short stories appeared as well, including *One More for the Road* (2002) and *The Cat's Pajamas* (2004). Perhaps the most important collection of this period, however, is *Summer Night, Summer Morning*, a handful of old stories and several new ones, published in 2008.

ANALYSIS

Ray Bradbury once said that he had not so much thought his way through life as he had done things and discovered what those things meant and who he was after the doing. This metamorphosis of experience under the aegis of memory also characterizes many of his stories, which are often transmogrifications of his personal experiences. He uses his stories as ways of hiding and finding himself, a self whose constant changes interested, amused, and sometimes frightened him. He believes that human beings are composed of time, and in many of his science-fiction stories, a frequent theme is the dialectic between the past and the future. For example, in several of his Martian stories, the invaders of the Red Planet have to come to terms with their transformation into Martians, since survival in an alien world necessitates the invader's union with the invaded. Aggression and submission might represent the initial dialectic, but survival or death becomes the determinative.

Even in stories in which Bradbury's characters and settings seem ordinary, this theme of metamorphosis is nevertheless present, because these stories often show ordinary people being transformed by extraordinary, sometimes bizarre situations. Sometimes Bradbury's purpose is to point out the enlightening power of the abnormal; sometimes he wants to reveal the limitations of the everyday and ordinary. His best works are often wrenching indictments of the dangers of unrestrained scientific and technical progress, though his work also encourages the hope that humanity will deal creatively with the new worlds it seems driven to make. His characters are changed by their experiences, particularly when they encounter great evil beneath the surface of seemingly normal life, but in other stories Bradbury gives the reader a window through which to see the positive meaning of life (these stories, usually sentimental, are life-affirming, permitting readers to believe that human dreams can be fulfilled). By helping readers to imagine the unimaginable, he helps them to think about the unthinkable. He speaks of his tales as "idea fiction," and he prefers to call himself a magical realist. Bradbury casts magic spells through his poetic words and highly imaginative visions, and because of

this aura of enchantment, some critics have seen his chief subject as childhood or the child hidden in the adult unconscious.

A danger exists, however, in treating Bradbury as a writer of fantasy suitable only for adolescents. This may be true for some of his works, but many of his stories exhibit emotional depths and logical complexities that call for a sophisticated dialectic between the adult and his buried childhood. The difference between fantasy and reality is not strongly developed in the child, whose experience of the world is minimal. Bradbury often plays with this tension between fantasy and reality in dealing with his principal themes--the power of the past, the freedom of the present, and the temptations and traps of the future. In the world of Bradbury's stories, fantasy becomes essential for a person existing in an increasingly technological era or with experiences that, like an iceberg, are nine-tenths buried below the surface. In these cases, the ability to fantasize about various alternatives or futures and to choose the best among them becomes necessary for survival.

Because of Bradbury's woefully inadequate knowledge of science and the lack of verisimilitude in the technological gadgetry of his science-fiction stories, many aficionados of the genre do not consider him a genuine science-fiction writer. He agrees. His science-fiction settings are backgrounds for characters with social, religious, and moral dilemmas. Like fellow science-fiction writer Isaac Asimov, Bradbury believes that science fiction's value lies in helping humans to visualize and solve future problems before they actually occur; unlike Asimov, Bradbury has a deep suspicion of the machine and a great faith in the human heart's capacity to perceive, do good, and create beauty. Because of this attitude, many critics view Bradbury as essentially a romantic. Since F. L. Lucas once counted 11,396 definitions of "romanticism," however, perhaps Bradbury's brand of romanticism should be more fully articulated. He has expressed an attraction for spontaneity of thought and action, and he actively has cultivated his own unconscious. He believes deeply in the power of the imagination, and he accepts Blaise Pascal's sentiment that the heart has reasons about which reason knows nothing.

In making an assessment of Bradbury's contribution to modern American literature, one must come to terms with the role he has played in popularizing science fiction and making it critically respectable. Bradbury once stated that, for him, science fiction is "the most important literature in the history of the world," since it tells the story of "civilization birthing itself." He has also said that he considers himself not a science-fiction writer but an "idea writer," someone who loves ideas and enjoys playing with them. Many of his science-fiction critics would concur in this characterization, as they have had problems categorizing this man who knows so little about science as a traditional science-fiction writer. When asked whether the Mariner mission's revelations about the inhospitability of Mars to humankind had invalidated his stories about the planet, Bradbury responded that these discoveries in no way affected them, because he had been composing poetic myths, not scientific forecasts.

In addition to their lack of scientific verisimilitude, his stories have other weaknesses. Few of his characters are memorable, and most are simply vehicles for his ideas. He has said frankly that he devises characters to personify his ideas and that all of his characters--youths, astronauts, and grotesques--are, in some way, variations on himself. Other critics have noticed failures in Bradbury's imaginative powers, particularly in his later stories. The settings and images that seemed fresh when first used in the early stories have become stale as they continued to be used in the later ones. Thomas Disch complained that Bradbury's sentimental attachments to his past themes "have made him nearly oblivious to new data from any source."

Despite these criticisms, Bradbury's stories possess great strengths. If his characters are made negligible by the burden of the ideas that they are forced to carry, these same ideas can open readers to his enchanting sense of wonder. These readers can be inspired by his enthusiasm for new experiences and new worlds. They may also be uplifted by the underlying optimism present even in his most pessimistic work and come to share his belief that humans will overcome materialism, avarice, and obsession with power to achieve the expansion of what is best in the human spirit.

DARK CARNIVAL

Many of these characteristics, along with Bradbury's penchant for the grotesque and macabre, can be seen in his first collection of stories, *Dark Carnival*. August Derleth, a Wisconsin writer who had established Arkham House to publish stories of fantasy and horror for a limited audience, had read Bradbury's stories in the pulp magazine *Weird Tales*, recognized their quality, and suggested that Bradbury collect them in a book. *Dark Carnival* was successful in its specialized market, and its three thousand copies were quickly sold and soon became collectors' items. The book's title was aptly chosen, since the stories often deal with the dark and strange. Several stories make use, albeit in highly altered forms, of emotions and events in Bradbury's life. For example, "The Small Assassin" depicts an infant, terrified at finding himself in a hostile world, taking revenge on his parents. Bradbury uses this metamorphosis of a supposedly innocent newborn into an assassin to explore some of the feelings he had as a child.

Death is a motif that appears often in these tales, but unlike Poe, whom he admired, Bradbury uses the morbid not for its macabre fascination but rather to shift readers onto a different level, from where they can see reality in a new and enlightening way. In most of these tales, more happens in the imaginations of Bradbury's characters than happens in their lives. He has the ability to reach down into the labyrinthine unconscious of his characters and pull out odd desires, strange dreams, and horrendous fears. For example, in "The Next in Line," a story that grew out of his own experience on a trip to Guanajuato, northwest of Mexico City, a young American woman is simultaneously frightened and fascinated by the rows of propped-up mummified bodies in a Guanajuato catacomb. After her traumatic ordeal, she finds herself increasingly immobilized by her alienation from the death-haunted Mexican society and by her fear that her own body is a potential mummy. Another story, "Skeleton," has a similar theme. A man is obsessed by the horrible bones that he carries within him, but when a strange creature crawls down his throat and consumes the bones that were the source of his obsession, he is transformed into a human jellyfish. These and other fantasies and horrors serve as exorcisms through which the devils of one's unconscious are expelled. The best of these stories leave the reader cleansed and transformed, with an expanded consciousness and control of the fears that can make people prisoners of their hidden emotions.

THE MARTIAN CHRONICLES

Some critics see the twenty-six stories collected in *The Martian Chronicles* as the beginning of the most prolific and productive phase of Bradbury's career. Like *Dark Carnival*, this collection resulted from the suggestion of an editor, but in this case Bradbury added passages to link together his stories about Mars. These bridge passages interrelate the stories but they do not make them into a unified novel. This places *The Martian Chronicles* into a peculiar literary category--less than a novel but more than a collection of short stories. Despite difficulties in categorizing this book, it is commonly recognized as Bradbury's most outstanding work. When it was first published, it was reviewed widely and read by people who did not ordinarily read science fiction. The writer Christopher Isherwood, for example, praised the book for its poetic language and its penetrating analysis of human beings forced to function on the frontier of an alien world. Within twenty years of its publication, *The Martian Chronicles* sold more than three million copies and was translated into more than thirty languages.

The Martian Chronicles is not unrelated to *Dark Carnival*, since Bradbury's Mars is a fantasy world, a creation not of a highly trained scientific imagination but of a mythmaker and an explorer of the unconscious. Within the time frame of 1999 to 2026, Bradbury orders his stories to give the reader a sense of the coherent evolution of the settling of Mars by earthlings. The early stories deal with the difficulties the emigrants from Earth have in establishing successful colonies on Mars. The fifteen stories of the middle section explore the rise and fall of these colonies. The stories in the final section are concerned with the possible renovation of the human race on Mars after an annihilating nuclear war on Earth.

In several of the stories in *The Martian Chronicles*, Bradbury is once again fascinated by the subject of death. Earthlings who make the mistake of trying to duplicate Earth's culture on Mars meet difficulties and death. This theme is particularly clear in "The Third Expedition," a story that was originally titled "Mars Is Heaven" and that deeply impressed the critic and writer Jorge Luis Borges. In "The Third Expedition," Captain John Black and his crew constitute a third attempt by Earthlings to create a successful settlement on Mars, this time in a town that bears a striking resemblance to traditional midwestern American towns of the 1920's. It turns out that the Martians have deceived the earthlings by using telepathic powers to manufacture this counterfeit town in their receptive imaginations. Captain Black and his crew have such a deep desire to believe in what they think they see that they delude themselves into seeing what the Martians want them to see. This mass hypnosis produced by the Martians capitalizes on the crew's self-delusion and on its members' need to re-create their past. When each earthling is securely locked within what he believes is his home, he is murdered by the Martians. Trapped by their past and unable to resist, the earthlings are destroyed. Illusion and reality, time and identity, change and stability are the themes that intertwine in Bradbury's treatment of this story (one can understand why Borges liked it so much, since his own work dwells on the theme of the Other as an inextricable element in one's own identity).

THE ILLUSTRATED MAN

Soon after *The Martian Chronicles* appeared, Bradbury published another book of interlinked stories, *The Illustrated Man*. Most of its eighteen stories had been published in various magazines between 1947 and 1951, but some had been written specifically for this book. The framing device, which is neither as consistent nor as unifying as the bridge passages in *The Martian Chronicles*, derives from tattoos that completely cover the skin of a running character. The tattoos, however, do not grow out of the personality of this character, as would be expected for a real tattooed man whose likes and dislikes would be represented in the permanent images with which he chooses to decorate his body. Instead, each tattoo embodies a Bradburian idea that comes alive in a particular story. The otherwise unrelated stories fall into several categories: tales of robots, space travel, Mexicans, and Martians. Four of the stories are set on Bradbury's Mars, and two of these are closely related to *The Martian Chronicles*. Some of the stories have themes related to those initially developed in *Dark Carnival*. For example, like "The Small Assassin," "The Veldt" concerns the revenge of children against their parents, this time in a futuristic setting. The children, obsessed with a room-filling television device that can depict scenes with three-dimensional realism, choose to watch an African veldt inhabited by lions gorging themselves on carcasses. The parents, who try to get their children to control their television addiction, end up as food for the lions. In this story, Bradbury makes use of a favorite theme: the blurred distinction between illusion and reality. Other stories in *The Illustrated Man* are animated by such social concerns as racism and with ethical and religious dilemmas derived from modern science and technology. For example, "The Fire Balloons" focuses on a religious missionary's discovery that the only surviving Martians have metamorphosed from human forms to floating balls of blue flame (reminiscent of the fire balloons in Earth's Fourth of July celebrations). After undergoing this transformation, these Martian flames are no longer capable of sin. Bradbury implies that a new planet means a new theology, the fall is reversible, and a state of innocence can be regained.

THE GOLDEN APPLES OF THE SUN

Bradbury's fourth collection, *The Golden Apples of the Sun*, used neither linking passages nor a frame narrative to interrelate the twenty-two stories. Instead, this book initiated the Bradburian potpourri of stories that would characterize most of his later collections: nostalgic, satiric, and humorous stories whose settings could be Mars, Mexico, or the Midwest and whose genre could be fantasy, science fiction, crime, or horror. He would use this variety of approach, setting, and genre to cast a revelatory light on aspects of modern life that conventional fiction was avoiding. Although the critical reception of *The Golden Apples of the Sun* was largely favorable, some critics found several of the stories disappointing and noted a falling-off from the high level of quality of *The Martian Chronicles* and *The Illustrated Man*. Despite the divided opinions, general agreement existed on the success of several of the stories--for example, "Sun and Shadow," which was set in Mexico and which won both praise and

awards. Another story, "The Fog Horn," became the basis of a film, *The Beast from Twenty Thousand Fathoms* (1953). It is about a lonely dinosaur who is attracted by the sound of a fog horn, interpreting it as the mating call of a potential companion (he dies of a broken heart when he swims to shore and discovers his error). The story "A Sound of Thunder" develops a favorite Bradburian theme of the profound effect of the past on the future. It depicts what happens when a time traveler steps on a butterfly in the past and inadvertently changes the future (this will remind modern readers of the "butterfly effect" in chaos theory, in which the beating of a butterfly's wings in a Brazilian rain forest may cause a tornado in Kansas via a long chain of cause and effect).

THE OCTOBER COUNTRY

The October Country, a collection that has as its core the stories of *Dark Carnival* along with four new stories, appeared appropriately in October of 1955. Bradbury described the country of the title as a place "whose people are autumn people, thinking only autumn thoughts" and whose steps "at night on the empty walks sound like rain." In the light of the earlier success of *Dark Carnival*, it is surprising that several critics were not as kind to this collection as they had been to Bradbury's earlier ones. For example, Carlos Baker, Ernest Hemingway's biographer, predicted in his review that the only route that Bradbury's writings could follow if he continued in the direction that he had chosen was down. Some critics did see Bradbury trying, in this and later collections, to develop new subjects, themes, and approaches. For them, his imagination was still nimble, his mind adventurous, and his heart sensitive. They also noticed his increased emphasis on social issues and his desire to treat the joyous side of human nature. For most critics, however, Bradbury's later collections of stories were repetitive mixes of ideas, themes, and treatments that he had used many times before.

A MEDICINE FOR MELANCHOLY

The problems sensed by these critics can be seen in the collection of twenty-two stories titled *A Medicine for Melancholy*. In addition to the expected stories of fantasy and science fiction, *A Medicine for Melancholy* includes tales from the lives of the Irish,

Mexicans, and Mexican Americans. The title story explores the awakening womanhood of an eighteenth century London girl who is cured of melancholia by the visit of what she interprets as Saint Bosco but who is in reality a dustman. Two of the stories in this collection, "Icarus Montgolfier Wright" and "In a Season of Calm Weather," led to films, and others, "A Fever Dream," for example, are reminiscent of films. In "A Fever Dream," aliens invade Earth not externally but by taking over the minds and hearts of their Earth victims (the film analogue is the 1956 *The Invasion of the Body Snatchers*). Derivative, too, seems the story "All Summer in a Day," about a group of children on cloud-enshrouded Venus who get to see the sun only once every seven years (the analogue here is Asimov's classic story "Nightfall").

THE MACHINERIES OF JOY

In the 1960's and 1970's, Bradbury's career entered a new phase, characterized by a decreasing output of short stories and novels and an increasing output of plays and poetry. When he did bring out short-story collections, the majority of critics saw little suggesting artistic growth, though a minority actually preferred his new stories, interpreting them as examples of a mature writer whose stories had acquired humanity, depth, and polish. These latter critics are also the ones who were not attracted to his tales about corpses, vampires, and cemeteries and who preferred his new optimism and his emphasis on civil rights, religion, and morality. Many of the stories in *The Machineries of Joy* provide good examples of these new tendencies. There are still stories characteristic of the old Bradbury, such as the science-fiction tale in which the explorers of a new planet find themselves possessed by a resident intelligence and a horror story in which raising giant mushrooms gets out of hand. Many of the stories, however, contain the epiphanic appearance of human warmth in unexpected situations. For example, in "Almost the End of the World," when sunspots destroy television reception, a world addicted to this opiate of the mind and heart is forced to rediscover the forgotten joys of interpersonal communication.

I SING THE BODY ELECTRIC!

Bradbury's next collection, *I Sing the Body Electric!*, also met with a mixed critical response. Academic critics and readers who had formed their taste for Bradbury on his early works found this potpourri of seventeen stories pretentious and a decline from his best science-fiction, fantasy, and horror stories. Some stories are slight, indeed, little more than anecdotes: In "The Women," for example, a man experiences the sea as a woman and his wife as her rival. On the other hand, some critics found Bradbury's new stories enthralling and insightful, with the unexpected--a robotic Abraham Lincoln, Ernest Hemingway's spirit, and an automated Martian city--confronting the reader at every turn of the page. The stories of *I Sing the Body Electric!* certainly contain some of Bradbury's favorite themes: the dialectic between past and future, reality and illusion. For example, the title story concerns a robot grandmother ideally programmed to meet the needs of the children of a recently motherless family. This electrical grandmother embodies the past (she has all the sentiments humans conventionally associate with this figure) and the future (she is a rechargeable AC-DC Mark V model and can never die). Another story that deals with the presentness of the past is "Night Call, Collect." In this tale, an old man alone on a deserted Mars receives a telephone call from himself when he was much younger (he has forgotten that he devised this plan many years earlier in order to assuage the loneliness of his old age). His young self battles with his old self, and as the old man dies, past, present, and future commingle in an odd but somehow enlightening amalgam.

LONG AFTER MIDNIGHT

Long After Midnight contains twenty-two stories, several of which had been written in the late 1940's and early 1950's but never anthologized. Some critics found the new stories aimless, uninspired, and self-indulgent, but others believed that many of them were poignant, sensitive, and touching. These latter critics thought that several of these stories represented Bradbury's new grasp of the power of love to overcome evil and to make permanent valued moments from the past. A few of the stories broke new ground in terms of subject matter: "The Better Part of Wisdom" is a compassionate and restrained treatment of homosexuality, and "Have I Got a Chocolate Bar for You!" deals gracefully with a relationship between a priest and a penitent.

THE STORIES OF RAY BRADBURY

In 1980, Bradbury collected one hundred stories from three decades of his work in *The Stories of Ray Bradbury*. Many reviewers treated this book's publication as an opportunity to analyze Bradbury's lifetime achievement as a short-story writer. Some found much to praise, comparing his body of work to that of Guy de Maupassant. Disch, however, in an influential essay in *The New York Times Book Review*, denigrated Bradbury's stories as "schmaltzy" and "more often meretricious than not." Unlike those critics who praised Bradbury's early work and saw a decline in the quality of his later stories, Disch stated that early and late are "meaningless distinctions" in Bradbury's output. He criticized Bradbury condescendingly as a child manqué, attributing his success to the fact that, "like Peter Pan, he won't grow up."

THE TOYNBEE CONVECTOR

To those who thought that Bradbury was using *The Stories of Ray Bradbury* to bid farewell to the form that had been his home for most of his life as a writer, another collection, *The Toynbee Convector*, showed that they were mistaken. Like his other late collections, this, too, contained the familiar blend of science fiction and gothic horror as well as sentimental tales of Ireland and Middle America, but it broke little new ground.

QUICKER THAN THE EYE

Most of the twenty-one stories in *Quicker Than the Eye* are loaded with symbols and metaphors about look-alikes, death, doors that open to the unknown, revelations from the unconscious mind, and psychic connections to the past and future. Magicians have always fascinated Bradbury. They pretend to do something, the audience blinks, and "quicker than the eye, silks fall out of a hat." Bradbury performs magic with words, and stories "fall out" of his imagination.

In "Quicker Than the Eye," the narrator and his wife watch a magician saw a woman in half and make her disappear. Men in the audience laugh. Then, Miss Quick, a pickpocket, nimbly removes wallets and other personal items from ten unsuspecting male volunteers.

Miss Quick particularly humiliates one volunteer, who looks exactly like the narrator, by stripping him "quicker than the eye." The angry narrator identifies with his "double's" vulnerability, but his wife laughs.

Several stories have themes of revenge and death. In "The Electrocution," carnival worker Johnny straps Electra in the Death Chair, blindfolds her, and pulls the switch. Blue flames shoot from her body, and, with a sword, she touches and "connects" with a fascinated youth in the crowd. After Electra and her lover meet secretly, Johnny, in a jealous rage, beats him up. The next time he "electrocutes" Electra, he turns up the voltage and says, "You're dead!" She replies, "Yes, I am."

Some doors that open to the unknown are better left closed. The title "Dorian in Excelsus" is wordplay on the liturgical phrase *Gloria in excelsis* and refers to Oscar Wilde's *The Picture of Dorian Gray* (1890 serial, 1891 expanded). A handsome youth invites the aging, dissipated narrator to become a Friend of Dorian at a spa. Behind golden doors, the narrator discovers how Friends of Dorian shed age and become physically beautiful. To regain youth, he must wrestle in Dorian's gym with hundreds of lustful men. Dorian is a "gelatinous, undulant jellyfish, the sponge of men's depravity and guilt, a pustule, bacteria, priapic jelly." He lives by breathing the sweaty stench of human passion and sin. The horrified narrator refuses Dorian's offer and scratches him with a fingernail. Dorian screams as noxious gases escape, and he and his Friends die.

Psychic connections to the past and future are recurring themes in *Quicker Than the Eye*. The title character in "That Woman on the Lawn" awakens a teenage boy with her crying. Her picture is in his family album. He directs her to an address down the street, and they agree to meet in three years; he is her future baby.

SUMMER MORNING, SUMMER NIGHT

Summer Morning, Summer Night, published when the author was eighty-eight years old, is an unusual book, partly an anthology of previously published tales and partly a presentation of new stories. Although nowhere nearly as engaging and impressive as his most celebrated collections of short fiction, such as *The Martian Chronicles* and *The Illustrated Man*, the book is nevertheless interesting as a genre exercise and as a capstone for Bradbury's lengthy career.

In *The Martian Chronicles*, the short stories constitute a history of the conquest of Mars by humans and the eventual extermination of the planet's indigenous people and culture, while *The Illustrated Man* has a frame device, much like that of Geoffrey Chaucer's *The Canterbury Tales* (1387-1400): Each story is symbolized by a tattoo on the body of the title character. In *Summer Morning, Summer Night*, the connective element is that of place: all the stories, old and new, are set in fictitious Green Town, Illinois, a version of Bradbury's hometown of Waukegan and the setting of two of his most acclaimed novels, *Dandelion Wine* and *Something Wicked This Way Comes*. In this regard, *Summer Morning, Summer Night* is reminiscent of James Joyce's short-story collection *Dubliners* (1914), in that the volume presents a suite of short pieces of fiction taking place in the same town and roughly in the same era, which for Bradbury is late nineteenth to early twentieth century. A problem with the collection, though, is that the previously published works in the first third of the book are far superior to most of the new pieces. "End of Summer" (1948) and "The Great Fire" (1949) are exquisite evocations of the sort of romantic small-town nostalgia that Bradbury conjures up so effectively in *Dandelion Wine*, while "The Screaming Woman" (1951), about a girl who psychically hears the subterranean shrieks of a woman beaten and buried alive by her abusive husband is, along with "Small Assassin" and "Skeleton," among his best horror tales.

Nothing new in *Summer Morning, Summer Night* is as good as these classic Bradbury stories, though two come close: "Arrival and Departure" and "I Got Something You Ain't Got!" The former is a gently humorous story about aging, in which an elderly couple, Mr. and Mrs. Alexander, emerge from their home after a long spell of illness and convalescence. As they walk through Green Town, shopping and reacquainting themselves with friends, Bradbury's sentimental depiction of small-town life and the beauty of summer in a bucolic setting rivals that in *Dandelion Wine*. The story ends with a melancholy lesson on humanity's propensity for inertia and routine, though: Upon returning home, the Alexanders give up their plans to go out to a film that evening. Instead, they end up sitting around the house and going to bed early, succumbing to old, comfortable habits, even though their health has improved. The best story in the collection, "I Got Something You Ain't Got!," is a fine example of Bradbury's ability to depict the dark, unsentimental side of childhood, as he does in *Something Wicked This Way Comes* and *The Halloween Tree* (1972). In "I Got Something You Ain't Got!", two little girls get into a rivalry based on one becoming jealous of the other, who is thought to be dying of tuberculosis, something the healthy child "Ain't Got."

Despite these two well-wrought stories, the new material in *Summer Morning, Summer Night* is not likely to impress readers who are not already devoted fans of Bradbury. Most of the second half of the book consists of brief sketches, some only a page or so in length, many of which read like jejune fragments from his early works set in Green Town. Nevertheless, the book serves as a summary work for Bradbury's long and intense preoccupation with small-town Americana.

OTHER MAJOR WORKS

LONG FICTION: *Fahrenheit 451*, 1953; *Dandelion Wine*, 1957; *Something Wicked This Way Comes*, 1962; *Death Is a Lonely Business*, 1985; *A Graveyard for Lunatics: Another Tale of Two Cities*, 1990; *Green Shadows, White Whale*, 1992; *From the Dust Returned: A Family Remembrance*, 2001; *Let's All Kill Constance*, 2003; *Farewell Summer*, 2006; *Now and Forever: Somewhere a Band Is Playing and Leviathan '99*, 2007.

PLAYS: *The Anthem Sprinters and Other Antics*, pb. 1963; *The World of Ray Bradbury: Three Fables of the Future*, pr. 1964; *The Day It Rained Forever*, pb. 1966; *The Pedestrian*, pb. 1966; *Dandelion Wine*, pr. 1967 (adaptation of his novel); *Madrigals for the Space Age*, pb. 1972; *The Wonderful Ice Cream Suit, and Other Plays*, pb. 1972; *Pillar of Fire, and Other Plays for Today, Tomorrow, and Beyond Tomorrow*, pb. 1975; *That Ghost, That Bride of Time: Excerpts from a Play-in-Progress*, pb. 1976; *The Martian Chronicles*, pr. 1977; *Fahrenheit 451*, pr. 1979 (musical); *A Device Out of Time*, pb. 1986; *On Stage: A Chrestomathy of His Plays*, pb. 1991.

SCREENPLAYS: *It Came from Outer Space*, 1952 (with David Schwartz); *Moby Dick*, 1956 (with John Huston); *Icarus Montgolfier Wright*, 1961 (with George C. Johnson); *The Picasso Summer*, 1969 (with Ed. Weinberger).poetry: *Old Ahab's Friend, and Friend to Noah, Speaks His Piece: A Celebration*, 1971; *When Elephants Last in the Dooryard Bloomed: Celebrations for Almost Any Day in the Year*, 1973; *Where Robot Mice and Robot Men Run Round in Robot Towns: New Poems, Both Light and Dark*, 1977; *The Bike Repairman*, 1978; *Twin Hieroglyphs That Swim the River Dust*, 1978; *The Aqueduct*, 1979; *The Haunted Computer and the Android Pope*, 1981; *The Complete Poems of Ray Bradbury*, 1982; *Forever and the Earth*, 1984; *Death Has Lost Its Charm for Me*, 1987; *Dogs Think That Every Day Is Christmas*, 1997 (illustrated by Louise Reinoehl Max); *With Cat for Comforter*, 1997 (illustrated by Louise Reinoehl Max); *I Live By the Invisible: New and Selected Poems*, 2002.

NONFICTION: *Teacher's Guide to Science Fiction*, 1968 (with Lewy Olfson); *"Zen and the Art of Writing" and "The Joy of Writing": Two Essays*, 1973; *Mars and the Mind of Man*, 1973; *The Mummies of Guanajuato*, 1978; *The Art of the Playboy*, 1985; *Zen in the Art of Writing: Essays on Creativity*, 1989; *Yestermorrow: Obvious Answers to Impossible Futures*, 1991; *Bradbury Speaks: Too Soon from the Cave, Too Far from the Stars*, 2005.

CHILDREN'S LITERATURE: *Switch on the Night*, 1955; *R Is for Rocket*, 1962; *S Is for Space*, 1966; *The Halloween Tree*, 1972; *Fever Dream*, 1987; *Ahmed and the Oblivion Machines: A Fable*, 1998.

EDITED TEXTS: *Timeless Stories for Today and Tomorrow*, 1952; *The Circus of Dr. Lao, and Other Improbable Stories*, 1956.

BIBLIOGRAPHY

Bolhafner, J. Stephen. "The Ray Bradbury Chronicles." *St. Louis Post-Dispatch*, December 1, 1996. An interview with Bradbury on the occasion of the publication of his collection of short stories *Quicker Than the Eye*. Bradbury reminisces about the beginnings of his career, talks about getting over his fear of flying, and discusses *The Martian Chronicles* as fantasy, mythology, and magical realism.

Bradbury, Ray. "Sci-fi for Your D: Drive." *Newsweek* 126 (November 13, 1995): 89. In this interview-story, Bradbury discusses why he is putting his most widely acclaimed short-story collection, *The Martian Chronicles*, on CD-ROM. Bradbury also discusses the role of imagination in technology, the space program, and his favorite literary figures.

Greenberg, Martin Henry, and Joseph D. Oleander, eds. *Ray Bradbury*. New York: Taplinger, 1980. This anthology of Bradbury criticism is part of the Writers of the Twenty-first Century series. Some of the articles defend Bradbury against the charge that he is not really a science-fiction writer but an opponent of science and technology; other articles defend him against the charge that he is mawkish. Includes an extensive Bradbury bibliography compiled by Marshall B. Tymn and an index.

Johnson, Wayne L. *Ray Bradbury*. New York: Frederick Ungar, 1980. Although this volume is the work of a fan rather than a critic, it provides a good general introduction to Bradbury's stories of fantasy and science fiction. Johnson's approach is thematic rather than chronological (he uses the categories of magic, monsters, and machines to facilitate his discussion of Bradbury's principal approaches, ideas, and themes). Index.

Mogen, David. *Ray Bradbury*. Boston: Twayne, 1986. This brief introduction to Bradbury's career centers on analyses of the literary influences that shaped the development of his style and the themes whose successful embodiment in his short stories and novels shaped his reputation. The detailed notes at the end of the book contain many useful references. Bibliography and index.

Shaftel, David. "Vintage Bradbury, Packaged Anew." *The New York Times*, August 27, 2007. Insightful interview that provides a glimpse of Bradbury's writing habits.

Slusser, George Edgar. *The Bradbury Chronicles*. San Bernardino, Calif.: Borgo Press, 1977. This booklet is part of a series, Popular Writers of Today. Intended for young students and general audiences, this brief work discusses summarily some of Bradbury's most important writings. Bibliography.

Touponce, William F. *Naming the Unnameable: Ray Bradbury and the Fantastic After Freud*. Mercer Island, Wash.: Starmont House, 1997. Touponce finds the psychoanalytic ideas of Sigmund Freud and Carl Jung helpful in plumbing the effectiveness of much of Bradbury's work (though in a letter to the author, Bradbury himself denies any direct influence, since he has "read little Freud or Jung"). Nevertheless, Touponce believes that Bradbury has presented stories of a modern consciousness that often forgets its debt to the unconscious.

Weller, Sam. *The Bradbury Chronicles: The Life of Ray Bradbury*. New York: HarperPerennial, 2005. A thorough and engaging biography of Bradbury with an excellent bibliography and index and many good photographs from throughout the author's long life.

Robert J. Paradowski; Martha E. Rhynes
Updated by Thomas Du Bose

CATHERINE BRADY

Born: Chicago, Illinois; January 1, 1955

PRINCIPAL SHORT FICTION
The End of the Class War, 1999
Curled in the Bed of Love, 2003
The Mechanics of Falling, and Other Stories, 2009

OTHER LITERARY FORMS

Catherine Brady wrote a biography in 2007, *Elizabeth Blackburn and the Story of Telomeres: Deciphering the Ends of DNA*, about the important molecular biologist. Brady's book *Story Logic and the Craft of Fiction* was published in the fall of 2010.

ACHIEVEMENTS

The End of the Class War was a finalist for the 2000 Western States Book Award and was a Book Sense 76 selection. *Curled in the Bed of Love* was the cowinner of the Flannery O'Connor Award for Short Fiction and was a finalist for the 2003 Binghamton University John Gardner Fiction Book Award. Catherine Brady also won the 2001 Zoetrope All Story Short Fiction Prize and the Brenda Ueland Prose Prize. In 2010, the Northern California Book Awards named *The Mechanics of Falling, and Other Stories* as the year's best work of fiction by a California author. Brady's stories have appeared

in anthologies, such as *The Best American Short Stories 2004*, and in numerous magazines, including *Other Voices*, *The Missouri Review*, *The Kenyon Review*, and *Redbook*.

BIOGRAPHY

One of six daughters of Irish immigrants who came to the United States in the early 1950's, Catherine Brady began writing stories when she was seven. A graduate of Northwestern University, she received her M.A. from Hollins College in Roanoke, Virginia. Brady spent three years at the University of Massachusetts, Amherst, working on her M.F.A. degree. Brady later said of her time at Amherst, "I think I really became a serious writer at UMass. My first semester there, I was living on almost no income, and I had to choose between buying a winter coat or buying a typewriter. I bought the typewriter."

Being a teaching assistant at Amherst influenced Brady to explore the teaching of writing as a career. "I started out as a volunteer, teaching writing to school kids and to pregnant teens and teens in group foster care," Brady said. She became a professor, teaching rhetoric and composition and in the M.F.A. program at the University of San Francisco.

Though Brady has three collections of short stories and two works of nonfiction to her credit, she still sometimes thinks about quitting writing. "One of the hardest things about writing, for me, is that you're always haunted by disappointment. I've never written anything as well as I've intended to write it, and, ironically, the impulse to quit stems from the same place as the impulse to persist--the feeling of having failed at a piece, and being tormented by that, so that you either have to throw in the towel or try again, in case you can get any closer to that beautiful thing you've envisioned."

ANALYSIS

In her review of Catherine Brady's second short-story collection, *Curled in the Bed of Love*, Joyce Carol Oates, writing in *The New York Review of Books*, stated, "It is rare for a writer to explore with such subtlety and respect the curious symbiosis of the needy and the needed as Brady does." Brady's short stories are like relationship peep-shows. For a short time, the veil is lifted and the reader sees naked, unaltered, raw coping between sisters, between spouses, between lovers, between parents and children. Suddenly, time runs out, the view is gone. Nobody dies; nobody achieves inner peace. The characters simply appear, and, with voyeuristic pleasure, the reader sees a slice of reality while it lasts.

Brady's strength as a writer progresses through her three short-story collections. The first collection, *The End of the Class War*, has recurring characters, a large family with several daughters, perhaps modeled on the author's family. While the women in her stories are drawn with considerable perception, the men seem one-dimensional. In fact, Brady uses the same image of a man in multiple stories, hunched over his plate at the dinner table, shoving food onto his fork with a knife. In this collection of stories the men are short-tempered, drunk, lascivious, and intolerant.

Brady's second collection, *Curled in the Bed of Love*, is the best of the three collections. The author does not rely on stock characters, and she presents complicated, even messy relationships that defy easy answers. In these stories, people are not always rational actors; damaged in some way, they maintain the scars even as they cling to sanity and desire a return to "normal."

Brady's third collection, *The Mechanics of Falling, and Other Stories*, continues the themes and mastery demonstrated in the second volume, but the stories have a regional, Northern California air to them. These stories focus on aging and loss: Characters mourn for their youth and recognize disappointments accumulated over the years. This collection demonstrates a mature but also a backward-looking author.

"AND THE SHIN BONE'S CONNECTED TO THE KNEE BONE"

In *The End of the Class War* is "And the Shin Bone's Connected to the Knee Bone." In this story, Liz comes from a family that is dominated by her cop father and her successful brothers. The only daughter, Liz is a meter maid. She drives around the city in her Cushman, marking tires, writing tickets, occasionally fending off angry drivers who demand that she tear up the ticket she has just written. Once a ticket is written, Liz explains, it has to be accounted for.

Michael is a bread truck driver, making his deliveries around the city. He and Liz meet one day when a bread cart overturns and packages of cinnamon rolls fly everywhere. Liz helps to clean up the mess, and she and Michael share some rolls from a damaged package. Before long, the two are dating, and Liz brings Michael home to meet the family.

Michael is unlike Liz's father and brothers; he is sensitive and respectful of women. After the men berate Liz over dinner, Michael comes to her defense and offers Liz's father and brothers tips on etiquette and the proper way to speak to a woman. For this, Michael is immediately branded a loser. "I hope you're not sleeping with him," one of her brothers says to Liz.

Liz breaks up with Michael over the phone. Michael takes it hard; he adores Liz. Too slow and out of shape to make the police force, Liz has failed to become a cop like her dad, failed to fit in and win respect. Her job as a meter maid is a family joke. One afternoon, Liz has an especially unpleasant argument with a man whose car she has ticketed. Feeling shaken and with nowhere to turn, she thinks of Michael. Though she has never been to his apartment, she knows his address. She thinks she is going to apologize in person to him for breaking up with him over the phone.

Instead, Liz and Michael are soon making love in Michael's apartment. Liz is astonished at Michael's gentleness and obvious admiration of her, something Liz has never experienced.

"Nothing to Hide"

In *Curled in the Bed of Love* is "Nothing to Hide." In this story, Maizie is an alcoholic, attending Alcoholics Anonymous (AA) meetings, living in a nice house with a wonderful, supportive husband and two beautiful children. She is a sneak. Alone in the basement with just the washer, the dryer, and a bottle of wine, Maizie had reveled in hiding her addiction to alcohol. Thanks to joining AA, she sneaks only cigarettes, trying to hide the odor from her critical daughter Hannah. Hannah is not fooled. Maizie drinks a lot of coffee, attends a lot of meetings, volunteers for too many projects at Hannah's school in order to keep her hands and mind occupied. Maizie hangs out with her AA friends, crying, hugging, and understanding.

Walter is another alcoholic. He is divorced and lives alone. He resents Maizie, who seems to want to hide from herself, lie about the severity of her addiction, pretend it was not really as bad as all that. Walter knows she is a liar.

Slowly, by degrees, Walter seduces Maizie. First, he asks for rides home, tells her he would love to see where she lives, invites her up to his place for coffee, and asks her to sit at the edge of his bed while he drifts off to sleep. Loneliness and silence can be difficult for a recovering alcoholic to bear. Maizie understands.

Maizie has an affair with Walter, just another guilty pleasure, just another vice to hide. Jay, her wonderful, supportive husband, and her two beautiful children are not enough. Maizie needs a pleasure that is only hers, separate and shameful.

"Light, Air, Water"

In *Curled in the Bed of Love* is "Light, Air, Water." In this story, Elena is disconnected, a young woman wandering alone in rural Northern California. A recent graduate from an Ivy League college; she has been abruptly dumped by her longtime boyfriend. She finds

a community of ex-hippies in Marin County, and she goes to work at a greenhouse owned by a woman who has a daughter named Nuala and a man named Vince. Vince is Nuala's father and lives nearby in a separate house.

The woman, the narrator, sees the inevitable. Vince will seduce Elena, even though she is less than half his age. The woman accepts this as common enough in her experience, but she worries Elena will be hurt.

Elena works at the greenhouse, learns to love and care for Nuala and her mother. Vince, who for several years has wandered in and out of the woman's life, wanders back in at the wrong time. Elena learns about plants, about treating insects, about watering. Meanwhile, Vince studies Elena and is irresistibly drawn to her youth and beauty.

Elena does not fit in with the adults. She has more in common with Nuala. One night Elena disappears. The woman and Vince find her alone in a greenhouse, where she has been cutting herself. The woman bandages Elena's arms with gauze from a first-aid kit.

"Scissors, Paper, Rock"

In *The Mechanics of Falling, and Other Stories* is "Scissors, Paper, Rock." In this story, Natalie is an aging legend at the local newspaper, a photographer whose talent was exceeded only by her beauty. In her day, the rules that applied to everyone else at the paper did not apply to Natalie. Editors looked the other way, charmed in her presence and awed by her talent.

As the years go by, Natalie's visits to the newspaper office become less frequent. Newer, younger staff members marvel at the strange lady who comes in carrying a little dog named Charlie and behaving as if she owns the place. Though the times had changed, Natalie had not changed along with them. While everyone else uploads digital photographs and manipulates them online, Natalie still haunts the paper's darkroom, timing exposures, dipping prints in developer and fixer, hanging prints on a wire with clothespins.

The days when Natalie's talents and charms could buy her tolerance and indulgence from editors are gone. Natalie is a newspaper relic, like an X-ACTO knife or a light board. However, Liz, a graphic designer, has been at the paper long enough to remember when Natalie was all the rage. For the sake of what once was, for the sake of another time and place, for the sake of an artist who never left that time and place, Liz indulges Natalie, respects her legend, and enables her illusions.

"LAST OF THE TRUE BELIEVERS"

In *The Mechanics of Falling, and Other Stories* is "Last of the True Believers." In this story, there is an abandoned car outside Neil's house. Nobody comes to tow the car away, and Neil is losing patience.

Neil lives with his wife and three daughters in rural Northern California. He works mornings at a local radio station, where he hosts a call-in show and gives his opinion on topics of national, state, and local importance. Neil's wife is a gardener. Both she and Neil are protective of their daughters, especially Molly, the oldest at fourteen, who wears a brace on her leg, a result of a bicycle accident. Molly will always need the brace, which makes her passage through puberty even more difficult on her parents, as Molly strives even more to demonstrate her independence from them.

Things are not going well at the radio station for Neil. New owners frown on the leftover leftist ideology of the 1960's that has long permeated the station's views. Neil finds himself verbally attacking the new owners on the air, striking a blow for the workingman. Molly knows it is just a matter of time before Neil loses his job. Molly's little sisters, Carrie and Emma, go to school each day, oblivious to their father's crusade.

The abandoned car continues to sit outside their house. Neil has called all the responsible local authorities and delivered a petition signed by members of the community. Some anonymous government representative finally has a boot placed on the car so it cannot be driven away. With this, Neil becomes both annoyed and amused.

As Molly suspected he would, Neil loses his job at the radio station. One morning the family wakes up to find the abandoned car outside the house in flames. A fire engine comes and puts out the fire. Neil seeks assurance from the fireman, "You'll tow this mess away, right?" The fireman assures Neil that it is not the fire department's job to tow away vehicles. No one confesses to setting the fire.

OTHER MAJOR WORKS

NONFICTION: *Elizabeth Blackburn and the Story of Telomeres: Deciphering the Ends of DNA*, 2007; *Story Logic and the Craft of Fiction*, 2010.

BIBLIOGRAPHY

Moloney, Caitriona, and Helen Thompson. *Irish Women Writers Speak Out: Voices from the Field.* Syracuse, N.Y.: Syracuse University Press, 2003. Brady is one of seventeen Irish women writers interviewed; includes bibliographical references.

Oates, Joyce Carol. *Uncensored: Views and (Re)views.* New York: Harper Perennial, 2006. In an essay, Oates assesses Brady's work, noting that Brady's "stories celebrate the ordinary humanity of small sins."

Tuch, Rebecca. "Ways of Loving." *Women's Review of Books* 21, no. 6 (March, 2004): 22-23. This work reviews two books about the different ways of loving. One of the books is Brady's collection *Curled in the Bed of Love.*

Randy L. Abbott

RICHARD BRAUTIGAN

Born: Tacoma, Washington; January 30, 1935
Died: Bolinas, California; September, 1984

PRINCIPAL SHORT FICTION

Trout Fishing in America, 1967
Revenge of the Lawn: Stories 1962-1970, 1971
The Tokyo-Montana Express, 1980

OTHER LITERARY FORMS

The fragmented prose style of Richard Brautigan (BROWT-ih-guhn) makes any effort to classify his work into long and short fiction difficult and somewhat arbitrary. Brautigan himself called all of his prose works novels, with the single exception of *Revenge of the Lawn*, but critics have understandably referred to his books as "un-novels" or "Brautigans," works that seem approachable only on their own terms because they deliberately confront the realistic tradition of the novel by disregarding causality and character development.

Nevertheless, *Trout Fishing in America* and *The Tokyo-Montana Express* can be grouped with *Revenge of the Lawn* as examples of Brautigan's short fiction. Although arguably unified by point of view, setting, theme, and recurrent characters, *Trout Fishing in America* and *The Tokyo-Montana Express* lack any semblance of coherent plot, and many of the individual selections that compose each book possess an integrity independent of context. Brautigan's other novels are distinguished by at least a thin strand of continuous narrative. The most important of these longer fictions are *A Confederate General from Big Sur* (1964), *In Watermelon Sugar* (1968), and *The Abortion: An Historical Romance* (1971). The best known of his poetry collections are *The Pill Versus the Springhill Mine Disaster* (1968), *Rommel Drives on Deep into Egypt* (1970), and *June 30th, June 30th* (1978).

ACHIEVEMENTS

When Don Allen's Four Season Foundation published *Trout Fishing in America* in 1967, it became a favorite of the counterculture movement that was peaking that year during the "summer of love." In the following year, Richard Brautigan was awarded a grant from the National Endowment for the Arts, and *Trout Fishing in America* became a best seller, eventually selling more than two million copies in twelve languages.

Trout Fishing in America was Brautigan's first fictional work and established his success and reputation. In a sense, it became the standard against which his later works would be judged. Unfortunately, it associated him closely with the counterculture movement, giving rise to popular and even critical misconceptions. Brautigan was not, as some supposed, a spokesman for the hippie movement; rather, the counterculture simply became his first sizable audience. In actuality, Brautigan's roots were more in the Beat poetry movement, which influenced his prose style, and he has even been considered a precursor to the metafictionalists of the 1970's.

In any case, Brautigan brought a special quality to his fiction, a style of expression that, although deceptively simple and direct, teems with figures of speech that often seem to defy the bounds of language. Early critics seemed to miss, ignore, or disparage exactly these distinctive formal qualities. Often, Brautigan's subject matter--the dead-end fixity of materialism, outworn myths, or the decay of the American dream--places him at home in the tradition of twentieth century American writers. What made Brautigan's fiction attractive to his early psychedelic audience, however, was something new: Implicit in his nontraditional structure and distended metaphors was the suggestion that experience could be transformed by imagination. The pursuit of shimmering, elusive instances of imaginative insight might possibly offer a personal alternative to the stultification of culture amid the grotesque remnants of

American myth. Many postmodern writers have read Brautigan; W. P. Kinsella has referred to some of his own short works as "Brautigans." At the very least, these writers have been alerted to the possibilities suggested by Brautigan's work. His influence may be greater than anyone could have guessed.

BIOGRAPHY

Richard Gary Brautigan was born in Tacoma, Washington, in the midst of the Great Depression. Very little is known about his early life. Although Brautigan apparently drew on his childhood experiences in his fiction, his idiosyncratic attitude toward his past made him reluctant to discuss actual details with anyone. From anecdotal fragments confided to a few persons close to him, a far less than idyllic picture emerges that includes a pattern of abandonment and mistreatment at the hands of stepfathers. Deprivation seems to have been a part of his heritage, and Brautigan would claim throughout his life that he never graduated from high school.

In 1956, Brautigan moved to San Francisco and became peripherally aligned with the Beat poets. He wrote and published several volumes of poetry, but none sold well. He also met an educated young woman, Virginia Adler, who became his first wife and the mother of Ianthe, their daughter. Adler supported the family by doing secretarial work. Problems arose when Brautigan continued his bachelor habits of haunting bars and bringing his friends home for further revels. In time, Virginia became involved with one of Brautigan's drinking friends and ran away with him to live in Salt Lake City in 1963. Although he was devastated, Brautigan wrote one of his best novels, *In Watermelon Sugar*, in 1964.

Success showered on Brautigan with the publication of *Trout Fishing in America* in 1967. Fame and money afforded him opportunity for a period of more or less unbridled hedonism. After purchasing a ranch in Montana, Brautigan spent portions of the year entertaining friends, and, perhaps, cultivating a lifestyle that quickly became an unfortunate blend of egoism and dissipation. Although his friends would fondly recall their early days with Brautigan, heavy drinking and a mordant sense of paranoia began to estrange

Richard Brautigan (Library of Congress)

most of them. Brautigan's later work was beginning to suffer at the hands of critics, his counterculture audience was dispersing, and sales in the United States were down. In Japan, however, his translated work was creating a wave of interest. In 1977, he married one of his Japanese admirers, Akiko. There was a brief period of happiness while they lived together in San Francisco, and Brautigan began to write *The Tokyo-Montana Express* in 1978. Unfortunately, Akiko, like so many others, was unable to cope with the peculiar stresses of a relationship with Brautigan; she left him. Brautigan tried the lecture circuit in 1980, but it was an unhappy venture. Sometime near the end of September, 1984, Richard Brautigan shut himself up in his house in Bolinas, California, and took his own life with a handgun. His body was discovered on October 25, 1984.

ANALYSIS

Richard Brautigan's short fiction explores the imagination's power to transform reality. In some stories, this means contrasting a gritty, naturalistic portrait of cheap materialism, personal defeat, and latent violence with a vision of the lost American Eden or a nostalgic remembrance of childhood's innocence. Collectively, the stories describe a search for good in contemporary America, but because they sympathize with the defeated, they suggest that such a search is futile. Brautigan's stories stoically accept the conditions of existence, withholding judgment while suggesting that the imagination holds the only possible hope for transcendence.

The stories are self-consciously artificial, continually calling attention to the process of their creation. The typographical experimentation, outrageous figures of speech, extreme compression, and deceptively simplistic syntax work through a disengaged narrative voice to create prose that has been compared to skywriting. The conscious artificiality of Brautigan's stylistic mannerisms has led some critics to dismiss his work as whimsical, coy, naïve, and self-indulgent.

TROUT FISHING IN AMERICA

Although *Trout Fishing in America* became popular as a counterculture book during the late 1960's, it was written in 1961 as a late expression of the San Francisco Beat movement. Brautigan, like other Beats, had been conditioned by the experience of the Great Depression and World War II, historical examples of deprivation and violence, and he saw in these experiences deep truths that belied America's complacent prosperity. In contrast to the radicals of the 1930's and the New Left of the 1960's, Brautigan and other Beats sought social change not through collective action but through personal transformation.

Thus, *Trout Fishing in America* is an antididactic book, an effort to document America from a disengaged, thoroughly nonpolitical point of view. Although the America it documents is spiritually decayed, the forty-seven stories that compose *Trout Fishing in America* do not promote a program of social reform. Instead, the book's underlying philosophy, derived from Zen Buddhist belief, assumes that life is essentially determined and that social progress is an illusion. Brautigan espouses a politics of the imagination in which social activism is supplanted by the individual imagination's ability to create a vision of freedom, a vision of an America that is "often only a place in the

mind." To this extent, the explicit theme of Kurt Vonnegut's *Mother Night*, which was published in 1961, as *Trout Fishing in America* was being written, suits Brautigan's book: "We are what we pretend to be, so we must be careful what we pretend to be." Brautigan's unnamed narrator uses his imagination to "fish" for something of value in the stream of contemporary America, but like his comically failed fisherman Alonso Hagen in "Fishing on the Streets of Eternity," his effort becomes "an interesting experiment in total loss."

Stylistically, *Trout Fishing in America* seems without literary precedent, a documentary collage of prose poems and cultural references (like Henry David Thoreau) are juxtaposed with references to historical figures (Richard Nixon, "Pretty Boy" Floyd, Andrew Carnegie, Caryl Chessman, Deanna Durbin) and the signatures of popular culture (bumper stickers, diaries, tombstone engravings, recipes, warning signs). Woven through this cultural stew is the protean phrase "Trout Fishing in America," which is applied to people, places, a hotel, a pen nib, a state of mind, and the book itself.

"The Cover for Trout Fishing in America," the opening piece, exemplifies the book's self-consciousness and introduces Brautigan's ironic view of America. By describing the book's cover photograph, Brautigan reminds his reader that *Trout Fishing in America* is itself an artifact, a component of the society he is documenting. He then juxtaposes a statue of Benjamin Franklin, the prototypical American optimist, to the derelicts who sadly wait in the park hoping for a handout. Although the concluding quotation from Franz Kafka, "I like the Americans because they are healthy and optimistic," is ironic, Brautigan's matter-of-fact presentation prevents the piece from being read as social protest. Instead, the book implies that optimism, no matter how ill-founded, is a part of the American condition.

"THE KOOL-AID WINO"

In a complementary way, "The Kool-Aid Wino" demonstrates the imagination's power to overcome the limitations of existence. The Kool-Aid Wino is a child who is restricted from picking beans or engaging in active play by a hernia. His family is too poor to afford an operation or even a truss, so the

Kool-Aid Wino spends his days lovingly preparing a watered-down, sugarless version of Kool-Aid "like a famous brain surgeon removing a disordered portion of the imagination." Through his ceremonious preparation and consumption he creates "his own Kool-Aid reality" and is "able to illuminate himself by it." The story celebrates the human capacity to transcend reality while simultaneously portraying the sad deprivations that make such imaginative escape necessary.

In "Trout Fishing on the Bevel," Brautigan's narrator describes fishing a stream that runs past two graveyards, one for the rich and one for the poor. Like many of Brautigan's short fictions, "Trout Fishing on the Bevel" meditates on loneliness, poverty, death, and the desire to transcend them. The narrator describes the weathered boards, "like heels of stale bread," that mark the graves of the poor and imagines darkly humorous inscriptions ("Beloved Worked-to-Death Mother Of") that disclose the painful reality usually disguised by euphemisms. In contrast, the graves of the rich are marked with "marble hors d'oeuvres like horses trotting up the fancy paths to the sky." Admittedly "bothered" by "the poverty of the dead," the narrator has "a vision of going over to the poor graveyard and gathering up grass and fruit jars and tin cans and markers and wilted flowers and bugs and weeds and clods and going home and putting a hook in the vise and tying a fly with all that stuff and then going outside and casting it up into the sky, watching it float over clouds and then into the evening star." It is one of Brautigan's clearest statements of his artistic purpose, expressing his desire to construct from the forgotten or overlooked bits of life an art that can imaginatively free his narrator and his reader from the particular loneliness of existence.

"THE CLEVELAND WRECKING YARD"

"The Cleveland Wrecking Yard" is placed near the end of *Trout Fishing in America*, and it provides a caricature of America's obsessive materialism. At the Cleveland Wrecking Yard, a microcosm of America, the narrator finds a trout stream for sale, stacked up in lengths beside toilets and other used plumbing supplies, but he does not condemn this outrageous "commodification" of nature; instead, he

sees the Cleveland Wrecking Yard as a repository for tarnished dreams that can only be revitalized with imagination. Indeed, the process by which discarded items can be recycled parallels the way in which Brautigan salvages the scraps of American culture to construct *Trout Fishing in America*.

"REVENGE OF THE LAWN"

Many of the stories collected in *Revenge of the Lawn* deal with childhood, portraying it as a fragile refuge, a time when people are more open to the transforming power of imagination. The stories contrast this freedom with the crippling disillusionments that accompany maturation and the sadder ways adults use imagination to escape reality.

The title story, however, shows Brautigan at his most playful, demonstrating an ability to use comic misdirection and a deadpan narrative voice in the manner of Mark Twain. This rambling, autobiographical remembrance focuses on his grandmother, his grandfather, and a man named Jack. The grandfather, "a minor Washington mystic," went mad after he correctly "prophesied the exact date when World War I would start." In his madness he returns to an eternal childhood in which he is six years old. He is replaced by Jack, an itinerant salesman of lots in Florida, who hawks "a vision of eternal oranges and sunshine." These contrasting visionaries are set against the grandmother, a bootlegger, who sells a utilitarian sort of bottled vision. The action of the story revolves around Jack's relationship to nature--specifically the lawn that he has destroyed by driving on it, a pear tree that grows in the yard, the bees that are attracted to the pears, and the grandmother's geese. The geese eat some fermenting mash and pass out in the yard. The grandmother, comically assuming that the geese are dead, plucks them. They recover and are standing about "like some helpless, primitive American advertisement for aspirin," when Jack, distracted by the sight, drives into the house. In a concluding note, the narrator writes that his earliest memory is an image of Jack setting fire to the tree "while the fruit was still green on the branches." "Revenge of the Lawn" demonstrates Brautigan's ability to write comic narrative while satirizing man's foolish attempts to manage nature.

"CORPORAL"

"Corporal" is a bittersweet inverted Horatio Alger story in which the narrator recounts his wartime involvement in a paper drive. The young patriots were to earn military ranks according to the amount of paper they collected. The narrator's initial eagerness was thwarted, however, when he realized that "the kids who wore the best clothes and had lots of spending money and got to eat hot lunch every day" had an unfair advantage, for these kids "were already generals," and "they strutted their military airs around the playground." Like so many of Brautigan's characters, the narrator admitted defeat and entered "the disenchanted paper shadows of America where failure is a bounced check or a bad report card or a letter ending a love affair and all the words that hurt people when they read them." "Corporal" evokes the opposing worlds of good and bad paper, the childlike creative dream and the stifling economic and social reality. The story painfully portrays the disappointments that constitute so much of life, and emphasizes, in a manner that is particularly relevant for an author who places imaginative creation at the center of life, the precariousness of a life lived in the mind.

"THE WORLD WAR I LOS ANGELES AIRPLANE"

The last piece in *Revenge of the Lawn* is one of the most openly autobiographical. "The World War I Los Angeles Airplane" is Brautigan's response to the death of his father-in-law, but this piece, despite its specificity, effectively communicates Brautigan's general sense of life as a process of attrition. "The World War I Los Angeles Airplane" exemplifies Brautigan's disregard for traditional narrative method and his love of lists, for after a brief introduction, the story presents a numbered catalog of thirty-three separate thoughts. In an elliptical manner, these distinct statements chronicle the life of a defeated man. Most suggestive is the contrast between his father-in-law's experience as a pilot in World War I, when "he had been followed by a rainbow across the skies of France," and the quiet alcoholism of his final years of inactivity, when he watched daytime television and "used sweet wine in place of life because he didn't have any more life to use." The father-in-law's retreat from life parallels the Kool-Aid Wino's, except that in "The World War I Los Angeles Airplane" there is no intimation that the escape is illuminating.

THE TOKYO-MONTANA EXPRESS

During the 1970's, Brautigan announced his intention to write a novel parodying a popular genre each year. *The Hawkline Monster: A Gothic Western* (1974), *Willard and His Bowling Trophies: A Perverse Mystery* (1975), *Sombrero Fallout: A Japanese Novel* (1976), and *Dreaming of Babylon: A Private Eye Novel, 1942* (1977) were critical disasters for Brautigan. By the time he published *The Tokyo-Montana Express* in 1980, his literary reputation had been ruined, and he had been deserted by most of his readers. His status as a counterculture hero, which was always based on a misunderstanding of his work, had become irrelevant, except as another barrier standing between him and the readers of the 1980's. Although Brautigan resumed lecturing to promote *The Tokyo-Montana Express*, he was unable to recapture the broad acceptance that had made him a best-selling author a decade before. Nevertheless, *The Tokyo-Montana Express*, for all of its unevenness, marked a healthy return to the effective short fiction evident in *Trout Fishing in America* and *Revenge of the Lawn*.

The Tokyo-Montana Express contains 131 individual prose pieces. A few of these approximate the traditional form of the short story, but most would more accurately be called anecdotes, vignettes, or prose poems. Overall, Brautigan's tendency toward compression is more evident in *The Tokyo-Montana Express* than in his earlier work. He is also more restrained in his use of bizarre figures of speech, and the disengaged flatness of his prose is more consistent.

As in all of his short fiction, Brautigan's primary concern in *The Tokyo-Montana Express* is the imagination. In *Trout Fishing in America*, he figuratively "fishes" for a vision of America; in *The Tokyo-Montana Express*, he travels an imaginary trans-Pacific railroad, a vehicle for the metaphysical commutation of ideas between East and West. Written after a period during which he spent most of his time either in Japan or on his farm in Montana, Brautigan's collection examines the cultures of East and West, repeatedly showing the ironic similarities and in the end suggesting that Montana's big sky country may be a geographically appropriate setting for the philosophy of Japan.

In *The Tokyo-Montana Express*, Brautigan's involvement with Zen Buddhist thought is more explicit than in his earlier work, expressing itself in the stoic attitude of the narrative voice he employs. One paradox expressed in the collection is that while all experiences are equally worthy of examination, all experiences are also ultimately insignificant. The narrator's emotional disengagement cannot disguise a sadness that is much more prevalent here than in Brautigan's earlier work. Indeed, the narrator in *The Tokyo-Montana Express* expects very little of life, accepts the inevitable process of attrition, assumes that any meaning must originate in the individual imagination, and exhibits great faith in the integrity of that imagination.

"ANOTHER TEXAS GHOST STORY"

"Another Texas Ghost Story" recounts the life of a man who, while growing up on a remote Texas ranch, is visited at night by a ghost. Forty years later at a family reunion, he accidentally admits his childhood experience to his brother and two sisters only to discover that they too had seen the apparition when they were children. They were all afraid to mention it at the time because they were afraid they would be thought crazy. In "Another Texas Ghost Story," Brautigan connects childhood and imagination and implies that societal pressure makes people less receptive to the wonder around them.

"Werewolf Raspberries" is an example of the extreme compression of many pieces in *The Tokyo-Montana Express*. Its seventy-nine words, interrupted by ellipses, seem like the fragmented remains of a more complete narrative, yet this abbreviated prose poem manages to communicate a complex story. Set in the spring of 1940 with a Glenn Miller recording playing in the background, the narrative voice in "Werewolf Raspberries" addresses a young man whose single-minded romantic desire to give his girl "a great big kiss" has been inexplicably thwarted by the raspberries' "little teeth shining in the moonlight." The piece concludes with the ironic remonstrance that "If you had played your cards right, you could have been killed at Pearl Harbor instead." On one level, this brief prose poem expresses a nostalgic feel for dreams lost to the inevitable imperfections and accidents of existence, but the final comment ironically compares the harmless adolescent dream of romance with the lethal, but equally adolescent, dream of glory.

"THE MENU/1965"

"The Menu/1965" is the longest piece in *The Tokyo-Montana Express*, and it shows Brautigan extracting significance from a strange but mundane object, in this case the monthly menu prepared for residents of San Quentin's Death Row. The narrator resists judging the significance of this artifact; instead, he reports several other people's reactions to this strange juxtaposition of dining and death. At the end, the narrator and the intellectual father of a friend become entranced in "a long conversation where the menu became a kind of thought diving bell going deeper and deeper, deeper and deeper until we were at the cold flat bottom of the sea, staring fish-like at the colored Easter eggs that were going to be served next Sunday on Death Row." The allusion to Easter portrays the condemned prisoners as Christlike sacrifices, but the primary focus of the story is the fascination of the object and the manner in which it triggers the imagination.

All of Brautigan's short fictions are meant to become "thought diving bells" for the reader, and often, as in "The Menu/1965," the process of mental exploration begins with the contemplation of a simple object or event. In the end, Brautigan's creative process stands as an exemplum of a method for confronting life's attrition.

OTHER MAJOR WORKS

LONG FICTION: *A Confederate General from Big Sur*, 1964; *In Watermelon Sugar*, 1968; *The Abortion: An Historical Romance*, 1971; *The Hawkline Monster: A Gothic Western*, 1974; *Willard and His Bowling Trophies: A Perverse Mystery*, 1975; *Sombrero Fallout: A Japanese Novel*, 1976; *Dreaming of Babylon: A Private Eye Novel 1942*, 1977; *So the Wind Won't Blow It All Away*, 1982; *An Unfortunate Woman*, 2000 (wr. 1982; first pb. in French as *Cahier d'un Retour de Troie*, 1994).

POETRY: *The Return of the Rivers*, 1957; *The Galilee Hitch-Hiker*, 1958; *Lay the Marble Tea: Twenty-four Poems*, 1959; *The Octopus Frontier*, 1960; *All*

Watched over by Machines of Loving Grace, 1967; *Please Plant This Book*, 1968; *The Pill Versus the Springhill Mine Disaster*, 1968; *Rommel Drives on Deep into Egypt*, 1970; *Loading Mercury with a Pitchfork*, 1976; *June 30th, June 30th*, 1978.

MISCELLANEOUS: *The Edna Webster Collection of Undiscovered Writings*, 1995.

BIBLIOGRAPHY

Abbott, Keith. *Downstream from "Trout Fishing in America."* Santa Barbara, Calif.: Capra Press, 1989. Abbott recounts his memories of Brautigan from their first meeting in San Francisco in 1966, through the Montana years, and back to 1982 in San Francisco. Abbott's last chapter, "Shadows and Marble," is a critical essay devoted to Brautigan's language and strategy of fiction.

Barber, John F., ed. *Richard Brautigan: An Annotated Bibliography*. Jefferson, N.C.: McFarland, 1990. A good source of materials for students of Brautigan.

_____. *Richard Brautigan: Essays on the Writings and Life*. Jefferson, N.C.: McFarland, 2007. The thirty-two essays in this book are written by friends and colleagues of Brautigan who knew and respected the author and his work. Many of the pieces here are previously unpublished, while others have appeared in literary journals. Altogether, they serve as a loving tribute to Brautigan, who was greatly admired by the essayists on both a personal and a literary level. Includes previously unpublished photographs and artwork.

Brautigan, Ianthe. *You Can't Catch Death: A Daughter's Memoir*. New York: St. Martin's Press, 2000. Brautigan's daughter recalls her childhood spent bouncing between her two bohemian parents' homes. She describes her father, who committed suicide when she was twenty-four years old, as a "dignified, brilliant, hysterically funny, and sometimes difficult" man.

Chénetier, Marc. *Richard Brautigan*. New York: Methuen, 1983. A semiotic examination of Brautigan's approach to structure and elements of style that generate meaning. This slender volume touches on several works, with particular attention to *Trout Fishing in America*.

Foster, Edward Halsey. *Richard Brautigan*. Boston: Twayne, 1983. This blend of biography and criticism deals primarily with Brautigan's work within his own cultural ambience, referring to other contemporary fiction, the Beat movement, and Zen Buddhism as an overall influence. Not always flattering, Foster discusses most of Brautigan's short fiction and novels.

Horvath, Brooke. "Richard Brautigan's Search for Control Over Death." *American Literature* 57 (October, 1985): 435-455. Horvath explores possible limits to Brautigan's response of imagination as a strategy for countering the basic issue of death in his four early novels and one of the stories in *The Tokyo-Montana Express*.

Hume, Kathryn. "Brautigan's Psychomachia." *Mosaic: A Journal for the Interdisciplinary Study of Literature* 34, no. 1 (March, 2001): 75. Describes Brautigan as a "narrative aesthetician," examining the Zen-based strategies that allow him to balance extreme emotional tension with simple form. Analyzes the nature of Brautigan's narrative technique and his solicitation of an unusual reader response modeled upon Zen observation.

Iftekharuddin, Farhat. "The New Aesthetics in Brautigan's *Revenge of the Lawn: Stories 1962-1970*." In *Creative and Critical Approaches to the Short Story*, edited by Noel Harold Kaylor. Lewiston, N.Y.: Edwin Mellen Press, 1997. Iftekharuddin examines Brautigan's literary innovation and other literary critics' analyses of Brautigan's work.

Palo, Brenda M. "Melancholia and the Death Motif in Richard Brautigan's Short Fiction." In *The Postmodern Short Story: Forms and Issues*, edited by Farhat Iftekharrudin, et al., under the auspices of the Society for the Study of the Short Story. Westport, Conn.: Praeger, 2003. Analyzes some of Brautigan's short stories in *Revenge of the Lawn*, focusing on his use of death as both an image and a theme.

Stull, William L. "Richard Brautigan's *Trout Fishing in America*: Notes of a Native Son." *American Literature* 56 (March, 1984): 69-80. Stull approaches general themes in *Trout Fishing in America* by examining some of the book's many allusions to other literature and Americana. A good introduction to Brautigan's work.

Wright, Lawrence. "The Life and Death of Richard Brautigan." *Rolling Stone*, April 11, 1985, p. 29. A biographical sketch, noting Brautigan's early fame and cult following, the decline of his reputation, and his suicide. Notes that when friends describe him, he seems to be two different people; at one point he was diagnosed as a paranoid schizophrenic.

Carl Brucker
Updated by Mary Rohrberger

KATE BRAVERMAN

Born: Philadelphia, Pennsylvania; February 5, 1950

PRINCIPAL SHORT FICTION

Squandering the Blue, 1990
Small Craft Warnings, 1998
"Cocktail Hour," 2005
"Science of Navigation," 2006
"In the Neutral Zone," 2009

OTHER LITERARY FORMS

Kate Braverman (BRAY-vur-mihn) first made her literary reputation as a poetess; her first volume of poetry, *Milk Run,* was published in 1977. It was followed quickly by three other volumes of verse. She then turned to the novel genre, with *Lithium for Medea* in 1979. This, too, made a strong impression on critics and readers and solidified her reputation as a serious literary figure in the Los Angeles area. She did not take up short fiction seriously until the late 1980's.

ACHIEVEMENTS

Kate Braverman's short stories have been widely acknowledged, especially within California, as being exceptionally poetic in their language and extremely disturbing in their portrayal of drug-induced states. Her language seeks to mirror states of consciousness, especially by confusing the senses. Her writing received early recognition. Two of her four volumes of poetry were nominated for Pulitzer Prizes. Her short stories "Tall Tales" and "Pagan Night" won a Best American Short Story Award for 1991 and 1998, respectively, and an O. Henry Award for 1992. "Mrs. Jordan's Summer Vacation" was the Editor's Choice for the Raymond

Carver Award for 2006, and "Cocktail Hour" won a Pushcart Prize for 2007. Other awards include *The Economist* of London Prize in 2003 for her essays, the Isherwood Fellowship for 2004, and a Recognition Award from the California Legislative Assembly.

BIOGRAPHY

Kate Braverman was born to Irving and Millicent Braverman, both of Eastern European Jewish descent. Although of limited education themselves, they were keen readers and encouraged their children to follow the same path. Kate Braverman is the elder of two children. The family lived in Philadelphia for the first seven years of her life, then moved to Los Angeles. The move was disastrous financially, and the family was forced to rely on public assistance and to move to a public housing project. The parents divorced.

Braverman's father was in poor health and often involved in criminal activities; her mother gained a position in a talent agency, and through her own efforts finally co-owned it, becoming a millionaire in the process. However, Braverman and her brother were left largely to fend for themselves. Writing had been a creative activity for Braverman from childhood. At thirteen, she submitted work to a writing workshop at the University of California, Los Angeles (UCLA), and was admitted. Soon after, she moved to the San Francisco Bay area, finishing her schooling at Berkeley High School, and later entered the University of California, Berkeley. This was at the height of the hippie movement, and Berkeley was a center of the student-protest movement.

Braverman majored in anthropology and graduated in 1971. She returned to Los Angeles and quickly became part of the literary life of the city. She was a founding member of the Venice Poetry Workshop, and her work first was published in small poetry magazines and later in better-known journals. During the 1970's she taught extension classes at UCLA and did editing and reviewing. Her first book of poetry was *The Milk Run*. She also wrote fiction, and her first novel, *Lithium for Medea*, appeared two years later. The novel attracted widespread attention, and her reputation as a feminist writer became established within California.

Braverman's daughter Gabrielle was born in 1981. At the time Braverman was a single parent, although later she married Alan Goldstein, a professor at Alfred University in New York, who adopted the child. The marriage meant Braverman had to move to the Allegheny Mountains in upstate New York. Later still, she moved to New Mexico. However, the subject of her writing remained California, especially the Los Angeles area. She has continued to teach and run poetry and creative-writing workshops. Over the course of her career, she has concentrated increasingly on writing fiction, although using poetic techniques in her prose style.

ANALYSIS

Kate Braverman's short stories are noted for three characteristics. First, the narrative, often in a modified form of stream of consciousness, approximates the language of free verse. Thus, her stories can be seen as types of prose poems. Second, the autobiographical elements, in terms of setting, characters, and actions, mimic Braverman's life and the culture of 1960's, 1970's, and 1980's California, especially the hippie-drug milieu. Third, consistency of story marks Braverman's work, which is retold in numerous guises. Some stories obviously mesh, and others rework the autobiographical details in parallel ways rather than in consecutive ways.

These features are immediately apparent in Braverman's first short-story volume, *Squandering the Blue*. Blue is a color that resonates for Braverman. It is not only the color of the California sky and the Hawaiian sea but also the color of the night, of drugs, of emotions, and of the spiritual inheritance or capital each human is given. Blue is basic; other colors are introduced as contrasts--the red-orange of sunsets, for example, or the vivid green of Hawaiian jungles. Blue is a motif that runs through nearly all the stories.

The two main autobiographical features that recur are the three generations of women, daughter-mother-grandmother, and the drug culture, in terms of either addiction or recovery. Recovery is often represented by Alcoholics Anonymous (AA) meetings, the attendance at which marks stages of grace or falling away from sobriety. The drug-induced consciousness is Braverman's central mode, blurring the senses in synesthesia and blurring the language in fluid imagery. The drug consciousness also introduces the sense of a parallel universe that the main characters inhabit, not dissimilar to that in another California fiction, Thomas Pynchon's *The Crying of Lot 49* (1966).

In the three-generations motif, Braverman typically is the mother, being bypassed or marginalized by daughter and grandmother, especially in the mother's drug-handicapped state. The mothers tend to live in this parallel universe. Sometimes, however, Braverman takes the child's perspective, either by going back to the Los Angeles projects she lived in as a child or projecting her own quarrels with her mother on to the daughter.

The stories are feminist, in that the men are shown to be inadequate, emotionally and spiritually, and also oppressive. Sometimes Braverman's horror at her father's illness, criminality, and desertion leaps out in vivid episodes. Mostly, however, the men are spineless

The shift in *Small Craft Warnings*, Braverman's second collection, is toward characters close to the end of their tether. The three-woman structure is breaking down, and the narrow focus on autobiography is blurred. The reader senses the obituary of the once-vibrant hippie culture of the 1960's and early 1970's. Drugs are wiping out the last vestiges of the free spirit; what is left is trash. The characters begin to sense that they inhabit a sordid, meaningless world. In the stories written after *Small Craft Warnings*, the settings move away from California and follow

Braverman to her new homes in New York's Alleghenies and in New Mexico.

"SQUANDERING THE BLUE"

The characters in "Squandering the Blue" are the typical daughter-mother-grandmother of many of Braverman's stories. This time the grandmother has a name, Dominique, and the story is told from the young daughter's point of view. Having been dragged though her mother's hippie roamings through Mexico and Hawaii, the daughter is drawn to the stability of her grandmother's Beverly Hills house, with the order of a school uniform and a routine schedule.

In her grandmother's house, her mother is marginalized, as she desperately seeks sobriety through AA. The girl's lack of a father, a severe social handicap, is also a demerit against her mother. The mother's efforts to write and to become sober do not amount to much, and the girl disrespects her. In the end, however, the mother emerges as a real person, only to die of breast cancer. After her mother's death, the daughter realizes that her grandmother's "order" is merely a social sham and worth nothing. Her mother was at least pursuing something in her wanderings. For the first time the girl understands her mother's love for her.

As in many stories, Beverly Hills represents the false society against which the hippies were rebelling; Hawaii is the paradise they briefly inhabit with the help of drugs, a world of the imagination, a parallel universe. The girl has to weigh the two worlds and the borders or margins that define them.

"TALL TALES FROM THE MEKONG DELTA"

This short story, "Tall Tales from the Mekong Delta," has won several awards, yet it is atypical of the stories in the first volume. Although there is a central unnamed mother character, typically attending AA meetings and trying to get her life in order, there is also a strong, violent man, Lenny. He claims to be a Vietnam veteran and a drug dealer with lots of money. He waylays the mother, wanting to begin an affair with her. He seems to know all about her and has soon undermined her attempts to regain sobriety. In the end, he disappears, but not before she is drinking, smoking, and doing drugs as before.

Lenny is a threatening presence, with no attractive qualities. Nevertheless, he is successful in seducing the woman. The story is perhaps best read as an allegory of the power of drugs. The inner voice of the drugs conveyed in other stories becomes externalized in Lenny. He knows all about her and her drug habit; he knows to what she will succumb, and in the end she does. However, there is no longer an attraction to the drugs or him. The promises made are fleeting and give nothing of worth. The story seems to represent Braverman's final disillusionment with the hippie drug world.

"THESE CLAIRVOYANT RUINS"

"These Clairvoyant Ruins" is the last story in the volume *Squandering the Blue*. It links with two early stories, "Desert Blues" and "Falling in October," both of which include Diana, Diana's friend Carlotta, and Diana's daughter Annabell. As is typical of Braverman's women characters, Diana is in the thirty-nine to forty-one-year-old age bracket (that is, about Braverman's age). In the early stories, Diana has been the helpless, drugged, and drunken mother going to AA, and Carlotta has been her supporter. In short, their roles are reversed.

The drama in this story, however, is between mother and daughter. Diana attends Annabell's school Christmas concert, in which Annabell plays the violin and has a small acting part. The concert is an unqualified disaster, and they both know it. References to the story "Tall Tales" are remembered, as the woman of that story becomes almost an alter ego for Diana. The Los Angeles sunset reminds her of Hawaii and the whole drug scene. The drug voice takes other forms. Diana no longer succumbs, but what has she gained to replace the old life? A superficial and second-rate performance, it would appear. She has to learn to walk in the darkness of this knowledge. At least there is a real relationship with her daughter.

"THEY TAKE A PHOTOGRAPH OF YOU WHEN YOU FIRST GET HERE"

"They Take a Photograph of You When You First Get Here" is the second story in Braverman's second volume of short stories, *Small Craft Warnings*. The story is told by a would-be recovering alcoholic in a rehabilitation unit, to which she has just been admitted.

She never gives her name, though her counselor, Susan, frequently asks for it. Part of the story consists of flashbacks to a time in Hawaii, again a typical locus of Braverman stories, which she spent with her lover, Sapphire--a blue gem, of course, though in this story the name of a man of indeterminate status. Blue comes into the story in other forms, as a swimmer in the sea, as chastity, and as the coldness of the rehabilitation unit.

The woman is totally withdrawn. Finally she admits to herself her lover is dead. Her parents come to visit her, but she has nothing to say to them. The story ends bleakly, with no apparent progress made in the woman's condition. The counseling and twelve-step programs seem unable to reach her, yet what has made her so withdrawn remains a mystery. She has become one of the living dead, a final dreadful memorial to the promise of the drug culture of earlier decades.

"PAGAN NIGHT"

"Pagan Night" has won particular recognition and awards. It follows "They Take a Photograph of You When You Get Here" in Braverman's second volume. The title refers to a rock band that had been successful during the hippie days, but, unlike such long-lasting groups as the Who, this group broke up after making a single tour. The story centers on two survivors, Sunny and Dalton. They drift in and out of San Francisco. Sunny gets pregnant and has a child. They move up to Oregon, where they live destitute in a van.

When Dalton can earn, legally or otherwise, some money, they buy drugs. Food comes from scavenging or from illegally fishing in the river. There is a growing unspoken agreement that they can no longer keep the baby. However, the only way they can think of to dispose of the baby is to abandon it, perhaps by the riverside. The story ends before they do this.

This story strikes a darker, more somber note than previous Braverman stories. The Oregon town is broken down. Its small zoo symbolizes the seedy remnants of a once-thriving hippie culture. Sunny and Dalton are the last unrehabilitated survivors, doomed to sink without trace into a colorless and meaningless future.

OTHER MAJOR WORKS

LONG FICTION: *Lithium for Medea*, 1979, 2002; *Palm Latitudes*, 1988, 2003; *Wonders of the West*, 1993; *The Incantation of Frida K.*, 2002.

POETRY: *Milk Run*, 1977; *Lullaby for Sinners*, 1980; *Hurricane Warnings*, 1987; *Postcard from August*, 1990.

NONFICTION: *Dropping In: Putting It All Back Together*, 1972; *Frantic Transmissions to and from Los Angeles: An Accidental Memoir*, 2006.

BIBLIOGRAPHY

Fujii, Hikari. "Los Angeles, I'm Yours." *Rising Generation* 154 (March, 2009). Deals with Braverman's attachment to Los Angeles in her fiction and poetry.

Gellfant, Blanche, ed. "Kate Braverman." In *Columbia Companion to the Twentieth Century American Short Story.* New York: Columbia University Press, 004. Reviews Braverman's earlier short stories.

Goldstein, Bill. "Squall Lines." *The New York Times*, January 24, 1999. Review of Braverman's collection *Small Craft Warnings* lauds her "beautiful language" and "sharp observations."

Guthmann, Edward. "In Los Angeles, Kate Braverman Starved for Culture Until S.F. Called Her Back Home." *San Francisco Chronicle*, January 30, 2006, p. E1. Frank and revealing interview with Braverman, in which she talks about her manic depression, her drug addictions, and her revolutionary life.

David Barratt

KEVIN BROCKMEIER

Born: Hialeah, Florida; December 6, 1972

PRINCIPAL SHORT FICTION

Things That Fall from the Sky 2002
The View from the Seventh Layer, 2008

OTHER LITERARY FORMS

Kevin Brockmeier (BRAHK-mi-ur) published two novels, *The Truth About Celia* (2003), about a science-fiction writer who comes to terms with the disappearance of his daughter through creating stories, and *The Brief History of the Dead* (2006), a contrapuntal narrative that juxtaposes two stories set during a plague that decimates Earth (one tells of a fabulous city where the recently dead go to await the crossover to the afterlife, and the other is a grim narrative of a research scientist who must struggle for her survival after she is marooned in Antarctica as part of an outlandish Coca-Cola marketing campaign). Brockmeier also published two books for young readers: *City of Names* (2002), in which a kid mistakenly chances upon a strange map that reveals an alternative world under his town, and *Grooves: A Kind of Mystery* (2006), in which a seventh-grader gets entangled in the nefarious schemes of a local millionaire jeans manufacturer after the kid hears messages through the creases in his jeans and the ridges of potato chips.

ACHIEVEMENTS

Kevin Brockmeier brings to short fiction a signature blend of fantasy and realism. His fiction disturbs boundaries and upends assumptions that readers may make about the texture and logic of narrative itself. His groundbreaking work has been recognized for its audacity and for its elegant proseline. A career academic, Brockmeier has been awarded numerous grants, including a Guggenheim Fellowship and a National Endowment for the Arts grant. His short stories have received three O. Henry Award citations, including a first prize. "A Day in the Life of Half of Rumpelstiltskin"--a bizarre fractured fairy tale that takes as its premise that after the churlish dwarf split in half after his name was guessed by the queen, both halves continued to live--won a coveted Italo Calvino Short Fiction Award in 2001, which was named for the pioneering Italian fabulist whose work influenced Brockmeier's. In 2003, Brockmeier received a first prize of five thousand dollars in the Nelson Algren Award competition, which is presented annually by *The Chicago Tribune* in recognition of outstanding works of short fiction. In 2007, the prestigious journal *Granta*, long respected for its promotion of cutting-edge literature, listed Brockmeier among the most promising writers under the age of forty.

BIOGRAPHY

Kevin Brockmeier, although known for his love of Arkansas, was born just outside Miami, Florida, in Hialeah. His father, an insurance agent, was transferred to Little Rock when Brockmeier was three. By then, Brockmeier had demonstrated a remarkable proclivity for words (he spoke in complete sentences before he was two). Early on, he loved fairy tales, drawn particularly to the dark stories of the Brothers Grimm. Brockmeier read voraciously. When his parents divorced, he found consolation in comic books, science fiction (particularly the alternate-world works of Madeleine L'Engle), and fantasy (particularly the fabulous narratives of Roald Dahl and Daniel Pinkwater). By eight, Brockmeier was writing his own stories; his first was a mystery that centered on a kid who disappears into an alternative universe. Although a daydreamer who often found the classroom dull, Brockmeier was an honors student in high school. He discovered a flair for forensics and a talent for acting, which caused him to toy briefly with the idea of pursuing theater. He secured a full scholarship to study honors arts at nearby Southwest Missouri State University (now Missouri State University). In the summers, he returned to Little Rock, where he worked at a nursery school and enthralled kids with his made-up-on-the-spot fantastic stories. Graduating in 1995 with a B.A. in philosophy, creative writing, and theater, he studied in Ireland for a year, reading widely in contemporary experimental fiction, which pushed traditional boundaries of narrative and upended expectations of mimesis, particularly the Magic Realism of Calvino and Gabriel García Márquez and the flamboyant postmodern experiments of Donald Barthelme. Brockmeier began to hone his own creative-writing skills, determined to pursue a career in writing.

On the strength of his growing portfolio of strikingly original stories, Brockmeier was admitted to the prestigious Writers' Workshop, the M.F.A. program at the University of Iowa. There he thrived, distinguishing himself to a faculty that included Frank Conroy and Pulitzer Prize winner Marilynne Robinson. By his graduation in 1997, Brockmeier had published his first short story, "A Day in the Life of Half of Rumpelstiltskin." With more than a dozen stories either completed or in draft, Brockmeier returned to Little Rock, confident that its relatively remote location would be no impediment to his career. To support himself, he taught basic composition courses part time at Pulaski Technical College and at the University of Arkansas's regional campus. As his stories found publication in a range of prestigious forums, notably *The Georgia Review* and *The New Yorker*, Brockmeier accepted a full-time position in creative writing on the faculty of the University of Arkansas, Little Rock. Despite his commercial and critical success, Brockmeier maintained his commitment to the classroom, encouraging fledgling writers to explore the possibilities of reconfiguring assumptions about narrative elements.

ANALYSIS

Thematically, Kevin Brockmeier's short fictions explore the sort of ideas that have long compelled traditional fiction: the nature of identity, the pressing negotiations of family, the tragicomedy of emotional distance, the perilous urge to fall in love, the oppressive push of time, the yearning ache of loneliness, the function of the imagination, the nature of childhood. Nevertheless, Brockmeier produces anything but traditional stories. Not content with the recycled conventions of mimetic realism and engaged by the reach and audacity of the imagination, Brockmeier, in his signature work, freely introduces elements of fairy tale or fantasy fiction into realistic narratives. Events happen without the reassuring logic of causality, characters engage in phenomena that shatter the norm, and the narrative lines break out into self-reflexive exercises that ask the reader to participate in the telling. With the sincere delight of a child willing to renegotiate the boundaries of reality, Brockmeier takes readers into a kind of parallel universe that has no compulsion to abide by the pedestrian rules of expectation.

In keeping with his pushing of assumptions about reality, Brockmeier's signature stylistic device--the elaborate, precise metaphor that stuns with its figurative energy--takes for granted that an ordinary world can be revivified through the tonic energy of the imagination, the world of "as if." Although capable of creating poignant, realistic narratives with richly drawn sympathetic characters, Brockmeier finds far more intriguing the challenge of redrawing readers' conceptions of possibility by ushering readers into worlds that only resemble theirs. In an era in which serious short fiction reflects either the limited range of domestic realism or the gimmicky self-reflexive tricks of postmodernism, Brockmeier has merged the two imperatives with fictions that respond to the profound dilemmas of everyday life but reflect a playful willingness to upend narrative elements to produce fictions that are startlingly new.

THINGS THAT FALL FROM THE SKY

At turns whimsical in their evocation of the playful, magical atmosphere of fairy tales (with prose that is deceptively accessible, like bedtime stories) and poignantly compassionate in their depiction of small lives crowded by ordinary anxieties, Brockmeier's stories in his initial collection neatly suggest his bicameral vision. Restless with realistic fiction, he edges his narratives into the improbable, the unexpected, even the inexplicable, but he never loses his driving curiosity about characters engaged in what readers recognize as dilemmas common to all people. These are quirky and highly engaging stories that use the special reach of the fabulous to explore the everyday

In the opening tale, "These Hands," recognized with an O. Henry Award, a first-person narrator, a shy, bookish writer of fairy tales, struggles with the implications of his growing infatuation with the sweet innocence and uncomplicated beauty of an infant girl he babysits. In the title story, a middle-aged librarian is just beginning to accept her life of diminished possibilities caring for two emotionally handicapped adult sons and a mother dying in a rest home. She meets an eccentric old man in the stacks of the library who reminds her of the possibilities of living in expectation of wonder (he offers her a list of news events that report bizarre things that have fallen from the sky on unsuspecting people). In a moment of self-determination, she abruptly quits her job and departs with the odd little man into the sheer openness of possibility. In "The Ceiling," another O. Henry Award winner and perhaps the collection's signature piece, a man whose marriage is floundering into routine and whose wife is drifting away from him into inconsequential infidelities watches with growing alarm as the sky itself begins to lower. Brockmeier uses the license of Magical Realism to reinvigorate the cliché about Chicken Little's apprehension over a sky that is falling.

Brockmeier commands as well the parameters of psychological realism. In the collection's harrowing closing story, readers learn of a small girl who lives in the woods with her guardian-father. The story reads like a Brothers Grimm fairy tale, and readers accept the father's calm explanations to his child about a world that has just collapsed. However, just as readers assume the premise of a charmed life in a magic woods, the police swarm the shack, and readers discover that the child in fact has been abducted by her deranged father and that the mother has been searching for her lost child for years. In a poignant twist, even as the daughter must leave her magic home, the only home she has known, the child resists and refuses to let go of her father's hand.

THE VIEW FROM THE SEVENTH LAYER

The edgy stories from Brockmeier's second collection reflect a far more mature writer, who confidently positions characters along the boundary between realism and fantasy, and the boundary itself becomes problematic. Brockmeier reconfigures readers' assumptions about the nature of reality, using his imaginative forays into the fantastic to provoke a sense of enchantment over the possibilities of the pedestrian real.

In the title story, for instance, Olivia is a traditional character familiar to readers of psychological realism: At midlife, she runs a gift shop for tourists, selling refreshments, maps, and condoms, on a remote wooded island. Her life is uncomplicated by passion or emotion or commitment, yet she recollects (or perhaps dreams of?) her experience of being abducted by aliens from the seventh layer of the universe, whom she hopes will someday return to take her back with them. It is an unsettling intrusion of the fantastic, one readers are never sure is entirely unreliable. In "Father Melby and the Ghost of Ann Elizabeth," an unprepossessing minister, known for doctrinely sound sermons that seldom impress his indifferent congregation, is suddenly gifted with the power to dazzle his parishioners. His sudden charisma is the result not of the infusion of the Holy Spirit but rather of his possession by the lonely ghost of a long-dead woman in search of love. Using the speculative suggestion of the paranormal, Brockmeier renders an entirely original take on the importance of passion and the profound regret over its neglect.

Fascinated by the parameters of genre fiction, Brockmeier offers four tales he forthrightly labels as fables, charming and evocative stories that read with the sweet, effortless accessibility of bedtime stories and that use exotic situations and archetypal imagery to offer gentle Aesop-like wisdom. In "A Fable Ending in the Sound of a Thousand Parakeets," the first story in the collection, a mute who loves music lives in a city where everyone loves to sing. Of course, he cannot sing, but he keeps parakeets in his parlor until over the years he has hundreds of birds. He loves their simple melodies. The birds in turn learn to mimic the sounds of the man's daily life, the beat of his footsteps, the whistle of his tea kettle, the whoosh of the water faucet when he does his dishes. When he dies and the towns-people come to his house, they are enthralled by the rich harmonies of the housebirds, which are in fact the beautiful songs of the lonely man's ordinary life.

Perhaps the most original selection is the sixty-page exercise in reader interaction called "The Human Soul as a Rube Goldberg Device: A Choose-Your-Own-Adventure Story." Written in the invitatory second person, "you" put milk back in the refrigerator and head upstairs to brush your teeth, and then you, the reader, begin a series of decisions, each of which leads to a different narrative path on a different page, thus providing Brockmeier's simple premise with dozens of different narrative permutations and enthralling the reader like a child discovering the joy of storytelling.

With the deft authority of a writer certain of his craft, these stories alter perceptions of what is termed "reality" but refuse to be simply gimmicky or transparently fantastic. Brockmeier never abdicates the traditional responsibility of narrative to illuminate the absurd sorrows and the too-rare joys of the everyday. It is as much Franz Kafka as it is *The Wonderful Wizard of Oz* (1900). However, if some critical response found the stories a bit tiresome and overplayful, what critics universally admired was Brockmeier's mature prose, his confident use of figurative language, and his dazzling way with language that has the accessibility and immediacy of children's books, belying Brockmeier's sobering themes.

OTHER MAJOR WORKS

LONG FICTION: *The Truth About Celia*, 2003; *The Brief History of the Dead*, 2006; *The Illumination*, 2010.

CHILDREN'S LITERATURE: *City of Names*, 2002; *Grooves: A Kind of Mystery*, 2006.

EDITED TEXT: *Real Unreal: Best American Fantasy 3*, 2010.

BIBLIOGRAPHY

Benson, Stephen. *Contemporary Fiction and the Fairy Tale*. Detroit, Mich.: Wayne State University Press, 2008. A valuable and highly readable exploration of Brockmeier's signature genre, which examines his postmodern reimaginings of the familiar elements.

Bowers, Maggie Ann. *Magic(al) Realism: The New Critical Idiom*. London: Routledge, 2004. A scholarly work that stakes out the elements of contemporary fiction that, like Brockmeier's, take significant license with the parameters of realism.

Brockmeier, Kevin, ed. *Real Unreal: Best American Fantasy 3*. Portland, Oreg.: Underland Press, 2010. A telling selection of tales along with a reader-friendly introduction that defines Brockmeier's sense of how realism and fantasy are ultimately fluid.

Morrison, Rusty, and Ken Keegan, eds. *ParaSpheres: Extending Beyond the Spheres of Literary and Genre Fiction: Fabulist and New Wave Fabulist Stories*. Richmond, Calif.: Omnidawn, 2006. Important context for Brockmeier's fiction with a wide range of writers, who, like Brockmeier, are fascinated by disturbing genre boundaries.

Weiss, Beno. *Understanding Italo Calvino*. Columbia: University of South Carolina Press, 1993. An accessible and valuable introduction to a writer of short fiction important to any approach to Brockmeier.

Joseph Dewey

HAROLD BRODKEY

Born: Alton, Illinois; October 25, 1930
Died: New York, New York; January 26, 1996
Also Known As: Aaron Roy Weintraub

PRINCIPAL SHORT FICTION

First Love and Other Sorrows, 1957, 1986
Women and Angels, 1985
Stories in an Almost Classical Mode, 1988
*The World Is the Home of Love and Death:
    Stories,* 1997

OTHER LITERARY FORMS

For more than three decades, Harold Brodkey (BRAHD-kee) worked on a sprawling, Proustian novel with a working title of "A Party of Animals," based on his life from birth to the end of college. Portions of the novel, under contract to Farrar, Straus and Giroux since 1961, appeared first in *The New Yorker, Esquire,* and *New American Review.* Two of the three segments of *Women and Angels,* "Ceil" and "Angel," were taken from this projected novel, which ran to more than two thousand pages in length. The novel was finally published in 1991 as *The Runaway Soul.* Brodkey also published works of nonfiction, including *This Wild Darkness: The Story of My Death* (1996) and *Sea Battles on Dry Land: Essays* (1999).

ACHIEVEMENTS

Harold Brodkey is best appreciated as a writer who produced three dozen stories that are so intricately presented as to make readers experience the smallest details. His greatest strength lay neither in plot construction nor in thematic development, but rather in his ability to capture and report authentically the exact, second-by-second occurrences about which he writes.

Brodkey received both the Prix de Rome (Magazine Award) and the Brandeis Creative Arts Award in 1974. He received first prize in the O. Henry short-story awards in 1975 and again in 1976. Brodkey was a fellow of the American Academy in Rome, of the John Simon Guggenheim Memorial Foundation, and of the National Endowment for the Arts.

BIOGRAPHY

Harold Roy Brodkey was born Aaron Roy Weintraub across the Mississippi River and slightly to the northeast of St. Louis, Missouri, in Alton, Illinois, in 1930. His father, a junk man, was illiterate. Brodkey's mother--who was bright, bookish, and fluent in five or six languages--died when Harold was an infant, and the father, unable to care for the child, allowed Joseph and Doris Brodkey to adopt him. They changed his name to Harold and gave him their surname.

In Brodkey's fiction, Joseph and Doris Brodkey become Leila and S. L. (perhaps to suggest St. Louis) Cohn. Their daughter, somewhat older than Harold, is Nonie in Brodkey's stories. Brodkey has kept the details of his personal life private except as they are revealed in his stories.

When he was six, Brodkey's high intelligence quotient was recognized, and special training was recommended for him. His birth father took him from his adoptive parents when he learned this but could not cope with the boy and returned him the next day. Having lost his real mother so early that he could not remember her, Brodkey created the mother he dreamed she was, reconstructing her from scraps of information gleaned from her acquaintances. By inventing her in his own imagination, Brodkey unleashed the earliest stirrings of his ability to create credible characters and situations.

Brodkey lost his adoptive parents when he was a teenager. Joseph Brodkey had a stroke when Harold was nine and was an invalid thereafter. He lived for five years, requiring constant attention. One year before her husband died, Doris Brodkey developed cancer and died during Harold's early days at Harvard University.

His Harvard scholarship and a small inheritance enabled Brodkey to live outside the Midwest. His first collection of stories, *First Love and Other Sorrows*, became an alternate selection of the Book-of-the-Month Club. The three segments of *Women and Angels*, published in 1985, were taken from *A Runaway Soul*, as were many of the stories found in *Stories in an Almost Classical Mode*. This book was also a Book-of-the-Month Club alternate selection.

Brodkey married Joanne Brown in 1952, and they had a daughter, Amma Emily, in 1953; the couple divorced in 1962. He married novelist Ellen Schwamm in 1980, and they settled in New York City. He taught writing and literature at Cornell University and at the City College of the City University of New York. Harold Brodkey died in New York City on January 26, 1996.

ANALYSIS

Harold Brodkey writes about people and places that most readers recognize and consider unexceptional. It is attention to detail, to the slow, agonizingly detailed unfolding of the commonplace, that has distinguished Brodkey as a chronicler of what it is like to grow up-- Jewish and adopted--in the Midwest. In the early stories, the cast of characters is identical: an adoptive mother and father, an older sister given to tormenting, and her younger brother, the autobiographical character, the first-person and occasionally third-person narrator.

The first three stories of *First Love and Other Sorrows* are really the beginning of what seems to be an embryonic bildungsroman. They detail the childhood of the first-person narrator, a child who longs for love but cannot attract it. The narrator was adopted by his foster parents in part because he was very attractive, but in "The State of Grace," the first story in the volume, he is thirteen years old, six feet tall, 125 pounds, and his ears stick out. He is displeased with the way he looks, extremely conscious of being the gangly teenager new to adolescence.

The first three stories in the first collection reveal the themes that his later work pursued and presage the focus of *A Runaway Soul*. A recurrent theme in Brodkey's work is that true selflessness as such does not exist. In his stories, as presumably in his early life, all Brodkey's characters have self-serving motives. This attitude may seem cynical, but in Brodkey's work it emerges as realistic. Sometimes Brodkey confuses reciprocity with selfishness, as, for example, in "Innocence," one of the later stories in *Stories in an Almost Classical Mode*, in which the first-person narrator is determined to give Orra Perkins her first orgasm, not so much to provide her with pleasure as to get a stronger hold on her and increase the intensity of his own sexual pleasure with her. It is difficult in this story to determine the line between selfishness and selflessness.

Brodkey's stories are essentially concerned with providing descriptive details about places and emotions. His prose style has been shaped considerably by the style of *The New Yorker*, in which many of his stories appeared. The prose is unadorned, lean and direct, carefully calculated, and assiduously polished. Brodkey succeeds best when he writes about his midwestern childhood in University City, Missouri, in an uncomplicated way, in a style that reports commonplaces.

FIRST LOVE AND OTHER SORROWS

The title story of *First Love and Other Sorrows* takes place in the springtime, when its narrator is sixteen years old and confronts a budding sexuality that raises many questions within him. He lives with his adoptive mother and his twenty-two-year-old sister, who seems no more pleased with herself physically than the narrator is with himself. The adoptive father is dead.

The boy's mother warns him against playing too hard and getting overheated. This admonition is a veiled warning that the heat of youthful sexuality can be as dangerous as the heat of April. The boy feels that such is the case, as a subplot that can be interpreted in a homosexual context makes clear. The sister dates Sonny Bruster, son of the town banker. The romance between them is not free of hazards. At one point, they stop seeing each other, but they reconcile and, before the story ends, are engaged. The boy feels like an intruder in the house of his mother, who makes it clear that she cooks only because he is there. The family situation is not hostile so much as vacant. The mother, a controlling woman, is vitally concerned with having her daughter marry someone prosperous. She, somewhat like Amanda Wingfield in Tennessee Williams's *The Glass Menagerie* (pr. 1944, pb. 1945), had experienced genteel living but has been reduced to living more humbly.

The story ends with the narrator's sister engaged to Sonny Bruster. Her mother is composing letters at night to inform all her relatives of the engagement. The boy and his sister come into the kitchen, and the mother offers to heat up some soup for them. Her eyes fill with tears of emotion, and the three embrace and kiss. This story is typical of Brodkey's early work and gives a strong indication of the course of his succeeding work. Nothing much happens in the story except that an adolescent boy makes tentative moves toward growing into manhood. He is uncertain and fearful of rejection. The story deals with situations and emotions but has little plot. It is filled with the carefully observed, well-presented sights, sounds, and textures that characterize Brodkey's writing.

"SENTIMENTAL EDUCATION"

"Sentimental Education," included in *First Love and Other Sorrows*, was first published in *The New Yorker* only one month after "First Love and Other Sorrows" appeared in the same magazine. It marks a tentative step toward "Innocence," which it predates by sixteen years. Set in Cambridge, Massachusetts, where the nineteen-year-old protagonist, Elgin Smith, is an undergraduate at Harvard, the story's only other character is Caroline Hedges, a freshman at Radcliffe College. Both are virgins. As the story progresses, they have a passionate affair.

The action takes place within an academic year, during which Elgin and Caroline are forced to reassess their values. They are caught in a paradoxical situation, never fully resolved because, at school year's end, they part, although they do not break up decisively. They agree to meet again in the fall, but platonically. During their last five weeks before summer, the two abjure sex. They kiss, they touch, but they hold back. Finally, Caroline catches the night train to Baltimore and later goes to Europe for the summer. This story is different from the others in the collection. It is, unlike the first three, a third-person, author-omniscient narrative. It is the only story in the collection not directly related to any of the others and perhaps the most delicately presented story in *First Love and Other Sorrows*.

"INNOCENCE"

"Innocence," unlike many of Brodkey's stories in *Stories in an Almost Classical Mode*, was not first published in *The New Yorker* but appeared in *American Review*, presumably because of *The New Yorker*'s reluctance to publish the four-letter word used vulgarly to indicate copulation. "Innocence" is a story of young lust--as opposed to young love--in which the protagonist, a Harvard undergraduate, achieves what he feared was the unachievable, a sexual encounter with a much sought-after Radcliffe nymphet, Orra Perkins.

Orra has never achieved an orgasm because, according to her, she is too sexual to have orgasms. She is not distressed by this omission and strenuously discourages the narrator from trying to give her the orgasm that he wants her to experience. His motive is twofold: He thinks that he will, in a way, own Orra if he achieves his end. He also thinks that his own sexual pleasure with her will be enhanced if she can respond fully.

This story, generally considered to be among Brodkey's best, is some thirty pages long, twenty pages of it devoted to presenting a highly detailed account of how Orra is brought to the pinnacle of passion that the narrator wants for her. Before the story is over, Orra not only has her long-awaited orgasm but also, mulling it over, has another, multiple orgasm. Despite all the explicit physical detail that the story contains, the result is not prurient, but neither is it clinical. Rather it is realistic, direct, and detailed--detailed, indeed, to the point that the reader longs for Orra to climax.

This longing is part of Brodkey's technique. He does not seek to titillate his readers but to walk them through the experience, to exhaust them as Orra becomes exhausted. As the two participants in the event strain through what seems an endless encounter to achieve orgasm, readers are dragged along, worn down by the detailed narration of the event, to the point that they feel as physically spent as the perspiring participants when the moment of ecstasy finally arrives. Brodkey's theme concerns dependency and achieving union through weakness--in this case, Orra's previous lack of sexual fulfillment. The narrator's ability to bring her to the point of climax makes her dependent upon him in ways that she has never been before.

"CEIL"

It is difficult to say definitively whether "Ceil," one of the three stories in *Women and Angels*, is a success. Some would question whether it is a story or merely a musing, a recollection, a jotting of fragments. "Lila" and "Largely an Oral History of My Mother," both depictions of Brodkey's mother by adoption, are more complete works and provide a more coherent picture of their subject than "Ceil" does.

Despite this caveat, "Ceil" is among Brodkey's most important works. It reveals more than any other story the inner Brodkey, the Brodkey yearning to establish a link with his past, the Brodkey searching for home, straining to walk behind the curtain that separates him from his shadowy heritage. Although the writing in "Ceil" is uneven, it contains some of Brodkey's best images, particularly his writing about the great plains of the Midwest near Staunton, where his mother lived.

Ceil, the youngest of what Brodkey vaguely refers to as twenty or twenty-five children, was the offspring of a charismatic, brilliant rabbi and his long-suffering, remarkably fertile wife. Born near Odessa, Ceil was her father's favorite. He arranged a marriage for her, but she refused. She was a bright, independent girl who, when her father simultaneously forgave and put a curse upon her, left Russia for the United States.

Ceil disembarks from the ship and goes directly to a beauty shop. She does not like the way her hair looks afterward, and, within an hour, she is in a beauty salon having it redone. Not only do appearances matter to Ceil, often described by Lila as queenlike, but also she values success. She moves quickly from being a waitress to being a housemaid to being a successful business woman. She marries Max, a man much beneath her, originally from around Odessa. She is his superior in every way. Her success becomes legendary. Her self-satisfaction culminates with the birth of her son. Then,

Ceil dies after an abortion, leaving Lila to become surrogate mother to two-year-old Wiley.

THE WORLD IS THE HOME OF LOVE AND DEATH

Published a year after his death, *The World Is the Home of Love and Death* is an unfortunate epitaph to the work of Harold Brodkey. Blasted by reviewers for its careless pretentiousness--several stories so loose and rambling that they seem like unedited rejects from his novel *The Runaway Soul*--the book's eleven stories are an uneven testimony to Brodkey's brilliance. Brodkey's self-proclaimed brilliance is just one of the reasons this final collection of stories was met with hostility by some reviewers and caution by others; even Brodkey's admirers warned Brodkey newcomers that this was not the place to begin. As one critic said, the book is for hardened Brodkey veterans.

Most of the stories focus on Brodkey's childhood persona Wiley Silenowicz (a central character in *The Runaway Soul*) growing up in Missouri during the Depression. Other members of the Silenowicz family featured in these loosely related stories are Wiley's adoptive mother, Lila, and her husband, S. L. Arrogantly intelligent, Wiley is not always an easy character to tolerate. His sense that he had been "a phenomenally pretty child" recalls Brodkey's own immodest admission once of being the "best living writer in English . . . the equivalent of a Wordsworth or a Milton."

In one of the most self-indulgent stories in the collection, "Waking," the young Wiley, mute and ill with shock after the death of his mother, confronts a new life with Lila, his adoptive mother. The only event in this long story is a bath Lila gives the boy as she tries to heal him by gentleness and coy wooing. Lila's theatrics and flirtation with the child are bound up with her genuine effort to rescue him from his grief and enable him to function in the world.

Most reviewers have singled out "Bullies" as the most subtle and sustained performance in the book. Although the story is forty pages long and primarily depends on reported dialogue between Lila and a neighbor named Ida, Brodkey manages to create a sensitive account of a long conversation filled with the nuances of forbidden flirtation between the two women. Wiley marvels at their ability to balance their talk in such a way as never to step over the taboo line: "Both women are controlled--and full of signals--so many that I don't see how they can keep track of what they are doing in the world. . . . "

As one reviewer has noted about this collection, Brodkey can seem needlessly self-indulgent and downright dull to any reader still interested in the old-fashioned pleasures of plot. Indeed here style, rather than mere event, is the heart of the matter. However, as it always was with Oscar Wilde, that most famous proponent of the superiority of style over mundane everyday reality, with Brodkey one is never quite sure if one is in the presence of genius or the consummate con man.

OTHER MAJOR WORKS

LONG FICTION: *The Runaway Soul*, 1991; *Profane Friendship*, 1994.

NONFICTION: *Avedon: Photographs, 1947-1977*, 1978 (with Richard Avedon); *This Wild Darkness: The Story of My Death*, 1996; *Sea Battles on Dry Land: Essays*, 1999.

MISCELLANEOUS: *My Venice*, 1998.

BIBLIOGRAPHY

Alumit, Noel. "'First Love and Other Sorrows: Stories' (1958), Harold Brodkey." In *Fifty Gay and Lesbian Books Everybody Must Read*, edited by Richard Canning. New York: Alyson Books, 2009. Alumit analyzes Brodkey's short-story collection, which is included in this discussion of "essential titles in the canon of gay and lesbian literature."

Bawer, Bruce. "A Genius for Publicity." *The New Criterion* 7 (December, 1988): 58-69. Bawer comments on how well known Brodkey had become, even though his major work, *The Runaway Soul*, had not yet appeared.

Bidney, Martin. "A Song of Innocence and of Experience: Rewriting Blake in Brodkey's 'Piping Down the Valleys Wild.'" *Studies in Short Fiction* 31 (Spring, 1994): 237-245. Argues that Brodkey's story is a reformulation of William Blake's poem into a sophisticated study of innocence that is maintained because of experience. Maintains that, like Blake, Brodkey sees innocence as filled with tension that will be more fully revealed by experience.

_____. "An Unreliable Modern Mariner: Rewriting Coleridge in Harold Brodkey's 'The State of Grace.'" *Studies in Short Fiction* 31 (Winter, 1994): 47-55. Argues that Brodkey's story is a remaking of Samuel Taylor Coleridge's *The Rime of the Ancient Mariner*. Maintains the story is balanced between witty takeoffs of Mariner themes and the seriousness of the protagonist's dilemma. Examines how in the story the Mariner motifs deflate the protagonist's self-deception.

Brodkey, Harold. "Harold Brodkey: The Art of Fiction." Interview by James Linville. *Paris Review* 33, no. 121. (Winter, 1991): 50. An insightful interview about Brodkey's style and methods.

_____. "In the Space of a Sentence." Interview by James Linville. *Harper's Magazine* 285 (August, 1992): 33. Discusses the ways in which good writing creates a unique perception in the reader's mind regarding public settings.

Garrison, Deborah Gottlieb. "The True Lover." *The New Yorker* 72 (October 7, 1996): 85. Notes that Brodkey often wrote about the problems associated with love during and after the sexual revolution. Provides a biographical sketch leading up to Brodkey's announcement that he was infected with the virus that causes acquired acquired immunodeficiency syndrome (AIDS).

Howard, Richard. "Almost Classic." *The New Republic* 209 (July 12, 1993): 10-11. Claims that Brodkey's AIDS disclosure constituted a blatant attempt to mythologize himself. Calls the announcement a cruel and propagandistic assertion of artistic privilege, making death a matter of public relations. Insists that Brodkey's self-disclosure is obscene, for the cost of the publicity he seeks is paid for by millions of others who are suffering in dignity and silence.

Iannone, Carol. "The Brodkey Question." *Commentary* 87 (April, 1989): 58-61. Iannone questions why Brodkey has achieved the reputation that he has. She notes the lack of "artistic restraint" but credits him with sensitivity in his observations. She contends that he is "smashing the graven idol of aestheticism."

Kakutani, Michiko. "First-Person Stories, Tidy and Not." *The New York Times*, September 14, 1988, p. C25. Kakutani points to some unevenness in Brodkey's largely autobiographical stories.

Kermode, Frank. "I Am Only Equivocally Harold Brodkey." Review of *Stories in an Almost Classical Mode*, by Harold Brodkey. *The New York Times Book Review*, September 18, 1988, p. 3. In this review of *Stories in an Almost Classical Mode*, Kermode provides valuable observations about Brodkey's unique style.

Mano, D. Keith. "Harold Brodkey: The First Rave." *Esquire* 87 (January, 1977): 14-15. Mano is particularly compelling in his comments about Brodkey's "tyrannical use of punctuation," one of the writer's salient characteristics.

Shiras, Mary. "Accessible Dreams." *Commonweal* 67 (February 7, 1958): 493-494. This early assessment of Brodkey's *First Love and Other Sorrows* is essentially favorable, commenting on the exceptional details that the author presents.

Shulevitz, Judith. "Was It Good for You?" *The New York Times Book Review*, February 24, 2002, 23. Discusses how Brodkey's story "Innocence" and "Time of Her Time," by Norman Mailer, not only "rank among the writers' best" works but also "made history" because of the unprecedented specificity with which the writers describe an act of sexual intercourse.

Smith, Denitia. "The Genius: Harold Brodkey and His Great (Unpublished) Novel." *New York* 21 (September 19, 1991): 54-66. The fullest and most important article on Brodkey. Smith provides illustrations and uncovers countless details of Brodkey's life available in no other source.

Weiseltier, Leon. "A Revelation." Review of *Women and Angels*, by Harold Brodkey. *The New Republic* 192 (May 20, 1985): 30-33. In one of the few reviews of *Women and Angels*, Weiseltier praises the new story, "Angel," but calls the other two stories "platitudinous."

R. Baird Shuman
Updated by Charles E. May.

Jason Brown

Born: Hallowell, Maine; May 30, 1969

Principal short fiction

Driving the Heart, and Other Stories, 1999
Why the Devil Chose New England for His Work, 2007

Other literary forms

In 2007, Jason Brown told an interviewer that he was working on a novel about a remote fishing island off the Maine and Canadian coasts and taking notes on another novel entitled *The Island of the Ipswich Sparrow* about an island off Nova Scotia.

Achievements

Jason Brown's story "Driving the Heart" won a fiction prize from *The Mississippi Review* and was chosen for the 1996 *Best American Short Stories*. In 1997, he won a Wallace Stegner Fellowship at Stanford University.

Biography

Jason Brown was born in a small town in Maine, on May 30, 1969. Because of his dyslexia, Brown was classified as a slow learner in grade school, and he began drinking alcohol when he was twelve. When his mother suffered from depression and his parents were going through a divorce, he was sent to a boarding school at age fifteen. However, his continued drinking got him expelled, and he returned to Portland, Maine, where his parents lived, and enrolled in Deering High School.

After writing a one-act play that won a regional contest, Brown was accepted at Bowdoin College, because, as he has said, Bowdoin did not require scores from the Scholastic Aptitude Test (SAT). Once he entered college, Brown decided to stop drinking and to start working hard at his writing. Because Bowdoin did not have a creative-writing program, he took an independent study course in writing under Frank Burroughs, who taught medieval English literature. After graduation, Brown continued to meet with Burroughs, who encouraged Brown in his work. He attended Alcoholics Anonymous regularly and worked at odd jobs, including a stint driving a delivery van transporting body parts to hospitals, on which he based the title story of his first book, "Driving the Heart."

After college, Brown sent several stories to literary journals, getting his first break when *Georgia Review* accepted and published "Animal Stories." Based on this success, he was accepted into the M.F.A. program at Cornell University, where he studied under novelist Alison Lurie. Two of his stories were published in the collection *Twenty-five and Under*, and "Driving the Heart" won a *Mississippi Review* fiction prize and a *Best American Short Story* award for 1996. In 1997, he was a Wallace Stegner Fellow at Stanford University and later was named Jones Lecturer in Fiction in Stanford's English Department.

In 2004, Brown accepted a position teaching creative writing in the English Department at the University of Arizona in Tucson, where he says he loves the Hispanic culture. His wife, of Hispanic ancestry from New Mexico, grew up the Tucson area from the time she was eight years old. Brown, who is working on a novel based in the Portland, Maine, area, has said: "When you go and live in places different from where you're from, it throws your background into sharp relief. It also allows you to see more clearly where you're coming from as a writer."

ANALYSIS

A debut collection of short stories by a young male author who has attended an M.F.A. program is apt to show a schism between the subject matter and the technique. Jason Brown's first collection, *Driving the Heart, and Other Stories*, is filled primarily with what

might be called "wild young man stories"--doing and detoxing from drugs, driving fast cars and having sex, dealing with dysfunctional or divorced parents, and trying to come to terms with psychic imbalance. However, for all this gritty realism, there is an academic quality about the style of Brown's early stories, all tightly controlled by parallel symbolic actions and ironic-comic situations. This quality is apparent immediately in the self-consciously catchy opening lines: "When my mother removed her shirt in front of third-period honors English, I was in the classroom next door taking a test"; "Someone broke into our house one afternoon and glued all my mother's shoes to the floor of the closet"; "She was having the best game of her life the day our father fell from the sky." There are imitative echoes of other contemporary young male writers in these stories: Denis Johnson's druggy ambulance-drivers, David Leavitt's men-with-their-mothers, Christopher Tilghman's focus on the family.

However, Brown's second collection, *Why the Devil Chose New England for His Work*, pushes beyond such predictability. Set in northern Maine, the stories are linked, but not self-consciously so, as they are in some "novel-in-stories" collections. They are all independent entities, united primarily by characters haunted by the past and tormented by the imagination. Brown's characters in this book are more varied and their backgrounds are more complex than in his first collection, and his stories have more of the ragged feel of reality and less of the formal control of the well-schooled student. Many of the characters are plagued by guilt for past misdeeds, haunted--as the title of the collection suggests--by something akin to a Puritan sense of original sin. Many others are precise evocations of two occupations characteristic of the coast of Maine: logging and seafaring. In "River Runner," for example, a man who runs logs is plagued by guilt for once beating his pregnant wife and thus causing the death of his unborn child. He lives in a haunted fantasy of his wife being alive and still pregnant. In "Afternoon of the Sassanoa," a young boy accompanies his father on a sailing journey from an island where his family is vacationing to the mainland, but the father neglects the care an experienced seaman exercises with disastrous results.

One of the significant signs of Brown's developing maturity as a writer is his shift of the locale of his stories away from the self-indulgent mind of his young male characters in *Driving the Heart* to his sympathetic identification with a variety of characters haunted by their individual demons in the fully realized world of the town of Vaughn, Maine, in *Why the Devil Chose New England for His Work.*

"DRIVING THE HEART"

Brown said in the contributors' notes to the 1996 edition of *Best American Short Stories* that he wrote the title story of his first collection when he was twenty-two, living in a condemned building with no heat and working the night shift for a company called Bits and Pieces Delivery, which delivered, among other things, body parts. In obvious reference to the name of the company he worked for, Brown said that he believes the story is about trying to hold it all together, adding, "I think writing the story helped me hold it together."

Told in first person, the story recounts one episode in the life of two men who deliver body parts to hospitals. On this particular night they are delivering a heart for a woman about to die from some disease or accident, stopping every hour at designated places to call the hospital to make sure the woman is still alive. The narrator, who has had his share of troubles in the past--arrested for armed robbery and for driving under the influence and assaulting a police officer--is the more experienced of the two men. His aide, Dale, who is learning the job, does not take his work as seriously as the narrator does. In much of the story, the narrator, who says he has seen some strange things, tells anecdotes about his own experiences. Believing his greatest accomplishment is that he can be both obsessed and relaxed at the same time, he lives his life according to a number of rules: do not have a telephone, do not own too many things, live on the first floor. His most important rule--the one that dominates the story--is: when in doubt, drive on.

At one of the stops to call the hospital, while Dale is in a variety store, two men drive up and point a shotgun at the narrator, demanding money. When he tells them he has none, they drive away, and Dale returns, saying he cannot get through to the hospital. When they reach the hospital, they are told they are too late; the narrator

contemplates that the hardest part of the job is trying to explain to Dale how they have driven all this way "with a heart for which, in the end, there is no life." Basically, "Driving the Heart" is a story about time, about literally running for one's life, not only for the life of the woman awaiting a heart but also for the life of the narrator, who finds his job gives him a sense of significant purpose. Believing that he has cared deeply about the wrong things, the narrator tries to find some way to rescue himself by rescuing others. The story is a carefully organized structure of ironic, comic-pathetic situations about a man who is racing calmly against someone else's diminishing time.

"ANIMAL STORIES"

This is Brown's first published story, which appeared in *Georgia Review* and was chosen for *Twenty-five and Under/Fiction*, a book of fifteen stories by American writers twenty-five years old and younger. This first-person story is recounted by a young man who admits that he is prone to bursts of self-destructiveness and lapses in concentration, qualities he gets from his mother, who he learns has a brain tumor, noting, "Any man's mother is a source of grief until she dies." The narrator, who has never been successful with work or women, says his mother's tumor has got him to thinking about what's important in life.

Since she has been in the hospital, the mother also has been thinking about what's important and has decided to write a book on how animals remember. The narrator talks about his childhood dyslexia and how he finally stopped caring about improving his life. The narrator's tone, when he tells about his mother's eccentric behavior and his own erratic conduct, is usually self-effacing and comic. He says his mother is in a flowering of her life because her own past has been replaced by the most pleasant memories from other people's lives, concluding that his own story is about what "happens to sadness after it grows weary and forgets itself."

"SHE"

One of the most complex stories in *Why the Devil Chose New England for His Work* is "She," about a beauty who has bloomed too early and who falls in love with a junior high school tough sought after by older girls. When the two disappear for a time, their fellow students and the rest of the town fantasize about their relationship to such an extent that they become mysterious iconic characters, like the famous child lovers Romeo and Juliet, who come to represent the beginnings of the complex link between love and sex. The narrator, a classmate of the two, says anything he and his friends had called love was like a mockery in the face of the couple's sudden "flight from reason." When one of the mothers says they are too young, she is thinking about their bodies, but she growls the word "love . . . as if the creature had risen from her dreams."

In this highly stylized, almost mythic, story, when the young couple experience their first passionate embrace in the back seat of a car, they are not quite sure what has happened. However, the girl knows that when she wakes up the next morning and looks at him sleeping with his mouth open that she is no longer in love with him and never would be. The story ends with a chase sequence, reminiscent of film scenes of angry villagers chasing a monster. When a shotgun goes off accidentally, the girl, hearing the shot, thinks the boy has been killed and imagines that in court she will absolve everyone but herself. She thinks she was a fool when she said she did not love him and believes she has lost everything. In its combination of realism and myth, the story is an ambitious attempt to explore the adolescent nature of romantic love, as the two young lovers becomes projections of the fantasies of the community.

"TREES"

Less complex, but equally as subtle, is the story "Trees," about a widow named Lucy, who tries to hold on to a stand of trees that she associates with her dead husband. She is visited weekly by her nephew Robbie, a young man who constantly tries to convince her to allow him to thin out the trees while they are still worth money to her. Since Lucy is childless, the trees will be inherited by Robbie when she dies. However, Robbie is engaged to an impatient young woman and does not want to wait. He ignores Lucy's protests and proceeds

as if she agrees with him, arriving one morning with a friend and chain saws. Lucy panics, but she does not know what to do or where to get help. She visits an old lover, who lives in a broken-down house with half the windows boarded over and the sink filled with tin cans and filthy dishes. At the end of the story, she goes down to the woods and finds that all but a few thin birches and maples have been cut down; she knows it will take a lifetime for them to grow back. She has always known the nephew would cut them down, but she thinks it seems such a little thing to ask that he would wait until she is gone. Evoking a sense of helplessness, lack of communication, and loss, the story is typical of Brown's work at its best.

BIBLIOGRAPHY

Kellogg, Carolyn. "Down Town." *Los Angeles Times*, December 23, 2007, p. 7. In this important review of *Why the Devil Chose New England for His Work*, Kellogg says the stories are characterized by a current of duty and betrayal, as if the characters were born into debts, like a Puritan sense of original sin that they do not fully understand. She calls the book "beautiful" and "devastating."

Lannin, Joanne. "Message in a Bottle for Jason Brown." *Portland Press Herald*, May 30, 1999, p. 1E. Informative biographical sketch in Brown's hometown newspaper, which discusses his early problems with alcohol, his undergraduate and graduate training in writing, and his emergence as a well-reviewed and highly praised writer of short fiction.

Mundow, Anna. "Dissecting New England's Long Shadows." *The Boston Globe*, November 18, 2007, p. E7. Interview with Brown in which he talks about the linked stories in *Why the Devil Chose New England for His Work*, explains the source of the book's title from the works of New England preacher Cotton Mather, and discusses the personal experiences that gave rise to several of the stories.

Charles E. May

LARRY BROWN

Born: Oxford, Mississippi; July 9, 1951
Died: Near Oxford, Mississippi; November 24, 2004

PRINCIPAL SHORT FICTION

Facing the Music, 1988
Big Bad Love, 1990

OTHER LITERARY FORMS

Larry Brown published five novels in his lifetime: *Dirty Work* (1989), *Joe* (1991), *Father and Son* (1996), *Billy Ray's Farm* (1997), *Fay* (2000), and *The Rabbit Factory* (2003); *A Miracle of Catfish: A Novel in Progress* (2007) was published three years after his death. Brown adapted *Dirty Work* for the prestigious *American Playhouse* series aired by the Public Broadcasting Service. He also wrote the nonfiction books *On Fire* (1994), a collection of autobiographical essays from his days as a firefighter in Oxford, Mississippi, and *Coyotes and Canaries: Characters Who Made the West Wild and Wonderful!* (2002).

ACHIEVEMENTS

In 1990, Larry Brown received the Award for Literature from the Mississippi Institute of Arts and Letters for his story "Facing the Music." Brown has had stories anthologized in *The Best American Short Stories* in 1989 and 1992. He was the first two-time winner of the Southern Book Critics' Circle award for fiction, receiving the honor in 1992 for *Joe* and in 1997 for *Father and Son*; *Joe* also was selected by the American Library Association as one of the twelve best fiction books of 1991. In 2000, the State of Mississippi granted Brown the Governor's Award for Excellence in the Arts.

BIOGRAPHY

Born in Oxford, Mississippi, on July 9, 1951, to Knox and Leona (Barlow) Brown, William Larry

Brown spent most of his life in that area. Brown was a Marine from 1970 until 1972 during the Vietnam conflict, but he remained stateside. On August 17, 1974, he married Mary Annie Coleman, and they had two sons, Billy Ray and Shane, and one daughter, LeAnne.

Brown did not attend college until 1982, when he took a class in creative writing at the University of Mississippi (Ole Miss) after years of writing convinced him that he still needed to find his voice. Author Ellen Douglas at Ole Miss more fully introduced him to the world of literature and simultaneously helped him forge that voice. In 1982, Brown's first short story was published in *Easyriders*, a magazine for motorcyclists, but his short story "Facing the Music," published in 1987 in *The Mississippi Review*, captured the attention of Algonquin Books editor Shannon Ravenel and won national acclaim.

From the time he left the Marines, Brown held a variety of jobs, from his first job with a stove company to his final and most significant job as a firefighter with the Oxford Fire Department, from which he retired as captain in 1990 in order to spend all his energy on his writing. Brown died at his home near Oxford, Mississippi on November 24, 2004.

ANALYSIS

When Algonquin Books was first marketing Larry Brown, it used his status as fireman-turned-writer to the firm's advantage, and, indeed, Brown's educational background is not the one usually associated with a writer. Brown's self-education enabled him to stay true to himself and his art and follow his inclinations wherever they led him. Where they led him is into the same realm to which they led the major writer William Faulkner, who also came from Oxford, Mississippi, and into those "eternal verities of the human heart" of which Faulkner spoke so eloquently and which any enduring artist must plumb. Indeed, Brown denied the "Faulknerian" influence on his work, and it is not there in any but a superficial way. In an interview with *Publishers Weekly*, Brown, though flattered by the comparison with Faulkner, quite accurately pinpointed one of the major ways in which his work departs from Faulkner's when he said that Faulkner "wrote about so much that went back before his time. I don't get into that. I write about the here and now." In fact, stylistically, Brown is far afield from Faulkner and reads much more like minimalist writer Raymond Carver, whose influence Brown readily acknowledges.

Sometimes difficult to pigeonhole--ranging as they do from the realism of "Facing the Music" to the humor of "Waiting for the Ladies" to the absurdist satire of "Discipline"--Brown's stories nonetheless are of a piece when it comes to their clearheadedness and lack of sentimentality. Often criticized as bleak and violent, they mirror the isolation and lack of communication that characterize modern society. Despite the dark vision they frequently portray, Brown's works also show the possibility of redemption and hope. As he said in an interview in *The Southern Quarterly*, his "fiction is about people surviving, about people proceeding out from calamity."

FACING THE MUSIC

In an essay published in *Publishing Research Quarterly* and written with Brown and others, Shannon Ravenel notes that *Facing the Music*, Brown's first book-length publication, was a departure for the publishing company, as it was a collection of short stories rather than a novel. The strength of the title story alone, however, allowed the editors to ignore "conventional wisdom." Too harsh and biting to have been accepted by either *The New Yorker* or *Esquire*, the unconventional stories in the collection are varied, gritty, and, to use one of the terms most commonly associated with Brown's work, "honest." Spanning a number of voices--from that of an isolated husband refusing to deal with his wife's mastectomy in "Facing the Music" to that of a young, African American, alcoholic mother in "Kubuku Rides (This Is It)" to that of Mr. Parker, jobless and friendless after his wife has him kill their dog in "Old Frank and Jesus" to that of a cynical (former) lover in "The End of Romance"--the stories all deal ultimately with what Brown, in an interview in *The Chattahoochee Review*, calls "the truths of the human heart."

The most poignant story of the collection, "Facing the Music" is the interior monologue of a husband who still loves his wife after her mastectomy yet detaches himself from her, choosing rather to watch old films or even commit adultery rather than admit that he, too, has been hurt by her cancer. In the end, as she reaches for him in the dark, he recalls their honeymoon, the sweetness of their love for each other as he realizes, "your first love is your best love, that you'll never find any better." The story stops short of promising an easy healing of their relationship. The love for and of her family also encompasses but is unable to heal Kubuku in "Kubuku Rides (This Is It)." Still recovering from a drunk-driving accident, Kubuku rides into the dark at the end of the story to procure more alcohol as her husband turns out the porch light, which had always symbolically shone for her return. Pain is present throughout the collection, though frequently peppered with cynicism.

In "Samaritans" the narrator, a young, "white trash" woman, emerges from a Rambler filled with kids and her mother, uses a tale of woe to weasel thirty dollars from a man whose wife has left him, and then spends it so she and her mother can get drunk. "Boy you a dumb sumbitch," her son tells her at the end of the story. "Leaving Town" presents a split narrative, focusing on an unhappily married carpenter and an older divorcée, who almost make a connection but are unable to because of her fears. "The End of Romance," the final story in the collection, is the most violent and darkest of all. In the midst of their breakup, the narrator and his girlfriend drive up to a convenience store and witness a shooting. When he returns to his girlfriend, who is waiting in the convertible outside, she screeches, distraught, "I WOULDN'T LEAVE YOU NOW FOR NOTHIN," as the wounded man flops on their car. She proceeds to tell him how they can heal their relationship ("maybe we should watch more TV together"), when the cops arrive and prepare to fire at the shooter. The narrator then calmly raises his hands, points to her, and says, "She did it."

BIG BAD LOVE

The three parts of *Big Bad Love* are linked by stories about writers, "The Apprentice," "Discipline," and *Ninety-two Days*. "The Apprentice" relates the story of a husband and wife who are almost driven apart by her need to write. His acceptance of her compulsion and his deep love for her keep their marriage intact. The satire "Discipline," quite different from Brown's other stories, is the mock-trial of a plagiarist, or at best, a literary imitator. Actually a novella, *Ninety-two Days* chronicles the stops and starts of the narrator as he attempts to write and publish and live something of a life in the meantime.

The other stories in the collection are more about the hits and misses of living itself. The narrator in "Big Bad Love" leaves his house to go drinking in order to avoid burying his dead dog, spends his time at the bar contemplating the fact that he is not sexually endowed enough to satisfy his wife, and returns to find she has left with a man who "has the equipment to take care" of her problem. Though he sees this as a possible new beginning, the loneliness sets in. "Old Soldiers" is a fond look at old soldiers who need one another to understand the horrors they have lived through, and "Sleep" traces the insomnia of an older couple who keep each other up at night with their fears. Perhaps the most interesting of the stories in the collection, "Waiting for the Ladies," highlights, in a rather unexpected manner, the need for connection and communication. When the narrator's wife tells her husband that someone exposed himself to her at the dumpster, he is incensed and goes to investigate the situation. Making a mental picture of the exhibitionist (fiftyish, living with his mother, on welfare, impotent), the narrator fails to note the similarity to himself, as he has quit his job and is suspicious of his wife's long lunches with her boss. After tracking down the exhibitionist, who is at home with his mother, the narrator enters, gun under his arm, and then sits down with the terrified mother and son only to tell them "what my life then was like."

OTHER MAJOR WORKS

LONG FICTION: *Dirty Work*, 1989; *Joe*, 1991; *Father and Son*, 1996; *Billy Ray's Farm*, 1997; *Fay*, 2000; *The Rabbit Factory*, 2003; *A Miracle of Catfish: A Novel in Progress*, 2007.

NONFICTION: *On Fire*, 1994; *Coyotes and Canaries: Characters Who Made the West Wild and Wonderful!*, 2002; *Conversations with Larry Brown*, 2007 (Jay Watson, editor).

BIBLIOGRAPHY

Applebome, Peter. "Larry Brown's Long and Rough Road to Becoming a Writer." *The New York Times*, March 5, 1990, p. C11. Tracing what Barry Hannah called Brown's "miracle" in which "he became his own genius," the article examines Brown's apprenticeship, his numerous rejections, and the amazing determination that led him to publication and success.

Bass, Rick. "Larry Brown: A Tribute." Southern Review44, no. 1 (Winter, 2008): 52-61. Bass, himself a writer, offers a tribute to his friend Brown. Bass focuses on Brown's novels, which he describes as "novels of manners" expressing deeply moral values and describing actions that have profound consequences.

Brown, Larry. *Conversations with Larry Brown*. Edited by Jay Watson. Jackson: University Press of Mississippi, 2007. Compilation of interviews that Brown conducted between 1988 and 2004. Includes an interview with Kay Bonetti, originally published in *Missouri Review*, in which Brown discusses his background, the writers who influenced him, his belief that writing is an acquired skill, and the themes and motifs in his works. An interview with Susan Ketchin, originally published in *The Southern Quarterly*, focuses on his short-story collection *Facing the Music*, emphasizing the philosophical underpinning of his writings. In "Larry Brown: The Former Firefighter Talks About His Long Apprentice as a Writer," an interview conducted by Bob Summer for *Publishers Weekly*, Brown discusses his views of writing and his literary influences, denying much, if any, similarity to William Faulkner.

_____. "Interview with Larry Brown: Breadloaf '92." Interview by Dorie LaRue. *The Chattahoochee Review* 13 (Spring, 1993): 39-56. Brown traces his career as a writer to his love of reading as a child. Noting Homer and Mark Twain as early influences, he cites Raymond Carver, Lewis Nordan, and Paul MacCormac as current favorites. He discusses the stories in *Big Bad Love* in some detail, mentioning that he gave many of the characters his initials and, more significantly, that he attempted to make his characters memorable and potentially redeemable.

Cash, Jean W., and Keith Perry, eds. *Larry Brown and the Blue-Collar South*. Jackson: University Press of Mississippi, 2008. Collection of essays analyzing all Brown's novels and short stories, as well as providing a general assessment of his works. Two essays pertain directly to his short fiction: *"Facing the Music*: What's Wrong with All Those Happy Endings," by Darlin' Neal, and "Saving Them from Their Lives: Storytelling and Self-Fulfillment in *Big Bad Love*."

Farmer, Joy A. "The Sound and the Fury of Larry Brown's 'Waiting for the Ladies.'" *Studies in Short Fiction* 29 (Summer, 1992): 315-322. Examining the influence of structure and theme of Faulkner's *The Sound and the Fury* (1929), Farmer sees a correspondence between "N" in Brown's "Waiting for the Ladies" and the three Compson males of Faulkner's novel. Farmer makes her case that this story is a "reworking" of the novel, albeit a comic one.

Gelfant, Blanche H., ed. *The Columbia Companion to the Twentieth-Century American Short Story*. New York: Columbia University Press, 2000. Includes a chapter in which Brown's short stories are analyzed.

Lyons, Paul. "Larry Brown's *Joe* and the Uses and Abuses of the 'Region' Concept." *Studies in American Fiction* 25 (Spring, 1997): 101-124. Although this essay deals with a novel, its placement of Brown's writing in a regional, cultural context is highly informative and also applicable to his short fiction.

Jaquelyn W. Walsh

BLISS BROYARD

Born: Greenwich, Connecticut; September 5, 1966

PRINCIPAL SHORT FICTION
My Father, Dancing: Stories, 1999

OTHER LITERARY FORMS

In addition to her collection of short stories, Bliss Broyard has written "My Father's Daughter," an essay appearing in *The Art of the Essay* (1999). In 2007, she published *One Drop: My Father's Hidden Life, a Story of Race and Family Secrets*, a chronicle of her father, writer and literary critic Anatole Broyard's, African ancestry. She traveled throughout the country to conduct research and interview her relatives for this book, and in 2001, she organized a family reunion in New Orleans that brought together her black and white relatives for the first time.

Broyard has also published essays and reviews in *The New York Times*, *The Washington Post*, and other periodicals. She was a producer and writer for "The Real World," a television series that airs on Music Television (MTV).

ACHIEVEMENTS

My Father, Dancing: Stories was a *New York Times* Notable Book of 1999 and was listed as a *Boston Globe* Best Book of 1999. *One Drop* was designated a Best Book of the Year by the *Chicago Tribune*, was selected as the Humanist Book of the Year by the Louisiana Endowment for the Humanities, and was a finalist for numerous prizes. Her short story "Mr. Sweetly Indecent" was chosen for *The Best American Short Stories 1998*. Broyard's work has also been included in the 1994 edition of *The Pushcart Prize*.

BIOGRAPHY

Bliss Broyard's father, the late Anatole Broyard, was an author and longtime literary critic and book review editor for *The New York Times*. Anatole Broyard exerted a profound influence on his daughter, and many of the stories in her first collection were inspired by her relationship with him.

An imaginative child and a voracious reader, who had been writing poems and stories for years, Bliss Broyard did not seriously consider becoming a writer herself until around the time her father was diagnosed with terminal prostate cancer. A friend from the elder Broyard's days in the Greenwich Village neighborhood of New York City came to visit him in the hospital and to pay an old debt, which was divided between Broyard's two children. With her share of the money ($250), Bliss Broyard enrolled in a fiction writing course at Harvard University. She eventually earned a master of fine arts in fiction writing from the University of Virginia, from which she received a fellowship and where she subsequently taught. In 1996, Broyard settled in Brooklyn, New York.

ANALYSIS

Bliss Broyard's first short-story collection, *My Father, Dancing: Stories*, generally garnered high praise as an auspicious debut. She was especially commended for her depiction of a young woman's coming-of-age and for her cool, economical style. Most important is her theme of a father's effect on a growing daughter, who sees him as the first and possibly the most important man, a theme particularly evident in the title story "My Father, Dancing," which was based on Broyard's thoughts and life. Some of the other father-daughter stories also have their sources in Broyard's own life, including her feelings as her father lay dying in the hospital.

The voice and the perspective of each story are those of a young woman, and whether named Lily, Kate, Pilar, or Lucy, these characters are essentially the same young woman with the same perspective. In addition, their situations, while sometimes comical, also provoke considerable apprehension. Furthermore, all the fathers in this collection share a close kinship--if not always famous, they are consistently handsome, suave, and overwhelming. Many of the stories feature fathers whose roguish, seductive sexuality has a powerful effect on their impressionable daughters. The bond between these often slick and breezy fathers and their adoring daughters is depicted in these stories as both a blessing and a curse, so that it is difficult to decide whether such a bond is an advantage or a catastrophe.

Many of her stories also depict the problems Broyard's young women have with men their own age, who often rate a poor second compared to the charming fathers of the previous generation. The psychological issues involving fathers and lovers are compounded by the difficulties involved in coming-of-age in a social world marked by permissive sexuality, divorce, blended families, and infidelity.

MY FATHER, DANCING

In *My Father, Dancing*, five of the eight stories concern a daughter's intense relationship with an adored, charming, and successful father. In the title story, a young woman named Kate reviews her life with her father as he lies dying from cancer. Central to these

Bliss Broyard (Getty Images)

memories is her father's love of dancing with her to popular songs of the day at home or in clubs, even in preference to his dancer-wife, Kate's mother. There is considerable apprehension and genuine grief over the impending loss of her father, but when Kate returns to her family living room after her father dies and has a vision of her father as he was the first time he ever danced with her, when she was but a toddler, she realizes that their intense bond has, in an almost magical way, survived his death.

Kate's father is the first in a series of charismatic fathers in this collection. In the second story, "Mr. Sweetly Indecent," however, the charming father is associated with out-of-bounds sexual behavior. In this story, the daughter, while leaving a sexual liaison with a virtual stranger, spies her father kissing a woman with whom he has obviously also spent the night. The parallels between their behavior disturb her, but she also sees that her father, as a married family man, is the more culpable. Her father breezily alleviates his daughter's sense of betrayal, assuring her that this adulterous incident is superficial and will never endanger the love he has for her mother. His daughter is less mollified by these assurances than by her knowledge of the continued, mysterious bond between her mother and father, in which her mother appears as the stronger and wiser figure. However, she has also discerned a talent for deception in her womanizing father and is struck by the fact that she herself evinces promiscuous tendencies.

A beloved father also appears in "At the Bottom of the Lake" as the long-expected guest of a young woman named Lucy who has invited him to stay with her at the family cabin on a lake. When her father finally returns to the cabin for a visit accompanied by his alcoholic second wife Victoria, Lucy's hopes of a family reunion that would heal the pain of her parents' devastating divorce are dashed. The weekend is cut short by a quarrel between Lucy and the temperamental Victoria, but it is Victoria who wisely warns Lucy that her behavior is alienating her patient fiancé Sam. Although Lucy comes to realize she cannot bring back the past, her affection for the cabin indicates her longing for the kind of love and family life she enjoyed when she was her father's adored little girl.

Fathers are also central to the plot of "The Trouble with Mr. Leopold." Here, an insecure schoolgirl named Celia asks her talented and literary father to help her write one of her papers. Her suburban prep school's headmaster, detecting the deception, promptly gives her a low grade. The rivalry between the headmaster, Mr. Leopold, and Celia's rather pompous father, both of whom come from similar working-class backgrounds in Brooklyn, and both of whom have risen in the world, seems to take precedence over Celia's own needs. Inappropriate sexuality, a dominant theme in this collection, also surfaces in this story in the person of Mr. Leopold, whose interest in his female students concentrates as much on their bodies as on their minds.

Two other stories feature a young girl's attachment not to her father but to an older and more successful man. In "Loose Talk," a girl named Pilar finds that her relationship with her devoted boyfriend is compromised by her infatuation with a famous musician, a magical, larger-than-life figure. In "Ugliest Faces," a college student named Bridget is in a relationship with one of her former teachers, who is eight years older than she is. His rival is Spike, a drunken fraternity boy whom Pilar accidentally runs down with her automobile, and who insists that Pilar compensate him for his injuries through sexual favors. Fearful of losing her pride of place with her older lover, Pilar finds herself building an ugly, secret life centering on the thuggish Spike and the debt she owes him.

A young girl's dissatisfaction with her peers is also a subject of the last two stories, "A Day in the Country" and "Snowed In," which both feature a young girl named Lily. In "A Day in the Country," the barely teenage Lily is pressured by her best friend into an unwelcome sexual situation with a boy her own age. While the boy in question possesses little charm, Lily's father, a well-known conductor, effortlessly draws women to him, including a neighboring mother and daughter, as well as Lily's friend Kelly. Lily's father also seems to be casually seducing a woman who has arrived as the date of one of his house guests. "Snowed In," the last story, is once again set in Connecticut and also features Lily, who is now a young woman. Trapped by a snowstorm in an upscale suburban house with a party of her friends, Lily also seems trapped in a peer culture dominated by the preferences of the boys in the house for alcohol and a pornographic film they find in the video collection of the parents who own the house. Lily is simultaneously repelled and attracted by the pornography, which leads to a joyless sexual episode with one of the boys, Bobby Callahan. Whether it is the insensitive Bobby, or the more devoted but dull boyfriends of other stories, these boys are devoid of the swashbuckling charm of the fathers of the previous generation. Whereas the first and title stories in the collection concern the exciting bond between a magical father and his captivated daughter, the final story, by way of contrast, gives the reader a portrait of a young girl utterly disappointed with the romantic prospects offered to her by the boys of her own generation.

OTHER MAJOR WORKS

NONFICTION: *One Drop: My Father's Hidden Life, a Story of Race and Family Secrets*, 2007.

BIBLIOGRAPHY

Bellafonte, Gina. "Windows into Life." *Time*, August 2, 1999, 91. This review of collections by four emerging short-story writers includes *My Father, Dancing*. Describes Broyard's writing as "spare and lovely" and praises her for elegantly exploring the bond between father and daughter.

Goodman, Allegra. "I Remember Papa." *The New York Times Book Review*, August 15, 1999, 7. Goodman's review of *My Father, Dancing* praises the collection for its accurate documentation of the trials of girlhood and especially for the distinctive examination of fathers and daughters.

Grossinger, Harvey. "Bliss Broyard Debuts with Heartfelt Stories." Review of *My Father, Dancing*, by Bliss Broyard. *Houston Chronicle*, October 24, 1999, p. 14. Praises the stories as well-crafted and tautly paced; singles out the father-daughter stories as most compelling. Especially lauds the title story as the product of an overflow of genuine sorrow and loss but praises all the stories as "unaffected and heartfelt." Provides an especially perceptive discussion of "The Trouble with Mr. Leopold" and "Loose Talk."

.Lehmann-Haupt, Christopher. "Flawed Fathers, Daughters Who Love and Learn." Review of *My Father, Dancing*, by Bliss Broyard. *The New York Times*, July 29, 1999, p. E9. Describes the book as a sharply observed collection of stories and praises Broyard's prose as having considerable power. However, Lehmann-Haupt faults Broyard's dialogue as too stiff and lacking in variety. Also comments on the theme of the seductive and overwhelming father.

Lenhard, Elizabeth. "Bloodlines, Not Plot Lines Carry Weight in 'Dancing'."*Atlanta Journal-Constitution*, August 8, 1999, p. L11. Describes *My Father, Dancing* as awkward and unsophisticated and is critical of Broyard's dependence on her father both as subject and as an entree to the literary world. Lenhard notes what she describes as the distasteful "overindulged Electra complex" in many of the stories but does praise Broyard for occasionally creating a lovely episode.

Linfield, Susie. "Stories of Father Obsession and Betrayal." Review of *My Father, Dancing*, by Bliss Broyard. *Los Angeles Times*, August 26, 1999, p. 5. Perceptively notes that these stories are essentially about one girl with one story to tell. Describes the young women narrators as obsessed with their fathers and as disturbingly passive. Argues that despite their many virtues, the stories suffer from a narrowness of vision.

Malkin, Marc S. "Ignorance Is Bliss."*New York* 36, no. 21 (June 23, 2002): 9. Reports on the research that Broyard was conducting for her second book, *One Drop*, in which she explored her family's African American heritage. Broyard discusses this book and how she was inspired to write it by her father, literary critic Anatole Broyard.

Schillinger, Lizza. "Daughters and Rebels." Review of *My Father, Dancing*, by Bliss Broyard. *The Washington Post*, August 15, 1999, p. 5. Describes the book as a coming-of-age collection that will particularly appeal to like-minded women. Discusses the dominant role of the father-daughter relationship in the stories, but notes that the young heroines have a worrisome combination of sexual precocity and emotional fragility. Praises the final story, "Snowed

In," as the best of the collection because it is not dominated by a father figure and instead perceptively portrays a group of world-weary but emotionally vulnerable children of wealthy suburbanites who are going bad.

Margaret Boe Birns

PEARL S. BUCK

Born: Hillsboro, West Virginia; June 26, 1892
Died: Danby, Vermont; March 6, 1973
Also known as: Pearl Sydenstricker, Pearl Comfort Sydenstricker, John Sedges, Sai Zhenzhu

PRINCIPAL SHORT FICTION

The First Wife, and Other Stories, 1933
Today and Forever, 1941
Twenty-seven Stories, 1943
Far and Near, Stories of Japan, China, and America, 1947
American Triptych, 1958
Hearts Come Home, and Other Stories, 1962
The Good Deed, and Other Stories, 1969
Once upon a Christmas, 1972
East and West, 1975
Secrets of the Heart, 1976
The Lovers, and Other Stories, 1977
The Woman Who Was Changed, and Other Stories, 1979

OTHER LITERARY FORMS

Pearl S. Buck's reputation rests primarily on her novels about China, most notably *The Good Earth* (1931), and on her biographical and autobiographical writings. In awarding her the Nobel Prize in Literature in 1938, the selection committee singled out for special praise *The Exile* (1936) and *Fighting Angel: Portrait of a Soul* (1936), her biographies of her missionary parents. She also wrote a number of essays, plays, and children's books and translated a classic Chinese novel.

ACHIEVEMENTS

Pearl S. Buck's writings have indelibly shaped many Western readers' images of the Far East and especially of China, where she spent the first half of her life. Her portrayal of the life of the Chinese peasants in *The Good Earth* won her the Pulitzer Prize in 1932 and was a major factor in making her the first American woman to receive the Nobel Prize in Literature. Buck's best work provides a moving, realistic portrayal of her characters in their struggles to survive in the midst of natural disasters and social turmoil. Even when her fiction is slick and sentimental, she provides her readers with provocative themes to consider. In both her books and her extensive humanitarian activities, her major concern was to improve understanding among those of different sexes, ages, races, and nationalities.

BIOGRAPHY

Pearl Sydenstricker spent her childhood and young adult years in China with her missionary parents, where she attended mission schools and studied with a Confucian tutor. Then she attended Randolph-Macon Woman's College in Virginia before returning to China, where she married John Lossing Buck, an American agricultural expert. She received her M.A. in English literature from Cornell in 1926, and she soon began publishing extensively. She divorced John Lossing Buck in 1935 and later that same year married Richard J. Walsh, president of the John Day publishing firm. Elected to the National Institute of Arts and Letters in 1936, she won the Nobel Prize in 1938. She founded the East and West Association, an organization working toward greater international understanding, and the Pearl Buck Foundation, an agency supporting homeless Amerasian children throughout Asia. Proceeds from her publications continued to fund the agency. Buck died from lung cancer on March 6, 1973. She had published more than one hundred works and had received hundreds of humanitarian awards.

ANALYSIS

Pearl S. Buck's best-known stories were typically published first in large circulation magazines, then included in collections of her short fiction. "The Enemy," "Hearts Come Home," and "The Good Deed" are examples reflecting Buck's international themes. By depicting characters in exotic or potentially threatening surroundings, Buck heightens cultural contrasts and emphasizes common human characteristics. The outsiders she presents may meet a Good Samaritan figure, fall in love and marry, or achieve greater understanding of others and themselves as Buck foregrounds the power of human beings, however weak and short-sighted they may be, to transform one another intellectually and emotionally.

In her short fiction, as in her novel *The Good Earth*, universal human experiences dominate: love, marriage, birth of children, death of loved ones, threats of natural disaster, and the encroachment of new ways on old culture that creates major conflicts. The stories, however, often lack the realism of the novels, and occasionally they become sentimental and didactic. Still, their color and simplicity of style enabled Buck to succeed in reaching the wide audience she felt literature should serve.

"THE ENEMY"

In "The Enemy," a story set in Japan during World War II, a wounded American washes up on the beach near the home of a respected Japanese surgeon, who finds both his daily activities and traditional attitudes transformed by the encounter with the American. Before the American's appearance, Dr. Sadao Hoki and his family live according to the old Japanese ways despite his modern profession. Their home has the traditional inner and outer courts and gardens tended by servants; Dr. Hoki's father had lived with them until his death. The Hokis' marriage, too, is traditional, for although they met in America where both were students, they waited to fall in love until after their marriage had been parentally arranged in Japan. Mrs. Hoki remains respectfully silent much of the time she is in her

husband's presence; she eats only after he has eaten his own meal. The narrative voice reveals that Dr. Hoki has many tender feelings for her because of her devotion to the old ways.

The exposition of the story is complete after the narrator describes Dr. Hoki's thoughts as he stands gazing at the islands beyond his home. These were, according to his old father, "stepping stones to the future for Japan," a future for which he prepared his son with the best American education available. When Mrs. Hoki arrives to tell her husband that the meal has been prepared, a figure appears in the mists along the rocky coast. As the man staggers, finally collapsing unconscious, they rush toward him, expecting to find an injured fisherman. With fear and horror, however, they discover that he is a white man, and they cannot decide at first what they should do with him.

They are unable to put the man back into the sea although they realize that for fear of the authorities they should do just that. When they move the injured man to safety, their servants leave for both political and superstitious reasons because they believe it is wrong to harbor an enemy. Only Mrs. Hoki remains to aid her

Pearl S. Buck (©The Nobel Foundation)

husband when he discovers a bullet lodged near the wounded man's kidney. She washes the man's body, which she cannot bear for her husband to touch at first; then she manages to administer the anesthetic, although the sight of the man's wound sickens her. Her husband, on the other hand, marvels that the young man has survived this long and strives at length to remove the bullet without creating paralysis. Indeed, throughout the surgery Dr. Hoki cannot help speaking to the patient, addressing him as a friend despite his foreign appearance. They realize in the course of their ministrations that the man is an American, probably an escaped prisoner of war, for his body shows signs of abuse.

The surgery is successful, and the couple settle into a period of hope and fear as they await the patient's recovery. When soldiers appear with a summons, the doctor is terrified until he learns that he is needed to treat an ailing Japanese general. After the general begins to recover, the doctor confesses to him that he has helped a wounded American who would have surely died without his help and that now he cannot bear to execute the American after having spent so many years with Americans when he was in medical school. The general agrees to send assassins who will, within the next three days, murder the American even as he lies in the doctor's house.

The days and nights pass, and the Hokis note only the American's recovery of strength and his deep gratitude toward them. Again they confront an opportunity to save him; the doctor gives him a boat, clothing, and food so that he may escape to a neighboring island and wait for a fishing boat. Days later, the doctor confesses to the general that the American has somehow escaped, and in a strange reversal, the general realizes with considerable anxiety that he has forgotten his promise to the doctor. The general then begs the doctor not to reveal their secret to the authorities, and the doctor willingly swears to the general's loyalty before returning home to discover his servants returned and peace restored.

Remaining somehow troubled, Dr. Hoki turns to face the island "steppingstones" of progress as he recalls the ugly faces of all the white people he has ever known and ponders why he could not kill the young white enemy. This resolution to the story suggests that

although no dramatic change has occurred in the lives of the Japanese family, an awakening has perhaps been achieved as they discovered that they must for human reasons help the injured American.

"HEARTS COME HOME"

In "Hearts Come Home," a modern young businessman of China finally affirms the old ways of his culture. David Lin, a manager in a printing house, discovers to his surprise a young woman of simple beauty and individuality in the unlikely setting of a sophisticated modern dance in the home of a wealthy banker. The girl turns out to be the banker's daughter, visiting her father briefly before returning to school. Sensing in her a kindred spirit, Lin falls desperately in love with her because she is so different from the other sophisticated women of Shanghai.

Throughout David Lin's pursuit of Phyllis, the atmosphere, dialogue, and actions of their courtship heighten cultural contrasts between old and new in China. David spares no expense in treating her to the finest modern entertainment: They dance, drive about in the car, enjoy imported foods, and converse in a fashionable mixture of Chinese and American slang. The two, however, eventually grow distant from each other; although they exchange kisses in the American fashion, David perceives Phyllis withdrawing from him, hiding her true personality more and more as the days pass.

He learns why one day when she suddenly asks him in Chinese whether he actually enjoys what they are doing, dancing in such a foreign and unrestrained style. Discovering that they share a dislike for dancing, she opens her heart to him, revealing to his pleased surprise that foreign things disgust her and that she does them only to please him.

The love for tradition that David and Phyllis share brings them close to each other in a new way. They exchange their traditional Chinese names, and before they know it they find themselves describing a Chinese marriage in which the old ways are celebrated. No longer will they kiss, wear foreign clothes, or eat foreign foods; their single-story house will have many courts and gardens filled with happy children. David, however, does not propose. He merely speaks of an arrangement that must soon be completed by their parents. Phyllis bids him a respectful goodbye according to the appropriate Chinese formula, and David leaves, peacefully contemplating their future.

"THE GOOD DEED"

"The Good Deed" portrays the impact of cultural changes on several generations, a common theme in Buck's work. Like "Hearts Come Home," this story suggests that the old ways can be valuable and satisfying. Mr. Pan, a Chinese emigrant to America, brings his aging mother to live with his wife and children in Chinatown in 1953. He discovers, however, that in saving her from the marauders destroying her native village, he has only brought her to another kind of suffering, for she becomes sickened at the rebellion of his children, his wife's inability to speak her native tongue, and the loneliness of life in a busy city. Although Mr. Pan and his wife can supply the aged woman with excellent Chinese food and physical comforts, her spirit weakens daily.

The Pans decide in desperation that a visitor may help, and they invite Lili Yang, a young Chinese social worker, to visit old Mrs. Pan. Lili listens with interest as the old woman describes her native village, which lies in a wide valley from which the mountains rise as sharply as tigers' teeth. A gentle friendship develops between the two women, but a conflict emerges when old Mrs. Pan discovers that Lili, twenty-seven years old, remains unmarried. The aged one is shocked and troubled as she concludes that Lili's parents had been remiss in their duties by failing to arrange a satisfactory marriage for their daughter before their deaths. Lili weeps for the children she has always wanted, although she tries to hide her loneliness from old Mrs. Pan.

Once Lili has returned to her work, old Mrs. Pan presents her son with the responsibility of securing a husband for Lili. Indeed, the aged one decides that she herself will serve as Lili's parent, if her son will only supply her with a list of appropriate prospects. Such a good deed will be counted well in heaven for all concerned. Through the succeeding weeks old Mrs. Pan's life reflects her newfound purpose. With renewed energy she commands Mr. Pan to seek out unattached men of good character so that she may contact their parents, a project he finds most amusing as he recalls secretly that even he and his wife had fallen in love

first, then allowed their parents to arrange a marriage later. He strives to explain to his mother that life in America is different, yet old Mrs. Pan remains determined.

Although she may do little else on her own, old Mrs. Pan stares daily out a window at the strangers passing along the street, hardly a suitable method of securing a mate for Lili, but at least a means of examining the young men of Chinatown. She develops an acquaintanceship with a young man who manages his father's pottery shop directly across the street. Learning from her son that this son of old Mr. Lim is wealthy and educated, she fixes upon him as an excellent prospect for Lili. Her son laughs at this possibility and tries to convince her that the young man will not submit to such an arrangement: He is handsome and educated, but Lili is plain and of simple virtue. At this argument, old Mrs. Pan becomes angry, reminding him that often women who lack beauty have much kinder hearts than their more attractive peers. She gives up her argument and makes plans of her own.

In order to meet the young man and perhaps at least introduce him to Lili, old Mrs. Pan waits until her son and his wife are gone and then asks one of the children to lead her across the street so that she may buy two bowls. The child dislikes her, however, and abandons her as soon as they reach the curb in front of the pottery shop. Fortunately, the young son of Mr. Lim rescues her, helping her into the shop and pleasantly conversing with her in excellent Chinese as she rests briefly. He then helps her find the bowls she seeks and they converse at greater length concerning the complexity of life in a large city. She finds herself confessing that if it had not been for Lili Yang, she would never have even looked out the window. When he asks who Lili Yang may be, she will not speak of her, for it would not be proper to discuss a virtuous young woman with a young man. Instead old Mrs. Pan goes into a lengthy speech on the virtues of women who are not beautiful. When he concludes that Lili must not be beautiful, old Mrs. Pan merely says that perhaps he will meet Lili some day and then they will discuss the matter of her beauty. Old Mrs. Pan, satisfied that she has made a point, leaves with graciousness and dignity.

Returning home with the purchased bowls, she informs her son that she has spoken with old Mr. Lim's son and found him indeed pleasant. Her son realizes immediately what she has been doing and secretly cooperates by inviting Lili to visit them again, providing Mrs. Pan with an opportunity to introduce the young people. Old Mrs. Pan, however, achieves much more satisfaction than she expects, for in taking Lili with her to buy more pottery, old Mrs. Pan meets old Mr. Lim. While Lili and young James Lim are conversing in English, she and the aged father agree quietly that perhaps a match is possible and that certainly to arrange a marriage is the best of all good deeds under heaven. Observing the young people together, they set a date to have the horoscopes of the children read and to arrange the match; the date they choose, the reader learns, is the day of Lili and James's first American-style date.

A final theme appearing late in Buck's work is the search for female identity. In several early novels, including *East Wind: West Wind* (1930) and *This Proud Heart* (1938), she presents women struggling to fulfill their potential in antagonistic cultural settings. In the novella *The Woman Who Was Changed* (1979), Buck depicts a woman who succeeds in expressing herself in the artistic and personal spheres. A particularly contemporary concern, women's struggles appear also in Buck's autobiography, *My Several Worlds: A Personal Record* (1954).

OTHER MAJOR WORKS

LONG FICTION: *East Wind: West Wind*, 1930; *The Good Earth*, 1931; *Sons*, 1932; *The Mother*, 1934; *A House Divided*, 1935; *House of Earth*, 1935; *This Proud Heart*, 1938; *The Patriot*, 1939; *Other Gods: An American Legend*, 1940; *China Sky*, 1942; *Dragon Seed*, 1942; *The Promise*, 1943; *China Flight*, 1945; *Portrait of a Marriage*, 1945; *The Townsman*, 1945 (as John Sedges); *Pavilion of Women*, 1946; *The Angry Wife*, 1947 (as Sedges); *Peony*, 1948; *Kinfolk*, 1949; *The Long Love*, 1949 (as Sedges); *God's Men*, 1951; *Bright Procession*, 1952 (as Sedges); *The Hidden Flower*, 1952; *Come, My Beloved*, 1953; *Voices in the House*, 1953 (as Sedges); *Imperial Woman*, 1956; *Letter from Peking*, 1957; *Command the Morning*, 1959; *Satan Never Sleeps*, 1962; *The Living Reed*,

1963; *Death in the Castle*, 1965; *The Time Is Noon*, 1967; *The New Year*, 1968; *The Three Daughters of Madame Liang*, 1969; *Mandala*, 1970; *The Goddess Abides*, 1972; *All Under Heaven*, 1973; *The Rainbow*, 1974.

NONFICTION: *East and West and the Novel*, 1932; *Fighting Angel: Portrait of a Soul*, 1936; *The Exile*, 1936; *The Chinese Novel*, 1939; *Of Men and Women*, 1941 (expanded 1971); *American Unity and Asia*, 1942; *What America Means to Me*, 1943; *China in Black and White*, 1945; *Talk About Russia: With Masha Scott*, 1945; *Tell the People: Talks with James Yen About the Mass Education Movement*, 1945; *How It Happens: Talk About the German People, 1914-1933, with Erna von Pustau*, 1947; *American Argument: With Eslanda Goods*, 1949; *The Child Who Never Grew*, 1950; *My Several Worlds: A Personal Record*, 1954; *Friend to Friend: A Candid Exchange Between Pearl Buck and Carlos F. Romulo*, 1958; *A Bridge for Passing*, 1962; *The Joy of Children*, 1964; *Children for Adoption*, 1965; *The Gifts They Bring: Our Debt to the Mentally Retarded*, 1965; *The People of Japan*, 1966; *To My Daughters with Love*, 1967; *China as I See It*, 1970; *The Kennedy Women: A Personal Appraisal*, 1970; *Pearl S. Buck's America*, 1971; *The Story Bible*, 1971; *China Past and Present*, 1972.

TRANSLATION: *All Men Are Brothers*, 1933 (of Shih Nai-an's novel).

CHILDREN'S LITERATURE: *The Young Revolutionist*, 1932; *Stories for Little Children*, 1940; *The Chinese Children Next Door*, 1942; *The Water-Buffalo Children*, 1943; *The Dragon Fish*, 1944; *Yu Lan: Flying Boy of China*, 1945; *The Big Wave*, 1948; *One Bright Day, and Other Stories for Children*, 1952; *The Man Who Changed China: The Story of Sun Yat-Sen*, 1953; *Johnny Jack and His Beginnings*, 1954; *The Beech Tree*, 1954; *Fourteen Stories*, 1961; *The Little Fox in the Middle*, 1966; *The Chinese Story Teller*, 1971.

BIBLIOGRAPHY

Bentley, Phyllis. "The Art of Pearl S. Buck." *English Journal* 24 (December, 1935): 791-800. Analyzes Buck's early works from a technical perspective, focusing on setting, style, characterization, plot, and theme. Concludes that the great strength of Buck's

Critical Survey of Short Fiction

fiction is its emphasis on the "continuity of life" from generation to generation.

Cevasco, George A. "Pearl Buck and the Chinese Novel." *Asian Studies* 5 (December, 1967): 437-450. Provides important insights into Buck's understanding of the novel as a form for the general public, not the scholar, and shows her debt to Chinese beliefs about the function of plot and characterization in fiction.

Conn, Peter. *Pearl S. Buck: A Cultural Biography.* Cambridge, England: Cambridge University Press, 1996. Attempts to revise the "smug literary consensus" that has relegated Buck to a "footnote" in literary history. Conn does not rehabilitate Buck as a great author but shows how her best work broke new ground in subject matter and is still vital to an understanding of American culture.

Dickstein, Lore. "Posthumous Stories." *The New York Times Book Review*, March 11, 1979, 20-21. Praises Buck's best work as having subject matter with a universal appeal and an easy, graceful style. Finds the late stories, however, to be excessively didactic and sentimental.

Doyle, Paul A. *Pearl S. Buck.* Boston: Twayne, 1980. A valuable survey of Buck's literary achievements, strengths, and weaknesses. Contains a biographical chapter and excellent bibliographies of both primary and secondary materials.

_____. "Pearl S. Buck's Short Stories: A Survey." *English Journal* 55 (January, 1966): 62-68. One of the few critical works devoted exclusively to Buck's short fiction. Her best stories, Doyle maintains, contain realistic description, clearly delineated characters, and narrative interest. Too often, however, she wrote slick magazine fiction, excessively sentimental or filled with improbable incidents.

Gao, Xiongya. *Pearl S. Buck's Chinese Women Characters.* Selinsgrave, Pa.: Susquehanna Press, 2000. Examines the treatment of Chinese women characters in Buck's work by focusing on five of her novels. Provides a general overview of Buck's work and discusses the critical response to her writing, how her work was influenced by her experiences in China, and the position of women in Chinese society at the time Buck's books appeared.

Leong, Karen J. *The China Mystique: Pearl S. Buck, Anna May Wong, Mayling Soong, and the Transformation of American Orientalism.* Berkeley: University of California Press, 2005. Focuses on three women who were associated with China in the 1930's and 1940's--Buck, actor Anna May Wong, and Soong Mei-ling, the wife of Chinese leader Chiang Kai-shek--to describe how they altered Americans' perceptions of what it meant to be American, Chinese American, and Chinese.

Liao, Kang. *Pearl S. Buck: A Cultural Bridge Across the Pacific.* Westport, Conn.: Greenwood Press, 1997. Examines Buck's political and social views and her means of expressing them. Studies the East-West cultural divide in her fiction.

Spurling, Hilary. *Pearl Buck in China: Journey to the Good Earth.* New York: Simon & Schuster, 2010. Comprehensive biography that correlates Buck's experiences in China to her fiction. Although it focuses on her novels, the book discusses some of her short stories, particularly "A Chinese Woman Speaks."

Stirling, Nora. *Pearl Buck: A Woman in Conflict.* Piscataway, N.J.: New Century, 1983. A balanced, well-researched biography that provides important insights into Buck's personality and the experiences that shaped her writings.

Chapel Louise Petty
Updated by Elizabeth Johnston Lipscomb

JAMES LEE BURKE

Born: Houston, Texas; December 5, 1936

PRINCIPAL SHORT FICTION

The Convict, and Other Stories, 1985
Jesus Out to Sea, 2007

OTHER LITERARY FORMS

James Lee Burke has written eighteen mystery novels starring Louisiana detective Dave Robicheaux, four mysteries starring Texas attorney Billy Bob Holland, seven miscellaneous novels, and two anthologies of acclaimed short fiction. Two Robicheaux novels have been made into motion pictures: 1988's *Heaven Prisoners* (1996, starring Alec Baldwin) and 1993's *In the Electric Mist with Confederate Dead* (2009, released as *In the Electric Mist,* starring Tommy Lee Jones). Burke's Western *Two for Texas* (1982) was made into a 1998 feature film, starring Kris Kristofferson.

ACHIEVEMENTS

James Lee Burke has been awarded a number of literary prizes. His novel *The Lost Get-Back Boogie* (1986) was rejected 111 times before being published and nominated for the Pulitzer Prize in 1987. He received the Edgar Allan Poe Award for best mystery novel from the Mystery Writers of America (MWA) twice, for *Black Cherry Blues* (1989) and for *Cimarron Rose* (1997). His novel *Sunset Limited* (1998) won the Crime Writers Association (CWA) Macallan Gold Dagger Award for Fiction in 1998. Burke also received the Louisiana Writer Award in 2002. His short story "Why Bugsy Siegel Was a Friend of Mine" won a Pushcart Prize in 2007. The MWA awarded him the Grand Master Award in 2009. Three of his other novels also have been nominated for literary prizes: *Jolie Blon's Bounce* (2002), *Pegasus Descending* (2006), and *The Tin Roof Blowdown* (2007).

BIOGRAPHY

James Lee Burke was born and raised in Houston, Texas, but for a good part of his childhood he lived in New Iberia, Louisiana, an area that provides the main stage for the Robicheaux series and many of Burke's other writings. Graduating in 1960 in creative writing from the University of Missouri, Burke tried a number of jobs, from truck driver to university professor, which all feature in his prose, before he became a writer. Another personal experience that features prominently in his writings is his bout with alcoholism, which he overcame using a twelve-step program. After initial success, Burke failed to publish anything from 1971 to 1984, when he came back with his first collection of short stories, *The Convict,* published by Louisiana State University Press. In 1987, he published his first mystery novel, *The Neon Rain,* which introduced Louisiana detective Robicheaux. With the success of the series, Burke became a full-time writer in 1989. He married and had four children; his daughter Alafair Burke became a successful writer of mysteries. With his wife, Pearl, Burke settled in two homes, one in New Iberia and the other in Missoula, Montana.

ANALYSIS

While James Lee Burke is principally known as the creator of the detective Robicheaux, he has published two collections of short stories, which were released originally in various magazines, such as *Esquire, The Atlantic Monthly,* and *The Southern Review,* and in compilations, such as *The Best American Short Stories* and *The Best American Mystery Stories.* Anthologies of his work *The Convict* and *Jesus Out to Sea* share three stories: "Water People," "Texas City, 1947," and "In Winter Light." Characters from his stories, such as the Holland family, also appear in his novels and vice versa. Burke admits that basically he is writing the same story, the search for the Holy Grail, over and over again. Consequently, as in his novels, two themes dominate Burke's short stories. First is the search for social justice. Social injustices prevalent in the United States are the source of conflicts in Burke texts. A Jeffersonian liberal who expects people to take responsibility for their own actions, Burke tackles various issues facing American society, such as racism, the environment, and the aftermath of Hurricane Katrina. His protagonists fight against a system of social injustice that keeps poor people, regardless of race, uneducated and convinced that the destruction of their environment is just a part of their lives. The conflicts arising from this are often violent, but the violence in Burke texts is always realistic and serves the author's political message. The second prominent theme in Burke's short stories is the search for redemption. His protagonists are always flawed, troubled by alcoholism, by the loss of family members, or by the sins of the past. Often these protagonists have experienced the horrors of war and the violence that comes with it. The Vietnam War (in which Burke did not serve), World War II, the Korean War, and the American Civil War figure in his texts, either as story background or as part of the troubled past of the protagonists, which they relive in flashbacks. However, in spite of all their shortcomings, the protagonists are always searching for redemption and a metaphorical Holy Grail, and references to the Bible and other literary texts are commonly found in Burke's writings.

The setting of Burke texts is the American South, mostly Louisiana and Texas, and his work is full of vivid descriptions of these areas, including the regional language, the local music and food, and the native vegetation, notably the live oak trees in Louisiana. These images of the South often carry a sense of lost innocence and times gone by. Burke's language is full of colorful metaphors and regional vocabulary, creating a convincing portrait of the South.

"Uncle Sidney and the Mexicans"

In this story from *The Convict*, the first-person narrator Hack Holland is a high school kid. In 1947, he is picking tomatoes on the farm of a judgmental racist priest, while staying with his uncle, Sidney, a flawed but ultimately good character. The priest humiliates an alcoholic veteran of World War II, Billy Haskel, and refuses to pay his wages after the priest finds Haskel

drinking on the job. Hack also experiences various kinds of racism, like getting beaten up in a drive-in, because he is falling in love with the Mexican girl Juanita. Uncle Sidney is accused by the local growers' association of working with communist Mexicans, so Sidney decides to fight back and hires workers from the union led by Juanita's father, who are likewise being ostracized. After a burning cross is planted in front of Sidney's house, he puts the cross in the back of his pickup, driving it around town and shaming both the growers' association and the priest, who subsequently has to pay the wages of Haskel. Hack takes the cross and Juanita to the drive-in, where he becomes the talk of the town, in a rather happy ending. In this story, told in a lighter tone than later texts, a victory against social injustice is won by nonviolent means.

"When It's Decoration Day"

This story, also from *The Convict*, takes place during the Civil War. Sixteen-year-old Wesley Buford is a member of a small troop of Confederate soldiers, who retreat after the fall of Atlanta in 1864 into Alabama. Other members include an aloof lieutenant, a sergeant, two released convicts, and other enlisted men. On their desolate march, tensions arise between the lieutenant and his men and between the convicts and Buford. Meanwhile, the sergeant tries to keep Buford alive until the end of the war.

Buford's memories of a happy childhood in the South that does not exist anymore sharply contrast with the horrors of war. The sergeant and others are killed or horribly wounded before the remainder of the group meets a Confederate hospital train. The whole train is then massacred by federal troops, and the lieutenant dies in a last heroic charge, while Buford is blown to pieces by federal artillery, thinking he is being anointed by God the moment he dies, in this brutally realistic story.

"Texas City, 1947"

A story published in both *The Convict* and *Jesus Out to Sea*, "Texas City, 1947" features a first-person narrator, Billy Bob Sonnier, who lives with his three siblings, Weldon, Lyle, and Drew, and his parents in southern Louisiana. His mother abruptly leaves the family after a fight with his father, whom she accuses of having an affair with Mattie, a bar maid and former prostitute. His mother dies in a car accident right after leaving home, and Mattie, an abusive drug addict, comes to live with the family. Billy Bob also suffers from rheumatic fever, and the only adult trying to help him is Sister Roberta, his fifth-grade teacher, who herself is burdened with family troubles, when her brother kills a black child while driving drunk. After Billy Bob's father is reported missing in an industrial accident, Mattie becomes even more abusive, especially against Drew, the sister, so the three brothers try to kill Mattie by setting her on fire. Billy Bob lights the match. Mattie survives, and when Sister Roberta comes to try to find foster homes for the children, she destroys all the evidence of the assault on Mattie. Years later, Billy Bob meets a man who might be his father and remembers his childhood in 1947. Once again, the story revolves around the themes of lost innocence and social injustice, but memories of the narrator's violent childhood are dominant.

"WINTER LIGHT"

In "Winter Light," from *The Convict* and *Jesus Out to Sea*, Roger Guidry is a divorced, retired university

James Lee Burke (AP Photo/Brad Kemp)

professor who is living alone on his property, which controls the access to a national forest; he refuses to grant access to anyone, however. One day he denies two redneck hunters the use of his road to the forest, already sensing that this argument will lead to a conflict. Across the creek his former colleague and rival from the university, Waldo Gates, likewise owns a home. Guidry retired because he was disgusted at Gates's manipulative politics, which also includes sexual harassment of a graduate student, Gretchen. The hunters, who turn out to be Gates's friends, return, killing a doe and shooting at Guidry's dog. Guidry fantasizes about killing the hunters with a knife, but instead of enacting such bloody revenge he steals the body of the deer and vandalizes the hunters' car. He returns to his property, burying the deer before Gates and the hunters arrive. The story ends with the narrator about to become a victim of both academic and lower-class perpetrators, illustrating that education alone does not guarantee moral superiority and that power in any form is likely to be abused.

"WHY BUGSY SIEGEL WAS A FRIEND OF MINE"

This story from *Jesus Out to Sea* was selected for *The Best American Mystery Stories, 2006* and *The Pushcart Prize XXXI* anthologies. The first-person narrator Charlie and his best friend, Nick Hauser, by accident meet gangster Bugsy Siegel in 1947, while practicing with their Cheerio yo-yos. Siegel is a big fan of these toys and asks them to teach him.

Meanwhile, Charlie's antisocial neighbors, the Dunlops, make life difficult for him, for the children at his school, and for one of his schoolteachers, Sister Felice, who has become an alcoholic following a personal tragedy. Charlie tries to enlist Siegel's help by infuriating him with the story of how the Dunlops chased away the Cheerio yo-yo vendor, but Siegel never makes good on his promise to take action against Charlie's enemies, although Charlie vividly dreams about it. In a surprising turn of events, Charlie confronts the Dunlops' abusive son Vernon and beats Vernon in a fistfight. However, Siegel somehow redeems himself when he calls the archdiocese on behalf of Sister Felice, who gets reinstated at her old school, which is why Charlie considers Siegel his friend. The character of the troubled but helpful nun returns in this story, which mixes fond memories of the narrator's youth with the fight against social injustice, with real-life gangster Siegel the narrator's surprising ally.

"Jesus Out to Sea"

In the title story from *Jesus Out to Sea*, the first-person narrator, who, together with his friend Miles Cardo, stayed in New Orleans during its destruction by Hurricane Katrina, describes in the present tense the traumatic scenes in the city after the storm, contrasting them with memories of his youth. He recalls how, with Miles, he became a jazz musician and later a drug addict, while Tony, Miles's brother and a character from Burke's *A Morning for Flamingos* (1990), became involved with the mob but nevertheless always helped the narrator and Miles in times of need. Waiting to be rescued from a rooftop, the narrator does not want to believe that the president flew over the disaster area without bothering to land. Juxtaposing his experiences of the government failures and the suffering of innocent people in Vietnam, where he, Tony, and Miles fought together, with the failures of government to rescue the inhabitants of New Orleans, the protagonist realizes that not everyone will be rescued this time, either. Becoming more and more delusional, they start to think that Tony, who was supposedly shot by the Drug Enforcement Agency, will come to their rescue. As the wood carving of Jesus on his cross from his neighborhood church drifts by, the narrator realizes that, with Miles and Jesus, and with Tony waiting for them in the beyond, he could not be in better company waiting for the end.

According to Burke, this text was inspired by the true story of a priest, who, after he decided to stay with his parishioners in the Lower Ninth Ward in New Orleans during Hurricane Katrina, got washed out to sea and was never found. This story also became the opening of Burke's novel *The Tin-Roof Blowdown* (2007). With *Jesus Out to Sea*, enhanced by his rare use of the present tense, and *The Tin Roof Blowdown*, Burke made a strong political statement, which resulted in not only in critical acclaim but also in hateful reactions.

Other major works

LONG FICTION: *Half of Paradise*, 1965; *To the Bright and Shining Sun*, 1970; *Lay Down My Sword and Shield*, 1971; *Two for Texas*, 1982 (also known as *Sabine Spring*); *The Lost Get-Back Boogie*, 1986; *The Neon Rain*, 1987; *Heaven's Prisoners*, 1988; *Black Cherry Blues*, 1989; *Present for Santa*, 1989; *Spy Story*, 1990; *Texas City, 1947*, 1992; *A Morning for Flamingos*, 1990; *A Stained White Radiance*, 1992; *In the Electric Mist with Confederate Dead*, 1993; *Dixie City Jam*, 1994; *Burning Angel*, 1995, *Cadillac Jukebox*, 1996; *Cimarron Rose,* 1997; *Sunset Limited*, 1998; *Heartwood*, 1999; *Purple Cane Road*, 2000; *Bitterroot,* 2001; *Jolie Blon's Bounce*, 2002; *White Doves at Morning*, 2002; *Last Car to Elysian Fields*, 2003; *In the Moon of Red Ponies*, 2004; *Crusader's Cross*, 2005; *Pegasus Descending*, 2006; *The Tin Roof Blowdown*, 2007; *Rain Gods*, 2009; *The Glass Rainbow*, 2010.

NONFICTION: *Ohio's Heritage*, 1989

BIBLIOGRAPHY

Bogue, Barbara. *James Lee Burke and the Soul of Dave Robicheaux: A Critical Study of the Crime Fiction Series*. Jefferson, N.C.: McFarland, 2006. Study examining Burke's Robicheaux novels, their autobiographical elements, and how the author deals with various issues of modern society. Includes an interview with the author.

Burke, James Lee. "A City of Saints and Sancho Panza." *Los Angeles Times*, September 18, 2005. Burke's commentary on Hurricane Katrina is an ode to New Orleans.

Engel, Leonard, ed. *A Violent Conscience: Essays on the Fiction of James Lee Burke*. Jefferson, N.C.: McFarland, 2010. Collection of essays examining the way Burke's works go beyond the traditional mystery genre. Includes an essay on the short story "Jesus Out to Sea" and an interview with the author, in which he comments on the short story "Winter Light."

Trachtenberg, Jeffrey. "The Craze After the Storm." *The Wall Street Journal*, August 17, 2007. An interview with Burke that discusses his theory of creativity, the nature of Robicheaux, and the linkage among the spirit, the body, and divinity.

Stefan Buchenberger

FREDERICK BUSCH

Born: Brooklyn, New York; August 1, 1941
Died: New York, New York; February 23, 2006

PRINCIPAL SHORT FICTION

Breathing Trouble, and Other Stories, 1973
Domestic Particulars: A Family Chronicle, 1976
Hardwater Country, 1979
Too Late American Boyhood Blues: Ten Stories,
    1984
Absent Friends, 1989
The Children in the Woods: New and Selected
    Stories, 1994
Don't Tell Anyone, 2000
Rescue Missions, 2006

OTHER LITERARY FORMS

Although he never wrote a "best seller," Frederick Busch (boosh) did write sixteen highly regarded novels. His first novel, *I Wanted a Year Without Fall,* was published in 1971. Generally his novels focused on contemporary life, except for two historically situated novels: *The Mutual Friend* (1978), an account of the last years of Charles Dickens, and *The Night Inspector* (1999), on Herman Melville. Busch also wrote nonfiction, beginning with *Hawkes: A Guide to His Fiction* (1973), on the work of John Hawkes; Busch wrote two books about writing and writers, *When People Publish* (1986) and *A Dangerous Profession* (1998). Busch edited *Letters to a Fiction Writer* (1999).

ACHIEVEMENTS

Frederick Busch was a prolific writer. In addition to novels and works of nonfiction, he published eight books of short stories. Highly regarded as a novelist, he was able to shift between writing novels and short stories. In fact some of his novels grew from characters created in the short stories. A master of the short story,

Busch was known as a "writer's writer," and he won many awards throughout his career. He won the National Jewish Book Award for Fiction for *Invisible Mending* (1984) and in 1986 the American Academy of Arts and Letters Fiction Award. In 1991, Busch was awarded the PEN/Malamud Award for his achievement in the short story.

BIOGRAPHY

Frederick Matthew Busch was born August 1, 1941, in Brooklyn, New York, the elder son of Benjamin J. Busch (originally Buschlowitz), an attorney, and Phyllis Schnell, a teacher, a naturalist, and an author of children's books. Both parents were immigrants, and Frederick Busch grew up in an ethnic, middle-class community. As early as fourth grade, Busch, who delighted in writing poems, wanted to be a writer. He graduated from Muhlenberg College in 1962 with a B.A. in English and went to Columbia University, as a Woodrow Wilson fellow, to study seventeenth century English literature. He left without earning his master's degree, and, between 1963 and 1965, he worked a number of jobs, including writing and editing for small magazines and teaching English at Baruch College in New York City. In 1966, he was hired to teach English at Colgate University in Hamilton, New York; he completed his M.A. in English from Columbia in 1967.

While teaching, Busch, who had given up writing poetry years before, also was writing fiction; his first long work, a novella, *There Is No Phenix,* was not published, nor was his second attempt, a novel called *Coldly by the Hand.* However, his third novel, *I Wanted a Year Without Fall,* a comic, contemporary version of the Beowulf legend, and his first collection of short stories, *Breathing Trouble, and Other Stories,* were published to general acclaim by critics. Novels, short stories, and awards followed.

Over his career, he continued to teach creative writing and fiction at Colgate and served as director of the Living Writers program, which he founded. He retired from teaching at Colgate in 2003. In 1978-1979, Busch served as the acting director of the University of Iowa's program in creative writing. In 1963, he married Judith Ann Burroughs, a teacher he met while they were students at Muhlenberg. They had two sons and lived near Sherburne, in upstate New York. Busch died of a heart attack in 2006.

ANALYSIS

Although admired by critics, Frederick Busch's short stories received little popular acclaim. His understated stories focus on domestic life and on relationships between men and women and parents and children. He portrays family life as it actually is: routine, with few earth-shattering incidents. The stories, fashioned with exquisite detail, are set in a variety of locales, both rural and urban, many in upstate New York. Some refer to past wars, others to current topics in the news. Stories vary in style; some are humorous, others verge on the poetic. Busch often included sentences with astounding impact. For example, the narrator in "I Am the News," describing the experience of cleaning out his dead father's house, says, "I ran into him two days after his death." Busch was a master of dialogue, showing the influence of Ernest Hemingway, one of Busch's literary idols, on his style. He varies his points of view with female and male narrators as well as children. People were his principal interest. He once said, "I write about characters I want to matter." Busch is particularly concerned with those who are vulnerable, especially children. His characters are not heroic in the sense of accomplishing great deeds, but they are memorable as they struggle within their world.

HARDWATER COUNTRY

Busch's third collection of short stories begins and ends with water. The thirteen stories have various points of views and focus on character and relationships. "Widow Water," the first story in the collection, is narrated by a plumber whose skill can fix a widow's pump and a professor's sump pump but not their pain. This story also incorporates one of Busch's themes: the importance of work, physical and intellectual. In "The

Lesson of the Hotel Lotti," the female narrator discovers a father in her mother's lover. A particularly moving story, told in diary format, is "The Old Man Is Snoring." The main character, whose wife had died four years before, provides diary entries detailing his daily life. They include his memories and reveal his determination to fill up his days. In "My Father, Cont." the narrator is a child who describes his father as "a doctor and an ex-convict." A conscientious objector during the Korean War, the father is not an easy person to live with, and the parents' marriage appears to be failing. The narrator, who is reading the tale of Hansel and Gretel, is troubled by how the father leaves his children in the woods. When a family trip into the woods turns into a possible disaster, the narrator is terrified, but his father tells him not to worry, "I'll get you out of the woods." Children who are lost, whether in the woods or by being abandoned in some way by parents, is a recurring Busch theme. The final story, "What You Might as Well Call Love," contrasts the menace of a flood outside with the security provided within the home by Ethan's parents.

Although *The New York Times* critic Anatole Broyard was not impressed with the collection, Robert Kiely, also writing for *The New York Times*, was more positive. He noted that the stories focus on "moments and details" in the daily lives of "mostly unexceptional" people and particularly enjoyed the first story of the failed pump as characteristic of "one of life's minor absurdities." Amy Wilentz, writing for *The Nation*, commented on how the stories convey different types of love and observed that Busch writes about "things that matter."

TOO LATE AMERICAN BOYHOOD BLUES

With a title that echoes a quote from Hemingway about men who stay boys too long, the ten stories in this collection focus on male relationships with parents, wives, lovers, and siblings. The first story, "The Settlement of Mars," is set in Maine and is narrated by a boy of nine, who discovers girls, comic books, and his parents "discontent" with each other. "Rise and Fall" focuses on two brothers, their early life in Flatbush, and the difficulties of that life. The brothers rise to become a lawyer and a doctor, achieving the American dream, but both experience failed marriages, in which kids get "broken." A character questions, "Was everyone born to be separate?" The problem of failed relationships is a major Busch theme. In "The News," the main character, Harry, has quit his position as a reporter with a newspaper to drive through a snowstorm because of what he thinks is a summons from Katherine, a woman he once loved. However, Katherine, like other women in Busch's stories, is no longer interested in a relationship; she wants to live life on her own. In "A History of Small Ideas," parent-child relationships, from an adult viewpoint, are portrayed on a trip to upstate New York to see Sidney's parents. He is particularly uptight about visiting his father, a doctor like himself. Father and son are the same characters Busch wrote about in "My Father, Cont.," but the child is an adult.

Critic Broyard notes that in this collection, it is the men, not the women, who are sentimental. The men seem to struggle to hold on to something that the women have let go. Looking at the settings of the stories that are often rural, Broyard sees Busch wanting to prove that life in small towns can be just as "disheveled" as life in big cities.

THE CHILDREN IN THE WOODS

The focus of this collection, nominated for the 1995 PEN/Faulkner Award, is the story of Hansel and Gretel, which intrigued Busch for years. Stories included are from books or were previously published works in various publications and revised for this volume. All twenty-three relate to parents and children. "Bread," originally published in *The Gettysburg Review*, shows adult children going through the possessions of their parents who were killed in a plane crash. The children reflect on happy childhood memories and discover their parents' "secrets" were their pride in their son and daughter, neither of whom has been able to maintain a relationship. The son is divorced, and his sister has left her lover. However, the son finds evidence of how they were cherished by their parents and leads his sister, as Hansel once led Gretel, out of the woods by following the crumbs of memory toward realization of their own value and the acceptance of their loss. The second story in the collection, "Bring Your Friends to the Zoo," originally published in *Breathing Trouble*, has a unique style. The reader is addressed in the second person,

"you," and informed of what to see and experience at the London Zoo. The detailed, expository writing is interspersed with the dialogue of an unnamed male and female, who are meeting at the zoo. Their emotional conversation reveals a scandal in the United States, how the man has followed the woman home to London, and how her husband has kicked her out. An explanation of the darkness of an area of the zoo, designed for creatures living in the dark, complements the darkness of the couple's future.

An important story in the collection, "Ralph the Duck," originally published in *Absent Friends*, was a selection in *The Best American Short Stories, 1989*. The story begins with a dog, throwing up something he ate, but "he loved what made him sick." That line relates to the young woman in the story, who falls in love with her literature professor, is disappointed, and tries to kill herself. The title refers to a story the narrator, "the oldest college student in America," wrote about a duck and its mother for the same professor. The mother duck saves Ralph by keeping him warm, just as the narrator saves the student by keeping her warm, but he could not save the life of his own child. Intrigued by the characters he created, Busch continued the story in his novel *Girls* (1997). The final story, "Berceuse," begins with Kim, the narrator who has had a miscarriage and is continually reading books about lost children "who sometimes come home." A Jewish cousin visits and describes an exhibit of Hansel and Gretel editions. Then the cousin equates the fairy tale to the Holocaust, with the Nazis being the witch. She compares the gold the children find with the looted money taken from the Jews and the witch's oven to the ovens used during the Holocaust. Her final, cruel comparison is with Kim, who is not Jewish, being responsible for the death of Jews and of her own child. Critic Patrick McGrath notes that the story relates to all people who are "children in the woods," looking for that trail of bread crumbs that will lead them from the darkness into the light.

RESCUE MISSIONS

The collection of ten stories is Busch's final published book. In an interview, he described the book as being about people taking journeys to help out loved ones, former lovers, children, and parents. However, those characters are also in need of rescue from their own emotional or psychological peril. The first story, titled "The Rescue Mission," begins in a trailer, located in a parking lot in Syracuse, New York. Edward, the narrator, a graduate student, is working there and accepts donations to aid the needy. A young woman comes in, looking for "a little warmth," and introduces herself as "a waitress and a punching bag." Edward has already seen the physical signs of her abuse because of his experience over the years trying to help his mother. He had come to Syracuse to identify the body of his mother, who had been battered to death by her boyfriend wielding a steam iron. Edward wishes he had confronted the man who beat his mother to death. Unable to rescue his mother, he tries to rescue Jill. However, Jill will not accept his help and leaves his protection. Edward stays in Syracuse, hoping to someday help someone, still unable to move on with his own life.

Many of the rescues in this volume are unsuccessful. In "Good to Go," a separated mother and father unite to help their son Patrick, who has been injured fighting in Iraq. His physical injury is healing but not his emotional wounds. The situation is tense because Patrick has purchased a gun, and his mother is concerned about his safety. Haunted by not being able to rescue a friend and fellow soldier in Falluja, Patrick feels responsible for the friend's death. At the conclusion of the story, as Patrick, armed with a loaded gun, lurches toward his parents, it is clear that he is certainly not "good to go." However, in "The Hay Behind the House," the outcome is more positive. Cara, fleeing a failed relationship, is attempting to "rescue" her parents. She had driven to upstate New York, allegedly to comfort her parents, who are worried about the other dying and therefore being alone. However, it is the parents, particularly her mother, who "rescue" Cara. In "I Am the News," Busch again has children return to a family home after a parent's death. The story begins with a statement about rescue, "nobody got left behind. . . . Everyone came home." In this case, the reference is to the Marine code of bringing back their dead. The narrator, an attorney, estranged from his father for years, rediscovers him while looking at items in the father's study, particularly a picture of him as a Marine. He listens to a tape the father made of an incident when he was in Korea, a gunnery sergeant, fighting his way out of enemy territory and carrying the dead. The narrator is with his younger brother, Sonny, who is always in trouble, and the older brother's attempt to "rescue" Sonny fails. However, the narrator is rescued by being reconciled, albeit through memories, with his father.

OTHER MAJOR WORKS

LONG FICTION: *I Wanted a Year Without Fall*, 1971; *Manual Labor*, 1974; *The Mutual Friend*, 1978; *Rounds*, 1979; *Take This Man*, 1981; *Invisible Mending*, 1984; *Sometimes I Live in the Country*, 1986; *War Babies*, 1989; *Harry and Catherine*, 1990; *Closing Arguments*, 1991; *Long Way from Home*, 1993; *Girls*, 1997; *The Night Inspector*, 1999; *A Memory of War*, 2003; *North: A Novel*, 2005.

NONFICTION: *Hawkes: A Guide to His Fiction*, 1973; *When People Publish: Essays on Writers and Writing*, 1986; *A Dangerous Profession: A Book About the Writing Life*, 1998.

EDITED TEXT: *Letters to a Fiction Writer*, 1999.

BIBLIOGRAPHY

Busch, Frederick. *A Dangerous Profession: A Book About the Writing Life*. New York: St. Martin's Press, 1998. Part one includes background information about his short stories, particularly the collection *The Children in the Woods*.

Gray, Paul. "Down a Bumpy Road." *The New York Times*, November 12, 2006, p. 8. Detailed review of *Rescue Missions*.

Martin, Douglas. "Frederick Busch, Author of Poetic Fiction, Dies at Sixty-Four." *The New York Times*, February 25, 2006, p. A12. An obituary that includes commentary on Busch as an author of short stories.

Walker, Charlotte Zoë. "An Interview." *Five Points* 3, no. 2 (1999): 40-78. A lengthy interview of Busch in 1998 and in 1999. He discusses how he writes and what he believes are the qualities of a good short story: "It starts and ends with great language."

Marcia B. Dinneen

ROBERT OLEN BUTLER

Born: Granite City, Illinois; January 20, 1945

PRINCIPAL SHORT FICTION
A Good Scent from a Strange Mountain, 1992
Tabloid Dreams, 1996
Had a Good Time: Stories from American Postcards,
  2004
Severance, 2006
Intercourse, 2008

OTHER LITERARY FORMS

Although Robert Olen Butler (OH-luhn BUHT-lur) has received particular praise for his short stories, his work mostly has been in the novel genre, where his special interest has been in the Vietnam experience. *The Alleys of Eden* (1981), *Sun Dogs* (1982), and *Deep Green Sea* (1997) all deal with this subject. His novel *They Whisper* (1994) has received substantial critical attention. His novel *Mr. Spaceman* (2000) had its seed in a story from the *Tabloid Dreams* collection.

ACHIEVEMENTS

Several of Robert Olen Butler's stories have been selected for the annual publication *The Best American Short Stories*; he also has received a Rosenthal Foundation Award from the American Academy of Arts and Letters, a John Simon Guggenheim Memorial Foundation Fellowship in fiction, and a grant from the National Endowment for the Arts. In 1987, the Vietnam Veterans of America gave him the Tu Do Chinh Kien Award for outstanding contributions to American culture by a Vietnam veteran. In 1993, he received the Pulitzer Prize for *A Good Scent from a Strange Mountain*. He received a fellowship from the National Endowment for the Arts in 1994. He has twice won National Magazine awards for short fiction (in 2001 and 2005) given by the American Society of Magazine Editors.

BIOGRAPHY

Robert Olen Butler was born on January 20, 1945, in Granite City, Illinois; he received a B.A. in theater from Northwestern University in 1967 and an M.A. in playwriting from the University of Iowa in 1969. He served with the U.S. Army in counterintelligence from 1969 to 1972; part of that time was spent in Vietnam, where he also served as an interpreter.

Although Butler had written plays during college, after his Vietnam experience he turned to narrative fiction, completing his first three novels during the hours he spent on a train commuting from his home to his editorial job for *Energy User News* in Manhattan. His experience in Vietnam furnished him with fertile subject matter and a desire to tell stories about it. However, his first published novel, *The Alleys of Eden* (1981), went through twenty-one rejections before it finally found a publisher. He has said of his earlier, unpublished fiction that it now serves as spare parts for his current work.

In 1985, Butler began teaching creative writing at McNeese State University, in Lake Charles, Louisiana (the setting for one of the stories from *A Good Scent from a Strange Mountain*), a congenial location in part because of its community of Vietnamese. Butler once said that he finds that much fiction about Vietnam fails to portray the Vietnamese people with sufficient depth, perhaps because it focuses primarily on military action. His task, he believes, is to write whatever books are given to him to write, regardless of their subjects or critical reception. In 1993, he began teaching at Florida State University, where he took the position of Michael Shaara Professor of Creative Writing.

ANALYSIS

Robert Olen Butler's literary concerns have focused on human relationships, especially those between men and women; on American culture; and on Vietnam. Butler's Pulitzer Prize-winning collection, *A*

Good Scent from a Strange Mountain, deals with the Vietnamese who came to America after the war: first with American attitudes toward the country's unsuccessful efforts to halt communism in Vietnam, and second with the problems of people living in an alien culture and trying to adapt to their new country while maintaining their Vietnamese values and customs. Butler has great sympathy for these displaced persons--for their sensitivity, the rich culture they left behind, and their hardships in America. He treats them, from the Saigon "bar girl" to the newly successful businessman, with respect.

Tabloid Dreams utilizes the device of the shocking headlines often used by tabloids to lure readers: invasions from outer space, dead presidents found to alive on desert islands, bizarre love relationships. Butler presents the bizarre claims literally; a *Titanic* victim is present as a spirit inhabiting a waterbed. The effects are sometimes comic--a dead husband returns as a parrot to spy on his wife--but often even the comedy has a serious edge, as Butler views the American culture that takes such headlines seriously.

Butler's willingness to use a "device" as a start point for short fiction is also evident in *Had a Good Time: Stories from American Postcards*, *Severance*, and *Intercourse*. In *Severance*, Butler records the last ninety seconds of consciousness of an array of people, mostly historical figures, who have been decapitated; each miniature story uses exactly two hundred and forty words. *Intercourse* also draws on historical figures, pairs in this case, to record their thoughts during sexual intercourse. In *Had a Good Time*, Butler uses the brief messages on a collection of postcards from early in the twentieth century to start fictions concerning the lives of the writers.

"CRICKETS"

"Crickets," from *A Good Scent from a Strange Mountain*, represents in miniature many of the themes of this collection. In the story, the narrator and his wife escape during Saigon's fall to the North Vietnamese and at present live in Lake Charles, Louisiana. Still, the narrator feels like an outsider; he is smaller than most American men, and he dislikes his American name, Ted. Worrisome, in addition, is his son's complete assimilation into American culture. Young Bill

speaks no Vietnamese and acts like his American-born schoolmates. His father, eager to connect the boy with his cultural past, suggests a game he himself once played--cricket fighting. They spend a happy morning looking for the large charcoal crickets and for the small brown fire crickets. Bill, however, worries about getting his new Nike sneakers dirty and at last wanders off, bored. Moreover, they never find any fire crickets, the small, tenacious fighters most admired by children in Vietnam. The fire crickets not only suggest Ted's youth but also, in their willingness to battle the larger charcoal crickets, recall the outnumbered South Vietnamese army. They even embody the comparatively small stature of the Vietnamese in America. Ted's final "See you later" to his son indicates his resigned acceptance of Bill's identity as an American boy.

"THE AMERICAN COUPLE"

The ironies of "The American Couple" are many layered: Butler examines the relationship between a Vietnam-born couple and their American-born counterparts, who find themselves staying at the same resort hotel in Puerto Vallarta, Mexico. (The two wives have

Robert Olen Butler (Getty Images)

won their trips on that most American of television experiences, a game show.) Gabrielle Tran wishes to give her husband, Vinh, a successful entrepreneur in America, a restful vacation. Acutely sensitive to others' moods and attitudes, she makes a game of reading the subtexts of others' conversations, particularly those of their new acquaintances, Frank Davies and his wife Eileen. Like Vinh, Davies fought in Vietnam, an experience so crucial to him that he talks about it constantly. When the couples explore the forest to see the abandoned set of the film *Night of the Iguana* (1964), the two husbands end up in a sort of war game in which Vinh injures Frank. The backdrop of American culture--game shows, the Elizabeth Taylor-Richard Burton romance that flourished during the filming of *Night of the Iguana*, the war in Vietnam--warns the reader that the Vietnamese couple may be at least as American as Frank and Eileen. During the holiday, Gabrielle goes parasailing, rising above the resort and bay in a parachute, leaving behind all ties to earthly business. For a few moments, she is a soul freed from nationality. Significantly, Frank plays no part in this freedom.

"A Good Scent from a Strange Mountain"

In this title story from the collection, Đao, a hundred-year-old Vietnamese man now living with his children in Louisiana, is visited on several successive evenings by the spirit of Ho Chi Minh, the onetime leader of North Vietnam, whom Đao had met in 1917 in Paris, where Ho Chi Minh, long before he turned his attention to politics, was studying under a famous pastry chef. Now Ho Chi Minh visits his old friend with his hands still fragrant from handling sugar as in the old days. He seems to be marking the Vietnamese tradition that in the last days of one's life one receives friends and relatives. The fact that Ho Chi Minh is long dead makes no difference.

In their conversations, the two old men delicately discuss the different directions their lives have taken; Ho Chi Minh has chosen revolutionary politics and Đao has pursued the simplest form of Buddhism, the form represented by four Chinese characters that translate into the story's title: a good scent from a strange mountain--the key to the simple mystery of joy. The story's title contrasts with Ho Chi Minh, who confesses that he is not at peace in the afterlife. In New Orleans,

Đao's daughter and son-in-law murmur about the recent murder of a local Vietnamese journalist, who, though still a patriot, has written that Vietnamese Americans should accept the reality of a communist Vietnam. The son-in-law's conversation implies that he and Đao's grandson were involved in the murder, a sour smell in the growing fragrance of the old man's impending death.

Tabloid Dreams

In this collection, Butler uses tabloid-style titles--"Boy Born with Tattoo of Elvis," "Doomsday Meteor Is Coming"--as premises for stories that take the titles' outlandish claims seriously. The results are sometimes humorous, sometimes serious. In the first story of the collection, "*Titanic* Victim Speaks Through Waterbed," the narrator has undergone a series of watery incarnations, the last one as part of a waterbed's filling. As he talks, he begins to sense how he wasted his life in pompous conformity and avoided all chances for love. An emblem of all he has missed, two people make love on the bed above him during this self-revealing narrative.

Most of the stories deal with human relationships, especially with love and marriage, fidelity and betrayal. In two stories-- "Woman Uses Glass Eye to Spy on Philandering Husband" and "Jealous Husband Returns in Form of Parrot"--spouses find comic means of checking on their mates' love affairs. The parrot story makes particularly good use of its narrator's reincarnation as a parrot. Butler gives the angry bird a parrotlike point of view, so that while he is outraged by his lover's new boyfriends, he also feels smug about the beauty of his plumage and frustrated by the limitations of his few words to communicate with the woman who has betrayed him.

One of the collection's strongest stories is "Help Me Find My Spaceman Lover," narrated by the naïvely folksy voice of Edna, who meets her spaceman (she calls him "Desi" because, like Desi Arnaz of the *I Love Lucy* television show, he speaks with an accent) in the parking lot of the Bovary, Alabama, Wal-Mart. As she describes their delicate courtship, the reader realizes that Edna is a sort of comic Madame Bovary, repressed by the conservative small-mindedness of her family and community. Desi, with no lips and with fingers that end in geckolike round pads, teaches her to see things from a wider point of view until, in the midst of the story's humor, the reader shares her sense of loss when they are parted. "How many chances do you have to be happy?" she asks.

SEVERANCE

In the *Severance* collection, Butler works from the premise that a severed head maintains consciousness for ninety seconds before lack of oxygen leads to its death. He couples that with the idea that an agitated person can speak one hundred sixty words a minute; thus each of the miniature stories in this collection, utterances from the various victims, is exactly two hundred and forty words long. The results are more like prose poems than narrative fiction, as the words tumble in an unpunctuated rush from the soon-to-die. Each "story" is preceded by a notation indicating the speaker and the date and means of death. Thus "Mud," the earliest in the collection, dies when he is beheaded by a saber-toothed tiger around 40,000 B.C.E. The march of victims moves on through Medusa and John the Baptist through the Apostles Paul and Matthew, the dragon that St. George beheaded, and then St. George himself. The Renaissance is a rich territory for decapitation: Anne Boleyn, Catherine Howard, Mary Stuart, Walter Ralegh. Other time periods include the French Revolution and the wars in Vietnam and Iraq. Aside from the political executions of the twentieth and twenty-first centuries, a number of accidental deaths (elevators are a surprisingly common means of beheadings) including car accidents (actor Jayne Mansfield) and murders (Nicole Brown Simpson). The last in the collection is Butler himself, whimsically portrayed as an elevator victim. In most cases, the victims speak as if their lives pass in front of them, often merging images of their deaths with sexual imagery. One of Butler's great strengths as a writer is his ability to create a distinctive voice for his characters. His dragon speaks with the limited perceptions of a dragon interested mostly in food and a bit bemused by the shiny skin of St. George in his armor. Sir Walter Ralegh dies recalling lovemaking with Queen Elizabeth I. A homeless man, decapitated by a train, dies remembering his father's brutality.

INTERCOURSE

Similarly in *Intercourse* Butler represents the thoughts during sex of lovers from history, ranging from Adam and Eve to Bill and Hillary Clinton. Each pair is introduced with their names and ages and the occasion and location of their coupling. Some of these interior monologues are humorous: comic Milton Berle thinks of old vaudeville jokes while making love with evangelist Aimee Semple McPherson, who thinks of herself as Mary Magdalene joining with Jesus. Mary Magdalene is represented in the volume, thinking of Jesus' compelling gaze while coupling for money with a Roman soldier, who is thinking of the harshness of military life. Violence permeates many of these musings and pleasure is a rare commodity, making the volume seem thin, despite Butler's skill in giving voice to his characters.

HAD A GOOD TIME

Butler's skill with voices is the showpiece of *Had a Good Time, Stories from American Postcards*. Butler takes a collection of postcards from the early twentieth century and reproduces at the start of each story the card's picture and scrawled message. Then he creates a story, with most being told in the voice of the card writer. In "Hotel Touraine," the first story of the collection, Butler creates a touchy young bellhop on his fifth day of employment, who is already resentful of the moneyed people he serves. When he meets a troubled guest, the bellhop is conscious of the social barrier between him and the guest, even though the latter seems oblivious to their different worlds. Throughout, the bellhop speaks with the breezy language of an ambitious young man, even as he talks himself into taking the guest's hat. In "Hiram the Desperado" Butler creates another breezy young man, this time a twelve-year-old, the bad boy of his school, who spends his time shaking down younger children for the cigarettes with which Hiram bribes the older students. Hiram's occupation as a junior gangster is humorous at first, but gradually he emerges as an abused youngster who has fallen in love with one of his teachers. His voice is full of bravado, but the reader comes to see that Hiram is too innocent to understand that his young teacher is seeking an abortion.

Some of the stories in this collection evoke the sentimentality of the early twentieth century. "Christmas, 1910," for example, gives voice to a lonely daughter of a South Dakota homesteader who finds solace only in her horse. In "Carl and I," a young wife mourns the impending death of her husband in a tuberculosis sanitarium. In "No Chord of Music," a woman asserts her independence to take her husband's new motor car out for a solo adventure.

One of the collection's most ambitious stories is "The One in White." Here a journalist reports on the arrival of a German shipload of munitions in Vera Cruz, Mexico. The journalist gives a detailed account of the intervention of American forces and the resultant bloodshed, while at the same time describing his attempt to court the young woman who does his laundry. On his postcard, an inked arrow indicates her picture in the background, while he is shown walking unconcernedly by a dead body. As a journalist, he knows that any story lies with the living, not the dead. Another lengthy story is "The Grotto." Here a timid middle-aged woman from a small town has joined a tour of Egypt with her local literary society. Her life has been devoted to caring for her mother and garden. Now the middle-aged woman finds herself alone and frightened at Egypt's noise, its smells, its foreignness. Only a public garden with familiar flowers seems reassuring, until she wanders into a grotto and has an experience that recalls events in E. M. Forster's novel *A Passage to India* (1924). She meets an Egyptian guard and discovers that they share a similar grief while at the same time remain essentially unknown to each other.

OTHER MAJOR WORKS

LONG FICTION: *The Alleys of Eden*, 1981; *Sun Dogs*, 1982; *Countrymen of Bones*, 1983; *On Distant Ground*, 1985; *Wabash*, 1987; *The Deuce*, 1989; *They Whisper*, 1994; *The Deep Green Sea*, 1997; *Mr. Spaceman*, 2000; *Fair Warning*, 2002; *Hell*, 2009.

NONFICTION: *From Where You Dream: The Process of Writing Fiction*, 2005 (Janet Burroway, editor).

BIBLIOGRAPHY

Benfey, Christopher. "He Got Mail." *The New York Times Book Reviews* (August 15, 2004): 6. In the review of *Had a Good Time*, Benfey argues that the stories lack empathy and that the many deaths in the stories suggest that America itself met a death of innocence at the start of the twentieth century.

Butler, Robert Olen. "An Interview with Robert Olen Butler." Interview by Michael Kelsay. *Poets and Writers* (January/February, 1996): 40-49. A meaty interview in which Butler discusses his life and work. He talks about his distaste for being called a "Vietnam" novelist and describes how he came to write *A Good Scent from a Strange Mountain*. He discusses the importance of the concrete world to the novelist. Kelsay includes some brief analyses of Butler's themes.

Butler, Robert Olen, and Tobey C. Herzog. *Writing Vietnam, Writing Life: Caputo, Heinemann, O'Brien, Butler.* Iowa City, Iowa: University of Iowa Press, 2008. This lengthy interview includes biographical material, discussion of Butler's Vietnam concerns, and his use of research for stories, such as those in his *Had a Good Time* series.

DeHaven, Tom. "In Flagrante Delicto." *The New York Times Book Reviews*, August 10, 2008, p. 13L. DeHaven argues that the blustering, mean; and self-centered women of the stories suggest a mean-spirited quality in the writer's approach.

Ewell, Barbara. "*Tabloid Dreams*." *America* 176 (May 17, 1997): 28-29. Ewell argues that a main theme of the collection considers the problem of determining what is fakery in the world. She links the strangeness of these stories to the strangeness that the Vietnamese characters in *A Good Scent from a Strange Mountain* found in America.

Ryan, Maureen. "Robert Olen Butler's Vietnam Veterans: Strangers in an Alien Home." *The Midwest Quarterly* (Spring, 1997): 274-295. Ryan discusses Butler's early Vietnam novels--*The Alleys of Eden*, *Sun Dogs*, and *On Distant Ground*. Ryan argues that the shared experiences of the novels' central characters make the works a trilogy. She also examines the theme of the difficulty of the veterans' reassimilation into American life.

Written and updated by Ann Davison Garbett

MICHAEL BYERS

Born: Seattle, Washington; 1971

PRINCIPAL SHORT FICTION

The Coast of Good Intentions: Stories, 1998

OTHER LITERARY FORMS

Michael Byers has published two novels since his first book, the short-story collection *The Coast of Good Intentions*, appeared in 1998. His first novel, *Long for This World* (2003), is a contemporary family drama; his second novel, *Percival's Planet* (2010), is a fictionalized account of the search for the former planet Pluto. In addition to fiction, he has published nonfiction pieces in *The Wall Street Journal*, *The Washington Post*, *Best American Travel Writing*, and other publications.

ACHIEVEMENTS

Michael Byers was a Wallace Stegner Fellow at Stanford University between 1996 and 1998. His story "Settled on the Cranberry Coast" was selected for *Prize Stories: The O. Henry Awards* in 1995; "Shipmates Down Under" was chosen for the annual publication *The Best American Short Stories* in 1997. *The Coast of Good Intentions* was a finalist for the PEN/Hemingway Award and won both the Sue Kaufman Prize from the American Academy of Arts and Letters and the Whiting Writers Award (1999), given to emerging writers of exceptional talent and promise. *The Coast of Good Intentions* was also a *New York Times* Notable Book, as was *Long for This World*, which also received the annual fiction prize from the Friends of American Writers, won the Virginia Commonwealth University First Novel Award, and was a finalist for the Washington State Book Award.

BIOGRAPHY

Michael Byers was born and raised in Seattle, Washington, graduating from Garfield High School in 1987. He received his B.A. degree from Oberlin College in Ohio and taught elementary school in Louisiana for two years in the Teach for America program. He received a master of fine arts degree from the University of Michigan and enrolled in the writing program at Stanford University before moving back to Seattle. In 2010, he was a faculty member in the University of Michigan's MFA in Creative Writing Program.

ANALYSIS

The stories of Michael Byers belong to the contemporary short-story tradition represented by Ethan Canin's 1988 collection *Emperor of the Air* and Christopher Tilghman's *In a Father's Place* (1990). Like Canin and Tilghman, Byers affirms, in a seemingly simple, matter-of-fact way, the solid, unsentimental values of family, commitment, and hope for the future. This is the kind of fiction that John Gardner urged in his book *On Moral Fiction* (1978) and that Raymond Carver embodied in his 1983 collection *Cathedral*, hailed as mellower and more hopeful than his earlier, so-called minimalist stories.

Byers focuses primarily on men who, although certainly not simple, are simply trying hard to do their best. They are, like the retired schoolteacher in "Settled on the Cranberry Coast," still looking hopefully to the future, or, when they do look to the past, are like the elderly couple in "Dirigibles," reaffirmed rather than disappointed by where they have been. When Byers takes on the persona of a woman, as he does in "A Fair Trade," the past is perceived without regret, the present is accepted with equanimity, and the future is looked forward to with hope. Even the self-absorbed father in "Shipmates Down Under," who should take responsibility for his troubled marriage, and the young widower in "Spain, One

Thousand and Three," who has, for ego's sake, treated women as conquests, ultimately are simply human with all the frailties to which humans are heir.

Such understanding, loving, and forgiving values are hard to resist, but they are also hard to present without either irony or sentimentality. Byers manages to avoid both, giving the reader characters who are neither perfect nor petulant, neither ironically bitter nor blissfully ignorant, but rather who are complex and believable human beings simply doing their best, which, Byers seems to suggest, is the most human thing anyone can do.

"SETTLED ON THE CRANBERRY COAST"

A satisfying story about second chances or the pleasant realization that it is never too late to live, "Settled on the Cranberry Coast" is narrated by Eddie, a bachelor who has just retired after teaching high school for twenty-seven years and has taken up part-time carpentry work. When Rosie, an old high school acquaintance who has also never married, hires him to repair an old house she has just bought, the story focuses quite comfortably on their inevitable gravitation toward each other. Rosie fills Eddie's need for a caring companion, while her six-year-old granddaughter Hannah, who lives with her, gives him the child he has never had.

As Eddie makes Rosie's house sturdier, their relationship grows as well, gradually affirming Eddie's opening sentence in the story: "This I know; our lives in these towns are slowly improving." Eddie can imagine moving in with Rosie and Hannah, thinking that people do not live their lives so much as come to them, as people and things "collect mysteriously" around them. At the end of the story, Eddie invites Hannah to go to the next town with him to buy radiators. In a simple scene handled perceptively and delicately by Byers, Eddie stands under a parking lot overhang in the rain, smoothing the sleeping child's hair, her head "perfectly round" on his shoulder. In a Carveresque final sentence, he thinks he is "on the verge of something" as he waits there, listening to Hannah's easy, settled breathing.

"DIRIGIBLES"

Because Byers was only in his twenties when he wrote these stories, reviewers have made much of his understanding of older characters, such as Eddie in "Settled on the Cranberry Coast." In "Dirigibles," Howard and Louise, in their late sixties and retired, are visited by James Couch, a friend from the old days, who is stopping on his way from Seattle to Montana. Couch talks about his daughter hang gliding in outer space, and Howard realizes that Couch has "gone a little way around the bend, and he [is not] coming back." When Howard sets up a film projector to show Couch old home films from the time when they were friends, it turns out he has put in the wrong film; what they see instead is a very brief scene of Louise, young and thin and almost all legs, running naked from one doorway to another. Howard and Louise both laugh, remembering when he returned from service in the Navy, and she came to the door nonchalantly nude.

After putting Couch to bed, the couple lie awake, and Howard says he played the greatest concert halls in Germany before the war, with ten thousand women waiting on his every need; he tells Louise to think of him like that, and she says, "Yes." He tells her he flew "great dirigibles of the age" over the "great nations of the earth," and she says, "Yes." In the last line, when he says "It's true. Everything is true," she says, "Oh, Howard. Howard." The conclusion is a great affirmative paean to love and union, much like the end of Molly Bloom's famous soliloquy in James Joyce's *Ulysses* (1922).

"SHIPMATES DOWN UNDER"

This story focuses on the protagonist's relationship with his nine-year-old son, who seems principled and controlled; with his six-year-old daughter, who becomes mysteriously ill; and with his wife, who feels an outsider to his connection with the children. Because the daughter's illness threatens to dominate the story, the underlying marital conflict, which is its real subject, does not become apparent until the end when the child improves just as mysteriously as she fell ill.

The boy, who intuits the unspoken conflict between the parents, says he is writing a sequel to a boys' adventure book his father recommended and urges his father to take his mother on a vacation, as their planned vacation to Perth, Australia, the father's home, has been canceled because of the daughter's illness. When the protagonist talks to his wife about this, she calls him "Mister Distant, Mister Nowhere, Mr. Say Nothing," accusing him of living in his own little world with the children while pretending she does not exist. Although he denies this, when he sees the first sentence of his son's sequel-- "My father and I live in Perth in a tiny white house with a wall around the garden"--he feels a "little bloom of secretive joy" in his heart. The story ends with his thinking that he will apologize to his wife and they will overcome their difficulties. However, when he imagines them finally taking their disrupted trip to Australia, what he thinks of is the children remembering the experience, the hotel standing strong and unchanged, "the solid keeper of my precious cargo, these two damaged packages of my detailed dreams."

"IN SPAIN, ONE THOUSAND AND THREE"

The central character in this story, Martin Tuttleman, tries to cope with the loss of his wife at age twenty-five to cancer. A computer game designer, he has been away from work so long because of her illness that now, at least temporarily, he works in the support department, giving phone advice to kids playing the game he helped design. The primary focus of the story is Martin's constant sexual fantasies about women. Before his marriage, he slept with every woman he could, and he thinks of himself as having had more sex than anyone he knows. Now that his wife, who completely filled his sexual desire during their marriage, is dead, he has begun to fantasize about other women again.

The central crucial event in the story is an ambiguous encounter with his mother-in-law in his wife's old bedroom. When he takes one of his shirts out of her closet, the mother embraces him, and he compares the feel of her body to that of his wife. They begin rubbing against each other like "shy dancers" and then abruptly push apart. The story ends with his father-in-law angrily confronting him, demanding that he apologize. When he does so, he feels good, as if he were saying he is sorry to all the women he ever seduced.

"A FAIR TRADE"

This is the longest story in the collection, and it covers the longest span of time, nearly the whole life of the central character Andie, beginning at age fourteen with her trip to live with her aunt for a period after her father's death and her mother's emotional breakdown, and ending with a visit to her aunt some forty years later when she is in her fifties. However, most of the story focuses on the time Andie lived with her Aunt Maggie; the rest of her life is recounted in brief summary. During this period, Andie has fantasies about a mysterious European man who works for an elderly couple who live across the road. The only real plot complications occur when Maggie's unscrupulous boyfriend, who is trying to get the elderly couple's farm, threatens to tell the authorities that the man has made sexual advances toward Andie; when Maggie finds out, she sends the boyfriend packing.

The last part of the story covers Andie's life after she returns to her mother--summarizing her marriage, divorce, her daughter's going off to college, and finally her move back to Seattle when she is fifty-five. Seeing her aunt's old boyfriend, now in his eighties, on television prompts a visit to her aunt, who has adopted a gay man and has a new boyfriend in his seventies. Although her aunt tells her she should have a man, Andie looks forward to twenty more years of being alone. She feels she has made a "fair trade," that her way is not a bad way to live. As she sits in a restaurant with her aunt and her adopted son, she shuffles her feet under the table, thinking that from other tables she may appear to be dancing.

OTHER MAJOR WORKS

LONG FICTION: *Long for This World*, 2003; *Percival's Planet*, 2010.

BIBLIOGRAPHY

Byers, Michael. "How to Convey Nonverbal Cues: Follow Examples of Masters of the Technique to Add Depth and Subtlety to Your Own Fiction." *Writer* 112, no. 6 (June, 2009): 40-55. An excerpt from *Faking Shapely Fiction*, Byers's collection of fourteen essays about the craft of writing that can be accessed at http://michaelbyers.org/wp-content/uploads/2009/11/FAKING-SHAPLEY-FICTION-2009.pdf.

Dyer, Richard. "Short Stories Long on Empathy, Resonance." *The Boston Globe*, August 5, 1998, p. C5. Notes that although most of Byers's stories are direct and intimate, they are also technically accomplished, with complex patterns of mirrors and receding reverberations. Says Byers's writing is so good it is patronizing to call him promising, for he has already arrived.

Marshall, John. "Seattle's Michael Byers Wins Whiting Award." *Seattle Post-Intelligencer*, November 6, 1998, p. 21. A biographical sketch and interview story. Byers credits Charles Baxter, under whom he studied at the University of Michigan, as being one of his most important inspirations, saying he likes Baxter's scrupulousness and generosity and his moral approach to fiction.

"Michael Byers' *The Coast of Good Intentions*." *Kirkus Reviews* (May 11, 1998). Calls *The Coast of Good Intentions* a strong debut collection of graceful tales about unresolved lives; says that the crab factories, cranberry bogs, and fog-shrouded shores of the Pacific Northwest are the settings for quiet but astonishing emotional epiphanies.

Seligman, Craig. "Ordinary Beauty." *The New York Times*, May 10, 1998, p. 7, 19. Discusses how Byers's technically seamless prose depicts men for whom life has not worked out the way they would like. Emphasizes that although Byers has some of the bleakness of the early Raymond Carver, his optimism shows though. Describes his writing as both melancholy and hopeful, characterized by the unexpected beauty of the ordinary.

Smyth, Charles. "Byers' Pitch Is True." *January Magazine* (October, 1998). Praises Byers for his mature and tender compassion for his characters; says his stories are about people coming to terms with what life has dealt them. Claims that comparisons to Raymond Carver do not hold up, for Byers is less turbulent and more pensive; whereas Carver liked a spare, clean style, Byers likes longer, more leisurely sentences.

Wanner, Irene. "Byers Reveals Much About His Characters." *The Seattle Times*, May 10, 1998, p. M2. Praises Byers for his ability to portray older adults and small children with convincing detail and to reveal character through carefully controlled dialogue. Calls his stories carefully crafted examples of tight, modern American short stories.

Charles E. May

SARAH SHUN-LIEN BYNUM

Born: Houston, Texas: February 14, 1972

PRINCIPAL SHORT FICTION

Ms. Hempel Chronicles, 2008
"The Erlking," 2010

OTHER LITERARY FORMS

Sarah Shun-Lien Bynum (shun LEE-ehn BI-nuhm) published her first novel, *Madeleine Is Sleeping*, in 2004. A Victorian-style fairy tale, it was described by one reviewer as "stoned Lewis Carroll."

ACHIEVEMENTS

Sarah Shun-Lien Bynum's novel *Madeleine Is Sleeping* was a finalist for the National Book Award in 2004 and won the Janet Heidinger Kafka Prize. Bynum received the Whiting Writers Award for fiction in 2005. Her story "Accomplice" was chosen for *Best American Short Stories, 2004*, and her story "Yurt" was chosen for *Best American Short Stories, 2009*. Her collection *Ms. Hempel Chronicles* was a finalist for the PEN/Faulkner Award in 2009. She was named one of "Twenty Under Forty" fiction writers by *The New Yorker* in 2010.

BIOGRAPHY

Sarah Shun-Lien Bynum, daughter of a Caucasian father and a Chinese mother, is a graduate of Brown University and the University of Iowa Writers' Workshop. She taught seventh and eighth grades at Park Slope's Berkeley Carroll School in Brooklyn for three years. She attended the famous MacDowell Colony in 2004 and the Ledig House International Writers' Colony. She moved to Los Angeles with her husband and daughter and began teaching writing and literature at the University of California, San Diego, where she became the director of the M.F.A. program.

ANALYSIS

Sarah Shun-Lien Bynum first came to public attention in 2004 when she was one of the five nominees for the National Book Award who became famous because they were so obscure. Two of the books nominated for an award usually given to a novel--Kate Walbert's *Our Kind* (2004) and Joan Silber's *Ideas of Heaven* (2004)--were actually collections of short stories, and Bynum's *Madeleine Is Sleeping* was reluctantly termed a novel, with *The New York Times* reviewer, Laura Miller, saying a more accurate term for the book would be "novel-ish." Bynum's refusal to yield to the popular demand for a clear-cut novel, preferably a realistic one, is also evident in her book *Ms. Hempel Chronicles*, which has been dubbed a "novel-in-stories," if for no other reason than the same central character appears in all of the stories in the book.

Caught between two worlds, the protagonist in all the stories in *Ms. Hempel Chronicles*, teacher Beatrice Hempel, is young enough to understand the lyrics of her middle school students' favorite songs but old enough to feel she should be shocked by them. Although she loves her job and her young charges, she worries that she is not a good teacher and fears she may be doomed to always repeat the seventh grade. Bynum, one of those precocious University of Iowa Writers' Workshop graduates, like her alter ego, Ms. Hempel, served a brief term teaching seventh and eighth grades before moving on to graduate school. *Ms. Hempel Chronicles* is a collection of fine stories, tightly organized, lyrical in style, metaphoric and mysterious, linked by their focus on the pains and pleasures of the

schoolteacher who gives the book its name. Some of the stories deal with Hempel's past relationship with her father (who has died), her younger brother Calvin, and her fiancé Amit, but most of them focus on her interactions with, and attitudes toward, her students, with whom she identifies more than is comfortable for her.

"ACCOMPLICE"

"Accomplice," which recounts Hempel's experience teaching the book Tobias Wolff's *This Boy's Life* (1989) and her experiment allowing the students to write self-evaluations, was chosen for the 2004 *Best American Short Stories.* In the contributor's notes to that anthology, Bonum says she wrote this story in an effort to understand how a well-conceived assignment managed to "go awry," adding that she was puzzled that worldly, educated parents could take reports that were so obviously written by their children to be those of the teacher. She adds that it was only when she imagined Hempel's relationship with her father that she began to grasp what it might be like, as a parent, to be the only one who recognizes one's child's talents.

The story begins with Hempel's concern about doing for her students "anecdotals"--detailed personal accounts of their progress--a task that she takes seriously, spending a couple of hours on each one; however, it is a task that she has little confidence she does well. This chore becomes interconnected with her seventh-grade class studying Wolff's *This Boy's Life*, which contains many four-letter words. When she meets with parents on the dreaded Parents' Night, and one of the parents questions the language in the book, she makes a speech about how, when she teaches J. D. Salinger's *Catcher in the Rye* (1951) in eighth grade, her students experience a shock of recognition. She wants the seventh graders to experience that also. This causes the parents to confess that they are pleased at how much their children are enjoying and relating to the Wolff book. In the days that follow, Hempel listens to how her students sympathize with the young protagonist of the book (who is treated badly by his stepfather) and how Wolff's success as an author constitutes a sweet revenge on the man. Hempel talks about her desire to be a teacher and tells her students about her own experiences in school, when her teachers scolded her for having a lot of potential that she does not fulfill.

Hempel gets the idea to have her students write their own anecdotals from *This Boy's Life*, when the protagonist forges his letter of recommendation to a boarding school. Afterward, she sends a letter to all the parents, telling them about her decision and sharing with them how enthusiastic the students were about writing their own letters. She recalls how when she was a child and took home an essay to her father that had earned a C+, her father had, instead of merely signing his name that he had read it, wrote comments critical of the teacher's remarks, praising the essay instead of criticizing it, crossing out the C+ and giving it a grade of A- instead. She also recalls a story she told about her father at his funeral, when he would pick her up after play rehearsals and let her off at the back door before parking the car in the garage, clicking his headlights off and on at her before she went in.

The story ends with one parent expressing her deep disappointment that the anecdotals were only a assignment, because she had been waiting for a long time for someone else to finally discover what she had always

Sarah Shun-Lien Bynum (AP Photo/Kathy Willens)

known about her son. The story ends with Hempel again recalling her little story at her father's funeral, which her aunt interprets as her father making sure she was safe. However, for Hempel, the gesture of flicking the lights off and on was really about their being "accomplices," plotting to prove that everyone else was woefully mistaken about her failure to "fulfill her potential."

"TALENT"

"Talent" describes Hempel's attendance at a talent show in which her students fill her with wonder but make her consider if she has stifled her talents. One of the students has choreographed a dance piece to Ludwig van Beethoven's "Moonlight Sonata," using glow-in-the-dark stars from her bedroom ceiling taped to her leotard. Hempel tries to see the student as a sylvan nymph, but finally decides that the child is lovely on the inside and that someday the outside will catch up. The funniest act features three ninth graders dancing to a song whose lyrics are about a man's penis becoming erect while dancing with someone he likes. Hempel is not sure that the parents understand the lyrics, realizing that she, like her students, has not really developed sensitivity to what is appropriate and what is inappropriate

The act that most delights Hempel is one of her students, Edward Ashe, playing an Australian didgeridoo. As he plays the giant wooden tube, the students shout out their approval, and Hempel recognizes the miracle of how he has grown into himself. The final act is by Harriet Reznik, who does sleight-of-hand magic tricks--making coins disappear and reappear--and card tricks. The story ends when Harriet does a trick in which she tries to identify a card and seems to fail, until the final moment when the card miraculously appears in the back pocket of the father who has chosen it. When the entire audience applauds loudly, Harriet opens a cardboard box and releases a large crow that flies out over the audience. As Harriet stands on the stage, marveling at what she has unleashed, the crow flies toward Hempel, and the teacher lifts her arm, stretches out her fingers, and touches it.

In many ways, this story is one of the most complex in the book, not only because it introduces Hempel's insecurity and sadness at the loss of her childhood and her talents but also because it introduces her fascination with, and love for, her students, admiring their talents and seeing them ultimately as magical and miraculous. Her efforts to be a good teacher, although she is never quite sure this is what she is meant to do, are heartfelt and convincing. She will make readers remember fondly teachers they loved.

"Yurt"

In the contributors' notes to the 2009 edition of *Best American Short Stories*, Bonum describes in some detail the source of the central character of this story, a teaching colleague she used to drink with after school in a pub in Brooklyn. She admits that she had never written a story that in its detail is so close to the person on whom it is based, but Bonum says she could not bring herself to change the details that she believes are central to the story: Yemen, the yurt, and the meat puppets, and particularly those qualities of her friend--inventiveness as a teacher, a sense of adventure, and a readiness to completely reimagine one's life. Hempel's colleague, Ms. Duffy, has returned from time off in Yemen, triumphantly pregnant. Much of the story focuses on Hempel's learning about Duffy's back story and future plans--that the father of the child is a kite artist she met when she returned from Yemen, that they plan to move upstate and live in a Mongolian-style yurt--and Duffy's dissatisfaction with how her replacement has managed her classroom. However, the central thematic focus of the story is Hempel's admiration for Duffy's sense of adventure and her courage to strike out in new directions, qualities that Hempel believes she lacks.

"The Erlking"

This story, published in *The New Yorker* series "Twenty Under Forty," was originally written for a collection of fairy tales. Based on Johann Wolfgang von Goethe's poem of the same name, "The Erlking" seems to follow many of the basic fairy-tale conventions, although it does not take place "once upon a time," but rather in the present world of anxieties experienced by a mother and her child (in Goethe's poem, it is a father and son). The mother suffers the common stresses of getting her daughter into the best schools, trying to manage money, and wanting to be loved by her child. The child, named Ondine (a mermaid), prefers the ordinary name Ruthie. Kate, the mother, wants magic for her daughter, but the daughter is not quite sure about magic and the mysterious, for she seems to be at that in-between point, where she is no longer a child but not quite yet an adult.

At a local fair, Ruthie sees a man in a cape--the perennial mysterious man in fairy tales who comes to take the child away from her parents--but he is not the same man that her mother sees. Ruthie knows from the look on the man's face that her mother does not have to come along. Ruthie believes the man is going to give her a present, and when she opens it she will be the kindest, luckiest, prettiest person in the world, "Not for pretend--for real life." She is angry with her mother for identifying the mystery man and thus somehow deflating the adventure. Ruthie believes the man is able to do things her mother cannot, such as let her live in a castle in a beautiful tower and have a little kitten and pet butterflies. The story also focuses on racial difference: Kate hopes there will be a brown doll among all the white ones, and Ruthie thinks the man will paint her skin so it is bright rather than brown and put her hair in braids like Dorothy in *The Wonderful Wizard of Oz* (1900).

The final paragraph of the story focuses on Ruthie's feeling that her surprise is turning into something other than a beautiful secret, a thing she knows will happen whether she wants it or not. While her mother looks at the prices of the dolls, Ruthie wets her pants, and while the puddle gets bigger, her mother squeezes her hand, "which is impossible, actually, because Ruthie, clever girl, kind girl, ballet dancer, thumb-sucker, brave and bright Dorothy, is already gone." "The Erlking" is a fairy tale in the sense that it deals in a magical way with that inevitable separation between the adult and the child--the mother-daughter or father-son--in which the parent feels a sense of the child's otherness.

Other major works

LONG FICTION: *Madeleine Is Sleeping*, 2004.

BIBLIOGRAPHY

Brosnan, Michael. "Ah, the Teaching Life." *Independent School* 68 (Spring, 2009): 126-127. Brosnan says *Ms. Hempel Chronicles*, which he calls a novel rather than a collection of stories, is carried not by a driving plot, but rather by separate scenes and images. Calls it a novel about a multifaceted woman that "hums with honesty and insight."

See, Carolyn. "The Teacher's Life Lessons." *Washington Post*, September 5, 2008, p. CO3. In this important appreciative review of *Ms. Hempel Chronicles*, See says that the teacher of middle school students is in her own kind of middle school, trying to make a transition from unformed adolescent--her father's favorite child--to grown-up who hates giving up her youth.

Tran, Madalena. "Sarah Shun-Lien Bonum." *Theme Magazine* (August 31, 2008). In this interview, Bonum says her collection of stories is about how complicated, painful, and fuzzy the change from childhood to adulthood can be. She also talks about the insights she gained from her students and from her stay at the MacDowell Colony in 2004.

Watrous, Malena. "Review of *Ms. Hempel Chronicles*." *San Francisco Chronicle*, September 16, 2008, p. E2. Watrous says that although many books called a "novel in stories" fail to satisfy either as novels or stories, Bonum succeeds, for she manages to write stories that seem dramatically complex and emotionally satisfying but that, taken together, create a total picture of the central character.

Charles E. May

C

GEORGE WASHINGTON CABLE

Born: New Orleans, Louisiana; October 12, 1844
Died: St. Petersburg, Florida; January 31, 1925

PRINCIPAL SHORT FICTION
Old Creole Days, 1879
Strong Hearts, 1899
Posson Jone' and Père Raphaël, 1909
The Flower of the Chapdelaines, 1918

OTHER LITERARY FORMS

George Washington Cable's published books include several novels and collections of essays in addition to his short stories. His first novel, *The Grandissimes* (1880), captured national attention and widespread praise. His essays, although less popular, delineated and criticized social, economic, and political conditions in the South.

ACHIEVEMENTS

George Washington Cable achieved distinction for his realistic portrayal of New Orleans and Louisiana in his novels and short fiction. His Creole works abound with rich details of setting and character, and his attention to the varieties of dialect mark him as a brilliant local colorist. His work, however, also defies this narrow classification. Cable's concern for the rights of African Americans and social conditions in general in the postbellum South inspired a number of essays. He also collaborated with Mark Twain on a series of lecture tours. His novels combine traditional forms, such as romance and melodrama, with the freshness of Creole detail and careful consideration of the looming social issues of the late nineteenth century. One of the finest regional writers of his day, Cable introduced the exotic Creole South to the rest of the country. He paved the way for later writers, such as William Faulkner, who likewise surpass mere regional identification to present intensely absorbing stories of the human condition.

BIOGRAPHY

After the death of his father, George Washington Cable left school at the age of twelve and worked in a warehouse. During the years he should have been in college he was a Confederate soldier. Ever eager to learn, he read incessantly while in the service. After the war he was a reporter for a short time, then a clerk for a cotton firm while continuing to publish personal essays signed "Drop Shot" for the New Orleans *Picayune*. In 1873, he met Edward King, who carried copies of his stories to the editors of *Scribner's Monthly*. In October of that year Cable's first story was published. Desiring to be closer to literary circles, Cable left the South and settled with his family in Northampton, Massachusetts. He loved the energetic atmosphere of the North, but much of what he wrote about the South after the move lacked the clarity and fire of his earlier work. During a return trip to the South in 1925, Cable died, leaving stories of a period that would never be again.

ANALYSIS

By the 1880's, much of the passion that had divided the country during the Civil War had been displaced by a growing interest in life in other regions of the newly rejoined republic. No longer separated by political and economic differences, people began not only to accept cultural differences but also to express keen interest in them, and the fiction of local color was perfectly suited to these readers. Stories of the day tended to emphasize verisimilitude of detail within scenic elements: Settings were often colorful extravaganzas; characters were typically drawn to emphasize peculiarities of their region or culture yet were often poorly developed; and plots were often thin.

These characteristics are reflected in George Washington Cable's stories of New Orleans: Settings sparkle with picturesque detail and rich imagery, and character descriptions emphasize the cultural or regional peculiarities of speech, manner, and thought. Cable's characters are rarely developed beyond the superficial, being distanced by narrative perspective, vague in motivation, and frequently shrouded in mystery. Plots are sketchy events, lacking causal relationships and frequently relying on melodrama. Given these general characteristics, Cable's stories could be pigeonholed as merely more local color; but then much that is specifically Cable's richness would be lost. Deeper elements of Cable's unique literary perspective, however, play an important role in the total artistic impact of his stories. His New Orleans still retained much of its international flavor and embraced a unique mixture of races, clashing cultures, opposing values, old loyalties, and old hatreds; poverty and wealth coexisted; and caste systems were accepted and propagated. Cable's strongly developed social consciousness directed his writing talents to portray these elements sensitively. Thus, while preserving the picturesque, Cable probed the ramifications of racial juxtaposition and of social problems, capturing more completely the spirit of his literary domain. This added dimension of circumstantial reality, born out of Cable's personality and New Orleans's uniqueness, distinguishes Cable's powerful stories from the mass of local-color fiction of his day.

"'SIEUR GEORGE"

Cable's first story, "'Sieur George," reflects characteristics typical both of local-color fiction and of Cable's fiction. The standard picturesque setting, in this case an old tenement building, rises before readers as the narrator masterfully describes it: "With its gray stucco peeling off in broad patches, it has the solemn look of gentility in rags, and stands, or, as it were, hangs, about the corner of two ancient streets, like a faded fop who pretends to be looking for employment." The simile of inanimate object to animate one is precise, and the images reinforce each other to create a subtle atmosphere of age and decay. Through its doors are seen "masses of cobwebbed iron . . . overhung by a creaking sign" into a courtyard "hung with many lines of wet clothes, its sides hugged by rotten staircases that

seem vainly trying to clamber out of the rubbish." The neighborhood has been "long since given up to fifth-rate shops." The setting is thus vividly drawn by a composite of details each artistically contributing to a subtle atmosphere of time and ruin vital to the story's texture.

It is not unusual for Cable's characters to echo the atmosphere of the setting, giving it an organic quality that continues the link of inanimate to animate. When 'Sieur George first appeared, both he and the neighborhood were "fashionable." At the time of the story, some fifty years later, he is a reclusive "square small man" draped in a "newly repaired overcoat." No longer fashionable and usually drunk, 'Sieur George stumbles home

> never careening to right or left but now forcing himself slowly forward, as if there was a high gale in front, and now scudding briskly ahead at a ridiculous little dogtrot, as if there was a tornado behind.

The descriptive detail is visually vivid and continues the image of time and its erosion.

George Washington Cable (Library of Congress)

As is typical of local-color fiction, however, 'Sieur George is rather superficially portrayed, and this weakens the story. His actions are related by the omniscient narrator, whose detached perspective never allows readers to experience any genuine sympathetic involvement with 'Sieur George. The reader hears about him but never knows his thoughts or feelings; consequently, he seems little more than a cardboard cutout. His motivations are vague, and his daily drunks continue only to be interrupted unexpectedly by surprising events. One day 'Sieur George shocks the neighborhood as he emerges from his apartment in full regimentals and marches off to the Mexican War, leaving his sister behind to become the new occupant of his rooms. Several years later, he suddenly reappears with battle scars and a tall dark companion. 'Sieur George and the stranger visit the sister weekly until her marriage to the stranger is announced by her appearance in bridal array. With the newlyweds gone, 'Sieur George returns to his rooms and drunken habits until the pattern is again interrupted when he returns home with the couple's infant. Since her mother had died and her drunken father had drowned in the river, 'Sieur George attentively raises the girl until it would violate proprieties for her to stay; finally, in a senseless moment, he blurts out that the only way for her to stay is for her to become his wife. She utters a mournful cry, runs to her room, and early the next morning leaves for a convent. 'Sieur George returns to drunkenness and finally becomes a penniless, homeless drifter searching the prairie "to find a night's rest in the high grass"-- "and there's an end."

Not only are his motivations vague, but he is also shrouded in Cable's frequent cloak of mystery. After 'Sieur George has lived in the neighborhood for about a year, "something happened that greatly changed the tenor of his life." "Hints of a duel, of a reason warped, of disinheritance, and many other unauthorized rumors, fluttered up and floated off." Soon he begins to display the "symptoms of decay" stumbling home, and "whatever remuneration he received went its way for something that left him dingy and threadbare." The artistically interwoven pictures of him recycle the images of decay and ruin, but the only thing the reader knows that 'Sieur George cares about, and strongly so, is the

mysterious small hair trunk he carefully guards. Even 'Sieur George's implied heroism is dubious and unconvincing. The reader hears about him marching off to war, returning with battle scars, and bravely directing the infant to womanhood; yet each admirable event on the one hand is treated only summarily, and on the other is undercut by his return to drunkenness. He is not a great man who, in a weak moment, has fallen prey to vicious evils; neither he nor his vices have any true tragic element. Finally, he is not a tragic man inspiring sympathy but merely a man in a pathetic situation, and it is the feeling for his situation with which the reader is left.

It is 'Sieur George's landlord, Kookoo, who emerges most vividly from this story. Like his tenant and his building, Kookoo also shows the effects of time, for the "ancient Creole" has grown "old and wrinkled and brown." He is vividly sketched by three descriptive strokes: "He smokes cascarilla, wears velveteen and is as punctual as an executioner." The reader's perception of Kookoo is enhanced by the narrator's attitude toward him as a "periodically animate mummy" possessing "limited powers of conjecture." Kookoo's favorite pastimes are to eavesdrop on his tenants, watch the habits of 'Sieur George, and revel in the mystery of 'Sieur George's small hair trunk. His personality emerges through his actions, clearly motivated by nosiness and curiosity. Moreover, the reader becomes a partner to his consciousness as 'Sieur George leaves for war, taking the omniscient narrator with him. It is Kookoo, driven by a fifty-year-old curiosity and taking advantage of 'Sieur George's open door and drunken stupor, who leads the reader to the mysterious trunk and a final revelation about its owner: "The trunk was full, full, crowded down and running over full, of the tickets of the Havanna Lottery!"

The plot of "'Sieur George" is thin, often vague, and finally melodramatic; and the climax is less than satisfying because the ramifications of compulsive gambling have not been portrayed in 'Sieur George's superficial development. It is not uncommon for Cable, with his social consciousness, to give social problems an antagonistic role, but the problem here is that neither 'Sieur George nor his vices stand out clearly enough against the images of Kookoo and Creole life; thus, their possible impact is lost in the collage. What holds the reader's attention, however, is the sustained suspense created by the adroit changes in the angle of narration. The perspective shifts back and forth between the omniscient narrator and Kookoo: The narrator, who initially dominates the reader's perspective of 'Sieur George, demonstrates a vast knowledge with a detached precision; when 'Sieur George is absent, however, the reader becomes partner with Kookoo, whose perspective is limited but allows deeper involvement. When 'Sieur George returns, so does the perspective of the omniscient narrator. Not only does the reader know both "sides" of the story, but also the suspense of Kookoo's curiosity is sustained as the narrator continues. This technique and its adroit management create a sustained suspense that holds the reader to the end. Cable's changing angles of narration, along with the scenic setting and glimpses of Creole life, are the final salvation of the story. The reader may well be disappointed by the less than satisfying climax, but reaching it is a fine experience, and the final praise of the story is that it is so well told.

"JEAN-AH POQUELIN"

In a later story, "Jean-ah Poquelin," Cable uses basically the same techniques, but much more effectively. The story begins in a time when the "newly established American Government was the most hateful thing in Louisiana--when the Creoles were still kicking at such vile innovations as the trial by jury, American dances, antismuggling laws, and the printing of the Governor's proclamation in English." This atmosphere of conflict is quickly followed by a sense of impending doom as the narrator centers the reader's attention on the stark details of the old Poquelin plantation: standing above the marsh, "aloof from civilization," "lifted up on pillars, grim, solid, and spiritless," "like a gigantic ammunition wagon stuck in the mud and abandoned by some retreating army." Two dead cypress trees "dotted with roosting vultures" and crawling waters filled with reptiles "to make one shudder to the ends of his days" create around the home an atmosphere of foreboding. This atmosphere is continued as the description of Jean Marie Poquelin unfolds. He was "once an opulent indigo planter, standing high in the esteem" of his friends but is "now a hermit, alike shunned by and shunning all

who had ever known him." Typically reflecting the setting's atmosphere, Jean is yet somewhat unique among local-color characters because of his multifaceted and full development.

His personality is discovered through a series of flashbacks to happier times. Jean had been "a bold, frank, impetuous, chivalric adventurer," but there was no trait for which he was better known than "his apparent fondness" for his little brother, Jacques. Jacques, thirty years Jean's junior and really a half-brother, was "a gentle studious book-loving recluse." Together "they lived upon the ancestral estate like mated birds, one always on the wing, the other always in the nest." The brothers' tranquil relationship is abruptly interrupted when Jean returns from a two-year slaving expedition apparently without Jacques, who, unable to tolerate his brother's long absence, had begged to go along. Jean remained silent on this issue, but rumor was that Jacques had returned "but he had never been seen again," and "dark suspicion" fell upon Jean as his name "became a symbol of witchery, devilish crime, and hideous nursery fictions." Rumors of blood-red windows, owls with human voices, and the ghost of the departed brother keep the plantation and Jean shrouded in mystery while children viciously taunt him in the streets, calling names and throwing dirt clods with youthful expertise, as ignorant adults blame him for all their misfortunes. Old Jean betrays his silence as latent boldness responds to this ill treatment; "rolling up his brown fist" he would "pour forth such an unholy broadside of French imprecation and invective as would all but craze" the Creole children "with delight." His actions are justified, and readers cheer him on as they become personally involved in the story.

Time passes, and immigrants flood New Orleans, forcing growing pains on the city. Greedy non-Creole American land developers and displaced Creoles begin to encroach on Jean's lonely home. Through Jean's reaction to these forces, the reader learns more about him and becomes more deeply involved in his plight. Hoping to stop the invaders, Jean appeals to the governor, and, in doing so, he projects much of his personality: He stands proudly with his large black eye "bold and open like that of a war horse, and his jaw shut together with the fierceness of iron." His open-neck shirt reveals "a herculean breast, hard and grizzled," yet there is "no fierceness of defiance in his look" but rather a "peaceful and peaceable fearlessness."

Jean's heroic stature is sensitively human, for on his face, "not marked in one or another feature, but as it were laid softly upon the countenance like an almost imperceptible veil, was the imprint of some great grief"--faint "but once seen, there it hung." In broken English, Jean protests the invasion of his privacy, but the reader senses the futility of his attempt as he is answered by questions about the wicked rumors. His temper flares as he declares, "I mine me hown bizniss." Jean's motivations may still be vague, but the strength of his convictions as to his rights and his powerful presence inspire the reader's respect.

Although he marches from the officials' rooms, Jean is kept ever present as he is discussed by the American and Creole developers. Old stories are retold, and Jean gains nobility as the greedy invaders callously plan how to oust him so that they can replace his home with a market. Their shallow commercialism and ignorant superstitions are illuminating foils to Jean's deep-seated desire to preserve his home. Jean's only champion, Little White, only temporarily stalls a mob determined to "chirivari" him, and ultimately they rush forward only to be met by Jean's only slave, an African mute, carting a draped coffin through the front gate. Old Jean is dead, and the crowd stands silent, except for its unanimous gasp at seeing the white figure slowly walking behind the cart. The cause of so many rumors and cruelties is the "living remains--all that was left--of little Jacques Poquelin, the long-hidden brother--a leper, as white as snow." The African adjusts the weight of the coffin on his shoulders, and "without one backward glance upon the unkind human world, turning their faces toward the ridge in the depth of the swamp known as Leper's Land, they stepped into the jungle, disappeared and were never seen again."

Melodramatic touches are frequent as the story turns on Jean's selfless devotion. The climax brings the reader's compassion to a peak well supported by all that has been learned about Jean: how his friends have spoken so well of him; the knowledge of his loving relationship with Jacques; and his justifiable responses to

the jeering children, Creole cruelty, and non-Creole American aggression. Although his motivations are vague until the end, and he is shrouded in mystery, the rightness of his actions and speeches assures the reader of his innate goodness.

Cable again employs a changing angle of narration, but Jean is ever the subject of other characters' thoughts and actions; thus, he is ever kept before the reader. All the elements of the story are clearly aimed at telling the story of Jean and his doomed resistance. Compassion for Jean and his brother remains strong after the conclusion of the story, one of the few in which Cable beautifully balances his romantic fiction and social criticism. The story succeeds as both; it is a haunting "ghost" story while it attacks ignorant prejudice and makes a touching plea for human compassion.

Cable was the first literary voice of the New South. Writing within the realm of local-color fiction, he enriched his stories with the circumstantial reality of local history; he preserved the beautiful detail of colorful New Orleans in impressionistic backgrounds peopled by unique characters; and he was the first writer to bring the crude patois of the Creoles accurately to print. Cable's stories are a unique blend of romantic elements and circumstantial reality drawn from his literary domain. Although many of his stories are hampered by a lack of clear direction, the cluttering, often paragraphic glimpses of different cultures are rewarding reading; and where Cable achieved a precise utility of a story's elements, the total impact is unforgettable.

OTHER MAJOR WORKS

LONG FICTION: *The Grandissimes*, 1880; *Madame Delphine*, 1881; *Dr. Sevier*, 1884; *Bonaventure*, 1888; *John March, Southerner*, 1894; *The Cavalier*, 1901; *Bylow Hill*, 1902; *Kincaid's Battery*, 1908; *Gideon's Band*, 1914; *Lovers of Louisiana*, 1918.

NONFICTION: *The Creoles of Louisiana*, 1884; *The Silent South*, 1885; *Strange True Stories of Louisiana*, 1889; *The Negro Question*, 1890; *The Busy Man's Bible*, 1891; *A Memory of Roswell Smith*, 1892; *The Amateur Garden*, 1914.

MISCELLANEOUS: *The Cable Story Book: Selections for School Reading*, 1899.

BIBLIOGRAPHY

Bikle, Lucy Leffingwell Cable. *George W. Cable: His Life and Letters*. New York: Charles Scribner's Sons, 1928. This biography of Cable, written by his daughter, has the advantage of immediacy to, and intimacy with, the subject. Bikle covers the life of Cable primarily through the many letters that he wrote. The book is arranged chronologically, but the lack of an index makes finding specific information difficult at times.

Butcher, Philip. *George W. Cable*. New York: Twayne, 1962. This literary biography studies the life of Cable in the context of his work, and vice versa. Like other biographies in the Twayne authors series, it provides a useful general introduction. Butcher covers the major phases of Cable's life--from New Orleans and *Old Creole Days* to the friendship with Mark Twain to his social and political involvement--in an honest, engaging fashion.

Cleman, John. *George Washington Cable Revisited*. New York: Twayne, 1996. A revision of an earlier critical introduction to Cable's life and work. Discusses Cable's major work and the social context that frames it. Includes chapters devoted to Cable's advocacy of civil rights for African Americans, his political writing, and his later works of "pure fiction."

Ekstrom, Kjell. *George Washington Cable: A Study of His Early Life and Work*. New York: Haskell House, 1966. Ekstrom focuses on Cable's Creole fiction, giving much historical, literary, and cultural background to Cable's early work. In addition to the biographical information on Cable's early years, Ekstrom also discusses literary and nonliterary sources for the Creole short stories and novels.

Elfenbein, Anna Shannon. *Women on the Color Lines: Evolving Stereotypes and the Writings of George Washington Cable, Grace King, Kate Chopin*. Charlottesville: University Press of Virginia, 1989. Argues that Cable identified racism with sexism and classism and subverted the traditional literary categories that have segmented white women and women of color. Discusses how in the story "Tite Poulete" Cable moves beyond racism to a consideration of the shared oppression of all women.

Jones, Gavin. "Signifying Songs: The Double Meaning of Black Dialect in the Work of George Washington Cable." *American Literary History* 9 (Summer, 1997): 244-267. Discusses the interaction of African American and French-Creole culture in Cable's works. Argues that African American dialect, song, and satire were transmitted to the white community subversively.

Ladd, Barbara. *Nationalism and the Color Line in George W. Cable, Mark Twain, and William Faulkner*. Baton Rouge: Louisiana State University Press, 1996. Argues that racial thinking about the lower Mississippi River area, on which Cable focused, is colonialist and assimilationist.

Payne, James Robert. "New South Narratives of Freedom: Rereading George Washington Cable's 'Tite Poulette' and *Madame Delphine*." *Melus* 27, no. 1 (Spring, 2002): 21. Concentrates on the themes of emancipation and racism in two of Cable's works, the short story "Tite Poulette" and the novel *Madame Delphine*. Examines the characters in the works, Cable's fictional technique, his religious preoccupations, and the manner in which he discusses the possibility of transforming traditional Southern values and cultural practices regarding racial and gender roles.

Robinson, Owen. "Truly Strange New Orleans: The Unstable City in George Washington Cable's *Strange True Stories of Louisiana*." *European Journal of American Culture* 26, no. 2 (2007): 97-108. Argues that the stories in Cable's *Strange True Stories of Louisiana* depict New Orleans as being as much a Caribbean city as an American one, with European influence an equally important element in the city's identity. Maintains that while Cable creates a chronological narrative of the city and the wider regions, he also presents a multitude of voices merging and clashing with one another, blurring the boundaries of fact and fiction as they obscure the boundaries of identity.

Rubin, Louis D., Jr. *George W. Cable: The Life and Times of a Southern Heretic*. New York: Pegasus, 1969. This critical biography focuses on Cable's position within the tradition of southern writers, while also noting that Cable--atypically for

Southerners of the time--supported campaigns to give African Americans equal rights in the post-bellum period. Rubin provides a number of excellent readings of, and insightful commentaries on Cable's works, including a chapter on *Old Creole Days*. The select bibliography is useful for locating more information on Cable's fiction.

Turner, Arlin. *George W. Cable: A Biography*. Durham, N.C.: Duke University Press, 1956. Turner's thoroughly researched biography in many ways set the

standard for further Cable studies. Turner discusses in great detail not only Cable's life but also his literary work, political involvement, geographical contexts, and the important historical events that affected Cable's life and work. Like the rest of this biography, the index and bibliography are extensive.

Kathy Ruth Frazier
Updated by Ann A. Merrill

JAMES M. CAIN

Born: Annapolis, Maryland; July 1, 1892
Died: University Park, Maryland; October 27, 1977

PRINCIPAL SHORT FICTION

"*Pastorale,*" 1928
"*The Taking of Monfaucon,*" 1929
"*Come-Back,*" 1934
"*Brush Fire,*" 1936
"*Dead Man,*" 1936
"*Hip, Hip, the Hippo,*" 1936
"*The Birthday Party,*" 1936
"*Coal Black,*" 1937
"*Everything but the Truth,*" 1937
"*The Girl in the Storm,*" 1940
Career in C Major, and Other Stories, 1943
"*Payoff Girl,*" 1952
"*Cigarette Girl,*" 1953
"*Two O'Clock Blonde,*" 1953
"*The Visitor,*" 1961
The Baby in the Icebox, and Other Short Fiction,
    1981 (posthumous, Roy Hoopes, editor)
Career in C Major, and Other Fiction, 1986
    (Hoopes, editor)

OTHER LITERARY FORMS

James M. Cain wrote novels, plays, screenplays, and magazine articles, in addition to short stories. The Mystery Writers of America designated him a Grand Master in 1970. His major novels include *The Postman*

Always Rings Twice (1934), *Mildred Pierce* (1941), and *Double Indemnity*, originally serialized in a magazine in 1936 and published as a book in 1943. Earlier in his writing career, he was a reporter and an editorial writer.

ACHIEVEMENTS

Though sometimes included among the top writers of hard-boiled crime fiction, James M. Cain himself scorned this label. Critical opinion has swung around to his view that, indeed, he wrote about murders, from the criminal's point of view, but he did not write crime fiction. What makes his writing so gripping is not the typical pull to resolve a puzzle but the fascination of ordinary people suddenly finding themselves making a wish come true, a concept that Cain described as terrifying and that he compared to opening Pandora's box. The influential existentialist writer Albert Camus claimed that his own novel *L'Étranger* (1942; *The Stranger*, 1946) was influenced by Cain's *The Postman Always Rings Twice*.

BIOGRAPHY

James Mallahan Cain was the oldest of five children of Rose Mallahan Cain, a singer, and James William Cain, a professor at St. John's College in Annapolis, Maryland. His grandparents were Irish immigrants who settled in New Haven, Connecticut, where his father attended Yale University. Cain was eleven when his father became the president of Washington College.

Cain enrolled there at the age of fifteen, was graduated in 1910, received a master's degree in 1917, and taught math and English for a year after giving up his ambition to become an opera singer. He was a reporter for several newspapers and taught journalism at St. John's before he spent seventeen years writing screenplays in Hollywood. His fourth marriage, to opera singer Florence Macbeth Whitwell in 1947, was a happy one, which encouraged him to write about music in four of his novels. The literary figure who exerted the single greatest influence on his career was H. L. Mencken, with whom he corresponded and who published his work in his periodical, the *American Mercury*.

ANALYSIS

James M. Cain's characters are ordinary people--capable of decency, passion, and crime--caught up in situations from which they seem incapable of extricating themselves. Cain valued the commonplace person and prided himself on writing the way people talk. In order to write accurately about the vagrants in *The Moth* (1948), for example, he visited the missions in Los Angeles where tramps gathered and interviewed many of them. He keeps up a relentless pace in his stories with a minimum of description and with blunt, brisk, and fast-paced dialogue.

Lack of exposition, typical of Cain's narrative style, also helps maintain the momentum. The reader is immediately confronted with an action in the present; in only one of Cain's twelve novels is there any flashback to explain the protagonist's background. What mattered to Cain's readers was not his characters' appearance. Cain's editors usually had to ask him to be more explicit about what his people looked like; the most he ever gave them was a film-star approximation: "Like Clark Gable [or some other movie star]--fill it in yourself." What mattered to Cain was a character's "presence" as expressed in action. It was probably this virile approach to storytelling that endeared him to the French existentialists and the postwar Italians, who favored such a style.

"BRUSH FIRE"

The opening scene of "Brush Fire" depicts a group of men wielding shovels against a forest fire, coughing from the smoke and cursing. They have come up from the railroad yards on the promise of money to be made; they have been fed a ration of stew in army mess kits, outfitted in denims and shoes, and taken by truckloads from Los Angeles to the hills to fight this brush fire. Readers do not learn the protagonist's name until well into the story when the Civilian Conservation Corps (CCC) man calls out the roll; readers never learn the name of his girlfriend. The one introspective moment in the story expresses the protagonist's regret at leaving her:

They parted--she to slip into the crowd unobtrusively; he to get his mess kit, for the supper line was already formed. As he watched the blue dress flit between the tents and disappear, a gulp came into his throat; it seemed to him that this girl he had held in his arms, whose name he hadn't even thought to inquire, was almost the sweetest human being he had ever met in his life.

By the end of the story he has committed murder for the sake of this nameless girl, and the man he kills in the evening is the same man whose life he had saved in the morning. The reporters who have covered both events are struck with the inherent ironies, but the protagonist, who moves unthinkingly from blind impulse, is unaware of ironies; such abstractions are foreign to him.

Cain keeps the story moving by not stopping to examine motivations; he simply carries the reader along in the rushing momentum of the story. The third shift is summoned for roll call and told to turn over their shovels to the fourth shift that is arriving. They assemble with singed hair, smoke-seared lungs, and burned feet. At the same moment that readers learn the protagonist's name, they learn the antagonist's also.

As each name was called there was a loud "Yo" so when his name, Paul Larkin, was called, he yelled "Yo" too. Then the foreman was calling a name and becoming annoyed because there was no answer. "Ike Pendleton! Ike Pendleton!"

Instantly Larkin races up the slope toward the fire where "a cloud of smoke doubled him back." He retreats, sucks in a lungful of air, then charges to where a body lay face down. The action is tersely rendered in taut, lean prose. "He tried to lift, but his lungful of air was spent: he had to breathe or die. He expelled it, inhaled, screamed at the pain of the smoke in his throat."

Critics complain that Cain's characters are so elemental that they seem stripped down to an animal vitality; in fact, it is precisely to this quality that Pendleton's survival is attributed. "He fought to his feet, reeled around with the hard, terrible vitality of some kind of animal." The men are fed and paid fifty cents an hour, and then the visitors, newspaper reporters, and photographers arrive. When they ask if there were any casualties, someone remembers that a man, whose name no one can remember, has been rescued. Paul is interviewed and has his picture taken as a crowd gathers. A girl, kicking a pebble, says, "Well, ain't *that* something to be getting his picture in the paper?" They talk, he buys her an ice-cream cone, they go for a walk, they embrace, and he brings her back to the camp without ever having exchanged names.

Later he sees Ike Pendleton, with doubled fists, cursing her, and the girl, backing away, crying. The explanation of the conflict is given by an anonymous choric figure. Cain claims that this technique of communicating information through dialogue--a mode of narration that effaces the narrator, and that Ernest Hemingway is usually credited as having invented--was his invention; he says that he arrived at this method of minimal exposition independently, before he had ever read any Hemingway. Its effectiveness can be judged by the shock with which the reader realizes that the girl is Mrs. Pendleton.

The fight accelerates; Paul intervenes and tension mounts toward the inevitable conclusion. That Cain can convince the reader that such an improbable event could seem inevitable is a mark of his storytelling skill. The reader is not given time to think about it as these characters act out their basest, most primitive impulses.

> He lunged at Ike with his fist--missed. Ike struck with the knife. He fended with his left arm, felt the steel cut in. With his other hand he struck, and Ike staggered back. There was a pile of shovels beside him, almost tripping him up. He grabbed one, swung, smashed it down on Ike's head. Ike went down. He stood there, waiting for Ike to get

up, with that terrible vitality he had shown this morning. Ike didn't move.

This, then, is the meaning of death, that the animal motions cease, and this is the end of the story, in which its meaning is embodied in its action without any philosophic implications, without any cultural pretensions, a brutal depiction of sexual and aggressive drives in men too crude to sublimate them and too hungry to repress them.

OTHER MAJOR WORKS

LONG FICTION: *The Postman Always Rings Twice*, 1934; *Double Indemnity*, 1936, serial, 1943, book; *Serenade*, 1937; *The Embezzler*, 1940; *Mildred Pierce*, 1941; *Love's Lovely Counterfeit*, 1942; *Past All Dishonor*, 1946; *Sinful Woman*, 1947; *The Butterfly*, 1947; *The Moth*, 1948; *Jealous Woman*, 1950; *The Root of His Evil*, 1951 (also pb. as *Shameless*, 1979); *Galatea*, 1953; *Mignon*, 1963; *The Magician's Wife*, 1965; *Rainbow's End*, 1975; *The Institute*, 1976; *Cloud Nine*, 1984; *The Enchanted Isle*, 1985.

PLAYS: *Crashing the Gates*, pr. 1926; *Theological Interlude*, pb. 1928 (dialogue); *Trial by Jury*, pb. 1928 (dialogue); *Citizenship*, pb. 1929 (dialogue); *Will of the People*, pb. 1929 (dialogue); *The Governor*, pb. 1930; *Don't Monkey with Uncle Sam*, pb. 1933 (dialogue); *The Postman Always Rings Twice*, pr. 1936 (adaptation of his novel); *7-11*, pr. 1938.

SCREENPLAYS: *Algiers*, 1938; *Stand Up and Fight*, 1938; *Gypsy Wildcat*, 1944.

NONFICTION: *Our Government*, 1930; *Sixty Years of Journalism*, 1986 (Roy Hoopes, editor).

MISCELLANEOUS: *The James M. Cain Cookbook: Guide to Home Singing, Physical Fitness, and Animals (Especially Cats)*, 1988 (essays and stories; Roy Hoopes and Lynne Barrett, editors).

BIBLIOGRAPHY

Cain, James M. "An Interview with James M. Cain." Interview by John Carr. *The Armchair Detective* 16, no. 1 (1973): 4-21. In this 1973 interview, Cain reveals interesting highlights of his career as a reporter and explains the influence of Vincent Sergeant Lawrence, a journalist and screenwriter, on his work. His comments on his three major novels are particularly valuable.

Contains an annotated list of people important in Cain's life and a bibliography of Cain's writings.

Forter, Gregory. "Double Cain." *Novel* 29 (Spring, 1996): 277-298. Argues that the primitive sense of smell is a powerful force in Cain's fiction; maintains that for Cain smell overcomes resistance and enslaves one to the other.

Hoopes, Roy. *Cain*. New York: Holt, Rinehart and Winston, 1982. This comprehensive biography on Cain is divided into four chronological parts. Covers his years in Maryland and France, New York, Hollywood, and Hyattsville. Includes an afterword on Cain as newspaperman. Supplemented by extensive sources and notes, a list of Cain's publications, a filmography, and an index.

Horsley, Lee. *The Noir Thriller*. New York: Palgrave, 2001. A scholarly, theoretically informed study of the thriller genre and its embrace of the dark thematic material that lent itself to adaptation into film noir. Cain is prominently featured. Bibliographic references and index.

Madden, David. *James M. Cain*. New York: Twayne, 1970. An excellent introductory volume that accepts Cain's varied reputation as an excellent, a trashy, an important, and an always popular writer. Approaches every major aspect of his work on several levels, including his life in relation to his writing, analyses of his characters, and his technical expertise. Complemented by notes, a bibliography of primary and secondary sources, and an index.

Marling, William. *The American Roman Noir: Hammett, Cain, and Chandler*. Athens: University of Georgia Press, 1995. An intriguing exercise in literary criticism that links the hard-boiled writing of Dashiell Hammett, James M. Cain, and Raymond Chandler to contemporary economic and technological changes. Marling sees the authors as pioneers of an aesthetic for the postindustrial age.

_____. "James M. Cain." In *A Companion to Crime Fiction*, edited by Charles J. Rzepka and Lee Horsley. Malden, Mass.: Wiley-Blackwell, 2010. An overview of Cain's life, work, and career that includes information on some of his short stories. Marling describes how Cain "changed forever how American crime fiction was written."

Nyman, Jopi. *Hard-Boiled Fiction and Dark Romanticism*. New York: Peter Lang, 1998. Examines the fiction of Cain, Dashiell Hammett, Ernest Hemingway, and Horace McCoy.

Oates, Joyce Carol. "Man Under Sentence of Death: The Novels of James M. Cain." In *Tough Guy Writers of the Thirties*, edited by David Madden. Carbondale: Southern Illinois University Press, 1968. Approaches Cain's novels as significant for the light they throw on his relationship with the American audience of the 1930's and 1940's. A brief but broad-ranging essay.

Pelizzon, V. Penelope, and Nancy M. West. "Multiple Indemnity: Tabloid Melodrama, Narrative Mobility, and James M. Cain." In *Tabloid, Inc.: Crimes, Newspapers, Narratives*. Columbus: Ohio State University Press, 2010. Chronicles how tabloid newspaper coverage of a sensational murder case, in which a woman and her lover killed the woman's husband, influenced Cain's fiction. The plot of a woman scheming to kill her husband was featured in Cain's short story "Pastorale" and later in his novels *Double Indemnity* and *The Postman Always Rings Twice*.

Skenazy, Paul. *James M. Cain*. New York: Continuum, 1989. A comprehensive study of Cain's work. Skenazy is more critical of his subject's writing than is David Madden but acknowledges Cain's importance and his continuing capacity to attract readers.

Wilson, Edmund. "The Boys in the Back Room." In *Classics and Commercials*. New York: Farrar, Straus & Giroux, 1950. A personal essay by an astute social and cultural commentator. Groups Cain with John Steinbeck, John O'Hara, William Saroyan, and other writers in the 1930's and 1940's who were influenced by Ernest Hemingway. Considers Cain to be the best of these writers.

Ruth Rosenberg
Updated by Shakuntala Jayaswal

ERSKINE CALDWELL

Born: White Oak, Georgia; December 17, 1903
Died: Paradise Valley, Arizona; April 11, 1987

PRINCIPAL SHORT FICTION

American Earth, 1931
Mama's Little Girl, 1932
Message for Genevieve, 1933
We Are the Living: Brief Stories, 1933
Kneel to the Rising Sun, and Other Stories, 1935
Southways: Stories, 1938
Jackpot: The Short Stories of Erskine Caldwell, 1940
Georgia Boy, 1943
*Stories by Erskine Caldwell: Twenty-four Represen-
tative Stories,* 1944
Jackpot: Collected Short Stories, 1950
The Courting of Susie Brown, 1952
Complete Stories, 1953
Gulf Coast Stories, 1956
Certain Women, 1957
When You Think of Me, 1959
Men and Women: Twenty-two Stories, 1961
Stories of Life: North and South, 1983
The Black and White Stories of Erskine Caldwell,
1984

OTHER LITERARY FORMS

The corpus of Erskine Caldwell's work includes
more than fifty-five volumes published in forty-three
languages, with more than eighty million copies sold.
Caldwell wrote more than twenty novels, works of social criticism, travel sketches, two autobiographies,
two books for children, "photo-text" coffee-table
books, and various pieces as a newspaper correspondent. His novel *Tobacco Road* (1932) was adapted to
the stage by Jack Kirkland and ran for 3,182
performances.

ACHIEVEMENTS

Erskine Caldwell is finally regaining his place as
one of the United States' important writers. In a remarkable literary career that covered more than six decades, Caldwell gained fame in the early 1930's for his
novels *Tobacco Road* and *God's Little Acre* (1933). He
became one of the country's most controversial,
banned, and censored authors, as well as one of the
most financially successful. For some years it even became fashionable to denigrate his work, and he lapsed
into relative obscurity for a time, but the 1980's witnessed a revival. Caldwell, who always preferred a
quiet life, lived long enough to see the change in public
opinion. He remains first and foremost a southern
writer who belongs to the naturalistic tradition. He was
instrumental in promoting a realistic portrayal of life in
the United States, particularly the South. His style of
writing is always simple and direct. Caldwell often has
been associated with Tennessee Williams and William
Faulkner as one of the South's celebrated authors. In
fact, Faulkner once praised Caldwell for his fiction.
Caldwell's wide range of literary output is remarkable
and encompasses short stories, novels and novellas,
text-picture documentaries, and children's books.
Throughout his life Caldwell received a number of
awards ranging from the *Yale Review* award for fiction
in 1933 to the Republic of Poland's Order of Cultural
Merit in 1981. Two years later he was given the Republic of France's Commander of the Order of Arts and
Letters and the following year was elevated to the select body of the American Academy of Arts and
Letters.

BIOGRAPHY

The son of a well-known Presbyterian minister, Erskine Preston Caldwell spent his boyhood in rural
Georgia and South Carolina as his father moved from
church to church. In 1920, he attended Erskine College
for a year and a half; in 1923, he spent a year at the

University of Virginia; and in 1924 he spent a summer at the University of Pennsylvania studying economics. After working for a brief time as a reporter for the Atlanta *Journal*, he left Georgia for Maine to devote his energies to full-time writing in 1926. Caldwell wrote nearly a hundred stories and novels before placing his first major publication with Maxwell Perkins and *Scribner's Magazine*. His novels in the 1930's, known primarily for their sexual suggestiveness and violence, firmly established him as a best-selling author. In 1937, in conjunction with the famous photographer Margaret Bourke-White, Caldwell published the remarkable *You Have Seen Their Faces*, a "photo-text" depicting the plight of the southern poor that deserves to be ranked as one of the finest examples of that genre. Caldwell was a war correspondent in Russia in 1942 and one of the few American journalists to cover the invasion of Russia. His later work is generally not as good as his early work (Faulkner once said that it "grew toward trash"), but the serious reader would do well to pay attention to *Call It Experience: The Years of Learning How to Write* (1951), his autobiography, and *Deep*

Erskine Caldwell (Library of Congress)

South: Memory and Observation (1968), a nonfictional study of southern religion. In his later years, Caldwell turned more to nonfiction and autobiography. A lifelong smoker, he had two operations for lung cancer. Caldwell finally succumbed to the disease in 1987 at the age of eighty-three.

ANALYSIS

Erskine Caldwell's reputation as a short-story writer rests mainly on the collections published in the 1930's: *American Earth, We Are the Living: Brief Stories, Kneel to the Rising Sun, and Other Stories*, and *Southways: Stories*. Most of these stories reflect a social protest against the racial and economic oppression in the South during the Great Depression. Along with writers such as John Steinbeck and James T. Farrell, Caldwell wrote of the struggles of the poor and is therefore a favorite of Marxist critics; he was also highly regarded in the Soviet Union. Although Caldwell's fiction deals with social injustice, he is not overtly didactic or doctrinaire. He may have written of the violence of racial prejudice, the hypocritical state of fundamentalist religion, or the economic agonies of sharecropping worn-out farmland, yet his first concern as a writer was always with the portrayal of individual characters rather than with lofty social issues. His ideology did not interfere with his art, and the result is a clean, stark narrative that often exhibits the ultrareal qualities of nightmare.

Good literature always bears the burden of altering the comfortable preconceptions of the world, and Caldwell's best fiction produces a disturbing effect on the reader. He is fond of placing his characters in complex situations, yet he has them react to these situations with the simple tropisms of instinct or the unthinking obedience to social custom. At the heart of one of his stories may be a profound moral point--such as a white dirt farmer's choice between defending his black friend or else permitting an unjust lynching--but Caldwell's characters face moral predicaments with the amoral reflexes of an automaton. There is rarely any evidence that Caldwell's characters grasp the seriousness of their situation. They do not experience epiphanies of self-redemption or rise to mythic patterns of suffering, but rather continue to submit, unaffected, to the agonies and absurdities of their world. For this reason,

Caldwell's work was frequently banned in the 1930's as pornographic and for appearing to promote gratuitous violence.

"SATURDAY AFTERNOON"

"Saturday Afternoon," for example, is the story of an offhand killing, by a mob of whites, of a black man named Will Maxie for supposedly talking to a white girl. The fact that Will Maxie is innocent is never in question. Everyone admits that he is a "smart Negro," always properly deferential and a hard worker, but the whites hate him anyway because he makes too much money and has no vices. Will is chained to a sweet-gum tree and burned alive. "Saturday Afternoon" is a compelling story, not because of its sensational violence, but rather because of the chilling indifference shown by the two central characters, Tom the town butcher and Jim his helper. The story opens in the back of the fly-ridden butcher shop as Tom is settling down for an afternoon nap on the butcher block, a slab of rump roast as a pillow. Jim bursts in and tells him that a lynching party is being formed, and they hurry out to join it. The two, however, are merely following the social instinct of herding animals rather than exercising any overt malice toward Will, and even the tone of the actual killing is casual, almost nonchalant: The local druggist sends his boy to sell sodas to the crowd, and Tom and Jim are as interested in swapping slugs of moonshine as they are in Will's death. Once the spectacle is over, they return to the butcher shop for the Saturday afternoon rush, business as usual. The violence may seem gratuitous, but Caldwell's carefully controlled tone undercuts its severity and reinforces the theme that mindless indifference to brutality can be more terrifying than purposeful evil. The moral impact of the story bypasses the consciousness of the characters but catches the reader between the eyes.

"KNEEL TO THE RISING SUN"

In "Kneel to the Rising Sun," the title story of Caldwell's 1935 collection, he shows that both racial oppression and economic oppression are closely linked. The central conflict in the story is between the white landowner Arch Gunnard and his two sharecroppers--Lonnie, a white, and Clem, a black. It is late afternoon and Lonnie has come to Arch's gas station to ask for extra food because he is being "short-rationed."

The black tenant Clem has asked for extra rations and gotten them, but Lonnie cannot be so bold. The unspoken rules of the caste system are strong, even between a white tenant and a white landowner. As Lonnie tries to make his request, Arch calmly takes out his jackknife and cuts the tail off Lonnie's dog. Lonnie leaves hungry and emasculated, his tailless dog following behind. In the second part of the story, Lonnie awakens in the night to find his old father gone from his bed. Clem helps him with the search, and they find his father trampled to death in Arch's hog pen where, in a fit of hunger, he went looking for food. As all three men view the torn body, Clem again shows the courage that Lonnie cannot by openly accusing Arch of starving his tenants. An argument ensues, and Arch leaves to drum up a lynching party. Lonnie is torn between loyalty to Clem as a friend and loyalty to his own race. He promises to lead the mob away from Clem's hiding place, but once Arch arrives, Lonnie leads him to Clem in stunned obedience. Clem dies in a hail of buckshot, and Lonnie returns home to his wife, who asks if he has brought extra food. "No," Lonnie quietly replies, "no, I ain't hungry."

The institutional enemy in Caldwell's fiction, as in much of his social criticism, is not so much racial bigotry as the economic system that fosters it, for bigotry is a by-product of an agrarian system that beats down the poor of both races. Like the plantation system it replaced, cotton sharecropping enriches the few at the expense of the many, and the violence of Clem's death in "Kneel to the Rising Sun" is no worse than the starvation visited upon Lonnie's family. Blacks are beaten into submission, and whites are evicted from the land. As one cotton-field boss says in *You Have Seen Their Faces*, "Folks here wouldn't give a dime a dozen for white tenants. They can get twice as much work out of blacks. But they need to be trained. Beat a dog and he'll obey you. They say it's the same with blacks." Caldwell treats the same issues, although in more melodramatic fashion, in the stories "Wild Flowers" and "A Knife to Cut the Cornbread With."

"THE GROWING SEASON"

Caldwell's prose style is plain and direct, and his method of narration depends entirely on concrete details and colloquial dialogue. It is not a method conducive to presenting symbolic import or psychological introspection, and Caldwell's critics often accuse him of creating flat characters. Caldwell's carefully controlled manipulation of external descriptions, however, can give rise to intense states of psychological unrest, as in one of his best stories, "The Growing Season." In the story, Jesse, a cotton farmer, has been working in the fields all morning trying to keep the wire grass away from his crop. He has made little headway because twelve acres of cotton is too much for one man to work. As he breaks at midday, his eyes burning bloodshot from the sun, Jesse hears "Fiddler" rattle his chain. Jesse cannot eat, and his attention repeatedly turns to the wire grass in his cotton and the rattling of Fiddler's chain. Unable to bear the heat and the weeds and the noise of the chain any longer, he herds Fiddler into a gully and brutally kills him with his shotgun and ax. The violence done, Jesse sharpens his hoe and returns to the fields, optimistic that he can save his crop. Caldwell never specifies what kind of creature "Fiddler" is, but after several close readings, it becomes clear that he is not a dog or a mule but a human being--perhaps a retarded child or a black.

Jesse's psychological state is externalized; he is what he sees and feels, and the surreal qualities of the outer world reflect his psychosis. He rubs his knuckles in his eye sockets as the sun blinds him, he cannot eat or sleep, and even Fiddler changes color. Caldwell's characters often experience a disruption of physical appetite and sensory perception as they engage in headlong pursuit of their bizarre idiosyncrasies. Furthermore, Fiddler's death produces a cathartic effect on Jesse. Caldwell implies that the choking circumstances that beat heavily on the poor require sure action to overcome them--even if that action is a violent one.

"CANDY-MAN BEECHUM"

Although Caldwell's plain prose style eschews most of the traditional literary devices, the rhetorical structure of his fiction uses the varied repetition of details and dialogue. In "Candy-Man Beechum," Caldwell incorporates the repetitions of colloquial black speech patterns to give the story the oral rhythms of a folk ballad in prose. The narrative line of the story is simple and episodic: Candy-Man leaves the rural swamp where he works as a sawmill hand and heads for town on a Saturday night to see his gal. The language of "Candy-Man Beechum," however, is the language of the tall tale, and the opening of the story ascribes to Candy-Man the larger-than-life qualities of the folk hero: "It was ten miles out of the Ogeechee swamps, from the sawmill to the top of the ridge, but it was just one big step to Candy-Man." At each stop on his journey to town, someone asks the question, "Where you going, Candy-Man?" and he supplies various boastful answers. These questions and answers give structure to the story in much the same way that a verse and refrain give structure to a popular ballad, and, again like a popular ballad, they move toward a tragic end. As Candy-Man nears the white folks' town, the questions become more ominous until a white-boss policeman asks the final question, "What's your hurry, Candy-Man?" Candy-Man, however, will not compromise his vitality by acquiescing to his demands and is shot down in the street; even in death he maintains his own exuberant sense of identity. Caldwell uses similar kinds of repetition to heighten the erotic effect of other stories, such as "August Afternoon" and "The Medicine Man."

Caldwell is often referred to as a local-color writer of the "southern gothic" school, but the range of his work shows him to be one of the most diverse and voluminous (and neglected) writers of the twentieth century. If the subject matter of his short fiction seems somewhat limited, it is only because Caldwell insisted on writing about what he knew best by firsthand observation. He once said in an interview:

> I grew up in the Great Depression in Georgia. I know how poverty smells and feels. I was poor as to eating. Poor as to clothes. Poor as to housing. And nearly everybody else was too, and you can't know about poverty any better way. You don't like it and nobody else does but you can't help yourself. So you learn to live with it, and understand it and can appreciate how others feel about it.

It is this genuine "feel" of poverty and its accompanying themes of violence, bigotry, frustration, and absurd comedy that ensure a lengthy survival of Caldwell's best works.

OTHER MAJOR WORKS

LONG FICTION: *The Bastard*, 1929; *Poor Fool*, 1930; *Tobacco Road*, 1932; *God's Little Acre*, 1933; *Journeyman*, 1935; *Trouble in July*, 1940; *All Night Long: A Novel of Guerrilla Warfare in Russia*, 1942; *Tragic Ground*, 1944; *A House in the Uplands*, 1946; *The Sure Hand of God*, 1947; *This Very Earth*, 1948; *Place Called Estherville*, 1949; *Episode in Palmetto*, 1950; *A Lamp for Nightfall*, 1952; *Love and Money*, 1954; *Gretta*, 1955; *Claudelle Inglish*, 1958; *Jenny by Nature*, 1961; *Close to Home*, 1962; *The Last Night of Summer*, 1963; *Miss Mamma Aimee*, 1967; *Summertime Island*, 1968; *The Weather Shelter*, 1969; *The Earnshaw Neighborhood*, 1972; *Annette*, 1974.

NONFICTION: *Some American People*, 1935; *Tenant Farmer*, 1935; *You Have Seen Their Faces*, 1937 (with Margaret Bourke-White); *North of the Danube*, 1939 (with Bourke-White); *Say! Is This the U.S.A.?*, 1941 (with Bourke-White); *All-Out on the Road to Smolensk*, 1942 (with Bourke-White; also known as *Moscow Under Fire: A Wartime Diary*, 1941); *Russia at War*, 1942 (with Bourke-White); *Call It Experience: The Years of Learning How to Write*, 1951; *The Humorous Side of Erskine Caldwell*, 1951; *Around About America*, 1964; *In Search of Bisco*, 1965; *In the Shadow of the Steeple*, 1967; *Deep South: Memory and Observation*, 1968; *Writing in America*, 1968; *Afternoons in Mid-America*, 1976; *With All My Might: An Autobiography*, 1987; *Conversations with Erskine Caldwell*, 1988; *Erskine Caldwell: Selected Letters, 1929-1955*, 1999.

CHILDREN'S LITERATURE: *Molly Cottontail*, 1958; *The Deer at Our House*, 1966.

MISCELLANEOUS: *The Caldwell Caravan: Novels and Stories*, 1946.

BIBLIOGRAPHY

Arnold, Edwin T., ed. *Conversations with Erskine Caldwell*. Jackson: University Press of Mississippi, 1988. Contains more than thirty articles and interviews with Caldwell on a wide range of subjects. Provides a good insight into Caldwell the writer and the individual. Includes a useful introduction, a chronology, and final thoughts.

Caldwell, Erskine. *With All My Might: An Autobiography*. Atlanta: Peachtree, 1987. Caldwell's second autobiography is his final work and was published a month before his death. A chatty and informative style suffuses the book and affords an interesting glimpse of Caldwell's career.

Devlin, James E. *Erskine Caldwell*. Boston: Twayne, 1984. Provides a good but limited introduction to Caldwell's literary career. Contains an interesting overview on the writer's career, five chapters covering individual works, and a final assessment. Supplemented by a chronology, notes and references, and a select bibliography.

Gelfant, Blanche H., ed. *The Columbia Companion to the Twentieth-Century American Short Story*. New York: Columbia University Press, 2000. Includes a chapter in which Caldwell's short stories are analyzed.

Klevar, Harvey L. *Erskine Caldwell*. Knoxville: University of Tennessee Press, 1993. A detailed discussion of Caldwell's life, focusing on the South and Caldwell's relationship to it as reflected in his work.

Korges, James. *Erskine Caldwell*. Minneapolis: University of Minnesota Press, 1969. Examines Caldwell's early work and argues that he has a great comic vision and is one of the United States' most important writers. Augmented by a select bibliography.

MacDonald, Scott, ed. *Critical Essays on Erskine Caldwell*. Boston: G. K. Hall, 1981. An excellent collection of critical essays on Caldwell that spans almost fifty years of the writer's life. Arranged chronologically, the anthology constitutes a good introduction to Caldwell with seventy-five articles and more than thirty essays, including eight by the writer himself.

McDonald, Robert L., ed. *The Critical Response to Erskine Caldwell*. Westport, Conn.: Greenwood Press, 1997. Includes reviews of Caldwell's major works, scholarly discussions of his themes and techniques, and academic analyses of the image of the South presented in his fiction.

Miller, Dan B. *Erskine Caldwell*. New York: Alfred A. Knopf, 1995. A biography of Caldwell, focusing on his first forty years. Details Caldwell's life and his growing up in the context of southern culture.

Rachels, David. "Erskine Caldwell's Short Stories: Teetering on the Edge of the Canon." In *Reading Erskine Caldwell: New Essays*, edited by Robert L. McDonald.Jefferson, N.C.: McFarland, 2006. In addition to Rachels's essay focusing on Caldwell's short fiction, another essay in the collection discusses "Cubist strategies" in literature from William Carlos Williams's poem "The Red Wheelbarrow" to Caldwell's story "Yellow Girl." Other essays examine Caldwell as a novelist, a humorist, and a modernist.

Silver, Andrew. "Laughing over Lost Causes: Erskine Caldwell's Quarrel with Southern Humor." *The Mississippi Quarterly* 50 (Winter, 1996/1997): 51-68. Discusses some of the characteristics of nineteenth century American frontier humor inherited by Caldwell, such as the narrator as cultured observer of frontier rustics. Argues that Caldwell subverts southern humor and critiques Depression-era capitalism.

Stevens, C. J. *Storyteller: A Life of Erskine Caldwell.* Phillips, Maine: John Wade, 2000. Comprehensive biography traces the details of Caldwell's life and discusses his "complicated personality." Describes how he wrote his novels and other works and summarizes their contents.

Robert J. McNutt
Updated by Terry Theodore

HORTENSE CALISHER

Born: New York, New York; December 20, 1911
Died: New York, New York; January 13, 2009

PRINCIPAL SHORT FICTION

In the Absence of Angels: Stories, 1951
Tale for the Mirror: A Novella and Other Stories, 1962
Extreme Magic: A Novella and Other Stories, 1964
"The Railway Police" and "The Last Trolley Ride," 1966
The Collected Stories of Hortense Calisher, 1975
Saratoga, Hot, 1985
The Novellas of Hortense Calisher, 1997

OTHER LITERARY FORMS

Although Hortense Calisher (CAL-ihsh-ur) first became known as a short-story writer, she published several novels and novellas, including *False Entry* (1961) and *In the Slammer with Carol Smith* (1997), an autobiography, and articles and reviews for *The New Yorker, Harper's Magazine, Harper's Bazaar, Mademoiselle, The New York Times, The American Scholar, The New Criterion, Ladies' Home Journal, The Saturday Evening Post, The Kenyon Review*, and *The Nation*, among others.

ACHIEVEMENTS

Twice a John Simon Guggenheim Memorial Foundation Fellow and once a Hurst Fellow, Hortense Calisher also received an American Specialist's Grant from the U.S. Department of State, a National Council of the Arts Award, an Academy of Arts and Letters Award, four O. Henry Awards, and National Book Award nominations in 1962 for *False Entry* (1961), in 1973 for *Herself* (1972), and in 1976 for *The Collected Stories of Hortense Calisher* (1975). She was president of the PEN Club and of the American Academy of Arts and Letters, and she won a Lifetime Achievement Award from the National Endowment for the Arts in 1989. The artistry of her prose earned her standing as a "writer's writer," especially in the carefully structured novellas and short stories.

BIOGRAPHY

After graduating from Barnard College in 1932 with a B.A. in English, Hortense Calisher worked at a variety of jobs in New York, including sales clerk, model, and social worker for the Department of Public Welfare. In 1935, she married Heaton Bennet Heffelfinger, an engineer, and had two children. Her first marriage ended in divorce in 1958, and in 1959 Calisher married Curtis Harnack, a writer. Calisher's family history as a

New York City native born of middle-class Jewish parents, a southern father and a German mother, provides the material for many of her stories; other stories are informed by her later life experiences as a suburban housewife. She taught creative writing and literature courses at a number of colleges and universities, including Barnard College, Iowa State University, Sarah Lawrence College, Brandeis University, the University of Pennsylvania, Columbia University, the State University of New York at Purchase, and the University of California at Irvine. She lectured in West Germany, Yugoslavia, Romania, and Hungary. Calisher died in New York City on January 13, 2009, at the age of ninety-seven.

ANALYSIS

Hortense Calisher described the short story as "an apocalypse, served in a very small cup," thus indicating her Jamesian penchant for intense psychological portrayals presented within the aesthetic confines of brevity of style and economy of emotional impact. After "A Box of Ginger," her first published story, appeared in *The New Yorker* in 1948, critics praised Calisher's writings for their complexity of theme, verbal intricacy, and strength and multiplicity of evocation. She has been compared with Henry James and Gustave Flaubert in her passion for precision and craftsmanship and with Marcel Proust in her motifs of the many-sided psychological levels of human experience.

Calisher has been described as a spokesperson for the "middle ground" of the ordinary, rather than the extreme, the unusual, or the bizarre. Her most convincing characters are, by and large, observers of the mysteries of human existence, seeking viable modes of action and belief in their own individual progressions toward the development of self-identity. The existential themes of choice and commitment and the search for meaning through self-definition are pervasive in her writings, as is the influence of phenomenology. Her short stories, in fact, can be seen as exemplifications of art in Edmund Husserl's definition of the phenomenological *epochē* (suspension of judgment) as the capacity of a single moment of experience to unfold itself into endless perspectives of reality.

The themes of Calisher's stories focus on bonding, the need for individual lives to merge in moments of appreciation, empathy, or love to assuage the emptiness, alienation, and apparent meaninglessness of much of human existence. The progression in her writings is generally outward, toward a merging or a reconciliation based upon understanding and new insight. Her stories also assert the power of illusions over everyday life and the reluctance with which fantasy is surrendered for the stark obduracy of reality. Primarily depictions of the complexity of human experience, Calisher's stories are presented via a poetic concern with language and imagery for communicating the subtleties of characters' insights into their experience. She has been praised for the insights into the psychology of women in her works and for her own contributions to women's literature.

"IN GREENWICH THERE ARE MANY GRAVELLED WALKS"

"In Greenwich There Are Many Gravelled Walks," a story many critics consider a modern classic, is an example of Calisher's themes of bonding and insight, both often attained against a background of psychological suffering and a sense of the amorphous character of life in the modern world. On an afternoon in early August, Peter Birge returns to the small apartment he shares with his mother after taking her to the Greenwich sanatorium she had to frequent at intervals to discover that "his usually competent solitude had become more than he could bear." He is a victim of defeated plans; the money he had saved from his Army stint for a trip abroad will now have to be spent on his mother's psychiatric treatment. His mood is one of disheartenment and isolation. Recalling taking his mother to the sanatorium on this bright, clear summer day, he senses the irony of his own plight--anyone "might have thought the two of them were a couple, any couple, just off for a day in the country." He is aware that much insanity in the modern world passes for sanity and that beneath the seeming calm of most lives lie secrets and potential complexities known only to the participants themselves.

Peter's estrangement from his mother is complete; Greenwich has claimed her through the sanatorium as it had through the Village. In the Village, she had become a fixture, a "hanger-on" in the bars in the presence and superficial camaraderie of would-be painters, philosophers, and poets, until alcoholism and a steady routine of safe and predictable fantasy--"a buttery flow of harmless little lies and pretensions"--became all that she had subsisted on for more than twenty years. Arriving at the sanatorium was like playing out one more fantasy scene from the bars, a safe world of protection and illusion. For the son, however, no illusions are left to comfort him. "It was just that while others of his age still shared a communal wonder at what life might hold, he had long since been solitary in his knowledge of what life was."

Finding being alone unbearable, Peter is prompted by his loneliness to visit his friend, Robert Vielum, for the same reason that many others stopped by, "because there was likely to be somebody there." Robert is "a perennial taker of courses" who derives a "Ponce de Leon sustenance from the young." Buttressed by family fortunes, he has ambled his way through academics, gathering up a troupe of enchanted devotees fascinated by his adirectional philosophy of hedonism and apathy. Watching him closely, Peter discovers that Robert is very much like his mother; they are "charmers, who if they could not offer you the large strength, could still atone for the lack with so many small decencies." People are drawn to Robert as they are to Peter's mother, for the exhilarating excitement of "wearing one's newest façade, in the fit company of others similarly attired."

Peter discovers that he has arrived in the midst of a homosexual love triangle; Robert has abandoned his plans to go to Morocco with Vince in order to go to Italy with Mario Osti, a painter. Robert is charmingly aloof, totally insensitive and unresponsive to Vince's emotional sufferings over being abandoned and rejected. A fight ensues, and Vince retreats to the bedroom as Robert's daughter, Susan, arrives to spend the summer in her father's apartment. When Mario looks out the window into the courtyard and discovers that Vince has committed suicide, Robert's carefully poised game of facades and practiced indifference is shattered by the reality of human despair.

Mario's self-protecting "I'd better get out of here!" is in direct contrast to Peter's compassion and empathy for Susan, whom he feels to be a fellow survivor of the carelessness and emptiness of the chaos of other people's lives. "I don't care about any of it, really," Susan tells him, "my parents, or any of the people they tangle with." Peter finds this a feeling with which he can empathize, and he agrees even more fully with her statement: "I should think it would be the best privilege there is, though. To care, I mean." The bond of mutual understanding of what has been lost and what is missing and needed is established between Peter and Susan as he realizes that they are alike in their same disillusionment with the world. The story ends on a note of muted optimism as Peter tells himself that "tomorrow he would take her for a drive--whatever the weather. There were a lot of good roads around Greenwich." If one envisions Greenwich in the story, both the sanatorium and the Village, as symbols of the sterility and insanity of most modern existence, then the journey "around Greenwich" may well be an affirmation that the two young people can avoid the

Hortense Calisher (Library of Congress)

dissipation of their parents' lives through the bond of caring the couple has established.

"IF YOU DON'T WANT TO LIVE I CAN'T HELP YOU"

"In Greenwich There Are Many Gravelled Walks" is roundly critical of the self-destructive waste of emotional abilities most people's lives become, a viewpoint even more heavily endorsed in one of Calisher's more moralistic stories, "If You Don't Want to Live I Can't Help You." On the day that Professor Mary Ponthus, a teacher at a New England college and a scholar of some repute, is to receive an honorary doctorate of letters, she pays a visit to her nephew, Paul. Paul has lived off the trust fund that Mary has administered for twenty years, and his life has become cankered with dissipation. "Foredoomed to the dilettante," he has dabbled in painting, writing, and love affairs because "these were good ways to pass the time--and of time he had so much to pass."

Now, too, as Mary reflects, he is dabbling in disease. Suffering from tuberculosis, her death- and failure-obsessed nephew refuses to take care of himself. When Mary arrives, she finds him hung over and ill from a night of wild partying. Further, she discovers that Paul's lover of several years, Helen Bonner, has left him because of his manipulative and dissolute state. Mary wants to call the doctor, but Paul tells her that his doctor has given up on him because Paul refuses to enter a sanatorium and to care for himself properly. Paul pleads, instead, for Mary to call Helen and draw her back to him. "I can't manage," Paul says, seeing his own plight. "The best I can do is to cling to someone who can." Paul collapses, and Mary calls the doctor, who arrives to take Paul to the hospital. Paul tells the doctor, "I'm just like everyone else. I don't want to die." To which the doctor responds, "Maybe not. But if you don't want to live I can't help you." The thematic crux of the story is thus established. When it comes to life itself, the doctor tells Mary, there are "the ones who are willing, and the ones who will have to be dragged."

Attending the graduation ceremonies at which she will receive her honorary doctorate, Mary contemplates the doctor's words with a deep sense of despair. Surrounded by young college students with eager, bright views of their future, she feels her own age weighing upon her and feels suddenly out of place, useless, and defeated. At the reception later, she notices that her usual enthusiasm for the quick and keen intelligence of the young has waned. A phone call to Helen to ask her to return to Paul has failed, and Mary considers giving up her own plans to devote the rest of her life to Paul. "People like Paul can be looked after quite easily out of duty," she reflects, "the agony comes only when they are looked after with hope."

A young graduate student comes up to converse with Mary, and she feels a deep sense of his brilliance of mind and high ethical character. He stands in such marked contrast to Paul, who wasted all of his abilities, that Mary is drawn to the student and to unlocking his potential. "I can't help it," Mary reflects. "I'm of the breed that hopes. Maybe this one wants to live." Her resurgence of faith and her renewed energies for survival and purpose reveal to her that this is the crux of the human situation. "We are all in the dark together, but those are the ones who humanize the dark." The ending is existential in upholding the "dark" puzzle of existence but compassionate in asserting that those who will to live with strength and dignity humanize the darkness for everyone.

"THE MIDDLE DRAWER"

The necessity for strengths of the heart is reiterated in "The Middle Drawer," a story of mother-daughter conflicts and their partial resolution through compassion. Published in a periodical in 1948, this is Calisher's first autobiographical story. After her mother's death from cancer, Hester is about to begin the process of going through her mother's most personal effects, locked in the middle drawer of her dresser. The gravity of exposing her mother's life to inspection for the final time causes Hester to reflect upon the course of their relationship and how flawed by failed communication their lives together had been.

Hester had come to know the drawer's contents gradually, through the course of a lifetime. She had begun peering over the drawer's edge as a baby, had played with the opera glasses and string of pearls she had found inside as a child, and had received from the drawer for her wedding the delicate diamond chain that had been her father's wedding gift to her mother. It is a small brown-toned photograph in the back of the drawer, however, that most held Hester's attention as she was growing up. The photograph was of her mother, Hedwig, as a child of two, bedecked in the garments of respectable poverty as she grew up in the small town of Oberelsbach, Germany, motherless since birth and stepmothered by a woman who had been "unloving, if not unkind." Hester senses that her mother was one of a legion of lonely children "who inhabited the familiar terror-struck dark that crouched under the lash of the adult."

Life "under the lash of the adult" had created in Hedwig an emotional reserve that precluded any open demonstration of love to Hester. Over the years, "the barrier of her mother's dissatisfaction with her had risen imperceptibly" until the two women stood as strangers, with bitter hurts and buried sorrows the only communion they had known. Hester's misery is that "she was forever impelled to earn her mother's approval at the expense of her own." Always, Hester had known, there had been buried the wish to find "the final barb, the homing shaft, that would maim her mother once and for all, as she felt herself to have been maimed."

The opportunity for the barb is given to Hester when she is called home to visit her mother after her mother's sudden operation for breast cancer. Hester discovers that her mother is suffering from a deep fear of the revulsion of others and a horror at what has been done to her. She has taken to sleeping alone at night and to eating from separate utensils from her family. It is clear to Hester that her father and her brother have not been successful in concealing their revulsion from Hedwig, thus contributing further to her isolation and anxiety.

One evening, when they are in her mother's bedroom, Hedwig begins to discuss her operation with Hester and asks her if she would like to see the incision, which no one has seen since she left the hospital. Hester tells her mother that she would very much like to see it and recalls intensely the times that she had stood as a child before her mother, "vulnerable and bare, helplessly awaiting the cruel exactitude of her displeasure." Her mother reveals the mastectomy scar to Hester, and Hester, with infinite delicacy, draws her fingertips along the length of the scar "in a light, affirmative caress, and they stood eye

to eye for an immeasurable second, on equal ground at last." Hester's discovery about her mother and herself in that moment of tender union is a freeing answer: "She was always vulnerable, Hester thought. As we all are. What she bequeathed me unwittingly, ironically, was fortitude--the fortitude of those who have had to live under the blow. But pity--that I found for myself." The opportunity for the barb of hurt and rejection has been replaced by the empathy of understanding.

The story's ending blends poignancy with realism and psychological insight, for Hester knows that, however tender the moment of communion "on equal ground," her struggle to win her mother's approval would have continued and that the scars from their troubled relationship remain in Hester's psyche. Her own life is in the middle drawer she is about to open. She has been made who she is by her mother's influence and by the fact that her own grandmother died too soon to leave the imprint of love upon Hedwig. Like her mother, Hester has been scarred by an absence of love that worked its way through two generations and is, even now, affecting Hester's relationship with her own daughter. She realizes that the living carry "not one tangible wound but the burden of innumerable small cicatrices imposed upon us by our beginnings; we carry them with us always, and from these, from this agony, we are not absolved." With this recognition, Hester opens the middle drawer to face and absorb whatever truth her life and her mother's life might contain.

Like many of Calisher's short stories, "The Middle Drawer" builds to a phenomenological *epochē* that reveals numerous multifaceted insights into the characters of the stories, the psychology of human motivations, and the metaphysics of human actions, especially actions springing from an ethical or a compassionate base. Calisher is not a facile optimist; she believes in strongly and portrays quite graphically the pain pervading most human lives. She does assert, however, an unwavering faith in the strength of the human will and in the necessity for commitment to ethical principles. Like Mary Ponthus in "If You Don't Want to Live I Can't Help You," Calisher affirms that humankind must "humanize the dark."

THE NOVELLAS OF HORTENSE CALISHER

Published in 1997, this collection contains seven stories, of which only one had been unpublished previously. In the book's introduction, Calisher defines a novella as being "not merely a shorter novel, of less wordage than commonly. It is a small one, tenaciously complete."

In order of publication, *Tale for the Mirror* (1962) is a gently ironic study of ethnic and cultural misunderstanding set in an old-money ingrown New York suburban community. The Hudson River setting is disturbed by the arrival of an eccentric Indian neurologist, Dr. Bhatta, who takes possession of a lavish estate and is viewed with suspicion by his neighbors. He is surrounded by an entourage of subservient females, client disciples, and an apparent madwoman living in his summer house. Whether Dr. Bhatta is a phony or merely a man who arranges the facts of his life into a story he can tell himself remains unresolved, for, in the last analysis, he too may be as much a victim seeking truth in the night as a criminal.

Extreme Magic (1964) revolves around Guy Callendar, who has lost his family in a house fire and tries to rebuild his life as a small-town antique dealer. He finally finds understanding with a battered wife whom he rescues from her alcoholic, suicidal, innkeeper husband through a miraculous intervention. *The Railway Police* (1966) is the story of an heiress and social worker to whom men are attracted by the colorful wigs she wears, only to be repelled by the discovery of her hereditary baldness. Seeing a vagrant being tossed off a train, she jettisons her fake hair and thus her life of pretense, gives all her money to needy clients, and goes off to live in the streets as an anonymous discard, a vagabond, obliterating all evidence of her place in the world.

Saratoga, Hot (1985) is about the fortunes and obsessions of a married couple in the upstate New York horse-racing resort of Saratoga Springs. The wife, a painter now healed from a crippling accident caused by the man who later married her, and her spouse encounter all types of characters, some sinister and some not, but all devoted to horses--gamblers, jockeys, aficionados, and mafiosi--who come with the territory. *The Man Who Spat Silver* (1986) is about a woman translator who escapes her daily solitude by taking long walks in the streets of New York City where she becomes obsessed with a salesman who intially attracts her attention by spitting on the sidewalk.

In all these stories, Calisher unfolds sagas of coming-of-age, infidelities, spousal abuse, mental illness, alcoholism, money troubles, and especially loneliness. Even so, they frequently celebrate mere existence through dedicated living and the inability of people to live in the present. Despite the frequent density of her prose, occasionally baffling plots, and too-intricate analyses of personality and motivation, a number of stories achieve Calisher's stated purpose of creating "an apocalypse in a very small cup."

OTHER MAJOR WORKS

LONG FICTION: *False Entry*, 1961; *Textures of Life*, 1963; *Journal from Ellipsia*, 1965; *The New Yorkers*, 1969; *Queenie*, 1971; *Standard Dreaming*, 1972; *Eagle Eye*, 1973; *On Keeping Women*, 1977; *Mysteries of Motion*, 1983; *The Bobby-Soxer*, 1986; *Age*, 1987; *The Small Bang*, 1992 (as Jack Fenno); *In the Palace of the Movie King*, 1993; *In the Slammer with Carol Smith*, 1997; *Sunday Jews*, 2002.

NONFICTION: *Herself*, 1972; *Kissing Cousins: A Memory*, 1988; *Tattoo for a Slave*, 2004.

BIBLIOGRAPHY

Aarons, Victoria. "The Outsider Within: Women in Contemporary Jewish American Fiction." *Contemporary Literature* 28, no. 3 (1987): 378-393. Examines the ways in which women characters portrayed in fiction by Jewish American women writers reflect the position of women in a male-dominated tradition.

Calisher, Hortense. "The Art of Fiction: Hortense Calisher." Interview by Allen Gurganus, Pamela McCordick, and Mona Simpson. *The Paris Review* 29 (Winter, 1987): 157-187. This insightful interview with Calisher explores her various approaches to creative writing.

_____. Introduction to *The Novellas of Hortense Calisher*. New York: The Modern Library, 1997. The author explains how a novella differs from a novel.

Gelfant, Blanche H., ed. *The Columbia Companion to the Twentieth-Century American Short Story*. New York: Columbia University Press, 2000. Includes a chapter in which Calisher's short stories are analyzed.

Hahn, Emily. "In Appreciation of Hortense Calisher." *Wisconsin Studies in Contemporary Literature* 6 (Summer, 1965): 243-249. A close reading of the early fiction, identifying themes such as the friction between generations, which Calisher explores so sensitively in her stories.

"*Saturday Review* Talks to Hortense Calisher." *Saturday Review* 11 (July/August, 1985): 77. In this biographical sketch, based on an interview, Calisher says she considers the Bible a major influence on her style and the New York environment a major force in her artistic development.

Shinn, Thelma J. *Radiant Daughters: Fictional American Women*. Westport, Conn.: Greenwood Press, 1986. Includes an examination of the female characters in Calisher's fiction from the short stories collected since 1951 through the novel *Mysteries of Motion* in 1983. Particularly relates her fiction to contemporary American writers of the 1950's.

Snodgrass, Kathleen. *The Fiction of Hortense Calisher*. Newark: University of Delaware Press, 1993. Discusses the central dual theme of rites of passage and extradition in Calisher's fiction. Argues that her style is not something imposed on the subject matter but the perfect embodiment of this dual theme. The first chapter discusses twelve autobiographical stories, mostly focused on the narrator and protagonist Hester Elkin.

Christina Murphy
Updated by Thelma J. Shinn and Peter B. Heller

ETHAN CANIN

Born: Ann Arbor, Michigan; July 19, 1960

PRINCIPAL SHORT FICTION

Emperor of the Air, 1988
The Palace Thief, 1994

OTHER LITERARY FORMS

In addition to his acclaimed short-story collections, Ethan Canin is the author of the novels *Blue River* (1991), *For Kings and Planets* (1998), *Carry Me Across the Water* (2001), and *America America* (2008).

ACHIEVEMENTS

Ethan Canin received the the Houghton Mifflin Literary Fellowship (1988), the Henfield/*Transatlantic Review* Award (1989), two National Endowment for the Arts grants (1989 and 1996), the California Book Award/Silver Medal in Fiction (1994), the Lyndhurst Prize (1994-1996), and a Guggenheim Fellowship (2010).

BIOGRAPHY

Ethan Andrew Canin's talents as a writer were first recognized by popular romance author Danielle Steel, who taught at Canin's private high school before her own novels became successful. After high school, Canin attended Stanford University, where he studied physics and then switched to English. After graduating from Stanford in 1982, he went on to get an M.F.A. from the prestigious writing program at the University of Iowa. Discouraged by his experience at the Iowa workshop, where he learned about many of the negative aspects of a writer's life, and feeling a need to be useful, Canin elected to attend Harvard's medical school. He was in the midst of his exams at medical school when the publishing company Houghton Mifflin proposed that he prepare a collection of short stories. This volume, *Emperor of the Air*, became a best seller, rare among short-story collections. Canin's success has been such that he has published every story he wrote from his first acceptance in 1987. Although he received his M.D. from Harvard in 1992 and was a resident at a San Francisco hospital for a time, Canin left medicine to devote himself exclusively to writing. In 1998, he joined the faculty of the Iowa Writers' Workshop.

ANALYSIS

Ethan Canin's short stories are characterized by a humorous and empathic approach to his characters and their situations and by a polished literary style. Family life is a favorite subject, although the members of Canin's families are almost always at odds with one another. Often Canin's stories turn on the exploration of two characters who, even if friends or members of the same family, approach life with differing values and modes of perception. As the paths of these characters diverge, Canin introduces a larger, more reflective aspect to his stories that allows the reader to consider such issues as sanity and normality, delinquency and conventionality, science and art.

The construction of a viable male identity is a strong concern in Canin's work. Whether they are concerned with fathers and sons, students and teachers, peers or brothers, Canin's stories often portray men whose characters or values clash. Of special concern is the contrast between the man who conforms to a fairly traditional role and the man who has chosen a more offbeat and unconventional way of life. Canin's mavericks can be frightening or they can be inspiring, but they always exist as a possibility in the psyche of his male characters.

The contrast between a scientific, secular America, whose primary value is material well-being, and a more imaginative, rebellious, or spiritual vision of life is also an important theme in Canin's work. In this theme readers can see the exquisite contrast between the medical and literary sides of Canin himself. In exploring the tensions in contemporary American life, however, Canin avoids an easy, journalistic topicality, so that his stories engage larger moral and philosophical issues and begin to function as timeless parables.

EMPEROR OF THE AIR

Although the stories in *Emperor of the Air* feature characters suffering from heart disease, epilepsy, and birth defects, these illnesses serve larger themes involving the tensions between father and son and between the practical mind and the poetic imagination. In

"Star Food," a young boy must resolve his father's wish that he help in his grocery store and learn to work for a living with the encouragement to dream coming from his mother, who feels that the time the boy spends on the roof looking at the stars will one day make him a great man. Competing perspectives are also the subject of "American Beauty." In this story, which features characters that return in Canin's novel *Blue River*, tensions between the creative Darienne and her two brothers, who are more interested in motorcycle mechanics, also contrast romantic and practical views of the world. Whereas the young boy in "Star Food" is able to balance these two perspectives, the divisions in Darlene's family end with revelations of psychopathology on the part of the older, dominant brother, who claims his brutal behavior as one of the prerogatives of masculinity.

Male role models are also the topic of "The Year of Getting to Know Us." The father's philandering and preoccupation with work and golf have made him an inaccessible parent, and his son reacts with acts of vandalism. Nevertheless, the remote father suggests that his emotional distance is actually, sadly, teaching his son how to be a man. The title story, "Emperor of the Air," gives readers a brighter look at the father-son relationship but once again explores the tensions between realistic and romantic perspectives. In this story, an old man suffering from heart disease fights to rescue an unhealthy old elm tree from his neighbor, a young man who wants to sacrifice it in the interests of three saplings growing in his yard. This contest between the old generation and the new is complicated by the fact that the old man is a former high school science teacher who has had no children, whereas the young father, who knows nothing about science, has a son. The young father invents for his son a magical story about one of the constellations in the sky, which he identifies as a sword that belongs to "the emperor of the air"; the future, in this story, seems to belong to the imaginative storyteller and not to the realistic man of science. A similar tribute to the poetic imagination, "We Are Nighttime Travelers," features a retired couple who have grown apart but who rediscover the love that brought them together when the husband begins writing poetry.

Ethan Canin (Time & Life Pictures/Getty Images)

THE PALACE THIEF

Canin's second collection consists of four long stories, each featuring two men who are linked in one way or another but who represent contrasting perspectives and whose lives have widely diverged. "Accountant" is told from the perspective of Abba Roth, whose careful, even voice reveals a deeply conventional man with a steady, if dull, life as an accountant and family man. His opposite is Eugene Peters, a boyhood friend whose free spirit and enthusiasm for auto mechanics have provided him with a lucrative business. In middle age, Roth and Peters both attend a fantasy baseball camp overseen by the great former baseball player Willie Mays. Although Roth is an excellent ballplayer, his inability to get into the spirit of the game ends in Mays's awarding a pair of prized baseball socks not to the tiresome Roth but to the lively Peters. A resentful Roth steals one of the socks, but this one act of uncharacteristic daring cannot change the fact that he knows he has traded a life with a potential for passion, spontaneity, and adventure for a life of material security and comfort.

"Batorsag and Szerelem" returns to one of Canin's favorite themes--namely, the tensions between a brilliant and eccentric young man and his admiring kid brother. The title refers to words invented by the older brother, Clive, a math prodigy who has developed a secret language he shares only with his best friend Eddie. The words in the title are eventually associated with sexual secrets in Clive's life that so shock and upset his previously indulgent parents that their discovery begins what Clive's brother describes as "the great unturning," in which he becomes the favored son and the free-spirited Clive the outcast whose great promise is never fulfilled.

Like "Accountant," the third story, "City of Broken Hearts," features both baseball and a defeated, middle-aged businessman. Wilson Kohler, who has lost his wife to someone higher up in the company, is a lonely man who seeks consolation by devoting himself to the fortunes of the Boston Red Sox baseball team. Wilson is baffled by the life of his son Brent, an idealistic college student who wears an earring and whose sensitivity to the feminine side has led him to work during his summer vacation at a shelter for battered women. Representative of a new and different generation of men, Brent also has an almost magical role in the life of his father, gently bringing his father out of the past and into a love affair that will give him a new lease on life.

The title story, "The Palace Thief," is narrated by Hundert, a retired history teacher at a fashionable West Virginia preparatory school. Although he prides himself on his integrity and his role as the molder of the young, Hundert was once manipulated by a powerful senator into making allowances for his ne'er-do-well son, whom Hundert knows to have cheated and whose dishonesty he has never exposed. The unscrupulous son in turn becomes a powerful political and economic force in the state, and he manipulates the now-retired professor into helping him become elected senator. Hundert constantly draws on analogies between his situation and the Augustan age of the Roman Empire, but he does not realize that, far from being a principal player, he is merely a slave, serving the interests of the wealthy and the powerful.

OTHER MAJOR WORKS

LONG FICTION: *Blue River*, 1991; *For Kings and Planets*, 1998; *Carry Me Across the Water*, 2001; *America America*, 2008.

EDITED TEXT: *Writers Harvest 2*, 1996.

BIBLIOGRAPHY

Aarons, Victoria. "Ancient Acts of Love and Betrayal: Ethan Canin's 'Batorsag and Szerelem.'" In *What Happened to Abraham? Reinventing the Covenant in American Jewish Fiction*. Newark: University of Delaware Press, 2005. An analysis of one of Canin's short stories. Aarons argues that Canin draws from a "long tradition of Jewish storytelling," and she describes him as a writer "for whom the past, grafted upon the present, is itself the medium for the unfolding" of place and character.

Canin, Ethan. "A Conversation with . . . Ethan Canin." Interview by Lewis Burke Frumkes. *Writer* 113, no. 5 (May, 2000): 19. Canin discusses his novel *For Kings and Planets*, how he incorporates his medical knowledge into his fiction, and his future plans. He also provides advice for young writers.

Crawford, Andrea. "For Writers, the Doctor's Definitely In." *Poets and Writers* 37, no. 1 (January/February, 2009): 16-20. Reports on the growing number of physicians writing fiction, singling out Canin as the most prominent among them. Canin explains why medical doctors are becoming creative writers.

Frucht, Abby. "Grand Delusions." *The New York Times*, February 20, 1994. Review of *The Palace Thief* discusses each of the four stories in detail. Although Frucht terms the stories highly intellectual, she does not feel that this distracts from their effectiveness in depicting lives that are disintegrating. She characterizes all four protagonists as "anti-heroes" who seem either foolish or delusional about their lives and find that, instead of the expected safety and security, they are in the midst of a vast psychological minefield.

Gurewich, David. "Breaking Away from the Brat Pack." *The New Leader* (March 21, 1988): 21-22. This review of *Emperor of the Air* examines several stories in detail, pointing out their depiction of the American family as troubled and unsettled.

Gurewich does not feel Canin is a trailblazer, noting the similarity to the stories of John Cheever, but also describes Canin as a "postminimalist" who moves the short story into the future.

Leavitt, David. "As Children and Others See It." *The New York Times Book Review*, February 14, 1988, 7. In this mixed review of *Emperor of the Air*, Leavitt, a well-known novelist and short-story writer, discusses a number of the stories in this collection. While suggesting the stories are overly artful and sentimental, Leavitt also praises Canin's talent as prodigious and admits that he admires his skill and imagination.

Lehmann-Haupt, Christopher. *Emperor of the Air*. *The New York Times*, January 23, 1988, p. C34. Important review by the noted critic discusses a number of the stories from *Emperor of the Air* in detail, praising the stories as remarkable and as preoccupied with matters of ultimate concern--life and death, youth and age, wealth and poverty.

_____. "Errors in Judgment and Ripples Thereof." *The New York Times*, February 3, 1994. Review of *The Palace Thief* singles out the first story, "The Accountant," as the best of the four and provides a lengthy analysis of it. Notes that although the subject matter is contemporary, characters and plots are traditional. Applauds the collection as a commanding performance that surpasses Canin's two previous books and calls him one of the most satisfying writers on the contemporary scene.

Michener, Charles. "*The Palace Thief*." *The New York Times*, March 21, 1994, p. 76. Describes the stories as old-fashioned tales that echo past masters Henry James and John O'Hara but praises Canin's natural assurance of voice, his acuity, the steadiness of his moral compass, and his often humorous detail.

Slay, Jack, Jr. "(Re)Solving the (Math) Problems in Ethan Canin's 'Batorsag and Szerelem.'" *Critique* 47, no. 1 (Fall, 2004): 27-30. Provides solutions to the math problems included in this short story. Also discusses the story's characters, setting, and closing scene.

Yardley, Jonathan. "Canin's Mature Miracles." *The Washington Post*, January 20, 1988, p. C2. An important review of *Emperor of the Air* by one of the

United States' most influential literary critics, this essay praises Canin's maturity. Pointing out especially his insights into the relationship between father and son and also into the mysteries of the solitary, individual psyche, Yardley sums up his

achievement by saying that in studying the health of the body, Canin has also discovered much about the human heart.

Margaret Boe Birns

MARY CAPONEGRO

Born: Brooklyn, New York; 1956

PRINCIPAL SHORT FICTION

Tales from the Next Village, 1985
The Star Café, and Other Stories, 1990
Five Doubts, 1998
The Complexities of Intimacy, 2001
All Fall Down, 2009

OTHER LITERARY FORMS

Mary Caponegro (cah-poh-NEH-groh) works in the area of experimental fiction. She writes only short fiction. Her short stories and novellas are nontraditional works she creates in multilayers; her creative process does not lend itself to the writing of longer fictional works. As a scholar of fiction writing, she also writes literary criticism. She is a contributing editor to the literary journal *Conjunctions*, published by Bard College. The journal includes original experimental fiction, poetry, drama, and literary criticism.

ACHIEVEMENTS

Mary Caponegro is recognized as one of the most innovative of the experimental fiction writers. She has contributed significantly to redefining fiction and its components. Rejecting the traditional novel form, which relies on plot and character, she uses syntactic complexity, voice, and texture to create fiction in which fantasy and reality mesh into an irreality and invites the reader to explore that irreality. Her talent as a writer was first acknowledged in 1988 when she received the General Electric Foundation Award for Younger Writers. This recognition was followed by the Rome

Prize in Literature (1991) and the Charles Flint Kellogg Award in Arts and Letters given by Bard College (1994). In 1997, she was awarded the Bruno Arcudi Award. In 2006, Caponegro was chosen as a recipient of a Lannan Residency Fellowship.

BIOGRAPHY

Mary Caponegro was born in Brooklyn, New York, in 1956. She began her academic career as a creative-writing student at Bard College in Annandale-on-Hudson, New York. She graduated with a bachelor of arts degree, and she began graduate study at Brown University. There she took courses with John Hawkes and Robert Coover, two important experimental fiction writers who took the novel in new directions and found focuses for fiction other than plot and character. Caponegro earned a master's degree from Brown. She taught English at Hobart and William Smith Colleges, then she became a faculty member at Syracuse University in the creative writing program. In 1994, she was visiting artist at the American Academy in Rome. She published her first collection of short fiction, *Tales from the Next Village*, in 1985, and in 1988 she received the General Electric Foundation Award for Younger Writers. Her second collection, *The Star Café, and Other Stories*, appeared in 1990. Marc Chénetier translated it into French in 1994.

In 1991, Caponegro received the Rome Prize, which enabled her to spend eleven months at the American Academy in Rome, where she acquainted herself with the art and culture of Italy. In 1994, she returned to the academy as a visiting artist. Her third collection of short fiction, *Five Doubts*, which appeared in 1998, comprises narrative meditations anchored in Italian art and culture. Although Caponegro reveals her Italian heritage and her close link to Italy in her inclusion of Italian art, settings, and language in her fictional works, she was not encouraged to acknowledge this heritage as a child. Her paternal grandparents emigrated from Italy. Her grandfather was from the Calabria region and her grandmother was from Arpino, a small town in central Italy. Her family did not live in an American Italian community, and her father sought to suppress their Italian heritage. At one time, she even considered changing her last name, which she thought was too Italian.

In 2001, she published *The Complexities of Intimacy* and "Because I Could Not Stop for Death," a fictional encounter between Joseph Cornell and Emily Dickinson in *A Convergence of Birds: Original Fiction and Poetry Inspired by Joseph Cornell*, edited by Jonathan Safran Foer. (In 2010, this work was performed at the Kyiv International School in Kyiv, Ukraine, in a Celebration of Women's History.) In 2002, Caponegro became the Richard B. Fisher Family Professor in Literature and Writing at Bard College. In March, 2010, a conference devoted to her fiction was held at the University of Siena, and in May, 2010, ODELA (Observatoire de littérature americaine) held a meeting in Paris that centered on her fiction. In addition to publishing collections of short fiction, Caponegro is both an editor of and a contributor to Brown University's literary journal *Conjunctions*, and she contributes to various other journals of literary criticism, including *Review of Contemporary Fiction*, *Iowa Review*, *Epoch*, *Sulfur*, and *Gargoyle*. Translator Daniela Daniele is translating her work into Italian. The first book of her work to be published in Italian is titled *Materia Prima*.

ANALYSIS

Mary Caponegro writes fiction that is described as experimental, avant-garde, metafiction, fabular, or postmodern, which, in contrast to traditional fiction, is not focused on plot, character, setting, and chronology. These elements still appear in the fiction but are not the driving forces of the narratives. Language no longer serves merely as a vehicle to express what happened to whom and where and how it happened. Language, its structure, its multilayered meanings, and its musical properties are developed and appreciated as the focal

point of the work. This genre of fiction does not follow a set of novel-writing rules and is a rebellion against both the realistic and the romantic novel. At Brown University, Caponegro studied creative writing with Hawkes and Coover, major writers in the field of nontraditional fiction. For Caponegro, who was fascinated with language as an entity in its own right, with its properties of syntax, meaning, and multilayers, the approach of these author-teachers to writing opened for her the path that she wished to take in creating fiction. She recognizes them as her mentors; however, her work is not merely an imitation or pastiche of theirs. What she took from them was neither form nor content, but rather the courage to experiment and create her unique fiction.

In her short fiction, Caponegro explores the minds, thoughts, and psychological being of characters who function as entrances into ideas, abstractions, and emotions. Voice and texture of the narration are more important than character, plot, or setting. Her fiction reverses the roles of the elements of traditional fiction. Plot, character, and setting serve to present and develop voice and texture; language becomes a foremost element. How something is said by a character is as, or even more, important than what is said in conveying nuances of meaning. Both the sounds and the rhythms of language, which differ greatly from language to language, from dialect to dialect, are important in her fiction. In "Sebastian" and in "The Translator," she incorporates series of words from various languages and considerations of how a word is pronounced. In "El Libro dell'Arte," the introductory story of *Five Doubts*, the rhythm that she creates in the language of the narrative reflects the chaos, the excessive preoccupation, and the constant need to be busily rushing about and working that imbues the misguided lives of the artist's apprentice and his assistant.

Emotion in the form of eros plays a major role in her fiction, and consequently gender becomes a significant aspect of her work. The sexual as self-identity, self-comprehension, and interaction with individuals is a major focus of many of her fictions, including "The Star Café," "The Complexities of Intimacy," and "The Last Resort Retreat." In her narratives, Caponegro often deconstructs established beliefs and attitudes by using derision and absurdity in their portrayal. Domesticity, marriage, family, and religion all come under attack. Her work also is imbued with a comic vein, which tends toward black comedy, as reality, fantasy, and absurdity are intermingled. The multilayering of her writing enhances and transforms the comic in her narrations, such that the fiction is comic, tragic, horror inspiring, and unsettling at the same time. Her story "Junior Achievement" in the collection *All Fall Down*, which portrays neglected children running an abortion clinic, is an excellent example of this aspect of her fiction. Caponegro avoids reliance on autobiographical elements and does not re-create fictionally her experience of life but rather maintains her fiction in the realm of invention, idea, and abstraction.

"SEBASTIAN"

In "Sebastian," Caponegro portrays two characters: Sebastian, an English businessman who has immigrated to the United States, and Sarah, a Jewish American artist. They are a couple planning to marry, yet the only aspect of their relationship that works is the sexual. The story begins with Sebastian on his way to the airport for a business trip. Sarah had picked up his suit at the dry cleaners, but somehow the trousers were left behind. He decides to stop and pick them up. He arrives at the cleaners to find it closed, with a scrawled sign indicating the owner will return in ten minutes.

At this point Caponegro transfers the narration into Sebastian's thoughts. He decides to wait, but is highly annoyed at the vagueness of the sign. Ten minutes? Ten minutes from when? Why did the owner leave? Did something happen to the owner after leaving? The fiction then explores Sebastian's anxieties about himself, his relationship with Sarah, his discomfort with American culture, and his abhorrence of how Americans, including Sarah, deform the English language. Sarah and Sebastian are incompatible opposites, except in their sexual relationship. Language plays an important role in their antagonistic interaction. Sebastian constantly corrects her pronunciation. English is to be respected and properly spoken. Sarah plays with his name. She manipulates it and calls him SeBastard or simply SB. She continuously alludes to Saint Sebastian, the martyr.

Toward the end of the story, Sebastian arrives, or imagines that he arrives, at Sarah's studio. There he enters into a world in which Sarah has turned him into art and once again exploited the fact that his name is that of a martyred saint. Insisting that she is busy, she puts him into a decrepit service elevator to descend to the street and go home. Once on the street, Sebastian decides to go back up to the studio in the elevator. The story ends with Sebastian trapped in the elevator between floors. Does the elevator really exist and is he really trapped, or is the elevator in his mind and his entrapment in his self-preoccupation? Caponegro leaves the reader as confused as Sebastian.

"LAST RESORT RETREAT"

Norm and Martha are in a totally unsatisfying marriage. At Martha's insistence, they go to the Last Resort Retreat, where counselors and facilitators will help them save their marriage. On the way, Norm hits and kills a deer, which becomes a means of drawing the story into a realm that may be reality, as he hallucinates, or may be fantasy; whichever it is, it is totally immersed in the absurd. Both Norm and Martha connect Martha to the deer. Norm reads the eulogy that Martha has written for him as part of the retreat activities. In the eulogy, Martha takes responsibility for the deer's death because she screamed and Norm swerved. She expresses her grief for what their relationship was and the impossibility of regaining it. She compares the deer's carcass to their empty sexual involvement and says the eulogy is her own. Norm decides to go out into a snowbank, weep, and freeze to death. The freezing-cold Norm then sees Martha coming toward him in her wedding gown, her puffy down jacket, and her L.L.Bean boots. She is surrounded by white deer and carries a pen, to sign divorce papers or to reaffirm marriage vows. Norm stands on his head, falls, and makes snow angels. The story ends with Norm reaching toward Martha and calling her name.

The comic in a dark coloration is also a key element of the story. Caponegro brutally parodies commercial standardized programs that solve problems for a price. The activities, including a food fight, a mock trial for Norm accused of murdering Martha, and symbolic husband castration and wife choking with objects made of a kind of foam, reduce the participants to a less-than-adult stage. The rebellious Norm makes a fool of himself wearing the props as deer antlers.

"THE TRANSLATOR"

"The Translator" is one of Caponegro's most layered and complex stories. The story starts with a series of translations into English. The list is completed with an English phrase that the translator in the story finds untranslatable. Much of the story, through the commentary and digressions of the translator, deals with language in its multiple definitions. Language is the means of spoken and written communication, but words have multiple meanings and can deceive. Language is also a specific set of words, grammar, and syntax used in a specific country, and each of these has levels from formal to dialect to slang. Translators often compound rather than clarify misunderstanding. The translator takes up the task of teaching Italian to Liza, a young American whom he has met in an English bookstore and invited to share his living quarters. Using this action, Caponegro includes series of Italian verbs and nouns throughout the text.

Another layer of the story concentrates on Italian art and architecture. As Liza explores Rome, the story acquires elements of a tourist guidebook. Her activities also bring her in contact with Italian mores and customs, and the story becomes a book of what to expect and what to do when in Italy.

Another layer of the story deals with the relationship between Liza and the translator. He is sexually attracted to her; yet he not only maintains a platonic relationship with her, although they share his bed at night, but also encourages her to become sexually involved with Giorgio, a young man she met in an appliance store. The translator is obsessed with translating in the sense of transforming Liza into an Italian. Finally, Caponegro transforms the medium of visual image into her story.

The description of Liza going about the streets in her short sheath dress, her bag over her shoulder, becomes a motif as it repeats and repeats. The reader has the sense of watching a film.

BIBLIOGRAPHY

Gardaphé, Fred L. *Italian Signs, American Streets: The Evolution of the Italian American Narrative.* Durham, N.C.: Duke University Press, 1996. Epilogue treats Caponegro's work as opening a new direction for Italian American narratives. Discusses how Italian influence is different in her work since she did not grow up in an Italian community.

McLaughlin, Robert L. "Mary Caponegro." *Review of Contemporary Fiction* 21, no. 3 (Fall, 2001): 111-150. Discusses Caponegro as an experimental novelist but recognizes that her work incorporates elements from other approaches to fiction writing.

Pipino, Mary Frances. *"I Have Found My Voice": The Italian American Woman Writer.* New York: Peter Lang, 2000. Chapter 5, "The Third Generation Narratives of Lisa Ruffolo, Mary Caponegro, and Carole Maso," gives good insights into Caponegro as a writer of Italian heritage.

Ponce, Pedro. "Defamiliarizing the Family: Mary Caponegro's *The Complexities of Intimacy.*" In *Narratives of Community: Women's Short Story Sequences*, edited by Roxanne Harde. Newcastle, England: Cambridge Scholar, 2007. Examines the presentation and function of female identity in Caponegro's work in contexts of social, literary, and family community.

Shawncey Webb

TRUMAN CAPOTE

Born: New Orleans, Louisiana; September 30, 1924
Died: Los Angeles, California; August 25, 1984
Also Known As: Truman Streckfus Persons

PRINCIPAL SHORT FICTION

A Tree of Night, and Other Stories, 1949
Breakfast at Tiffany's: A Short Novel and Three Stories, 1958
One Christmas, 1983
I Remember Grandpa: A Story, 1986
The Complete Collected Stories of Truman Capote, 2004

OTHER LITERARY FORMS

In addition to stories and short novels, Truman Capote (kah-POH-tee) wrote travel sketches and various kinds of nonfiction, much of which has been collected, along with some of Capote's short stories and novellas, in *A Capote Reader* (1987). The volume *Local Color* (1950) is a collection solely of travel essays. Capote also did some screenwriting, including critically well-received scripts for *Beat the Devil* (1954) and *The Innocents* (1961), a film adaptation of the Henry James story *The Turn of the Screw* (1898).

In Cold Blood (1966), probably his most famous work, is a "nonfiction novel," a documented recreation of the murder of a family in Kansas. The novel was both a critical and a popular success, and the television film version won an Emmy Award in 1967. Capote's last work, another nonfiction novel, *Answered Prayers: The Unfinished Novel* (1986), set off a social scandal with its gossipy revelations. Capote finished his writing career in ignominy.

ACHIEVEMENTS

The best of Truman Capote's writing is regarded as elegant prose, noted for its lucidity, although at its worst it became an example of vain excess and gossip. Capote was one of the United States' leading post-World War II writers. He pioneered the genre of the "nonfiction novel" with *In Cold Blood* and gained renown for his short stories and novellas. His story "Miriam" won the O. Henry Memorial Award in 1943, and "Shut a Final Door" won the same prize in 1946. Although much of his work has been both critically and popularly praised, Capote was rarely formally recognized during his writing career.

BIOGRAPHY

Truman Streckfus Persons, who would later become Truman Capote, was born in New Orleans, Louisiana, on September 30, 1924. Because his parents were divorced when he was four years old, Capote was reared by aunts and cousins in a small town in Alabama. At seventeen, he moved to New York City and worked his way up from mailroom clerk to feature writer for *The New Yorker*. Capote's early promise seemed fulfilled with the success of *In Cold Blood*, and he spent many years traveling around the world as a celebrated author. He became the pet celebrity for a number of high-society women, most notably Barbara "Babe" Paley and Lee Bouvier Radziwill, sister of Jacqueline Kennedy Onassis. His charmed life seemed to fade, however, under the pressure of trying to produce another successful novel. During the 1970's and early 1980's, Capote's health was ruined by alcoholism and drug dependency.

The downslide began in 1975, however, when *Esquire* magazine published Capote's story "La Côte Basque: 1965." The story was a thinly veiled exposé of the scandals of the rich and famous, and its targets did not appreciate the publicity. Capote's friends immediately ostracized him, and he became persona non grata in many of the places he had previously frequented. Depressed by the reaction that his story generated, Capote became reclusive. His work deteriorated even more, and he did not produce anything to rival his earlier writing before he died at the home of his longtime friend Joanne Carson in 1984.

ANALYSIS

Truman Capote's stories are best known for their mysterious, dreamlike occurrences. As his protagonists try to go about their ordinary business, they meet with unexpected obstacles--usually in the form of haunting, enigmatic strangers. Corresponding to some childhood memory or to someone the protagonist once knew, these people take on huge proportions and cause major changes in the character's life. The central figures of these stories are usually people who have left their hometowns, who travel, or who live alone, for they seem most vulnerable to chance encounters. Their isolation gives them the time, and their loneliness gives them the motivation to see these experiences through to their conclusions--and often with great risk.

Capote was a careful craftsman. His words are meticulously chosen for their evocative power, and, at their best, they create highly charged images and symbols. His descriptions of the seasons or weather further heighten the effects he wants to create. Snow, rain, dusk, and sunlight serve to separate the particular setting from a larger landscape, thus reinforcing the self-reflexive nature of his stories. Attics, kitchens, one-room walk-ups, and isolated apartments are typical locations that also provide sequestered settings. The atmospheres, locations, characters, and events present a touching but often chilling and ominous beauty. The combination of reality and dream also produces an eerie beauty.

"A TREE OF NIGHT"

In "A Tree of Night," one of his finest stories, Kay is a young, attractive student returning to college after the funeral of an uncle. It is late on a winter night, bare and icy, when she boards the train from the deserted platform. Taking the only available seat, she sits opposite an odd-looking couple. The woman is in her fifties, with a huge head and a dwarfish body, while the man is mute, with marblelike eyes and an expressionless face. Although Kay is initially polite, she hopes to be left alone, but the woman wants company and conversation. Kay tries to remain distant,

but the woman and man are persistent and aggressive. Without any warning, the man reaches toward Kay and strokes her cheek. Her reaction is immediate but confused: She is repelled by the boldness of the gesture while, at the same time, she is touched by the delicacy.

From this point on, Kay seems to view the man and woman as harbingers of danger. Capote's style remains realistic and his tone objective, but the couple behave as though they are part of Kay's nightmare. The woman talks endlessly, always wanting a response from her listener. She forces Kay to drink liquor with her and even grabs her wrist. As in a nightmare, Kay wants to scream and awaken the other passengers, but no sounds come out. Trying to escape from the woman's irritating voice, Kay has a reverie as she stares into the void face of the man, and suddenly his face and her uncle's dead face blend. She sees, or imagines that she sees, a shared secret and a stillness. This association of the stranger with someone from her past is deadly, preparing the reader for the end of the story.

Truman Capote (Library of Congress)

By degrees, the man assumes control over Kay. He takes from his pocket a peach seed and fondles it gently. The woman insists that he only wants Kay to purchase it as a good-luck charm, but Kay is frightened, interpreting his action as some kind of warning. Trying to avoid the man, she leaves her seat for the observation platform and fresh air, but soon she senses someone beside her and knows that it must be the man. Now, without the distracting annoyance of the woman, Kay understands why she finds him so threatening. Unable to speak or to hear, he is like her uncle, dead, and the dead can haunt. She further recognizes him as a figure from her childhood dreams, the boogeyman, the "wizard-man," the mysterious personage that could bring alive "terrors that once, long ago, had hovered above her like haunted limbs on a tree of night." Kay's submission is unquestionable, but precisely what she submits to is left ambiguous. Together, she and the man return to their seats, and she gives him money for the peach seed. Then the woman takes possession of Kay's whole purse and, although Kay wants to shout, she does not. Finally the woman takes Kay's raincoat and pulls it "like a shroud" over her head. No longer struggling, Kay sinks into a strange passivity.

"A Tree of Night" raises many questions but provides few answers. The characters are realistically presented, but eccentric, to say the least. Kay is not wholly convincing, yet is still three-dimensional. It is rather the events themselves that appear unlikely and nightmarish, but since Capote delights in paradox, his story cannot be classified as either pure dream or simple reality. Why does Kay not protest? To what extent do she and the mute actually communicate? Is the submission of the young girl carefully planned by the couple? Are the two travelers real passengers who want to do her harm, or can they be projections from Kay's psyche?; or are they merely two unique strangers to whom Kay attributes much more power than they really have? These ambiguities are the source of both the story's weaknesses and its strengths; they enrich the encounter and abstract it, but they also leave the reader feeling baffled. Nevertheless, Capote seems to imply that human beings are extremely vulnerable to destructive instincts. Perhaps beginning with a memory or fear from deep within the psyche, one projects it and expands it until it acquires a frightening degree of reality. In fact, it may become a deadly kind of reality. Kay essentially wills herself first into isolation from other passengers and finally into submission. She returns from the observation platform accompanied by the stranger. She chooses neither to change her seat nor to scream. Eventually, she chooses not to struggle. Human beings are delicate creatures, and the power of the "wizard-man" is enough to cause Kay to sink into nightmarish and unnecessary helplessness.

"MASTER MISERY"

The mysterious realm of dream can invade the workaday world and then consume it. This is precisely what happens in "Master Misery" when Sylvia leaves her hometown of Easton to stay with married friends who live in New York City. Soon she becomes frustrated with her daily routine and her "namby-pamby, bootsy-totsy" friends. Hoping to earn money to find her own apartment, Sylvia overhears a conversation in the Automat. As unlikely as it sounds, a certain Mr. Revercomb purchases dreams. Intrigued, Sylvia visits his Fifth Avenue brownstone and discovers that Mr. Revercomb does indeed purchase dreams for cash. As she continues to visit his office, events take an unfortunate turn. The more Sylvia sees him, the more he seems eccentric, even unnatural. One time as she whispers her dream, Mr. Revercomb bends forward to brush her ear with his lips, apparently in a sexual approach.

Sylvia becomes so obsessed with selling her dreams that everything else in her life loses significance. She cuts off communication with her married friends, quits her office job, and rents a dingy studio apartment. Her only friend is Oreilly, a former clown whom she meets in Mr. Revercomb's waiting room. They have much in common, for Oreilly also used to sell his dreams, but now Mr. Revercomb has no use for them. Although he spends most of his time drunk, Oreilly has the foresight to warn his new companion against the man he calls the Master of Misery, who is so adept at convincing people that parting with a dream is worth five dollars. He explains to Sylvia that she must not lose her independence or her private world of memory and dream, and he compares Mr. Revercomb with the demon of childhood nightmare, the ominous figure who haunted the trees, chimneys, attics, and graveyards of make-believe. Like the mute in "A Tree of Night," Revercomb is "a thief and a threat," for after he appropriates one's dreams, it is a short passage to one's subconscious and one's soul.

Sylvia's life contracts to unhappy proportions. She moves from Revercomb's waiting room back to Oreilly, her waiting companion, who commiserates with her shrinking self before consuming the liquor she buys with her dream-money. He does, however, advise her to ask Revercomb for her dreams back, provided that she gradually returns the money over a period of time. Sylvia agrees, for her life has become miserable and isolated, but this is a Faustian story, and what was spent cannot be retrieved. Revercomb informs Sylvia that under no circumstances would he return what she has sold and, besides, he has already used them up. Walking home in the falling snow, Sylvia acknowledges that she is no longer her own master and has no individuality; soon she will not have even Oreilly, who will go his own way. Thinking she used Revercomb, it turns out that he has used her, and now they are inseparable--until he discards her as he did Oreilly. The story concludes as Sylvia overhears footsteps following behind. There are two boys, who have followed her from the park and continue to do so. Sylvia is frightened, but like Kay in "A Tree of Night," she becomes passive and submissive, for there is "nothing left to steal."

As in much of Capote's short fiction, the individual tacitly gives a stranger enormous power. Once Sylvia abdicates full responsibility for herself and enters Revercomb's world, she becomes vulnerable and he becomes omniscient. Gradually she is emptied of friends, an orderly routine, ambition, desire, and, finally, of self-possession. The reader can never be sure who Revercomb is or what he does with dreams, but Sylvia, not the Master of Misery, is the focus of interest. She allows him to create her misery, leaving her with no one, not even her former self.

Capote's early work especially makes use of the gothic tradition, but because the details remain realistic and controlled, the mysterious elements are subtle and therefore even more insidious. The "wizard-man" is Capote's archetype--the mute in "A Tree of Night," Mr. Revercomb in "Master Misery," the young girl in "Miriam," Mr. Destronelli in "The Headless Hawk."

This figure transforms the actual world of the protagonist, usually in undesirable and irreversible ways. Whether the encounter with this stranger is a final retreat into narcissism or a submission to a purely external presence may not be clarified, but the fragility of the human psyche is all too clear.

OTHER MAJOR WORKS

LONG FICTION: *Other Voices, Other Rooms*, 1948; *The Grass Harp*, 1951; *A Christmas Memory*, 1956 (serial); *In Cold Blood*, 1966; *The Thanksgiving Visitor*, 1967 (serial); *Answered Prayers: The Unfinished Novel*, 1986; *Summer Crossing*, 2005 (found manuscript).

PLAYS: *The Grass Harp: A Play*, pr., pb. 1952 (adaptation of his novel); *House of Flowers*, pr. 1954 (with Harold Arlen).

SCREENPLAYS: *Beat the Devil*, 1954 (with John Huston); *The Innocents*, 1961.

NONFICTION: *Local Color*, 1950; *The Muses Are Heard*, 1956; *Observations*, 1959 (with Richard Avedon); *The Dogs Bark: Public People and Private Places*, 1973; *Portraits and Observations: The Essays of Truman Capote*, 2007.

MISCELLANEOUS: *Selected Writings*, 1963; *Trilogy: An Experiment in Multimedia*, 1969 (with Eleanor Perry and Frank Perry); *Music for Chameleons*, 1980; *A Capote Reader*, 1987; *Too Brief a Treat: The Letters of Truman Capote*, 2004 (Gerald Clarke, editor).

BIBLIOGRAPHY

Bibler, Michael P. "Making a Real Phony: Truman Capote's Queerly Southern Regionalism in *Breakfast at Tiffany's: A Short Novel and Three Stories*." In *Just Below South: Intercultural Performance in the Caribbean and the U.S. South*, edited by Jessica Adams, Bibler, and Cécile Accilien. Charlottesville: University of Virginia Press, 2007. Argues that each story in the book concerns "problems of difference, identity and classification." Focusing on *Breakfast at Tiffany's*, Bibler maintains that Holly Golightly's recreation as a sophisticated, cosmopolitan woman depends upon her hiding her Southern background, making her a "real phony" who resists classification.

Brinnin, John Malcolm. *Truman Capote: Dear Heart, Old Buddy*. Rev. ed. New York: Delacorte Press, 1986. This expansion on an earlier memoir of Capote (which can be found in Brinnin's *Sextet*, 1981) chronicles Capote's life from before the success of *In Cold Blood* to his ruin from alcoholism and drugs. Particularly useful for the insight into the literary circles in which Capote moved. Includes an index.

Clarke, Gerald. *Capote: A Biography*. New York: Simon & Schuster, 1988. Probably the definitive biographical work on Capote, this lengthy text covers all the ups and downs of his career. In particular, Clarke recounts the effect that the short story "La Côte Basque: 1965" (later published as part of *Answered Prayers: The Unfinished Novel*) had on his life. Contains copious references and an index.

Dunphy, Jack. *"Dear Genius": A Memoir of My Life with Truman Capote*. New York: McGraw-Hill, 1987. In this biography, Dunphy reminisces about Capote and discusses the self-destructive streak that perhaps led the writer to alienate almost everyone who loved him. Supplemented by an index.

Garson, Helen S. *Truman Capote: A Study of the Short Fiction*. New York: Twayne, 1992. An introduction to Capote's short fiction, arranged chronologically. Provides brief analyses of his major stories and includes critical essays by a number of other critics.

Gelfant, Blanche H., ed. *The Columbia Companion to the Twentieth-Century American Short Story*. New York: Columbia University Press, 2000. Includes a chapter in which Capote's short stories are analyzed.

Grobel, Lawrence. *Conversations with Capote*. 1985. Reprint. New York: Da Capo Press, 2000. Biographical work draws on in-depth interviews with Capote. Topics covered include events of the author's childhood and his eventual fall from society's good graces. Chapter 4, "Writing," discusses Capote's writing career and the authors he believed had the greatest influence on him.

Inge, M. Thomas, ed. *Truman Capote: Conversations*. Jackson: University Press of Mississippi, 1987. A collection of interviews with Capote conducted by interviewers who range from Gloria Steinem to George Plimpton to Capote himself, in a section called "Self-Portrait." The index allows the reader to find specific references to individual short stories.

Long, Robert Emmet. *Truman Capote, Enfant Terrible*. New York: Continuum, 2008. Brief work combines biographical information and literary criticism. Examines Capote's fiction, screenplays, and nonfiction. Discusses how the southern gothic elements of his early work relate to his later work.

Plimpton, George. *Truman Capote: In Which Various Friends, Enemies, Acquaintances, and Detractors Recall His Turbulent Career*. New York: Doubleday, 1997. As the subtitle warns, this work is about a controversial author. As an oral biography based on interviews, it provides dramatic, primary information, but it also must be checked against the more reliable biography by Gerald Clarke. Includes biographies of contributors and a chronology.

Vickery, John B. "Perspectives on the Self: Malcolm Lowry's *Under the Volcano*, Truman Capote's *Breakfast at Tiffany's*, and Joan Didion's *Play It as It Lays*." In *The Prose Elegy: An Exploration of Modern American and British Fiction*. Baton Rouge: Louisiana State University Press, 2009. Vickery examines the form that the elegy has taken in the twentieth century. He compares *Breakfast at Tiffany's* with two other works and concludes that Capote views memory, which can quickly disappear, as inherently sad.

Windham, Donald. *Lost Friendships: A Memoir of Truman Capote, Tennessee Williams, and Others*. New York: William Morrow, 1987. A friend of the major literary lights of the 1950's and 1960's, as well as a novelist himself, Windham dedicates the first half of *Lost Friendships* to his relationship with Capote and its subsequent decline. No reference material is included.

Miriam Fuchs
Updated by Jo-Ellen Lipman Boon

ORSON SCOTT CARD

Born: Richland, Washington; August 24, 1951

PRINCIPAL SHORT FICTION

Capitol: The Worthing Chronicle, 1979

Unaccompanied Sonata, and Other Stories, 1981

Cardography, 1987

The Folk of the Fringe, 1989

*Maps in a Mirror: The Short Fiction of Orson Scott
Card,* 1990

The Worthing Saga, 1990

Magic Mirror, 1999 (illustrated by Natahn Pinnock)

Keeper of Dreams, 2008

OTHER LITERARY FORMS

A prolific author in many forms, Orson Scott Card has written, in addition to many short stories, more than a dozen novels, as well as plays, poetry, video and audiotape productions, nonfiction books, and essays on biography, history, Mormonism, the craft of writing, computing, science fiction, and fantasy, and other topics. His honored works are series of novels, especially a science-fiction series that consists of *Ender's Game* (1985), *Speaker for the Dead* (1986), *Xenocide* (1991), *Children of the Mind* (1996), *Ender's Shadow* (1999), *A War of Gifts: An Ender Story* (2007), *Ender in Exile* (2008), and a fantasy series, *Tales of Alvin Maker,* the first volumes of which are *Seventh Son* (1987), *Red Prophet* (1988), *Prentice Alvin* (1989), *Alvin Journeyman* (1995), *Heartfire* (1998), and *The Crystal City* (2003).

ACHIEVEMENTS

Within the genres of fantasy and science fiction, Orson Scott Card achieved eminence early in his career. Before his fortieth birthday, he not only had joined the small group of science-fiction writers to receive both the Nebula and Hugo Awards--the most prestigious in the field--for the same work, *Ender's Game,* but also had become one of only two writers to capture both awards two years in a row, when *Speaker for the Dead* won them in 1986. Card won the Hugo Award again in 1991 for his nonfiction work *How to Write Science Fiction and Fantasy* (1990). In 1996, he won a Locus Award for *Alvin Journeyman* (1995) and a Whitney Lifetime Achievement Award in 2008.

Science fiction and fantasy tend to gain relatively little attention from critics whose reviews appear in general-circulation media. Card, like Ursula K. Le Guin, is one of the few authors to attract a wider readership and receive the notice of critics outside the science-fiction and fantasy magazines and journals.

BIOGRAPHY

Orson Scott Card was born on August 24, 1951, in Richland, Washington, the son of Willard Richards, a teacher, and Peggy Jane Park Card, an administrator. He earned his B.A. at Brigham Young University in 1975, interrupting his studies to spend two years as a Mormon missionary in Brazil, from 1971 to 1973. His experience in Brazil is reflected in several of his stories and novels, perhaps most vividly in *Speaker for the Dead,* though more literally in the short story "America." He married Kristine Allen on May 17, 1977.

Card began his artistic career at Brigham Young University, writing and producing a number of plays on Mormon themes during his college years. After college, he began publishing short stories in science-fiction and fantasy magazines. Completing his M.A. in 1981, he began a doctoral program in literature at the University of Notre Dame with the idea of becoming a teacher and writer, but he abandoned this program to devote himself to writing fiction. When Card won the Hugo and Nebula best novel awards two years in a row, 1985 and 1986, he was firmly established as one of the best young writers in science fiction. The appearance of the first volume of *Tales of Alvin Maker* in 1987 won for him a wider audience, especially among younger readers and their teachers. He has published three collections of his short fiction, *Maps in a Mirror*, *First Meetings in Ender's Universe* (2003), and *Keeper of Dreams*. In these he brings together stories that had appeared in ephemeral sources or that had been absorbed into his novels, as well as his best stories that were no longer in print. During the 1990's and on into the twenty-first century, Card has continued to add to both the Ender saga and the Alvin Maker series. He also completed the five-volume Homecoming series and branched out into historical fiction: *Stone Tables* (1997), the supernatural thriller *Homebody* (1998), the modern fantasy *Enchantment* (1999), and the illustrated fairy tale *Magic Mirror*. Card and his wife settled in Greensboro, North Carolina, with their five children: Geoffrey, Emily, Charles, Zina Margaret, and Erin Louisa. His son Charles died of cerebral palsy soon after his seventeenth birthday and Erin Louisa died in infancy.

Orson Scott Card (Pawel Supernak/epa/Corbis)

ANALYSIS

Orson Scott Card is most often praised as an absorbing storyteller. He creates characters of great depth and places them in morally complex situations. The result is fiction that grips and entertains the reader in the ways expected in popular fiction, while provoking thought about his major themes: a religious view of humanity and the cosmos, the exploration of ideal conceptions of human community and the struggles of individuals to realize such communities, examination of the forms of spiritual poverty that repeatedly threaten individual fulfillment, and the realization of living communities. In interviews, Card made clear his commitment to Mormonism, and his reviewers noted how Card's religious beliefs permeate his work. Michael R. Collings compares Card's work to that of an important influence on Card, C. S. Lewis in his seven-volume Chronicles of Narnia series, showing that both writers produce stories that are enriched by their religious beliefs without being explicitly didactic.

Card's short fiction includes a variety of styles, though most stories fall within popular genres. He divides *Maps in a Mirror* into groups of horror stories, speculative fiction, fables and fantasies, religious tales, and a miscellaneous group that includes stories and a poem that have grown into novels as well as several exemplary stories for religious, family readers. The stories in *The Worthing Saga* are closer to traditional science fiction, while those in *The Folk of the Fringe* speculate about a postnuclear holocaust world in the Mormon West. While nearly all these stories have been well received, the most interesting and moving of them tend to be the fantasies and speculative fiction that explore themes of human spirituality.

"KINGSMEAT"

"Kingsmeat" was first published in 1978 and later collected in *Maps in a Mirror*. Though it is a story of the liberation of a conquered human colony on another planet, these events are not the central interest of the story. The story of the conquest and release is revealed at the human shepherd's trial for collaboration with the alien king and queen. The king and queen are multi-limbed alien life forms with an advanced technology that allows them to dominate human colonists. Their usual procedure is to conquer a colony, feed off it, eating the humans until they are gone, and move to another colony. At some point, they reproduce a large number of new pairs to spread the species. The shepherd discovers a way to save the human colony from this fate. He succeeds in communicating with the king and queen and persuades them to accept a procedure by which he will provide them an endless supply of human flesh. He thereby preserves the colony until its rescue by cutting off body parts of the colonists, using tools provided by the king and queen that allow painless surgery, and saving the colonists' lives at the cost of their physical wholeness.

On the day the king and queen are defeated, the shepherd supplies their order of breast-in-butter by cutting off the breasts of a fifteen-year-old mother of a newborn, then overseeing the cooking and serving of this delicacy. After a rescue party destroys the king and queen, there is a trial of the collaborators, mainly the shepherd, whom the colonists have hated and feared for years. The trial supplies the reader with the background of the conquest and with a detailed account of how the shepherd came to occupy his position. The trial is conducted by telepathic means, there being a machine for this purpose. As a result, the entire colony and the accused participate, and every participant feels what the witnesses and the accused feel as they remember these events. The court is moved to compassion by the shepherd's story. While it is true he has committed atrocities, his doing so saved lives, for the shepherd never took a life. The court decides that for his sacrifice, the shepherd is to be preserved, cared for, and honored by the colonists.

The story ends, however, with what proves to be its most horrific image. The colonists cannot forgive the shepherd for having remained whole while he dismembered them. Therefore, they remove all of his limbs and his genitals. They carry out the court's order to the letter, caring for him, preserving his life, and honoring him annually with visits and gifts. They leave him his tongue, because he never speaks, and his eyes, because they want him to see them smile as he once smiled when he was their shepherd.

"Kingsmeat" is a powerful tale that suggests meanings on several levels. The testimony in the trial can hardly fail to evoke images of the Jewish Holocaust of

World War II, specifically the problem of collaborating with evil to mitigate it. The narrative voice of the story is always sympathetic to the shepherd, emphasizing how much he tries to be kind to his flock, even as he makes them into food, and how he endures their hatred and fear in order to save them. His final fate suggests a living crucifixion, the figure of a savior who cannot be forgiven for his necessary actions. Card says that as he developed this story, he found himself focusing on "an area of unbearable ambiguity. . . . [T]he one who suffered and died to save others is depicted as one who also inflicts suffering; it is a way to explicitly make the Christ figure take upon himself, in all innocence, the darkest sins of the world."

The final image is so horrifying because those he saved prove unable to show him the same mercy he won for them. In the end, they prove more vicious than the king and the queen, whose morality did not require that they value humans any more than humans value the animals they use and eat. By obeying the letter rather than the spirit of the law, his tormentors fail to understand their human condition, revealing that they need but do not deserve the mercy they deny the shepherd.

Card said in the extensive commentary included in *Maps in a Mirror* that he considered science fiction the ideal genre for dealing with basic religious questions. While he was not always aware that this was happening in his fiction, the more experience and success he gained, the clearer it became to him that he preferred science fiction, in part because it allowed him to explore metaphysical issues without having to choose or favor the point of view of a particular religion. In "Kingsmeat," Card is able to explore aspects of the problem of the affirmation of community values--life, wholeness, suffering, and sacrifice--in an ultimate, yet fictional, situation. The reader is given a means of thinking about these issues concretely but without having to connect them to historical events or institutions that often demand loyalties that would fix a reader's perspective.

"THE PORCELAIN SALAMANDER"

Card considers science fiction an ideal genre for the exploration of religious issues because the genre as a whole is committed to a scientific worldview at the same time that it is open to the representation of alien cultures. Fantasy, because it usually occurs in a world where supernatural powers operate, is less well suited to the exploration of religious questions. Nevertheless, Card considers fantasy ideal for the creation of myths about the values by which communities are defined. One of Card's best stories of this kind is "The Porcelain Salamander," first published in 1981 and collected in *Maps in a Mirror*.

"The Porcelain Salamander" tells how a curse is spoken and then lifted. It takes place in a beautiful land, where all are said to be as happy as humans can be. However, Princess Kiren is singled out for special unhappiness. Because her father's much-beloved wife dies in giving birth to Kiren, he curses the child: "May you never move a muscle in your life, until you lose someone you love as much as I loved her!" In Kiren's world, magic and curses work, but partially and unpredictably. Kiren is not paralyzed, but she is so weak that she can move only with great difficulty and is soon exhausted by any activity. Though he almost immediately regrets his curse, her father is unable to take it back, so Kiren lives for eleven years in enforced passivity.

Her father travels to foreign lands for relief from his guilt, and on one of his trips meets a magician, Irvass, who sells him a cure for the curse, a porcelain salamander magically endowed with motion and, as Kiren learns later, the power of speaking to her alone. Should the salamander ever stop moving, her father tells her, it will be frozen forever, as an ordinary piece of porcelain. The salamander changes her life, helping her to become more lively by the cheerfulness of its constant motion and by talking to her. Eventually, she comes to love it more, she says, than her father or even the dream of her mother. This declaration brings Irvass to her door to reclaim the salamander. Irvass does not simply take it away but creates a magical situation: A wall encloses Kiren and her pet while they are playing in the forest and gradually squeezes in upon them, until the salamander tells her that she can escape only by standing on him, and she can stand on him only if he holds still. Instantly, he becomes a porcelain statue. When she climbs over the wall, it and the salamander disappear, and she becomes physically whole.

The story does not end, however, with her cure, for to achieve it, she has had to suffer exactly what her father suffered upon losing his wife. This, it turns out, was the real curse, and how she deals with her grief becomes a central theme of this fable, opening it out to all readers who will suffer bereavement as an inheritance of mortality. When Irvass comforts Kiren for her loss, he offers the usual platitudes that, at first glance, are not particularly consoling to the bereaved: The salamander, always in motion, needed and welcomed rest; the salamander's life ended with the motives of a generous action frozen in its memory; it will live more vibrantly in her memory now than had it continued longer. As Kiren grows older, she comes to understand this more deeply, and she learns in this way what her father forgot when he cursed her: "The moment when he [the salamander] decided, without love, that it would be better for his life, such as it was, to end than to have to watch Kiren's life end. It is such a moment that can be lived with for eternity." She has her father's grief but not his guilt, and he would have been happier had he known or remembered this. Grief cannot be avoided, but it is better to suffer alone than to cause another to suffer.

"The Porcelain Salamander" is a charming fable, told in an intimate and humorous voice. Its moral content is complex, even though the tale seems simple, and it is subtly conveyed, allowing the reader the pleasure of discovery. Furthermore, it is structured to allow for repeated discoveries of meaning on several levels. For example, charming and humorous as it is, the story is absolutely uncompromising in its presentation of the inevitability and pain of the loss of loved ones. Not a living being, not capable of love, the salamander will give up its claim to life rather than suffer bereavement, yet the human characters cannot choose death over grief, because to do so bereaves the others who love them. Card considered this to be one of his three best stories: "If my career had to be encapsulated in only three stories, I believe I would choose 'The Porcelain Salamander,' 'Unaccompanied Sonata,' and 'Salvage' as the three that did the best job, together, of saying all I had to say."

MAGIC MIRROR

Magic Mirror is a contemporary adult fable disguised as an illustrated children's fairy tale. It epitomizes one of Card's primary themes, the family in crisis. His stories often demonstrate how family members influence one another and should be the primary source for solving life's problems. On the surface, *Magic Mirror* is the tale of Heather, who, as a young princess, dreamed of contributing to the success of her dashing prince, Richard. Now that her children have grown, she laments her lonely existence as a stay-at-home queen. In order to placate her, Richard gives her a magic mirror that allows her to communicate with their son, Jason, who is away at school. Lonely and despondent, Heather turns to the mirror to fill the hours of her life, first for news and information, finally for companionship. Stephen, a compassionate wizard, becomes her true friend and confidant. Then Heather's life is upended when Stephen reveals that Richard has taken a mistress.

What seems like an ordinary, even mundane fantasy is given a contemporary interpretation by means of Nathan Pinnock's illustrations. Working from detailed descriptions provided by Card, Pinnock provided illustrations that interpret the story by combining ingeniously medieval and modern settings. Heather's home is a cross between a castle and a suburban house, but anachronisms are used for both time periods. In an illustration depicting a mostly modern setting, some conveniences are replaced by medieval devices (a gnome washing dishes instead of a dishwasher), while a mostly medieval setting contains modern devices (a luxury sedan instead of a gallant steed). King Richard fights corporate battles but slays real dragons. The magic mirror is a computer wired to the Internet. Card's fairy tale is thereby a metaphor for the destructive forces facing the contemporary family. For example, the so-called evidence of Richard's affair is actually a series of digital images manipulated by a vengeful enemy pretending to be a wise confidant.

Nowhere, however, does Card decry the obvious. He does not lament the modern family. Contemporary challenges are presented as simple facts of life. Instead, Card's tale is redemptive. It is never too late

for family members to recognize the forces that have separated them and to make decisions that enable their relationships to heal.

First Meetings in Ender's Universe consists of four stories that fill in some of the gaps in the Ender Wiggins saga. "The Polish Boy" is about Ender's father, John Paul Wieczorek. He is five years old, a brilliant Polish child who is tested for intellectual and military aptitude by the International Fleet (IF) authorities. John Paul's family are noncompliant. Catholics who have not obeyed the population control laws; consequently, they are placed under severe legal handicaps. In exchange for John Paul's agreement to attend the IF Battle School, he is able to manipulate the authorities into resettling the family in the United States under the surname Wiggin. The discriminatory laws are circumvented. Two of Card's major concerns emerge in this tale: how unwise or unjust laws can disrupt family life and how accurately children perceive reality, much more so than adults give children credit for. In "Teacher's Pest," John Paul is of college age. He meets and falls in love with his Human Communities instructor, Theresa Brown. She is the daughter of an eminent but controversial military strategist who has been forced into retirement both for his unconventional views and for his Mormon refusal to comply with the population laws. The byplay between John Paul and Theresa is both clever and wonderfully written--some of the best writing in Card's canon. Although the protagonists are only at the beginning of their relationship, it is clear that they will marry and have children, one of whom will be Ender Wiggin, the central character of the entire Ender saga. It is also made plain that the whole development, culminating in Ender's birth, has been foreseen and subtly prompted by the Battle School leaders.

"Ender's Game" is the short-story version of the original Ender tale, the basis for Card's best-known and most successful novel. In "Investment Counselor," Card explains how Ender meets "Jane," the computerized "person" who is to be his helper and invisible companion in the later Ender books. In the course of the story Jane is able to discomfit and punish a corrupt tax official by manipulating computer files, another expression of Card's concern with ethical behavior.

Keeper of Dreams is a collection of twenty-one of Card's short stories. He divides them into five categories: science fiction, fantasy, literary, Hatrack River (part of the Alvin the Maker series), and Mormon stories. Although the line between science fiction and fantasy is often blurry, in fantasy, magic is an important element. Card's central themes as a writer are present, found in each of the categories. The dominant moral thrust of these stories is to celebrate individual ethical judgment as the important force in human life as opposed to great historical trends. In quite a few of the stories, Card deplores cruelty, especially to children. He sees happiness and achievement grounded in a warm and stable family life.

Many of Card's protagonists are children or teenagers. In "Dust," one of the fantasy stories, Enoch Hunt is a twelve-year-old whose mother is ill. Enoch somehow finds his way into a magical world in which he meets a girl named Maureen. After some harrowing adventures he is able to secure "healing dust," which enables him to cure his mother's illness. He is also able to choose between two magical elixirs, one of which gives wisdom and the other love. He has matured enough to choose the latter, and he and Maureen--she turns out to be in his class at school--drink it. As usual, the adventure that Card recounts is engaging and well done, but the story's underlying significance is Enoch's wisdom in choosing between the elixirs. Affection and kindness are more important than "wisdom." Another parental rescue story is "Space Boy," in which a boy rescues his mother from an adjoining universe into which she has fallen accidentally and from which she has been unable to escape. Here, as in "Dust," the child's courage and wit result in reuniting the family.

An upstanding family life is at the center of "Feed the Baby of Love," one of the stories Card has classified as "literary." Rainie Pinyon, formerly a noted singer and songwriter, travels from one town to another, working anonymous short gigs as a waitress in diners. She stops in a small town in Utah, likes the people she finds there, and stays on much longer than has been her custom. She falls in love with a young Mormon, who is married. He recognizes her from her past days of fame. He loves her and her music, but just as their relationship is to be physically consummated

he understands that the qualities that have attracted her to him--his warmth with his family and his loyalty to it--will be lost if he gives in to his passion. He backs off, and Rainie leaves town the next morning without even going back to the diner. However, she really cared for him, and for loving him she is rewarded by being able to write and perform a song that gets her back onto the charts. This is an old-fashioned story, neither fantasy nor science fiction, but in Card's capable hands, the celebration of virtue is neither corny nor cloying.

Another motif found in several stories in this collection is death. Card sees death as a normal and an ultimately desirable part of life. "Geriatric Ward" and "Heal Thyself" both deal with this theme. Moreover, in "Homeless in Hell" he posits an afterlife in which people are suspended between heaven and hell, having been neither good enough for heaven nor wicked enough for hell. However, in this middle ground it is still possible for them to do some good works, although their power over the physical universe is limited.

Each story in this collection is accompanied by explanatory notes, telling about the genesis of the story, its publication history, and often the story's reception. These notes broaden the reader's understanding of Card's intent for each story and add to the interest of this eclectic collection.

Card pointedly writes for a popular audience, yet he is uncompromising in his moral seriousness. Like "Kingsmeat," "The Porcelain Salamander," and *Magic Mirror*, most of his fiction is accessible to young and adult readers alike. The stories encompass humor, epic adventure, and human suffering, sometimes in its darkest hues, as when the shepherd removes the young mother's breasts or when those he saved through atrocity come to mock him. Card's creation of interesting stories that speak profound truth have made him one of the best writers to work in the genres of fantasy and science fiction.

OTHER MAJOR WORKS

LONG FICTION: *A Planet Called Treason*, 1979 (revised as *Treason*, 1988); *Songmaster*, 1980; *Hart's Hope*, 1983; *The Worthing Chronicle*, 1983; *A Woman of Destiny*, 1984 (also as *Saints*, 1988); *Ender's Game*, 1985; *Speaker for the Dead*, 1986; *Seventh Son*, 1987;

Wyrms, 1987; *Red Prophet*, 1988; *Prentice Alvin*, 1989; *The Abyss*, 1989; *Xenocide*, 1991; *Lost Boys*, 1992; *The Memory of Earth*, 1992; *The Call of Earth*, 1993; *Lovelock*, 1994; *The Ships of Earth*, 1994; *Alvin Journeyman*, 1995; *Earthborn*, 1995; *Earthfall*, 1995; *Children of the Mind*, 1996; *Pastwatch: The Redemption of Christopher Columbus*, 1996; *Treasure Box*, 1996; *Stone Tables*, 1997; *Heartfire*, 1998; *Homebody*, 1998; *Enchantment*, 1999; *Ender's Shadow*, 1999; *Sarah*, 2000; *Rebekah*, 2001; *Shadow of the Hegemon*, 2001; *Shadow Puppets*, 2002; *The Crystal City*, 2003; *Rachel and Leah: Women of Genesis*, 2004; *Magic Street*, 2005; *Shadow of the Giant*, 2005; *Empire*, 2006; *Invasive Procedures*, 2007 (with Aaron Johnston); *Ender in Exile*, 2008; *Hidden Empire*, 2009.

NONFICTION: *"Listen, Mom and Dad . . . : Young Adults Look Back on Their Upbringing*, 1977; *Saintspeak: The Mormon Dictionary*, 1981; *Ainge*, 1982; *Characters and Viewpoint*, 1988; *How to Write Science Fiction and Fantasy*, 1990; *A Storyteller in Zion: Essays and Speeches*, 1993.

BIBLIOGRAPHY

Collings, Michael R. *In the Image of God: Theme, Characterization, and Landscape in the Fiction of Orson Scott Card.* New York: Greenwood Press, 1990. Dealing mainly with Card's major novels, Collings's book is a good introduction to Card's themes, interests, aims, and influences. There is considerable attention to ways in which Mormonism influences his work. Collings quotes and summarizes generously from Card's interviews and essays. Includes bibliographies of Card's works and of secondary writing about Card.

DeCandido, GraceAnne Andreassi, and Keith DeCandido. *Publishers Weekly* 237 (November, 1990): 54-55. Discusses *Maps in a Mirror: The Short Fiction of Orson Scott Card*, noting that he writes stories

that turn on issues of moral choice. Card discusses the importance of challenging readers in science fiction and contends that, at its best, the genre changes the world's moral imperatives.

Hantke, Steffen. "Surgical Strikes and Prosthetic Warriors: The Soldier's Body in Contemporary Science Fiction." *Science Fiction Studies* 25 (November, 1998): 495-509. Discusses how the technologically augmented body in the science fiction of Card and others raises issues about what it means to be male or female, or even human, since the use of prosthetics to heal or strengthen the body is accompanied by the dissolution of the body.

Heidkemp, Bernie. "Responses to the Alien Mother in Post-Maternal Cultures: C. J. Cherryl and Orson Scott Card." *Science-Fiction Studies* 23 (November, 1996): 339-354. Discusses Card's use of the Queen Mother archetype as a literary manifestation of the pre-Oedipal mother figure. Argues that in his work protagonists react as infants to this archetypal mother image in gendered ways.

Tyson, Edith. *Orson Scott Card: Writer of the Terrible Choice.* Lanham, Md.: Scarecrow Press, 2003. Analysis of Card's works, emphasizing his religious faith and his ethical posture.

Van Name, Mark L. "Writer of the Year: Orson Scott Card." *Science Fiction and Fantasy Book Review Annual*, edited by Robert A. Collins and Robert Latham. Westport, Conn.: Meckler, 1988. This combination interview-review essay provides an introduction to Card's career as well as helpful insights into his ideas about life and writing. The richest source of such information, however, remains *Maps in a Mirror*, which includes long and interesting introductions and afterwords for each group of stories.

Terry Heller; Gerald S. Argetsinger
Updated by Robert Jacobs

RON CARLSON

Born: Logan, Utah, September 15, 1947

PRINCIPAL SHORT FICTION

The News of the World, 1987
Plan B for the Middle Class, 1992
The Hotel Eden, 1997
At the Jim Bridger, 2002
A Kind of Flying: Selected Stories, 2003

OTHER LITERARY FORMS

Although Ron Carlson has been a preeminent short-story writer in the United States for the past twenty-five years, he began his career as a novelist, publishing *Betrayed by F. Scott Fitzgerald* in 1977 and *Truants* in 1981. Carlson mostly focused on short fiction for the next twenty years; and he adapted several of his short stories into plays, including *Bigfoot Stole My Wife*, produced in 1986, and *This Guy Wrote the Book of Love* in 1990. His play *Our First Water Problem* was produced in 2006. In 2003, he published a young adult novel, *The Speed of Light*, dealing with an adolescent character similar to the graduate student narrator of *Betrayed by F. Scott Fitzgerald.* Despite his success as a short-story writer and director of prominent creative-writing programs, Carlson enjoyed his most significant mainstream success with the publication of his 2007 novel *Five Skies.* He published *The Signal*, another novel, in 2009.

ACHIEVEMENTS

Ron Carlson earned a Connecticut Arts Commission grant in 1978. He was a Bread Loaf fellow in 1983 and won a fellowship from the National Endowment for the Arts in 1985. His short stories won Pushcart Press prizes in 1998 and 2000, and his work has been chosen for *The Best American Short Stories*

anthologies--in 1983 for "Milk" and in 2000 for "The Ordinary Son." In 2001, he won an O. Henry Award for short fiction. He is also a recipient of the Aspen Literary Award.

BIOGRAPHY

Ron Carlson was born in Logan, Utah, on September 15, 1947. His parents spent time as teachers, and his mother worked as a part-time editor and slogan writer. The family moved to Salt Lake City when Carlson was three, so his father could take a position as a welder and eventually as a contractor. When Carlson was in high school, the family relocated to Houston, Texas; after attending the University of Houston for one year, he returned to the University of Utah to be closer to his high school girlfriend, Elaine Craig, whom he would marry after graduation. After working at several small jobs, Carlson returned to the University of Utah for his master's degree. During his time completing his master's, Carlson wrote several stories he called "the Larry Stories," which would serve as the basis for his first novel, *Betrayed by F. Scott Fitzgerald.*

Upon graduating with his master's degree, Carlson and his wife moved to Connecticut, where he began teaching for the Hotchkiss School, a preparatory and boarding school in Lakeville. During his time there, he began composing *Betrayed by F. Scott Fitzgerald*, which was published in 1977. He finished his second novel, *Truants*, two years later during a sabbatical year, and he left Hotchkiss in 1981, the year the novel was published. Over the next few years his wife worked as an editor, while Carlson wrote and worked as an artist-in-residence at various institutions. In 1985, he earned a National Endowment for the Arts fellowship, and he and his wife adopted two sons, Nick and Colin. A year later, he became a professor of creative writing at Arizona State University, where he remained until 2003. He served as the director of the Master's of Fine Arts in Creative Writing program at Arizona State for many years. While there he would occasionally serve as the visiting writer at other institutions, including the University of Hawaii and Beloit College, and during that tenure he published four collections of short fiction. In 2003, Carlson and his wife divorced, and he became the director of the creative writing program at the University of California, Irvine. That year his selected stories, *A Kind of Flying*, and his first novel in more than twenty years, *The Speed of Light*, were published.

ANALYSIS

Since the publication of his first collection of short stories, Ron Carlson has been one of the American literary scene's best-kept secrets. Although his stories often have appeared in some of the most prestigious literary magazines on the market, including *The New Yorker*, *Harper's*, *Esquire*, *McCall's*, and *Tin House*, like many writers who focus primarily on short fiction he toiled in relative obscurity until the publication of his novel *Five Skies*. Carlson's body of work is distinctive for a variety of reasons. Foremost, he eschews the mundane realism of suburban writers, such as John Updike and John Cheever, and the grim minimalism of Raymond Carver in favor of stories with more heart. As one reviewer has pointed out, Carlson is one of the few writers of contemporary literary fiction who can master happy endings without having them devolve into sentimentality or wish fulfillment. Carlson often writes with a wry sense of humor that is gentle rather than biting, and at times his sense of whimsy propels stories into original circumstances. For example, in his collection *The News of the World*, one story ("Bigfoot Stole My Wife") tells how a man lost his wife to the legendary creature; Bigfoot himself is rejoined in a later story from Bigfoot's point of view. Similarly, "What We Wanted to Do" (from *The Hotel Eden)* is told from the point of view of a medieval castle dweller who has failed in repelling a siege, telling his story in a tone evocative of an incident report of a failed experiment or product trial.

On a more sophisticated level, a number of Carlson stories are about the ephemeral and elusive nature of innocence. Characters are challenged not so much by intruders stealing their way into paradise as by serpents uncoiling in their own hearts. Similarly, he often writes

of characters whose lives are in disarray and who must strive to piece things back together again. Carlson's gentle sense of humor and genuine human interest in his characters allow him to paint poignant, funny, and honest portraits in limited spaces. For example, his story "Keith" (in *The Hotel Eden*), at some level, seems familiar and perhaps cliché: A quirky science geek is paired as a lab partner with a beautiful cheerleader and develops a crush on her. However, Carlson is able to redeem the most despised character in the world of fiction--the head cheerleader--and make her story a human and a redemptive one. Similarly, "At Copper View" in *At the Jim Bridger* seems to pull from the same world of familiar teen angst when a young man attends a dance at a rival high school. In Carlson's deft hands, however, this becomes a tale about boundaries, risk taking, and spreading wings.

THE NEWS OF THE WORLD AND PLAN B
FOR THE MIDDLE CLASS

The News of the World, published in 1987, introduced many of Carlson's recurring tropes. For example, in "The H Street Sledding Record," the father of

Ron Carlson (Getty Images)

an eight-year-old girl worries that she is growing up too quickly; to ensure that she hold on to childhood (and her innocence) a little longer, at Christmastime he throws manure on the roof so that she will think Santa's reindeer were there. In "Life Before Science," an art teacher goes to great lengths, even trying a kind of sympathetic magic, in order to help his wife who cannot conceive. Instead of their marriage fracturing (surely a common story in contemporary literature), he takes heroic steps to cement their bond. Similarly, in the title story for *Plan B for the Middle Class*, published in 1992, a newspaper columnist whose column is being canceled takes a last trip with his wife while reminiscing about the other time of great change in his life--finishing high school--and again Carlson's story is about recognizing the strengths of the characters' relationships. In this case, the narrator's bond with his wife is beautifully compared to his parents' long relationship. "Blazo," on the other hand, tells of a father who, as an alcoholic, was often absent from the life of his son; recovered, the father travels to Alaska, where his son has died, to try to make some sense of his son's life and to provide his own a direction. As in *The News of the World*, *Plan B for the Middle Class* occasionally gives Carlson rein to indulge his whimsical side, as shown by the story "On the U.S.S. *Fortitude*," about a mother trying to raise a large family on their aircraft carrier.

THE HOTEL EDEN

The stories of *The Hotel Eden* not only show Carlson at the peak of his talents but also demonstrate the development of even greater depths in his short fiction. His interest in the theme of innocence lost is on display in the two best stories in the collection, "The Hotel Eden" and "Oxygen." "The Hotel Eden" tells of a young couple, Mark and Allison, who are attending graduate school in Oxford, England. While there, they meet a legendary local character, Porter, whom Mark discovers has a bit of a sinister reputation. Even as the two are manipulated by Porter, Mark realizes that Porter's ultimate game is to seduce Allison and that Porter may well be successful in the matter. Like many of Carlson's characters, Mark understands that the innocence of paradise--or Eden--is brief and fleeting, just like a stay in a hotel. This realization is profoundly

complicated in Carlson's marvelous "Oxygen." David is a young man home from college for the summer, working for an oxygen company; as the summer grows hotter, David delivers oxygen tanks to elderly patients. On one such run he meets Elizabeth Rensdale, the daughter of a client; soon David and Elizabeth begin a heated sexual affair. David is astounded and eventually sickened at the lengths he is driven to by lust, and by the end of the story he feels he has "spent the summer as someone else, someone [he] didn't care for." David goes on to say that "I would be glad when he left town. We would see each other from time to time, but I also knew he was no friend of mine."

Carlson's maturity as a writer is perhaps even better displayed in "Keith" and "Down the Green River," which tells of a fishing trip down a canyon river with the narrator Jack; a divorced woman, Glenna (a college friend of Jack's ex-wife); and her young son, Toby. Even as Jack unconsciously becomes a surrogate father to Toby, Glenna is unable to accept the trajectory of her life. Despite the complexity of some of its stories, *The Hotel Eden* continues to display Carlson's taste for the humorous and unique. "A Note on the Type" tells of a convict who invents his own type font and who finds love as a fugitive. "The Chromium Hook" turns the scary urban legend about a prowling killer with a hook into a hilarious melodrama of romantic reconciliation with lost loves. "Zanduce at Second" is perhaps the most successful of these kinds of stories; it tells of a major league batter whose foul balls have killed eleven spectators and who has become a cult hero of sorts. Despite the absurdity of the premise, Carlson grapples with the problems of celebrity culture and with the avaricious mentality of crowds.

AT THE JIM BRIDGER

Carlson's fourth collection picks up where *The Hotel Eden* lets off; its stories again show a remarkable range and an extraordinary ability to evoke real people with real hopes, dreams, and personal tragedies. "The Clicker at Tips" tells of a man having drinks with a former lover and her bitterness over his lack of willingness to commit; it is yet another story of people gently trying to regain control. The title story juxtaposes a man's rescue of a blizzard victim with his later extramarital affair and the realization that, in some ways, the protagonist's old life is over. *At the Jim Bridger* also introduces a recurring theme, that of isolation and the way humans separate themselves. "Towel Season" is about a suburban father who is a mathematical and engineering genius, who becomes lost in a difficult problem in search of a solution. One day he simply has enough of it and slowly allows himself to reemerge into his family's suburban life. "The Ordinary Son," similarly, tells of a young man, Reed, from a family of geniuses: His father is an engineer for the National Aeronautics and Space Administration (NASA), his mother is an activist and poet, his sister is a chemical theorist, and his brother was admitted to college at eight years of age. Reed is not resentful that he did not turn out to be a genius; rather, he is relieved, opting instead to drive fast cars and go fishing with his friend. The narrative makes clear at one point that Reed, too, has the makings of genius in him, but he suppresses it with an act of will so that he may be integrated into a normal life.

OTHER MAJOR WORKS

LONG FICTION: *Betrayed by F. Scott Fitzgerald*, 1977; *Truants*, 1981; *The Speed of Light*, 2003; *Five Skies*, 2007; *The Signal*, 2009.

PLAYS: *Bigfoot Stole My Wife*, pr. 1986; *The Tablecloth of Turin*, pr. 1987; *Two Monologues: "Madame Zelena Finally Comes Clean" and "The Time I Died,"* pr. 1988; *This Guy Wrote the Book of Love*, pr. 1990; *Our First Water Problem*, pr. 2006.

NONFICTION: *Ron Carlson Writes a Story*, 2007.

BIBLIOGRAPHY

Boyer, J. "About Ron Carlson." *Ploughshares* 32, no. 3 (Fall, 2006): 202-208. An excellent overview of Carlson's body of work, including a brief biographical sketch.

Dishner, Jackie. "Deep in the Fictional Landscapes of Ron Carlson." *The Writer* 120, no. 7 (July, 2007): 17-20. A discussion of Carlson's development as a writer and a conversation with the writer about his use of workingmen and blue-collar work in his fiction.

Haworth, Kevin. "Conversation with Ron Carlson." *Another Chicago Magazine* 38 (2001): 222-228. An interview with Carlson that stresses the interests that influence his short fiction.

Pitt, Matthew. "Skywriter." *Poets and Writers Magazine* 35, no. 4 (2007): 42-47. A discussion of Carlson's transition from years spent primarily as a short-story writer back to being a novelist again.

Wootten, Leslie A. "Shadows and Light: An Interview with Ron Carlson." *Bloomsbury Review* 5, no. 1 (September/October, 1997): 15-16. A brief interview with Carlson that discusses his interest in juxtaposing the comic with the tragic.

Scott D. Yarbrough

JOHN DICKSON CARR

Born: Uniontown, Pennsylvania; November 30, 1906
Died: Greenville, South Carolina; February 27, 1977
Also known as: Carr Dickson, Roger Fairbairn,
   Carter Dickson

PRINCIPAL SHORT FICTION

The Department of Queer Complaints, 1940 (as
   Carter Dickson; also as *Scotland Yard: Depart-
   ment of Queer Complaints*)
Dr. Fell, Detective, and Other Stories, 1947
The Third Bullet, and Other Stories, 1954
The Exploits of Sherlock Holmes, 1954 (with Adrian
   Conan Doyle)
The Men Who Explained Miracles, 1963
The Door to Doom, and Other Detections, 1980

OTHER LITERARY FORMS

John Dickson Carr's prolific and lengthy career produced seventy-one novels, four novelettes, several
radio plays, two nonfiction works, and numerous articles in addition to six short-story collections (one of
which was compiled posthumously by Douglas G.
Greene). His work has been translated into at least a
dozen languages--everything from the standard French,
German, Italian, and Spanish to the more exotic Greek,
Hungarian, Serbo-Croatian, and Turkish.

ACHIEVEMENTS

John Dickson Carr is best known for his contribution
to the genre of detective fiction, specifically, to the tiny
subgenre known as "impossible crime." Under his
pseudonym Roger Fairbairn, Carr is also credited with
having been among the first to write a historical detective novel, *Devil Kinsmere* (1934). One of his early
radio plays, *Cabin B-13* (1943), for the Columbia
Broadcasting System series *Suspense,* later became the
basis of a film called *Dangerous Crossing* (1953), which
starred Michael Rennie and Jeanne Crain.

Carr was the recipient of many honors for his work,
including an award from *Ellery Queen's Mystery Mag-
azine* for "The Gentleman from Paris," a 1949 Edgar
Allan Poe Award for *The Life of Sir Arthur Conan
Doyle* (1949), and a 1962 Grandmaster Award from the
Mystery Writers of America.

BIOGRAPHY

Born in Uniontown, Pennsylvania, John Dickson
Carr came from a respectable, well-to-do family. His
father, Wood Nicholas Carr, was a lawyer and, later, a
postmaster who also enjoyed a career in politics: He
was elected to the House of Representatives, as a Dem-
ocrat, in 1912. The family spent four years in Washington, D.C., from 1913 to 1916. Perhaps inspired by
his grandfather, who was a partial owner of a newspaper in Uniontown, Carr began writing articles on
court proceedings and murder cases at the age of
eleven. By age fifteen, he had his own column--about
boxing.

From 1921 to 1925, Carr attended a preparatory
school called the Hill School, where he wrote for the
literary magazine. In 1925, he started at Haverford
College, in Haverford, Pennsylvania. There, he became associate editor (in April, 1926) and then editor
(in June of the same year) of *The Haverfordian,* although most of his literary contributions have been described as "tales of historical adventure." English and
European history remained among Carr's principal interests, although he also commanded detailed knowledge about true crime, fencing, and other, as one critic
called them, "curious bits of learning."

In 1928, Carr went to Paris, ostensibly to attend the
Sorbonne, but it was during this time that Carr wrote
Grand Guignol (1929), a short novel that served as the
basis for his later *It Walks by Night* (1930). After the
success of the latter novel, Carr married an English-
woman named Clarice Cleaves, and the couple moved
to England, where Carr instituted his now-legendary

                         **

regimen of producing three to five novels a year. He and Clarice had three daughters, Julia (named for his mother), Bonita, and Mary.

ANALYSIS

John Dickson Carr's abundant output throughout his writing career is best characterized by his reply to a friend who asked if he had much trouble with inventing plots: "I've had exactly a hundred and twenty complete plots outlined, for emergencies, since I was eleven years old." This natural propensity for puzzles perhaps explains why Carr always restricted his writing to the locked-room murder in particular or the "impossible crime" in general, rather than branching out into other categories of mystery writing.

Carr was influenced at an early age by the Father Brown stories of G. K. Chesterton. In fact, Carr himself said that one of his most popular detectives, Dr. Gideon Fell, was based on Chesterton, as that author and his Father Brown series were the idols of Carr's boyhood.

Detective fiction for Carr was a "hoodwinking contest, a duel between author and reader" as he wrote in his essay "The Grandest Game in the World." He despaired at the turn writers in the genre had taken by the 1960's. He believed that the authors were not taking enough care to craft a fair and reasonable story that would not purposely mislead the reader. Carr believed that all the writer had to do was to state his or her evidence, "and the reader [would] mislead himself."

Carr's oeuvre is most easily divided by detective. His three most famous creations were Henri Bencolin, prefect of police and later juge d'instruction in Paris; Dr. Gideon Fell, whose career as an amateur detective spanned twenty-three novels and five short stories, as well as a number of radio plays; and Sir Henry Merrivale, a genteel chief of the Military Intelligence Department in the War Office. There were various other detectives whom Carr tried over the years but usually discarded after one or two outings.

Henri Bencolin is unique as a Carr creation in that he is the only detective whom Carr created who is officially connected with the police department. He appeared in only a few stories and novels before being retired by Carr. According to critic Douglas G. Greene, in 1937 Carr revived Bencolin in *The Four False*

Weapons to demonstrate that "the original Bencolin of the short stories was the genuine version of the detective."

"THE SHADOW OF THE GOAT"

In "The Shadow of the Goat," Bencolin, while vacationing in England, becomes involved in a case unofficially when a Frenchman is murdered. Carr sets the scene for the story complete with thick London fog and swirls of tobacco smoke. Bencolin calls on his English friend Sir John Landervorne, a man with unofficial connections to both Whitehall and Scotland Yard, to see if he can glean more details about the murder of Monsieur Jules Fragneau.

The supernatural aspects to this story are emphasized by Carr's own clues to the reader. Sir John states that the probable murderer was locked in a room while he himself (as well as some others) watched the door and that "nobody had either entered or left that door." Carr finishes that section of the story with the italicized line,"And, as later events proved, Sir John spoke the absolute truth." The conclusion is that the explanation to this story's puzzle is most likely one beyond the ken

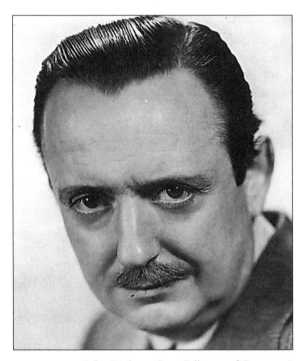

John Dickson Carr (Library of Congress)

of rationality. Few of Carr's stories, however, ever bear out that conclusion. Most of the time, as in "The Shadow of the Goat," the murderer proves to be all too human.

"THE DOOR TO DOOM"

In "The Door to Doom," Carr does incorporate the supernatural as at least partial explanation for foul play. Instead of using one of his more famous detectives, Carr introduces the character of Peter Maynard, a hapless American tourist lost on the road to Chartres. Advised by two local peasants to take a shortcut through the woods, Maynard finds himself staying at a most peculiar inn called the Inn of the Beautiful Prospect, although its original name seems to have been something much less enticing.

Despite its name, this inn turns out to be less than salubrious for Maynard's future. He ends up in a struggle against the innkeeper and his friends, who lure unsuspecting American and English guests to a "crushing" end. They then take the tourists' money, making it look as if they have been crushed by falling into the local ravine and thus lulling any police suspicions. Fortunately for Maynard, help arrives in a form that proves to be Carr's trump card in this story, for it appears that vengeance on the perpetrators is taken from beyond the grave, and Carr's ending does not dispute this supernatural interpretation.

Not all Carr's stories are so overtly violent. In his Department of Queer Complaints stories, for example, Carr's detective Colonel March takes pride in handling situations that hint at foul play, although in "William Wilson's Racket," there is not even a murder to solve. In "The Empty Flat," the Department of Queer Complaints' Colonel March handles a bona fide death, but the question arises as to whether it was murder.

"ALL IN A MAZE"

"All in a Maze" (originally entitled "Ministry of Miracles" when first published in *Housewife*, in 1955) is a long short story that showcases the talents of Sir Henry Merrivale, generally known by his admirers as "the old man" or "H. M." Merrivale holds an ambiguous government position in a somewhat mysterious department that technically is called Central Office Eight but that goes by the nom de guerre of the Ministry of Miracles.

Merrivale, however, is not ostensibly the main protagonist of the story. Carr has his detective take a backseat to two characters, Tom Lockwood and Jennifer Holden, one of whom is the actual victim and the other of whom is the seemingly intended victim of a ventriloquist-murdering Frenchman. Merrivale does manage to get at least a mention, however, even in the scenes in which he does not actually appear. For example, upon first hearing the suggestion that she should seek help from Merrivale, Jenny cries, "But he is awful! He is fat and bald, and he swear [sic] and carry on and throw people out of windows."

Ultimately, however, Merrivale is asked to handle the case and proceeds to dispatch the mysteries that keep developing. He does so with such prosaic solutions that he himself admits to the disappointment that people feel upon discovering that the miracle is merely a tawdry work of human design--which only adds to the humor of his character.

"THE INCAUTIOUS BURGLAR"

It is Carr's detective Dr. Fell who features in "The Incautious Burglar" (originally entitled "A Guest in the House" when it was first published in *Strand Magazine*, in 1940). Fell is an idiosyncratic detective, as different from Henri Bencolin as possible. Physically, Fell is similar to Rex Stout's Nero Wolfe--that is, he is impressively large. In "The Incautious Burglar," he "settled back massively in the wicker settee, so that its frame creaked and cracked like a ship's bulkhead in a heavy sea." Carr himself, however, has said that the inspiration for Fell came from G. K. Chesterton, creator of the Father Brown mysteries. In "Invisible Hands" (originally entitled "King Arthur's Chair" when it was first published in *Lilliput*, in 1957), Carr writes about Dr. Fell: "Into the room, wheezing and leaning on a stick, lumbered a man so enormous that he had to maneuver himself sideways through the door. . . . His big face would ordinarily have been red and beaming, with chuckles animating several chins."

"The Incautious Burglar" is noteworthy not only for Fell's appearance but also for Carr's careful setup of the murder victim as a criminal. The description of the murdered man implies that art collector Marcus Hunt set out to steal his own collection but was murdered in the process. Both his attire and his fatal wound are carefully described, and with these clues, Carr gives the reader--and Dr. Fell--enough to solve the mystery. The brilliance of Carr's stories lies in their simplicity; Carr always lays out his hand for the careful reader to study.

OTHER MAJOR WORKS

LONG FICTION: *Grand Guignol*, 1929; *It Walks by Night*, 1930; *Castle Skull*, 1931; *The Lost Gallows*, 1931; *The Corpse in the Waxworks*, 1932 (also known as *The Waxworks Murder*); *Poison in Jest*, 1932; *The Bowstring Murders*, 1933 (first edition as Carr Dickson and subsequent editions as Carter Dickson); *Hag's Nook*, 1933; *The Mad Hatter Mystery*, 1933; *The Blind Barber*, 1934; *Devil Kinsmere*, 1934 (as Roger Fairbairn; revised as *Most Secret*, 1964); *The Eight of Swords*, 1934; *The Plague Court Murders*, 1934; *The White Priory Murders*, 1934; *Death-Watch*, 1935; *The Red Widow Murders*, 1935; *The Three Coffins*, 1935 (also known as *The Hollow Man*); *The Unicorn Murders*, 1935; *The Arabian Nights Murder*, 1936; *The Magic-Lantern Murders*, 1936 (also as *The Punch and Judy Murders*); *The Burning Court*, 1937; *The Four False Weapons*, 1937; *The Peacock Feather Murders*, 1937 (also as *The Ten Teacups*); *The Third Bullet*, 1937 (as Carter Dickson); *The Crooked Hinge*, 1938; *Death in Five Boxes*, 1938; *The Judas Window*, 1938 (also as *The Crossbow Murder*); *To Wake the Dead*, 1938; *Fatal Descent*, 1939 (with John Rhode, pseudonym of Cecil John Charles Street, and as Carter Dickson; also as *Drop to His Death*); *The Problem of the Green Capsule*, 1939 (also as *The Black Spectacles*); *The Problem of the Wire Cage*, 1939; *The Reader Is Warned*, 1939; *And So to Murder*, 1940; *The Man Who Could Not Shudder*, 1940; *Nine--and Death Makes Ten*, 1940 (also as *Murder in the Submarine Zone* and *Murder in the Atlantic*); *Death Turns the Tables*, 1941 (also known as *The Seat of the Scornful*); *The Case of the Constant Suicides*, 1941; *Seeing Is Believing*, 1941 (also as *Cross of Murder*); *The Emperor's Snuff-Box*, 1942; *The Gilded Man*, 1942 (also as *Death and the Gilded Man*); *She Died a Lady*, 1943; *He Wouldn't Kill Patience*, 1944; *Till Death Do Us Part*, 1944; *The Curse of the Bronze Lamp*, 1945 (also as *Lord of the Sorcerers*); *He Who Whispers*, 1946; *My Late Wives*,

1946; *The Sleeping Sphinx*, 1947; *The Skeleton in the Clock*, 1948; *Below Suspicion*, 1949; *A Graveyard to Let*, 1949; *The Bride of Newgate*, 1950; *Night at the Mocking Widow*, 1950; *The Devil in Velvet*, 1951; *Behind the Crimson Blind*, 1952; *The Nine Wrong Answers*, 1952; *The Cavalier's Cup*, 1953; *Captain Cut-Throat*, 1955; *Fear Is the Same*, 1956; *Patrick Butler for the Defence*, 1956; *Fire, Burn!*, 1957; *The Dead Man's Knock*, 1958; *Scandal at High Chimneys: A Victorian Melodrama*, 1959; *In Spite of Thunder*, 1960; *The Witch of the Low-Tide: An Edwardian Melodrama*, 1961; *The Demoniacs*, 1962; *The House at Satan's Elbow*, 1965; *Panic in Box C*, 1966; *Dark of the Moon*, 1967; *Papa Là-Bas*, 1968; *The Ghosts' High Noon*, 1969; *Deadly Hall*, 1971; *The Hungry Goblin: A Victorian Detective Novel*, 1972; *The Dead Sleep Lightly*, 1983; *Crime on the Coast*, 1984 (with others).

RADIO PLAYS: *The Bride Vanishes*, 1942; *The Devil in the Summerhouse*, 1942; *Will You Make a Bet with Death?*, 1942; *Cabin B-13*, 1943; *The Hangman Won't Wait*, 1943; The Phantom Archer, 1943.

NONFICTION: *The Murder of Sir Edmund Godfrey*, 1936; *The Life of Sir Arthur Conan Doyle*, 1949; *The Grandest Game in the World: A Brilliant Critique*, 1963.

EDITED TEXTS: *Maiden Murders*, 1952; *Great Stories*, 1959 (by Sir Arthur Conan Doyle).

BIBLIOGRAPHY

Greene, Douglas G. "John Dickson Carr." In *Critical Survey of Mystery and Detective Fiction.* edited by Carl Rollyson. Pasadena, Calif.: Salem Press, 2008. Provides a biography and an overview of Carr's mystery and detective fiction.

_____. *John Dickson Carr: The Man Who Explained Miracles.* New York: Otto Penzler, 1995. A brief biographical sketch, followed by a survey of Carr's works, commenting on the high consistency of his fiction, his focus on the locked-room mystery convention, and the romantic and fantastic atmosphere that distinguishes his books from those of other detective writers.

_____. "A Mastery of Miracles: G. K. Chesterton and John Dickson Carr." *Chesterton Review* 10 (August, 1984): 307-315. Pays homage to Carr's work, particularly as it relates to that of G. K. Chesterton. Greene concentrates on Carr's short fiction but also includes some biographical information. Notes on sources are given at the end of the article.

Joshi, S. T. *John Dickson Carr: A Critical Study*. Bowling Green, Ohio: Bowling Green State University Popular Press, 1990. Joshi's text is the main full-length critical study available. He discusses in detail Carr's short fiction while also including some biographical information. Joshi gives publishing information for Carr's individual stories, as well as for the collections. His detailed notes, bibliographies (both primary, including translations, and secondary), and index make this text an excellent starting place for research.

Malmgren, Carl D. *Anatomy of Murder: Mystery, Detective, and Crime Fiction*. Bowling Green, Ohio: Bowling Green State University Popular Press, 2001. Includes readings of four of Carr's novels. Bibliographic references and index.

Panek, LeRoy. *An Introduction to the Detective Story*. Bowling Green, Ohio: Bowling Green State University Popular Press, 1987. References to Carr's work--in particular, his short fiction--are scattered throughout this text. Good for setting Carr in the context of his time. An index and a list of reference works are given at the end, and a separate list of history and criticism texts is also included.

_____. "John Dickson Carr." In *Watteau's Shepherds: The Detective Novel in Britain, 1914-1940*. Bowling Green, Ohio: Bowling Green University Popular Press, 1979. Despite Carr's nationality, he is considered one of the finest British mystery writers. Panek devotes a detailed chapter to Carr, covering his most famous detectives and works, including both long and short fiction. An appendix outlines the structure of the detective story. Supplemented by a chronology of Carr's works, notes on the Carr chapter, and an index.

Taylor, Robert Lewis. "Two Authors in an Attic, Part I." *The New Yorker* 27 (September 8, 1951): 39-44, 46, 48.

_____. "Two Authors in an Attic, Part II." *The New Yorker* 27 (September 15, 1951): 36-40, 42, 46, 48, 51. This pair of articles is extremely useful for detailed biographical information, as well as for Carr's own thoughts on his writing. Carr discusses with Taylor which writers influenced him most and goes into detail about his political and philosophical views. Invaluable for getting a personal look at Carr, despite its lack of references.

Jo-Ellen Lipman Boon

RAYMOND CARVER

Born: Clatskanie, Oregon; May 25, 1938
Died: Port Angeles, Washington; August 2, 1988

PRINCIPAL SHORT FICTION

Put Yourself in My Shoes, 1974
Will You Please Be Quiet, Please?, 1976
Furious Seasons, and Other Stories, 1977
What We Talk About When We Talk About Love, 1981
Cathedral, 1983
Elephant, and Other Stories, 1988
Where I'm Calling From, 1988
Short Cuts: Selected Stories, 1993
Collected Stories, 2009

OTHER LITERARY FORMS

Raymond Carver (CAR-vur) distinguished himself as a short-story writer and poet, and he wrote in both forms until his death. His poetry has been published in the following collections: *Near Klamath* (1968), *Winter Insomnia* (1970), *At Night the Salmon Move* (1976), *Two Poems* (1982), *Fires: Essays, Poems, Stories* (1983), *If It Please You* (1984), *This Water* (1985), *Where Water Comes Together with Other Water* (1985), *Ultramarine* (1986), and *A New Path to the Waterfall* (1989).

ACHIEVEMENTS

Raymond Carver's greatest achievement was overcoming his economically and culturally disadvantaged background to become an author of world renown. He made the short story a viable literary form; since Carver, short-story collections became a marketable commodity in the book trade. Both as a model and as a teacher, he had such an influence on younger fiction writers that author Jay McInerney could truthfully say (alluding to a famous statement that Fyodor Dostoevski made about Nikolai Gogol) that there is hardly a single American short-story writer younger than Carver who did not "come out of Carver's overcoat."

With only a bachelor's degree and mediocre grades, Carver was invited to teach at distinguished universities and became a professor of English at Syracuse University in 1980. He received many honors during his lifetime, including a Strauss Living Award, which guaranteed him an annual stipend of thirty-five thousand dollars and enabled him to devote all his time to writing during the last years of his life. Just before his death, he received a doctorate of letters from the University of Hartford.

BIOGRAPHY

Raymond Carver grew up in a sparsely populated corner of the Pacific Northwest. This rustic environment had an indelible effect on his character and writing. Like Ernest Hemingway, one of the writers who influenced Carver, he loved the purity and freedom of the American wilderness, and he also respected the simplicity, honesty, and directness of the men and women who earned meager and precarious livelihoods in that primitive setting. He married young and had two children to support by the time he was twenty. He had wanted to be a writer from the time he was in the third grade, but the responsibilities of parenthood made it extremely difficult for him to find time to write. His limited education forced him to take menial jobs, for which he was unsuited temperamentally. He was unable to consider tackling anything as ambitious as a full-length novel, so he spent his odd free hours writing short stories and poetry. He managed to get some of his work published in little magazines, but these publications paid little or nothing for his work, so he was haunted by financial problems for much of his life.

One of the most important influences in Carver's life was John Gardner (1933-1982), who taught creative writing at California State University at Chico and said, "You cannot be a great writer unless you feel greatly." The idealistic Gardner introduced his students to the literary magazines that represented the cutting edge in contemporary American fiction and poetry, and he urged them to write honestly about what they knew, as opposed to turning out formula fiction in an attempt to make money. This is exactly what Carver did, and, ironically, he found that the hardships and distractions that were preventing him from writing were the very things that provided him with material to write about. This may account for the characteristic stoical humor to be found in many of his stories.

Another profound influence in his life was alcohol. One of Carver's distinguishing traits as a writer was his astonishing candor, and anyone who reads a dozen of his short stories will get a good idea of what his life was like for nearly two decades. His drinking caused serious domestic and financial problems, which led to feelings of guilt and more drinking. Amazingly, his strong constitution and unwavering motivation enabled him to continue producing stories and poems.

With the publication of *What We Talk About When We Talk About Love* in 1981, Carver achieved critical and popular fame. His financial problems were ameliorated because he received valuable grants and teaching assignments, and he sold his work to high-paying magazines, such as *Esquire, Harper's Bazaar, Playgirl,* and *The New Yorker*. Collections of his short stories sold well, and he earned money teaching creative-writing courses and appearing as a featured attraction at many workshops and seminars.

By the late 1970's, Carver had separated from his first wife and was living with the poet and teacher Tess Gallagher. She helped him cope with his drinking problem and provided a much-needed stabilizing influence. Carver, always a heavy cigarette smoker, died of lung cancer in 1988. By that time, his works had been published all over the world in more than twenty languages.

ANALYSIS

Nearly everything written about Raymond Carver begins with two observations: He is a minimalist, and he writes about working-class people. Even when the critic is sympathetic, this dual categorization tends to stigmatize Carver as a minor artist writing little stories about inconsequential people. Although it is true that most of Carver's characters

Raymond Carver (Sophie Bassouls/Sygma/Corbis)

belong to the working class, their problems are universal. Carver writes about divorce, infidelity, spiritual alienation, alcoholism, bankruptcy, rootlessness, and existential dread; none of these afflictions is peculiar to the working class, and, in fact, all were once common to members of the high social classes.

Carver was a minimalist by preference and by necessity. His lifelong experience had been with working-class people, and it would have been inappropriate to write about simple people in an ornate style. Furthermore, his limited education would have made it impossible for him to do so effectively. The spare, objective style that he admired in some of Hemingway's short stories, such as "The Killers" and "Hills Like White Elephants," was perfectly suited to Carver's needs.

The advantage and appeal of minimalism in literature are that readers are drawn into the story by conceptualizing missing details. One drawback is that minimalism allows insecure writers to imply that they know more than they know and mean more than they are saying. This was true of the early stories that Carver collected in *Will You Please Be Quiet, Please?* Carver's literary strengths and weaknesses may be found in a short story titled "Fat" in that volume.

"FAT"

As the title suggests, "Fat" is about a fat man. It is little more than a character sketch; nothing happens in the story. Throughout his career, Carver based stories and poems on people or incidents that he observed or scraps of conversation that he overheard; he imbued these living metaphors and symbols with broader implications. Carver frames his story by setting it in a restaurant and by describing the fat man from the point of view of a waitress. She says that she has never seen such a fat person in her life and is somewhat awestruck by his appearance, by his gracious manners, and by the amount of food that he consumes at one sitting. After she goes home at night, she is still thinking about him. She says that she herself feels "terrifically fat"; she feels depressed and ends by saying, "My life is going to change. I feel it."

The reader can feel it, too, but might be hard pressed to say what "it" is. The story leaves a strong but an ambiguous impression. No two readers would agree on what the story means, if anything. It demonstrates Carver's great talent for characterization through dialogue and action. Both the waitress and her fat customer come alive as people, partially through the deliberate contrast between them. Carver's treatment of the humble, kindly waitress demonstrates his sensitivity to the feelings of women. His former wife, Maryann Carver, said of him, "Ray loved and understood women, and women loved him."

"Fat" also shows Carver's unique sense of humor, another trait that set him apart from other writers. Carver could not help seeing the humorous side of the tragic or the grotesque. His early experimental short stories most closely resemble those of William Saroyan, reprinted in *The Daring Young Man on the Flying Trapeze, and Other Stories* (1934) and subsequent collections of his stories that appeared in the 1930's. Saroyan is perhaps best remembered for his novel *The Human Comedy* (1943), and it might be said that the human comedy was Carver's theme and thesis throughout his

career. Like the early stories of Saroyan, Carver's stories are the tentative vignettes of a novice who knows very well that he wants to be a writer but still does not know exactly what he wants to say.

"NEIGHBORS"

Will You Please Be Quiet, Please? includes the tragicomic "Neighbors," the first of Carver's stories to appear in a slick magazine with a large circulation. Gordon Lish, editor of the men's magazine *Esquire*, recognized Carver's talent early but did not immediately accept any of his submissions. Lish's welcome encouragement, painful rejections, and eventual acceptance represented major influences in Carver's career. "Neighbors" deals with ordinary people but has a surrealistic humor, which was to become a Carver trademark.

Bill and Arlene Miller, a couple in their thirties, have agreed to feed their neighbors' cat and water the plants while they are away. The apartment of Jim and Harriet Stone holds a mysterious fascination, and the Millers find excuses to enter it more often than necessary. Bill helps himself to the Chivas Regal scotch, eats food out of the refrigerator, and goes through the Stones' closets and dresser drawers. He tries on some of Jim's clothes and lies on their bed to masturbate. He goes so far as to try on Harriet's brassiere and panties and then a skirt and blouse. Arlene also disappears into the neighbors' apartment on her own mysterious errands. The Millers fantasize that they have assumed the identities of their neighbors, whom they regard as happier people leading fuller lives. The shared guilty adventure arouses both Bill and Arlene sexually, and they have better lovemaking than they have experienced in a long while. Then disaster strikes: Arlene discovers that she has inadvertently locked the Stones' key inside the apartment. The cat may starve; the plants may wither; the Stones may find evidence that the Millers have been rummaging through the Stones' possessions. The story ends with the frightened Millers clinging to each other outside their lost garden of Eden.

This early story displays some of Carver's strengths: his sense of humor, his powers of description, and his ability to characterize people through what they do and say. It also has the two main qualities that editors look for: timeliness and universality. It is therefore easy to understand why Lish bought this piece after rejecting so many others. "Neighbors" portrays the alienated condition of many contemporary Americans of all social classes.

"Neighbors," however, has certain characteristics that have allowed hostile critics to damn Carver's stories as "vignettes," "anecdotes," "sketches," and "slices-of-life." For one thing, readers realize that the terror they briefly share with the Millers is unnecessary: They can go to the building manager for a passkey or call a locksmith. It is hard to understand how two people who are so bold about violating their neighbors' apartment should suddenly feel so helpless in the face of an everyday mishap. The point of the story is blunted by the unsatisfactory ending.

What We Talk About When We Talk About Love

The publication of the collection titled *What We Talk About When We Talk About Love* made Carver famous. These short, rather ambiguous stories also saddled him with the term "minimalist." Carver never accepted that label and claimed that he did not even understand what it meant. He had a healthy mistrust of critics who attempted to categorize writers with such epithets: It was as if he sensed their antagonism and felt that they were trying to "minimize" him as an author. A friend of Carver said that he thought a minimalist was a "taker-out" rather than a "putter-in." In that sense, Carver was a minimalist. It was his practice to go over and over his stories, trying to delete all superfluous words and even superfluous punctuation marks. He said that he knew he was finished with a story when he found himself putting back punctuation marks that he had previously deleted. It would be more accurate to call Carver a perfectionist, not a minimalist.

"Why Don't You Dance?"

One of the best short stories reprinted in *What We Talk About When We Talk About Love* is "Why Don't You Dance?" It is one of the most representative and "Carveresque" of all the writer's short stories. A man who is never given a name places all of his furniture and personal possessions outside on the front lawn and whimsically arranges them as if they are still indoors. He runs an extension cord from the house and hooks up lamps, a television, and a record player. He sits outside

drinking whiskey, totally indifferent to the amazement and curiosity of his neighbors. One feels as if the worst is over for him: He is the survivor of some great catastrophe, like a marooned sailor who manages to salvage some flotsam and jetsam.

A young couple, referred to throughout the story as "the boy" and "the girl," drive by and assume that the man is holding a yard sale. They stop and inquire about prices. The man offers them drinks. The boy and girl get into a party spirit. They put old records on the turntable and start dancing in the driveway. The man, anxious to get rid of his possessions, accepts whatever they offer. He even makes them presents of things that they do not want. Weeks later, the girl still talks about the man, but she cannot find the words to express what she really feels about the incident. Perhaps she and her young friends will understand the incident much better after they have worked and worried and bickered and moved from one place to another for ten or twenty years.

"Why Don't You Dance?" is a humorous treatment of a serious subject, in characteristic Carver fashion. The man's tragedy is never spelled out, but the reader can piece the story together quite easily from the clues. Evidently there has been a divorce or a separation, following financial problems, and the man has been evicted. Judging from the fact that he is doing so much drinking, alcoholism is either the cause or the effect of his other problems. The man gives up all hope and now sees hope only in other people, represented by this young couple just starting out in life and trying to collect a few pieces of furniture for their rented apartment.

Divorce, infidelity, domestic strife, financial worry, bankruptcy, alcoholism, rootlessness, consumerism as a substitute for intimacy, and disillusionment with the American Dream are common themes throughout Carver's stories. The man sitting outside on his front lawn, drinking whiskey and surrounded by all his worldly possessions, which are soon to be scattered to the four winds, is a striking symbol of modern human beings. It is easy to acquire possessions but nearly impossible to keep a real home.

Carver, who did not witness such an event but had a similar episode described to him by a friend, eventually used it in this story. A glance at the titles of some of Carver's stories shows his penchant for finding in his mundane environment external symbols of subjective states: "Fat," "Gazebo," "Vitamins," "Feathers," "Cathedral," "Boxes," "Menudo." The same tendency is even more striking in the titles of his poems, for example, "The Car," "Jean's TV," "NyQuil," "My Dad's Wallet," "The Phone Booth," "Heels."

In his famous essay "The Philosophy of Composition," Edgar Allan Poe wrote that he wanted an image that would be "emblematical of Mournful and Never-ending Remembrance," so he created his famous raven perched on the bust of Pallas Athena and croaking the refrain "nevermore." To highlight the difference in Carver's method, Carver might have seen a real raven perched on a real statue, and it would have suggested mournful and never-ending remembrance. This kind of "reverse symbolism" seems characteristic of modern American minimalists in general, and Carver's influence on their movement is paramount.

Poe states that he originally thought of using a parrot in his famous poem but rejected that notion because it did not seem sufficiently poetic and might have produced a comical effect; if Carver had been faced with such a choice, he probably would have chosen the parrot. What distinguishes Carver from most minimalists is a sense of humor that is impervious to catastrophe: Like the man on the front lawn, Carver had been so far down that everyplace else looked better. He would have concurred heartily with William Shakespeare's often-quoted lines in *As You Like It* (1599-1600):

> *Sweet are the uses of adversity,*
> *Which, like a toad, ugly and venomous,*
> *Wears yet a precious jewel in his head*

On a different level, "Why Don't You Dance?" reflects Carver's maturation as a person and an author. The responsibilities of parenthood as well as the experience of teaching young students were bringing home to him the fact that his personal problems could hold instructional utility for others. As a teacher of creative writing, placed more and more in the limelight, interacting with writers, editors, professors, and interviewers, he was being forced to formulate his own artistic credo. The older man in the story sees himself in his young yard-sale customers and wants to help them along in life. Consequently, the story is not merely an autobiographical protest or a lament, such as some of Carver's earlier works, but is designed to deliver a message--perhaps a warning--for the profit of others. The melancholy wisdom of Carver's protagonist reflects Carver's own mellowing as he began to appreciate the universally tragic nature of human existence.

"Where I'm Calling From"

"Where I'm Calling From" is a great American short story. It originally appeared in the prestigious *The New Yorker*, was reprinted in the collection titled *Cathedral*, and appears once again as the title story in the best and most comprehensive collection of Carver's stories, *Where I'm Calling From*. The story is narrated by an alcoholic staying at a "drying-out facility," an unpretentious boardinghouse where plain meals are served family style and there is nothing to do but read, watch television, or talk. The bucolic atmosphere is strongly reminiscent of the training-camp scenes in one of Hemingway's most brilliant short stories, "Fifty Grand."

The narrator in Carver's story tells about his drinking problems and interweaves his life story with that of a friend the narrator makes at the drying-out facility, a man he refers to as J. P. The only thing unusual about their stories is that J. P. is a chimney sweep and is married to a chimney sweep. Both J. P. and the narrator ruined their marriages through their compulsive drinking and are now terrified that they will be unable to control their craving once they get out of the facility. They have made vows of abstinence before and have not kept them. They have dried out before and gone right back to the bottle.

Carver manages to convey all the feelings of guilt, remorse, terror, and helplessness experienced by people who are in the ultimate stages of alcoholism. It is noteworthy that, whereas Carver's alcoholic protagonists in his early stories were often isolated individuals, the protagonist-narrator of "Where I'm Calling From" not only is actively seeking help but also is surrounded by others with the same problem. This feature indicates that Carver had come to realize that the way to give his stories meaning--something that they had previously lacked--was to suggest the existence of large-scale social problems of which his characters are victims. He had made what author Joan Didion called "the quantum leap" of realizing that his personal problems were social problems. The curse of alcoholism affects all social classes; even people who never touch a drop can have their lives ruined by it.

"THE BRIDLE"

"The Bridle" first appeared in *The New Yorker* and was reprinted in *Cathedral*. It is an example of Carver's mature period, a highly artistic story fraught with social significance. The story is told from the point of view of one of Carver's *faux-naïf* narrators. Readers immediately feel that they know this good-natured soul, a woman named Marge who manages an apartment building in Arizona and "does hair" as a sideline. She tells about one of the many families who stayed a short while and then moved on as tumbleweeds being blown across the desert. Although Carver typically writes about Northern California and the Pacific Northwest, this part of Arizona is also "Carver Country," a world of freeways, fast-food restaurants, laundromats, mindless television entertainment, and transient living accommodations, a homogenized world of strangers with minimum-wage jobs and tabloid mentalities.

Mr. Holits pays the rent in cash every month, suggesting that he recently went bankrupt and has neither a bank account nor credit cards. Carver, like minimalists in general, loves such subtle clues. Mrs. Holits confides to Marge that they had owned a farm in Minnesota. Her husband, who "knows everything there is about horses," still keeps one of his bridles, evidently symbolizing his hope that he may escape from "Carver Country." Mrs. Holits proves more adaptable: She gets a job as a waitress, a favorite occupation among Carver characters. Her husband, however, cannot adjust to the service industry jobs, which are all that are available to a man his age with his limited experience. He handles the money, the two boys are his sons by a former marriage, and he has been accustomed to making the decisions, yet he finds that his wife is taking over the family leadership in this brave new postindustrial world.

Like many other Carver males, Holits becomes a heavy drinker. He eventually injures himself while trying to show off his strength at the swimming pool. One day the Holitses with their young sons pack and drive off down the long, straight highway without a word of explanation. When Marge trudges upstairs to clean the empty apartment, she finds that Holits has left his bridle behind.

The naïve narrator does not understand the significance of the bridle, but the reader feels its poignancy as a symbol. The bridle is one of those useless objects that everyone carts around and is reluctant to part with because it represents a memory, a hope, or a dream. It is an especially appropriate symbol because it is so utterly out of place in one of those two-story, frame-stucco, look-alike apartment buildings that disfigure the landscape and are the dominant features of "Carver Country." Gigantic economic forces beyond the comprehension of the narrator have driven this family from their farm and turned them into the modern equivalent of the Joad family in John Steinbeck's classic novel *The Grapes of Wrath* (1939).

There is, however, a big difference between Carver and Steinbeck. Steinbeck believed in and prescribed the panacea of socialism; Carver has no prescriptions to offer. He seems to have no faith either in politicians or in preachers. His characters are more likely to go to church to play bingo than to say prayers or sing hymns. Like many of the contemporary minimalists, he seems to have gone beyond alienation, beyond existentialism, beyond despair. God is dead; so what else is new?

Carver's working-class characters are far more complicated than those in Steinbeck's Joad family. Americans have become more sophisticated in the past fifty years as a result of radio, motion pictures, television, the Internet, educational opportunities, improved automobiles and highways, cheap air transportation, alcohol and drugs, more leisure time, and the fact that their work is less enervating because of the proliferation of labor-saving machinery. Many Americans have also lost their religious faith, their work ethic, their class consciousness, their family loyalty, their integrity, and their dreams. Steinbeck saw it happening and showed how the Joad family split apart after being uprooted from the soil; Carver's people are the Joad family a half-century down the road. Oddly enough, Carver's mature stories do not seem nihilistic or despairing because they contain the redeeming qualities of humor, compassion, and honesty.

"Boxes"

Where I'm Calling From is the most useful volume of Carver's short stories because it contains some of the prominent stories that had been printed in earlier books plus a generous selection of his later and best efforts. One of the new stories reprinted in *Where I'm Calling From* is "Boxes," which first appeared in *The New Yorker*. When Carver's stories began to be regularly accepted by *The New Yorker*, it was an indication that he had found the style of self-expression that he had been searching for since the beginning of his career. It was also a sign that his themes were evoking sympathetic chords in the hearts and minds of *The New Yorker*'s middle- and upper-class readership, the people at whom that magazine's sophisticated advertisements for diamonds, furs, high-rise condominiums, and luxury vacation cruises are aimed.

"Boxes" is written in Carver's characteristic tragicomic tone. It is a story in which the *faux-naïf* narrator, a favorite with Carver, complains about the eccentric behavior of his widowed mother, who, for one specious reason or another, is always changing her place of residence. She moves so frequently that she usually has the bulk of her worldly possessions packed in boxes scattered about on the floor. One of her complaints is the attitude of her landlord, whom she calls "King Larry." Larry Hadlock is a widower and a relatively affluent property owner. It is evident through Carver's unerring dialogue that what the woman is bitter about is Larry's indifference to her fading charms. In the end, she returns to California but telephones to complain about the traffic, the faulty air-conditioning unit in her apartment, and the unconcerned manager. The son vaguely understands that what his mother really wants, though she may not realize it, is love and a real home. Sadly, she can never have these things again in her lifetime, no matter where she moves.

What makes the story significant is its universality: It reflects the macrocosm in a microcosm. In "Boxes," the problem is the rootlessness and anonymity of modern life and plight of millions of aging people, who are considered useless in their old age and a burden to their children. It was typical of Carver to find a metaphor for this important social phenomenon in a bunch of cardboard boxes.

Carver uses working-class people as his models, but he is not writing solely about the working class. Rather, it is simply the fact that all Americans can see themselves in his inarticulate and bewildered characters that makes Carver an important writer in the dominant tradition of American realism, a worthy successor to Mark Twain, Stephen Crane, Sherwood Anderson, Theodore Dreiser, Willa Cather, Steinbeck, and William Faulkner, all of whom wrote about humble people. Carver, despite the antipathy of certain critics, became one of the most important American fiction writers in the second half of the twentieth century.

Collected Stories

Collected Stories is primarily a reprint of the 1991 collection *No Heroics, Please*, padded out by a few essays from the 1983 miscellany *Fires*. It includes five early Carver stories and five previously unpublished stories. Carver's first story, "Furious Seasons," published in 1960 in a college literary magazine while he was studying under John Gardner, is an intense but misguided disarray of self-conscious Faulknerian syntax. "The Hair," published three years later in another undergraduate magazine, indicates that he had taken the advice Gardner once gave him to read Hemingway to get Faulkner out of his system; it is the one early piece that signals promise.

Of the five previously uncollected mature stories by Carver, three-- "Kindling," "Dreams," and "Vandals"--were discovered in a desk drawer by Tess Gallagher, Carver's widow and the main beneficiary of his legacy, and published in *Esquire*. The other two-- "What Would You Like to See?" and "Call If You Need Me," published in England--were found by William L. Stull, Carver's early critic and huge academic fan, in a collection of materials Carver sold to the Ohio State University Library.

"What Would You Like to See?" and "Vandals" are so syntactically cluttered and confused that it is obvious Carver never subjected them to the kind of obsessive rewriting for which he was known. The other three, however, are Carver at his most characteristic, although not Carver at his best. "Dreams" centers on a common Carver theme of trying futilely to identify with the suffering of someone one does not really know. However, either because it deals with the sentimentally risky subject of the death of children or because the dream theme is not integrated with the deaths, Carver probably decided to put it aside.

"Kindling" focuses on a Carver persona who has appeared in other stories, a writer named Meyers, who has just been released from a drying-out facility and whose wife has left him. He is "between lives," renting a room from an older couple, while trying to "get it together" and trying to write. As usual in Carver's stories, it often takes only a small good thing to get a man over a bad patch. In this case, it is the act of sawing, splitting, and stacking two cords of firewood. Only Carver's restrained style could make a reader believe that.

The title story is the best of the five new ones, but Carver likely decided not to publish it because two other stories-- "Chef's House" in *Cathedral* and "Blackbird Pie" in *Where I'm Calling From*--use similar material. All three deal with a couple's final, ineffectual effort to hold a marriage together. "Call If You Need Me" even uses the mystical nighttime appearance of horses in the yard that are the climax of "Blackbird Pie."

Carver had a profound knowledge of the short story, mostly from his study of Anton Chekhov, but Carver was not an intellectual writer. Consequently, with a few exceptions, the introductions, reviews, and occasional remarks that fill out this book are mostly commonsense comments about his own work and collegial praise for the work of others. However, the essay "On Writing" contains some of the most important comments he ever made about what he was trying to do.

OTHER MAJOR WORKS

SCREENPLAY: *Dostoevsky*, 1985.

POETRY: *Near Klamath*, 1968; *Winter Insomnia*, 1970; *At Night the Salmon Move*, 1976; *Two Poems*, 1982; *If It Please You*, 1984; *This Water*, 1985; *Where Water Comes Together with Other Water*, 1985; *Ultramarine*, 1986; *A New Path to the Waterfall*, 1989; *All of Us: The Collected Poems*, 1996.

EDITED TEXT: *American Short Story Masterpieces*, 1987 (with Tom Jenks).

MISCELLANEOUS: *Fires: Essays, Poems, Stories*, 1983; *No Heroics, Please: Uncollected Writings*, 1991 (revised and expanded as *Call If You Need Me: The Uncollected Fiction and Prose*, 2000).

BIBLIOGRAPHY

Adelman, Bob, and Tess Gallagher. *Carver Country: The World of Raymond Carver*. Introduction by Tess Gallagher. New York: Charles Scribner's Sons, 1990. Produced in the spirit of a photographic essay, this book contains excellent photographs of Carver, his relatives, people who served as inspirations for characters in his stories, and places that were important in his life and work. The photographs are accompanied by excerpts from Carver's stories and poems.

Barth, John. "A Few Words About Minimalism." *The New York Times Book Review*, December 28, 1986, p. 2. A prominent American writer, who is considered a leading exponent of the maximalist style of fiction writing, defines minimalism in art and concludes that there is a place for both maximalism and minimalism in literature. He regards Carver as the prime shaper of "the new American short story."

Bugeja, Michael. "Tarnish and Silver: An Analysis of Carver's *Cathedral*." *South Dakota Review* 24, no. 3 (1986): 73-87. Discusses the revision of an early Carver story, "The Bath," which was reprinted in *Cathedral* as "A Small Good Thing." The changes made throughout the story, and especially the somewhat more positive resolution, reflect Carver's evolution as a writer.

Campbell, Ewing. *Raymond Carver: A Study of the Short Fiction*. New York: Twayne, 1992. An introduction to Carver's stories that focuses on such issues as myth and archetype, otherness, and the grotesque. Discusses the difference between "early" and "late" versions of the same story, such as "So Much Water Close to Home" and "The Bath" and "A Small Good Thing." Includes Carver's own comments on his writing as well as articles by other critics who challenge the label of minimalist for Carver.

Carver, Raymond. "A Storyteller's Shoptalk." *The New York Times Book Review*, February 15, 1981, p. 9. In this interesting article, Carver describes his artistic credo, evaluates the work of some of his contemporaries, and offers excellent advice to aspiring young writers. The article reveals his perfectionism and dedication to his craft.

Gentry, Marshall Bruce, and William L. Stull, eds. *Conversations with Raymond Carver*. Jackson: University Press of Mississippi, 1990. A wide-ranging collection of interviews covering Carver's career from the early 1980's until just before his death.

Halpert, Sam, ed. *When We Talk About Raymond Carver*. Layton, Utah: Gibbs Smith, 1991. A collection of transcripts of interviews with ten writers who knew Carver on a personal basis, including a fascinating interview with Carver's first wife, Maryann, who provides a fresh perspective on the incidents on which many of Carver's stories were based.

Kesset, Kirk. *The Stories of Raymond Carver*. Athens: Ohio University Press, 1995. An intelligent discussion of Carver's stories, focusing on Carver's development of his own moral center.

Mullen, Bill. "A Subtle Spectacle: Televisual Culture in the Short Stories of Raymond Carver." *Critique* 39 (Winter, 1998): 99-114. Discusses the relationship between television--both as an influence on and a subject of--Carver's fiction. Argues that, in both structure and tone, Carver's stories constitute a critique of television culture based on the medium's ability to eliminate class consciousness; discusses "Will You Please Be Quiet, Please?"

Powell, Jon. "The Stories of Raymond Carver: The Menace of Perpetual Uncertainty." *Studies in Short Fiction* 31 (Fall, 1994): 647-656. Discusses the sense of menace Carver creates by leaving out or providing only clues to central aspects of his stories. Argues that this technique forces both the characters and the readers to try to understand what happens.

Runyon, Randolph Paul. *Reading Raymond Carver*. Syracuse, N.Y.: Syracuse University Press, 1992. Analyzes Carver's stories as "intratextual" and argues that they should be read in relationship to each other. Claims that in *Will You Please Be Quiet, Please?* and *Cathedral* each story is linked to the immediately preceding story and the one after it.

Saltzman, Arthur M. *Understanding Raymond Carver*. Columbia: University of South Carolina Press, 1988. A short overview of Carver's life and work, with an emphasis on Carver's short stories and one chapter devoted to his poetry. Contains a valuable bibliography of works by and about Carver.

Scofield, Martin. "Story and History in Raymond Carver." *Critique* 40 (Spring, 1999): 266-280. Shows how three late Carver stories-- "Intimacy," "Blackbird Pie," and "Elephant"--embody a new experimental technique for integrating fiction and autobiographical or historical events.

Sklenicka, Carol. *Raymond Carver: A Writer's Life*. New York: Scribner, 2010. A highly detailed and documented biography of Carver's early struggles, his problems with alcohol, and his rise to world fame before his early death from lung cancer.Stull, William L. "Raymond Carver." In *Dictionary of Literary Biography*, edited by Jean W. Ross. Detroit: Gale Research, 1985. This article covers Carver's life and work up until shortly before his death and attempts to analyze his poetry and fiction techniques. It contains a fairly comprehensive list of Carver's books and miscellaneous publications as well as a list of articles about Carver.

Wolff, Tobias. "Raymond Carver Had His Cake and Ate It Too." *Esquire* 112 (September, 1989): 240-248. A friend and fellow writer and teacher relates a series of anecdotes about Carver in his wild drinking days. The essay highlights Carver's zest for life, his kindly interest in people, and his unconcealed delight with the recognition that he received toward the end of his life.

Bill Delaney
Updated by Charles E. May

R. V. CASSILL

Born: Cedar Falls, Iowa; May 17, 1919
Died: Providence, Rhode Island; March 25, 2002

PRINCIPAL SHORT FICTION

15 X 3, 1957 (with Herbert Gold and James B. Hall)
The Father, and Other Stories, 1965
The Happy Marriage, and Other Stories, 1966
Collected Stories, 1989
The Unknown Soldier, 1991
Late Stories, 1995

OTHER LITERARY FORMS

Although R. V. Cassill has won high praise for his short stories, he also wrote more than twenty novels, the first of which, *The Eagle on the Coin*, was published in 1950. In addition, he wrote the nonfiction books *Writing Fiction* (1962) and *In an Iron Time: Statements and Reiterations, Essays* (1969), many articles, and more than one hundred book reviews for periodicals. As editor, he has worked on *The Norton Anthology of Short Fiction* (1977) and *The Norton Anthology of Contemporary Fiction* (1988). His most critically recognized novel is *Clem Anderson* (1961).

ACHIEVEMENTS

R. V. Cassill has been noted mainly for his short stories, the first of which, "The Conditions of Justice," won second place in the *Atlantic Monthly* "Firsts" contest for the short story in 1947. Despite the fact that he wrote many novels, the only one that received wide critical attention was *Clem Anderson*. It could perhaps be argued that the attention his short stories have been given has overshadowed such a collection of novels, but both genres demonstrate Cassill's diversity, range, and depth. His literary subjects explore the tensions between the individual and society, between the forces of moral conviction and practical expression, between power and sex. Cassill's own convictions have been expressed not only in his stories but also in his career. The protagonist of Cassill's novel *Clem Anderson*, which portrays the struggles of an American poet (Clem), in some ways represents Cassill's own struggle to fit a literary voice of integrity and moral conviction into a world becoming increasingly institutionalized and anonymous. The novel, like the writer, gives the literary world much to savor, much to consider, though critics may disagree on the true value of what Cassill has to offer.

BIOGRAPHY

Before World War II, Ronald Verlin Cassill studied art, planning to become a professional painter, and won some regional art contests in Iowa in 1939 and 1940. He began to write fiction after serving as an army officer in the South Pacific during the war. The beginning of his professional writing career was marked by his winning second place in the *Atlantic Monthly* "Firsts" contest of 1947. Several of his stories have been included in *The Best American Short Stories* and in *Prize Stories: The O. Henry Awards*. He earned B.A. and M.A. degrees from the University of Iowa, studied at the Sorbonne, and received a Fulbright fellowship, Rockefeller grant, and John Simon Guggenheim Memorial Foundation grant. He taught at Iowa, the New School for Social Research, and Purdue, Columbia, Harvard, and Brown Universities.

Although he wrote less in his later years, his long career as writer, editor, and professor of literature and fiction writing has assured his voice an echoing resonance across the landscape of twentieth century literature since World War II. He settled in Providence, Rhode Island, where he remained professor emeritus at Brown University until his death in 2002.

ANALYSIS

The writers whom R. V. Cassill especially admired were Gustave Flaubert, Henry James, D. H. Lawrence, and James Joyce. Their influence is not verifiable from the features of a given story so much as it is a cumulative force in Cassill's writing. His work often manifests the rich hues and texture of Flaubert's visual imagery, the complex internal conflicts of characters presented by Flaubert and James, the agonies of initiation from Joyce, and the energy and obsession of the characters of Lawrence. Considering his background in art, it is natural for Cassill to share the painterly qualities that all of these men, except the nearly blind Joyce, exhibited throughout their works. Cassill does not neglect color, shape, composition, and fine detail.

His stories, usually set in the Midwest, present rather common situations of youthful initiation, frustrated dreams, family conflict, and harbored delusion. The stories might be considered in terms of two broad types: those that examine the effects of youthful passions and those that reveal the destructiveness of self-delusion in adults. The most lyrical language and imagery in Cassill's short fiction appear in the stories of youthful initiation. Good examples of this type are "The Biggest Band" and "In the Central Blue," both of which present boyhood passions that are so strong that achieving them becomes the focal point of a boy's life. Given such a frame of mind, whatever happens to the boys in these stories is bound to be disappointing; either they fail to get what they want, or they succeed and find that the thing desired is not so valuable after all. Perhaps Cassill's most complex dramatic problems appear in the stories about adults, such as "The Crime of Mary Lynn Yager" and "The Sunday Painter." In both of these pieces the protagonists are unable to face inadequacies within themselves.

"THE BIGGEST BAND"

In most of the stories of the first type, locale is crucial, as is the case with "The Biggest Band." This story, Cassill's own favorite, grows out of the small-town environment and financial straits of Davisburg, Iowa, during the Depression. The reflective first-person narrator (called Buddy in childhood) speaks as an adult about his experiences with the Corn State Southern Band, and what he knows now strikes a telling contrast to what he felt as a boy.

The plan to assemble a state-wide band to travel to Chicago and play at the 1933 World's Fair is promoted by Lothar Smith, whose nominal resemblance to Lothario (deceiver and seducer) carries over into his character. He resembles Meredith Wlilson's "Music Man"; however, his ambition and musical ability far exceed those of "Professor" Harold Hill. A more important difference is that, despite all the appearances of a massive confidence game, the trip does take place, the band does play at the world's fair, and Smith goes broke realizing his dream. Finally, he appears to have been more a grand dreamer than a self-server. In this regard he and Buddy are alike.

The vital factor in the success of Smith's plan is the imagination of the people, and it is a historical commonplace that hard times produce ardent dreamers. Part of the plan is to sell instruments to people who want to make the trip but do not have an instrument and, therefore, usually cannot play one. Buddy's parents buy him a trombone that he must learn to play; he is later required to sell two "excursion tickets" in order to make the trip, and every appearance of a swindle is present. Buddy becomes so obsessed that he even suggests that his father should borrow money to buy the tickets. Buddy fails to sell the tickets, and his mother, who has known Smith since childhood, forces him to honor his initial promise. Buddy goes, the band plays at odd times and poorly, and the whole affair is a predictable failure. He does not discover what he expected, just as he fails to see the evasively nude Sally Rand; nevertheless, he learns more than he will admit, even in retrospect.

Buddy's selfish obsession with going to Chicago, like Smith's big plans, is presented negatively at first because both of them expect others to sacrifice for their personal fulfillment. In the end, however, Smith has given far more than he has taken, and Buddy feels "oddly free to do [his] best now that it didn't seem to count for anything." He narrates the story from adulthood and speaks laughingly of the band as "an altogether preposterous blunder committed against nature and a fine art," but he also admits the clean beauty of a performance given at dawn before a stadium populated only by a few janitors. He describes how he would have told the story to Mrs. Packer, who shared his dream, if she had been alive when he returned, and the story ends with a burst of images embodying youthful zeal and true art:

> From their staffs over the national pavilions the ultra-marine and lemon and scarlet pennants streamed out like dyes leaking out into an oceanic current. It was only the empty sky that watched us-- but my God, my God, how the drums thundered, how we blew.

"In the Central Blue" also deals with youthful obsession, this time the more common one of sex. The location is changed to Chesterfield, Nebraska, but the place is essentially similar. Also, as in "The Biggest Band," the proportions of the boy's desire exceed any gratification he might achieve. The first-person narrator says of the girl desired, "I loved her ignorantly, impurely and intermittently." However, his desire is far more than a physical one:

> But it was not a physical assault on her that I planned or needed. I was going to ravish her mind. With the aid of this powerful movie plus a few tickles and kisses and afterward, I was going to wheedle her mind right away into the realm of wish and nonsense, where I was so lonely all by myself.

What he really wants is escape from the fearful self-doubt and loneliness of adolescence, but, like the World War I aviator-heroes of films and, like all mortals, he finds himself condemned to "soaring in the central blue."

In the process of the story he discovers his identity as an uneasy inhabitant of the middle space between heaven and hell. More important than dealing with his frustrated desire to take "Hudson's blonde and titless cousin Betty" home and share kisses, tickles, and isolation is the discovery he makes about himself. Through the whim of his older brother, he is not allowed to go along in the car to take Betty home and fulfill his hopes. When he realizes what is being done to him, he puts up a fight to stay in the car and his father comes outside. His father, walking into the house with him, tells him he is too old to cry. In his frustration and his desire to be punished for his stupidity, he shouts back, "Well, I'm crying, you bastard." With obvious effort his father controls the urge to strike him, causing a discovery: "Maybe for the first time, I saw

him in his human dimension, bewildered and tugged in contrary directions like me." Even his father lives in the central blue of divided feelings. As in "The Biggest Band," the boy has not achieved what he was looking for, but he has found something more important in its place.

"THE SUNDAY PAINTER"

Representative of the other broad type of Cassill's stories is "The Sunday Painter," in which detail and delusion are interwoven to create a vivid, amusing, and ironic story. In this third-person narrative limited to the viewpoint of Joe Becker, businessman and unfulfilled amateur artist, there is a theme that works on at least two levels. First, Becker is self-deluded regarding his skill as a painter, thinking that "What had been so painful twenty years ago had mellowed and changed without being totally lost." Second, after months of painting works that are rendered with fine visual detail, Becker convinces himself that he has "explored art clean down to its sterile origin." Implicitly Cassill states that the sterility is not in art but in Becker himself. Quite like some artists in many forms of expression, Becker has transferred his own failing to art in general. In a comic and powerful final scene, he goes berserk and starts painting all over objects in his house and ends up painting the babysitter from next door. She, who mocked his serious earlier efforts for lacking the bizarre, quickly comes to his defense as the neighbors pull him off her: "I don't think you should persecute him. . . . Artists have enough troubles as it is." Her misunderstanding of art mirrors his. The story can also be viewed as a satire of those writers and artists who complain that traditional approaches to art have become "sterile" and meaningless. Interpreted along these lines, the story argues that the fault lies not with art but with the complaining artists themselves. In the reference work *Contemporary Novelists* (1972), Cassill comments, "As I grow older I love the commonplace of traditional thought and expression with growing fervor."

"THE CRIME OF MARY LYNN YAGER"

"The Crime of Mary Lynn Yager" presents the problem of self-deception in more serious terms. Clarissa Carlson, who plans to marry Joe Meadow and leave Iowa with him once he finishes his degree and begins his promising business career, has the course of her life altered when one of her second-grade children drowns. Mary Lynn Yager, the girl Clarissa always disliked, drowns on a school outing at the lake. When Clarissa finds that the drowned child is Mary Lynn and not one of her "good ones," she feels a relief that later leads to guilt. The guilt that engulfs Clarissa in the story emanates from her refusal to face the unfairness of her attitude toward Mary Lynn. The third-person point of view is slanted through Clarissa's perception in order to heighten the effect of her turmoil. Even though Clarissa has convinced herself that the child was a "wrong little girl," it becomes clear that there was very little basis for this attitude. The teacher blames Mary Lynn's contrary nature for causing the accident because she cannot admit her own prejudice and thereby remove her submerged guilt. She is doomed to struggle subconsciously with both her guilt over the child's drowning and her guilt over having misjudged her. An underlying question is implanted in the story as to whether people's lives can be fated by the attitudes of others.

The unconfronted guilt makes Clarissa quarrelsome, driving off Joe, and one problem leads to another. She marries LeRoy Peterson, who blames her for his business troubles just as she had unjustly blamed Mary Lynn. With her confidence destroyed by LeRoy's accusations, she wonders "what was to blame for the decay of her life" and begins to agree with him "that it was she who had brought it on them." Their marriage degenerates to "protracted hostility" and ends when LeRoy deserts her.

After years of absence, Clarissa returns to Iowa where she discovers that one of her "good children," Bobbie Tenman, is in trouble with the law. In fact, it becomes clear that he was better than Mary Lynn only in Clarissa's mind. She is relieved that he receives a suspended sentence for vandalism, feeling, "In the maimed frustration of her loneliness any evasion of just punishment [is] a sign of hope." As Mary Lynn was misunderstood, so is Clarissa when she kisses Bobbie in an attempt to keep him innocent and unblemished in her mind. Bobbie's wife, who also happens to be one of Mary Lynn's sisters, discovers Clarissa and shoves her to the ground. The girl has no idea who Clarissa is but

assumes the worst of her. In Clarissa's eyes, "Mary Lynn's play with her teacher's life had been foul play," when the foul play actually has been in Clarissa's self-deception. At the end of the story she is still haunted by a picture of Mary Lynn that she has long since destroyed, and she envies the child her peace in death.

In his conscientious presentation of characters caught up in their passions and delusions, Cassill has given much to the short story. He develops irony by setting his characters in a common milieu, then twisting them slightly on their axis to reveal their agony and their worth.

OTHER MAJOR WORKS

LONG FICTION: *The Eagle on the Coin*, 1950; *Clem Anderson*, 1961; *Pretty Leslie*, 1963; *The President*, 1964; *La Vie Passionnée of Rodney Buckthorne*, 1968; *Dr. Cobb's Game*, 1970; *The Goss Women*, 1974; *Hoyt's Child*, 1976; *Flame*, 1980; *Labors of Love*, 1980; *Patrimonies*, 1988.

NONFICTION: *Writing Fiction*, 1962; *In an Iron Time: Statements and Reiterations, Essays*, 1967.

EDITED TEXTS: *The Norton Anthology of Short Fiction*, 1977; *The Norton Anthology of Contemporary Fiction*, 1988.

BIBLIOGRAPHY

The Antioch Review 30, nos. 3-4 (1970). "Second thoughts" persuaded the editors to mention Cassill's novel *Dr. Cobb's Game*, which they admit they find "outrageous but nonetheless unforgettable." They conclude: "A repugnant reading experience--so be it. Evil is evil and must be nothing less than frightening."

Cassill, Kay, Orin E. Cassill, and Kurt Johnson, eds. *R. V. Cassill*. Chicago, 1981. A collection of articles, reminiscences, commentaries, and analyses of Cassill's work by friends, admirers, and members of his family.

Grumbach, Doris. "Fine Print: *The Goss Women*." *The New Republic* 170 (June 29, 1974): 33. Grumbach looks at this Cassill novel in the light of feminine sexuality, claiming that Cassill's female characters are "extrasexual perceptive." Although she finds the author's technical skills quite developed, she says the novel ultimately results in "ennui."

Lehmann-Haupt, Christopher. "R. V. Cassill, Novelist and Writing Teacher, Dies at 82." *The New York Times*, April 1, 2002, p. 7. Cassill's obituary provides an overview of his life and literary career.

Roberts, David. "The Short Fiction of R. V. Cassill." *Critique: Studies in Modern Fiction*, no. 1 (1966): 56-70. Roberts searches out "a continuous vision" in Cassill's short fiction. He studies Cassill's short stories, analyzing some of them individually, finds "excellence" in the body of short fiction as a whole, and concludes Cassill is "eminently deserving of further critical attention."

Yates, Richard. "R. V. Cassill's *Clem Anderson.*" *Ploughshares* 14, nos. 2-3 (1988): 189-196. A critical study of Cassill's most widely acclaimed novel. Analyzes the main character, Clem, as representative of Cassill's own struggle as writer and poet to find meaning in the academic world, and links that struggle to the author/narrator's search for new forms of expression.

James Curry Robison
Updated by David J. Thieneman

WILLA CATHER

Born: Back Creek Valley, near Gore, Virginia; December 7, 1873
Died: New York, New York; April 24, 1947
Also Known As: Wilella Sibert Cather

PRINCIPAL SHORT FICTION
"Paul's Case," 1905
The Troll Garden, 1905
Youth and the Bright Medusa, 1920
Obscure Destinies, 1932
The Old Beauty and Others, 1948
Willa Cather's Collected Short Fiction: 1892-1912, 1965
Uncle Valentine, and Other Stories: Willa Cather's Collected Short Fiction, 1915-1929, 1973

OTHER LITERARY FORMS

Willa Cather (KATH-ur) is best known as a novelist, but she wrote prolifically in other forms, especially as a young woman; she had been publishing short stories for more than twenty years before she published her first novel. Although her fame rests largely on her twelve novels and a few short stories, she has a collection of poetry, several collections of essays, and hundreds of newspaper columns and magazine pieces to her credit. Durning Cather's lifetime, only one of her books, *A Lost Lady* (1923), was adapted as a Hollywood film; after that one experience, Cather would not allow any of her work to be filmed again. Nevertheless, several of her novels have been adapted to the screen, stage, and television over the past two decades.

ACHIEVEMENTS

Willa Cather was one of America's first modern writers to make the prairie immigrant experience an important and continuing subject for high-quality fiction. Although her setting is often the American Western frontier, she masterfully locates the universal through the specific, and her literary reputation transcends the limitations of regional or gender affiliation. In her exploration of the human spirit, Cather characteristically defends artistic values in an increasingly materialistic world, and she is known for her graceful rendering of place and character.

Praised in the 1920's as one of the most successful novelists of her time, Cather was sometimes criticized in the next decade for neglecting contemporary social issues. Later, however, and especially since her death, she was recognized as a great artist and one of the most important American writers of the twentieth century. In 1923, she was awarded the Pulitzer Prize for the novel *One of Ours* (1922). She also received the Howells

Medal for fiction from the Academy of the National Institute of Arts and Letters in 1930, the Prix Fémina Américain for *Shadows on the Rock* (1931) in 1933, and the gold medal from the National Institute of Arts and Letters in 1944. With time, interest in Cather's fiction continued to increase, rather than diminish, and she enjoys appreciative audiences abroad, as well as in her own country.

BIOGRAPHY

Wilella Sibert Cather moved with her family from Virginia to Nebraska when she was only nine years old, a move that was to influence her mind and art throughout her life. As a student at the University of Nebraska, she wrote for various college magazines; she also became a regular contributor to the *Nebraska State Journal*, publishing book, theater, and concert reviews, as well as commentary on the passing scene. Even after she moved to Pittsburgh, Pennsylvania, to take an editorial job, she continued to send columns home to the *Nebraska State Journal*. Later she also began contributing to the Lincoln *Courier*. She taught English in Pittsburgh (an experience that became the source for one of her most famous short stories, "Paul's Case") and then moved to New York to take a position with *McClure's Magazine*. After the publication of her first novel, *Alexander's Bridge*, in 1912, she left *McClure's Magazine*, financially able to devote full time to her creative work. Over the next three decades, she published successfully and to critical acclaim.

ANALYSIS

Willa Cather was always conscious of a double urge in herself, toward art and toward the land. As long as her parents were living, she found herself torn between the Western prairie and the cultural centers of the East and Europe. That basic polarity appears again and again in her stories, some of which deal with the artist's struggle against debilitating influences, and some with both the pleasant and the difficult aspects of the prairie experience. Perhaps only in her work did Cather achieve a comfortable reconciliation of these polarities, by making the prairie experience the subject of her art.

All of Cather's work is consistently value-centered. She believed in characters who are good, artists who are true to their callings, people who can appreciate and use what is valuable from the past, and individuals who have a special relationship with the land. Her chief agony lay in what she saw as a general sellout to materialism--in the realm of art, in the prairie and desert, in the small town, and in the city.

The struggle of the artist to maintain integrity against an unsympathetic environment and the forces of an exploitative materialism is explored in three stories that are particularly important in the Cather canon. Two of them, "The Sculptor's Funeral" and "Paul's Case," have been widely anthologized and are well known. The third, "Uncle Valentine," is an important later story.

"THE SCULPTOR'S FUNERAL"

"The Sculptor's Funeral" is about the return in death of a world-renowned sculptor to the pinched little prairie town from which he somehow miraculously sprang. Harvey Merrick's body arrives by train in the dead of winter, accompanied by one of his former students.

Willa Cather (Library of Congress)

There to meet the coffin are several prominent townsmen, among them a brusque, red-bearded lawyer named Jim Laird. Only he can appreciate the magnitude of Harvey Merrick's achievement. The watchers around the body chuckle and snort over poor Harvey's uselessness as a farmhand, over his inability to "make it" in the only things that count for them--moneymaking ventures in Sand City. Jim Laird, in a storm of self-hatred for having become the scheming lawyer these harpies wanted him to be, enters the room and blasts them mercilessly. He reminds the town elders of the young men they have ruined by drumming "nothing but money and knavery into their ears from the time they wore knickerbockers." They hated Harvey, Laird says, because he left them and rose above them, achieving in a world they were not fit to enter. He reminds them that Harvey "wouldn't have given one sunset over your marshes" for all of their material properties and possessions. Laird is too drunk the next day to attend the funeral, and it is learned that he dies some years later from a cold he caught while "driving across the Colorado mountains to defend one of Phelps's sons who had got into trouble there by cutting government timber."

Harvey Merrick is not the tragic figure of the story, for he, thanks to a timid father who sensed something special about this one son, managed to escape destruction. He became the artist he was destined to be, in spite of his unlikely beginnings. The money-grubbing first citizens of Sand City can wag their tongues feebly over his corpse, but they cannot touch him or detract from his accomplishment. If there is a tragic element in the story, it is the life of Jim Laird. Like Harvey, he went away to school full of idealistic fire; like Harvey, he wanted to be a great man and make the hometown people proud of him. Instead, he says, "I came back here to practice, and I found you didn't in the least want me to be a great man. You wanted me to be a shrewd lawyer." He became that shrewd lawyer and lost his soul in the process. The dead artist, imposing and serene in his coffin, serves as a perfect foil for Jim Laird, and the story stands as one of Cather's most powerful treatments of the conflict between artistic ideals and materialistic value systems.

"PAUL'S CASE"

"Paul's Case" presents a somewhat different view of that conflict. Paul, a high school youngster, is not a practicing artist, but he has an artistic temperament. He loves to hang around art galleries and concert halls and theaters, talking with the performers and basking in their reflected glory. It is glitter, excitement, and escape from the dripping taps in his home on Pittsburgh's Cordelia Street that Paul craves. A hopeless "case," Paul is finally taken out of high school by his widowed father because his mind is never on his studies. Forced from his usher's job at the concert hall and forbidden to associate with the actors at the theater, he loses the only things he had lived for and cared about. When he is denied those vital outlets for his aesthetic needs and sent to do dull work for a dull company, he carries out a desperate plan. One evening, instead of depositing his firm's receipts in the bank, he catches a train for New York. With swift determination, he buys elegant clothes and installs himself in a luxurious suite at the Waldorf-Astoria Hotel, there to live for a few brief days the life for which he had always felt himself suited. Those days are lovely and perfect, but the inevitable reckoning draws near: He learns from a newspaper that his father is en route to New York to retrieve him. Very deliberately Paul plots his course, even buying carnations for his buttonhole. Traveling to the outskirts of town, he walks to an embankment above the Pennsylvania tracks. There he carefully buries the carnations in the snow, and when the appropriate moment comes, he leaps into the path of an oncoming train.

A sensitive youngster with limited opportunity, Paul is not an artist in the usual sense. His distinction is that he responds to art, almost any art, with an unusual fervor. To him, anything associated with the world of art is beautiful and inspiring, while anything associated with lower-middle-class America is ugly and common. He is wrong about both worlds. With eyes only for the artificial surface glitter that spangles the world of art, he never sees the realities of hard work and struggle that define the life of every artist. Clearly, Cordelia Street is not as bad as Paul imagines it to be; it is, in fact, a moderately nice neighborhood where working people live and rear their families. Cordelia Street, however, has inadvertently taught him that money is the answer to all desires, that it can buy all the trappings that grace the world of art. Cordelia Street's legendary heroes are the kings of Wall Street.

In spite of his blindness, Paul captures the reader's sympathies because he feels trapped in an aesthetic wasteland to which he cannot and will not return; the reader realizes at the end that perhaps Paul's only escape lies in his final choice. The Waldorf, after all, provided temporary breathing space at best. His only real home is, as Cather tells us, in the "immense design of things."

"UNCLE VALENTINE"

Valentine Ramsay, the title character in "Uncle Valentine," is like Paul in many ways: He is sensitive, charming, flighty, unpredictable, temperamental, and intolerant of commonness. Unlike Paul, however, Valentine is a true artist, a gifted composer; it is not the artificial shell of art that he values, but the very heart of it. After several years abroad, he decides to return to Greenacre, his family home in the lush Pennsylvania countryside. He feels that perhaps at Greenacre he can shut out the world and find the peace he needs to write music.

He and the neighbors next door, with whom he shares a special affection, both artistic and social, have a magnificent year together, a "golden year." They roam the fields and woods, they share music, and they increase in aesthetic understanding. Casting a tragic shadow over this happy group, however, is the figure of Valentine's uncle, who haunts the premises like a grieving ghost. A child prodigy, he had left home to pursue his art, but for reasons never disclosed, he gave up his music and returned, burying himself in the ashes of his ruined life.

As a young man, Valentine had made a bad marriage to a rich woman whose materialistic coarseness became a constant affront to him; her very presence beside him in a concert hall was enough to shatter his nerves and obliterate the music he came to hear. Valentine has escaped from her, but she is destined to destroy his peace once again. He and his neighbors discover that she has purchased the large piece of property next to theirs, the property they had loved and tramped through for endless days. She intends to move in soon, bringing her fortune, her brash assertiveness, and Valentine's only son. She, along with the encroaching factory smoke downriver, spells the end of the blessed life the little group of art fanciers

has known at Greenacre. Valentine is forced to flee again, and readers learn that he is killed while crossing a street in France.

Cather's message is clear. The important things in life--art and the sharing of its pleasures, friendships, a feeling for land and place, a reverence for the past--are too often destroyed in the name of progress. When economic concerns are given top priority, whether on the prairie or in Pennsylvania, the human spirit suffers. Happily, in a much-loved story called "Neighbor Rosicky," Cather affirms that material temptations can be successfully resisted. Valentine is defeated, but Rosicky and his values prevail.

"NEIGHBOR ROSICKY"

Anton Rosicky, recognizable as another rendering of Ántonia's husband in Cather's best-known novel *My Ántonia* (1918), has instinctively established a value system that puts life and the land above every narrow-minded material concern. For example, when his entire corn crop is destroyed in the searing heat one July day, he organizes a little picnic so the family can enjoy the few things they have left. Instead of despairing with his neighbors, Rosicky plays with his children. It is no surprise that he and his wife Mary agree without discussion as to what things they can let go. They refuse to skim the cream off their milk and sell it for butter because Mary would "rather put some colour into my children's faces than put money into the bank." Doctor Ed, who detects serious heart trouble in Rosicky, observes that "people as generous and warm-hearted and affectionate as the Rosickys never got ahead much; maybe you couldn't enjoy your life and put it into the bank, too."

"Neighbor Rosicky" is one of Cather's finest tributes to life on the Nebraska prairie, to a value system that grows out of human caring and love for the land. Rosicky had lived in cities for many years, had known hard times and good times there, but it occurred to him one lonely day in the city that he had to get to the land. He realized that "the trouble with big cities" was that "they built you in from the earth itself, cemented you away from any contact with the ground," so he made his decision and went west.

The only thing that disturbs his sleep now is the discontentment of his oldest son. Rudolph is married to a town girl, Polly, and he wants to leave the farm and seek work in the city. Rosicky understands Rudolph's restlessness and Polly's lonesomeness and looks for every opportunity to help the young couple find some recreation time in town. In spite of his efforts, however, Polly continues to dislike farm life and to find the Rosickys strange and "foreign." Then one day Rosicky suffers a heart attack near Rudolph's place. No one is there to care for him except Polly, and that day something lovely happens between the two of them: She has a revelation of his goodness that is "like an awakening to her." His warm brown hand somehow brings "her to herself," teaches her more about life than she has ever known before, offers her "some direct and untranslatable message." With this revelation comes the assurance that at last all will be well with Rudolph and Polly. They will remain on the land and Rosicky's spirit will abide with them, for Polly has caught the old man's vision. It is fitting that Rosicky's death a few months later is calmly accepted as a natural thing, and that he is buried in the earth he loved. That way there will be no strangeness, no jarring separation.

Rosicky is Cather's embodiment of all that is finest in the human character. He had been a city man, a lover of opera and the other cultural advantages of city life, but he found his peace in the simple life of a Nebraska farm. By contrast, Harvey Merrick, the sculptor, had been a country boy, a lover of the prairie landscape, but he found his peace in the art capitals of the world. Nevertheless, Merrick and Rosicky would have understood each other perfectly. One's talent lay in molding clay, the other's in molding lives.

Cather is sometimes accused of nostalgia, of denying the present and yearning for the past. What seems clear in her work, however, is not that she wants to live in the past, but that she deplores a total rejection of the values of the past. She fears a materialistic takeover of the human heart, or a shriveled view of human life. She is convinced that the desire for money and the things money can buy corrupts character, cheapens life, destroys the landscape, and enervates art. In her exploration of the conflicts engendered by a destructive materialism, in her celebration of art and the land,

Willa Cather's devotion to an enduring system that spans time and space to embrace the good, the beautiful, and the true is made evident.

OTHER MAJOR WORKS

LONG FICTION: *Alexander's Bridge*, 1912; *O Pioneers!*, 1913; *The Song of the Lark*, 1915; *My Ántonia*, 1918; *One of Ours*, 1922; *A Lost Lady*, 1923; *The Professor's House*, 1925; *My Mortal Enemy*, 1926; *Death Comes for the Archbishop*, 1927; *Shadows on the Rock*, 1931; *Lucy Gayheart*, 1935; *Sapphira and the Slave Girl*, 1940.

POETRY: *April Twilights*, 1903.

NONFICTION: *Not Under Forty*, 1936; *Willa Cather on Writing*, 1949; *Willa Cather in Europe*, 1956; *The Kingdom of Art: Willa Cather's First Principles and Critical Statements, 1893-1896*, 1966; *The World and the Parish: Willa Cather's Articles and Reviews, 1893-1902*, 1970 (2 volumes).

MISCELLANEOUS: *Writings from Willa Cather's Campus Years*, 1950.

BIBLIOGRAPHY

Arnold, Marilyn. *Willa Cather's Short Fiction*. Athens: Ohio University Press, 1984. Discusses all of Cather's known short fiction in chronological order. The detailed investigations will be helpful both for readers new to Cather's stories and those who are more familiar with them. The examinations of stories that have received little critical attention are especially useful. Includes a selected bibliography.

Birns, Nicholas, ed. *Critical Insights: Willa Cather*. Pasadena, Calif.: Salem Press, 2012. Collection of original and reprinted essays providing critical readings of Cather's work. Also includes a biography, a chronology of major events in Cather's life, a complete list of her works, and a bibliography listing resources for further research.

De Roche, Linda. *Student Companion to Willa Cather*. Westport, Conn.: Greenwood Press, 2006. Provides an introductory overview of Cather's life and work aimed at high school students, college undergraduates, and general readers. Although the book focuses on Cather's novels, one of its chapters provides a discussion of her short-story collection *The Troll Garden*.

Gelfant, Blanche H., ed. *The Columbia Companion to the Twentieth-Century American Short Story*. New York: Columbia University Press, 2000. Includes a chapter in which Cather's short stories are analyzed.

Gerber, Philip L. *Willa Cather*. Rev. ed. New York: Twayne, 1995. In this revised edition, Gerber focuses more on Cather's short fiction than in the first edition, and he also discusses the resurgence of criticism of her work. Examines the major themes of the experience of the artist and life in rural Nebraska in major Cather short stories.

Harris, Jeane. "Aspects of Athene in Willa Cather's Short Fiction." *Studies in Short Fiction* 28 (Spring, 1991): 177-182. Discusses Cather's conflict between her gender and her inherited male aesthetic principles and the way this conflict is reflected in some of her early short stories by "manly" female characters modeled after the Greek goddess Athene. Maintains that Cather's androgynous females represent her dissatisfaction with traditional notions of femininity and masculinity.

Madigan, Mark J. "Cather and the Short Story." In *The Cambridge Companion to Willa Cather*, edited by Marilee Lindermann.New York: Cambridge University Press, 2005. This essay focusing on Cather's short fiction is part of a collection of articles providing a comprehensive overview of Cather's life and works. In addition to analyses of the major novels, some of the other essays examine such topics as politics, sexuality, and modernism in Cather's writings.

Meyering, Sheryl L. *A Reader's Guide to the Short Stories of Willa Cather*. New York: G. K. Hall, 1994. Discusses individual Cather stories, focusing on publishing history, circumstances of composition, sources, influence, relationship to other Cather works, and interpretations and criticism. Deals with her debt to Henry James, the influence of her sexual orientation on her fiction, and the influence of Sarah Orne Jewett.

Murphy, John J., ed. *Critical Essays on Willa Cather*. Boston: G. K. Hall, 1984. Among the thirty-five essays in this substantial collection are reprinted reviews and articles by Eudora Welty, Katherine Anne Porter, Leon Edel, Blanche H. Gelfant, and Bernice Slote. Also includes original essays by David Stouck, James Leslie Woodress, Paul Cameau, and John J. Murphy. The introduction offers a history of Cather scholarship.

Porter, David. *On the Divide: The Many Lives of Willa Cather*. Lincoln: University of Nebraska, 2008. An overview of Cather's life and works focusing on the people and ideas that influenced her writing.

Rosowski, Susan J. *The Voyage Perilous: Willa Cather's Romanticism*. Lincoln: University of Nebraska Press, 1986. Interprets Cather's writing within the literary tradition of Romanticism. Although the main focus is on her novels (with a chapter devoted to each), the volume also investigates the stories in *The Troll Garden* and includes a chapter on her short-story collection *Obscure Destinies*.

Shanley, J. Lyndon. "Willa Cather's Fierce Necessity." *Sewanee Review* 102 (Fall, 1994): 620-630. Notes that Cather's stories are about ordinary people and that one of her most important themes is youthful dreams. Discusses Cather's clear prose and the apparent simplicity of her stories.

Skaggs, Merrill Maguire, ed. *Willa Cather's New York: New Essays on Cather in the City*. Madison, N.J.: Fairleigh Dickinson University Press, 2001. Collection of twenty essays that focuses on the work Cather produced after she moved to New York City, analyzing how the city influenced her life and writing. One of the essays discusses the story "Old Mrs. Harris," while another essay examines the short-story collection *Obscure Destinies*.

Thomas, Susie. *Willa Cather*. Savage, Md.: Barnes & Noble Books, 1990. This feminist study, which draws extensively on Cather's unpublished letters, focuses on the particular contributions Cather made as a woman writing about America and analyzes how her cultural awareness influenced the development of her style. Includes a short biography and chapters on Cather's major novels and works of short fiction.

Wasserman, Loretta. *Willa Cather: A Study of the Short Fiction*. Boston: Twayne, 1991. Wasserman focuses on selected short stories that he believes are the most challenging and lend themselves to different critical approaches. Includes interviews with Cather, one of Cather's essays on the craft of writing, samples of criticism, a chronology, and a select bibliography.

Woodress, James. *Willa Cather: A Literary Life*. Lincoln: University of Nebraska Press, 1990. This definitive biography extends previous studies of Cather, including Woodress's own earlier work (*Willa Cather: Her Life and Art*, 1970), with fuller accounts of Cather's life. Includes new and expanded critical responses to her work, taking feminist criticism into account. In preparing the volume, Woodress was able to use the papers of Cather scholar Bernice Slote. Scholars and students will appreciate the extensively documented sources. Contains photographs of Cather and of people and places important to her.

Marilyn Arnold
Updated by Jean C. Fulton

MICHAEL CHABON

Born: Washington, D.C.; May 24, 1963
Also known as: Leon Chaim Bach, Malachi B. Cohen, August Van Zorn

PRINCIPAL SHORT FICTION

A Model World, and Other Stories, 1991
Werewolves in Their Youth: Stories, 1999

OTHER LITERARY FORMS

Michael Chabon (SHAY-bohn) began his literary career in 1988 with the publication of his first novel, *The Mysteries of Pittsburgh*. He also published travel sketches in magazines such as *Vogue*, as well as essays in *The New Yorker* and *Civilization*. In 1995, his second novel, *Wonder Boys*, was published, followed by *The Amazing Adventures of Kavalier and Clay* (2000), *Gentlemen of the Road* (2007; originally published serially in *The New York Times Magazine*), and *The Yiddish Policemen's Union* (2007). Chabon is also the author of *Summerland* (2002), a fantasy novel for young adults and the nonfiction books *Maps and Legends: Reading and Writing Along the Borderlands* (2008) and *Manhood for Amateurs: The Pleasures and Regrets of a Husband, Father, and Son* (2009). He has edited two collections of short fiction, *McSweeney's Mammoth Treasury of Thrilling Tales* (2003) and *McSweeney's Enchanted Chamber of Astonishing Stories* (2004).

ACHIEVEMENTS

When Michael Chabon's adviser in the master of fine arts program at the University of California at Irvine submitted *The Mysteries of Pittsburgh* to an agency in 1987, the novel created such a sensation that the right to publish was sold at auction. The publisher William Morrow paid a record $155,000 for publication rights. Foreign publishers were eager to obtain rights, and by the time the novel appeared, Chabon was already at work under contract on a film adaptation. He wrote other screenplays, which were sold but not produced, and the film rights to *Wonder Boys* were purchased after that novel's release. In 1987, his short stories began to appear in *Mademoiselle* and *The New Yorker*, which subsequently bought most of the stories that appear in *A Model World, and Other Stories*.

The Amazing Adventures of Kavalier and Clay, the novel that many consider Chabon's magnum opus, became a *New York Times* best seller and received the Pulitzer Prize for fiction in 2001. *The Yiddish Policemen's Union*, a combination detective novel and alternative history, in which the Jews settle in Alaska instead of Israel, received the Nebula Award for Best Novel (2007), the Hugo Award for Best Novel (2008), and the Sidewise Award for Alternate History (2007).

BIOGRAPHY

Michael Chabon was born in Washington, D.C. He graduated with a B.A. from the University of Pittsburgh and went on to study creative writing as a Regents Fellow at the University of California at Irvine. He submitted his first novel, *The Mysteries of*

Pittsburgh, to his graduate adviser, novelist Mac-Donald Harris, who then recommended it to his literary agent. The book was accepted for publication when Chabon was twenty-three years old. Chabon subsequently completed his master of fine arts degree. The success of his first novel plunged Chabon into a glamorous world of endorsement offers (deals from the Gap and *People* magazine)--all of which he rejected. He settled with his first wife, Lolly Groth, in Seattle, Washington. After their divorce he married Ayelet Waldman, with whom he had four children and settled in Berkeley, California.

ANALYSIS

Michael Chabon's distinctive strength in story-telling is a command of style that reminds his reviewers of an engaging surface of epigrams, wit, and telling comparisons. His subjects are also similar to Fitzgerald's, dealing mainly with young people trying to find their way through morally ambiguous and confusing situations. Though his style calls attention to the surface of his stories, they are, nevertheless, moving, mainly because his characters are realized fully enough and their problems and dilemmas are serious enough to involve the reader. *A Model World* is divided into two parts. "Part 1: A Model World" contains six stories on varied subjects. "Part 2: The Lost World" is a group of five stories about Nathan Shapiro, a boy who grows up while dealing with his parents' divorce. Looking closely at three stories, "S ANGEL," "A Model World," and "The Little Knife," illustrates the characteristics of Chabon's work.

"S ANGEL"

In "S ANGEL," Ira Wiseman, a twenty-one-year-old senior drama student at the University of California, Los Angeles, goes to the wedding of his cousin, Sheila, in Los Angeles. A young romantic, Ira is waiting for fate to bring him together with the right woman: "Ira never went anywhere without expecting that when he arrived there he would meet the woman with whom he had been destined to fall in love." His ideas of falling in love are confused, a mixture of unsatisfied sexual desire and idealism, but the world that he finds at the wedding seems dominated by sexual exploitation and economics.

Michael Chabon (AP Photo/Seth Wenig)

At the reception following the wedding, Ira feels uncomfortable and lonely. A woman attracts his notice: "Her body had aged better than her fading face, which nonetheless he found beautiful, and in which, in the skin at her throat and around her eyes, he thought he read strife and sad experience and a willingness to try her luck." Is she attractive because suffering has deepened her character or her romantic appeal, or because she might prove willing to engage in sex? The narrative voice makes fairly clear that the advice that he gets from his lesbian cousin, Donna, is right; Carmen, a neurotic, abused divorcée, is not a good prospect for Ira's first love affair.

As Ira approaches, meets, and attempts to begin a friendship with Carmen, he witnesses events that sketch out his activities and attitudes. He sees, and others confirm, that after two hours of wedded bliss, Sheila remains uncertain that marrying is what she wants. He overhears a conversation in which a non-Jew, Jeff Freebone, who affects Jewish speech and mannerisms, and who has rapidly become wealthy in the real estate business, talks about firing an employee:

"I should have done it the day it happened. Ha ha. Pow, fired in her own bed." Later, this same man commands the "carnal" affections of the group of Jewish women at Ira's table, including Carmen, his wealth overcoming even the unabashed lesbianism of Donna and her girlfriend and Carmen's history of abuse by a husband not unlike Freebone. He takes them away from the reception to view Carmen's house, which she would like to sell. These and other incidents underline Ira's naïve attitudes toward sex and love. Left alone again, Ira receives the assignment of locating the bride, who is supposed to cut the cake but has disappeared. Ira finds her alone, and they sympathize with each other, seemingly renewing an old sexual attraction between them. The story ends with their kiss.

As the story of a young idealist looking for romantic love in what turns out ironically to be an inappropriate place, at a wedding, "S ANGEL" is light in tone. There are no great defeats or losses in the story, and Ira does not lose his sweet, idealistic side. Nevertheless, the threats to people such as Ira and Sheila are serious. They believe that they are looking for authentic relationships, untainted by sexual exploitation and the struggle for wealth and status, but virtually everyone around them seems to match the way Sheila feels at her wedding-- like "a big stupid puppet or something, getting pulled around." They may both be victims of rather silly romantic illusions about love. Chabon achieves this lightness of tone in part through his style, especially in sentences that carry readers over long thoughts containing interesting turns and amusing surprises. When Ira pretends to go to the bar in order to walk by Carmen's table for a closer look at her, he is described: "Ira swung like a comet past the table, trailing, as he supposed, a sparkling wake of lustfulness and Eau Sauvage, but she seemed not to notice him, and when he reached the bar he found, to his surprise, that he genuinely wanted a drink." Here, Chabon captures the contrast between Ira's dream of his attractiveness and Carmen's jaded response, which converts his pretense of going for a drink into a reality.

The story's title refers to a misfolded map of Los Angeles in Carmen's purse. Ira is following a metaphorical map of romantic love, believing that he knows the signposts: "He had yet to fall in love to the degree

that he felt he was capable of falling, had never written villanelles or declarations veiled in careful metaphor, nor sold his blood plasma to buy champagne or jonquils. . . . " This only begins his list of the signs of love. Carmen has the map in a disorganized purse that reflects her lost life, and she apparently used it to find the location of the wedding, whereas Ira got lost and was late in arriving. This metaphor implies that Carmen, abused, divorced, depressed, and still looking for another rich husband, knows the road much better than Ira.

"A MODEL WORLD"

"A Model World" shows Chabon setting up a complex social situation that might remind one of the parties that Fitzgerald created in *The Great Gatsby* (1925). Smith, the narrator, and his friend, Levine, are physics students at a Southern California university. Smith is working on subatomic particles with brief lives: "Evanescence itself was the object of my studies." Levine is working on cloud dynamics, research that should lead toward the ability to control internal cloud movements. Both areas of study involve modeling, attempting to describe phenomena that are virtually impossible to measure and manipulate. This motif of modeling parts of the world turns up in a variety of ways, from the central image of a model of the greenhouse effect on Baldwin's computer, through the modeling of social life in drama and on television, to the telling of stories, fictional models of human life. The story culminates in a dinner party at the home of Baldwin, Levine's thesis adviser. There, social tensions mount as in a storm cloud until Smith manages to give them the spin that eases tension and contributes to changing the course of several people's lives.

The tensions arise from the secrets shared between various pairs at the dinner party, secrets that amount to attempts to give shape to different aspects of the relationships among these people. Having lost the excitement of science while working on his dissertation, Levine discovers in a used bookstore an obscure study of Antarctic clouds that completely and persuasively demonstrates the thesis toward which he has been working. This book arouses his passion, for it seems to have suffered the fate that he fears: "It was the horror of death, of the doom that waited all his efforts, and it was this horror, more than anything else . . . that determined him to commit the mortal sin of Academe." The sin is to plagiarize the book. By doing so, he will escape the prison of his fruitless studies so that he can go to New Mexico to make ceramic wind chimes and forget about measuring and controlling wind in clouds. In the process of plagiarizing, however, "his faith in the stoic nobility of scientific endeavor" is restored, and he once again dreams of a scientific career. This leads him to want to confer with Baldwin, to learn whether he has any real chance of getting away with plagiarizing. At this point, an academic reader might wonder why Levine does not simply use the book in the usual way, giving the author credit for his or her work instead of stealing it.

Smith's dissertation is going well enough, but he has become interested in an attractive drama student, Jewel, who turns out to be Julia, Baldwin's wife. She is currently enthralled by a French Egyptian theater guru, Mehmet Monsour. When Levine is invited to the dinner party, Mrs. Baldwin asks that he bring his friend, Smith. The dinner party then consists of Monsour, Levine, Smith, Baldwin, and Julia. Monsour seems mainly interested in absorbing a variety of American experiences and transforming them into drama. Levine wants to find out whether his plagiarism will work without revealing that he has plagiarized. Smith wants a sexual encounter with Julia. Julia, it turns out, wants mainly to plague her husband. Baldwin wants to triumph over Julia in some way and, perhaps, to humiliate himself in the process, since he wants to confront and expose the affair that he has detected but that he mistakenly believes is between Julia and Monsour. During a private talk with Baldwin, Levine again despairs that he can get away with plagiarism, as he realizes that the book he is copying, though published by a vanity press and probably very rare, still exists for someone to find sometime. Out of this despair, he betrays Smith, revealing what he discovers in the course of his conversation with Baldwin, that Smith, not Monsour, is Julia's lover.

The dinner proceeds with all of these tensions in operation. Monsour observes and talks volubly; Smith is unaware of his danger but observes that Julia sees him as an instrument to use against her husband rather than

as a lover; Levine is aware that he can probably succeed in his plagiarism but that he has, perhaps, bought this security by betraying his friend; Baldwin thinks he has gained power over Julia with his knowledge that Smith is her lover. These tensions come to a crisis when, at Baldwin's instigation, Monsour begins a game that is one of his theater exercises, in which each person must tell, truthfully, the worst thing that he or she has ever done. Smith is chosen to go first. He says that he had good sense enough to tell the truth. From among the most obvious choices--acquiescing in plagiarism, adultery, being an instrument in a marital battle--he chooses none but instead remembers a childhood action that he has most regretted--the wanton, unmotivated destruction of a neighbor child's toy--depending on his undeserved reputation for goodness as a shield from discovery and punishment. He tells the story so well that no one believes him, perhaps in part because it concerns none of them and is not what they expected to hear. The immediate effect of the story, nevertheless, is to bring an end to the game, to the tensions, and to the evening. The longer-term effects are also interesting: an end to Smith's affair with Julia and the beginning of his own very successful theater career, the end of Levine's vacillation about plagiarism and the beginning of his rapid ascent in the academic study of meteorology.

Like "S ANGEL," this story is light in tone, though in the crisis the stakes for the main characters are fairly high. The tone is maintained in part by Chabon's witty style and in part by the distance that he maintains from the characters. In this story, the moral ambiguities of the social world that he presents seem foregrounded while the characters remain relatively flat, which is another similarity with some of the best-known fiction of Fitzgerald, such as *The Great Gatsby*. The central effect of the story seems to be the irony of a world in which truth seems like fiction, where plagiarism and social lies may lead just as surely to success as telling the truth. The complexity of this irony becomes clear when one considers that while Levine steals his dissertation, he also rescues from loss the valuable work of another scientist, and when one considers that although Smith may tell a true story from his childhood, it is a difficult matter to judge whether breaking a child's toy was worse than committing adultery or failing to report plagiarism.

"THE LITTLE KNIFE"

Chabon maintains his light surface tone even in the sad and moving story that begins his series about Nathan Shapiro as he lives through and adjusts to his parents' divorce. The contrast between subject and tone is exemplified in the opening sentence of "The Little Knife": "One Saturday in that last, interminable summer before his parents separated and the Washington Senators baseball team was expunged forever from the face of the earth, the Shapiros went to Nag's Head, North Carolina, where Nathan, without planning to, perpetrated a great hoax." This contrast parallels the ironic distance between ten-year-old Nathan's perceptions about that vacation and the reader's more adult view.

This vacation brings the elder Shapiros to the realization that their marriage has come to an end. Mrs. Shapiro, though she says that her husband is a liberal and generous man, is looking for means of fulfillment in addition to marriage, and Dr. Shapiro has come to see these explorations into yoga, bonsai, and real estate as affronts to himself. They have fights, overheard by Nathan and his little brother, Ricky, in which Dr. Shapiro buries his wife "under a heap of scorn and ridicule." The fight that cuts their vacation short at midweek leads her to assert herself and implies that the marriage is over as far as she is concerned. By the middle of the day, Dr. Shapiro seems to have realized and accepted this finality, too.

Nathan, however, as the point-of-view character, has a child's mixed and somewhat vague understanding of what is happening, his vision typified by the equation of separating parents and the demise of the Washington Senators. His first reaction to his parents' fighting is a wish to return home, a step in the development of the nostalgia that becomes one of his leading characteristics throughout the stories in this series. He feels his parents are coming apart and wants to return to, or somehow preserve, a past that he remembers as more comfortable, when he was not in danger of being abandoned.

He actually perpetrates two hoaxes on their last day at Nag's Head. In the first, he walks alone along the beach on his heels, leaving impossible tracks, then returns to the spot later with his parents. To divert them from the realization that they must separate, he points to these tracks, and they go along with his game, pretending not to know what monster made them, though Ricky realizes immediately and Nathan must stifle him. When they announce that they are "unwell" and must cut the vacation short, Nathan thinks--or perhaps pretends to believe--that the strange tracks are the cause of this decision. When he asks them not to leave and claims responsibility, they react to quite another message, for they believe that he understands they are going to separate and believes himself to blame. This hoax creates a complexly moving moment of family unity and probably leads him to commit the second hoax.

At breakfast, his mother admired an especially handy little knife that is part of the furnishing of their beach cottage. His father suggests that she just take it, and this sets off the latest explosion in this last phase of their disintegration. She says that she will not let Dr. Shapiro make her dishonest. Nathan does not know what this means, but he arranges to be alone to pack his things while the rest of the family takes a last walk on the beach. While they are gone, he gathers up the seashells that they have found in a shoe box and, finally, he puts in the little knife, "where it swam, frozen, like a model shark in a museum diorama." As he looks at it, he looks forward to his parents fighting over it: "He foresaw, recalled, and fondly began to preserve all the discord for which, in his wildly preserving imagination, he was and would always be responsible." At least in discord, they are all together, and his "wildly preserving imagination" wishes to hold that togetherness, even at the price of discord.

Chabon's control of imagery in this story is especially notable. For example, as the family walks on the beach, they give seashells to Dr. Shapiro to hold, so that they come to jingle in his hands like money. When Mrs. Shapiro repeats "never again," her husband lets the shells fall: "He rubbed his hands together and then stared at them as though waking from a dream in which he had been holding a fortune in gold." The depth of this image is enhanced when Nathan reads it in the same way the reader is told to read it and responds quickly with his first hoax.

"WEREWOLVES IN THEIR YOUTH"

The title story of *Werewolves in Their Youth* opens with: "I had known him as a bulldozer, as a samurai . . . as a Peterbilt truck . . . but it was as a werewolf that Timothy Stokes finally went too far." Timothy clings to the imaginative world of most boys with a greater tenacity, ultimately at greater risk to himself. The narrator, Paul Kovel, is Timothy's reluctant neighbor, a boy who tries to avoid him at any cost. Paul struggles with obesity and, most profoundly, a violent father whose wife has tossed him out of their home. Both the school administrators and Timothy's mother, Mrs. Stokes, rely on Paul to wrest the boy from his conviction that he is a werewolf.

Paul's mother, who used to take the time to make him healthy meals, is now out selling real estate. When Paul finds her in the basement ready to throw away the last of his father's belongings--his Panama hat, his experiments as a research chemist for the Food and Drug Administration--it is all too much for the boy. He calls his father at work and lies about getting expelled from school to trick him into coming to the house. Then Paul steals a box of his father's possessions, including the notebook containing the formulas for his experiments, and hides it outside Timothy's house.

When Paul goes to retrieve the box later, he runs into Timothy, who carries Paul's father's notebook and wears a "rifle strapped across his back and a plastic commando knife in his boot." Timothy, having decided that Paul's father has been poisoning his son slowly, offers him an antidote, Coca-Cola and something else that burns his throat going down. Returning to the Kovel house, the boys are shocked to see Paul's parents locked in an amorous embrace. They throw up the antidote, and Paul tells Mrs. Stokes that Timothy has a real gun; he then helps his father load the rest of his things in the car. The following morning, Paul watches Timothy board a bus bound for the "special school" for boys who do not fit in elsewhere.

"Werewolves in Their Youth" is redolent of those boyhoods in which parents are too busy with their own dilemmas to be of any significant use to their children.

Chabon reveals a masterful eye for detail, such as the pancakes that Mrs. Stokes makes for her disturbed son that "sounded okay until you found out that she put things in them like carrots and leftover pieces of corn." In less skillful hands, "Werewolves in Their Youth" could fall prey to vilifying the parents while painting the boys as hapless victims. It is not that simplistic, however. Chabon portrays Mrs. Kovel as a woman trying to do her best in an untenable situation. By the same token, Paul's father, although a drinker and wife beater, is limited by his own inability to confront his addiction and mercurial temper. The boys are both inventive and complex, funny and maddening. Such tales of domestic discord are Chabon's trademark.

OTHER MAJOR WORKS

LONG FICTION: *The Mysteries of Pittsburgh*, 1988; *Wonder Boys*, 1995; *The Amazing Adventures of Kavalier and Clay*, 2000; *The Final Solution: A Story of Detection*, 2004; *Gentlemen of the Road*, 2007; *The Yiddish Policemen's Union*, 2007.

NONFICTION: *Maps and Legends: Reading and Writing Along the Borderlands*, 2008; *Manhood for Amateurs: The Pleasures and Regrets of a Husband, Father, and Son*, 2009.

CHILDREN'S LITERATURE: *Summerland*, 2002.

EDITED TEXTS: *McSweeney's Mammoth Treasury of Thrilling Tales*, 2003; *McSweeney's Enchanted Chamber of Astonishing Stories*, 2004.

MISCELLANEOUS: *Michael Chabon Presents: The Amazing Adventures of the Escapist*, 2004 (2 volumes).

BIBLIOGRAPHY

Benedict, Elizabeth. "Sorrow at the Mall." Review of *A Model World, and Other Stories*, by Michael Chabon. *The New York Times Book Review*, May 26, 1991, 7. In this review of Chabon's first short-story collection, Benedict praises the author's narrative skills and descriptive powers. For Benedict, Chabon in the second half of the collection seems to be "delving below the surface of his fluent, astonishingly vivid prose and reaching deeper into his characters."

Bigelow, Gordon. "Nichael Chabon's Unhomely Pulp." *Literature Interpretation Theory* 19, no. 4 (October-December, 2008): 305-320. A critique of "In the Black Mill," one of the stories included in *Werewolves in Their Youth*. Explains how in the story Chabon is critical of Sigmund Freud and his essay "The Uncanny," and describes the story's examination of fear, disorientation, patriarchy, and other Freudian concepts.

Cahill, Bryon. "Michael Chabon: A Writer with Many Faces." *Writing* 27, no. 6 (April/May, 2005): 16-20. Presents a detailed examination of Chabon's developing interests and the inspirations behind many of his works.

Chabon, Michael. "Smashing the Dishes." Interview by Laurel Graeber. *The New York Times Book Review*, May 26, 1991, 7. This brief interview focuses on Chabon's art of storytelling. Basing his stories on "real episodes," Chabon explains that "you have these gives. But to write an interesting story you have to depart from them." Includes a photograph of Chabon.

Fowler, Douglas. "The Short Fiction of Michael Chabon: Nostalgia in the Very Young." *Studies in Short Fiction* 32 (Winter, 1995): 75-82. Suggests that Chabon's stories are best when he deals with memory and when he makes use of light comic irony and sophisticated prose. Argues that the tales in "The Lost World" sequence of *A Model World* are the best place to examine Chabon's exploration of the child within everyone.

Giles, Jeff. "He's a Real Boy Wonder." *Newsweek* 125 (April 10, 1995): 76-77. Describes Chabon's literary celebrity status in 1988 at the age of twenty-four after the publication of *The Mysteries of Pittsburgh*, which he wrote as a master's thesis. Discusses a number of Chabon projects, including screenplays.

See, Lisa. "Michael Chabon: Wonder Boy in Transition." *Publishers Weekly* 242 (April 10, 1995): 44-45. Discusses Chabon's rise to late 1980's "brat packer"; in this informal interview, Chabon describes his struggles with his second novel and the pressures of being a successful young writer.

Terry Heller
Updated by Nika Hoffman

RAYMOND CHANDLER

Born: Chicago, Illinois; July 23, 1888
Died: La Jolla, California; March 26, 1959

PRINCIPAL SHORT FICTION

Five Murderers, 1944
Five Sinister Characters, 1945
Finger Man, and Other Stories, 1946
Red Wind, 1946
Spanish Blood, 1946
The Simple Art of Murder, 1950
Trouble Is My Business, 1950
Pick-up on Noon Street, 1952
Smart-Aleck Kill, 1953
Pearls Are a Nuisance, 1958
Killer in the Rain, 1964 (Philip Durham, editor)
The Smell of Fear, 1965
The Midnight Raymond Chandler, 1971
The Best of Raymond Chandler, 1977
Stories and Early Novels, 1995
Collected Stories, 2002

OTHER LITERARY FORMS

Raymond Chandler is best known for his hard-boiled detective novels featuring Philip Marlowe. Chandler often used material from his short stories to create the novels, and Philip Marlowe's character grew out of the various detectives in the short tales. This archetypal hero has been further popularized through many major motion pictures. Chandler wrote screenplays for four works by others. His works were selected for Book-of-the-Month Club members, and his stories and novels were collected in a number of editions. He also wrote criticism on the art of detective fiction and, in his early years, conventional poems and essays.

ACHIEVEMENTS

Raymond Chandler may clearly be considered second only to Dashiell Hammett as the writer who raised the reputation of the hard-boiled detective novel from its humble origins in popular culture to the level of serious literature. The seven novels he wrote are classics of the genre; the many films made from his novels are equally well known. Together, the novels and films have made Chandler's major literary creation, Philip Marlowe, one of America's most popular icons. Cynical, tough, yet curiously sentimental and moral, this detective figure seems particularly appealing as a lone fighter against heavy odds in a violent world.

Chandler's screenplay *The Blue Dahlia* (1946) won the Edgar Allan Poe Award from Mystery Writers of America and an Academy Award nomination in 1946. One of his seven novels, *The Long Goodbye* (1953), won another Edgar Allan Poe Award in 1954.

BIOGRAPHY

Although he was born in Chicago and spent his first seven years in the Middle West, Raymond Thornton Chandler received an English Public School education (Dulwich College) when his mother took him to England after her divorce. He traveled in Europe, spent an unsatisfying few months in the British civil service, and set out to become a writer. After publishing a number of poems and essays, he returned to the United States in 1912. He worked at various jobs and in 1917 joined the Canadian army and served in France. After the war, he became a successful oil executive in California and married Cissy Pascal, who was eighteen years his senior. Chandler's dissatisfaction and drinking left him jobless in 1932. He turned to writing again and became the best of the *Black Mask* magazine pulp writers before turning to novels with *The Big Sleep* in 1939. He was a successful and highly paid Hollywood screenwriter throughout the 1940's. Following Cissy's death in 1954, Chandler resumed his rootless life and heavy drinking. He visited England several times. When he died of pneumonia, on March 26, 1959, he was president of the Mystery Writers of America and was at work on another Philip Marlowe novel.

ANALYSIS

Joseph T. Shaw, editor of *Black Mask*, the leading pulp detective magazine of the 1930's, remarked upon receiving Raymond Chandler's first story that the author was either a genius or crazy. He must have decided in favor of genius, for he accepted "Blackmailers Don't Shoot" in 1933 and paid Chandler the standard rate of a penny a word, or $180.

Chandler reveals in his letters that he taught himself to write for the pulps by reading back issues. He gives full credit to Dashiell Hammett, who wrote stories that commented on contemporary life using the detective story or puzzle framework. Chandler, however, surpasses his mentor in his use of the language. His ability to hear the American vernacular and to transfer it onto the printed page may be his strongest point as a writer. This trait helps to explain Chandler's often aimless sentences and strange word order. His classical education in England made him aware of the finer points of language and the uses of slang. His characters reveal themselves through their language. Since his fiction describes the interplay between levels or classes in society, the speech of his characters as identifying labels is paramount.

Chandler's major themes also deserve consideration. His close examination, in both short stories and novels, of society at large reveals a concern for humanity equal to that of Mark Twain. He wrote about human behavior in almost every work of fiction. True, his characters often came from the criminal element, but his works show that the criminal element (or at least the vices of that element) extends into all levels of society, that greed, pride, and violence have no basis in economic or social status. His revelation of Southern California of the 1930's to 1950's offers a view not found in other media of that era.

Chandler's ability to set a scene or mood is also remarkable. "Red Wind" takes its title from the prevailing weather phenomenon present at the time of the story.

There was a desert wind blowing that night. It was one of those hot dry Santa Anas that come down through the mountain passes and curl your hair and make your nerves jump and your skin itch. On nights like that every booze party ends in a fight. Meek little wives feel the edge of the carving knife and study their husbands' necks. Anything can happen.

Although the wind does not figure in the events of the story, it sets a mood in which the story seems plausible, in spite of several coincidences that the reader may wonder over. As if Chandler realizes this, he seems to joke with the reader:

"There's a hell of a lot of coincidences in all this business," the big man said.

"It's the hot wind," I grinned. "Everybody's screwy tonight."

Chandler never lets the reader wonder about a room or a house. The unusual Southern California locations for his scenes seem to be designed as if for a Hollywood set.

We sat down and looked at each other across a dark floor, on which a few Navajo rugs and a few dark Turkish rugs made a decorating combination with some well-used overstuffed furniture. There was a fireplace, a small baby grand, a Chinese screen, a tall Chinese lantern on a teakwood pedestal, and gold net curtains against lattice windows. The windows to the south were open. A fruit tree with a white-washed trunk whipped about outside the screen, adding its bit to the noise from across the street.

Chandler felt that such detail helped to build character as well as set the scene. He considered that many readers wanted more than the barest plot filled with action, and his success bears him out.

Chandler's humor is an important element of his work. Perhaps realizing that stories filled with violence and murder need some relief, he frequently allows his narration to entertain the reader. When a man is shot in a bar in "Red Wind," Dalmas relates that "the guy took a week to fall down." In describing the beautiful girl in the story, he tells readers: "She had brown wavy hair under a wide-brimmed straw hat with a velvet band and loose bow. She had wide blue eyes and eyelashes that didn't quite reach her chin." As a car leaves the scene of a murder, Dalmas "got its license number the way I got my first million." He doesn't "like being a witness" because "the pay's too low." The humor presented through the first-person narrator makes him human; he remains a believable, if somewhat exaggerated, character; and he remains a stabilizing force in an otherwise inhuman world. Chandler was aware of the extent of the exaggeration called for by the formula. He wrote "Pearls Are a Nuisance" as a deliberate parody of the type.

Chandler's private eyes invariably find much more action and a more involved plot than the reader suspects, a fact that makes his stories difficult to synopsize. The detective follows one lead to another and ends up walking a narrow path between the mob and the police as new characters appear on the scene. Although the citizen being protected is usually female, Chandler was not afraid to include a woman as the villain. Carol Donovan in "Goldfish" is meaner and tougher than her male rivals, but Carmady (another Marlowe prototype) is equal to the task. Someone else shoots Carol, but only after Carmady has slugged her in the jaw to provide the opportunity.

Raymond Chandler (Library of Congress)

Chandler is best known as a writer of detective fiction, and he deserves much credit for the phenomenal growth of the genre in popular literature, but his contributions to serious literature and film continue to be recognized by readers and scholars. His revelation of Southern California to the world is unique among his writing peers; his view of human behavior moves his stories into a context encompassing all of the corrupt world of his vision; and his influence will continue to be felt as long as detective stories and crime tales are written.

"BLACKMAILERS DON'T SHOOT"

In his early stories, Chandler attempted to master the hard-boiled style of writing while still saying something of value about society and human behavior. "Blackmailers Don't Shoot" is a story about an actress, Rhonda Farr, who is being blackmailed because of a bundle of reckless letters she wrote. The detective character in the story, Mallory, is hired by the actor-turned-gangster recipient of the letters to get them back and to identify the blackmailer. The chase leads Mallory, who is imported to Los Angeles from Chicago for the case, to crooked cops, Rhonda Farr's crooked lawyer, and assorted gangsters. Four men are killed in a short space of time; Rhonda Farr is kidnapped (by the blackmailers) and recovered (by Mallory). The actress turns out to want as much publicity as possible, and she seems only slightly penitent in her reaction to the beatings, killings, and trouble created by her letters. Landry, the actor-gangster, seems to have created the whole caper in an attempt to recapture the affections of Rhonda Farr. In the aftermath of this plot, two more hoods are killed and one wounded, and Mallory is wounded. He gets a clean slate from the local police, who manage to tie up all the loose ends with ease, including a complete cover-up of the illegal activities of their own men. Mallory decides that he might stay in Los Angeles instead of returning to Chicago.

The action of this story is fast, furious, and somewhat confusing. Mallory uses some deductive reasoning to figure out the details of the case, but he is much more involved in threatening, hitting, and shooting than in deducing. The story exposes the unreasonable desire for publicity in Hollywood, even bad publicity. "You don't know much about this

Hollywood racket, do you, darling?" Rhonda Farr chides Mallory. "Publicity has to hurt a bit out here. Otherwise nobody believes it."

The corrupt elements of society are also well represented here. Practically every character who enters the story has a gun and is willing to use force to have his way over someone else. Chandler wrote that it is the "smell of fear" in the detective tale that ties it to real life. His chief target for criticism seems to be those who, by whatever means, try to rule others unjustly. Since the world of the criminal is built around injustice--toward individuals, society, or its institutions--Chandler found a remarkable wealth of material about which to write.

In the midst of the chaotic world of Los Angeles crime and violence, there is always the good man, the man who tries to bring order. As Chandler wrote later: "Down these mean streets a man must go who is not himself mean, who is neither tarnished nor afraid." Mallory considers himself "the nearest thing to an honest stranger," and he is basically upright. The Chicago police verify that he has "a clean sheet--damn' clean."

Mallory is the direct predecessor of Philip Marlowe, Chandler's famous private eye. Marlowe did not appear as the central detective character until Chandler began writing novels in 1939. His detective in the earlier short stories--whatever his name--is, however, usually the same man. Chandler probably found it a minor task to change most of the names to Philip Marlowe in later stories and collected printings of the early stories.

"RED WIND"

In later printings, John Dalmas in "Red Wind" becomes Marlowe--the only change, made in the story. It is not true, as some have reported, that all book versions of the stories use the revised Marlowe name. The collection *Red Wind* (World Publishing Company, 1946), for example, keeps the original names used in magazine texts.

Chandler is a moral writer. His detective, even before Marlowe, is a man who sees the truth and works to set things right, often without pay and always alone. He is disappointed in himself and in the world when he is unable to succeed. John Dalmas in "Red Wind" suffers dejection at the breakup of a marriage, even though he

knows the husband and wife have been equally unfaithful. As a final act of decency, he protects the wife from the knowledge that her dead lover had been "just another four-flusher." Dalmas substitutes a set of obviously fake pearls for the seemingly real pearls given her. Dalmas/Marlowe protects her memory of her lover at considerable expense and trouble to himself. In so doing, he assumes the grief, which readers see as he throws the pearls into the Pacific one by one.

"GUNS AT CYRANO'S"

An unusual character for Chandler is Ted Malvern in "Guns at Cyrano's." Unlike the typical hard-boiled detective, Malvern is wealthy and essentially idle. He is generous with his wealth, because, as readers learn at the story's conclusion, he considers it "dirty money." The money is inherited from his father, who made it

> out of crooked sewerage and paving contracts, out of gambling concessions, appointment payoffs, even vice, I daresay. And when it was made and there was nothing to do but sit and look at it, he died and left it to me. It hasn't brought me any fun either. I always hope it's going to, but it never does.

Malvern compensates, in his own hard-boiled fashion, for living on his father's "crooked dough" by consorting with the rougher elements in society and helping to rid the world of at least one crooked politician.

THE CHANDLER DETECTIVE

Chandler's detective (even when he is not a licensed private investigator) works against tremendous odds to clean up a small corner of the world. He seldom gets paid, he almost never gets the girl, and he knows that the next case will involve him with just as many seedy and malevolent characters as the last case. He does not contemplate his old age or retirement. His violent world is not provided with such sureties. He knows he is alone and that he will probably remain so.

The hard-boiled formula as created by Dashiell Hammett and Chandler includes an almost automatic confrontation with the police. Thus the detective is the true guardian of morality, caught between abusive police and equally abusive criminals. He risks arrest and beatings from the former for not revealing his clients' interests, and he risks physical violence and death from the latter for daring to enter the nether world of mobsters and crooks--which he inevitably must do in the course of his work.

His home is not his castle. He lives alone, usually in a spare, if not spartan, apartment. He is likely to find either a pair of unfriendly and incompetent police detectives or a mob of violent gangsters in his living room when he arrives home intent only on a slug of whiskey and much-needed sleep. His office is equally spartan, with no secretary and no fellow workers. He has a waiting room, a desk--with an "office bottle" in one drawer--and a telephone.

Many writers of mystery and detective fiction have been influenced by Chandler. The violence visited upon Chandler's detective hero may be the source of the almost constant threats, beatings, and incarcerations used by writer Dick Francis. The security--or lack of it--of the home may help to explain the elaborate system of checks that Travis McGee has installed on his houseboat to see if anyone is or has been aboard. Robert B. Parker has said that he learned to write detective novels by reading Hammett and Chandler.

Chandler has placed the hard-boiled detective firmly in American literature as a remarkable and enduring character type. The many imitations, exaggerations, and developments based on Philip Marlowe speak well of Chandler's profound influence on fiction and the popular arts. Chandler's importance and his craft do not stop there, however; Chandler wanted to be considered a serious writer. He was pleased that the British critics considered him a major writer, and he would no doubt be pleased to know that he is ever being "discovered" by new generations of American readers and critics.

OTHER MAJOR WORKS

LONG FICTION: *Big Sleep*, 1939; *Farewell, My Lovely*, 1940; *The High Window*, 1942; *The Lady in the Lake*, 1943; *The Little Sister*, 1949; *The Long Goodbye*, 1953; *Playback*, 1958; *The Raymond Chandler Omnibus: Four Famous Classics*, 1967; *The Second Chandler Omnibus*, 1973; *Poodle Springs*, 1989 (incomplete manuscript finished by Robert B. Parker); *Later Novels and Other Writings*, 1995.

SCREENPLAYS: *And Now Tomorrow*, 1944 (with Frank Partos); *Double Indemnity*, 1944 (with Billy Wilder); *The Unseen*, 1945 (with Hager Wilde); *The Blue Dahlia*, 1946; *Strangers on a Train*, 1951 (with Czenzi Ormonde).

NONFICTION: *Raymond Chandler Speaking*, 1962 (Dorothy Gardiner and Katherine Sorely Walker, editors); *Chandler Before Marlowe: Raymond Chandler's Early Prose and Poetry*, 1973 (Bruccoli, editor); *The Notebooks of Raymond Chandler and English Summer*, 1976 (Frank MacShane, editor); *Raymond Chandler and James M. Fox: Letters*, 1978; *Selected Letters of Raymond Chandler*, 1981 (Frank MacShane, editor); *The Raymond Chandler Papers: Selected Letters and Non-fiction, 1909-1959*, 2000 (Tom Hiney and Frank MacShane, editors); *Philip Marlowe's Guide to Life: A Compendium of Quotations*, 2005 (Martin Asher, editor).

BIBLIOGRAPHY

Bruccoli, Matthew J., and Richard Layman, eds. *Hardboiled Mystery Writers: Raymond Chandler, Dashiell Hammett, Ross Macdonald*. New York: Carroll & Graf, 2002. Compilation of interviews, articles, letters, and previously published studies about the three writers. Lavishly illustrated with personal photographs, reproductions of manuscript pages, print advertisements, film promotional materials, dust jackets, and paperback covers.

Freeman, Judith. *The Long Embrace: Raymond Chandler and the Woman He Loved*. New York: Pantheon Books, 2007. Freeman maintains that Chandler's life was a greater mystery than his novels, so she traveled to the almost two dozen Southern California houses and apartments where he and his wife Cissy lived and uncovered information about Cissy, who played a crucial role in Chandler's understanding of women and of himself.

Hamilton, Cynthia S. "Raymond Chandler." In *Western and Hard-Boiled Detective Fiction: From High Noon to Midnight*. Iowa City: University of Iowa Press, 1987. Provides an unusual insight into Chandler's detective fiction from the historical and generic perspective of the American Western novel. Includes three chapters on the study of formula literature. Complemented by a bibliography and an index.

Hiney, Tom. *Raymond Chandler: A Biography*. New York: Atlantic Monthly Press, 1997. A brief biography of Chandler that discusses his education in England, his relationship to Los Angeles, and the plots and characters of his most important detective stories and novels.

Jameson, F. R. "On Raymond Chandler." In *The Poetics of Murder: Detective Fiction and Literary Theory*, edited by Glenn W. Most and William W. Stowe. San Diego, Calif.: Harcourt Brace Jovanovich, 1983. Observes that Chandler's English upbringing in essence gave him an outsider's view of American life and language. Provides a useful discussion of the portrait of American society that emerges from Chandler's works.

Knight, Stephen. "'A Hard Cheerfulness': An Introduction to Raymond Chandler." In *American Crime Fiction: Studies in the Genre*, edited by Brian Docherty. New York: St. Martin's Press, 1988. Discusses the values and attitudes that define Philip Marlowe and make him unusual in the genre of hard-boiled American crime fiction.

Lehman, David. "Hammett and Chandler." In *The Perfect Murder: A Study in Detection*. New York: Free Press, 1989. Chandler is represented in this comprehensive study of detective fiction as one of the authors who brought out the parable at the heart of mystery fiction. A useful volume in its breadth and its unusual appendixes, one a list of further reading, the other an annotated list of the critic's favorite mysteries. Includes two indexes, one of concepts and another of names and titles.

Moss, Robert F., ed. *Raymond Chandler: A Literary Reference*. New York: Carroll & Graf, 2003. Useful compilation of primary documents relating to Chandler's life and work. Includes letters, interviews, and other documents produced both by Chandler and by friends and colleagues. Includes extensive bibliographic resources and index.

Skinner, Robert E. *The Hard-Boiled Explicator: A Guide to the Study of Dashiell Hammett, Raymond Chandler, and Ross Macdonald*. Metuchen, N.J.: Scarecrow Press, 1985. Indispensable for the scholar interested in tracking down unpublished dissertations, as well as mainstream criticism. Brief introductions of each author are followed by annotated bibliographies of books, articles, and reviews.

Steiner, T. R. "The Origin of Raymond Chandler's 'Mean Streets.'" *ANQ*, n.s. 7 (October, 1994): 225-227. Suggests that the origin of the expression "mean streets" is Arthur Morrison's *Tales of Mean Streets*, a classic of late Victorian slum literature. The phrase referred to the lack of purpose and joy in the East End of London.

Van Dover, J. K., ed. *The Critical Response to Raymond Chandler*. Westport, Conn.: Greenwood Press, 1995. A collection of essays examining Chandler's literary output. Includes bibliographical references and an index.

Widdicombe, Toby. *A Reader's Guide to Raymond Chandler*. Westport, Conn.: Greenwood Press, 2001. Features entries, arranged alphabetically, on Chandler's works, characters, places, allusions, and major topics. The sections discussing the individual short stories are listed in the index under the name of each story.

Thomas D. Lane
Updated by Shakuntala Jayaswal

LAN SAMANTHA CHANG

Born: Appleton, Wisconsin; 1965

PRINCIPAL SHORT FICTION
Hunger: A Novella and Stories, 1998

OTHER LITERARY FORMS

Hunger: A Novella and Stories was Lan Samantha Chang's first book. She subsequently published two novels: *Inheritance* (2004) and *All Is Forgotten, Nothing Is Lost* (2010).

ACHIEVEMENTS

Lan Samantha Chang was awarded a Wallace Stegner Fellowship at Stanford University in 1993. "Pippa's Story" was selected for the annual publication *The Best American Short Stories* in 1994; "The Eve of the Spirit Festival" appeared in *The Best American Short Stories* in 1996. She won a Truman Capote Fellowship, a National Endowment for the Arts grant, and first place for fiction in The Bay Area Book Reviewers Association Awards. She received a Guggenheim Fellowship in 2008.

In 2010, Chang was a professor of English at the University of Iowa and the first Asian American writer to serve as director of the Iowa Writers' Workshop; she also taught at the Warren Wilson College MFA Program for Writers.

BIOGRAPHY

Lan Samantha Chang's parents both lived in China during the Japanese occupation of that country in World War II; they came to the United States separately, met in New York, and settled in Appleton, Wisconsin, where Chang was born in 1965. Following her parents' wishes, Chang attended Yale University as a premedical student but changed her mind and earned a degree in East Asian studies. She then attended Harvard University's Kennedy School of Government; however, after taking a number of classes in economics, she decided she wanted to be a writer and began taking creative writing classes in Boston and later earned an M.F.A. at the University of Iowa. She attended Stanford University for two years as a Wallace Stegner Fellow and stayed on there as a teacher.

ANALYSIS

Among the almost universally positive reviews that Lan Samantha Chang's first book received, there were some that inevitably compared her to other Asian women writers, such as Amy Tan and Maxine Hong Kingston. It is true that Chang charts some of the same thematic territory as have those established novelists, especially the familiar Asian American conflict between parents and children, the Old World and the New. However, those reviewers who liken Chang to Bernard Malamud or James Joyce are perhaps more accurate. Like those masters of the modern short story, Chang is a consummate stylist, more concerned with tightly structured aesthetic form than with abstract social issues, such as marginality, cultural diversity, and the status of the immigrant.

Also like past masters of the short story, Chang is often oblique in her narrative presentation, frequently situating the heart of the story in places other than where the reader first assumes it to be. Thus, while the title novella *Hunger* seems to be about the ambitious hunger of the husband, it is really about the lyrically implied hunger of the wife; likewise, while the prize-winning "Pippa's Story" seems to be about the escape of the daughter into the future, it is really about the hold the mother has on her through the past.

The fact that Chang's stories have been received with wide praise for their universality, lyricism, and formal control rather than for their cultural particularity and postcolonial political stance perhaps signals that, in the late 1990's, the multicultural and the marginal were not praised for exoticism alone; if Chang's reception is indicative, the focus in contemporary fiction seems to be on what unites people as human beings rather than what separates them as multicultural individuals.

HUNGER

More than half of Chang's first collection of stories is taken up by this novella of a Chinese immigrant violinist, his wife, and their two daughters. Although the plot focuses on Tian's "hunger" to be a professional musician in America, the psychological interest of the novella centers on the narrator, his wife Min, on whom Tian's passionate desire has the greatest impact. Tian's account of swimming half a mile across the Taiwan Strait from mainland China to a refugee ship, holding his precious violin out of the water, is a central image of the hunger at the core of the story, but Min's hunger, revealed indirectly by her simple, lyrical voice, resonates throughout the story and colors everything. Although Tian is obsessively passionate, first about playing the violin himself and then about compelling his daughters to learn to play, it is Min, hungry for the love denied to her by her self-obsessed family, who lives her life destined to receive very little of what her mother calls *yuanfen*-- "the apportionment of love" destined for one in the world.

What also makes the story more than a domestic tragedy of one man's unfulfilled immigrant ambitions is Min's sense of the magic and mystery of human passion and transcendent reality; she is like a finely tuned violin, quiescent until her own passion is evoked. When Tian gives up on becoming a professional musician and loses his job at the school where he has been teaching, he turns his attentions to Anna, the oldest daughter, only to discover that she has a poor ear for music. By next directing his teaching attentions to Ruth, the younger daughter, he puts Anna in the same situation Min has endured, yearning for his love. Min identifies both with Anna, who feels shut out, and with Ruth, who hates the violin and wants to leave their closed-in world for someplace else.

The story works itself out in classically tragic fashion: Ruth runs away; Tian dies unfulfilled; Anna seems destined to be alone; Min, ill with cancer, has

only the past from which to gain sustenance. However, in spite of this darkness at the end of *Hunger*, what remains is Min's endurance. Although she fears that there may come a time when no one will remember their lives, the story she has just told is a guarantee that this is not true.

"THE UNFORGETTING"

"The Unforgetting" is Chang's most explicit, almost parabolic, treatment of the familiar Asian immigrant story--the tension between hanging on to the traditions of the Old World and wholeheartedly embracing those of the New. The Hwangs are the prototypical Asian family, who move to the heartland of the Midwest to forget what they no longer need to know and learn what they do need to know. When their son Charles is born, they forget even more, replacing all useless memories with thoughts of him. Still, their memories persist, the world of their past growing larger and larger. When Charles decides to go away to school, the mother blames the father for making him like other Americans who leave their parents and create their own homes. In a bitter scene in which they blame each other for the

Lan Samantha Chang (AP Photo/Elise Amendola)

loss of Charles, the couple break every plate in the kitchen. At the end of the story, both realize that the world they once knew now lives only inside them and that they are the end of that world. "They had no solace, and no burden, but each other."

"THE EVE OF THE SPIRIT FESTIVAL"

Chang again presents the conflict between generations in this story, although not in such stark terms as in "The Unforgetting." The Chinese father has aspirations for academic promotion and invites his colleagues over for drinks, "watching the Americans and studying to become one." As in *Hunger*, two daughters are involved: Claudia, who narrates the story, and Emily, who berates her father for mimicking the Americans. Although Claudia tries to be a good daughter, Emily puts on makeup, dresses in pants, and goes out with boys against her father's wishes. After Emily has gone away to college and the father has died, the focus of the story shifts to the two sisters--the good daughter, who has stayed home, and the prodigal one, who has returned. In the climactic scene, Emily asks Claudia to cut off her long, black hair, and Claudia, who has scraggly, brownish hair, enjoys it. When she is awakened that night by Emily's screams, Claudia understands that her father's ghost will never visit her, but she lies awake waiting anyway.

"PIPPA'S STORY"

"Pippa's Story" is the only story in *Hunger* that is not based on immigrants in America. Although the plot centers on a young woman who leaves her Chinese village to work for a wealthy family in Shanghai, the thematic heart of the story is the relationship between the girl and her mother, who stays home. The mother works in charms and is a powerful figure in her village; the girl thinks she will disappear if she cannot escape her mother's shadow. When she leaves, the mother gives her a small stone and makes her promise to find the heart of the house where Wen, the man for whom she is going to work, lives and to hide the stone there. Although the girl does not know the story behind the promise, it is clear that even though she is leaving, the shadow of her mother accompanies her.

The daughter gets rid of the stone when she arrives, but later she hears the story behind it--how Wen desired her mother when they were young and murdered her

father just before she was born. Although she insists that she will not keep her promise to her mother, that none of the story has anything to do with her, she begins to think that even her flight from her mother fits into some incomprehensible design. She finds the stone and, when Wen sexually assaults a friend, hides it in his bed.

The story mixes history and folklore. When the Communists enter the city, they execute Wen, as a result of either the mother's curse or Wen's political leanings. The narrator says her story is a small one compared with the larger events of the Communist occupation of China. However, in its delicate treatment of the past's impingement on the present and in its complex combination of the political, the personal, and the supernatural, the story reflects, the narrator says, how individuals' buried pasts are like ginseng roots, all with different shapes.

OTHER MAJOR WORKS

LONG FICTION: *Inheritance*, 2004; *All Is Forgotten, Nothing Is Lost*, 2010.

BIBLIOGRAPHY

Carter, Emily. "Chang Debuts with Uneven Stories." *Minneapolis Star Tribune*, November 22, 1998, p. 18F. In practically the only negative review of *Hunger*, Carter says that Chang's writing is basic, writing-school fare and that her psychological insights are simple; argues that Chang stays close to the themes of assimilation and forgetfulness according to which immigrant parents want to escape the past while the children want to understand it.

Chang, Lan Samantha. "Memories That Reach Back into Consciousness." In *Illuminating Fiction: A Collection of Author Interviews with Today's Best Writers of Fiction*, conducted and edited by Sherry Ellis. Los Angeles: Red Hen Press, 2009. Chang discusses how she creates her fiction.

_____. "Out of Parents' Silence Comes a Daughter's Tales." Interview by Scott Martelle. *Los Angeles Times*, December 21, 1998, p. E3. In this interview/feature story, Chang talks about her parents' reticence about the past and her creation of stories that allowed her to work through questions about them. Martelle discusses the universality of the stories, which Chang says are about things that happen over and over again. Chang discusses the conflict in her stories between children who wish to know their parents and parents who want to make new lives in America for their children.

Kurjatto-Renard, Patrycja. "Metaphors of Hunger and Satiety in Patricia Chao's *Monkey King* and Lan Samantha Chang's *Hunger*." In *Transnational, National, and Personal Voices: New Perspectives on Asian American and Asian Diasporic Women Writers*, edited by Begoña Simal anjd Elisabetta Marino. Piscataway, N.J.: Transaction, 2004. Examines how the two works depict both the relationship of food to artistic creation and the generation and cultural gaps, which Kurjatto-Renard argues are "typical" themes of "immigrant fiction."

Messud, Claire. "A Hole in Our House." *The New York Times*, October 25, 1998, pp. 7, 24. In this review, Messud says that Chang offers no easy resolution for the immigrant experience; she maintains that Chang's stories express internal struggles in a complex way. Discusses several stories, praising Chang's ability to create concrete descriptions of the abstract.

Rubin, Sylvia. "A Hunger for Heritage." *The San Francisco Chronicle*, December 2, 1998, p. E1. In this biographical sketch/review/interview, Chang says she writes from a position of deep incomprehension; she discusses how her parents' secrets about their past have allowed her to use her imagination to re-create that past for herself. She also describes how her parents disapproved of her decision to be a writer rather than a doctor or a lawyer.

Ryan, Suzanne C. "Immigrants in *Hunger* Starved of Their Past." *The Boston Globe*, October 9, 1998, p. D10. Notes that while the stories focus on the Chinese immigrant experience, they could really be about any race or nationality; Ryan says the desire for love, prosperity, parental approval, and strong family ties in Chang's stories is universal. Discusses the common theme in the stories of well-meaning parents who, despite sacrifices, cannot give their children what they need most--a firm foundation of cultural and family history.

Salm, Arthur. "Author Taps into Immigrant Experiences." *The San Diego Union-Tribune*, November 15, 1998, p. E4. An interview/biographical sketch in which Chang talks about what she thinks is central to the immigrant experience--the artifacts of personal history--and laments that she has nothing to represent her grandparents' lives in China. Chang discusses the way she writes, the relationship between the short story and the novel, and her work on her first novel.

Wan, Helen C. "Children of Broken Dreams." *The Washington Post*, October 18, 1998, p. X11. Wan argues that Chang's stories go beyond the current appeal of ethnicity and are truly universal in their significance; she discusses how the stories focus on fragility and family relationships rather than merely the immigrant experience. Wan argues that the stories emphasize universal themes of loneliness, longing, unfulfilled ambition, love and loss, and memory and forgetting.

Charles E. May

DAN CHAON

Born: Omaha, Nebraska; June 11, 1964

PRINCIPAL SHORT FICTION

Fitting Ends, 1996
Among the Missing, 2001
"The Bees," 2003
"Five Forgotten Instincts," 2004
"Shepherdess," 2006

OTHER LITERARY FORMS

Dan Chaon (shawn) is the author of two novels: *You Remind Me of Me* (2004) and *Await Your Reply* (2009). Both novels are set in the same midwestern and Great Plains milieu that is featured in Chaon's short fiction, and both consist of interwoven narratives that suggest the influence of his short fiction on Chaon's longer works. *You Remind Me of Me* was a finalist for the National Book Award. *Await Your Reply* was named a notable book of the year by both the *San Francisco Chronicle* and *The Washington Post.* Chaon also has been recognized for personal essays, including an account of his late wife's battle with cancer, "What Happened to Sheila?"

ACHIEVEMENTS

Dan Chaon has been honored with four Pushcart Prizes for his stories "The Illustrated Encyclopedia of the Animal Kingdom" (2000), "Seven Types of Ambiguity" (2002), "I Demand to Know Where You Are Taking Me" (2003), and "Shepherdess" (2008). He received a second prize from the O. Henry Awards for "Big Me" in 2001. His contributions to *The Best American Short Stories* include "Fitting Ends" (1996) and "The Bees" (2003); "Five Forgotten Instincts" appeared in *The Best Nonrequired Reading* (2005). His story "Sorrow Comes in the Night," which first appeared in *Book,* was a finalist for the National

Magazine Award in 2002; "Shepherdess," which first appeared in the *Virginia Quarterly Review,* was a finalist in 2007. In recognition of his promise as a fiction writer, Chaon received an Academy Award in Literature from the American Academy of Arts and Letters in 2006.

BIOGRAPHY

Dan Chaon was raised by adoptive parents in Sidney, Nebraska, a rural community at the western edge of the Great Plains that becomes the fictional "Beck, Nebraska" in Chaon's well-known story "Big Me." His father was a construction worker and electrician. No one in his family had ever gone to college. At an early age, Chaon took an interest in issues of identity, and his own experiences eventually formed the impetus for his debut novel, *You Remind Me of Me,* which features a young mother who gives up her baby for adoption. Chaon says that he started reading *The New Yorker* at the age of ten and began submitting his fiction to magazines while in junior high school. One of the editors to whom he sent a manuscript while a teenager, Reginald Gibbons of *TriQuarterly,* urged Chaon to apply to Northwestern University. Chaon graduated from Northwestern with a degree in creative writing, where Gibbons served as his mentor, in 1986, and received his M.F.A. from Syracuse University in 1990.

One of Chaon's favorite teachers at Northwestern was the writer Sheila Schwartz, a former Stegner Fellow and an up-and-coming luminary in the world of literary fiction. The pair met at a Christmas party when Chaon was nineteen and Schwartz was thirty. They married four years later. (Chaon uses the subject of a student who hopes to marry his former college professor in "Late for the Wedding.") Schwartz followed Chaon to Syracuse, where she worked as a technical writer for Magnavox and taught intermittently. After Chaon's graduation, he followed her to Ohio, where she received an appointment to the English Department at Cleveland State University. The couple soon had two boys, Philip and Paul. Schwartz, who went on to publish a major collection of short stories, *Imagine a Great White Light* (1993), and a well-received novel, *Lies Will Take You Somewhere* (2009), died of ovarian cancer at the age of fifty-six. In the wake of her death, Chaon has written extensively about her life and legacy.

Chaon started drawing critical notice for his short fiction in the early 1990's as his work appeared in multiple prominent literary journals. *Ploughshares* published "Fraternity" in 1992, and *Triquarterly* published "Going Out" in 1989, "Rapid Transit" in 1994, and "Fitting Ends" in 1995. Other short stories debuted in *American Short Fiction* and *Story*, leading up to the publication of his first collection, *Fitting Ends, and Other Stories*, by Northwestern's *TriQuarterly Books* in 1996. By the time he rolled out his second collection, *Among the Missing*, five years later, Chaon was widely regarded as the master of the modern-day ghost story. He was among the distinguished judges of the coveted

Dan Chaon (Getty Images)

Story Prize in 2004. Chaon started teaching as a visiting instructor at Ohio University and, after a brief stint at Cleveland State, joined the faculty of Oberlin College as the Pauline Delaney Professor of Creative Writing.

ANALYSIS

Dan Chaon has confessed in interviews that he was fascinated by ghost stories as a child, and much of his short fiction is distinguished by the haunting menace of the supernatural. His short fiction contains both postmodern devices and elements of the paranormal, but his works are better classified as traditional realist stories with uncanny themes. He has a gift for lyrical yet matter-of-fact prose, perfectly pitched to capture the dreary world of the Nebraska prairie, and in that sense he is far more the heir to Willa Cather than he is the successor of Edgar Allan Poe or H. P. Lovecraft. Chaon's world is mysterious and often cold, an insular universe where all sorts of unspeakable horrors may occur. However, at the core of his writing is a fascination with childhood and adolescence, with the relationships of parents and siblings, with the search for identity in a world whose essence is constantly in flux. His stories reveal the disturbing message that people often know far less than they think about other human beings, even those dearest to them, and that truly transcending the barrier between people is the great challenge and illusion of existence.

"FITTING ENDS"

"Fitting Ends," which appeared in *The Best American Short Stories, 1996*, was the first of Chaon's stories to garner a national audience. The tale is narrated by Stewart, a college fund-raiser hailing from tiny Pyramid, Nebraska, whose brother, Del, was killed in a train accident as a teenager and whose death was later written up in a volume called *More True Tales of the Weird and Supernatural.* Prior to the night on which Del's truck broke down and he was struck by an oncoming locomotive while walking home, multiple train conductors during the course of several years had reported running over boys who matched his description on the same stretch of track, only to discover that these victims left behind no bodies. However, these ghost sightings merely provide a backdrop for a story far more important to Stewart--namely, how his relationship with his brother deteriorated prior to Del's death. Stewart and Del had never been close, and on one occasion Del had even attempted to strangle Stewart without provocation. Eventually, Del was sent on an Outward Bound wilderness program for juvenile delinquents.

The turning point in the brothers' relationship occurs shortly after a newly reformed Del returns from his Outward Bound trip, when the narrator nearly slips off a grain elevator and Del yanks Stewart to safety, saving his life. Rather than thanking Del, Stewart accuses his older brother of pushing him, an accusation that undermines Del's determination to reform. From that moment forward, Del treats Stewart as though he does not exist, in essence rendering him a ghost in their own home. Only then, too late, does Stewart realize that he had valued his relationship with his brother. When an adult Stewart, married and with a son of his own, reflects upon his false charge against Del, Stewart recognizes the harm that his lie has done to both himself and his family. As with many of Chaon's stories, "Fitting Ends" proves haunting, not because of its supernatural elements but because of its penetrating insights into domestic relationships. Another Chaon trademark also appears in the story: a first-person narrator willing to speak candidly of his own shortcomings. These include the scene in which Stewart uses the story of his brother's death to convince a college coed to sleep with him, and the disquiet he feels, while recalling a happy moment in which his father and brother assembled a model ship, that his relationship with his own son might disintegrate as quickly as did Del's with his parents.

"BIG ME"

In awarding Chaon's best-known work, "Big Me," an O. Henry Prize in 2001, novelist Michael Chabon described the unsettling story as one that evokes the horrors of having "wandered into the wrong life with no hope of escape." The protagonist, Andy O'Day, is another of Chaon's middle-aged male narrators looking back on the domestic conflict of his childhood. As an eight-year-old boy in Beck, Nebraska, O'Day had conjured a parallel fantasy universe in which he was Detective O'Day, solving crimes in a metropolis populated by larger-than-life characters based upon his relatives and neighbors. (A representative Chaon detail is that Mr. Karaffa, the seventh-grade science teacher in Beck, is a lycanthrope who preys upon junior high school girls in anti-Beck.) During the summer after sixth grade, Mr. Mickleson moves into one of the houses on the narrator's block. O'Day believes that Mickleson is actually the middle-aged version of himself, come from the future to deliver him a message, and O'Day repeatedly sneaks into the hard-drinking man's home to search for clues. Eventually, a drunken Mickleson catches him and discovers the notebook in which O'Day has recorded his fantastic suspicions. When Mickleson threatens to share with the narrator the secret that he has allegedly brought from the future, O'Day flees. Mickleson soon moves away, but the episode haunts O'Day into adulthood.

As with most of Chaon's stories of the supernatural, the narrative never deviates conclusively from reality. Instead, every event in the story can be read and understood within the rules of the known world, as a product either of childhood imagination or of distorted memory. This careful tightrope walk between realism and magical realism is a signature Chaon device, one that he uses to remind readers that his stories are far more personal tragedies than tales of the occult. In "Big Me," the adult O'Day compares notes with his brother, Mark, who insists that their childhood was one of relentless abuse and suffering. Readers learn that O'Day's parents eventually go bankrupt, then divorce, and that his erratic mother abandons her children for a second marriage in Mexico and is never heard from again. O'Day's sister suffers severe brain damage in an automobile accident and lives in a group home. Later, when talking with his father by phone, O'Day makes up a girlfriend whose adventures he narrates for months, as though she were real. Much as O'Day escapes the suffering of his childhood through his fantasy life, he continues to indulge in such escapism into adulthood. Underlying all of these incidents is the disquieting question of whether O'Day has become an adult that his childhood self would admire.

"THE BEES"

After the publication of his second collection, *Among the Missing*, Chaon's fiction took a sinister turn, and the hints of violence in his early work became more explicit. A dramatic example of this darker phase is "The Bees," in which a middle-aged father, Gene, finds the harmony of his family life haunted by the legacy of an earlier family that he had abandoned. The story begins with a rather straightforward domestic problem: Gene and Karen's five-year-old son, Frankie, is suffering from "screaming attacks" while he sleeps. As the family struggles to find a solution for these outbursts, however, the narrative reveals that Frankie is the same age as an earlier son, DJ, whom Gene deserted in a drunken rage years before. Gene arrives at the realization that his first wife, Mandy, and their son have died and that DJ has come back to revenge himself upon his father's happiness. Gene suspects that DJ is responsible for Frankie's nightmares, although Gene cannot explain how. The narrative veers into the ominous when a caller whose name Gene's wife cannot understand-- "BB or BJ"--leaves a message for Gene. As is often the case in Chaon's work, this call could indeed be a coincidence or a wrong number, but it also might be the dead son phoning to warn his father. Eventually, after Gene dreams that DJ has returned to destroy Gene's life, he wakes up to find the house aflame, his new wife and his son victims of the blaze. Frankie's mouth, in death, is frozen into a scream.

Unlike his earlier stories, which were mostly set on the Great Plains, Chaon settles on his adopted Cleveland as the setting for "The Bees," while allowing that Gene's first marriage disintegrated in Nebraska. In a change from many of the stories in his first two collections, which emphasize settings, geography plays a far less significant role in this narrative. Instead, the emphasis is on tight-knit, dialogue-driven scenes. The author has described this piece as a breakthrough story and has credited the influence of George Saunders, Kelly Link, and Kevin Brockmeier, among others, as having influenced this later phase of his writing. "The Bees" takes more chances than any of Chaon's earlier works, in terms of structure and emotion, and the result is both his deepest and his strangest story to date.

"SHEPHERDESS"

While Chaon has positioned himself as a master of ghostly realism, some of his stories, including "Shepherdess" and "Five Forgotten Instincts,"

display a ruminative quality that contrasts with the matter-of-fact nature of his prior work. Humor also becomes more apparent in his stories. In "Shepherdess," for example, a man relates, through a series of interlocking scenes, both the tragedy of his mother's recent death and the minor crisis that ensues when his girlfriend, while attempting to break up with him, accidentally falls out of a tree. The first-person narrator in "Shepherdess" echoes the earnest narrators of "Fitting Ends" and "Big Me," but this man has departed Nebraska for Los Angeles, and he is more edgy than his predecessors. He is also able to make the reader laugh at his own expense, as when he concedes that his minor celebrity (he plays the voice of "Fuzzy the Fieldmouse" on television) will not gain him any special privileges in the hospital emergency room. Rather than uncanny, "Shepherdess" is haunting in a bittersweet and philosophical way. It features an oblique ending, as does "Five Forgotten Instincts," which distinguishes it structurally from the extremely direct, often overpowering endings of stories such as "Big Me" and "The Bees." In addition, the story reprises two symbolic Chaon details that first appear in "Big Me," a deaf mother and the threat of falling from an elevated height, although in "Shepherdess," the narrator is unable to prevent his girlfriend from toppling to the ground.

OTHER MAJOR WORKS

LONG FICTION: *You Remind Me of Me*, 2004; *Await Your Reply*, 2009.

NONFICTION: "What Happened to Sheila?" 2009.

BIBLIOGRAPHY

Charles, Ron. "Web of Lies: Identity Crises in the Internet Age." *The Washington Post*, August 26, 2009. A review of Chaon's novel *Await Your Reply* that describes his use of horror and suspense, which permeate his short stories.

Handley, Derek. "Interview: Dan Chaon." *Hot Metal Bridge* (Spring, 2007). An interview in which Chaon discusses his childhood and his short-story collections.

Leahy, Anna. "*Among the Missing.*" *Prairie Schooner* 77, no. 1 (Spring, 2003): p. 184-186. An insightful review of Chaon's short-story collection.

Lowry, Beverly. "The Disappeared." *The New York Times*, August 5, 2001. Review of *Among the Missing*, which describes Chaon's themes.

Jacob M. Appel

FRED CHAPPELL

Born: Canton, North Carolina; May 28, 1936

PRINCIPAL SHORT FICTION
Moments of Light, 1980
More Shapes Than One, 1991
The Lodger, 1993
Ancestors and Others: New and Selected Stories, 2009

OTHER LITERARY FORMS

Fred Chappell (CHAP-uhl) is an award-winning poet whose works include the four-volume *Midquest* cycle and two collections of critical essays on poetry. He has written eight novels, including a quartet featuring the multigenerational Kirkman family: *I Am One of You Forever* (1985); *Brighten the Corner Where You Are* (1989); *Farewell, I'm Bound to Leave You* (1996); and *Look Back All the Green Valley* (1999).

ACHIEVEMENTS

Fred Chappell has been honored with grants from both the Rockefeller Foundation and the National Institute of Arts and Letters. He was awarded the Prix de Meilleur des Lettres Étranger by the French Academy in 1971 for his novel *Dagon* (1968), the Sir Walter Raleigh Award in 1973 for his novel *The Gaudy Place* (1972), and the Bollingen Prize in poetry from the Yale University Library in 1985. He received the Ragan-Rubin Award from the North Carolina English Teachers Association and the Thomas H. Carter Prize for the Essay. He is also a recipient of the Ingersoll Foundation's T. S. Eliot Prize for Creative Writing and a two-time recipient of the World Fantasy Award for short fiction (1992, 1994). His poetry is the subject of a

tribute anthology of essays, *Dream Garden: The Poetic Vision of Fred Chappell* (1997).

BIOGRAPHY

Fred Davis Chappell was born in Canton, North Carolina, on May 28, 1936, and was raised on his grandparents' farm in the mountains outside Asheville. He attended Canton High School and enrolled at Duke University, but he was expelled at the beginning of his junior year for misconduct. In 1959, he married his high school sweetheart, Susan Nicholls, and the following year their son, Heath, was born. He returned to Duke to finish his studies and graduated with a B.A. in English in 1961.

Chappell enrolled in the graduate English program at Duke on a three-year National Defense Education Act fellowship and was completing his master's thesis when he was approached by a New York publisher to write a novel. *It Is Time, Lord*, which he wrote in six weeks, was published in 1963. The following year he published his first short story in *The Saturday Evening Post* and received his M.A. *The World Between the Eyes*, the first of more than a dozen volumes of his poetry, was published in 1971. Chappell began teaching English at the University of North Carolina in Greensboro, a position he was offered while still a graduate student at Duke, and where he taught for forty years until his retirement in 2004. In 1997, Chappell was appointed the Poet Laureate of North Carolina, a post he held until 2002.

ANALYSIS

Like his contemporaries Reynolds Price and Peter Taylor, Fred Chappell draws on his rural southern background for much of his fiction. However, Chappell is not easily pigeonholed as a "southern writer." His short fiction includes, in addition to tales in the southern folk tradition, period stories with European settings and tales of the supernatural. The forms Chappell's stories take also vary widely, from realistic drama to biblical allegory, gothic fantasy, and whimsical humor.

Most of Chappell's stories are character-driven and concerned with personal ideals challenged by private experience. John Lang, in his essay "Illuminating the Stricken World: Fred Chappell's *Moments of Light*," locates the dramatic core of Chappell's stories in the "conflict between transcendent and temporal values" that ensues when characters cling to noble beliefs that are either naïve or outmoded in the world at large. This conflict manifests as a tension between opposites incarnated in the story's different characters: the traditional and the modern, the sacred and the profane, the civilized and the primitive, the artistic and the scientific, the rational and the irrational. Chappell's stories often focus on family relationships, notably fathers and sons embarked on rites of passage from childhood innocence to adult experience. Notwithstanding the "fallen world" that Lang feels this clash of values presupposes, Chappell's outlook is essentially optimistic. His innocent characters are rarely crushed by their experiences. They emerge edified, rather than disillusioned, and with a broadened base of experience.

"THE MAKER OF ONE COFFIN"

"The Maker of One Coffin" is typical of Chappell's tales in the southern folk tradition, presenting a slice of rural life with gentle humor that softens its account of young Jess's passage from childhood innocence to adult experience through an early encounter with death. Uncle Runkin, a visiting relative from Jess's mother's side of the family, is a death-obsessed man who sleeps in a coffin and reads tombstone epitaphs for amusement. Joe Robert, Jess's practical-minded father, teases Uncle Runkin relentlessly for his morbidness. Uncle Runkin and Joe Robert represent the opposite extremes of attitudes toward death between which Jess must choose or find a middle ground. As a joke, Jess and his father put a skeleton borrowed from the local school in the coffin, hoping to scare Uncle Runkin.

The next day, Runkin gives no clue that the prank has worked, but the skeleton is missing. Jess sneaks into Runkin's room to look for the skeleton and,

attracted to Runkin's coffin, climbs into it and has a comforting vision of death, which is interrupted when the startled Runkin walks in on him. Uncle Runkin leaves the next day, to his and the family's relief, and the mystery of the skeleton is solved when it is discovered that he has disarticulated it and secreted all of the bones in 3,034 hiding places around the house. An older Jess muses how, for the next twenty years, "When you went looking for a Mason jar rubber or a length of string you would turn up a toebone or a metacarpal"--a lesson, perhaps, that even when we choose to ignore it, death *is* an inescapable part of life.

"BLUE DIVE"

The themes of Chappell's stories often resonate with myth and legend, giving them a timelessness. "Blue Dive," set in a southern roadhouse in the 1970's, is a variation on the folktale of John Henry, in which Chappell explores the clash of traditional and modern values. Elderly African American blues guitarist Stovebolt Johnson arrives in a small southern town to take a job offer made three years earlier to perform regularly at the Blue Dive roadhouse. The roadhouse has since been sold to Locklear Hawkins, a progressive young African American man, who prefers a jukebox for music. Stovebolt offers to provide an evening of free entertainment to prove that he can outplay the jukebox. He gives an inspired performance that pleases the Blue Dive patrons, but Locklear is implacable: He wants nothing to do with Stovebolt and the old ways of southern blacks that Stovebolt and his blues music represent. Stovebolt leaves dejected but dignified, knowing that, like John Henry, he has outperformed the machine. The story ends with him composing a blues song about his trial at the Blue Dive, adding a new chapter of his own to the legacy of misery and suffering memorialized in the blues.

"MOMENTS OF LIGHT"

"Moments of Light" is one of several period stories in which Chappell uses compassionate and sympathetic portraits of historical personalities to explore universal human concerns and ideals. Events center on a meeting between the composer Franz Joseph Haydn and his contemporary, astronomer William Herschel, both expatriate Germans living in England in the latter half of the eighteenth century. Both men are geniuses in their fields and share similar tastes and interests, but Haydn postpones the much anticipated meeting with the astronomer out of his unspoken fear that Herschel's perspective-shifting discoveries are inimical to the principles of harmony on which Haydn's music is based. At the meeting, Haydn finds Herschel a gracious host with a genuine respect for what he calls "the Harmony of the Universe." When Herschel treats Haydn to a demonstration of his telescope, Haydn feels his spirit drawn from his body to the remote celestial body he is viewing. There he discovers a world of indescribable beauty that supports a harmonious music equivalent to his own. Back in his own body, Haydn realizes that Herschel's discoveries describe a vast and orderly cosmic score in which Haydn's art and Herschel's science contribute equally to the harmonic music of the spheres. Coincidentally or not, Haydn composes some of his most inspired music in the years that follow.

"THE LODGER"

Winner of the World Fantasy Award, "The Lodger" is a humorous fantasy that allegorically addresses one of Chappell's favorite themes, the challenges that the mundane world poses to the creative spirit. Librarian Robert Ackley is an average man with ordinary tastes and a boring job transferring card catalog entries to a computer system. A book lover with wide-ranging interests, he chances upon a volume of verse by the obscure early twentieth century poet Lyman Scoresby and accidentally resurrects his spirit. Scoresby, an arrogant man with an exaggerated sense of his own importance, lodges in Ackley's subconscious and tries to turn Ackley into an appropriate vessel for Scoresby's soul by subliminally cultivating decadent passions, such as a taste for absinthe and a desire for unconventional sex. Ackley attempts to exorcise Scoresby by indulging in behavior that Ackley hopes will disgust the poet: eating junk food, watching bad television programs, and reading poetry worse than Scoresby's. Ackley succeeds only when he begins reading postmodern literary criticism that is more impenetrable and self-important than Scoresby's verse. Surprisingly, Ackley discovers a latent talent for such writing and becomes a critic himself. Having exorcised the poet from his soul, he becomes a crippled version of the poet he might have been.

MORE SHAPES THAN ONE

The title of *More Shapes Than One* derives from John Milton's essay *Areopagitica* (1644) and refers to the variety of forms truth takes in the world. The majority of the stories in the book are fantasies, yet, as the title suggests, fantasy is but one of a variety of possible approaches Chappell uses to explore the ideas that inform his fiction.

A theme that predominates in the thirteen stories is the fallen world in which ideals of beauty and order have been subverted. Characters who seek to transcend the corrupted forms of these ideals find themselves thwarted and often forced to make compromises. The first story, "Linnaeus Forgets," sets the tone for the tales that follow. It tells of eighteenth century botanist Carl Linnaeus, who is ridiculed by his colleagues as being prurient for his sexual classifications of plants. Linnaeus is vindicated during an experience he later dismisses as a dream, in which he studies an exotic plant and discovers an entire world in its leaves that transcends human notions of morality. This theme finds exquisite expression in the World Fantasy Award-winning story "The Somewhere Doors," about an underappreciated writer of fantasy and science-fiction stories who is told by a mysterious visitor that sometime in the future he will be given a choice of two doors, each of which leads to a different reality. The writer spends much of his life waiting expectantly to see the doors, only to realize years later that he has already explored the possibilities each offers but at the expense of "the entrance to the world in which he already lived." Although much has passed him by, he remains hopeful that "much awaited him still."

The book's sober efforts are counterbalanced by an equal number of comical treatments of the same ideas. In "The Adder," a book of occult knowledge manifests its corrupting power by poisoning the text of any book shelved next to it, turning Milton's beautifully measured verse into drunken doggerel that gets laughably worse each time the narrator inspects it. "Mankind Journeys Through Forests of Symbols" grapples with the idealized in a banal setting, imagining some of the problems a rural police force might encounter trying to get rid of a symbolist who materializes in the middle of the main highway leading into town.

ANCESTORS AND OTHERS

Unlike Chappell's previous large collection of work, *The Fred Chappell Reader* (1987), which contained short fiction, novel excerpts, and poems, *Ancestors and Others* consists exclusively of short stories. Most of the stories have appeared elsewhere, as part of *I Am One of You Forever*, *Moments of Light*, and *More Shapes Than One*. Of the more recent work, five have appeared in literary journals in the past few years. The stories of this collection are set mainly in the historical yet mythic Appalachian setting that characterizes much of Chappell's work. However, the range of story genres demonstrates Chappell's mastery: character sketches, folk fables, ghost stories, science fiction, and tall tales. Many of Chappell's best-known pieces are present, including "Moments of Light," "The Somewhere Doors," and "The Lodger." Only two stories, "Ember" and "Duet," have never before appeared in print. In the ghost story "Ember," a fugitive flees up Ember Mountain, where he is given harbor by the very object of his horror. In "Duet," which also takes place near Ember Mountain, folk musician Kermit Wilson is asked to play at the funeral of his best friend, who has just met a violent and sudden death, and where to his undoing he is discovered by a record company agent. Of the other stories that appeared in journals, "Christmas Gift!" and "Tradition" both take place in the same western North Carolina setting as the poetry cycle *Midquest* and the Kirkland family fiction quartet. Both concern the relationship between Jerry, a recent college graduate returned home who seems similar to the Jesse Kirkland of the earlier stories, and Curly Spurling, a salty-but-wise older man who recalls Virgil Campbell, mentor to Jesse in the stories, and the "Fred" narrator of *Midquest*: "Curly was a good twenty years Jerry's senior and treated his young co-worker as a pupil. . . . Curly felt the young man needed instruction now and again--and so did Jerry." While "Christmas Gift!" is a comedy that gets further and further out of hand, "Tradition" is a tragedy in which the aftermath of war haunts a hunting party. "Bon Ton" is a darkly clever take on the role of the sin-eater, where a visitor hears the gossip spilling from a small-town community. The current fascination with genealogy is parodied in the title story, "Ancestors": "Harry and Lydie were enduring their

third ancestor and finding it a rum go . . . and now they regretted the hour they had joined the Ancestor Program of the Living History Series." "Gift of Roses" is a solid tale of the supernatural for which Chappell is so renowned, where gifts are often burdens, though no less readily accepted. As in much of Chappell's work, these stories betray a tension between the rural Appalachian culture in which Chappell was raised, and yet for which he has evident nostalgia, and the intellectual traditions in which he was classically educated and for which he served as an educator for more than forty years.

OTHER MAJOR WORKS

LONG FICTION: *It Is Time, Lord*, 1963; *The Inkling*, 1965; *Dagon*, 1968; *The Gaudy Place*, 1973; *I Am One of You Forever*, 1985; *Brighten the Corner Where You Are*, 1989; *Farewell, I'm Bound to Leave You*, 1996; *Look Back All the Green Valley*, 1999.

POETRY: *The World Between the Eyes*, 1971; *River*, 1975; *The Man Twice Married to Fire*, 1977; *Bloodfire*, 1978; *Awakening to Music*, 1979; *Wind Mountain*, 1979; *Earthsleep*, 1980; *Driftlake: A Lieder Cycle*, 1981; *Midquest*, 1981 (includes *River*, 1975); *Castle Tzingal*, 1984; *Source*, 1985; *First and Last Words*, 1989; *C: Poems*, 1993; *Spring Garden: New and Selected Poems*, 1995; *Family Gathering*, 2000; *Backsass*, 2004; *Shadow Box*, 2009.

NONFICTION: *Plow Naked: Selected Writings on Poetry*, 1993; *A Way of Happening: Observations of Contemporary Poetry*, 1998.

EDITED TEXT: *Locales: Poems from the Fellowship of Southern Writers*, 2003.

MISCELLANEOUS: *The Fred Chappell Reader*, 1987.

BIBLIOGRAPHY

Bizzarro, Patrick. *Dream Garden: The Poetic Vision of Fred Chappell*. Baton Rouge: Louisiana State University Press: 1997. A collection of essays mainly on Chappell's poetry, which also includes an interview with the author; an essay, "Chappell's Aesthetic Agenda," which examines the larger project of the connected poetry cycle *Midquest* to the four Jess Kirkland novel/story collections; and a survey of the collected Fred Chappell Papers at Duke University by Alex Albright.

Broughton, Irv. "Fred Chappell." In *The Writer's Mind: Interviews with American Authors*. Vol. 3. Fayetteville: University of Arkansas Press, 1990. Far-ranging interview in which Chappell discusses influences on his writing and the differences between writing fiction and poetry. Discussion of his short fiction touches upon his historical short stories as attempts to liberate historical personalities from the history books and make them seem living human beings.

Campbell, Hilbert. "Fred Chappell's Urn of Memory: *I Am One of You Forever*." *Southern Literary Journal* (Spring, 1993): 103-112. Discusses the title work (which is often called a novel, though it is a series of ten linked short stories) and others in terms of Chappell's preoccupation with the problem of recapturing one's past in some way that is meaningful to the present.

Chappell, Fred. "First Attempts." *Turnstile* (1992): 71-84. Discusses the changes that being objective about subjective feelings makes in a writer and how a young writer comes to appreciate this. As a young man, Chappell wrote science-fiction stories because "plotting real experiences proved impossible; plotting what I made up proved to be fairly easy." Once he learned how to combine analysis with vision, his interest shifted from stories of the fantastic to stories based on his personal life.

_____. "Fred Chappell." Interview by Tersh Palmer. *Appalachian Journal* (Summer, 1992): 402-410. Interview that touches on all aspects of Chappell's creative efforts, including his poetry and novels. Of his short fiction, Chappell observes that critics tend to divide his work into realistic stories and fantasies, but he sees "no need to distinguish between what is imaginary and what is objective . . . both ways of writing are ways to try to deal with reality on the plane of literature."

Dillard, Annie. Foreword to *Moments of Light*. Raleigh, N.C.: New South, 1980. Critical exegesis of the stories in Chappell's first collection, which Dillard interprets as a history of human experience. In Dillard's view, the parable-like stories in the first half of the book establish a theoretical and historical framework for the morally complex stories with contemporary settings that make up the second half. Recurring themes in the stories include one's search for a just moral order in a fallen world, one's longing for transcendence of the temporal world, and one's use of art to reconcile the "hope of harmony with his experience of chaos."

Dziemianowicz, Stefan. "Fred Chappell." In *The St. James Guide to Horror, Ghost, and Gothic Writers*, edited by David A. Pringle. Detroit: St. James, 1998. Brief exploration of Chappell's weird fiction and his debt to H. P. Lovecraft in his novel *Dagon* and his short stories "Weird Tales" and "The Adder." Discusses Chappell's work as an extension of the southern gothic tradition.

Hyde, Gene. "The Southern Highlands as Literary Landscape." *Southern Quarterly* (Winter, 2002): 86-99. An interview with Chappell and Donald Harington in which they discuss their friendship, careers, and their views on the nostalgic versions of the Appalachians.

Lang, John. "Illuminating the Stricken World: Fred Chappell's *Moments of Light*." *South Central Review* (Winter, 1986): 95-103. Close reading of Chappell's first short-fiction collection, *Moments of Light*, the eleven stories of which the author views as interrelated by the themes of lost innocence and the quest for justice. Follows the arc the stories describe as they move from biblical allegory to historical parable and finally to contemporary realism. Concludes that Chappell's stories all elaborate the concept of a fallen world in which humanity is forever seeking transcendence.

Stefan Dziemianowicz
Updated by Heidi K. Czerwiec

JOHN CHEEVER

Born: Quincy, Massachusetts; May 27, 1912
Died: Ossining, New York; June 18, 1982

PRINCIPAL SHORT FICTION

The Way Some People Live, 1943
The Enormous Radio, and Other Stories, 1953
"The Country Husband," 1954
The Housebreaker of Shady Hill, and Other Stories,
    1958
Some People, Places, and Things That Will Not
    Appear in My Next Novel, 1961
The Brigadier and the Golf Widow, 1964
The World of Apples, 1973
The Stories of John Cheever, 1978
Thirteen Uncollected Stories, 1994
Collected Stories, and Other Writings, 2009

OTHER LITERARY FORMS

Believing that "fiction is our most intimate and acute means of communication, at a profound level, about our deepest apprehensions and intuitions on the meaning of life and death," John Cheever (CHEE-vur) devoted himself to the writing of stories and novels. Although he kept voluminous journals, he wrote only a handful of essays and even fewer reviews, and only one television screenplay, *The Shady Hill Kidnapping,* which aired January 12, 1982, on the Public Broadcasting Service. A number of Cheever's works have also been adapted by other writers, including several early short stories such as "The Town House" (play, 1948), "The Swimmer" (film, 1968), "Goodbye, My Brother" as *Children* (play, 1976), and "O Youth and Beauty," "The Five-Forty-Eight," and "The Sorrows of Gin" (teleplays, 1979). Benjamin Cheever has edited selections of his father's correspondence, *The Letters of John Cheever* (1988), and journals, *The Journals of John Cheever* (1991).

ACHIEVEMENTS

A major twentieth century novelist, John Cheever has achieved even greater fame as a short-story writer. He published his first story, "Expelled," in *The New Republic* when he was only eighteen. Reviewers of his first collection, *The Way Some People Live*, judged Cheever to be a promising young writer. Numerous awards and honors followed: two John Simon Guggenheim Memorial Foundation grants (1951, 1961), a Benjamin Franklin award for "The Five-Forty-Eight" (1955), an O. Henry Award for "The Country Husband" (1956), election to the National Institute of Arts and Letters in 1957, elevation to the American Academy in 1973, a National Book Award in 1958 for *The Wapshot Chronicle* (1957), the Howells Medal in 1965 for *The Wapshot Scandal* (1964), cover stories in *Time* (1964) and *Newsweek* (1977), the Edward MacDowell Medal in 1979, a Pulitzer Prize and a National Book Critics Circle award (both in 1978), an American Book Award (1979) for *The Stories of John Cheever*, and the National Medal for Literature (1982). Nevertheless, Cheever's achievements cannot be measured only in terms of the awards and honors that he has received (including the honorary doctorate bestowed on this high school dropout), for his most significant accomplishment was to create, with the publication of *The Stories of John Cheever*, a resurgence of interest in, and a new respect for, the short story on the part of public and publishers alike.

BIOGRAPHY

The loss of his father's job in 1930, followed by the loss of the family home and the strained marital situation caused, John Cheever believed, by his mother's growing financial and emotional dependence, all had a lifelong effect on Cheever. When he was expelled from Thayer Academy at the age of seventeen, Cheever was already committed to a writing career. His career, however, would do little to assuage his sense of emotional and economic insecurity. Although he liked to claim that "fiction is not crypto-autobiography," from the beginning his stories were drawn from his personal experiences. They have even followed him geographically: from New England, to New York City, through his military service, to the suburbs (first Scarborough, then Ossining), with side trips to Italy (1956-1957), the Soviet Union (on three government-sponsored trips), and Sing Sing prison, where he taught writing (1971-1972). The stories have, more importantly, followed Cheever over hazardous emotional terrain, transforming personal obsessions into published fictions: alcoholism, bisexuality, self-doubts, strained marital relations, and the sense of "otherness." The stories also evidence the longing for stability and home that manifested itself in three of the most enduring relationships of his fifty-year career: with the Yaddo writers' colony in Saratoga Springs, New York, beginning in 1934; with *The New Yorker*, which began publishing his work in 1935; and with his wife Mary Winternitz Cheever, whom he met in 1939 and married two years later, and with whom he bickered over the next forty years.

Cheever did not become free of his various fears and dependencies--including his nearly suicidal addiction to alcohol--until the mid-1970's. After undergoing treatment for alcoholism at Smithers Rehabilitation Center, he transformed what might well have become his darkest novel into his most affirmative. *Falconer* (1977) was both a critical and a commercial success. Like its main character, Cheever seemed for the first time in his life free, willing at least to begin talking about the private life that he had so successfully guarded, even mythified before, when he had played the part of country squire. The triumph was, however, short-lived: two neurological seizures in 1980, a kidney operation and the discovery of cancer in 1981, and, shortly after the publication of his fifth novel, the aptly and perhaps whimsically titled *Oh. What a Paradise It Seems* (1982), his death on June 18, 1982.

ANALYSIS

John Cheever has been called both "the Chekhov of the exurbs" and "Ovid in Ossining"--which suggests both the variety and the complexity of the man and his fiction. Accused by some of being a literary lightweight--a writer merely of short stories and an apologist for middle-class life--he has been more often, and more justly, praised as a master chronicler of a way of life that he both celebrates and satirizes in stories that seem at once conventional and innovative, realistic and fantastic. His stories read effortlessly, yet their seeming simplicity masks a complexity that deserves and repays close attention. The line "The light from the cottage, shining into the fog, gave the illusion of substance, and it seems as if I might stumble on a beam of light," for example, only appears simple and straightforward. It begins with a conventional image, light penetrating darkness, thus illuminating the way to truth, but the next five words undermine the "illusion" first by calling attention to it, then by paradoxically literalizing the metaphor, making this substantive light a stumbling block rather than a source of spiritual and/or philosophical truth.

"A MISCELLANY OF CHARACTERS THAT WILL NOT APPEAR IN MY NEXT NOVEL"

Nothing in Cheever's fiction of stark contrasts--light and dark, male and female, city and country--ever exists

John Cheever (Getty Images)

independent of its opposite. His stories proceed incrementally and contrapuntally, at times in curiously indirect ways. In "A Miscellany of Characters That Will Not Appear in My Next Novel," for example, Cheever's narrator banishes seven kinds of characters and situations from his fiction, including alcoholics, homosexuals, and "scornful descriptions of American landscapes." However, not only did his next novel, as well as much of the rest of his fiction, include all three, but also the very act of listing them in this "miscellany" confirms their power, giving them a prominence that far outweighs their hypothetical banishment from any later work. This play of voices and positions within individual works also exists between stories.

The same narrative situations appear in various Cheever stories--handled comically in some, tragically in others. In effect, the stories offer a series of brilliant variations on a number of basic, almost obsessive themes, of which the most general and the most recurrent, as well as the most important, is the essential conflict between his characters' spiritual longings and social and psychological (especially sexual) nature. "What I wanted to do," one of his narrator-protagonists says, is "to grant my dreams, in so incoherent a world, their legitimacy," "to celebrate," as another claims, "a world that lies spread out around us like a bewildering and stupendous dream." Their longings are tempered not only by the incoherence of their world but also by a doubt concerning whether what they long for actually exists or is only an illusion conjured out of nothing more substantial than their own ardent hopes for something or someplace or someone other than who, what, and where they presently are. Even when expressed in the most ludicrous terms possible, the characters' longings seem just as profound as they are ridiculous, as in the case of "Artemis the Honest Well Digger" searching "for a girl as pure and fresh as the girl on the oleomargarine package." The line seems both to affirm and to qualify the yearning of a character who may confuse kitsch with Kant, advertising copy with lyrical longings, but who nevertheless seems as much a holy fool as a deluded consumer.

Whether treated comically or tragically, Cheever's characters share a number of traits. Most are male, married, and white-collar workers. All--despite their Sutton Place apartments or, more often, comfortable homes in affluent Westchester communities--feel confused, dispossessed, lost; they all seem to be what the characters in Cheever's Italian stories actually are: expatriates and exiles. Physical ailments are rare, emotional ones epidemic. Instead of disease, there is the "dis-ease" of "spiritual nomadism." They are as restless as any of Cheever's most wayward plots and in need of "building a bridge" between the events of their lives as well as between those lives and their longings. Trapped in routines as restricting as any prison cell and often in marriages that seem little more than sexual battlefields, where even the hair curlers appear "bellicose," his characters appear poised between escaping into the past in a futile effort to repeat what they believe they have lost and aspiring to a lyrical future that can be affirmed, even "sung," though never quite attained. Even the latter can be dangerous. "Dominated by anticipation" (a number of Cheever's characters hope excessively), they are locked in a state of perpetual adolescence, unwilling to grow up, take responsibility, and face death in any form. Although their world may lie spread out like a bewildering and stupendous dream, they find it nevertheless confining, inhospitable, even haunted by fears of emotional and economic insecurity and a sense of personal inadequacy and inconsequentiality, their sole inheritance, it seems, from the many fathers who figure so prominently in the stories, often by virtue of their absence from the lives of their now middle-aged sons. Adrift in an incoherent world and alone in the midst of suburbs zoned for felicity, they suffer frequent blows to their already fragile sense of self-esteem, seeing through yet wanting the protection of the veneer of social decorum and ceremoniousness that is the outward and visible sign of American middle-class aspiration and which Cheever's characters do not so much court as covet.

"THE ENORMOUS RADIO"

The thinness of that veneer is especially apparent in "The Enormous Radio," a work that shows little trace of the Ernest Hemingway style that marks many of Cheever's earlier stories. The story begins realistically enough. Jim and Irene Westcott, in their mid-thirties, are an average couple in all respects but one: their above-average interest in classical music (and, one assumes, in the harmony and decorum that such music represents). When their old radio breaks down, Jim generously buys an expensive new one to which Irene takes an instant dislike. Like their interest in music, which they indulge as if a secret but harmless vice, this small disruption in their harmonious married life seems a minor affair, at least at first. The radio, however, appearing "like an aggressive intruder," shedding a "malevolent green light," and possessing a "mistaken sensitivity to discord," soon becomes a divisive, even diabolical presence, but the evil in this story, as in Nathaniel Hawthorne's "Young Goodman Brown," to which it has often been compared, comes from within the characters, not from without (the radio). When the radio begins to broadcast the Westcotts' neighbors' quarrels, lusts, fears, and crimes, Irene becomes dismayed, perversely entertained, and finally apprehensive; if she can eavesdrop on her neighbors' most intimate conversations, she thinks that perhaps they can listen in on hers. Hearing their tales of woe, she demands that her husband affirm their happiness. Far from easing her apprehensiveness, his words only exacerbate it as he first voices his own previously well-guarded frustrations over money, job prospects, and growing old, and as he eventually exposes his wife's own evil nature. As frustration explodes into accusation, the illusion of marital happiness that the Westcotts had so carefully cultivated shatters.

Like so many Cheever stories, "The Enormous Radio" has its origin in biographical fact: While writing in the basement of a Sutton Place apartment house, Cheever would hear the elevator going up and down and would imagine that the wires could carry his neighbors' conversations down to him.

"GOODBYE, MY BROTHER"

"Goodbye, My Brother" derives from another and far more pervasive biographical fact--Cheever's relationship with his elder brother, Fred, the father figure to whom he developed too close an attachment. Fred turned to business and for a time supported Cheever's writing but, like Cheever, eventually became an alcoholic. Beginning with "The Brothers" and culminating

in the fratricide in *Falconer*, relations between brothers figure nearly as prominently in Cheever's fiction as those between spouses. Just as stories such as "The Enormous Radio" are not simply about marital spats, "Goodbye, My Brother" is not just about sibling rivalry. Just as the relationship between Irene and the malevolent radio is actually about a condition within the marriage and more especially within Irene herself, the external relationship between the story's narrator and his brother Lawrence is actually about the narrator's own Dr. Jekyll and Mr. Hyde personality--in psychological terms, a matter of split personality and projection. The narrator objectifies in Lawrence his own fears, frustrations, and self-loathing.

Lawrence and the narrator are two of the Pommeroys who have gathered on Laud's Head in August for their annual family vacation. Like his sister, just back after her divorce, and their widowed mother, who drinks too much while trying to keep up the family's upper-crust pretensions, the narrator needs these few weeks of respite from the grind of his dead-end teaching job. Together they swim, play cards and tennis, drink, and go to costume dances, where in an almost Jungian freak of chance, all the men come dressed as football players and all the women as brides, as eloquent a statement of the sadness of their blighted but still aspiring lives as one can imagine.

Lawrence partakes in none of it. A lawyer moving from one city and job to another, he is the only family member with prospects and the only one unable to enjoy or even tolerate the illusion of happiness that the family seeks to maintain. He is also the only one willing, indeed eager, to detect the flaws and fakery in the Pommeroys' summer home, its protective sea wall, and its equally protective forms of play. Gloomy and morose as well as critical, Lawrence is, to borrow the title of another Cheever story, the worm in the Pommeroy apple. He is the messenger bearing the bad news, whom the narrator nearly kills with a blow to the head as the two walk along the beach. He strikes not only to free himself from his brother's morbid presence but also to extirpate the Lawrence side of his own divided self: Cain and Abel, murderer and good Samaritan.

Once Lawrence and his sickly looking wife and daughter leave, the narrator turns to the purifying water and the triumphant vision of his mythically named wife and sister, Helen and Diana, rising naked from the sea. The story closes on a lyrically charged note that seems both to affirm all that the Pommeroys have sought and, by virtue of the degree of lyrical intensity, to accentuate the gap between that vision and Lawrence's more factual and pessimistic point of view.

"O YOUTH AND BEAUTY"

"O Youth and Beauty" makes explicit what virtually all Cheever's stories imply--the end of youth's promise, of that hopeful vision that the ending of "Goodbye, My Brother" sought to affirm. Thus it seems ironically apt that "O Youth and Beauty" should begin with a long (two-hundred-word) Whitmanesque sentence, which, in addition to setting the scene and establishing the narrative situation, subtly evokes that Transcendental vision that Walt Whitman both espoused and, in his distinctive poetic style, sought to embody. Beginning "At the tag end of nearly every long, large Saturday night party in the suburb of Shady Hill," it proceeds through a series of long anaphoric subordinate clauses beginning with the word "when" and ending with "then Trace Bearden would begin to chide Cash Bentley about his age and thinning hair." The reader is thus introduced to what, for the partygoers, has already become something of a suburban ritual: the perfectly named Cash Bentley's hurdling of the furniture as a way of warding off death and reliving the athletic triumphs of the youth that he refuses to relinquish.

When Cash, now forty, breaks his leg, the intimations of mortality begin to multiply in his morbid mind. Although he may run his race alone, and although the Lawrentian gloominess that comes in the wake of the accident may make him increasingly isolated from his neighbors and friends, Cash is not at all unique, and his fears are extreme but nevertheless representative of a fear that pervades the entire community and that evidences itself in his wife's trying to appear younger and slimmer than she is and her "cutting out of the current copy of *Life* those scenes of mayhem, disaster, and violent death that she felt might corrupt her children." It is rather ironic that a moment later she should accidentally kill her husband in their own living room with the

starter's pistol, as he attempts to recapture the past glories of all those other late Saturday night races against time and self in an attempt always, already doomed, to recapture the past glories of his days as a young track star. The track is in fact an apt symbol for Cash's circular life, in which instead of progress one finds only the horror of Nietzschean eternal recurrence.

"THE FIVE-FORTY-EIGHT"

Upon first reading, "The Five-Forty-Eight" seems to have little in common with the blackly humorous "O Youth and Beauty." A disturbed woman, Miss Dent, follows Blake, whose secretary she had been for three weeks and whose lover she was for one night, some six months earlier. She trails him from his office building to his commuter train. Threatening to shoot him, she gets off at his stop and forces him to kneel and rub his face in the dirt for having seduced and abandoned her six months earlier. One of Cheever's least likable characters, Blake gets what he deserves. Having chosen Miss Dent as he has chosen his other women (including, it seems, his wife) "for their lack of self-esteem," he not only had her fired the day after they made love but also took the afternoon off. Miss Dent fares considerably better, for in choosing not to kill Blake she discovers "some kindness, some saneness" in herself that she believes she can put to use. Blake too undergoes a change insofar as he experiences regret for the first time and comes to understand his own vulnerability, which he has heretofore managed to safeguard by means of his "protective" routines and scrupulous observance of Shady Hill's sumptuary laws. Whether these changes will be lasting remains unclear; he is last seen picking himself up, cleaning himself off, and walking home, alone.

"The Five-Forty-Eight" is quite literally one of Cheever's darkest stories; only the dimmest of lights and the faintest of hopes shine at its end. Although it too ends at night, "The Housebreaker of Shady Hill" is one of Cheever's brightest and most cheerful works, full of the spiritual phototropism so important in *Falconer*, the novel that *Newsweek* hailed as "Cheever's Triumph." The housebreaker is thirty-six-year-old Johnny Hake, kindly and comical, who suddenly finds himself out of work, at risk of losing his house, his circle of friends, and the last shreds of his self-esteem.

Desperate for cash, he steals nine hundred dollars from a neighbor, a theft that transforms his vision of the world. Suddenly, he begins to see evil everywhere and evidence that everyone can see him for what he now is. The "moral bottom" drops out of his world but in decidedly comic fashion: Even a birthday gift from his children--an extension ladder--becomes an acknowledgment of his wrongdoing (and nearly cause for divorce). Chance, however, saves Johnny. Walking to his next victim's house, he feels a few drops of rain fall on his head and awakens from his ludicrous nightmare, his vision of the world restored. Opting for life's simple pleasures (he is after all still unemployed), he returns home and has a pleasant dream in which he is seventeen years old. Johnny cannot get his youth back, but he does get his job, and he does return the money he has stolen. The happy endings proliferate as the story slips the yoke of realism and romps in the magical realm of pure fairy tale, where, as Cheever puts it far more sardonically in his third novel, *Bullet Park* (1969), everything is "wonderful wonderful wonderful wonderful."

"THE COUNTRY HUSBAND"

Comic exaggeration and hyperbolically happy endings characterize many of Cheever's stories of the late 1950's and early 1960's. In "The Hosebreaker of Shady Hill," it is losing his job that starts Johnny Hake on his comical crime spree; in "The Country Husband," it is nearly losing his life that sends Francis Weed on an ever more absurdly comical quest for love and understanding. Weed has his brush with death when his plane is forced to make an emergency landing in a field outside Philadelphia. The danger over, his vulnerability (like Blake's) and mortality (like Cash Bentley's) established, the real damage begins when Weed can find no one to lend a sympathetic ear--not his friend, Trace Bearden, on the commuter train, not even his wife, Julia (too busy putting dinner on the table), or his children (the youngest are fighting and the oldest is reading *True Romance*). With his very own True Adventure still untold, Weed goes outside, where he hears a neighbor playing "Moonlight Sonata," rubato, "like an outpouring of tearful petulance, lonesomeness, and self-pity--of everything it was Beethoven's greatness not to know," and everything it will now be Weed's comic misfortune to experience as he embarks upon his own

True Romance with the rather unromantically named Anne Murchison, his children's new teenage babysitter.

Playing the part of a lovesick adolescent, the middle-aged Weed acts out his midlife crisis and in doing so jeopardizes his family's social standing and his marriage. The consequences are potentially serious, as are the various characters' fears and troubles (Anne's alcoholic father and Julia's "natural fear of chaos and loneliness," which leads to her obsessive partygoing). What is humorous is Cheever's handling of these fears in a story in which solecisms are slapstick, downfalls are pratfalls, and pariahs turn out to be weeds in Cheever's suburban Garden of Eden. When Francis finally decides to overcome his Emersonian self-reliance, to confide in and seek the help of a psychiatrist (who will do what neither friends nor family have thus far been willing to do--that is, listen), the first words Weed tearfully blurts out are, "I'm in love, Dr. Harzog." Since "The Country Husband" is a comedy, Weed is cured of his "dis-ease" and able to channel his desires into more socially acceptable ways (conjugal love and, humorously enough, woodworking). The story ends with a typically Cheeveresque affirmation of Fitzgerald-like romantic possibilities, no less apparent in Shady Hill than in the *Great Gatsby*'s (1925) West Egg. It is an affirmation, however, tempered once again by the tenuousness of the characters' situation in a "village that hangs, morally and economically, from a thread."

"THE DEATH OF JUSTINA"

The thread will break--although still comically--in "The Death of Justina." Here, the focus is double, on the parallel plights of the authorial narrator, a fiction writer, and the protagonist-narrator of the story that he writes (like "The Housebreaker of Shady Hill," in oral style), also a writer (of advertising copy). Briefly stated, their shared predicament is this: how (for the one) to write about and (for the other) to live in a world that seems to grow increasingly chaotic and preposterous. As the authorial narrator explains, "Fiction is art and art is the triumph over chaos (no less) and we can accomplish this only by the most vigilant exercise of choice, but in a world that changes more swiftly than we can perceive there is always the danger that our powers of selection will be mistaken and that the vision we serve will come to nothing."

The authorial narrator then offers Moses' account of the death of his wife's cousin Justina as "one example of chaos." Ordered by his doctor to stop smoking and drinking and by his boss to write copy for a product called Elixircol (something of a cross between Geritol and the Fountain of Youth), Moses suddenly finds himself at a complete loss when he tries to arrange for Justina's funeral, for Justina has died in his house and his house is an area of Proxmire Manor not zoned for death. No doctor will issue a death certificate, and the mayor refuses to sign an exemption until a quorum of the village council is available, but when Moses threatens to bury Justina in his yard, the mayor relents. Victorious but still shaken, Moses that night has a strange dream set in a vast supermarket where the shoppers stock their carts with unlabeled, shapeless packages, which are then, much to their shame, torn open at the checkout counters by brutish men who first ridicule the selections and then push the shoppers out the doors into what sounds much like Dante's inferno. The scene is amusing but, like the ludicrously comical scenes in Franz Kafka's works, also unsettling. The story does not affirm the shoppers any more than it does the village council that drew up the zoning laws, but it does understand what compels them even as it sympathetically satirizes the inadequacy of their means. As Moses points out, "How can a people who do not mean to understand death hope to understand love, and who will sound the alarm?"

"THE BRIGADIER AND THE GOLF WIDOW"

"The Brigadier and the Golf Widow" makes a similar point in a similar way. Here too, the authorial narrator is perplexed, wondering what the nineteenth century writers Charles Dickens, Anton Chekhov, Nikolai Gogol, and William Makepeace Thackeray would have made of a fallout shelter bizarrely decorated and disguised with gnomes, plaster ducks, and a birdbath. He also understands, however, that fallout shelters are as much a part of his mid-twentieth century landscape as are trees and shrubbery. The shelter in question belongs to Charlie Pastern, the country club general who spends his time calling loudly for nuclear attacks on any and all of his nation's enemies. His world begins to unravel when, by chance, he begins an affair with a neighbor whose own fears and insecurity lead her first

to promiscuity and then to demanding the key to the Pasterns' shelter--a key that the local bishop also covets. Apparently the last words of "The Death of Justina," taken verbatim from the Twenty-third Psalm, about walking through the shadow of the valley of death and fearing no evil, no longer apply.

For all the good cheer, hearty advice, biblical quotations, comical predicaments, and lyrical affirmations, there lies at the center of Cheever's fiction the fear of insufficiency and inadequacy--of shelters that will not protect, marriages that will not endure, jobs that will be lost, threads that will not hold.

"THE SWIMMER"

That the thread does not hold in "The Swimmer," Cheever's most painstakingly crafted and horrific work, is especially odd, for the story begins as comedy, a lighthearted satire, involving a group of suburban couples sitting around the Westerhazys' pool on a beautiful midsummer Sunday afternoon talking about what and how much they drank the night before. Suddenly Neddy Merrill, yet another of Cheever's middle-aged but youthfully named protagonists, decides to swim home pool to pool. More than a prank, it is for him a celebration of the fineness of the day, a voyage of discovery, a testament to life's romantic possibilities. Neddy's swim will cover eight miles, sixteen pools, in only ten pages (as printed in *The Stories of John Cheever*). Although he encounters some delays and obstacles--drinks graciously offered and politely, even ceremoniously, drunk, a thorny hedge to be gotten over, gravel underfoot--Neddy completes nearly half the journey in only two pages (pages 3-4; pages 1-2 are purely preparatory). The story and its reader move as confidently and rapidly as Neddy, but then there are a few interruptions: a brief rain shower that forces Neddy to seek shelter, a dry pool at one house, and a for-sale sign inexplicably posted at another. Midway through both journey and story, the point of view suddenly and briefly veers away from Neddy, who now looks pitifully exposed and foolishly stranded as he attempts to cross a divided highway. His strength and confidence ebbing, he seems unprepared for whatever lies ahead yet unable to turn back. Like the reader, he is unsure when his little joke turned so deadly serious. At the one public pool on his itinerary, he is assaulted by crowds, shrill sounds, and harsh odors. After being nearly stalled for two pages, the pace quickens ever so slightly but only to leave Neddy still weaker and more disoriented. Each "breach in the succession" exposes Neddy's inability to bridge the widening gap between his vision of the world and his actual place in it. He is painfully rebuffed by those he had previously been powerful enough to mistreat--a former mistress, a socially inferior couple whose invitations he and his wife routinely discarded. The apparent cause of Neddy's downfall begins to become clear to the reader only as it begins to become clear to Neddy--a sudden and major financial reversal--but Neddy's situation cannot be attributed to merely economic factors, nor is it susceptible to purely rational analysis. Somewhere along Neddy's and the reader's way, everything has changed: The passing of hours becomes the passage of whole seasons, perhaps even years, as realism gives way to fantasy, humor to horror as the swimmer sees his whole life pass before him in a sea of repressed memories. Somehow Neddy has woken into his own worst dream. Looking into his empty house, he comes face to face with the insecurity that nearly all Cheever's characters fear and the inadequacy that they all feel.

The stories (and novels) that Cheever wrote during the last two decades of his life grew increasingly and innovatively disparate in structure. "The Jewels of the Cabots," for example, and "The President of the Argentine" match the intensifying disunity of the author's personal life. Against this narrative waywardness, however, Cheever continued to offer and even to extend an affirmation of the world and his protagonists' place in it in a lyrically charged prose at once serene and expansive ("The World of Apples," *Falconer*). In other words, he continued to do during these last two decades what he had been doing so well for the previous three: writing a fiction of celebration and incoherence.

OTHER MAJOR WORKS

LONG FICTION: *The Wapshot Chronicle*, 1957; *The Wapshot Scandal*, 1964; *Bullet Park*, 1969; *Falconer*, 1977; *Oh, What a Paradise It Seems*, 1982; *Complete Novels*, 2009.

TELEPLAY: *The Shady Hill Kidnapping*, 1982.

NONFICTION: *The Letters of John Cheever*, 1988 (Benjamin Cheever, editor); *The Journals of John Cheever*, 1991; *Glad Tidings, a Friendship in Letters: The Correspondence of John Cheever and John D. Weaver, 1945-1982*, 1993 (with John D. Weaver).

BIBLIOGRAPHY

Bailey, Blake. *Cheever: A Life*. New York: Knopf, 2009. Comprehensive and lengthy biography partly based on Cheever's unpublished journals and interviews with his friends and family. Reveals the details of Cheever's personal life, including his struggle with alcoholism and his bisexuality.

Bloom, Harold, ed. *John Cheever*. Philadelphia: Chelsea House, 2004. Compilation of previously published essays that analyze Cheever's short stories, including "Goodbye My Brother," "The Enormous Radio," The Five-Forty-Eight," "The Country Husband," and "The Swimmer." Includes a plot summary and a list of characters for each of the stories.

Bosha, Francis J, ed. *The Critical Response to John Cheever*. Westport, Conn.: Greenwood Press, 1994. A collection of reviews and critical essays on Cheever's novels and short-story collections by various commentators and critics.

Collins, Robert G., ed. *Critical Essays on John Cheever*. Boston: G. K. Hall, 1982. Reprints an excellent sampling of reviews, interviews, and early criticism, including many dubbed "new" that are in fact only slightly reworked older pieces. Of the items dubbed new, three deserve special mention: Collins's biocritical introduction, Dennis Coale's bibliographical supplement, and particularly Samuel Coale's "Cheever and Hawthorne: The American Romancer's Art," arguably one of the most important critical essays on Cheever.

Dessner, Lawrence Jay. "Gender and Structure in John Cheever's 'The Country Husband.'" *Studies in Short Fiction* 31 (Winter, 1994): 57-68. Argues that the story is structured as a comedy with a farcical narrow escape and a tension between the domestic and the wild. Contends that the plot pattern dissolves pain into laughter.

Donaldson, Scott. *John Cheever: A Biography*. New York: Random House, 1988. Scrupulously researched, interestingly written, and judiciously argued, Donaldson's biography presents Cheever as both author and private man. Donaldson fleshes out most of the previously unknown areas in Cheever's biography and dispels many of the biographical myths that Cheever himself encouraged. The account is sympathetic yet objective.

_____, ed. *Conversations with John Cheever*. Jackson: University Press of Mississippi, 1987. Cheever was a rather reticent man until his final years, and he granted relatively few interviews. The most important ones are reprinted here, along with the editor's thorough chronology and brief but useful introduction.

Gelfant, Blanche H., ed. *The Columbia Companion to the Twentieth-Century American Short Story*. New York: Columbia University Press, 2000. Includes a chapter in which Cheever's short stories are analyzed.

Hipkiss, Robert. "'The Country Husband': A Model Cheever Achievement." *Studies in Short Fiction* 27 (Fall, 1990): 577-585. Analyzes the story as a prose poem filled with imagery of war, myth, music, and nature. Argues that the elaborate image pattern makes readers realize how the protagonist's final fate is deeply rooted in the American value system.

Meanor, Patrick. *John Cheever Revisited*. New York: Twayne, 1995. The first book-length study of Cheever to make use of his journals and letters published in the late 1980's and early 1990's. Focuses on how Cheever created a mythopoeic world in his novels and stories. Includes two chapters on his short stories, with detailed analyses of the stories in *The Enormous Radio* and *The Brigadier and the Golf Widow*.

Morace, Robert A., ed. *Critical Insights: John Cheever*. Pasadena, Calif.: Salem Press, 2012. Collection of original and reprinted essays providing critical readings of Cheever's work. Also includes a biography, a chronology of major events in Cheever's life, a complete list of his works, and a bibliography listing resources for further research.

O'Hara, James E. *John Cheever: A Study of the Short Fiction*. Boston: Twayne, 1989. In addition to reprinting five important reviews and critical essays and providing a detailed chronology and annotated selected bibliography, this volume offers a 120-page analysis of Cheever as a writer of short stories that goes well beyond the introductory level. O'Hara's discussion of the early unanthologized stories is especially noteworthy.

Salwak, Dale, and Paul David Seldis, eds. *Dragons and Martinis: The Skewed Realism of John Cheever*, by Michael D. Byrne. San Bernardino, Calif.: Borgo Press, 1993. Focuses on the style of Cheever's fiction. Includes bibliographical references and an index.

Simon, Linda. "Bewildering Love: John Cheever and the Legacy of Abandonment." In *Naming the Father: Legacies, Genealogies, and Explorations of Fatherhood in Modern and Contemporary Literature*, edited by Eva Paulino Bueno, Terry Caesar, and William Hummel. Lanham, Md.: Lexington Books, 2000. Examines how Cheever's fraught relationship with his father influenced his fictional treatment of men and of fatherhood.

Robert A. Morace

KELLY CHERRY

Born: Baton Rouge, Louisiana; December 21, 1940

PRINCIPAL SHORT FICTION

My Life and Dr. Joyce Brothers: A Novel in Stories, 1990
The Society of Friends, 1999
The Woman Who, 2010

OTHER LITERARY FORMS

Kelly Cherry is remarkable for her restless willingness to explore literary genres. She is an accomplished novelist, notably for *Augusta Played* (1979), a comic tour de force about a concert flutist and her tangled relationships, and *We Can Still Be Friends* (2003), a postmodern-styled text that experiments with multiple points of view in telling the story of a women's studies professor who, at midlife, decides it is time to have a baby. Cherry's early and most sustained work has been poetry, several volumes of at times metaphysical speculations about art and time and the self in sculpted lines that reveal her love of music and her remarkable ear for the deft lyricism of language (she is an accomplished translator). A career academic, Cherry has published a wide range of nonfiction, much of it gathered in 2009's *Girl in a Library: On Women Writers and the Writing Life,* provocative pieces that expose her emotional experiences, subtle readings of contemporary writers (essays that collectively provide critical insight into Cherry's aesthetic sensibility), and theoretical contemplations on the relationship between language and experience.

ACHIEVEMENTS

Kelly Cherry has been pigeonholed as a bold and frank feminist writer. Although the label has validity--female characters in her short fiction wrestle with expectations compromised by men who routinely disappoint--it does not entirely define her considerable body of work. Cherry grounds her best short fiction in the moral dilemmas of the emotional life, at times thinly veiled autobiography. That brutal honesty and passionate intensity give her work its immediacy and its appeal, defining with unflinching care and profound compassion the relationship between art and real life. She also has explored the role of the writer and the responsibility of the engaged reader. She delineates the rich and broad horizons of the creative process and details the work of responding to such aesthetic artifacts (often using the metaphors of music). Thematically, her characters engage the unsuspected depths of those perilous endeavors--finding love, sustaining a family, and ultimately confronting the reality of mortality--that define the world of everyday experience. Her fictions, which reflect her respect for both the psychological realism of Sherwood Anderson and the subtle layered minimalism of Raymond Carver, have been recognized with the Pushcart Prize and the O. Henry Prize. Her second collection, *The Society of Friends,* was awarded the Dictionary of Literary Biography Award for best short-story collection in 2000. Her poetry was awarded the Hanes Prize, given annually by the Fellowship of Southern Writers in recognition of the career achievement of a Southern poet.

BIOGRAPHY

Kelly Cherry was born December 21, 1940, in Baton Rouge, Louisiana. Because her parents, both accomplished violinists, struggled to make ends meet through a variety of academic postings, Cherry had a peripatetic childhood. From ages four to nine, her family lived in Ithaca, New York, while her father completed a music theory doctorate from Cornell; the family then moved to Richmond, Virginia, where her father taught at the Richmond Professional Institute. Although the family was economically strapped, Cherry grew up in the rich ambiance of the arts, sharing her parents' respect for the elegance of subtle harmonies and the work of crafted beauty. Much later, Cherry recalled her feelings of estrangement from her parents, of whom were consumed by the intensely private nature of their involvement with music. Trained in piano, Cherry grew to love language and literature; she was a voracious reader and wrote poetry, which she would sing aloud, in her early teens. She wrote her first story in high school, about a failed writer who contemplates suicide. Reading *Voyna i mir* (1865-1869; *War and Peace*, 1886) and *Moby Dick* (1851) in the same summer set her ambitions to be a writer. Something of a rebellious teen and determined not to pursue conservative career ambitions, she earned her B.A. in the relatively obscure discipline of philosophy from Mary Washington University in 1961 (there were few creative writing programs anywhere at the time); attended the University of Virginia as a DuPont Fellow, again in philosophy; and then completed her M.F.A. in creative writing from the University of North Carolina at Greensboro in 1967.

Her emotional life was tempestuous. In 1965, as a visiting scholar in the Soviet Union, she fell in love with a Latvian composer, although marriage was out of the question, given the hostile political climate. In her last year of study at Greensboro, she married a visiting art historian and decided to abandon her writing ambitions; in 1969 she divorced and returned to writing.

After a stint as a children's book editor in publishing houses first in Richmond and then in New York and tutoring emotionally disturbed adolescents, she accepted her first college teaching position at Southwestern Minnesota State College (now University). During that time, she never stopped writing. In 1975, after living in England for a year with her ailing parents and after her first novel was published, Cherry returned to the United States and accepted an appointment at the University of Wisconsin, Madison. A southerner by temperament, she overcame her initial feelings of displacement in the forbidding northern climate and grew to love the college community. Over the next two decades, Cherry distinguished herself as a passionate teacher and a prodigious writer. When Cherry retired from full-time teaching in 1999, she was the Eudora Welty Professor of English and the Evjue-Bascom Professor in the Humanities. She

moved to the northern Virginia farm country of her childhood and married novelist Burke Davis III. Cherry maintained her writing and her teaching, accepting writer-in-residence appointments at a variety of prestigious universities, including the University of Alabama, Colgate University, and Hollins College.

ANALYSIS

Long before she could even read, Kelly Cherry came to understand the aesthetic imperative through her exposure to classical music, particularly the Romantic repertoire, which taught her the central position of emotions in art and the dramatic importance of self-expression. Her short fiction deals frankly with her own emotional life, especially the complicated logic of attraction. Her undergraduate study in philosophy grounds her fiction in larger speculations. Her interest in the dynamics of relationships is always set against her fascination with time itself, how experience cools into memory and how memory shapes the present. Her characters--notably Nina Bryant, her fictional alter ego, a writer and academic at a large midwestern university--struggle with relationships and specifically with the tension between intentions and experience, how dreams of love are exposed to the vicissitudes of bad luck and chance. Defined within the model of iconic realist writers of the early twentieth century, such as Edith Wharton and Sherwood Anderson, and such contemporary proponents as Eudora Welty and Raymond Carver, Cherry's stories are formally conservative: Her central character undergoes a critical epiphany, and the text is replete with suggestive and layered symbols that help the reader piece together a psychological profile of that character.

MY LIFE AND DR. JOYCE BROTHERS

Interested in expanding the range of the single story, Cherry crafted what she termed a "novel in stories," in which the reader follows a single character's difficult emotional evolution to understand the perplexing motives of the heart and the human need to define the self. Nina Bryant is introduced as a middle-aged woman still reeling from the collapse of her long-term relationship with Cliff, a geneticist who has left her for a married woman. Only gradually, however, does the reader understand that Nina, despite being an accomplished academic who appears confident, even invulnerable, is crippled emotionally by a forbidding secret, which occurred on a night long ago when her older brother forced himself on her. The memory has savaged her self-esteem and left her feeling unworthy of love. Her brother has since careened into a life of promiscuity and self-destructive alcoholism (his death from liver complications occurs late in the story cycle). Shortly before his death, he stuns Nina by admitting the incest was more out of curiosity and really did not mean that much to him.

As the title suggests, with a reference to a trendy pop psychologist of the 1970's who specialized in damaged relationships, Nina has spent her life in therapy and support groups. She fears the implications of intimacy, even as she yearns for the security of a family, which ironically she never knew. In two heartbreaking stories--"Where She Was" and "That Old Man I Used to Know"--Nina renders accounts of her distant parents, both consumed by the egocentric demands of careers as concert musicians. The mother is shown as a young woman who retreats to the loneliness of the swampy Louisiana bayou to listen to splendid symphonies that play only in her head; the father is shown late in life, in the early stages of Alzheimer's, the disease robbing him of his memories, indeed his self, but not his music. When he listens to Ludwig von Beethoven's Violin Concerto on a radio broadcast, the old man still moves his fingers in accompaniment.

Abandoned by Cliff, Nina attempts artificial insemination ("What I Don't Tell People") but that sterile hospital procedure strikes her as a kind of death. In the collection's closing three stories, however, Nina is gifted with the child she so profoundly desires: Her brother's daughter, pregnant and unmarried at sixteen, comes to live with Nina, and in the process Nina becomes the de facto guardian of the baby, Tavy, and eventually its adoptive mother, as if the brother from the grave has righted his grievous wrong. The bonding between Nina and Tavy, captured in the poignant "Spacebaby" (Nina compares the swaddled newborn to an astronaut), lifts the collection toward its hesitatingly hopeful close. In the closing story, Nina runs into Cliff on the way to taking her new daughter to see Santa Claus and at last effects a goodbye. The collection closes with Nina telling a bedtime story to her daughter, a celebration of

the consoling power of storytelling, her words flying about the darkened bedroom like resilient butterflies.

THE SOCIETY OF FRIENDS

Published less than a decade after her first collection, Cherry's second volume nevertheless reveals a significant evolution in her artistic reach. Although Nina is at the center of six of the collection's thirteen stories, Cherry investigates the emotional turbulence of Nina's neighbors and colleagues in Josh Court, a neighborhood in a midwestern university town. In doing so, Cherry reveals the larger human hunger for love, the crushing weight of disappointment, and the difficult adjustment to loneliness. Using as her arch metaphor (introduced in the first story) the Quaker concept of the inner light that defines and elevates each individual, Cherry, like Sherwood Anderson in *Winesburg, Ohio* (1919), confidently inhabits the remarkably unremarkable dilemmas of these small-town misfits.

Of course, Nina inevitably dominates the story cycle. If in the first collection the character often appears self-involved and obsessively engaged by the relentless process of excavating her private traumas (as some critics charged), Nina in this volume accomplishes the difficult process of opening her scarred heart to others. Nina adjusts to the complicated responsibilities and the precarious joy of motherhood and the baffling wonder of her daughter, Tavy, finding emotional comfort in a bond with a raggedy tiny dog, Oscar, and in Nina's platonic relationship with a toy designer who lives next door. In "As It Is in Heaven," Nina takes her daughter to England to be with Nina's dying mother, and there confronts literally the ghost of her father, who sits in the kitchen, eats ice cream, and talks about the beauty of heaven. Nina hesitatingly begins a promising relationship with a history professor who understands that history is repetition, that time past is always present.

In other stories, characters make similar adjustments. A woman, a nurse who works in an acquired immunodeficiency syndrome (AIDS) ward, makes her peace with the reality that her daughter is a lesbian; a husband struggles to share bad medical news with his wife, but, unwilling to devastate her, he dances with her instead; devastated by the death of both his wife and his son, a career academic, new to Wisconsin, hires a graduate student and her mother to shovel his sidewalks in the depth of winter, while he retreats into the darkness of his empty house and the routine of chores; the owner of a failing bookstore fears his wife will leave him for her lesbian best friend. In the sumptuous closing piece, "Block Party," Cherry brings together her argument. Cherry reminds her readers that the devastations of the heart, recorded into stories, are what, in the end, create community. Nina nurses her beloved dog as he must be put down, his tiny body riddled with tumors. Returning from the veterinarian, a shattered Nina postulates an afterlife where all creatures transcend the tacky limits of the body; she contemplates her own finitude and then, emotionally exhausted, falls asleep. The last word is saved for the young Tavy, who joins her mother in bed. The child falls asleep to the mysterious sound of a distant calliope--the muse of poetry--Cherry suggesting that the perplexing and painful dilemmas of life are, in the end, elevated by being transcribed into the subtle, gorgeous music of language of stories.

OTHER MAJOR WORKS

LONG FICTION: *Sick and Full of Burning*, 1974; *Augusta Played*, 1979; *In the Wink of an Eye*, 1983; *The Lost Traveller's Dream*, 1984; *We Can Still Be Friends*, 2003.

POETRY: *Lovers and Agnostics*, 1975; *Relativity: A Point of View*, 1977; *Natural Theology*, 1988; *God's Loud Hand*, 1993; *Death and Transfiguration*, 1997; *Rising Venus*; 2002; *Hazard and Prospect: New and Selected Poems*, 2007; *The Retreats of Thought*, 2009.

NONFICTION: *The Exiled Heart: A Meditative Autobiography*, 1991; *Writing the World*, 1995; *History, Passion, Freedom, Death, and Hope: Prose About Poetry*, 2005; *Girl in a Library: On Women Writers and the Writing Life*, 2009.

BIBLIOGRAPHY

Anderson, Sherwood. *Winesburg, Ohio*. New York: Norton, 1995. Authoritative casebook, edited by Charles Modlin and Ray Lewis White, of Anderson's renowned 1919 collection, on which Cherry models her work. Helpful critical work explicates the genre of small-town realism and the genre of the novel-in-stories.

Cherry, Kelly. *Girl in a Library: On Women Writers and the Writing Life*. Kansas City, Mo.: Bookmark Press, 2009. Indispensable introduction to Cherry that includes her essays on the writers who influenced her and several lengthy autobiographical pieces.

Finkle, David. "Nature's Way of Recycling Men." *The New York Times*, May 27, 1990. Review of *My Life and Dr. Joyce Brothers* comments on Cherry's ability to portray psychological issues in lyrical language.

Welty, Eudora. *On Writing*. New York: Harper & Row, 2002. Reprint of seven now-classic essays about the construction of the short story and the vital importance of capturing the eccentricities of apparently ordinary characters by a writer whose influence Cherry readily acknowledges.

Joseph Dewey

CHARLES WADDELL CHESNUTT

Born: Cleveland, Ohio; June 20, 1858
Died: Cleveland, Ohio; November 15, 1932

PRINCIPAL SHORT FICTION

The Conjure Woman, 1899
The Wife of His Youth, and Other Stories of the Color Line, 1899

OTHER LITERARY FORMS

Charles Waddell Chesnutt achieved his literary reputation and stature as a short-story writer. His scholarly bent and indelible concern for human conditions in American society, however, occasionally moved him to experiment in other literary forms. Based on his study of race relations in the American South, he wrote the novel *The Marrow of Tradition* (1901). As a result of the critical acclaim for this and another novel, *The House Behind the Cedars* (1900), Chesnutt became known not only as a short-story writer but also as a first-rate novelist. He wrote six other novels, five of which were published posthumously.

In 1885, Chesnutt published several poems in *The Cleveland Voice.* The acceptance of his essay "What Is a White Man?" by the *Independent* in May of 1889 began his career as an essayist. Illustrating his diverse talent still further and becoming an impassioned voice for human justice, he wrote essays for a major portion of his life. Chesnutt demonstrated his skill as a biographer when he wrote *The Life of Frederick Douglass* (1899) for the Beacon biography series.

ACHIEVEMENTS

One of Chesnutt's most significant achievements was his own education. Self-taught in the higher principles of algebra, the intricate details of history, the linguistic dicta of Latin, and the tenets of natural philosophy, he crowned this series of intellectual achievements by passing the Ohio bar examination after teaching himself law for two years.

A man of outstanding social reputation, Chesnutt received an invitation to Mark Twain's seventieth birthday party, an invitation "extended to about one hundred and fifty of America's most distinguished writers of imaginative literature." The party was held on December 5, 1905, at Delmonico's, in New York City. Chesnutt's greatest public honor was being chosen as the recipient of the Joel E. Springarn Medal, an award annually bestowed on an American citizen of African descent for distinguished service.

BIOGRAPHY

Charles Waddell Chesnutt was born in Cleveland, Ohio, on June 20, 1858. He attended Cleveland public schools and the Howard School in Fayetteville, North Carolina. Having distinguished himself academically early in his schooling, Chesnutt was taken into the tutelage of two established educators, Robert Harris of the Howard School and his brother, Cicero Harris, of Charlotte, North Carolina. He later succeeded Cicero Harris as principal of the school in Charlotte in 1877 and followed this venture with an appointment to the Normal School in Fayetteville to train teachers for Negro schools.

On June 6, 1878, Chesnutt was married to Susan Perry. Shortly after his marriage, he began his training as a stenographer. Even at this time, however, his interest in writing competed for his energies. He spent his spare time writing essays, poems, short stories, and sketches. His public writing career began in December, 1885, with the printing of the story "Uncle Peter's House" in the *Cleveland News and Herald.* Several years passed and "The Goophered Grapevine" was accepted by *The Atlantic Monthly* and published in 1888. Continuing his dual career as a man of letters and a businessman and attorney for more than a decade after his reception as a literary artist, Chesnutt decided, on

September 30, 1899, to devote himself full time to his literary career. From that moment on he enjoyed a full and productive career as a man of letters.

At the beginning of the twentieth century, Chesnutt became more politically active as a spokesman for racial justice. He toured the South and its educational institutions, such as Tuskegee Institute and Atlanta University. He joined forces with black leaders, such as Booker T. Washington and W. E. B. Du Bois. In May, 1909, he became a member of the National Negro Committee, which later became the National Association for the Advancement of Colored People (NAACP). The last two decades of Chesnutt's life were less active because his health began to fail him in 1919. He was, however, elected to the Cleveland Chamber of Commerce in 1912. Chesnutt continued to write until his death on November 15, 1932.

ANALYSIS

The short fiction of Charles Waddell Chesnutt embraces traditions characteristic of both formal and folk art. Indeed, the elements of Chesnutt's narrative technique evolved in a fashion that conspicuously parallels the historical shaping of the formal short story itself. The typical Chesnutt narrative, like the classic short story, assumes its heritage from a rich oral tradition immersed in folkways, mannerisms, and beliefs. Holding true to the historical development of the short story as an artistic form, his early imaginative narratives were episodic in nature. The next stage of development in Chesnutt's short fiction was a parody of the fable form with a folkloric variation. Having become proficient at telling a story with a unified effect, Chesnutt achieved the symbolic resonance characteristic of the Romantic tale, yet his awareness of the plight of his people urged him toward an increasingly realistic depiction of social conditions. As a mature writer, Chesnutt achieved depth of characterization, distinguishable thematic features, and a rare skillfulness in creation of mood, while a shrewdly moralizing tone allowed him to achieve his dual goal as artist and social activist.

"THE GOOPHERED GRAPEVINE"

Chesnutt's journal stories constituted the first phase of his writing career, but when *The Atlantic Monthly* published "The Goophered Grapevine" in 1888, the

serious aspects of his artistic skill became apparent. "The Goophered Grapevine" belongs to a tradition in Chesnutt's writings that captures the fable form with a folkloric variation. These stories also unfold with a didactic strain that matures significantly in Chesnutt's later writings. To understand clearly the series of stories in *The Conjure Woman*, of which "The Goophered Grapevine" is one, the reader must comprehend the allegorical features in the principal narrative situation and the thematic intent of the mythic incidents from African American lore.

The Conjure Woman contains narratives revealed through the accounts of a northern white person's rendition of the tales of Uncle Julius, a former slave. This storytelling device lays the foundation for Chesnutt's sociological commentary. The real and perceived voices represent the perspectives he wishes to expose, those of the white capitalist and the impoverished, disadvantaged African American. The primary persona is that of the capitalist, while the perceived voice is that of the struggling poor. Chesnutt skillfully melds the two perspectives.

Chesnutt's two volumes of short stories contain pieces that are unified in theme, tone, and mood. Each volume also contains a piece that might be considered the lead story. In *The Conjure Woman*, the preeminent story is "The Goophered Grapevine." This story embodies the overriding thematic intent of the narratives in this collection. Chesnutt points out the foibles of the capitalistic quest in the post-Civil War South, a venture pursued at the expense of the newly freed African American slave. He illustrates this point in "The Goophered Grapevine" by skillfully intertwining Aunt Peggy's gains as a result of her conjurations and Henry's destruction as a result of man's inhumanity to man. Chesnutt discloses his ultimate point when the plantation owner, McAdoo, is deceived by a Yankee horticulturist and his grape vineyard becomes totally unproductive.

Running episodes, such as Aunt Peggy's conjurations to keep the field hands from consuming the grape crop and the seasonal benefit McAdoo gains from selling Henry, serve to illustrate the interplay between a monied white capitalist and his less privileged black human resources. McAdoo used Aunt Peggy to deny his field laborers any benefit from the land they worked, and he sold Henry every spring to increase his cash flow and prepare for the next gardening season.

The central metaphor in "The Goophered Grapevine" is the bewitched vineyard. To illustrate and condemn man's inhumanity to man, Chesnutt contrasts the black conjure woman's protection of the grape vineyard with the white Yankee's destruction of it. McAdoo's exploitation of Henry serves to justify McAdoo's ultimate ruin. Through allegory, Chesnutt is able to draw attention to the immorality of capitalistic gain through a sacrifice of basic humanity to other people.

"PO' SANDY"

Following the theme of inhumanity established in "The Goophered Grapevine," "Po' Sandy" highlights the abuse of a former slave laborer. Accordingly, a situation with a folkloric variation is used to convey this message. Sandy, Master Marabo's field hand, is shifted from relative to relative at various points during the year to perform various duties. During the course of these transactions, he is separated from his second common-law wife, Tenie. (His first wife has been sent to work at a distant plantation.) Tenie is a conjurer. She transforms Sandy into a tree, and she changes him back to his original state periodically so they can be together. With Sandy's apparent disappearance, Master Marabo decides to send Tenie away to nurse his ailing daughter-in-law. There is therefore no one left to watch Sandy, the tree. The dehumanizing effects of industrialization creep into the story line at this point. The "tree" is to be used as lumber for a kitchen at the Marabo home. Tenie returns just in time to try to stop this transformation at the lumber mill, but she is deemed "mad."

Sandy's spirit thereafter haunts the Marabo kitchen, and no one wants to work there. The complaints are so extensive that the kitchen is dismantled and the lumber donated toward the building of a school. This structure is then haunted, too. The point is that industrialization and economic gain diminish essential human concerns and can lead to destruction. The destruction of Sandy's marital relationships in order to increase his usefulness as a field-worker justifies this defiant spirit. In his depiction of Sandy as a tree, Chesnutt illustrates an enslaved spirit desperately seeking freedom.

"THE CONJURER'S REVENGE"

"The Conjurer's Revenge," also contained in *The Conjure Woman*, illustrates Chesnutt's mastery of the exemplum. The allegory in this work conveys a strong message, and Chesnutt's evolving skill in characterization becomes apparent. The characters' actions, rather than the situation, contain the didactic message of the story. Some qualities of the fable unfold as the various dimensions of the characters are portrayed. Consequently, "The Conjurer's Revenge" is a good example of Chesnutt's short imaginative sketch. These qualities are also most characteristic of Chesnutt's early short fiction.

"The Conjurer's Revenge" begins when Primus, a field hand, discovers the conjure man's hog alone in a bush one evening. Concerned for the hog and not knowing to whom the animal belongs, Primus carries it to the plantation where he works. Unfortunately, the conjurer identifies Primus as a thief and transforms Primus into a mule. Chesnutt uses this transformation to reveal Primus's personality. As a mule, Primus displays jealousy when other men show an attraction to his woman, Sally. The mule's reaction is one of shocking violence in instances when Sally is approached by other men. The mule has a tremendous appetite for food and drink, an apparent compensation for his unhappiness. Laying the foundation for his exemplum, Chesnutt brings these human foibles to the forefront and illustrates the consequences of even the mildest appearance of dishonesty.

The conjurer's character is also developed more fully as the story progresses. After attending a religious revival, he becomes ill, confesses his act of vengeance, and repents. During the conjurer's metamorphosis, Chesnutt captures the remorse, grief, and forgiveness in this character. He also reveals the benefits of human compassion and concern for other human beings. A hardened heart undergoes reform and develops an ability to demonstrate sensitivity. Nevertheless, the conjurer suffers the consequences of his evil deed: He is mistakenly given poison by a companion and he dies before he completely restores Primus's human features, a deed he undertakes after repenting. The conjurer dies prematurely, and Primus lives with a clubfoot for the rest of his life.

Features of Chesnutt's more mature writing emerge in the series of narratives that make up *The Wife of His Youth, and Other Stories of the Color Line*. The stories in this collection center on the identity crisis experienced by African Americans, portraying their true human qualities in the face of the grotesque distortions wrought by racism. In order to achieve his goal, Chesnutt abandons his earlier imaginative posture and embraces realism as a means to unfold his message. The dimensions of his characters are therefore appropriately self-revealing. The characters respond to the stresses and pressures in their external environment with genuine emotion; Mr. Ryder in "The Wife of His Youth" is no exception.

"THE WIFE OF HIS YOUTH"

"The Wife of His Youth" follows the structural pattern that appears to typify the narratives in the collection. This pattern evolves in three phases: crisis, character response, and resolution. The crisis in "The Wife of His Youth" is Mr. Ryder's attempt to reconcile his new and old ways of life. He has moved north from a southern plantation and entered black middle-class society. Adapting to the customs, traditions, and mores of this stratum of society is a stressful challenge for Mr. Ryder. Tensions exist between his old life and his new life. He fears being unable to appear as if he belongs to this "blue vein" society and exposing his lowly background. This probable eventuality is his constant preoccupation.

The "blue veins" were primarily lighter-skinned blacks who were better educated and more advantaged than their darker counterparts. Relishing their perceived superiority, they segregated themselves from their brothers and sisters. It is within this web of social clamoring and essential self-denial that Mr. Ryder finds himself. The inherent contradictions of this lifestyle present a crisis for him, although a resolution is attained during the course of the narrative.

Mr. Ryder's efforts to fit into this society are thwarted when his slave wife appears at his doorstep on the day before a major social event that he has planned. He is about to introduce the Blue Vein Society to a widow, Mrs. Dixon, upon whom he has set his affections. The appearance of Liza Jane, his slave wife, forces Mr. Ryder to confront his new life. This situation also allows Chesnutt to assume his typically moralizing tone. Mr. Ryder moves from self-denial to self-pride as he decides to present Liza Jane to his society friends instead of Mrs. Dixon. The narrative ends on a note of personal triumph for Mr. Ryder as he proudly introduces the wife of his youth to society.

"THE PASSING OF GRANDISON"

Chesnutt does not totally relinquish his allegiance to the use of myth in *The Wife of His Youth, and Other Stories of the Color Line*. The myth of the ascent journey, or the quest for freedom, is evident in several stories in the collection, among them "The Passing of Grandison" and "Wellington's Wives." Following the structured pattern of crisis, character response, and resolution, "The Passing of Grandison" is a commentary on the newly emerging moral values of the postbellum South. Colonel Owens, a plantation owner, has a son, Dick, who is in love with a belle named Charity Lomax. Charity's human values reflect the principles of human equality and freedom, and the challenge that she presents to Dick Owens becomes the crisis of the narrative.

Dick is scheduled to take a trip north, and his father insists on his being escorted by one of the servants. Grandison is selected to accompany his young master. Charity Lomax challenges Dick to find a way to entice Grandison to remain in the North and receive his well-deserved liberation. Charity's request conflicts with the values held by Dick and Grandison. Dick believes that slave/master relationships are essential to the survival of the South. Grandison holds that servants should be unequivocally loyal to their masters.

In spite of Dick's attempts to connect Grandison unobtrusively with the abolitionist movement in the North, the former slave remains loyal to Dick. Grandison's steadfastness perplexes Dick because his proposed marriage to Charity is at risk if he does not succeed in freeing Grandison. After a series of faulty attempts, Dick succeeds in losing Grandison. Dick then returns home alone and triumphant. Grandison ultimately returns to the plantation. He had previously proven himself so trustworthy that goodwill toward him is restored. To make the characterization of Grandison realistic, however, Chesnutt must have him pursue his freedom.

In a surprise ending typical of Chesnutt, Grandison plans the escape of all of his relatives who remain on the plantation. They succeed, and in the last scene of the narrative, Colonel Owens spots them from a distance on a boat journeying to a new destination. "The Passing of Grandison" successfully achieves the social and artistic goals of *The Wife of His Youth, and Other Stories of the Color Line*. Chesnutt creates characters with convincing human qualities and captures their responses to the stresses and pressures of their environment. While so doing, he advocates the quest for human freedom.

"UNCLE WELLINGTON'S WIVES"

"Uncle Wellington's Wives" contains several of the thematic dimensions mentioned above. The story concerns the self-identity of the African American and the freedom quest. Wellington Braboy, a light-skinned mulatto, is determined to move north and seek his freedom. His crisis is the result of a lack of resources, primarily financial, to achieve his goal.

Braboy is portrayed as having a distorted view of loyalty and commitment. He justifies stealing money from his slave wife's life savings by saying that, as her husband, he is entitled to the money. On the other hand, he denies his responsibility to his slave wife once he reaches the North. In order to marry a white woman he denies the legality of a slave marriage.

Chesnutt takes Braboy on a journey of purgation and catharsis as he moves toward resolution. After being subjected to much ridicule and humiliation as a result of his mixed marriage, Braboy must honestly confront himself and come to terms with his true identity. Abandoned by his wife for her former white husband, Braboy returns to the South. This journey is also a symbolic return to himself; his temporary escape from himself has failed.

Milly, Braboy's first wife, does not deny her love for him, in spite of his previous actions. Milly receives and accepts him with a forgiving spirit. Chesnutt capitalizes on the contrast between Braboy's African and Anglo wives. The African wife loves him unconditionally because she has the capacity to know and understand him, regardless of his foibles.

Braboy's Anglo wife was frustrated by what she considered to be irreparable inadequacies in his character and abandoned him.

"CICELY'S DREAM"

In his character development, Chesnutt repeatedly sought to dispel some of the stereotypical thinking about African Americans. An example of his success in this effort is found in "Cicely's Dream," set in the period of Reconstruction. Cicely Green is depicted as a young woman of considerable ambition. Like most African Americans, she has had very little education and is apparently limited in her capacity to achieve. She does have, however, many dreams.

Cicely's crisis begins when she discovers a wounded man on her way home one day. The man is delirious and has no recollection of who he is. Cicely and her grandmother care for the man until his physical health is restored, but he is still mentally distraught. The tenderness and sensitivity displayed by Cicely keep the stranger reasonably content. Over a period of time, they become close and eventually pledge their love to each other. Chesnutt portrays a caring, giving relationship between the two lovers, one that is not complicated by any caste system that would destroy love through separation of the lovers. This relationship, therefore, provides a poignant contrast to the relationships among blacks during the days of slavery, and Chesnutt thereby exposes an unexplored dimension of the African American.

Typically, however, there is a surprise ending: Martha Chandler, an African American teacher, enters the picture. She teaches Cicely and other black youths for one school term. During the final program of the term, the teacher reveals her story of lost love. Her lover had been killed in the Civil War. Cicely's lover's memory is jolted by the teacher's story, and he proves to be the teacher's long-lost love. The happy reunion is a celebration of purely committed love. Again, Chesnutt examines qualities in African Americans that had largely been ignored. He emphasizes the innate humanity of the African American in a natural and realistic way, combining great artistic skill with a forceful moral vision.

OTHER MAJOR WORKS

LONG FICTION: *Mandy Oxendine*, wr. 1897, pb. 1997; *A Business Career*, wr. 1898, pb. 2005 (Matthew Wilson and Marjan van Schaik, editors); *The House Behind the Cedars*, 1900; *The Marrow of Tradition*, 1901; *Evelyn's Husband*, wr. 1903, pb. 2005 (Matthew Wilson and Marjan van Schaik, editors); *The Colonel's Dream*, 1905; *Paul Marchand, F.M.C.*, wr. 1921, pb. 1998; *The Quarry*, wr. 1928, pb. 1999.

NONFICTION: *The Life of Frederick Douglass*, 1899; *The Journals of Charles W. Chesnutt*, 1993; *"To Be an Author": The Letters of Charles W. Chesnutt, 1889-1905*, 1997; *Charles W. Chesnutt: Essays and Speeches*, 1999; *Selected Writings*, 2001 (SallyAnn H. Ferguson, editor); *An Exemplary Citizen: Letters of Charles W. Chesnutt, 1906-1932*, 2002.

MISCELLANEOUS: *Stories, Novels, and Essays*, 2002; *The Portable Charles W. Chesnutt*, 2008.

BIBLIOGRAPHY

Chakkalakal, Tess. "Wedded to Race: Charles Chesnutt's Stories of the Color Line." *Studies in American Fiction* 36, no. 2 (Autumn, 2008): 155-176. A literary critique of the short-story collection *The Wife of His Youth, and Other Stories of the Color Line*. Describes how the legal issues and laws regarding marriage for former African American slaves in the United States play a prominent role in the stories. Argues that Chesnutt was critical of the need for former slaves to legally marry at the end of the Civil War.

Chesnutt, Charles Waddell. *"To Be an Author": Letters of Charles W. Chesnutt, 1889-1905*. Edited by Joseph R. McElrath, Jr., and Robert C. Leitz III. Princeton, N.J.: Princeton University Press, 1997. The six-part, chronological organization of this volume is particularly useful to a student of Chestnutt's fiction and of his career development. Also includes a comprehensive introduction and detailed index.

Delma, P. Jay. "The Mask as Theme and Structure: Charles W. Chesnutt's 'The Sheriff's Children' and 'The Passing of Grandison.'" *American Literature* 51 (1979): 364-375. Argues that the two stories exploit the theme of the mask, symbolizing the need to hide one's true personality and racial identity from oneself and others. Maintains that Chesnutt's use of the mask theme keeps these stories from being run-of-the-mill treatments of the long-lost-son plot.

Duncan, Charles. "Charles W. Chesnutt and the Fictions of a 'New America.'" In *A Companion to the American Short Story*, edited by Alfred Bendixen and James Nagel. Malden, Mass.: Wiley-Blackwell, 2010. An analysis of Chesnutt's short fiction, including the stories "A Matter of Principle," "Po' Sandy," "The Wife of His Youth," and "Her Virginia Mammy."

Filetti, Jean. "The Goophered Grapevine." *The Explicator* 48 (Spring, 1990): 201-203. Discusses the use of master-slave relationships within the context of storytelling and explains how Chesnutt's "The Goophered Grapevine" relates to this tradition. Indicates that one of Chesnutt's concerns was inhumanity among people, but the story is told from a humorous perspective with the newly freed slave outwitting the white capitalist.

Gleason, William. "Chesnutt's Piazza Tales: Architecture, Race, and Memory in the Conjure Stories." *American Quarterly* 51 (March, 1999): 33-77. Argues that in the second phase of the conjure tales, Chesnutt uses piazzas as a central imaginative space for African American memory. Argues that Chesnutt counters historical amnesia with concrete memories from the piazza that represent a simpler past.

Heermance, Noel. *Charles Chesnutt: America's First Great Black Novelist*. Hamden, Conn.: Archon Books, 1974. A good introduction to Chesnutt's overall life and themes. Discusses his short fiction, novels, and other writings, and asserts that Chesnutt was the first great African American novelist.

Izzo, David Garrett, and Maria Orban, eds. *Charles Chesnutt Reappraised: Essays on the First Major African American Fiction Writer*. Jefferson, N.C.: McFarland, 2009. Reevaluates Chesnutt's work from a twenty-first century perspective, applying contemporary scholarship to analyze his narrative strategies, dominant themes, and the political and social issues he raises by his depiction of race. Several of the essays focus on his short fiction, including discussions of "The Wife of His Youth" and *The Conjure Woman*.

Kulii, Elon A. "Poetic License and Chesnutt's Use of Folklore." *CLA Journal* 38 (December, 1994): 247-253. Discusses Chesnutt's use of the hoodoo tradition in "The Goophered Grapevine." Claims that Chesnutt communicates the inner tale as a story from the hoodoo tradition, but the episodic core of the tale is not of the oral tradition.

McFatter, Susan. "From Revenge to Resolution: The (R)evolution of Female Characters in Chesnutt's Fiction." *CLA Journal* 42 (December, 1998): 194-211. Discusses the theme of female revenge in Chesnutt's fiction, showing how female characters respond to racism and patriarchal paradigms in various ways. Argues that Chesnutt's women use their intelligence and instinct for survival in order to manipulate their repressive environments.

McWilliams, Dean. *Charles W. Chesnutt and the Fictions of Race*. Athens: University of Georgia Press, 2002. Examines Chesnutt's novels and short stories, describing how his fiction changed Americans' assumptions about race. Includes discussion of the black vernacular and race in the short stories and of Chesnutt's use of language in all of his fiction.

Render, Sylvia. *Charles W. Chesnutt*. Boston: Twayne, 1980. A good general introduction to the life and writing of Chesnutt. Discusses his major concerns with narrative technique, social justice, and the place of the African American in American society.

_____. *The Short Fiction of Charles Chesnutt*. Washington, D.C.: Howard University Press, 1974. Discusses the collected short fiction of Chesnutt and indicates that it came out of the storytelling tradition of African Americans and was written within the conventions of local humor that were popular at the time.

Sollers, Werner. "Thematics Today." In *Thematics Reconsidered: Essays in Honor of Horst S. Daemmrich*, edited by Frank Trommler. Amsterdam: Rodopi, 1995. A detailed discussion of the themes in "The Wife of His Youth." Argues that contemporary thematic readings that stress race and gender are less likely to identify other themes, such as marriage, fidelity, and age difference. Suggests that Chesnutt's special way of treating the race and age themes needs more attention.

Wonham, Henry B. "Plenty of Room for Us All? Participation and Prejudice in Charles Chesnutt's Dialect Tales." *Studies in American Fiction* 26 (Autumn, 1998): 131-146. Argues that the dialect tales deal in a subtle way with the restriction of African American rights in the post-Reconstruction South. Asserts that Chesnutt focuses on a historical moment between Reconstruction and the return of white racism.

Wright, Susan Prothro, and Ernestine Pickens Glass, eds. *Passing in the Works of Charles W. Chesnutt*. Jackson: University Press of Mississippi, 2010. Examines how the theme of black people "passing" for white people is a significant element in Chesnutt's works. While most of the essays focus on the novels, two of the articles are devoted to analysis of the short stories "Po' Sandy" and "The Passing of Grandison."

Patricia A. R. Williams
Updated by Earl Paulus Murphy

KATE CHOPIN

Born: St. Louis, Missouri; February 8, 1851
Died: St. Louis, Missouri; August 22, 1904
Also Known As: Katherine O'Flaherty

PRINCIPAL SHORT FICTION

Bayou Folk, 1894
A Night in Acadie, 1897

OTHER LITERARY FORMS

In addition to the short stories that brought her some fame as a writer during her own lifetime, Kate Chopin (SHOH-pan) published two novels, *At Fault* (1890) and *The Awakening* (1899). The latter was either ignored or condemned because of its theme of adultery and frank depiction of a woman's sexual urges. Chopin also wrote a few reviews and casual essays and a number of undistinguished poems.

ACHIEVEMENTS

Kate Chopin's short stories, which were published in contemporary popular magazines, won her fame as a local colorist with a good ear for dialect and as a writer concerned with women's issues, such as sexuality, equality, and independence. After the publication of *The Awakening* in 1899, however, her popularity waned, in part because of the furor over the open treatment of adultery and sex in the novel. She wrote few stories after 1900, and her work was largely neglected until the rediscovery of *The Awakening* by feminist critics. Criticism of that novel and new biographies have spurred a new interest in her Creole short stories, which have been analyzed in detail in terms of their regionalism and their treatment of gender. Influenced by Guy de Maupassant, Chopin did not exert any literary influence on later short-story writers, at least until the rediscovery of *The Awakening*.

BIOGRAPHY

Kate Chopin was born Katherine O'Flaherty in St. Louis, Missouri, in 1851. Her mother's family was Creole, descended from French settlers, and her father, a successful merchant, was an Irish immigrant. She was educated at the Academy of the Sacred Heart in St. Louis beginning in 1860, five years after her father's accidental death, and graduated in 1868. In 1870, she married Oscar Chopin, who took her to live in Louisiana, first in New Orleans and later in Natchitoches Parish, the setting for many of her stories. In 1882, Oscar died of swamp fever; Kate Chopin managed her husband's properties for a year and in 1884 returned to St. Louis. The next year her mother died, and in 1888 Chopin began writing out of a need for personal expression and to help support her family financially. Her stories appeared regularly in popular periodicals, and she published a novel, *At Fault*, in 1890. *Bayou Folk*, a collection of stories and sketches, appeared in 1894, the year her widely anthologized "The Story of an Hour" was written. *A Night in Acadie* followed in 1987, and she was identified as one of four outstanding literary figures in St. Louis by the *Star-Times*. Her celebrated novel, *The Awakening*, received hostile reviews that upset her, though reports about the book being banned were greatly exaggerated. She did, however, write relatively little after this controversy and died five years later in St. Louis, where she was attending the World's Fair.

ANALYSIS

Until the 1970's, Kate Chopin was known best literarily, if at all, as a "local colorist," primarily for her tales of life in New Orleans and rural Louisiana. Chopin manages in these stories (about two-thirds of her total output) to subtly bring to life the settings and personalities of her characters, usually Creoles (descendants of the original French settlers of Louisiana) or Cajuns (or Acadians, the French colonists who were exiled to Louisiana following the British conquest of Nova Scotia). What makes Chopin especially important for modern readers, however, is her insight into human characters and relationships in the context of their societies, whether Creole, Cajun, or Anglo-Saxon, and into the social, emotional, and sexual roles of women within these societies.

Chopin's desire and hope for female independence can be seen in two of her earliest stories, "Wiser Than a God" and "A Point at Issue!" (both published in 1889). In the first story, the heroine Paula Von Stoltz rejects an offer of marriage in order to begin a successful career as a concert pianist because music is the true sole passion of her life; it is an act that anticipates the actions of Edna Pontellier in *The Awakening*. In the second story, Eleanor Gail and Charles Faraday enter into a marriage based on reason and equality and pursue their individual careers in separate places. This arrangement works very well for some time, but finally each of the two succumbs to jealousy. In spite of this blemish in their relationship, Chopin's humorous tone also manages to poke fun at traditional attitudes toward marriage.

"THE STORY OF AN HOUR"

This questioning though humorous attitude is strongly evident in one of Chopin's most anthologized and best-known tales, "The Story of an Hour" (1894). Mrs. Mallard, a woman suffering from a heart condition, is told that her husband has been killed in a train accident. She is at first deeply sorrowful, but soon realizes that even though she had loved and will mourn her husband, his death has set her free: "There would be no powerful will bending hers in that blind persistence with which men and women believe they have a right to impose a private will upon a fellow-creature." As Mrs. Mallard descends the stairs, however, the front door is opened by her husband, who had never been on the train. This time her heart gives out and the cause ironically is given by the doctors as "the joy that kills."

"LA BELLE ZORAÏDE"

It is in her Louisiana stories, however, that Chopin's sympathy for female and indeed human longings emerges most fully, subtly blended with a distinct and evocative sense of locale and folkways. "La Belle Zoraïde" (1893) is presented in the form of a folktale

being told by a black servant, Manna-Loulou, to her mistress, Madame Delisle (these two characters also are central to the story "A Lady of Bayou St. John," published in 1893). The tale itself is the story of a black slave, Zoraïde, who is forbidden by her mistress to marry another slave with whom she has fallen in love because his skin is too black and her mistress intends her for another, more "gentlemanly" servant. In spite of this, and although the slave she loves is sold away, Zoraïde bears his child and refuses marriage to the other slave. Her mistress falsely tells Zoraïde that her child has been born dead, and the slave descends into madness. Even when her real daughter is finally brought back to her, Zoraïde rejects her, preferring to cling to the bundle of rags that she has fashioned as a surrogate baby. From then on,

> She was never known again as la belle Zoraïde, but ever after as Zoraïde la folle, whom no one ever wanted to marry. . . . She lived to be an old woman, whom some people pitied and others laughed at-- always clasping her bundle of rags--her 'piti.'

The indirect narration of this story prevents it from slipping into the melodramatic or the maudlin. Chopin's ending, presenting the conversation of Manna-Loulou and Madame Delisle in the Creole dialect, pointedly avoids a concluding moral judgment, an avoidance typical of Chopin's stories. Instead, readers are brought back to the frame for the tale and focused on the charm of the Creole dialect, even while readers retain pity and sympathy for Zoraïde.

"DÉSIRÉE'S BABY"

In spite of their southern locale, Chopin's stories rarely deal with racial relations between whites and blacks. One important exception is "Désirée's Baby" (1892). Désirée Valmondé, who was originally a foundling, marries Armand Aubigny, a plantation owner who is proud of his aristocratic heritage but very much in love with Désirée. He is at first delighted when she bears him a son, but soon begins to grow cold and distant. Désirée, puzzled at first, soon realizes with horror that her child has Negro blood. Armand, whose love for Désirée has been killed by "the unconscious injury she had brought upon his home and his name," turns her out of the house, and she disappears with her child into the bayou, never to be seen again. Later, in a surprise ending reminiscent of Maupassant, Armand is having all reminders of Désirée burned when he discovers a letter from his mother to his father that reveals his mother had had Negro blood. In this story readers see the continuation of Chopin's most central theme--the evil that follows when one human being gains power over another and attempts to make that person conform to preset standards or expectations.

As suggested earlier, Chopin finds that power of one person over another is often manifested in the institution of marriage. As even her earliest stories suggest, she does not always find that marriage necessarily requires that a wife be dominated by her husband, and she demonstrates that both men and women are capable of emotional and spiritual growth.

"ATHÉNAÏSE"

That possibility for growth is perhaps best seen in the story "Athénaïse" (1895). Athénaïse, an emotionally immature young woman, has married the planter Cazeau, but has found that she is not ready for marriage. She runs back to her family, explaining that she does not hate Cazeau himself:

> It's jus' being married that I detes' an' despise. . . . I can't stan' to live with a man; to have him always there; his coats and pantaloons hanging in my room; his ugly bare feet--washing them in my tub, befo' my very eyes, ugh!

When Cazeau arrives to bring her back, however, she finds that she has to go with him. As the couple rides home, they pass an oak tree that Cazeau recalls was where his father had once apprehended a runaway slave: "The whole impression was for some reason hideous, and to dispel it Cazeau spurred his horse to a swift gallop."

Despite Cazeau's attempt to make up and live with Athénaïse at least as friends, she remains bitter and unhappy and finally runs away again, aided by her romantic and rather foolish brother Montéclin. Cazeau, a sensitive and proud man, refuses to go after her again as though she too were a runaway slave: "For the companionship of no woman on earth would he again undergo the humiliating sensation of baseness that had overtaken him in passing the old oak-tree in the fallow meadow."

Athénaïse takes refuge in a boarding house in New Orleans where she becomes friendly with Mr. Gouvernail, a newspaper editor. Gouvernail hopes to make Athénaïse his lover, but he refrains from forcing himself on her: "When the time came that she wanted him . . . he felt he would have a right to her. So long as she did not want him, he had no right to her,--no more than her husband had." Gouvernail, though, never gets his chance; Athénaïse has previously been described as someone who does not yet know her own mind, and such knowledge will not come through rational analysis but rather "as the song to the bird, the perfume and color to the flower." This knowledge does come to her when she discovers that she is pregnant. As she thinks of Cazeau, "the first purely sensuous tremor of her life swept over her. . . . Her whole passionate nature was aroused as if by a miracle." Thus, Athénaïse returns to reconciliation and happiness with her husband.

Chopin's story illustrates that happiness in a relationship can come only with maturity and with mutual respect. Cazeau realizes that he cannot force his wife to love him, and Athénaïse finally knows what she wants when she awakens to an awareness of her own sexuality. If Cazeau has to learn to restrain himself, though, Mr. Gouvernail learns the need to take more initiative as well; not having declared his love for Athénaïse he suffers when she goes back home. The tone of the entire story is subtly balanced between poignancy and humor, allowing readers to see the characters' flaws while remaining sympathetic to each of them.

The importance of physical passion and of sexual self-awareness that can be found in "Athénaïse" can also be found in many of Chopin's stories and is one of the characteristics that make her writing so far ahead of its time. It is this theme that, as the title suggests, is central to her novel *The Awakening* and that was partly responsible for the scandal which that novel provoked. Chopin's insistence not merely on the fact of women's sexual desires but also on the propriety and healthiness of those desires in some ways anticipates the writings of D. H. Lawrence, but without Lawrence's insistence on the importance of male dominance.

"THE STORM"

Sexual fulfillment outside of marriage without moral judgments can be found in "The Storm," written in 1898, just before *The Awakening*, but not published until 1969. The story concerns four characters from an earlier tale, "At the 'Cadian Ball" (1892). In that earlier story, a young woman, Clarisse, rides out in the night to the 'Cadian Ball to declare her love for the planter Alcée Laballière. Alcée is at the ball with an old girlfriend of his, Calixta, a woman of Spanish descent. Clarisse claims Alcée, and Calixta agrees to marry Bobinôt, a man who has been in love with her for some time.

"The Storm" is set several years later. Calixta and Bobinôt have had a child, and Alcée and Clarisse have been happily married. One day, while Bobinôt and his son are out on an errand, a huge storm breaks out. Alcée takes refuge at Calixta's house, and the old passion between the two is rekindled; as the storm breaks about them in mounting intensity, the two make love, Calixta's body "knowing for the first time its birthright." While the storm mirrors the physical passion of the couple, neither it nor the passion itself is destructive. Where one would expect some retribution for this infidelity in a story, the results are only beneficial: Calixta, physically fulfilled, happily welcomes back her returning husband and son; Alcée writes to Clarisse, off visiting relatives, that he does not need her back right away; and Clarisse, enjoying "the first free breath since her marriage," is content to stay where she is for the time. Chopin's ending seems audacious: "So the storm passed and every one was happy."

Although written about a century ago, Chopin's stories seem very modern in many ways. Her concern with women's place in society and in marriage, her refusal to mix guilt with sexuality, and her narrative stance of sympathetic detachment make her as relevant to modern readers as her marked ability to convey character and setting simply yet completely. In the little more than a decade in which she produced most of her work, her command of her art grew ever stronger, as did her willingness to deal with controversial subjects. It is unfortunate that this career was cut short by the reaction to *The Awakening* and her early death, but it is fortunate that Chopin left the writing that she did, and that her work has been preserved.

OTHER MAJOR WORKS

LONG FICTION: *At Fault*, 1890; *The Awakening*, 1899.
NONFICTION: *Kate Chopin's Private Papers*, 1998.
MISCELLANEOUS: *The Complete Works of Kate Chopin*, 1969 (2 volumes; Per Seyersted, editor); *Complete Novels and Stories*, 2002.

BIBLIOGRAPHY

Arima, Hiroko. *Beyond and Alone! The Theme of Isolation in Selected Short Fiction of Kate Chopin, Katherine Anne Porter, and Eudora Welty*. Lanham, Md.: University Press of America, 2006. Examines how the common theme of isolation enables the three writers to address universal human and social issues.

Beer, Janet. *Kate Chopin, Edith Wharton and Charlotte Perkins Gilman: Studies in Short Fiction*. London: Macmillan, 1997. Includes three chapters on Chopin's short fiction. In one, Beer argues that Chopin's Louisiana is postcolonial rather than postbellum; in another, she discusses how erotic desire expresses the lives of women; and in the third, she examines the authorial voice in Chopin's short-shory fables.

Bloom, Harold, ed. *Kate Chopin*. Updated ed. New York: Chelsea House, 2007. Two of the critical essays in this volume focus on Chopin's short fiction: "Semiotic Subversion in 'Désirée's Baby,'" by Ellen Peel, and "'Local Color' Literature and *A Night in Acadie*," by Nancy A. Walker. Other essays provide a more general analysis of Chopin's fiction.

Boren, Lynda S., and Sara de Saussure Davis, eds. *Kate Chopin Reconsidered: Beyond the Bayou*. Baton Rouge: Louisiana State University Press, 1992. Although most of these essays focus on *The Awakening*, several discuss such stories as "Charlie," "After the Winter," and "At Cheniere Caminada." Other essays compare Chopin with playwright Henrik Ibsen in terms of domestic confinement and discuss her work from a Marxist viewpoint.

Brown, Pearl L. "Awakened Men in Kate Chopin's Creole Stories." *ATQ*, n.s. 13, no. 1 (March, 1999). Argues that in Chopin's Creole stories, in intimate moments women discover inner selves buried beneath socially imposed ones and men discover subjective selves buried beneath public personas.

Erickson, Jon. "Fairytale Features in Kate Chopin's 'Désirée's Baby': A Case Study in Genre Cross-Reference." In *Modes of Narrative*, edited by Reingard M. Nischik and Barbara Korte. Würzburg, Germany: Königshausen and Neumann, 1990. Shows how Chopin's story conflicts with the expectations set up by the fairy-tale genre on which it is based; for example, the prince turns out to be the villain. Argues that the ending of the story is justified, for in the fairy tale the mystery of origin must be solved and the villain must be punished.

Evans, Robert C., ed. *Kate Chopin's Short Fiction: A Critical Companion*. West Cornwall, Conn.: Locust Hill Press, 2001. Provides synopses of the short stories and summarizes the critical reception of these works. The appendixes reprint the stories "Caline" and "La Belle Zoraïde" and offer critical analyses of the two works.

Gale, Robert L. *Characters and Plots in the Fiction of Kate Chopin*. Jefferson, N.C.: McFarland, 2009. Contains alphabetically arranged entries that summarize the plots of Chopin's novels and short stories, identify her fictional characters, and relate these characters to her life experiences, family members, and friends. An introductory essay discusses Chopin's background and fiction.

Koloski, Bernard. *Kate Chopin: A Study of the Short Fiction*. New York: Twayne, 1996. Discusses Chopin's short stories in the context of her bilingual and bicultural imagination. Provides readings of her most important stories, examines her short-story collections, and comments on her children's stories. Includes excerpts from Chopin's literary criticism and brief discussions by other critics of her most familiar stories.

Ostman, Heather, ed. *Kate Chopin in the Twenty-First Century: New Critical Essays*. Newcastle, England: Cambridge Scholars, 2008. Some of the essays analyze theater in Chopin's short fiction; the short stories published in *Vogue* magazine; and religion, race, class, and gender in the shorter fiction, including her stories "The Storm," "The Godmother," and "At the 'Cadian Ball."

Rich, Charlotte. "Kate Chopin." In *A Companion to the American Short Story*, edited by Alfred Bendixen and James Nagel. Malden, Mass.: Wiley-Blackwell, 2010. Provides an overview and critical examination of Chopin's short fiction.

Seyersted, Per. *Kate Chopin: A Critical Biography*. Baton Rouge: Louisiana State University Press, 1980. In addition to providing invaluable information about the New Orleans of the 1870's, Seyersted's biography examines Chopin's life, views, and work. Provides lengthy discussions not only of *The Awakening* but also of her many short stories. Seyersted sees Chopin as a transitional literary figure, a link between George Sand and Simone de Beauvoir.

Shaker, Bonnie James. *Coloring Locals: Racial Formation in Kate Chopin's "Youth's Companion" Stories*. Iowa City: University of Iowa Press, 2003. Examines the treatment of gender, class, race, and ethnicity in Chopin's short stories for *Youth's Companion*, a family-oriented periodical in which her work was published in the late nineteenth century.

Skaggs, Peggy. *Kate Chopin*. Boston: Twayne, 1985. Focuses on the theme of the search for identity in Chopin's work, devoting two chapters to her short fiction. Includes a biographical chapter, a chronology, and a select bibliography. The book is indispensable for readers of Chopin's short fiction.

Stein, Allen F. *Women and Autonomy in Kate Chopin's Short Fiction*. New York: Peter Lang, 2005. Analyzes thirty of Chopin's short stories, focusing on the difficulties the women characters confront in their efforts to obtain autonomy amid the social constraints of marriage, courtship, and seeking to live independently.

Taylor, Helen. *Gender, Race, and Religion in the Writings of Grace King, Ruth McEnery Stuart, and Kate Chopin*. Baton Rouge: Louisiana State University Press, 1989. Taylor divides her chapter on Chopin between the novels and the short stories, some of which are given extensive feminist readings. Taylor focuses on Chopin as a local colorist who uses regional and historical themes to explore gender issues. The book is invaluable in its material on literary influences, particularly Guy de Maupassant, and the intellectual climate of the time.

Toth, Emily. *Kate Chopin*. New York: William Morrow, 1990. Toth's thoroughly documented, exhaustive work is the definitive Chopin biography. She covers not only Chopin's life but also her literary works and discusses many of the short stories in considerable detail. Toth updates Per Seyersted's bibliography of Chopin's work, supplies a helpful chronology of Chopin's life, and discusses the alleged banning of *The Awakening*. An excellent starting point for Chopin research.

_____. *Unveiling Kate Chopin*. Jackson: University Press of Mississippi, 1999. Using newly discovered manuscripts, letters, and diaries of Chopin, Toth examines the source of Chopin's ambition and passion for her art, arguing that she worked much harder at her craft than previously thought.

Donald F. Larsson
Updated by Thomas L. Erskine

SANDRA CISNEROS

Born: Chicago, Illinois; December 20, 1954

PRINCIPAL SHORT FICTION

The House on Mango Street, 1984
Woman Hollering Creek, and Other Stories, 1991

OTHER LITERARY FORMS

Sandra Cisneros is known for her poetry and long fiction, as well as for her short stories. She has published several collections of poems, including *Bad Boys* (1980), *My Wicked, Wicked Ways* (1987), and *Loose Woman* (1994); much of her poetry remains uncollected and unpublished, according to the author's wishes. Her novel *Caramelo: Or, Puro Cuento* appeared in 2002. Cisneros's other publications include a series of essays explaining her own creative processes as a writer that appeared in *The Americas Review* and *Hairs = Pelitos* (1994), a children's book illustrated by Terry Ybanez that expands on the chapter "Hairs" featured in *The House on Mango Street*.

ACHIEVEMENTS

Together with authors such as Ana Castillo, Denise Chávez, and Alma Villanueva, Sandra Cisneros is one of the literary voices that emerged in the 1980's and was responsible for securing for Chicana fiction a place in mainstream American literature. Her collection of short stories *Woman Hollering Creek, and Other*

Stories was the first work by and about Chicanas--that is, Mexican American women--to obtain a contract with a major publishing house (Random House). This collection received the PEN Center West Award for Best Fiction of 1991, the Anisfield-Wolf Book Award, the Lannan Foundation Literary Award, and the Quality Paperback Book Club New Voices Award. Her first collection of short fiction, *The House on Mango Street*, was awarded the Before Columbus American Book Award and the PEN Center West Award. *Caramelo* received the Premio Napoli and was selected as a notable book of the year by several journals, including *The New York Times*, *Los Angeles Times*, *Chicago Tribune*, *San Francisco Chronicle*, and *The Seattle Times*.

In addition Cisneros is a two-time recipient of a National Endowment for the Arts Fellowship for Creative Writers for her poetry and fiction. In 1984, she received a Dobie-Paisano Fellowship. She was granted a MacArthur Fellowship in 1995, and she subsequently organized a reunion where the Latino MacArthur Fellows--Los MacArturos--focused on community outreach. In 2003, she was awarded the Texas Medal of the Arts, and she has received many other honors and honorary degrees.

BIOGRAPHY

Sandra Cisneros was born in 1954 into a working-class family in Chicago, Illinois. With a Mexican American mother, a Mexican father, and six brothers, she described her circumstances as being similar to having seven fathers. Because of close familial and cultural ties with Mexico, the Cisneros family moved back and forth between a series of cramped apartments in Chicago and the paternal grandmother's home in Mexico City. The concept of home or the lack of one would later weigh heavily in Cisneros's writing. The combination of an uprooted lifestyle and an ever-changing circle of friends, schools, and neighborhoods, as well as the isolation that resulted from her brothers' unwillingness to let a girl join in their play, led Cisneros to turn inward to a life of books. That time spent alone allowed an observant, creative voice to take root in the author.

Cisneros considered her career as a professional writer to have begun in 1974--the year in which she enrolled in a writing class as a junior at Loyola University of Chicago, where she would later receive her bachelor of arts degree in English. However, it was her tenure at the University of Iowa Writers' Workshop, from which she earned a master of fine arts degree, that proved an invaluable aid in the formation of her own literary voice. During a discussion of Gaston Bachelard's *La Bétique de l'espace* (1957; *The Poetics of Space*, 1964), in which her classmates spoke of the house as a literary symbol complete with attics, stairways, and cellars of imagination and childhood, Cisneros realized that her experience was different from that of her college classmates. Her background was that of a multiethnic, working-class neighborhood complete with drunken bums, families sleeping on crowded floors, and rats. She ceased trying to make her style fit that of the perfect, white, and mostly male image that was foreign to her and, instead, began writing about that to which her classmates could not relate but was familiar to her.

Cisneros has used her education to foster change within the Chicano community. She taught high school dropouts for three years in a Chicano barrio. She has also worked as an administrative assistant at Loyola University, where she was involved in the recruitment of minority and disadvantaged students. In 1984, she was the literature director of the Guadalupe Cultural Arts Center in San Antonio, the city which she made her home. Cisneros served as writer-in-residence at the Michael Karolyi Artists Foundation in Vence, France,

Sandra Cisneros (AP Photo/Dana Tynan)

the University of Michigan in Ann Arbor, the University of California at Irvine, and the University of New Mexico in Albuquerque.

ANALYSIS

Sandra Cisneros has said that she writes about the memories that will not let her sleep at night--about the stories that are waiting to be told. Drawing on the memories of her childhood and her cultural identity--the run-down, crowded apartment, the double-edged sword of being American yet not being considered American, the sight of women in her community closed in behind apartment windows--Cisneros's fiction avoids any romantic clichés of life in the barrio. Despite the sobering themes upon which Cisneros touches--poverty, sexism, and racism--she tells her stories with a voice that is at the same time strong, playful, and deceptively simple. Cisneros's distinctive style is marked by the grace with which Spanish words and phrases are woven into her stories. Central to her stories is a preoccupation with the house, the community, and the condition of women. Her images are vivid and lyrical. She acknowledges that she was influenced in style by the mix of poetry and fiction in Jorge Luis Borges's *El hacedor* (1960; *Dreamtigers*, 1964). Indeed, while Cisneros herself classifies her fiction as stories that read like poems, critics have not reached an agreement, labeling her works *The House on Mango Street* and *Woman Hollering Creek, and Other Stories* alternatively as novels, short-story collections, series of vignettes, and prose poems.

THE HOUSE ON MANGO STREET

The series of sketches in *The House on Mango Street* offers a bittersweet view of life in a Chicago barrio. Readers follow the young adolescent narrator Esperanza--whose name (as explained in the story "My Name") means "hope" in Spanish and also implies too many letters, sadness, and waiting--as she makes the discoveries associated with maturing. She introduces the reader to her neighbors and her neighborhood, making them as familiar to the reader as they are to her. In the title story, Esperanza explains how her family came to live on Mango Street. The family had hoped that the house on Mango Street would be like the ones they had always dreamed of--with real stairs and several washrooms and a great big yard with trees and grass.

Esperanza sadly explains, however, that their house does not fulfill this wish at all. She is ashamed of her red brick house, as she has been of all of her family's previous dwellings. She succinctly describes the embarrassment that she felt when the family was living on Loomis and she had to show her apartment to a nun from her school. She pointed to the family's third-floor flat, located above a boarded-up laundry, and suffered the blow of the nun's disbelieving response, *"there?"* From that moment, Esperanza knew that she had to have a house--one that she could show with pride to people as if it were a reflection of herself. She was sure the family would have such a house soon, but the house on Mango Street is not that house.

Because Esperanza remarks that she wants a house "all my own. With my porch and my pillow, my pretty purple petunias. My books and my stories," Cisneros has been read as creating a grasping and selfish protagonist. However, the section titled "Bums in the

Attic" dispels this notion of untoward individualism. In this sketch--which resembles one of Cisneros's favorite children's stories, Virginia Lee Burton's *The Little House* (1942), in which the owners of a house on a country hill promise the house never to sell it--Esperanza speculates about the grand home on a hill that she will have someday. As much as she wants to leave Mango Street, however, she stresses that even in her country home she will not forget from where she came. She will not make her house a secured palace that locks out the world; she will instead offer her attic to the homeless so that they too will have a home.

In "Those Who Don't," the young Esperanza discusses in a matter-of-fact tone the concept of being the "other" in society. She knows that people who happen into her neighborhood think that her community is dangerous, but she knows her neighbors by name and knows their backgrounds. Among her Latino friends she feels safe. Esperanza, however, can understand the stranger's apprehension, for when she and her family venture out of the security of their neighborhood, their bodies get tense and their eyes look straight ahead.

Cisneros's concern for the place women hold in Latino society is evident in the powerful story "Alicia Who Sees Mice." Alicia, Esperanza's friend, must rise early every morning "with the tortilla star" and the mice in the kitchen to make her father's lunch-box tortillas. Alicia's mother has died, and, Esperanza remarks, young Alicia has inherited her mother's duty as the family caregiver along with her "rolling pin and sleepiness." Alicia has dreams of escaping this life of confinement and sacrifice, however, with a university education. She studies hard all night with the mice that her father says do not exist. With its precise imagery, "Alicia Who Sees Mice" is at once a criticism of patriarchal oppression of women and a beacon for those women who would struggle to break away from that oppression.

The theme of education and writing as a means whereby women can escape from the barrio is also found in "Minerva Writes Poems." Minerva is only a bit older than Esperanza, "but already she has two kids and a husband who left . . . and keeps leaving." Minerva's husband reappears sporadically, but their reunion usually ends in violence and abuse. Minerva cries every day over her bad situation and writes poems at night. In an act of artistic and sisterly solidarity, she and Esperanza read their poems to each other, yet at this point, Esperanza feels helpless, unable to stop the beatings. In her reply, "There is nothing *I* can do," there is a sense that Esperanza is inciting Minerva to take action for herself, as well as implying that society itself must change its attitudes.

This sisterly support for fulfillment through learning is echoed in "Edna's Ruthie." The title character is a talented but damaged woman who returns to her mother's home when she can no longer care for herself. Her own fondness for books--for hearing and telling a good story--inspires Esperanza in her own creative endeavors. Ruthie is moved to tears by Esperanza's recitation of children's stories, a response that conveys to the young girl the power of the word.

Esperanza's passage into adulthood is not without setbacks. In "Red Clowns," she goes to the amusement park with her friend Sally. When the sexually precocious Sally abandons Esperanza to slip away with a boy, Esperanza is molested and possibly raped by an older boy who tells her, "I love you Spanish girl, I love you." She is angry and sad and confused over the loss of her innocence. She cannot understand why everyone told her that sex would be so wonderful when, in fact, she found nothing pleasant about the perpetrator's dirty fingernails and sour breath. She wants to forget that degrading experience; she does not want to speak its horror. She yells at her friend Sally for leaving her, but she also directs her anger at a society that is partner to such an awful lie.

The fundamental conflict that besets Esperanza is resolved in "The Three Sisters." While Esperanza has repeatedly voiced her desire to escape the barrio and its double bind of racism and sexism that ensnares many women, she nevertheless loves her community and cannot come to terms with deserting it. Then three wise, eccentric, and decidedly feminist sisters settle the issue. Young Esperanza is strong, talented, and destined to "go very far," they tell her. Their encouraging words sanction her flight, yet the sisters also remind her of the need for loyalty:

When you leave you must remember to come back for the others. A circle, understand? You will always be Esperanza. You will always be Mango Street. You can't erase what you know. You can't forget who you are.

Young Esperanza can finally look to a life beyond the confines of her repressive environment.

WOMAN HOLLERING CREEK, AND OTHER STORIES

Likewise, *Woman Hollering Creek, and Other Stories* offers a glimpse into the lives of Chicanas who must confront daily the triple bind of not being considered Mexican, not being considered American, and not being male. Cisneros said that while the pieces of *Woman Hollering Creek, and Other Stories* function individually, there is a single, unifying thread of vision and experience that runs throughout the collection of twenty-two narratives. While the names of the narrators change with each work, each narrator retains a strong, determined, rebellious voice.

"ELEVEN"

In "Eleven," eleven-year-old Rachel's birthday prompts her to consider what it means to grow older. The wisdom of her eleven years has taught her that the years "underneath" the birthday, like the rings inside a tree trunk, make one a certain age. When people want to cry, she reasons, it is the part of them that is three that brings on tears; when they are scared, it is the part in them that is five that registers fear. For this reason, Rachel explains, she was not able to act eleven years old today in school when her teacher wrongly accused her of forgetting an ugly red sweater that had been in the coatroom for a month. All the years were welling up inside her, preventing Rachel from telling everyone that it was not her sweater. Instead, she was silent. She tries to be happy and remember that today she is eleven and that her mother will have a cake for her when she goes home. The part of Rachel that is three, however, comes out in front of the class instead. She wishes she were anything but eleven.

The narrator of the chilling "One Holy Night" is an adolescent girl who sells fruits and vegetables from her grandmother's pushcart. She meets a wanderer named Chaq who tells her that he is a descendant of a long line of Mayan kings. Intrigued by his story, the young woman begins to follow Chaq to his little room behind an automobile garage after she has sold each day's produce. Chaq spins mystic tales of the past and future greatness of his family's lineage as he entices the girl into her first sexual experience. She returns home to her grandmother and uncle a changed woman, barely able to contain her excitement. The young woman's secret, however, is soon discovered: She is pregnant. The family, in total disgrace, attempts to locate Chaq, who has since left town. Her uncle writes a letter in hope of finding the man who could correct his niece's ruined life. A response arrives from Chaq's sister. She explains that her brother's name is actually Chato, which means "fat-face"; he is thirty-seven, not at all Mayan, and not at all royal. The girl's family sends her to Mexico to give birth and to avoid disgrace. It is later learned that Chato has been captured and charged with the deaths of eleven women. The girl appears unfazed by the news, however, and continues to plan her dreams of children. She becomes indifferent to love.

"Never Marry a Mexican"

The title "Never Marry a Mexican" sums up the advice that the protagonist Clemencia was told as a young girl by her Chicana mother who regretted marrying a Mexican. Her mother's words ultimately consign Clemencia to cultural and social marginality. Clemencia scorns the working-class Latino men in her life and refuses to consider any of them as potential husbands. However, ironically, the white men whom she favors follow the same advice her mother has instilled in her: They will become sexually involved with a Chicana, but they will not marry outside of their own race.

Caught uncomfortably between cultures, Clemencia attempts to make the most of her difficult status. She prides herself on remaining unattached, a seductress who beds white, married men while their wives are in the throes of childbirth, but her pain and loneliness are palpable. She nurses affection for one white married lover for eighteen years, eventually gaining revenge on him by entering into a sexual relationship with his son. For Clemencia, the unhealthy relationship yields and yet perverts what she ostensibly disavows: marriage and motherhood. Sexual intercourse with the young man, she believes, links her to his father and mother's marital relations, of which he is the product, and her lover's relative youth allows her to "mother" him.

"Woman Hollering Creek"

The collection's title story is one of its strongest. It is a story of Cleófilas, a woman reared in a small town in Mexico not far from the Texas border. Cleófilas dreams of the romance and passion of the soap operas that she watches at her girlfriend's house. She believes her fantasy is realized when she meets Juan Pedro, a Texan who wants to marry her right away, "without a long engagement since he can't take off too much time from work." Cleófilas is whisked away across the border to Seguin, Texas, a town like so many others, with nothing of interest to walk to, "built so that you have to depend on husbands."

Life on "the other side" is, at first, a blessing for Cleófilas. Texas is the land of laundromats and dream homes. Running behind their new house is a creek that all call Woman Hollering. Cleófilas wonders if the odd name is connected to tales of La Llorona, the tragic mythical figure known to wail after drowning her children. Her enthusiasm for her new life ends quickly, however, with a slap to her face by Juan Pedro. That slap will start a long line of abuse and cause Cleófilas to think flatly, "This is the man I have waited my whole life for." Although she had always promised herself that she would not allow any man to hit her, Cleófilas, isolated at home, not allowed to correspond with her family, hindered by not knowing English, and afraid of Juan Pedro's rage, stays with him. When she begins to suspect that Juan Pedro is unfaithful, she thinks about returning to her native town but fears disgrace and does not act. Cleófilas had always thought that her life would be like a soap opera, "only now the episodes got sadder and sadder. And there were no commercials in between for comic relief." She becomes pregnant with their second child but is almost too afraid to ask Juan Pedro to take her to the clinic for prenatal care. Once at the clinic, Cleófilas breaks down and tells her plight to a sympathetic doctor who arranges a ride for her and her son to the bus station in San Antonio. The morning of their escape, Cleófilas is tense and frightened. As they pass over Woman Hollering Creek in a pickup truck, their spirited female driver lets out a Tarzan-like yell that startles her two passengers. On her way back to her father's home, Cleófilas catches a glimpse of what it is to be an autonomous woman.

OTHER MAJOR WORKS

LONG FICTION: *Caramelo: Or, Puro Cuento*, 2002.
POETRY: *Bad Boys*, 1980; *The Rodrigo Poems*, 1985;
My Wicked, Wicked Ways, 1987; *Loose Woman*, 1994.
CHILDREN'S LITERATURE: *Hairs = Pelitos*, 1994.
MISCELLANEOUS: *Vintage Cisneros*, 2004.

BIBLIOGRAPHY

Bloom, Harold, ed. *Sandra Cisneros's "The House on Mango Street."* New York: Bloom's Literary Criticism, 2010. Collection of essays providing various interpretations of the book, including discussions its literary continuity, its erotic depiction of feet, and its "dual"-ing images of La Malinche and the Virgin of Guadalupe.

Brady, Mary Pat. "The Contrapuntal Geographies of *Woman Hollering Creek, and Other Stories*." *American Literature* 71 (March, 1999): 117-150. Shows how Cisneros's narrative techniques challenge various spatial representations and lay bare hidden stories. Claims that Cisneros explores the various subtleties of violence of changing spatial relations.

Cisneros, Sandra. "Barbie-Q." In *The Art of the Short Story*, edited by Dana Gioia and R.S. Gwynn. New York: Pearson Longman, 2006. Cisneros's "Barbie-Q" is one of the short stories included in this anthology. The book also includes Cisneros's commentary on her story, a brief biography, and the editors' analysis of her work and its place within the literary tradition.

_____. "On the Solitary Fate of Being Mexican, Female, Wicked, and Thirty-Three: An Interview with Writer Sandra Cisneros." Interview by Pilar E. Rodríguez Aranda. *The Americas Review* 18, no. 1 (1990): 64-80. In an enlightening interview, Cisneros discusses her identity as a Chicana, her development as a writer, and her use of poetry and modern myth in her fiction. The interview focuses on the collections *My Wicked, Wicked Ways* and *The House on Mango Street*.

Doyle, Jacqueline. "More Room of Her Own: Sandra Cisneros' *The House on Mango Street*." *MELUS* 19 (Winter, 1994): 5-35. Discusses *The House on Mango Street* as a transformation of the terms of Virginia Woolf's vision in *A Room of One's Own*

(1929). Asserts Cisneros's work provides a rich reconsideration of the contemporary feminist inheritance as influenced by Woolf.

Gelfant, Blanche H., ed. *The Columbia Companion to the Twentieth-Century American Short Story*. New York: Columbia University Press, 2000. Includes a chapter in which Cisneros's short stories are analyzed.

Griffin, Susan E. "Resistance and Reinvention in Sandra Cisneros' *Woman Hollering Creek*." In *Ethnicity and the American Short Story*, edited by Julie Brown. New York: Garland Publishing, 1997. Discusses the role that Mexican popular culture and traditional Mexican narratives play in limiting women's sense of identity. Focuses primarily on the negative effects of popular romances in Mexico and televised soap operas.

Herrera-Sobek, María, ed. *Critical Insights: "The House on Mango Street," by Sandra Cisneros*. Pasadena, Calif.: Salem Press, 2011. Collection of original and reprinted essays providing critical readings of *The House on Mango Street* from several different perspectives. Includes a brief biography of Cisneros.

Lewis, L. M. "Sandra Cisneros." In *A Reader's Companion to the Short Story in English*, edited by Erin Fallon, et al., under the auspices of the Society for the Study of the Short Story. Westport, Conn.: Greenwood Press, 2001. Aimed at the general reader, this essay provides a brief biography of Cisneros followed by an analysis of her short fiction.

Matchie, Thomas. "Literary Continuity in Sandra Cisneros's *The House on Mango Street*." *The Midwest Quarterly* 37 (Autumn, 1995): 67-79. Discusses how *The House on Mango Street* uses Mark Twain's *Adventures of Huckleberry Finn* (1884) and J. D. Salinger's *The Catcher in the Rye* (1951) as literary models of adolescents growing up in a culturally oppressive world. Like Huck and Holden, Cisneros's protagonist is innocent, sensitive, and vulnerable, and she grows mentally in the process of the narrative.

Mullen, Harryette. "'A Silence Between Us Like a Language': The Untranslatability of Experience in Sandra Cisneros's *Woman Hollering Creek*."

MELUS 21 (Summer, 1996): 3-20. Argues that Spanish as a code comprehensible to an inside group and as a repressed language subordinate to English are central issues in *Woman Hollering Creek*.

Olivares, Julian. "Sandra Cisneros' *The House on Mango Street*, and the Poetics of Space." *The Americas Review* 15, nos. 3/4 (1987): 160-170. This essay is an in-depth analysis of the stories of *The House on Mango Street* in terms of Cisneros's distinctive use of the metaphor of a house situated in a Latino neighborhood. Contains bibliographical references pertinent to *The House on Mango Street*.

Rivera, Carmen Haydée. *Border Crossings and Beyond: The Life and Works of Sandra Cisneros*. Santa Barbara, Calif.: Praeger, 2009. Examines how Cisneros's writing and social activism reflect issues of cultural and racial identity. Describes her creative process when writing novels.

Sagel, Jim. "Sandra Cisneros: Conveying the Riches of the Latin American Culture Is the Author's Literary Goal." *Publishers Weekly* 238 (March 29, 1991): 74-75. In this informative interview, Cisneros speaks about the influence that her childhood had on her writing. The interview touches upon the personal side of the writer and includes a brief description of the genesis of the collection *Woman Hollering Creek, and Other Stories*.

Tokarczyk, Michelle M. "The Voice of the Voiceless: Sandra Cisneros." In *Class Definitions: On the Lives and Writings of Maxine Hong Kingston, Sandra Cisneros, and Dorothy Allison*. Selinsgrove, Pa.: Susquehanna University Press, 2008. Discusses the lives and work of the three authors, focusing on their shared traits as working-class writers, as evidenced by their concern with providing a voice for the voiceless. Includes a previously unpublished interview with Cisneros.

Thompson, Jeff. "'What Is Called Heaven?' Identity in Sandra Cisneros's *Woman Hollering Creek*." *Studies in Short Fiction* 31 (Summer, 1994): 415-424. States that the overall theme of the stories is the vulnerability of the female narrators. The vignettes should be read as symptomatic of a social structure that allows little cultural movement and little possibility for the creation of an identity outside the boundaries of the barrio.

Wyatt, Jean. "On Not Being *La Malinche:* Border Negotiations of Gender in Sandra Cisneros's 'Never Marry a Mexican' and 'Woman Hollering Creek.'" *Tulsa Studies in Women's Literature* 14 (Fall, 1995): 243-271. Discusses how the stories describe the difficulties of living on the border between Anglo-American and Mexican cultures and how the female protagonists of the stories struggle with sexuality and motherhood as icons that limit their identity.

Mary F. Yudin
Updated by Theresa Kanoza

WALTER VAN TILBURG CLARK

Born: East Orland, Maine; August 3, 1909
Died: Reno, Nevada; November 10, 1971

PRINCIPAL SHORT FICTION
The Watchful Gods, and Other Stories, 1950

OTHER LITERARY FORMS

In addition to his short stories, Walter Van Tilburg Clark wrote three novels--*The Ox-Bow Incident* (1940), *The City of Trembling Leaves* (1945), and *The Track of the Cat* (1949). The first and last of these were made into motion pictures. *Tim Hazard* (1951) is the enlarged version of *The City of Trembling Leaves*. Clark also produced an early book of poems, *Ten Women in Gale's House and Shorter Poems* (1932).

ACHIEVEMENTS

Although Walter Van Tilburg Clark is known primarily for his novels, his one volume of stories, as well as his uncollected short stories, have established him as a fine writer of short stories. In fact, his story "The Wind and the Snow of Winter" received the O. Henry Award in 1945. In their Western settings, their ambiguous depiction of the American dream, their concern about personal identity and oneness with nature, and their essentially tragic vision, the short stories are of a piece with his three novels. Unlike some "Western" writers, Clark used his landscape as both subject and backdrop for his own philosophical themes. Less concerned with characters--one story virtually omits them, concentrating instead on animals as "characters"--than with ideas, Clark used his characters, many of whom seem stereotypical, to embody and actualize his notions about the possibility of defining self and position in the cosmos.

BIOGRAPHY

Walter Van Tilburg Clark was born on August 3, 1909, in East Orland, Maine, the first child of Walter Ernest and Euphemia Abrams Clark. In 1917, his father, a distinguished economics professor, became president of the University of Nevada at Reno. Therefore, the family had to move when Clark was only eight. In Reno, Clark attended public schools and later received his B.A. and M.A. degrees in English from the University of Nevada. Clark married Barbara Morse in 1933, and they became the parents of two children, Barbara Ann and Robert Morse. The couple settled in Cazenovia, New York, where Clark began a career in high school and college teaching as well as creative writing. In the next several years, Clark continued writing and taught at several schools, including the University of Montana, Reed College, and the University of Nevada, where he resigned after protesting the autocratic tendencies of the administration. He eventually returned there, however, to teach creative writing. Clark was also director of creative writing at San Francisco State College from 1956 to 1962. He died of cancer on November 10, 1971, at the age of sixty-two.

ANALYSIS

Walter Van Tilburg Clark once wrote that the primary impulse of the arts has been religious and ritualistic--with the central hope of "propitiating or enlisting Nature, the Gods, God, or whatever name one wishes to give the encompassing and still mysterious whole." Certainly Clark's fiction attests to such a view. In a world in which thought is often confused and fragmented, he advocates for humanity a stance of intellectual honesty, an acceptance of instinctive values, and a belief in love. The key is human experience. As Max Westbrook so aptly put it in his study of Clark, "Clark's literary credo, then, is based on the capacity of the unconscious mind to discover and to give shape to objective knowledge about the human experience."

"THE BUCK IN THE HILLS"

"The Buck in the Hills" may be Clark's clearest reflection in his stories of the literary credo mentioned above. Writing more or less in the terse, almost brittle, style of Ernest Hemingway, Clark opens the story with vividly descriptive passages of mountain scenery. The narrator, whose name the reader never learns, has returned to this setting after five years. It is really more than a return for him; it is a pilgrimage to a sacred place. Like Hemingway's heroes, he feels a deep need to replenish his spirit, to reattach himself to things solid and lasting. The clear sky, the strong mountains, and the cold wind all serve as a natural backdrop for the spiritual ritual of his pilgrimage. As he climbs toward the peak of a mountain, he recalls with pleasure an earlier climb with a dark girl "who knew all the flowers, and who, when I bet her she couldn't find more than thirty kinds, found more than fifty." On that day, as on this, the narrator felt a clear sense of the majesty of the mountains and the "big arch of the world we looked at," and he recalls spending two hours another time watching a hawk, "feeling myself lift magnificently when he swooped up toward me on the current up the col, and then balanced and turned above."

When he returns to his campsite by a shallow snow-water lake, he swims, naked, and as he floats in this cleansing ritual, looking up at the first stars showing above the ridge, he sings out "an operatic sounding something." At this point, just when his spiritual rejuvenation is nearly complete, the ritual is broken by the appearance of Tom Williams, one of the two men whom he had accompanied on this trip to the mountains. The plan had been for Williams and the other man, Chet McKenny, to spend a few days hunting, leaving the narrator alone. As he watches Williams approach, the narrator unhappily expects to also see McKenny, a man he dislikes not because of his stupidity but because of something deeper than that. Williams, however, is alone.

After a while Williams tells the narrator of the experience he has just had with McKenny, whom he calls a "first-rate bastard." During their hunt McKenny had purposely shot a deer in the leg so that he could herd it back to their camp rather than carry it. When they arrived at the camp, he slit the deer's throat, saying, "I

never take more than one shot." Sickened by this brutal act, Williams drove off in his car, leaving McKenny to get out of the mountains as best he could. After Williams's story, both men agree that McKenny deserves to be left behind for what he did. In another cleansing ritual, they both take a swim, becoming cheerful later as they sit by their fire drinking beer. The next morning, however, it is snowing, and as they silently head back down the mountain, the narrator feels that there is "something listening behind each tree and rock we passed, and something waiting among the taller trees down slope, blue through the falling snow. They wouldn't stop us, but they didn't like us either. The snow was their ally."

Thus there are two contrasting moods in "The Buck in the Hills": that of harmony and that of dissonance. At the beginning of the story, the narrator has succeeded after five years in reestablishing a right relationship with nature and thus with himself, but at the end, this relationship has been destroyed by the cruel actions of McKenny. The narrator's ritual of acceptance of the primordial in human beings has been

Walter Van Tilburg Clark (Library of Congress)

overshadowed by McKenny's ritual of acceptance that human beings are somehow above nature. Ernest Hemingway's belief that morality is what one feels good after is in one sense reversed here to the idea that immorality is what one feels bad after; certainly the narrator and Williams, on their way down the mountain, feel bad. Human beings and nature in a right relationship is not a mere romantic notion to Clark. It is reality--indeed, perhaps man's only reality.

"THE PORTABLE PHONOGRAPH"

In "The Portable Phonograph" Clark ventures, if not into science fiction, at least into a kind of speculative fiction as he sets his story in a world of the future, one marked by the "toothed impress of great tanks" and the "scars of gigantic bombs." It seems a world devoid of human existence; the only visible life is a flock of wild geese flying south to escape the cold of winter. Above the frozen creek in a cave dug into the bank, however, there is human life: four men--survivors of some undescribed Armageddon--huddle before a smoldering peat fire in an image of primitive existence. Clark provides little background for these four almost grotesque men. One, the reader learns, is a doctor, probably of philosophy rather than of medicine. One is a young musician, quite ill with a cough. The other two are middle-aged. All are obviously intelligent. The cave belongs to the doctor, whose name is Jenkins, and he has invited the others to hear him read from one of his four books--the Bible, *Moby Dick*, *The Divine Comedy*, and William Shakespeare. In selfish satisfaction he explains that when he saw what was happening to the world, "I told myself, 'It is the end. I cannot take much; I will take these.'" His justification is his love for the books and his belief that they represent the "soul of what was good in us here."

When Jenkins finishes his reading from *The Tempest*, the others wait expectantly, and the former finally says grudgingly, "You wish to hear the phonograph." This is obviously the moment for which they have been waiting. Jenkins tenderly and almost lovingly brings out his portable phonograph and places it on the dirt-packed floor where the firelight will fall on it. He comments that he has been using thorns as needles, but that in deference to the musician, he will use one of the three steel needles that he has left. Since Jenkins will play only one record

a week, there is some discussion as to what they will hear. The musician selects a Claude Debussy nocturne, and as Jenkins places the record on the phonograph, the others all rise to their knees "in an attitude of worship."

As the piercing and singularly sweet sounds of the nocturne flood the cave, the men are captivated. In all but the musician there occur "sequences of tragically heightened recollection"; the musician, clenching the fingers of one hand over his teeth, hears only the music. At the conclusion of the piece, the three guests leave--the musician by himself, the other two together. Jenkins peers anxiously after them, waiting. When he hears the cough of the musician some distance off, he drops his canvas door and hurries to hide his phonograph in a deep hole in the cave wall. Sealing up the hole, he prays and then gets under the covers of his grass bed, feeling with his hand the "comfortable piece of lead pipe."

Structurally a very simple story, "The Portable Phonograph" is rich in its implications. In a devastated world four men represent what Jenkins refers to as "the doddering remnant of a race of mechanical fools." The books that he has saved symbolize the beauty of man's artistic creativity as opposed to the destructiveness of his mechanical creativity. Again, Clark portrays two sides of human nature, that which aspires to the heights of human spiritual and moral vision and that which drives him on to his own destruction. The cruel and bitter irony is that essentially man's imagination is at once his glory and his undoing. As the men kneel in expectation before the mechanical wonder of the phonograph, they worship it as a symbol of human ingenuity. The music that comes from the record provides for at least three of the men a temporary escape from their grim reality. Thus, man's drive for mechanical accomplishment--the same drive that has destroyed a world--now has also preserved the beauty of his musical accomplishment. This may well be what the musician understands as he lets his head "fall back in agony" while listening to the music. Human beings are forever blessed to create and doomed to destroy. That is why the piece of lead pipe is such a protective comfort to Jenkins as he closes "his smoke-smarting eyes." In order to protect what is left of art, he must rely on the very methods that have brought about its demise.

"THE INDIAN WELL"

In his novel *The Track of the Cat*, Clark takes the reader into the realm of human unconscious as Curt Bridges, the protagonist, is driven to his own death while tracking both a real and an imagined cougar. In the short story "The Indian Well," set in the desert in 1940, Jim Suttler also seeks to kill a cougar, and although the mythological and psychological implications are not developed as fully as they are in the novel, the story is still powerful in its total effect. In what must be one of the best word pictures of the desert and the creatures that inhabit it, Clark devotes six pages to the stark drama of life and death that takes place around a desert well; rattlesnakes, road runners, jackrabbits, hawks, lizards, coyotes, and a cow and her calf all play parts.

The story's only character is Jim Suttler, a grizzled old prospector who, with his mule Jenny, still seeks gold in abandoned and long-forgotten mines. Suttler is a man well attuned to life in the desert wilderness. Armed with a rifle, an old six-shooter, and primitive mining tools, he is not merely a stereotyped prospector; his red beard and shoulder-length red hair might lead some to see in him a resemblance to Christ, but Suttler is unlike Christ in several ways. Early in the story, Suttler and Jenny arrive at Indian Well. The history of Indian Well is recorded on the walls of the rundown cabin nearby; names and dates go back to the previous century. All had used the well, and all had given vent to some expression, ranging from "God guide us" to "Giv it back to the injuns" to a more familiar libel: "Fifty miles from water, a hundred miles from wood, a million miles from God, and three feet from hell." Before Suttler leaves, he too will leave a message.

Finding some traces of gold in an abandoned mine near the well, Suttler decides to stay for a while to see if he can make it pay off. It is a comfortable time, and both he and Jenny regain some of the weight lost during their recent travels. Two events, however, change the idyllic mood of their stay. The first occurs when Suttler kills a range calf that, along with its mother, has strayed close to the well. While he has some qualms about killing the calf, Suttler, enjoying the sensation of providence, soon puts them out of his mind. Next, a cougar kills Jenny. This event inflames Suttler with the desire

for revenge--even if "it takes a year"--so throughout the winter he sits up nights waiting for the cat to return. When he eventually kills it, he skins it and, uncovering Jenny's grave, places the skin over her carcass. His revenge complete, he cleanses himself at the well and leaves as a "starved but revived and volatile spirit." Thus, one more passerby has contributed to the history of Indian Well, and the life around the well goes on.

The basic element in "The Indian Well" is the ironic contrast between the beginning and the ending of the story, just as it is in "The Buck in the Hills." When they come upon Indian Well, Suttler and Jenny enter into a natural world that has its own ordered life and death, and they blend easily into it. Suttler appears to be a man at one with nature, yet at the end of the story, the death that he has inflicted upon the cougar stands as something apart from the ordered world of the well. It is a death that was motivated by the desire for revenge, a very human emotion. The reader might be suspicious when Suttler kills the calf, but he justifies such a killing on the basis of the meat that the calf provides. Killing the cougar, on the other hand, cannot be justified in any external way. The deep satisfaction that it brings to Suttler stands in opposition to any right relationship between human beings and nature; it is solely a part of Suttler's inner self. When the deed is done, Suttler can blend back into the natural world around him. For that one winter, however, as he lies in wait for the cougar, he exhibits man's all-too-common flaw of putting himself above the natural world. Still, because he knows what he has done and, moreover, accepts it, he is able once more to establish his relationship with the cosmic forces.

"HOOK"

In a very real sense, this establishing of a relationship with the cosmic forces is the goal of many of Clark's characters. Caught in the ambiguities of good and evil, of morality and immorality, they struggle to maintain a faith in humanity and to bring moral law into accordance with natural law, for only in that way can human beings be saved from their own destructive tendencies. Some critics, such as Chester E. Eisinger, see Clark as being rather pessimistic regarding the success of such a human attempt at unity and attribute to him a desire to retreat from other human beings. If this view is correct, then perhaps the story "Hook" is the best expression of what Clark wants to say. The main character in this story is a hawk who fulfills himself in flight, in battle, and in sex, until he is killed by a dog. His is a life cycle of instinct, and, as he lives it, he can easily enough be seen as an antihuman symbol. If Eisinger's view is wrong, however, then it is possible to see Clark as a writer who seeks not a retreat from other human beings but an explanation of humanity. Like the hawks that appear so often in Clark's stories, human beings are also a part of nature and because they are, it is possible to see their task as one of defining themselves in the context of the natural order of things. Whatever the outcome, Clark's characters do make the attempt.

OTHER MAJOR WORKS

LONG FICTION: *The Ox-Bow Incident*, 1940; *The City of Trembling Leaves*, 1945; *The Track of the Cat*, 1949; *Tim Hazard*, 1951.

POETRY: *Ten Women in Gale's House, and Shorter Poems*, 1932.

EDITED TEXT: *The Journals of Alfred Doten, 1849-1903*, 1973 (3 volumes).

BIBLIOGRAPHY

Benson, Jackson J. *The Ox-Bow Man: A Biography of Walter Van Tilburg Clark*. Reno: University of Nevada Press, 2004. First full-length biography of Clark. Describes his life as a writer and teacher and addresses his significant role in transforming Western literature. Chapter 8 provides analysis of *The Watchful Gods, and Other Stories*.

Clark, Walter Van Tilburg. *The Watchful Gods, and Other Stories*. Foreword by Ann Ronald. Reno: University of Nevada Press, 2004. In addition to Clark's short stories, this edition features Ronald's foreword in which she discusses Clark's life, work, and the individual stories in this collection.

Court, Franklin E. "Clark's 'The Wind and the Snow of Winter' and Celtic Oisin." *Studies in Short Fiction* 33 (Spring, 1996): 219-228. Examines the mythic pattern of Clark's story against the background of the Celtic legend of wandering Oisin.

Eisinger, Chester E. *Fiction of the Forties*. Chicago: University of Chicago Press, 1963. Eisinger regards Clark's short stories as having similar themes (the search for identity, the desire to merge with nature, and rejection by nature) as the novels. While several short stories are mentioned in passing, Eisinger includes lengthy analyses of "The Buck in the Hills," "Hook," and "The Watchful Gods."

Gelfant, Blanche H., ed. *The Columbia Companion to the Twentieth-Century American Short Story*. New York: Columbia University Press, 2000. Includes a chapter in which Clark's short stories are analyzed.

Kich, Martin. *Western American Novelists*. Vol. 1. New York: Garland, 1995. After a brief account of Clark's career, Kich provides an extensive, annotated bibliography, offering detailed commentary on reviews of virtually every significant work of prose fiction. Kich also annotates reference works with entries on Clark and books with chapters on his fiction.

Laird, Charlton, ed. *Walter Van Tilburg Clark: Critiques*. Reno: University of Nevada Press, 1983. A collection of eighteen pieces, some by Clark himself, on Clark's life, his major published work, and his literary craftsmanship. The book is most valuable for the essays on "The Watchful Gods" and "The Pretender," which portray Clark as a reviser/craftsman, and for the autobiographical information and the detailed chronology provided by his son.

Lee, Lawrence L. *Walter Van Tilburg Clark*. Boise, Idaho: Boise State College Press, 1973. In his monograph, Lee devotes a separate chapter to the short stories, which he believes repeat the themes of the novels but with greater clarity and insight. "The Portable Phonograph" and "The Watchful Gods" are discussed in some detail. Supplemented by a helpful bibliography.

Ronald, Ann. "Walter Van Tilburg Clark's Brave Bird, 'Hook.'" In *Reader of the Purple Sage: Essays on Western Writers and Environmental Literature*. Reno: University of Nevada Press, 2003. Ronald's essay on Clark's story "Hook," originally published in *Studies in Short Fiction* (Fall, 1988), discusses the complex irony of the story, arguing that critics have wrongly ignored it as a simple fable or animal tale for children.

Westbrook, Max. *Walter Van Tilburg Clark*. New York: Twayne, 1969. Westbrook's book remains the best overall assessment of Clark's literary work. In addition to a chronology of Clark's life, a biographical chapter, and a select bibliography, Westbrook includes a chapter on *The Watchful Gods, and Other Stories*, and several paragraph-length discussions of Clark's best short stories.

_____. "Walter Van Tilburg Clark and the American Dream." In *A Literary History of the American West*, edited by J. Golden Taylor. Fort Worth: Texas Christian University Press, 1987. Westbrook blends biography with criticism as he analyzes Clark's fiction and defines Clark's place in literary history. Using characters from Clark's stories and novels, Westbrook depicts the Clark "hero" as an idealistic dreamer incapable of practical action. As a result, the American dream, or its nightmarish counterpart, becomes a real concern for Clark.

Wilton Eckley
Updated by Thomas L. Erskine

EVAN S. CONNELL

Born: Kansas City, Missouri; August 17, 1924

PRINCIPAL SHORT FICTION

The Anatomy Lesson, and Other Stories, 1957
At the Crossroads: Stories, 1965
Saint Augustine's Pigeon: The Selected Stories of Evan S. Connell, 1980
The Collected Stories of Evan S. Connell, 1995
Lost in Uttar Pradesh: New and Selected Stories, 2008

OTHER LITERARY FORMS

Evan S. Connell's literary career extends across all forms and genres. He wrote a number of highly successful and acclaimed short stories and novels, including *Mrs. Bridge* (1959) and *Mr. Bridge* (1969), which have been recognized as minor modern classics, and *The Alchymist's Journal* (1991; expanded as *Alchymic Journals*, 2006) and *Deus lo Volt! A Chronicle of the Crusades* (2000). He also wrote book-length poems. In nonfiction, Connell produced studies of famous explorers in *A Long Desire* (1979), the essay collections *The White Lantern* (1980) and *The Aztec Treasure House: New and Selected Essays* (2001), and the biography *Francisco Goya: Life and Times* (2004). One of his most popular works is *Son of the Morning Star: Custer and the Little Bighorn* (1984), an acute, penetrating, and poetic meditation on the often tragic relationship between white settlers and Native Americans.

ACHIEVEMENTS

Evan S. Connell's first novel, *Mrs. Bridge*, was a best seller and was nominated for the National Book Award for Fiction in 1960. Connell's writing has earned him Saxton and John Simon Guggenheim Memorial Foundation Fellowships and a Rockefeller Foundation grant. *Son of the Morning Star* was a best seller and won for Connell a National Book Critics Circle Award. In 1987, he was honored with an American Academy and Institute of Arts and Letters Award. He was one of the nominees for the Man Booker International Prize in 2009. On April 23, 2010, Connell received the Robert Kirsch Award from the *Los Angeles Times*, which is presented annually in recognition of a distinguished body of work by a writer residing in or writing about the West.

BIOGRAPHY

Evan Shelby Connell, Jr., was born in Kansas City, Missouri, the son and grandson of physicians. He attended Southwestern High School in Kansas City and later Dartmouth College in Hanover, New Hampshire. Through his early college years, Connell intended to become a doctor; this ambition changed, however, after he left Dartmouth to serve in the United States armed forces during World War II. Leaving Dartmouth before he graduated, Connell joined the Navy, where he was assigned to flight school, becoming first a pilot and then, after completing his training, a flight instructor. During his time in the Navy, from 1943 through 1945, he saw no actual combat. When Connell completed his military service, he enrolled in the University of Kansas and finished his undergraduate education there with a degree in English. Further studies followed at Stanford University, Columbia University, and San Francisco City College (now San Francisco State University). In addition to enrolling in writing courses, Connell took courses in art, especially painting and sculpture.

Having embarked upon a literary career, Connell began publishing his short stories in various small and literary magazines. The quality of his work was recognized early, and his writings soon appeared in anthologies. His work was chosen for *Prize Stories: The O. Henry Awards* in 1949 and again in 1951, and his works were published in *The Best American Short Stories* in 1955. His first collection of stories, *The Anatomy Lesson, and Other Stories*, appeared in 1957, causing critics to take note of this new and strikingly different talent. Throughout most of Connell's career, his reputation among critics and other writers has been consistently higher than his recognition among the general public. Fairly early recognition of Connell's abilities also came in the form of grants, fellowships, and awards.

In addition to his own writing, Connell was active from 1959 through 1965 as the editor of *Contact*, a literary magazine published in California, where he then resided. One of Connell's earlier books, his novel *Mrs. Bridge*, was quickly recognized as a modern classic by a small but discerning group of readers. The companion work, *Mr. Bridge*, was also accorded the status of a cult classic. Connell's first real popular success was his 1984 study of Custer and the Indian wars, *Son of the Morning Star*. He spent four years conducting research for the book, reading firsthand accounts and visiting the battle site of the Little Bighorn four times. The *The Alchymist's Journal* also earned praise from critics as a "highly cerebral and wisdom-filled work." Connell eventu-

ally made his home in Santa Fe, New Mexico.

ANALYSIS

Evan S. Connell is a careful and precise writer, whose fictions capture and reveal their meanings through detail, observation, and implication. Settings and descriptions of how his characters dress and appear offer subtle but unmistakable clues to the inner lives of the individuals in his stories. Quite often these individuals appear to be conventional, even boring characters; Mr. and Mrs. Bridge, for example, appear at first to be almost numbingly normal. A closer and more sympathetic examination, however, shows that even the mask of midwestern, middle-American normality often covers passion, doubts, and dreams.

Connell is a master of the quotidian, the everyday or ordinary. Sometimes he uses the everyday settings in a satirical fashion, exposing the gap between modern culture's stated beliefs and its actions. This satire, however, is generally restrained, even muted, rather than being broad or forced. More open and pointed attacks are found not in Connell's prose fictions but in his long poems, especially *Points for a Compass Rose* (1973), which is overtly political.

Connell is most concerned with the people in his stories and in the baffling, mysterious fashions in which they fall in and out of love, rejoice over happy events, cry over sad ones, and, in essence, live their everyday but compellingly wonderful lives. Through an extensive but not obtrusive vocabulary and a lean, economical prose style, Connell reveals these everyday people and their lives as matters worth careful observation and consideration.

Each story by Connell creates, in the space of only a few pages, a world that is uniquely its own. This world may be, and often is, connected with the everyday world of modern American life, but inevitably it also carries with it the hint of other ways and other views, and these provide insight into more varied experiences. Often these alternate lifestyles are introduced by a character who disturbs the tranquil flow of the ordinary and then fades from the story. There is something more possible than ordinary life, these characters suggest, and this suggestion and the reactions of other figures in the story to it are central to Connell's fictions.

"THE FISHERMAN FROM CHIHUAHUA"

Sometimes this sense of otherness is presented obliquely, as in "The Fisherman from Chihuahua." In this story, the ordinary restaurant known as Pendleton's is visited by a tall, mysterious Mexican who suddenly, and for no explicable reason, begins to sing a piercing, meaningless dirge. Although at first annoyed, the owner and his regular patrons begin to look forward to the man's visits and his unearthly singing, which reveal a glimpse of something that they cannot name. When the tall Mexican abruptly ceases his visits, those who remain are left with a sense of loss.

"THE WALLS OF AVILA"

This division between necessary but boring life and romantic adventures is explored more explicitly in a pair of stories featuring the character known only by his initials, J. D. In "The Walls of Avila," J. D. returns to his hometown after years of wandering throughout Europe, Africa, and Asia. J. D. spins eloquent and elaborate tales of his adventures, and his stories are packed with such vivid detail that they make distant places, such as the ancient village of Avila, in Spain, seem as real as New York or as tangible as a suburban house. J. D.'s tales leave his childhood friends depressed and angry because they are now older, more "mature," and established but feel they have missed the adventures of life. J. D. has given them a glimpse of a romantic life that is denied to them, perhaps because of their own failures or fears.

"THE PALACE OF THE MOORISH KINGS"

These themes are explored in even greater detail in "The Palace of the Moorish Kings." Again, J. D. spins his wonderful yarns, and apparently the man has been everywhere: the Black Pagoda in Konorak, the islands of Micronesia, the painted caves of Altamira. Now, he wishes to return home, get married, and find a job. His friends are partly relieved by this decision, since it affirms that their choices and lives have been, after all, correct. At the same time, however, they sense that when J. D. settles down it will mark the end to their own dreams, even as lived through him. One of them attempts to explain their mixed feelings to J. D.: "It's simply that you have lived as the rest of us dreamed of living, which is not easy for us to accept."

"ARCTURUS"

One of Connell's most ambitious and fully realized flights in short fiction has been his series of stories about the Muhlbach family, who live across the river from Manhattan in a moderately exclusive New Jersey suburb. Like the Bridges, who appeared in short stories before receiving more extended treatment in novels, the Muhlbachs have appeared in both stories and novels, and one of the short stories, "The Mountains of Guatemala," later reappeared, revised, as the opening chapter of the novel *Double Honeymoon* (1976).

By returning to the same characters in successive stories, Connell is able to develop them more fully and completely. This gradual development is especially important for Karl Muhlbach, since his inner life and especially his emotional crises following the death of his wife are the central themes of all these stories. That death is signaled in typically indirect Connell fashion in the first of the Muhlbach stories, "Arcturus." This is a key story in the body of Connell's work for several reasons: First, it introduces the Muhlbach family; second, "Arcturus" is a high point in Connell's literary technique of presenting deeply emotional, disturbing events through oblique reference. In many ways, "Arcturus" is powerful precisely because of what is not said, what is left unexpressed. Finally, the story is one of the best pieces of American short fiction written during the second half of the twentieth century.

The plot of "Arcturus" is deceptively simple. Karl Muhlbach and his wife, Joyce, are expecting a guest, Sandy Kirk. Sandy is an old boyfriend of Joyce, and the reader learns through hints that he has been asked for a final visit because Joyce is dying. As the Muhlbachs wait, their children, Otto and Donna, drowse by the fireplace. Otto is aware that something is going to happen, that some tension pervades the room, but he cannot quite recognize it. Still, it troubles him throughout the evening, even after he is put to bed; later, when Sandy has left, Karl must reassure his son that everything will be well, but even as he says the words, he doubts them.

"Arcturus" is a story about perceptions. Connell structures his narrative so that the reader shares directly the thoughts of Karl and his son, and those of Sandy Kirk, but Joyce Muhlbach, the very center of the story, remains closed and unexplained. Her actions and remarks can be observed, but the reader must attempt to deduce their underlying causes with little assistance from the author. In a sense, this is the very position in which the men of the story find themselves, as they struggle to understand what Joyce is trying to tell them and to comprehend what she wants to hear.

Perceptions vary. Sandy, who at first seems to be so much more sophisticated and worldly than Karl, turns out to be the less imaginative and intuitive of the two men. Although he once thought that he was in love with Joyce, Sandy cannot understand her, and he leaves the Muhlbachs' house not only confused but also a little frightened. Karl, on the other hand, emerges as a much more generous and expansive soul, full of unexpected talents (such as speaking German) or knowledge (most notably of astronomy). Finally, Otto, being poised between childhood and adolescence, has the unique perspective which that precarious position brings; as noted, he recognizes the tension in the house but cannot comprehend its cause. "Are the stars falling?" he asks his father, his symbolic question for all disorder and confusion. In a sense, with the death of Joyce, the stars will fall for the family; still, Karl Muhlbach answers "no," and his son is reassured.

In this story, Connell deliberately echoes one of the great masterpieces of modern short fiction, James Joyce's "The Dead," an intention signaled even by the name of Mrs. Muhlbach, Joyce. The parallels between the two works are many and striking, and it seems clear that Connell is fashioning an answer to the earlier work. Both stories take place in winter, during a snowfall, and in each a husband must confront and react to his wife's earlier affections for another man. In "The Dead," the former lover is dead and buried, while in "Arcturus" it is the wife who will soon die. Even scenes are repeated, although with a twist, for in Joyce's story the husband stands at a second-story window looking out over a snow-covered landscape, while in Connell's it is Karl who stands on the ground, staring up at the windows of his own house. Despite these differences, both men experience a sense of loss and isolation and realize intuitively that it is not only death but also life itself that can make men and women as separate and distant as stars.

"SAINT AUGUSTINE'S PIGEON"

The next story about the Muhlbachs is "Saint Augustine's Pigeon," in which Karl Muhlbach attempts to adjust to the death of Joyce and construct a new life for himself and his two children. These attempts are fumbling, even slightly pathetic, as Karl's emotional needs are complicated by his sexual desires. In "Saint Augustine's Pigeon," Karl Muhlbach impulsively leaves his placid suburban home one evening to travel into New York, where he intends to find a mistress.

Muhlbach's efforts are both desperate and farcical. In Greenwich Village, he plays chess with a young bohemian girl who calls herself Rouge, but after Karl wins the game he finds himself forced into buying soup for Rouge and two of her friends. After the meal, the young people abruptly vanish, and Karl finds himself alone. He then takes a taxi to a tawdry night spot called Club Sahara. It is aptly named, for here Karl Muhlbach finds only sterile shows of sex and has his pocket picked. Later, he must call a sick friend out of bed to have a check cashed in order to spend the night, drunk, in a hotel. His trip into the city has been an unmitigated disaster, a descent into hell.

Unfulfilled desire is the essence of "Saint Augustine's Pigeon," and what is important in the story is not Karl Muhlbach's actions but his reasons for them and his emotional responses. The story gains its title, and opens with a quotation from, the early Church father Saint Augustine of Hippo, and throughout the story Karl Muhlbach's perceptions are filtered through Augustine's philosophy of humankind's inherently sinful and incomplete nature. Although he is not very sinful, except in intention, Karl Muhlbach is certainly incomplete.

"THE MOUNTAINS OF GUATEMALA"

This incomplete nature is further explored in the story "The Mountains of Guatemala," in which Muhlbach again fails to make the human connection that he so desperately needs. Once more, he meets a younger woman, named Lambeth. By coincidence, Karl and Lambeth arrive at a party together, and everyone assumes that they are a couple. The irony of this is not lost on Karl, and it makes his isolation more acute than ever. Throughout the story, he broods over a tourist brochure of Guatemala, which gives the story its title and functions as a symbol of Muhlbach's unrealized dreams.

"OTTO AND THE MAGI"

These dreams change to nightmares in the next story in the sequence, "Otto and the Magi," an exploration of the relationship between Karl Muhlbach and his son, Otto, whose own small failures and defeats are echoes of his father's. In the key central portion of the story, Karl and Otto look over a government pamphlet about fallout shelters. In fact, Karl has already constructed a shelter in his own yard, and later that night he sleeps there, having horrible dreams. He awakens to find that he is suffocating, because Otto has stuffed a potato into the shelter's air intake valve.

The shelter is a symbol of Karl's life since the death of his wife. He has withdrawn, psychologically and emotionally, and now he literally goes underground, sealing himself off from a world that he can neither understand nor control. What Otto does can be seen as an attempt, typically fumbled, to reestablish the fragile links between father and son. As the story ends, it is questionable whether these links can be reestablished, since Karl turns again to logic and reason, rather than emotion, to understand and resolve his dilemma. Logic and reason, the Muhlbach stories suggest, are bleak resources with which to manage tangled human relations.

The Muhlbach series displays Connell's mastery of short fiction. Actions are sparse, and everyday events fill the stage: People meet, talk, fail to connect, regret the past, plan vaguely for the future. The real actions in these stories, as in most of Connell's fiction, are internal, in the thoughts and emotions of his characters. These inner lives are deep and often philosophical, and even such a seemingly commonplace character as Karl reveals deep and unsuspected attributes, listening to Johann Sebastian Bach, speaking German, and quoting Saint Augustine. In these masterful stories, the quotidian world is shown to be full of human beings' deepest fears and most enduring dreams.

THE COLLECTED STORIES OF EVAN S. CONNELL

The Collected Stories of Evan S. Connell features an assemblage of fifty-six short stories written by the author between 1946 and 1995, including fifteen older stories and thirteen later ones never before published in book form. Arranged by common theme, the entries reflect the acerbic yet compassionate view the author

holds toward his protagonists. In "Madame Broulard," a hollow French landlady is described "as so much alone, trying to hold on to something, anything, that retains a shred of meaning," an observation that could be applied to any number of his characters. Connell is a master of measuring the impact of great events through the eyes of the bourgeoisie. Broulard herself is torn between playing the generous host to an American visitor and being a victim of occupational forces, from German troops to American tourists. In "The Cuban Missile Crisis," the international nuclear dance of death between the Soviet Union and the United States is played out in the mind of one individual as he passes time in a New York pool hall.

Interspersed throughout the stories are the random indignities suffered by individuals. In "Mademoiselle from Kansas City," a New York prostitute is connected by chance to a customer from her old hometown, an occasion that threatens to shatter her self-imposed state of detachment from the past. The comedic tone in a few of his stories can take on a dark quality, as in "The Short Happy Life of Henrietta," the tale of a naïve Nebraska tourist in Paris who, because of a language gap, meets a gruesome death as the result of a foolish misunderstanding.

Connell returns to the theme of a romantic life denied in "The Most Beautiful," the story of a young Hispanic man living in squalid surroundings, who copes with his condition by engaging in an imaginary love affair with a model whose picture he has lifted from a magazine. A similar theme is examined in "Succubus," when a distinguished elderly gentleman relates a tale of unrequited love during a shipboard romance, an incident that forever frames his view of love. In each case Connell instills in his characters a persona and passion unlike that of the typically sterile middle-class figures who populate his longer fictions. In so doing, he offers an ambiguity that gives full range to his entire body of work.

Altogether, the stories demonstrate Connell's skill in providing his narratives with precise points of view that allow the reader to easily identify with the author's protagonists as they struggle with the vagaries of life. A critic once commented that Connell's view of the world as reflected in his stories was that of a man who felt "like a refugee in a precarious place." This is a place in which his characters invariably find themselves and one they have little hope or capability of escaping with their dignity still intact.

OTHER MAJOR WORKS

LONG FICTION: *Mrs. Bridge*, 1959; *The Patriot*, 1960; *The Diary of a Rapist*, 1966; *Mr. Bridge*, 1969; *The Connoisseur*, 1974; *Double Honeymoon*, 1976; *The Alchymist's Journal*, 1991 (expanded as *Alchymic Journals*, 2006); *Deus lo Volt! A Chronicle of the Crusades*, 2000.

POETRY: *Notes from a Bottle Found on the Beach at Carmel*, 1963; *Points for a Compass Rose*, 1973.

NONFICTION: *A Long Desire*, 1979; *The White Lantern*, 1980; *Son of the Morning Star: Custer and the Little Bighorn*, 1984; *The Aztec Treasure House: New and Selected Essays*, 2001; *Francisco Goya: Life and Times*, 2004.

BIBLIOGRAPHY

Blaisdell, Gus. "After Ground Zero: The Writings of Evan S. Connell, Jr." *New Mexico Quarterly* 36 (Summer, 1966): 181-207. Contains helpful and revealing insight into Connell's earlier works, which include many of his formative short stories.

Brooke, Allen. "Introverts and Emigres." *New Criterion* 14 (October, 1995): 58-63. Brooke finds an uneven quality to Connell's short stories. He believes Connell reserves his best stories for conventional characters, while those that deal with fashionable types are narrow and pointless.

Connell, Evan S. "Evan S. Connell." Interview by Patricia Holt. *Publishers Weekly* 220 (November 20, 1981): 12-13. Connell speaks perceptively about his efforts and aims in his writing, with some interesting sidelights on his critical and popular reception.

_____. "Evan S. Connell, Jr." Interview by Dan Tooker and Roger Hofheins. In *Fiction: Interviews with Northern California Writers*. New York: Harcourt Brace Jovanovich, 1976. Connell is often cited by critics as the foremost of the Northern California writers, who created a literary movement that has had considerable impact on contemporary American fiction. Connell is articulate in presenting his views, especially on the themes and methods of his own writing.

Kirkus Reviews 76, no. 12 (June 15, 2008): 30. A review of Connell's collection *Lost in Uttar Pradesh: New and Selected Stories*.

Myers, Edward. "Notes from a Bottle Found on the Beach at Sausalito: An Interview with Evan S. Connell." In *The Muse upon My Shoulder: Discussions of the Creative Process*, edited by Sylvia Skaggs McTague. Madison, N.J.: Fairleigh Dickinson University Press, 2004. In this wide-ranging interview, originally published in *The Literary Review* in 1991, Connell discusses his literary influences and his interest in alchemy, the early West, and pre-Columbian art.

Sipper, Ralph B. "The Great Helmsman." Review of *The Collected Stories of Evan S. Connell*, by Evan S. Connell, Jr. *Los Angeles Times Book Review*, February 11, 1996, 3. Comments on the stories' urban settings as more barbarous than primitive ones, their characters who deny history, and closed-in beings with subdued passions ready to explode.

Wanner, Irene. "A Collection of Gems by Connell." *The Seattle Times*, March 3, 1996, p. M2. A review of *The Collected Stories of Evan S. Connell*. Explains the language and pace of his stories and his control of multiple conflicts. Discusses a number of the stories as finely wrought studies of human nature.

Michael Witkoski
Updated by William Hoffman

FRANK CONROY

Born: New York, New York; January 15, 1936
Died: Iowa City, Iowa; April 6, 2005

PRINCIPAL SHORT FICTION
Midair, 1985

OTHER LITERARY FORMS

Reviewer Terrence Rafferty praised Frank Conroy's first book, *Stop-Time* (1967), as a "terrifically original contribution to the autobiography-of-a-young-man genre." Conroy's only novel, *Body and Soul* (1993), is an old-fashioned, often refreshingly upbeat bildungs-roman, the history of a musical prodigy's development from humble beginnings to concert fame as a piano virtuoso. Conroy subsequently published two nonfiction works, *Dogs Bark, but the Caravan Rolls On: Observations Then and Now* (2002) and *Time and Tide: A Walk Through Nantucket* (2004); he also edited two anthologies, *The Eleventh Draft: Craft and the Writing Life in Iowa* (1999) and *The Iowa Award: The Best Stories, 1991-2000* (2001).

ACHIEVEMENTS

Frank Conroy received fellowships from the John Simon Guggenheim Memorial Foundation, the Rockefeller Foundation, the National Foundation for the Arts and Humanities, and the National Council for the Arts. He was named a Knight of the Order of Arts and Letters by the French government. *Stop-Time* was nominated for a National Book Award. Conroy directed the Iowa Writers' Workshop from 1987 through 2005, and he also taught writing at other workshops and universities, including the Massachusetts Institute of Technology, American University, Brandeis University, and George Mason University.

BIOGRAPHY

Frank Conroy was born in New York City in 1936 and attended Peter Stuyvesant High School. He won a scholarship to attend Haverford College, a small liberal arts-oriented school in suburban Philadelphia. Upon being graduated in 1958 with a B.A. in English, he married the daughter of a socially prominent family; the two met at a college soccer game. The couple had two sons, Danny and Will, before they divorced after thirteen years of marriage. Conroy dedicated his short-fiction collection *Midair* to "Maggie," his second wife, with whom he had a son, Tim.

In January, 1970, Conroy published his first story, "Car Games," in *The New Yorker*. That same year the magazine published "The Mysterious Case of R," and, in 1974 and 1984, respectively, "Celestial Events" and "Midair," the title story of his collection. Conroy considered himself primarily a teacher, a profession he entered at the renowned Writers' Workshop at the University of Iowa, where he became the director in 1987. Between his appointments there, he served as director of the Literature Program of the National Endowment of the Arts (NEA) from 1981 through 1987, during which he insisted on teaching at least one class.

For about four years, between college and his first teaching position, he worked full time as a jazz pianist in New York. While with the NEA, Frank Conroy, pianist, sat in with a group at the Georgetown Fish House in Washington, D.C. He wrote widely on the subject of jazz. Conroy died of colon cancer on April 6, 2005, in Iowa City, Iowa, at the age of sixty-nine.

ANALYSIS

As a story writer and fictional memoirist, Frank Conroy is a disciple of the early James Joyce, employing in his work the "showings-forth" of suddenly apprehended truths that Joyce called "epiphanies." In "The Sense of the Meeting," Conroy conveys epiphanic moments when a father recognizes in the setting of his old college on whose basketball team his son plays, that, looking at his son in the double vision of his own past and his maturing son's present, he is overcome by "a great rush of bitterness, protective love, a desire to shelter the boy against some vague, unnamed threat." Seemingly unrelated, the stories in *Midair* make up a composite that the title reinforces. Their strategy is a variation on Joyce's *A Portrait of the Artist as a Young Man* (1916), in which young Stephen Dedalus builds to an assured sense of high purpose. The reader finds in story after story that what is literally airborne--as in the title story, where a child is held out of a fifth-story window--must be perceived epiphanically. Writer Anne Tyler puts it well: "We begin to associate with that suspended instant that precedes a new comprehension, or a radical swerve in one's life." Maggie Conroy once urged her husband, if asked about the eighteen-year interval between his first and second books and the eight-year period between the second and third, to reply, "I've been doing errands."

To Conroy himself, it was quite logical that he had written only three books by 1993: "I really never thought of writing as a career. Although *Stop-Time* was a critical success, I never got any signals that I could make a living as a writer. So I had to look elsewhere to figure out how I was going to support myself."

"MIDAIR"

Most introspective persons experience dramas even in the quotidian, rethink such catalytic moments, and find themselves fashioning out of them a circuitry of remembered links. At the end of perhaps Conroy's finest story, an elevator slightly malfunctions between the sixty-third and sixty-fourth floors. The only other occupant with the protagonist, Sean, is a young man whom he takes momentarily for his son, who is away at college. The

> two ideas overlap--the idea of [son] Philip and the idea of the young man--and in that moment time seems to slow down. It is as if Sean had seen his son across a supernatural barrier--as if he, Sean, were a ghost haunting the elevator, able to see the real body

of his son but unable to be seen by him. An almost unbearable sadness comes over him.

That night, rethinking how he "saved" the frightened young man by assuring him he had experienced scares like this before (Sean had never been on that elevator before), he flashes back to an earlier time in the story when he was six and his improvident father, unexpectedly returned from a mental hospital, carried him out on the windowsill of their apartment five floors up. "Here, in the darkness, he can see the cracks in the sidewalk from more than forty years ago. He feels no fear--only a sense of astonishment." The story is told by the man who was once the small boy and who directly or obliquely is at the center. Whether describing Sean the boy asking why Sean the father is crying ("he has never felt as close to another human being") or conveying the signs by which Sean senses that his marriage is coming apart, Conroy evokes the powerful influence that events from the past can exert on the present. For him, all things have double meanings.

"GOSSIP"

This is the only story in *Midair* dealing with what Conroy calls his main calling: teaching. It may be one of the few in which a creative-writing professor's evolving relationship with a promising and beautiful woman who is his student does not lead to the inevitable tryst. Anne Tyler gives "Gossip" faint praise in her *New Republic* review, finding it "less successful" because it is about "writing and writing teachers." Like "Midair," the story moves deftly, often unexpectedly, among different periods in George's life. He discovers in early middle age that he is an effective teacher of writing, a discovery made in relation to a gifted and dedicated female student named Joan to whom George gives all of his teaching self:

> He spent week after week, month after month going after every weakness he could find in her prose, attacking from one direction after another, trying to tear the work apart in front of her eyes. She responded by writing better and better stuff, paradoxically with more and more confidence, until it became difficult for him to find any of the weaknesses she had originally exhibited.

The story builds to a tension that is a version of art-for-art's-sake. George must regard her writing as sacrosanct with a life of its own outside any other. When his wife suggests they invite some of his students, including Joan, to dinner, he awakens to the knowledge that Joan, though not his lover, has far transcended the tyro-tutor accommodation:

> She was important to him, and the degree of importance was a secret which he must keep to himself. Their relationship was based on the tacit understanding that they would remain always in their respective roles of teacher and student, and he needed her enough to want to do nothing to threaten that arrangement. Dinner, small talk, socializing, were full of imponderables, and the prospect made him nervous.

What makes George uneasy can be said in the title of this story--gossip, the subtly threatening waves of words that deluge people's lives with, as William H. Pritchard puts it, "power over the self and what others say about that self and its relationships." Gossip that enmeshes teacher and student--were they or were they not sleeping together?--takes its toll. Joan leaves school before the term ends; George is harassed by his wife, and yet Conroy can conclude: "Everyone was connected in a web, and yet despite it, people loved one another."

"THE SENSE OF THE MEETING"

In this father-son story Conroy takes a worn, often sentimentalized, donnée about a father returning to his alma mater to see his son play in the big game and, by staying inside the parent's head, endows the experience with a bittersweet flavor that few but this writer could bring off. Kirby, too thin and weak to play sports and medically excused from them in college, nevertheless introduced his son Alan to basketball early. At the moment of demonstrating successfully the hook shot, Kirby "saw a complex expression of pleasure, pride, and eagerness on the boy's face . . . at that precise moment . . . understood the force of his son's love." It is a Joycean/Conroyan epiphanic moment again. The reader is advised to remember it, for in the next paragraph the narrative flashes forward to Kirby's arrival by train in Philadelphia for the game in which his son will play. He is met by the six-foot-six Gus, his former roommate. Gus was captain of the basketball team, and Kirby was editor of the literary magazine. Conroy hints

at an athlete-versus-aesthete tension that is leavened by the arrival at the club of the third member of their coterie. Charley was thin, nervous, and self-conscious in college but is now self-possessed, well-spoken, handsome--a thriving Philadelphia lawyer. They reminisce over boilermakers until it is time for Kirby to be driven to Alan's dorm.

By bringing the son on stage, Conroy generates more interest than has been provided by the men's bleak hindsight that they have settled for less. The reader infers that the father's concern for his capable and resourceful son may be a reflex of his own disappointments. The subtexts of one dorm scene and of two basketball games--both wins--reveal Conroy at his best: "He was relieved to get out of the room. He didn't understand what came over him sometimes when he saw Alan on Alan's own turf, a great rush of bittersweet, protective love, a desire to shelter the boy against some vague, unnamed threat." After Alan's pass enables a teammate to hit a half-court shot just as time runs out, Alan's words, the last of the story, reinforce the connection between father and son: "I'm glad you saw it. . . . There's no way I could have told you." In fiction and in life, showing and doing counts more than telling. In the words of Terrence Rafferty, "the delicate texture of achieved expression can't always be willed-- that sometimes, unpredictably, the patterns just coalesce around us."

OTHER MAJOR WORKS

LONG FICTION: *Body and Soul*, 1993.

NONFICTION: *Stop-Time*, 1967 (autobiography); *Dogs Bark, but the Caravan Rolls On: Observations Then and Now*, 2002; *Time and Tide: A Walk Through Nantucket*, 2004.

EDITED TEXTS: *The Eleventh Draft: Craft and the Writing Life in Iowa*, 1999; *The Iowa Award: The Best Stories, 1991-2000*, 2001.

BIBLIOGRAPHY

Conroy, Frank. "Frank Conroy." Interview by Sybil S. Steinberg. *Publishers Weekly* (August 23, 1993): 44. Upholds *Publishers Weekly*'s tradition of high-quality interviews. Conroy discusses the difficulties of writing fiction in which music is central, why

Stop-Time came out at exactly the wrong time ("Everybody was taking drugs and making love, and here was this sort of neoclassical memoir"), and his meager output.

_____. "The Writer's Workshop." In *On Writing Short Stories*, edited by Tom Bailey. New York: Oxford University Press, 2000. Conroy discusses the prestigious writers' workshop that he directed, and he contradicts the belief that workshops "imprint themselves" upon their students' works: "Art cannot be made by committee. The student . . . should not be looking for solutions from the other students or from the teacher. The student should be looking for problems in the text that he or she had not been aware of."

Grimes, Tom. *Mentor: A Memoir*. Portland, Ore. Tin House Books, 2010. Grimes was a student at the Iowa Writers' Workshop when he met Conroy, his teacher in the program. Grimes's memoir recounts the long friendship that developed from this initial student-teacher relationship and describes Conroy's influence upon his own career as a writer.

Pritchard, William H. Review of *Midair*, by Frank Conroy. *The New York Times Book Review* 98, October 3, 1993, 12. While wondering "what Mr. Conroy has been up to as a writer" during nearly two decades of silence between *Stop-Time* and *Midair*, Pritchard connects the memoir and the stories by stressing Conroy's exceptional grasp of the pains of childhood and the relationship between sons and fathers, which are examined in the first and last stories, from the angle of each. Finds that Conroy's "reliance on the actual" does not rule out the abstract.

Rafferty, Terrence. Review of *Midair*, by Frank Conroy. *The Nation* 242 (January 11, 1986): 23-24. Sees *Midair* as, in part, a completion of *Stop-Time* and the two works together as "the best record we have of the ups and downs of writing as if your life depended on it." Favors "Car Games," Conroy's *New Yorker* debut story as *Midair's* best, a vicious parody of *Stop-Time*.

Tyler, Anne. Review of *Midair*, by Frank Conroy. *The New Republic* 193 (November 18, 1985): 48-50. Easily the most imaginative of *Midair's* reviews. Noting that all the characters are men, novelist Tyler identifies the underlying concerns of the seven stories: "How to live in the world as an adult male. How men connect with their sons and fathers, their old college roommates, their squash opponents. How they cling to their drinking rituals and their driving rituals."

Richard Hauer Costa

ROBERT COOVER

Born: Charles City, Iowa; February 4, 1932

PRINCIPAL SHORT FICTION

Pricksongs and Descants, 1969

The Water Pourer, 1972 (a deleted chapter from *The Origin of the Brunists*)

Charlie in the House of Rue, 1980

Hair o' the Chine, 1979 (novella/screenplay)

A Political Fable, 1980 (novella)

Spanking the Maid, 1981 (novella)

The Convention, 1981

In Bed One Night, and Other Brief Encounters, 1983

Aesop's Forest, 1986

A Night at the Movies: Or, You Must Remember This, 1987

Briar Rose, 1996 (novella)

The Grand Hotels (of Joseph Cornell), 2002 (vignettes)

Stepmother, 2004 (novella; illustrated by Michael Kupperman)

A Child Again, 2005

OTHER LITERARY FORMS

Besides his collections of short fiction and novellas and many uncollected short stories, Robert Coover's has written the novels *The Origin of the Brunists* (1966), *The Universal Baseball Association, Inc., J. Henry Waugh, Prop.* (1968), *The Public Burning* (1977), *Gerald's Party* (1985), *Pinocchio in Venice* (1991), *John's Wife* (1996), *Ghost Town* (1998), *The Adventures of Lucky Pierre: Directors' Cut* (2002), and *Noir* (2010). His other works include a collection of plays entitled *A Theological Position* (1972), which contains *The Kid, Love Scene, Rip Awake,* and the title play; another play, *Bridge Hound* (pr. 1981); the screenplays *On a Confrontation in Iowa City* (1969) and *After Lazarus* (1980); several poems, reviews, and translations published in journals; and theater adaptations of "The Babysitter" and *Spanking the Maid.* Coover also has published a few essays on authors he admires, such as Samuel Beckett ("The Last Quixote," in *New American Review,* 1970) and Gabriel García Márquez ("The Master's Voice," in *New American Review,* 1977).

ACHIEVEMENTS

Robert Coover is one of the authors regularly mentioned in relation to that slippery term "postmodernism." As a result of the iconoclastic and experimental nature of his fiction, Coover's work does not enjoy a widespread audience; his reputation among academics, however, is well established, and the reviews of his works have been consistently positive. Although in the beginning of his career he had to resort to teaching in order to support his family, he soon began to gain recognition, receiving several prizes and fellowships: a William Faulkner Award for Best First Novel (1966), a Rockefeller Foundation grant (1969), two John Simon Guggenheim Memorial Foundation Fellowships (1971, 1974), an Academy of Arts and Letters award (1975), a National Book Award nomination for *The Public Burning,* a National Endowment for the Humanities Award (1985), a Rea Award (1987) for *A Night at the Movies: Or, You Must Remember This,* a Rhode Island Governor's Arts Award (1988), and Deutscher Akademischer Austauschdienst Fellowship (1990). The publisher Alfred A. Knopf's rejection of *The Public Burning* after initial acceptance brought some notoriety to Coover. Since the novel deals with the trial of Ethel and Julius Rosenberg and presents former president Richard M. Nixon as its central narrator, the publisher thought it would be too controversial. Eventually, *The Public Burning* was published by Viking Press and became a Book-of-the-Month Club selection. Critical studies of Coover's work first appeared in the late 1970's. Still, in spite of the critical acclaim and the considerable amount of scholarship about his work, Coover's writing remains relatively unknown to the public, and some of his early novels are now out of print.

Robert Lowell Coover was born in Charles City, Iowa. His family soon moved to Indiana and then to Herrin, Illinois. His father managed the local newspaper, the *Herrin Daily Journal*, which prompted Coover's interest in journalism. His college education began at Southern Illinois University (1949-1951), but he transferred to Indiana University, where he received a B.A., with a major in Slavic studies, in 1953. After graduation, Coover was drafted and joined the United States Naval Reserve.

While in Spain, he met Maria del Pilar Sans-Mallafré, who became his wife on June 13, 1959. During these years, his interest in fiction began. His first published story, "Blackdamp," was the seed of his first novel, *The Origin of the Brunists*. He received an M.A. from the University of Chicago in 1965. During the following years, Coover and his family alternated stays in Europe with periods in the United States. The several awards he received during the 1970's made him financially secure and allowed him to continue writing.

Coover has held appointments at Bard College, the University of Iowa, Columbia University, Princeton University, and the Virginia Military Institute, and since 1979, he has been a distinguished professor at Brown University. He has also been writer-in-residence at Wisconsin State University. In spite of a large amount of time spent abroad in Europe and in South America and his outspoken need to take distance from his own country, Coover's production is very "American," since he often bases his fiction on American events, persons, and national myths. Coover often manipulates historical events for artistic purposes, but he has a solid knowledge of the facts.

In the late 1980's, Coover began teaching courses about electronic writing on computers. With the rise of the World Wide Web in the 1990's, he made significant progress in the use of hyperfiction. Hyperfiction, also referred to as hypertext fiction, tree fiction, nonlinear fiction, or electronic fiction, is fiction written with the capabilities of hypertext. Hyperfiction is truly nonlinear since it cannot be represented on a printed page. The reader takes an active role in hyperfiction, choosing which links to click on and which paths to follow. Thus, the narrative may be very different from one reading to the next, depending on the choices made by the reader. Readers can follow different characters, or points of view, or skip back and forth between different time zones. By clicking on an interesting name, place, event, or idea, the reader can be taken to a new page connected to that name, place, event, or idea.

Coover reads, writes, and reviews hyperfiction, and he teaches courses on electronic writing and mixed media at Brown University. The Hypertext Hotel is a collaborative hyperfiction that grew out of Coover's courses. During the 1990's, students, authors, and scholars have added to the fictional hotel text. Coover developed a course at Brown that introduces students to the possibilities of hyperfiction. He has also been known to encourage the use of hyperfiction and the software that makes it possible. Coover

Robert Coover (National Archives)

is the author of the now classic "The End of the Book," an article in which he explains hyperfiction and his general optimism that it will someday replace books.

Analysis

Robert Coover's central concern is the human being's need for fiction. Because of the complexity of human existence, people are constantly inventing patterns that give them an illusion of order in a chaotic world. For Coover, any effort to explain the world involves some kind of fiction-making process. History, religion, culture, and scientific explanations are fictional at their core; they are invented narratives through which human beings try to explain the world to themselves. The problem, Coover would say, is that people tend to forget the fictional nature of the fictional systems they create and become trapped by them, making dogmas out of the fictions. The artist's function, then, is to reexamine these fictions, tear them down, and offer new perspectives on the same material, in order to make the reader aware of the arbitrariness of the construct.

Coover's fiction often has been labeled "metafiction"--that is, fiction about fiction--and indeed most of his works are comments on previously existing fictional constructs. If in his longer works he examines the bigger metaphoric narratives, such as religion, history, or politics (which one of the theorists of postmodernism, Jean-François Lyotard, has called "metanarratives"), in his shorter works Coover turns to smaller constructs, usually literary fictions.

In the prologue to the "Seven Exemplary Fictions" contained in *Pricksongs and Descants*, Coover addresses Miguel de Cervantes as follows:

But, don Miguel, the optimism, the innocence, the aura of possibility you experienced have been largely drained away, and the universe is closing in on us again. Like you, we, too, seem to be standing at the end of one age and on the threshold of another.

Just as Cervantes stood at the end of a tradition and managed to open a door for a new type of fiction, contemporary authors confront a changing world in need of new fictional forms that can reflect this world's nature better. Just as Cervantes tried to stress the

difference between romance and the real world through the mishaps of Don Quixote, Coover wants to stress the fictionality and arbitrariness of some fictions that hold a tight grip on the reader's consciousness. Like Cervantes, Coover wants to free readers from an uncritical acceptance of untrue or oversimplified ideas that limit and falsify their outlook on life. Fictions, Coover and Cervantes would say, are not there to provide an escape by creating fantasies for the reader. When they do so, Coover continues writing in his prologue, the artist "must conduct the reader to the real, away from mystification to clarification, away from magic to maturity, away from mystery to revelations."

This quotation, coming from an author whose work is usually considered "difficult," might seem somehow odd. How does Coover's fiction clarify, or what does it reveal? His work often presents constantly metamorphosing worlds, which mimic the state of constant change in the real world. Just as the world is continuously changing, Coover's fictions also refuse to present stable, easily describable characters or scenarios. Coover also calls attention to the fictionality of fiction by focusing on the process and the means of creation rather than on the product. As he states in the prologue, the novelist turns to the familiar material and "defamiliarizes" it in order to liberate readers' imagination from arbitrary constraints and in order to make them reevaluate their reactions to those constraints. These are the main strategies of Coover's two collections of stories, *Pricksongs and Descants* and *A Night at the Movies: Or, You Must Remember This.*

Pricksongs and Descants

The title of Coover's first short-fiction collection refers to musical terms, variations played against a basic line (the basic line of the familiar narrative). As one character in one of the stories says, however, they are also "death-c-- and prick-songs," which prepares the reader for the sometimes shocking motifs of death and sex scattered throughout the stories. In *Pricksongs and Descants*, Coover turns to the familiar material of folktales and biblical stories. Using this material offers him the possibility of manipulating the reader's expectations. One of the ways in which Coover forces the reader to look at familiar stories from new perspectives is by retelling them from an unfamiliar point of view.

For example, the story "The Brother" is Coover's version of the biblical flood told from the point of view of Noah's brother, who, after helping Noah to build the ark, is left to drown. "J's Marriage" describes how Joseph tries to come to terms with his marriage to the Virgin Mary and his alternating moods of amazement, frustration, and desperation. Some of the stories of the same collection are based on traditional fairy tales: "The Door" evokes "Little Red Riding Hood," "The Gingerbread House," reminds one of "Hanzel and Gretel"; "The Milkmaid of Samaniego" is based on the Spanish folktale of the same title; and *Hair o' the Chine*, a novella, mocks the tale of the "Three Little Pigs and the Wolf." Coover subverts, however, the original narratives by stressing the cruelty and the motifs of sex, violence, and death underlying most folktales. Revealing the darker side of familiar stories is in fact one of Coover's recurrent techniques.

In other stories in *Pricksongs and Descants*, Coover experiments with the formal aspects of fiction-making. He reminds the reader of the artificiality of fiction by presenting stories that are repertoires of narrative possibilities. Often, Coover juxtaposes several different beginnings, or potential stories, but leaves them undeveloped. He interweaves the different story lines, some of which are complementary and some of which might be contradictory, as is the case in "Quenby and Ola, Swede and Carl" and in "The Magic Poker." In the "Sentient Lens" section and in "Klee's Dead," Coover explores the possibilities and the limitations of the narrational voice: In the first set of stories, Coover denies the possibility of an objective narrative voice by portraying a camera that constantly interferes with the events of the story; in "Klee's Dead," the supposedly "omniscient" narrator is unable to explain the reasons for artist Paul Klee's suicide.

In most of the stories of *Pricksongs and Descants*, the figures are types described with a flaunted lack of depth of characterization, which prevents the reader from identifying with them in any possible way. This contributes to the critical distance that Coover thinks is necessary to maintain toward fiction. As critic Cristina Bacchilega says in her article about Coover's use of the *Märchen* (folktales) in this collection, while the *Märchen* is symbolic of development, of a passage from immaturity to maturity, Coover's fictions present rather static characters . . . the only dynamic process allowed is in the reader's new awareness of the world as a construct of fictions.

The function of the artist in contemporary society is one of Coover's recurring concerns, which surfaces in "Panel Game," "Romance of Thin Man and Fat Lady," and "The Hat Act," all of which portray cruel and insatiable audiences who, in their thirst for entertainment, do not hesitate to exterminate the artists if their performance does not stand up to their expectations.

A NIGHT AT THE MOVIES

In *A Night at the Movies*, Coover probes the nature of filmic fictions, which present a greater danger of being taken for "real" because of the immediacy of filmic images. He approaches film from three perspectives. In the stories "Shootout at Gentry's Junction," "Charlie in the House of Rue," "Gilda's Dream," and "You Must Remember This," Coover demythologizes specific films and offers his own version of the story, usually baring the ideology of the original version. In "After Lazarus" and "Inside the Frame," he explores the conventions through which these fictions create an illusion of an independent world on the screen. In "The Phantom of the Movie Palace" and "Intermission," he challenges the ontological status of reality and film by making the characters cross the boundaries that separate these two realms.

"Shootout at Gentry's Junction" is a parody of the ideology and of the form of the Western film *High Noon* (1952). Coover parodies the narrative line and the easy identification of good and evil typical of most Westerns. The film celebrates the code of honor and personal integrity typical of the Western hero; abandoned by everybody, the sheriff of the film, played by Gary Cooper, has to fight alone with the villain and his gang. In the story, however, the protagonist is a fastidious, neurotic sheriff who is obsessed with fulfilling the role imposed on him. The villain is Don Pedro, the Mexican bandit, whose major talent is expressing himself by expelling intestinal gas. As in the film, the narrative progresses toward the confrontation of the villain and the sheriff. The tight structure of the film, however, is disrupted in the story by giving both characters a different kind of discourse. The sheriff's discourse has a traditional narrative line. It is narrated in the past tense and refers to formulas taken directly from the visual tradition of the Western. The Mexican's discourse is in the present tense and in broken English, influenced by Spanish. Furthermore, Coover makes the Mexican ubiquitous. Readers never really know where he is--he seems everywhere at the same time, raping the schoolmarm at the local school, cheating at cards in the saloon, and burning papers at the sheriff's office. After shooting the sheriff, the Mexican sets the town on fire and rides into the sunset.

The irreverence of Coover's version of the film *Casablanca* (1942) is even greater. *Casablanca* has become the epitome of the romantic melodrama, drawing like the Western upon codes of honor and heroic behavior. In "You Must Remember This," Coover gives his version of what might have happened between frames. Quite literally, Rick and Ilsa fall between frames and make furious love several times. The love story becomes a pornographic film. The disruption of the moral code of the film creates an avalanche of disruptions in other categories: Rick and Ilsa begin to sense that their senses of time and place are fading, and their identities become increasingly diffused. At the end of the story, the characters melt into nothingness after several desperate attempts to return to the mythic film.

Other stories in the collection *A Night at the Movies* aim at exposing the artificiality of the technical conventions of film. Written in the form of a screenplay, "After Lazarus" parodies the notion of the camera as the ultimately objective narrator. In the story, the camera "hesitates," "pauses," "follows back at a discreet distance," and rapidly moves back when frightened. "Inside the Frame" refers in its very title to film-related terms. If films construct a narrative through the sum of frames that all have a reason and a function in the global construct of the story, this story presents several possible beginnings of stories in one single frame. In "Inside the Frame," the reader gets glimpses of what could be potential stories: a woman stepping off a bus, an Indian with a knife between his teeth, a man praying at a grave, a singing couple, a sleepwalker. There is no development, no explanation of the images. "Lap

Dissolves" is a literary imitation of the film technique. The story fades from one film-related situation to the next, with the words giving the cues to the transformation of the scenario.

Coover disrupts the ontological boundaries between "reality" and fiction by making the protagonists of "The Phantom of the Movie Palace" and "Intermission" move between them. The mad projectionist of the first story lives in an abandoned motion-picture theater and plays with the reels of film, constructing films by cutting and pasting images of other films. Somehow, his experiments go awry, and he becomes trapped in the fictions he has been creating. The girl of "Intermission" enters a film-related fantasy when the film in the story ends and she steps into the lobby of the theater to buy a snack. Outside the theater, she is thrown into a series of situations directly drawn from Hollywood films: She moves from a car race with gangsters, to a tent with Rudolph Valentino, to the sea surrounded by sharks. In what is supposed to be "reality," she becomes a dynamic individual, but back in the cinema she returns to the passivity that Hollywood fictions seem to invite.

BRIAR ROSE

In *Briar Rose*, a novella and a retelling of the fairy tale of Sleeping Beauty, Coover travels deeply into the dreams of the sleeping princess and into the forest of briars and brambles that plague the prince as he tries to rescue her. The story centers on the powers of the human imagination and escalates to an erotic pace as sex and storytelling fuse together. As the prince fights his way to the princess's bed chamber to awaken her from a deathly enchanted sleep, Coover involves the reader by dangling numerous interpretative possibilities just below the surface of this brief narrative.

Coover's genius is displayed in his use of words, drifting back and forth between reality and dreams. His speculations about what makes a prince forge through the briars and what a princess dreams about while magically asleep for one hundred years are thought provoking, mysterious, compelling, and at times hilarious. As the tale unwinds, Coover exposes the masculine desire to prey on female beauty. In addition, he leads the reader to contemplate the necessity that women resist male yearnings that are projected onto them. The tale is a bit dull in places and lacks a definite ending with some culminating metaphor, but Coover constructs an intriguing story that is well known, turned in on itself, and explored to reveal different levels of human consciousness.

In his major collections of stories, Coover elaborates on his fundamental concern, --namely the necessity for the individual to distinguish between reality and fiction and to be liberated from dogmatic thinking. In order to do so, Coover emphasizes the self-reflexive, antirealistic elements of his fiction. The result is original, highly engaging, and energetic stories that probe human beings' relationships to the myths that shape their lives.

OTHER MAJOR WORKS

LONG FICTION: *The Origin of the Brunists*, 1966; *The Universal Baseball Association, Inc., J. Henry Waugh, Prop.*, 1968; *Whatever Happened to Gloomy Gus of the Chicago Bears?*, 1975 (expanded 1987); *The Public Burning*, 1977; *Gerald's Party*, 1985; *Pinocchio in Venice*, 1991; *John's Wife*, 1996; *Ghost Town*, 1998; *The Adventures of Lucky Pierre: Directors' Cut*, 2002; *Noir*, 2010.

PLAYS: *A Theological Position*, pb. 1972; *Love Scene*, pb. 1972; *Rip Awake*, pr. 1972; *The Kid*, pr., pb. 1972; *Bridge Hound*, pr. 1981.

SCREENPLAYS: *On a Confrontation in Iowa City*, 1969; *After Lazarus*, 1980.

BIBLIOGRAPHY

Andersen, Richard. *Robert Coover*. Boston: Twayne, 1981. A useful and very accessible introduction to Coover's production up to 1981. Andersen combines plot summary with commentary, helping the reader to make an initial acquaintance with Coover's work. Includes notes, select bibliography, and index.

Benson, Stephen. "The Late Fairy Tales of Robert Coover." In *Contemporary Fiction and the Fairy Tale*, edited by Benson. Detroit: Wayne State University Press, 2008. Examines Coover's use of the fairy tale in his fiction.

Coover, Robert. "Interview." *Short Story*, n.s. 1 (Fall, 1993): 89-94. Coover comments on the difference between the short story and the novel, the writing of *Pricksongs and Descants*, his use of sexuality in his fiction, his iconoclastic streak, postmodernism, and his use of the short story to test narrative forms.

_____. Interview by Amanda Smith. *Publishers Weekly* 230 (December 26, 1986): 44-45. Coover discusses the motivations that lie behind his experimental fiction. He says he believes that the artist finds his metaphors for the world in the most vulnerable areas of human outreach; he insists that he is in pursuit of the mainstream. What many people consider experimental, Coover argues, is actually traditional in the sense that it has gone back to old forms to find its new form.

_____. "Tale, Myth, Writer." In *Brothers and Beasts: An Anthology of Men on Fairy Tales*, edited by Kate Bernheimer. Detroit: Wayne State University Press, 2007. Coover, who has written short fiction that subverts traditional fairy tales, explains his artistic and emotional relationship to this genre.

Cope, Jackson. *Robert Coover's Fictions*. Baltimore: Johns Hopkins University Press, 1986. More sophisticated than Richard Andersen's book. Cope supposes that readers know Coover's work and uses several approaches to it, analyzing his techniques, his subject matter, and the critical theories that cast light on his writings. Contains an index.

Evenson, Brian K. *Understanding Robert Coover*. Columbia: University of South Carolina Press, 2003. Evenson explains the particularly dense style of Coover's metafiction in a comprehensive survey. He guides readers through Coover's postmodern fiction, which deals with myth- and story making and their power to shape collective, community action, which oftentimes turns violent.

Gelfant, Blanche H., ed. *The Columbia Companion to the Twentieth-Century American Short Story*. New York: Columbia University Press, 2000. Includes a chapter in which Coover's short stories are analyzed.

Gordon, Lois. *Robert Coover: The Universal Fiction-Making Process*. Carbondale: Southern Illinois University Press, 1983. Like Richard Andersen's book, this volume provides a friendly introduction and overview of Coover's work, placing him in the context of metafictional or postmodernist literature. Includes notes, select bibliography, and index.

Kennedy, Thomas E. *Robert Coover: A Study of the Short Fiction*. New York: Twayne, 1992. An introduction to Coover's short fiction. Discusses the postmodernist trend in fiction in the 1960's and Coover's place in this movement. Provides summary analyses of Coover's stories, as well as discussions of the critical reception of Coover's fiction. Also includes interviews with Coover, as well as previously published criticism, including William H. Gass's review of *Pricksongs and Descants*.

Maltby, Paul. *Dissident Postmodernists: Barthelme, Coover, Pynchon*. Philadelphia: University of Pennsylvania Press, 1991. A comparative look at these three writers and their fictions. Includes a bibliography and an index.

McCaffery, Larry. *The Metafictional Muse: The Works of Robert Coover, Donald Barthelme, and William H. Gass*. Pittsburgh: University of Pittsburgh Press, 1982. After describing what he considers a major current in contemporary American fiction, McCaffery discusses the metafictional traits of Coover's work and relates him to other important contemporary American writers.

_____. "Robert Coover on His Own and Other Fictions." *Genre* 14 (Spring, 1981): 45-84. A lively discussion in which Coover examines, among other things, the importance of stories about storytelling, the function of the writer in a world threatened by nuclear apocalypse, the fiction that has influenced his work, and popular culture.

"The Pleasures of the (Hyper)text." *The New Yorker* 70 (June/July, 1994): 43-44. Discusses Coover's Hypertext Hotel, the country's first online writing space dedicated to the computer-generated mode of literature known as hypertext. Describes Coover's writing class at Brown University and its use of hypertext.

Scholes, Robert. "Metafiction." *The Iowa Review* 1, no. 3 (Fall, 1970): 100-115. Initially theoretical, then descriptive, this article discusses four major metafictional writers: Coover, William H. Gass, Donald Barthelme, and John Barth. Scholes categorizes the different types of metafictional writing and classifies Coover's *Pricksongs and Descants* as "structural" metafiction, since it is concerned with the order of fiction rather than with the conditions of being.

Stengel, Wayne B. "Robert Coover." In *A Reader's Companion to the Short Story in English*, edited by Erin Fallon, et al., under the auspices of the Society for the Study of the Short Story. Westport, Conn.: Greenwood Press, 2001. Aimed at the general reader, this essay provides a brief biography of Coover followed by an analysis of his short fiction.

Carlota Larrea
Updated by Alvin K. Benson

JAMES GOULD COZZENS

Born: Chicago, Illinois; August 19, 1903
Died: Stuart, Florida; August 9, 1978

PRINCIPAL SHORT FICTION
Child's Play, 1958
Children and Others, 1964
A Flower in Her Hair, 1975

OTHER LITERARY FORMS

James Gould Cozzens (KUHZ-uhnz) published thirteen novels, two of which won special acclaim: *Guard of Honor* (1948) was awarded the Pulitzer Prize in fiction in 1949 and is widely regarded as one of the best American novels of World War II, and *By Love Possessed* (1957), recipient of the Howells Medal of the American Society of Arts and Letters in 1960, was a major best seller. One of Cozzens's volumes of short fiction, *Children and Others*, contains seventeen of his twenty-nine published stories. It was a Book-of-the-Month Club selection, as were five of his novels.

ACHIEVEMENTS

James Gould Cozzens was consistently neglected by the serious critics during his fifty-five-year writing career. He never received the proper recognition and honors accorded to his contemporaries, including Theodore Dreiser, William Faulkner, F. Scott Fitzgerald, Ernest Hemingway, and Sinclair Lewis. Cozzens is partly to blame because he lived such a reclusive life, avoiding close contact with people and devoting himself totally to the craft of writing. Another reason may be that his work fits no definite category in American fiction. He has become the least read and least taught of the major American writers enjoying the status of "cult author."

Cozzens launched his writing career at age twenty-one and did not involve himself in self-promotion. He always felt that the first objective of writers should be to perfect and master their art. Despite six Book-of-the-Month Club selections and a Pulitzer Prize, Cozzens's work remains largely unknown to the general public. With the exception of *By Love Possessed*, his books have never circulated widely as paperbacks and none was ever adopted as a classroom text. Critics have long regarded Cozzens as too highly intellectual a novelist, too detached in his writings, and lacking involvement with his characters. Cozzens is at his best creating traditional social novels with believable characters exhibiting a variety of weaknesses and strengths. Two important themes run throughout his work. He believes in the ultimate dignity of humans and in a moral order imposed on what seems to be a chaotic, meaningless world.

BIOGRAPHY

Born in Chicago, James Gould Cozzens grew up on Staten Island, New York, attended the Kent School in Connecticut, and then went to Harvard University in 1922, where he remained for two years. During the mid-1920's he served as a tutor of American children in Cuba and Europe. In 1927, he married Bernice Baumgarten, a New York literary agent; they had no children. In 1938, Cozzens was briefly a guest editor at *Fortune*. Upon the outbreak of World War II, he entered the U.S. Army Air Force, worked on various classified stateside assignments, and was discharged as a major in 1945. Cozzens was a member of the National Institute of Arts and Letters, received two O. Henry Awards for short fiction in 1931 and 1936, the Pulitzer Prize for fiction in 1949, and the Howells Medal of the American Society of Arts and Letters in 1960.

ANALYSIS

Although most of the stories collected in *Children and Others* were originally published between 1930 and 1937, three of them--including Cozzens's best, "Eyes to See"--were first published as late as 1964. This fact suggests that his continuing interest in and developing mastery of the short-story form complements and illuminates his career-long devotion to the novel.

Of the five sections into which the collection is divided, the first two, "Child's Play" and "Away at School," containing ten stories between them, are perceptive recollections of childhood experiences. Although Cozzens is rigorously impersonal in his fiction, readers may be pardoned for imagining that one of the children of his title is the young Cozzens. Readers see a little boy turned in on his own imaginative self, and later a student at Durham (modeled on the Kent School, which Cozzens attended)--precocious, self-conscious, and at times frightened. The third section, "War Between the States," is composed of two Civil War stories. In the late 1930's, Cozzens assembled material

James Gould Cozzens (Library of Congress)

for a Civil War novel but found that he could not write it, and perhaps in the stories the reader sees something of what that novel might have been. The fourth section, "Love and Kisses," with four stories, examines the complexity of inexorably changing relations between men and women. The seventeenth, last, and longest story, "Eyes to See," written in 1963, is Cozzens at his distilled best and hence deserves somewhat more extended consideration than its predecessors.

"TOTAL STRANGER"

"Total Stranger," from part 1, which received the O. Henry Memorial Award for the best story of 1936, develops--with typical indirection and understated humor--the process by which a boy begins to see his father in an entirely new light. John is being driven back to his New England prep school by his father, who is distinctly dissatisfied with his son's undistinguished academic performance there and does not accept the boy's self-serving explanations and ill-constructed defenses. John has never had trouble getting around his mother; with his father, however, who is authoritative, competent, and always right, it is a different matter.

They stop for the night at a bad but conveniently located hotel and there encounter, by chance, a "total stranger," a Mrs. Prentice. John finds her notably attractive and shortly discovers that the two adults know each other well from years before. John is curious and confused; Mrs. Prentice seems to know or remember an altogether different man, yet she says to his father, "Will, you haven't changed a bit!" Words such as "strange," "bewildering," and "astonishment" register the boy's evolving perception of his father and realization, finally, that before he himself had been born, before his father had known his mother, before Mrs. Prentice had met Mr. Prentice, the two of them had been in love. Leaving the next morning, John says, "Somehow it all fitted together. I could feel that."

In literal fact, it is Mrs. Prentice who is to the boy a "total stranger"; metaphorically and more important, however, it is his father--or much of his father's life-- which John has never before glimpsed. What John sees, hears, and intuits of his father and Mrs. Prentice might have evoked alarm, contempt, amusement, or jealousy. That the chance meeting with the stranger in fact strengthens the boy's love and admiration for his father is apparent in the story's last line, in which John confesses that he never did do much better at school, but that "that year and the year following, I would occasionally try to, for I thought it would please my father."

"FAREWELL TO CUBA"

"Farewell to Cuba," a second prize O. Henry Award winner in 1931, is set in Havana and focuses on Martin Gibbs, an American bank employee who is planning to leave the island the next day with Celia after twenty-two years of residence. Cozzens, who lived in Cuba in the 1920's, makes the island atmosphere an almost tangible force in the drama, with its heat, humidity, smells, noise, and the loneliness. Life there has worn Martin out and he is getting old, yet--much as he wants to--he is afraid to leave. He has always been a resident alien, and now, he feels, he is about to desert his home and venture into the unknown. He wonders both how he can do it and how he cannot do it.

Up in their hot, airless hotel room, Martin tries to comfort Celia. At least they have some money, he tells her. She is haggard, sick, drenched with sweat, and unable to eat. She is trying to rest, perhaps to sleep. Tomorrow, he assures her, they will be gone, heading north. At Celia's urging, and over his protestation that he will stay with her, Martin spends his last night with three old friends--Joe Carriker, a car dealer; George Biehl, a banker; and Homer Loran, a newspaper publisher. He has always had a good time with them, Martin reflects, even though he cannot really see much point in it, since he expects never to see them again, but where else can he go? Through the four friends' conversation Cozzens delineates the life Martin has led for too long. His friends offer advice, warnings, endless drinks, horror stories, even a loan if that will help. Why must he leave? Martin cryptically explains, "As it happens, I'm not alone. That's all."

That is not all, as readers discover shortly. Despite initial appearances, Celia is the wife of another man, a very powerful man from whom she has run away. On the stairs up to their room, with his friend George comatose in the lobby below, Martin wonders how his scheme can possibly work--it all seems a terrible mistake. He finds Celia as he left her, quiet on the bed, but there is an empty Veronal bottle on the bureau. Celia has taken an overdose; she could not live with her sickness and fear

or with her knowledge that Martin had taken ninety thousand dollars from the bank. All that remains is his confession and a call to the police. Martin has come suddenly and inescapably to the end of the road.

By withholding significant information--Celia's true identity, Martin's theft from the bank--Cozzens makes "Farewell to Cuba" in its conclusion a more overtly dramatic story than "Total Stranger," with its benign vision of familial relations. Almost from the beginning of "Farewell to Cuba," however, readers have known--or at least strongly suspected--that Martin's escape attempt will fail, that he will not live happily ever after with Celia. How--not whether--he will be thwarted and finally entrapped is the question. Martin, an intelligent, experienced man, does his best. He has planned and schemed for freedom for himself and the woman he loves, and readers are never allowed to regard him as a criminal; but in the end, for reasons he could not have anticipated, he is left bereaved, penniless, and facing a long prison sentence.

"EYES TO SEE"

"Eyes to See," a subtle and ambitious narrative forty-two pages long, is another story of parents and children, love and death, and a boy's coming-of-age. Cozzens's multiplex development of the first-person retrospective point of view is not only intimately related to but also a manifestation of theme. The story follows four days in the life of Dick Maitland, age fifteen, son of Dr. and Mrs. Charles Maitland, who on a football Saturday is summoned home from prep school owing to the wholly unexpected death of his mother, who--in the words of the title--he "never had eyes to see" as someone other than his mother. Plans are made; telegrams, flowers, and family members (expected and unexpected) arrive; the funeral and subsequent gatherings occur; conversations are listened to and overheard; and Dick is sent back to school. The narrator's retrospective inflections on Mrs. Maitland's extramaternal identities shortly expose his more essential concern: those difficult discoveries of self and others that will form the ground of his postadolescent identity.

In parts 1 and 2 of this thirteen-part story, Cozzens juxtaposes two worlds, the old and the new, waiting to be born, the terrible, paradoxical simultaneous existence with which young Maitland will soon have to grapple. In part 1, bad luck is followed by worse (or is it better?) as Dick's mother dies, her hopeless case aggravated by specialists. In part 2, at the school football game, bad luck (the star quarterback fumbles) is followed by a successful trick play that brings a touchdown. What these details collectively suggest is that the patterns and assumptions of the protagonist's sheltered, predictable childhood are breaking down. What is good, what is bad, and what is usual all require redefinition.

The new Maitland, as Cozzens first observes in part 3, feels more than he understands but not a great deal more. "That which was to be demonstrated lay beyond the then-grasp of my awareness; but only a little beyond." This is the essence of Cozzens's management of point of view: fully delineating the obliquities and never overtly violating the integrity of the "then-grasp" of his fifteen-year-old protagonist. The adult retrospective narrator easily coexists with his younger self, providing facts and cultural and other history, but, most important, reflecting upon and illustrating his younger self's growing but uneven powers of awareness and assimilation.

Two relatives on whom the latter half of the story focuses are Cousin Eben and Cousin Lois, strikingly handsome and beautiful, respectively, nominally son and daughter-in-law of Dick's great-aunt Margaret, who had, a generation before, scandalized the Maitlands and other respectable people by running off to join the Perfectionists of Oneida (New York) Colony, and whose practice of "complex marriage" (polygamy) places Cousin Eben's ancestry almost beyond young Dick's "then-grasp."

What is within his understanding by the end of the story has much to do with love (or sex) and death, his awareness that "henceforth anything could happen to anyone." From an early point in the story, from his construction of the facts of his mother's biography, the narrator notes his younger self's squeamishness about sex, his refusal of reason's syllogistic instruction that "All children are a result of sexual commerce. A child was begotten on my mother. Therefore. . . . "Before the story ends, young Dick not only receives that fact but also vicariously enacts it through the unknowing agency of Cousin Eben and Cousin Lois.

They, who have hitherto embodied mysteries of familial relations and antipathies and, obliquely, parentage, greatly embarrass their priggish young relative, himself now and forever an only child, by having produced three children in three years. As Dick is finally drifting off to sleep on the night of his mother's funeral, various words and phrases rise to consciousness. One is "Theophilus Pell," founder of the Oneida Colony; others are "complex marriage" and "bastard," which Cousin Eben has blithely admitted he is in the eyes of the law. Another is "exceptional children," first heard in Cousin Eben's discussion of the teaching of retarded children. Then Dick hears, shortly visualizes, and--despite prayerful forbearance--is excited to ejaculation by those exotic two in the next room making love: "I also, in extremis, had to give way. . . ."

"Eyes to See," in its lucid though formal prose, its self-assured handling of complex form, and its subtle and moving evocation of adolescent self-discovery, is Cozzens at his best in the short story. Although Cozzens once observed that he stopped writing short fiction when he no longer needed the money, and although he was more at ease and more impressive as a novelist, *Children and Others* is a memorable if uneven collection.

From the beginning of his career in the 1920's, Cozzens's stories and novels evoked sharply conflicting responses. Some critics set him down as a literary and social conservative, narrow in interests and sympathies, orthodox in technique, increasingly pedantic in style, and too often given to melodrama and pathos. Admirers, equally vigorous, found him unquestionably a major novelist, a master craftsman, and a superb social historian, whose hallmarks were his irony, worldly wisdom, and deadly penetration into individual character and the social environment. Adjudication of such critical extremes must await the passage of time, but Samuel Johnson's dictum-- "Nothing can please many, and please long, but just representation of general nature"--appears to be the aesthetic principle by which Cozzens would be content to be judged.

OTHER MAJOR WORKS

LONG FICTION: *Confusion*, 1924; *Michael Scarlett*, 1925; *Cock Pit*, 1928; *The Son of Perdition*, 1929; *S.S. San Pedro*, 1931; *The Last Adam*, 1933 (pb. in England as *A Cure of Flesh*, 1958); *Castaway*, 1934; *Men and Brethren*, 1936; *Ask Me Tomorrow*, 1940; *The Just and the Unjust*, 1942; *Guard of Honor*, 1948; *By Love Possessed*, 1957; *Morning, Noon, and Night*, 1968.

NONFICTION: *Just Representations: A James Gould Cozzens Reader*, 1978 (Matthew Bruccoli, editor); *A Time of War: Air Force Diaries and Pentagon Memos, 1943-1945*, 1984 (Matthew Bruccoli, editor); *Selected Notebooks, 1960-1967*, 1984 (Matthew Bruccoli, editor); *Dear Bill: Letters to His Publisher*, 2000.

BIBLIOGRAPHY

Bruccoli, Matthew J. *James Gould Cozzens: A Descriptive Bibliography*. Pittsburgh, Pa.: University of Pittsburgh Press, 1981. A thorough and scholarly listing of Cozzens's works that is indispensable to both the student and the scholar.

_____. *James Gould Cozzens: A Life Apart*. New York: Harvest/HBJ, 1983. Bruccoli has emerged as Cozzens's most ardent literary champion. His biography of the reclusive writer is a highly readable and interesting account of Cozzens's remarkable career. Working with limited cooperation from Cozzens, Bruccoli has critically examined the author's letters, diaries, and notebooks. Contains several appendixes, notes, and an index.

_____, ed. *James Gould Cozzens: A Documentary Volume*. Detroit: Gale, 2004. A compendium of material about Cozzens, including biographical information; writings regarding his critical reception; reproductions of book pages, advertisements, and other graphics; and some of his letters, notebook entries, and essays.

_____. *James Gould Cozzens: New Acquist of True Experience*. Carbondale: Southern Illinois University Press, 1979. Collection of ten varied essays on Cozzens that examine his work in general and specific novels. Bruccoli also includes a variety of short statements by well-known writers, such as Malcolm Cowley, James Dickey, and C. P. Snow, among others, who praise Cozzens's literary achievements.

Includes a complete list of publications by Cozzens.

Cozzens, James Gould. *Just Representations: A James Gould Cozzens Reader*. Edited by Matthew J. Bruccoli. New York: Harcourt Brace Jovanovich, 1978. Bruccoli has compiled a representative collection of Cozzens's writings over the decades from his short stories, novels, essays, letters, and a complete novella. The pieces provide the best example of Cozzens's autobiographical comments on his private life. A brief biography and notes from Cozzens are used to introduce the study.

Hicks, Granville. *James Gould Cozzens*. Minneapolis: University of Minnesota Press, 1966. A short study of Cozzens's literary career with primary emphasis on his major novels. Recommended for its brevity on the subject, but the study is very limited and highly selective in its overall critical appraisal. Hicks fails to examine Cozzens's short stories and nonfictional writings. Includes a select bibliography.

Michel, Pierre. *James Gould Cozzens*. Boston: Twayne, 1974. A good literary study of Cozzens that examines his short stories, early novels, transitional novels, and major work. Michel demonstrates a continuity and evolution of themes by Cozzens over the decades, as well as a ripening mastery of his craft. A good introduction to the writer. Includes a chronology and a select bibliography.

Mooney, Harry John, Jr. *James Gould Cozzens: Novelist of Intellect*. Pittsburgh: University of Pittsburgh Press, 1963. Mooney is an admirer of Cozzens and believes him to be the equal of the best novelists. After closely examining eight of Cozzens's novels, he defends the writer against the critics. Mooney speaks highly of Cozzens's growing literary mastery and his ability to work well within the mainstream framework of the American novel. He concludes that Cozzens is a deliberate and complicated artist.

Allen Shepherd
Updated by Terry Theodore

STEPHEN CRANE

Born: Newark, New Jersey; November 1, 1871
Died: Badenweiler, Germany; June 5, 1900

PRINCIPAL SHORT FICTION

The Little Regiment, and Other Episodes of the American Civil War, 1896
The Open Boat, and Other Tales of Adventure, 1898
The Monster, and Other Stories, 1899
Whilomville Stories, 1900
Wounds in the Rain: War Stories, 1900
Last Words, 1902
The Sullivan County Sketches of Stephen Crane, 1949 (Melvin Schoberlin, editor)

OTHER LITERARY FORMS

Stephen Crane began his brief writing life as a journalist, and he continued writing for newspapers, notably as a war correspondent, throughout his career, sometimes basing his short stories on events that he had first narrated in press reports. He also wrote raw-edged, realistic novels in which he employed journalistic techniques, most significantly in *Maggie: A Girl of the Streets* (1893) and *The Red Badge of Courage: An Episode of the American Civil War* (1895). By contrast, he composed wry, evocative, often cryptic poems, published in *The Black Riders, and Other Lines* (1895) and *War Is Kind* (1899), that seemed to reveal the philosophy behind the world created in his fiction.

ACHIEVEMENTS

Stephen Crane's fiction has proved difficult to classify--not, however, because he defies categorization, but because he worked in two nearly incompatible literary styles at once, while being a groundbreaker in both.

On the one hand, Crane founded the American branch of literary naturalism (this style had originated in France) in his early novels. These works emphasized the sordid aspects of modern life, noted the overpowering shaping influence of environment on human destiny, and scandalously discounted the importance of morality as an effective factor touching on his characters' behavior. In this style, he was followed by writers such as Theodore Dreiser and Frank Norris.

On the other hand, in these same early novels, Crane developed a descriptive style that made him a founder of American impressionism. While the naturalist component of his writing stressed how subjectivity was dominated by social forces, the impressionist component, through coloristic effects and vivid metaphors, stressed the heightened perceptions of individual characters from whose perspectives the stories were presented. The man closest to Crane in his own time in developing this impressionist style was Joseph Conrad, though, it will be recognized, this method of drawing from a character's viewpoint became a central tool of twentieth century literature and was prominently employed by authors such as William Faulkner, Virginia Woolf, and Henry James.

Crane took the unusual tack of both playing up his characters' points of view in presenting the world and downplaying the characters' abilities to influence that world. Although this combination of strategies could be made to work satisfactorily, later authors who have taken Crane's path have tended to develop only one of these strands. Moreover, many critics have found Crane's dual emphases to be jarring and incompletely thought through, particularly in his novels. In fact, many have felt that it is only in his short stories that he seemed thoroughly to blend the two manners.

BIOGRAPHY

To some degree, Stephen Crane's life followed a perverse pattern. He was acclaimed for the authenticity of his writings about events that he had never experienced and then spent the remainder of his few years experiencing the events that he had described in prose--often with disastrous consequences.

Born on November 1, 1871, in Newark, New Jersey, Crane was the last child in the large family of a Methodist minister, Jonathan Townley Crane. The family moved frequently from parish to parish and, in 1878, came to Port Jervis, New York, in forested Sullivan County, where Crane would set most of his early stories. Two years later, his father died, and his mother had to begin struggling to support the family, doing church work and writing for religious publications.

Crane determined to be a writer early in his life, and though he attended a few semesters at Lafayette College and then Syracuse University, his real interest in his college years was in soaking up the atmosphere of New York City lowlife and writing freelance articles for newspapers. In 1892, he completed his first novel, *Maggie: A Girl of the Streets*, the story of a young girl driven into streetwalking by a Bowery Romeo. This first novel was so shocking in tone and full of obscenity (in those days, this meant that it contained words such as "hell") that it was rejected by respectable publishers. Borrowing money, Crane printed the book himself, and though it went unread and unsold, it garnered the appreciation of two of the outstanding literary figures of the day, Hamlin Garland and William Dean Howells.

His next book, *The Red Badge of Courage*, a novel about the Civil War, brought him universal acclaim and celebrity status. In the year of the book's publication, however, as if living out his fiction, he defended an unjustly accused prostitute against the corrupt New York City police, just as he had defended the poor prostitute Maggie in prose, and found undeserved blight attached to his name. From then on, life would be made difficult for him in New York City by the angered police force.

Crane more or less abandoned New York at this point, easily enough since the authority of his army novel had placed him in much demand as a war correspondent. Going to Florida to wait for a ship to Cuba, where a rebellion against the Spanish colonialists was taking place, Crane met Cora Taylor, the madame of a house of ill repute who was to become his common-law wife. The ill-fated ship that he eventually boarded sank, and Crane

Stephen Crane (Library of Congress)

barely escaped with his life, though, on the positive side, he produced from the experience what many consider his greatest short story, "The Open Boat."

As if to show that he could describe real wars as well as he could imagine them, he began shuttling from battle to battle as a reporter, first going to the Greco-Turkish War and then back to view the Spanish-American War, ruining his health in the process. Between wars, he stayed in the manorial Brede Place in England, where he became acquainted with a number of other expatriates who lived in the area, including Joseph Conrad, Harold Frederic, and Henry James.

His problems with the police and the irregularity of his liaison with Cora Taylor--she could not get a divorce from her long-estranged husband--would have made it difficult for Crane to live in his homeland, so in 1899, he settled at the manor for good. Sick and beset with financial woes brought on by extravagant living and an openhanded generosity to visitors, he wrote feverishly but unavailingly to clear his debts. He died the next year from tuberculosis, after having traveled to the Continent to seek a cure.

ANALYSIS

Perhaps because his writing career was so short, critics have devoted much space to Stephen Crane's slight, decidedly apprentice series of sketches, collectively entitled *The Sullivan County Sketches*. One trait that the sketches do have in their favor is that they contain all the facets of style and theme that Crane was to use as his writing developed. The reader finds the overbearing power of the environment, the vivid descriptions, the premise that these descriptions reflect the heightened consciousness of a character or characters, and the idea that this very heightening involves a distortion of perception that needs to be overcome for the characters' adequate adjustment to, and comprehension of, reality. These stores are also significant because they are concerned with the actions of four campers and hence reflect not only on individual psychology but also on the psychology of group dynamics, which was to become a focus of Crane's writing.

"FOUR MEN IN A CAVE"

In one of the better pieces from this series, "Four Men in a Cave," a quartet of campers decides to explore a cave in order to have something to brag about when they return to the city. Their scarcely concealed fears about the expedition are rendered by Crane's enlivening of stalactites that jab down at them and stalagmites that shoot up at them from crevices. At the end of their path, they find a hermit who invites them to a game of poker, but their fear-stoked imaginations visualize the gamester as a ghoul or Aztec priest. Only later after escaping the cave, in a comic denouement, do they learn of the cave dweller's true identity, that of a mad farmer who took to solitude when he lost his land and wife through gambling. By this time, there seems to be little to brag about, since what has happened has exposed their cowardice and credulity.

The story provides an early example of the rough-and-ready combination of impressionist subjectivity, in how the descriptions in the piece are tinged by the campers' fears, and naturalist objectivity, in how the overwhelming environment of the cave, for part of the story, controls the men's action while dwarfing them. In addition, the piece indicates the way, as Crane sees it, emotions can be constructed collectively, as when each camper tells the others how he has misidentified the hermit, adding to the growing hysteria.

"AN EXPERIMENT IN MISERY"

In 1894, Crane published a more mature story, "An Experiment in Misery," in which he transposed the narrative of a cave journey into a serious study of urban social conditions. In the originally printed version of the piece, two middle-class men observe tramps and speculate about their motives and feelings. On impulse, the younger man decides to dress as a tramp in order to penetrate into their secrets. (Such a tactic, of disguising oneself to uncover hidden areas of society, was a common practice of crusading reporters at that time.)

In the later, revised version of this story, the one that is more commonly known, Crane removed the beginning and ending that reveal the protagonist to be slumming; yet, though his social origins are obscured, the story still concerns a neophyte who knows nothing of the life of the underclass and who is being initiated into the ways of the Bowery slums. The high point of the tale, corresponding to the cave exploration, is the hero's entrance into an evil-smelling flophouse. He has trouble sleeping in the noisome room, for his keyed-up fancy sees morbid, highly romanticized symbols everywhere. He understands the shriek of a nightmare-tossed sleeper as a metaphoric protest of the downtrodden.

Awakening the next morning, the protagonist barely remarks on the stench, and this seems to indicate that, merely through familiarity, some of the falsely romantic pictures that he has entertained about the life of the city's poorest have begun to rub off. Exactly what positive things he has learned and of what value such learning will be to him are never clear. Indeed, as Crane grew as a writer, while his stories still turned on the loss of illusions, they began to lose the dogmatic assurance that such a change is necessarily for the good.

The last scene of the sketch, though, does make a more definite point, this one about the nature of groups. The hero has begun to associate with a fellow tramp called the assassin. Now, after his initiatory night, he seems both adjusted to his new station and accepted by the tramp world, at least insofar as the assassin is willing to regale him with his life story. By abandoning his preconceptions about poverty, the protagonist has quite seamlessly fitted himself into the alien milieu, yet this joining of one community has a negative side effect of distancing him from another. The last tableau has the assassin and the hero lounging on park benches as the morning rush-hour crowd streams by them. Here, soon after the hero has had the comfortable feeling of being accepted in one society, he has the poignant realization that, as a bum, he no longer belongs to the larger American working world. There is even a sly hint, given by the fact that the youth begins employing the same grandiose, romanticized terms in depicting his separation from the business world that he had earlier used to depict the flophouse, that he has embarked on a new course of building delusions. In other words, his loss of illusions about the reality of tramp life has been counteracted (as if a vacuum needed to be filled) by the imbibing of a new set of illusions about the vast gulf between the classes. Each community one may join seems to have its own supply of false perspectives.

"THE OPEN BOAT"

In 1897, after his near death at sea, Crane produced "The Open Boat," which most critics consider his greatest short story and which some even rank as his supreme achievement, placing it above his novels. This story also involves four men. They are in a small boat, a dinghy, escapees from a sunken vessel, desperately trying to row to shore in heavy seas.

The famed first sentence establishes both the parameters of the fictional world and a new chastening of Crane's style. It reads, "None of them knew the color of the sky." Literally, the boat's occupants are too intent on staying afloat to notice the heavens; figuratively, in this godless universe the men cannot look to the sky for help but must rely on their own muscles and wits, which, against the elements, are little enough. Furthermore, the opening's very dismissal of color descriptions, given that much of Crane's earlier work, such as *The Red Badge of Courage*, depends heavily on color imagery, can be seen as the author's pledge to restrain some of the flashiness of his style.

This restraint is evident not only in a more tempered use of language here but also in the nature of the protagonists' delusions. In works such as the slum experiment, the romanticized preconceptions that determine the protagonist's viewpoint can be seen as trivial products of a shallow culture--that is, as marginal concerns--whereas

in the sea story, the men's illusions are necessities of life. The men in the boat want to believe that they must survive, since they have been fighting so hard. If they do not believe this, how can they continue rowing? The point is made wrenchingly at one moment when the men refuse to accept that they will drown, as it seems they will, in the breakers near the shore. Such illusions (about the meaningfulness of valor and effort) obviously have more universal relevance than others with which Crane has dealt, and that is why the story strikes so deep; the illusions also, ingeniously, tie in with the reader's expectations. As much as the reader begins to identify with the four men (and they are sympathetically portrayed), he or she will want them to survive and thus will be on the verge of agreeing to their illusions. Thus, Crane engineers a remarkable and subtle interlocking of readers' and characters' beliefs.

Furthermore, the functionality of the possibly delusive beliefs of the struggling men--that is, the fact that they need to believe that they will make it ashore to keep up the arduous fight for life--helps Crane to a fuller, more positive view of human community. The men in the cave were merely partners in error, but these toilers share a belief system that sustains them in their mutually supportive labor, which the characters themselves recognize as "a subtle brotherhood of men." The men's shared recognition of the supportive structure of human groups gives weight to the story's last phrase, which says, of the three survivors who have reached land, "and they felt that they could then be interpreters."

The story, written in the third person, is told largely from the viewpoint of one of the four, a newspaper correspondent. This is not evident at once, however, since the narrative begins by simply objectively reporting the details of the men's struggle to stay afloat and reproducing their laconic comments. In this way, the group is put first, and only later, when the correspondent's thoughts are revealed, does the reader learn of his centrality as the story begins to be slightly colored by his position. What the focus on his consciousness reveals, aiding Crane in deepening his presentation, is how the subtle brotherhood is felt individually.

After rowing near to the shore but not being able to attract anyone's attention, the crew settle down for a night at sea. While whoever is rowing stays awake, the others sleep like the dead they may soon become, and at this point the story dwells more intently on the correspondent's outlook as he takes his turn at the oars. The newspaperman reconsiders the beliefs that have been keeping them afloat, seeing the weakness in them and accepting, now that he is alone, the possibility of an ironic death--that is, one coming in sight of shore after their courageous struggle. His existential angst, an acknowledgment that there is no special heavenly providence, neither stops him from his muscle-torturing rowing nor diminishes his revived illusions on the morrow, when they again all breast the waves together.

If this line of reasoning shows him mentally divorcing himself from the collective ideology, another night thought implies that, in another direction, the correspondent is gaining a deeper sense of solidarity. He remembers a verse that he had learned in school about a legionnaire dying far from home with only a comrade to share his last moments. The correspondent had thought little of the poem, both because he had never been in extremis (and so saw little to the pathos of the case) and, as Crane notes, had formerly looked cynically at his fellows (and so had found unpalatable or unbelievable the care of one soldier for another). A day's experience in the dinghy has made him keenly aware of the two aspects of experience that he had overlooked or undervalued, and thus has given him a clear understanding of the networks (those of democratic brotherhood) and circumstances (a no-holds-barred fight against an indifferent universe) that underlie the human social world. This understanding can be applied in many ways--not only toward a grasp of group interaction, but also toward an interpretation of honest art.

Still, the most telling incident of his lonely watch is not any of his thoughts but is instead an action. The boat, the correspondent finds, has become a magnet for a huge shark. Achingly, he wishes that one of his fellow sailors were awake to share his fidgety vigil, yet he resists any impulse he has to rouse them or even to question aloud whether any of them is conscious for fear that he should waken a sleeper. Even if alone he cannot continue with the group illusion, he can, though alone, effortlessly maintain the group's implicit morality,

which holds that each should uncomplainingly shoulder as much of the burden as possible, while never revealing irritation or fear. Much later, the newspaperman learns that another of the four, the captain, was awake and aware of the predator's presence during what had been taken to be the correspondent's moment of isolated anguish. The hidden coexistent alertness of the captain suggests the ongoing mutuality of the group that undergirds even seemingly isolated times of subjectivity.

To bring this story in line with the last one mentioned, it is worth noting that the small group in the boat is contrasted to a group on shore, just as in "An Experiment in Misery" the hoboes are contrasted to the society of the gainfully employed. When the rowers are near the coast on the first day, they vainly hope to attract the ministering attentions of people on land. They do attract their attention, but the people, tourists from a hotel, merrily wave at them, thinking that the men in the dinghy are fishermen. The heedlessness, inanity, and seeming stupidity of the group on shore compare unfavorably with the hard-won, brave alertness of the boatmen, pointing to the fact that the small group's ethical solidarity is not of a type with the weaker unity found in the larger society. The men's deep harmony--beautiful as it is--is something that can be found only in pockets. The depiction of the community on the land foreshadows elements of Crane's later, darker pictures of community, as in "The Blue Hotel," where what sustains a group is not a life-enhancing though flimsy hope but a tacitly accepted lie.

"THE BRIDE COMES TO YELLOW SKY"

In the year that he wrote "The Open Boat" and the next year, Crane was to compose three other brilliant stories, two of which dealt with myths of the Old West. Both these Western tales were written in his mature, unadorned style, and both continued his focus on the belief systems of communities. What is new to them is a greater flexibility in the handling of plot. Previously, Crane had simply followed his characters through a continuous chronological sequence from start to finish; now, however, he began shifting between differently located character groups and jumping around in time.

In "The Bride Comes to Yellow Sky," the action begins on a train moving through Texas, carrying Yellow Sky's sheriff, Jack Potter, and his new wife back to town. Potter is apprehensive about his reception, since he has married out of town in a whirlwind courtship and none of the townspeople knows of his new status. The scene shifts to the interior of a Yellow Sky saloon, where the gathered, barricaded patrons have more immediate things to be apprehensive about than Potter's marriage. Scratchy Wilson, the local ruffian, has gotten drunk and is shooting in the main street, while, as the bar's occupants admit, the only man able to cow him is the absent sheriff. Scratchy Wilson himself, as the reader learns in another scene shift, not aware of Potter's trip, is truculently looking for the sheriff so that they can engage in a showdown. In truth, the reader, knowing of Potter's imminence, will probably share Wilson's expectation of a gun battle, which is not an unreasonable forecast of the plot's unfolding. This expectation is founded on a deeper belief that the West will always be an uncivilized place of outlaws and pistols. A chagrined Scratchy recognizes that this belief is invalid and that an era has passed when he finds that the sheriff has taken a wife. After meeting the couple, he holsters his guns and stalks off toward the horizon.

"THE BLUE HOTEL"

A tragic variation on similar themes of violence and community beliefs appears in "The Blue Hotel," a story that a few critics rank in importance above "The Open Boat." The tale concerns a fatalistic traveler, the Swede, who stops for the night in a hotel in Nebraska. (This protagonist's name will be picked up by Ernest Hemingway, a Crane admirer, for an equally fatalistic character in his short-story masterpiece "The Killers.") Through the Swede's conversation with the hotel owner, Scully, and other people staying at the hotel, it appears that, based perhaps on an immersion in dime novels, the Swede thinks that this town--or, for that matter, any town in the West--is a hotbed of bloodshed and mayhem. After his fears seem to be allayed by the officious owner, who assures him that he is mistaken, the Swede overreacts by becoming boisterous and familiar. His mood eventually dissipates when, involved in a game of cards, he accuses the owner's son of cheating. The pair engage in a fistfight, which the

Swede wins. He is now triumphant but can no longer find any welcome at the hotel. So, he wanders off to a nearby saloon, in which his even more high-strung and aggressive demonstrations lead to his death at the hands of an icy but violent gambler he had been prodding to drink with him.

At this point, the story seems a grim meditation on the truth or falsity of myths. What seemed to be the manifestly absurd belief of the Swede has been proven partially true by his own death. However, it appears this truth would never have been exposed except for the Swede's own pushy production of the proper circumstances for Western violence to emerge. There is, however, another turn of the cards. A final scene is described in which, months later, two of the hotel's card players, witnesses to the dispute between the Swede and Scully's son, discuss events of that fateful evening. One of them, the Easterner, claims that the whole group collected at the hotel that night is responsible for what led to the death since they all knew that the owner's son was cheating but did not back up the Swede when he accused the youth.

In one way, this final episode indicates that perhaps the Swede's suspicions were accurate in yet another sense: The whole town is made up, metaphorically, of killers in that the community is willing to sacrifice an outsider to maintain its own dubious harmony. From this angle, this Western town's particular violence merely crystallizes and externalizes any hypocritical town's underlying psychic economy. (Crane depicted this economy more explicitly in his novella *The Monster*.) In another way--and here the increasing complexity of Crane's thought on community is evident--even after the final episode, it still appears that the Swede's murder has some justification.

There are two points to be made in this connection. For one, throughout the story, Crane represents the frailty of human existence as it is established on the prairies in the depths of winter. The story begins by underlining the presumptuousness of Scully's hotel's bright blue color, not so much as it may be an affront to the other, staider buildings in town, but in its assertiveness against the grimness of the white wastes of nature surrounding and swamping the little burg. The insignificance of human beings measured against the universe is explicitly stated by Crane in an oft-quoted passage. He speaks of humans clinging to a "whirling, fire-smitten, icelocked, disease-stricken, space-lost bulb." He goes on to say that the "conceit of man" in striving to prevail in such conditions is "the very engine of life." It is true that they all killed the Swede in some sense, but the fragility of the human community, it may be surmised, demands that its members all practice respect and forbearance toward one another so that a common front can be presented against uncaring nature. If anyone consistently violates this unwritten code, as the Swede does, he must be eliminated for group self-preservation. It is significant in this light that the Swede, who demands a grudge match with the owner's son, would take the men away from the large, red-hot stove (symbol of the warmth of peaceful intercourse and home comfort) outside to fight in subzero weather. To restate this, for his own egotistical purposes, the Swede would drag everyone into a much greater exposure to a harsh environment than life in the community, were it running harmoniously, would ever make necessary.

The second point to be made is that Crane's portrait of the gambler, which interrupts the narrative at a high point and which seems at first sight a cumbersome miscalculation by the author, allows the reader a fuller understanding of the place of an outsider in this Western society. If the reader had been given only the Swede's treatment to go by, he or she would be forced to conclude that, whatever the necessity of the visitor's expulsion, this town has little tolerance for aberrant personalities. Such a position, however, has to be modified after Crane's presentation of the gambler, whose disreputable calling excludes him from the city's better social functions but whose behavior in other areas--he bows to the restrictions put on him with good grace and is a charitable family man who will not prey on the better citizens--conforms enough to standards to allow him to be generally accepted. Intervening at this point, Crane's portrayal of this second (relative) outsider is used to indicate that the community will permit in its midst a character who has not followed all of its rules, provided such a character does not, as the Swede does, insistently and continuously breach the accepted norms.

All this taken together does not, certainly, excuse a murder. What it does show is that Crane's understanding of how a community sustains itself has expanded beyond the understanding that he had at the time of the sea story. He indicates that the guiding principle of mutual support found in the dinghy has remained operative, even in a far less threatened situation, while adding that violations of this principle can lead to less happy consequences than might have been foreseen in the earlier story.

"DEATH AND THE CHILD"

In "Death and the Child," Crane produced an excellent story about war, the topic that had been both the most consistent and the least successful subject of his short pieces. The intertwined themes of the effect of illusions and the ways that an individual can be integrated into, or excluded from, a community--the most important themes of Crane's work--are again central. In this piece, the character who nurses illusions is Peza, a journalist who has decided to join the Greek side during the Greco-Turkish War, motivated by unrealistic ideas about the glories of classical Greece and the adventure of fighting. Once he reaches the battle lines, however, he finds it impossible to join the other combatants.

He is displeased by the nonchalance of the troops, who refuse to strike heroic poses, but what actually ends up turning him away from solidarity is his realization that to become part of the group he must accept not only a largely humdrum life but also the possibility of a prosaic death. In other words, it is not coming down to earth with the common men that ultimately scares him but the understanding that he may have to come down under the earth (into a grave) with them.

The story exhibits what had become the traits of Crane's mature style. He writes with a terse, crisp, subdued prose that is occasionally shot through with startling or picturesque imagery, this imagery being the residue of his initial, more flowery style. Crane also exhibits a mastery of plotting. This is brought out by the careful joining of Peza's emotional states to his gyrations around the battle camp as well as by the story's final encounter, where Peza comes upon an abandoned child, who, too young to comprehend war, still has a clearer view of reality than the distraught journalist.

This skill at plotting is not something that Crane possessed from the beginning, which brings up a last point.

It might be said that there is a chronological distinction between Crane's interests and his method of narration. While his thematic concerns were constant throughout his career, as he grew older his attention to how a community was created and sustained grew in weight, and his ability to construct complex plots is one that he picked up during the course of his creative life. There are authors who advance little after their first books, but in Crane's case it can definitely be said that there was a promise for the future that his short life never redeemed.

OTHER MAJOR WORKS

LONG FICTION: *Maggie: A Girl of the Streets*, 1893; *The Red Badge of Courage: An Episode of the American Civil War*, 1895; *George's Mother*, 1896; *The Third Violet*, 1897; *The Monster*, 1898 (serial), 1899 (novella; pb. in *The Monster, and Other Stories*); *Active Service*, 1899; *The O'Ruddy: A Romance*, 1903 (with Robert Barr).

PLAYS: *The Blood of the Martyr*, wr. 1898?, pb. 1940; *The Ghost*, pr. 1899 (with Henry James; fragment).

POETRY: *The Black Riders, and Other Lines*, 1895; *A Souvenir and a Medley*, 1896; *War Is Kind*, 1899.

NONFICTION: *The Great Battles of the World*, 1901; *The War Dispatches of Stephen Crane*, 1964.

MISCELLANEOUS: *The University of Virginia Edition of the Works of Stephen Crane*, 1969-1975 (10 volumes).

BIBLIOGRAPHY

Benfey, Christopher. *The Double Life of Stephen Crane*. New York: Alfred A. Knopf, 1992. This brief (294-page) biography of Crane makes a virtue out of necessity by translating the dearth of biographical information about Crane--who died at the age of twenty-eight--into the key to his character. For Benfey, Crane is "a man who . . . vanished into his own fictions," a writer who planned his life by writing about experiences before living them. Thus, for Benfey, Crane's life is not so much mysterious as it is "duplicate."

Berryman, John. *Stephen Crane*. New York: William Sloane Associates, 1950. Reprint. New York: Cooper Square Press, 2001. This combined biography and interpretation has been superseded as a biography, but it continues to be an absorbing Freudian reading of Crane's life and work. Berryman, himself a major American poet, eloquently explains the patterns of family conflict that appear in Crane's fiction. Furthermore, Berryman's wide-ranging interests allow him to tackle such large topics as Crane's influence on the birth of the short story, a form that, although existing earlier, came to prominence only in the 1890's. Includes notes and index.

Bloom, Harold, ed. *Stephen Crane*. New York: Bloom's Literary Criticism, 2009. Reprints critical essays about Crane's work, including his short-story collections *The Little Regiment, and Other Episodes of the American Civil War*; *The Open Boat, and Other Tales of Adventure*; *The Monster, and Other Stories*; *Whilomville Stories*; and *Wounds in the Rain*.

Colvert, James B. "Stephen Crane and Postmodern Theory." *American Literary Realism* 28 (Fall, 1995): 4-22. A survey of postmodern approaches to Crane's fiction. Summarizes the basic premises of postmodern interpretation, examining how these premises have been applied to such Crane stories as "The Open Boat," "The Upturned Face," and "Maggie"; balances such interpretive strategies against critics who affirm more traditional, humanistic approaches.

Davis, Linda H. *Badge of Courage: The Life of Stephen Crane*. Boston: Houghton Mifflin, 1998. Makes use of research to separate the real Crane from the legends, myths, and rumors about his life. Discusses his pioneering a new way of writing about war in *The Red Badge of Courage* and his short stories.

Halliburton, David. *The Color of the Sky: A Study of Stephen Crane*. Cambridge, England: Cambridge University Press, 1989. Though somewhat thematically disorganized, the author's philosophical grounding and ability to look at Crane's works from unusual angles make for many provocative readings. In his discussion of "The Blue Hotel," for example, he finds much more aggression directed against the Swede than may at first appear, coming not only from seemingly benign characters but also from the layout of the town. Notes, index.

Metress, Christopher. "From Indifference to Anxiety: Knowledge and the Reader in 'The Open Boat.'" *Studies in Short Fiction* 28 (Winter, 1991): 47-53. Shows how the structure of "The Open Boat" (made up of four key moments) creates an epistemological dilemma for readers, moving them from a position of indifference to a state of epistemological anxiety. By suggesting that the survivors have become interpreters, Crane implies that readers must get rid of their indifference to the difficulty of gaining knowledge and embrace the inevitable anxiety of that failure.

Monteiro, George, ed. *Stephen Crane: The Contemporary Reviews*. New York: Cambridge University Press, 2009. Reprints a representative selection of the reviews of Crane's works that appeared after their initial publication, including critiques of his short-story collections.

Nagel, James. *Stephen Crane and Literary Impressionism*. University Park: Pennsylvania State University Press, 1980. Nagel carefully delineates what he considers Crane's application of Impressionist concepts of painting to fiction, which involved Crane's "awareness that the apprehension of reality is limited to empirical data interpreted by a single human intelligence." This led Crane to emphasize the flawed visions of men and women and to depict the dangers of this natural one-sidedness in works such as *Maggie: A Girl of the Streets*; it also resulted in his depiction of characters who transcended this weakness through an acceptance of human inadequacies in such works as "The Open Boat." Notes, index.

Robertson, Michael. *Stephen Crane: Journalism and the Making of Modern American Literature*. New York: Columbia University Press, 1997. Argues that Crane's success inspired later journalists to think of their work as preparatory for writing fiction. Claims the blurring of fact and fiction in newspapers during Crane's life suited his own narrative experiments.

Sorrentino, Paul. "The Short Stories of Stephen Crane." In *A Companion to the American Short Story*, edited by Alfred Bendixen and James Nagel. Malden, Mass.: Wiley-Blackwell, 2010. Crane scholar Sorrentino provides an overview and critical examination of Crane's short fiction.

_____, ed. *Stephen Crane Remembered*. Tuscaloosa: University of Alabama, 2006. A more recent complementary volume to Stallman's still valuable biography of Crane. Sorrentino brings together nearly one hundred documents from Crane's acquaintances for a somewhat more revealing look at the writer Crane than has heretofore been available.

_____. *Student Companion to Stephen Crane*. Westport, Conn.: Greenwood Press, 2006. Includes chapters discussing Crane's life, literary heritage, his New York City stories and sketches, the tales of Whilomville, and his other short fiction.

Stallman, R. W. *Stephen Crane: A Biography*. New York: George Braziller, 1968. This definitive biography involves a thorough sifting of all the circumstances surrounding Crane's major fiction, a sifting that is especially impressive in the case of "The Open Boat." Stallman also gives the reader a feeling for Crane's times. Contains a meticulous bibliography (Stallman later composed a book-length bibliography), extensive notes, an index, and appendixes that include contemporary reviews of Crane's work and obituaries.

Wertheim, Stanley, and Paul Sorrentino. *The Crane Log: A Documentary Life of Stephen Crane 1871-1900*. New York: G. K. Hall, 1994. Stanley and Sorrentino, editors of *The Correspondence of Stephen Crane* (1988), have attempted to counter many of the falsehoods that have bedeviled analyses of Crane's life and work by providing a documentary record of the author's life. Opening with biographical notes on persons mentioned in the text and lavishly sourced, *The Crane Log* is divided into seven chapters, beginning with the notation in Crane's father's diary of the birth of his fourteenth child, Stephen, and ending with a newspaper report of Crane's funeral, written by Wallace Stevens.

Wolford, Chester L. *Stephen Crane: A Study of the Short Fiction*. Boston: Twayne, 1989. This overly brief but useful look at Crane's short fiction provides Wolford's sensitive readings, as well as commentary on the major points that have been raised in critical discussions of the Crane pieces. In describing "The Bride Comes to Yellow Sky," for example, Wolford explains his view of how the story fits into the archetypical patterns of the passing-of-the-West narratives, while also exploring why other critics have seen Crane's story as a simple parody. About half of the book is given over to selected Crane letters and extractions from other critics' writings on Crane's short pieces. Includes a chronology, bibliography, and index.

James Feast

MOIRA CRONE

Born: Goldsboro, North Carolina; August 10, 1952

PRINCIPAL SHORT FICTION
The Winnebago Mysteries, and Other Stories, 1982
Dream State, 1995
What Gets into Us, 2006

OTHER LITERARY FORMS

Known primarily for short stories that probe the ordinary lives of women struggling to make sense of love and commitment to family, Moira Crone (MOY-ra krohn) also published *A Period of Confinement* (1986), a novel that explores the difficult adjustments an unmarried Baltimore artist in her late twenties must make after the birth of her child. As a pioneering look at the psychology of postpartum depression (the woman will for a time abandon her new commitment), the novel succeeded as a character study, avoiding sentimentality and refusing to offer pat and easy solutions. In addition, Crone, a career academic in the field of creative writing, promoted the work of promising writers in her four-year stint (1997-2001) as senior editor of the University Press of Mississippi fiction series.

ACHIEVEMENTS

Moira Crone, in a steady output of short fiction across more than thirty years, has acquired a sterling reputation among critics, who see in her stories of mothers, daughters, and wives the generous compassion and probing psychology representative of the best of contemporary realistic fiction. Her works routinely have been included in a variety of best-of-the-year anthologies, and, as a creative-writing professor at Louisiana State University (LSU) for close to thirty years, she has received numerous academic grants and national fellowships and has accepted several writer-in-residence appointments. A southern writer born in North Carolina with career ties to Louisiana, Crone has been recognized twice by the Pirate's Alley Faulkner Society of New Orleans in nationwide competitions open to any unpublished work in a variety of genres, winning its award for short fiction in 1992 for "Dream State" and its William Faulkner/WilliamWisdom Prize for best novella in 2004 for "The Ice Garden." In 2009, the Fellowship of Southern Writers awarded Crone the prestigious Robert Penn Warren Award, a lifetime achievement award, for a body of work that with profound sympathy and lyrical prose worked to depict the emotional lives of people in the contemporary South.

BIOGRAPHY

Moira Crone was born in the heart of tobacco-rich rural east-central North Carolina, an hour south of Raleigh. Her father, an accountant, was a lifelong southerner who had met Crone's mother in New York City during World War II--thus, every summer Crone visited Brooklyn, where she fell under the spell of her maternal grandmother, a feisty, chain-smoking former flapper, who regaled the young Crone with lively stories of her own life. When Crone was sixteen, her grandmother retired and came to live in Goldsboro, and Crone promptly moved in with her. Years later, Crone would credit long nights of talking with her grandmother for teaching her the shape and sound of storytelling. Crone also was an inveterate reader. In high school, Crone was intrigued by the works of William Faulkner, finding particularly intoxicating the writer's fascination with the psychological life of the South and the stately music of his measured and often ornate prose line. In addition, growing up in a small rural town, Crone read with deep admiration the stories of Sherwood Anderson, which revealed the complex emotional lives of such characters.

Accomplished in the classroom, Crone accepted a scholarship in 1970 to study literature at Smith College, a private liberal arts college for women in Massachusetts. It was there she first began to experiment with writing short stories, under the tutelage of British writer V. S. Pritchett, one of the twentieth century's most accomplished masters of the short story. After graduating with high honors in 1974, Crone was accepted into the Creative Writing Graduate Program at Johns Hopkins University in Baltimore. Graduating in 1977 and drawn to teaching, she worked briefly as a tutor in reading and writing for the Enoch Pratt Free Library in Baltimore and then as a part-time lecturer in English at both Johns Hopkins and Goucher College in the Baltimore suburb of Towson. In 1981, she accepted an instructorship at Louisiana State University, where she would remain for more than thirty years, serving, beginning in 1987, as the director of its internationally renowned creative-writing program. In addition, she has pursued a tireless public agenda of readings from her own works, in which she enthralls audiences with the effortless charisma of her storytelling power. She and her husband, poet and scholar Rodger Kamenetz, who is also on the faculty of LSU, have long maintained a residence just north of New Orleans. In the aftermath of Hurricane Katrina in 2004, Crone was in the forefront of recording the emotional impact of the devastation and a significant figure in the extended campaign following the catastrophe to promote the resurgence of the area.

ANALYSIS

It is tempting to pigeonhole the short fiction of Moira Crone. She is, after all a local-color realist,

compelled by a generous compassion for apparently uneventful lives, a southern writer whose psychological realism is touched by (although not obsessed with) the gothic and the eccentric and animated by a subtle wit and sympathetic humor. That she is most engaged by the psychology of women, notably in the roles of mother and daughter, makes her a feminist writer as well. It is all the more tempting to approach her through established traditions because, as a university professor of creative writing, she has long defined her own influences, especially Ellen Gilchrist, Truman Capote, Sherwood Anderson, and William Faulkner.

Each is, of course, an element critical to understanding Crone's fictional sensibility. However, no single label entirely defines her work. She is primarily a storyteller, fascinated by the implications of setting down in language the events of lives otherwise spent in obscurity. From her early stories, the apprentice efforts gathered in *The Winnebago Mysteries, and Other Stories*, Crone investigates characters who come to fascinate the reader, with their confusions, their impulsive decisions, and their complicated needs. The title story of the first collection, for instance, tells of a college-aged woman, terrified of the implications of maturity, heading out on a quixotic road trip, uncertain of where she is going or when she will return and certain only of what she is leaving behind: the dead end of responsibility and adulthood. Such characters fascinate Crone. Hers is character-driven fiction, as her creations come to have the depth and feel of people the reader might meet.

Her fiction privileges the reader, as a kind of listener, to be part of the dynamic of storytelling. Readers are invited to sympathize with characters and to understand their disappointments, their struggles, and their loneliness. The reader invests enormous imaginative energy in responding to suggestive symbols, and Crone's alert eye is sensitive to the implications of the things surrounding her characters and how such things reveal difficult psychologies. Notable is Crone's meticulously created prose; its accessibility, with its unforced sense of how language is spoken rather than written, belies its subtle music. Significant are Crone's deft use of color, her rich sense of setting, and her pitch-perfect ear for the dialogue of her southern characters. In addition to examining the implications of the feminist experience, Crone has investigated the cultural diversity of the New South through the hybrid nature of her adopted Louisiana, bringing to her fiction a contemporary sense of cultural identity and cultural collisions. Never, however, does the fiction sound distant, as if Crone is measuring and defining a culture with the cool eye of an anthropologist. Without sentimentality, maintaining her edge as an observer, Crone makes her characters vivid and accessible and their experiences revealing and universal.

DREAM STATE

The eight stories, all published previously, gathered in Crone's breakthrough publication touch on themes that have become her signature. The stories center on thirtysomethings struggling to come to terms with the implications of a sudden strong passion in lives that had up to that point been wasted, lost in an emotional drift. The cultural makeup of Louisiana serves as a metaphor for the stories' protagonists, who come to the bayou country from the North, suggesting a peculiar sense of rootlessness.

In the title story, a real estate agent from up North, struggling in a financially depressed market, comes under the powerful spell of an aging Hollywood star, who hopes to find in New Orleans a graceful refuge from a career that has spiraled into memory. Crone deftly manipulates a contrapuntal narrative, as both characters move into emotionally unsatisfying marriages. In "I'm Eleven," Crone uses the first-person narrative vehicle of a child to examine the taut emotional crisis in a family, when the girl's older brother gets his girlfriend pregnant. Perhaps no story more catches Crone's sensitive perception of the emotional catastrophes of ordinary people than "Fever," in which a frustrated writer, long detached from his heart and ghostwriting a slick political biography for a hack Texas politician, gets caught up in a whirlwind affair with a girl at the neighborhood copy store, herself a frustrated café singer. Adjusting to the new responsibilities of fatherhood (he has been left for a week while his wife attends to business out of town), he finds himself pulled irresistibly to the enticing lure of the young girl (she was named for Camille, a devastating hurricane that caught the Louisiana coast unprepared).

Although in her fascination with small lives Crone reflects Anderson's sensibility, there is none of his cool sense of distance, how he clinically examines his emotional grotesques. What emerges from this collection is Crone's unwavering compassion for hearts suddenly, stunningly made aware of their power.

"ICE GARDEN"

The stories gathered in Crone's 2006 collection, *What Gets into Us*, represent an ambitious story cycle. The interrelated stories work off one another to reflect cumulatively the life of Fayton, a fictitious North Carolina rural town, and travel across nearly four decades through the lives of four families, primarily those of the mothers and daughters. These are stories of small-town life, of secrets that families struggle to keep quiet, of the powerful yearnings that take place behind doors, of hungers that residents never acknowledge publicly. Given the dynamic reach of Crone's stories, reaching from the 1950's to the 1990's, she also offers insight into how social issues--from civil rights to women's rights, from the Vietnam War to economic booms and busts--have shaped the lives of southerners. As such, she emerges as part of the post-Flannery O'Connor, post-Walker Percy generation of southern writers who define the New South.

"Ice Garden," the novella that leads off the collection, is perhaps the collection's best work, reflecting Crone's new maturity. In it, Crone reveals her fascination with postwar southern gothicism, particularly the atmospheric early stories of Capote and the lurid family narratives of O'Connor. The tale is told through the limited agency of a ten-year-old child, Claire McKinney, the daughter of woman in and out of mental treatment, plagued by a sense of her own fading beauty (set in the late 1950's, she fancies herself another Marilyn Monroe). The narrative explores the mother's deep paranoia and penchant for violent outbursts secondhand, through the eyes of a daughter struggling to love a disturbed and dangerous mother. The narrative explores a troubling and troubled woman and the implications of beauty lost. The prose is subtle, musical, and carefully cadenced to reflect the awareness of a child told through the perspective of the child grown up: It lends itself to recitation, reflecting Crone's love of storytelling, which she learned listening to her grandmother. The narrative device recalls convincingly the frame technique of Harper Lee's *To Kill a Mockingbird* (1960). Effortlessly, the narrative transforms common objects--a beauty parlor hairdo, diamond-shaped window panes, unmade beds, jars of Gerber baby food--into suggestive symbols that engage the reader while working to reveal Claire's growing maturity.

Claire, the child, understands she is not as pretty as her mother and contends with a growing animosity toward a mother who cannot show even the most meager maternal love. The mother fancies herself as privileged--hailing from the faded aristocracy of distant Charleston--and cannot accept a place among what she perceives to be the rural squalor of the Carolina hills. It is a riveting read, especially when the daughter rescues her baby sister from a bath that the mother had left running and the girl and the reader are left to fathom the implications of a mother who might have killed her own child. When the sudden descent of a rare Carolina winter storm sends the family out to the father's rundown farmhouse (it runs on gas and is not affected when ice brings down the town's power lines), Claire is drawn to the cold beauty of trees and houses laced with ice, which Crone deftly develops as a metaphor for the girl's growing distance from the mother. In the story's shattering climax, when the farmhouse's decrepit gas lines cause a devastating fire, the daughter, safely outside after rescuing her baby sister, hears her mother's screams for help but is unmoved. The frame of the story--an adult Claire, haunted by her memories, doomed to recall her mother's fiery death--gives the story its subtle and disturbing irony.

OTHER MAJOR WORKS

LONG FICTION: *A Period of Confinement*, 1986.

BIBLIOGRAPHY

Ciuba, Gary M. *Desire, Violence, and Diversity in Modern Southern Fiction: Katherine Anne Porter, Flannery O'Connor, Cormac McCarthy, and Walker Percy*. Baton Rouge: Louisiana State University Press, 2007. A critical look at the postwar southern fiction that influenced Crone, especially that of O'Connor. Explores the gothic sensibility and the immense importance of Faulkner's regionalism.

Gaudet, Marcia, and James C. McDonald, eds. *Mardi Gras, Gumbo, and Zydeco: Readings in Louisiana Culture*. Jackson: University Press of Mississippi, 2003. Engaging reading of the culture that shapes Crone's fictional sensibility. Provides helpful essays on the cultural diversity of the region and the conservative notions of family and the role of women.

Kinman, Eric. "Interview with Moira Crone." *Short Story* 3, no. 2 (1995): 81-90. Chatty interview in which Crone describes her writing process as a journey of discovery, in which she creates a character but, as Crone tells the story, the character reveals itself to her.

Nagel, James. *Contemporary American Short Story Cycle: The Ethnic Resonance of the Genre*. Baton Rouge: Louisiana State University Press, 2004. A helpful introduction to story collections that work more as novels. Although Crone's work is not addressed directly, the book defines the concept of concentricity and how stories work subtly off one another to create suspense and coherence.

Yaeger, Patricia. *Dirt and Desire: Reconstructing Southern Women's Writing*. Chicago: University of Chicago Press, 2003. Important and highly accessible study of the genre associated with Crone. Looks at issues specific to Crone: motherhood, the responsibilities of family, sexual politics, and the importance of identity.

Joseph Dewey